W9-CUQ-396

# THE KIDS' FAMILY TREE BOOK

Caroline Leavitt

Illustrated by Ian Phillips

Sterling Publishing Co., Inc.
New York

Special thanks are due to all those—family and friends—who provided information and gave permission for the use of many old and perhaps slightly more recent photographs in this book. Your help was invaluable.

Edited by Claire Bazinet
Design by Judy Morgan and Lucy Wilner

**Library of Congress Cataloging-in-Publication Data Available**

2  4  6  8  10  9  7  5  3  1
Published in paperback in 2007 by Sterling Publishing Co., Inc.
387 Park Avenue South, New York, NY 10016
© 2005 by Caroline Leavitt
Distributed in Canada by Sterling Publishing
℅ Canadian Manda Group, 165 Dufferin Street
Toronto, Ontario, Canada M6K 3H6
Distributed in the United Kingdom by GMC Distribution Services
Castle Place, 166 High Street, Lewes, East Sussex, England BN7 1XU
Distributed in Australia by Capricorn Link (Australia) Pty. Ltd.
P.O. Box 704, Windsor, NSW 2756, Australia

*Manufactured in China*
*All rights reserved*

Sterling ISBN-13: 978-1-4027-0942-5 Hardcover
ISBN-10: 1-4027-0942-0
ISBN-13: 978-1-4027-4715-1 Paperback
ISBN-10: 1-4027-4715-2

*For information about custom editions, special sales, premium and corporate purchases, please contact Sterling Special Sales Department at 800-805-5489 or specialsales@sterlingpub.com*

# CONTENTS

FOREWORD    4

Chapter 1
GENEALOGY IS YOU!    5

Chapter 2
GETTING STARTED    9

Chapter 3
YOUR FAMILY TREE    12

Chapter 4
DIGGING FOR YOUR ROOTS    19

Chapter 5
GETTING ORGANIZED    27

Chapter 6
SEARCHING ONLINE    35

Chapter 7
TRACKING YOUR ANCESTORS    40

Chapter 8
HERALDRY    47

Chapter 9
MAKING THE CONNECTIONS    52

Chapter 10
WINDOWS ON THE PAST    56

Chapter 11
THE GEOGRAPHY OF GENEALOGY    60

Chapter 12
FAMILY HISTORY STORIES    66

Chapter 13
THE WAY THEY WERE    71

Chapter 14
FAMILY TRADITIONS    76

Chapter 15
A FAMILY REUNION!    81

Chapter 16
KEEPING IN TOUCH    88

Chapter 17
BACK TO THE FUTURE    91

AFTERWORD—PLANT A FAMILY TREE    95

INDEX    96

# FOREWORD

Do you have a family tree? No, don't look around for a big trunk topped with green leaves. That's not the kind of tree we're talking about. When you are born, you become a living and growing part of your own family tree. Your parents and brothers and sisters, and your aunts and uncles and other relatives, all play their parts in helping the branches of your family tree spread out and grow strong. Are you ready to put them in their honored places in your family tree? It's time to learn about and meet your ancestors. And it all begins with a word you may have heard: genealogy.

# Chapter 1
# GENEALOGY IS YOU!

## WHAT MAKES YOU YOU?

Ever wonder how you became who you are? Why you are tall or short? How your hair got to be curly or straight? Your skin dark or pale or olive?

How you got to be the way you are is due, in large part, to your family genealogy. Look at members of your family and you might notice things you all share, beyond the same last name and hometown. Your father might be tall the way you are and have the same springy dark hair. Your mother's brown eyes might be the same chocolate shade as yours. If you have siblings, maybe your brother has your same strong nose, or your sister shares your lopsided smile. If you are one of identical twins, it's like looking in a mirror!

It's not only "looks" that families share. Talents, such as a beautiful singing voice or being able to draw wonderful pictures, can also run in families. So can medical problems, such as being colorblind or sneezing around cats or dogs or at certain times of the year. You might also be much different in some ways from your parents and your siblings. Maybe you are short while they are all tall or you enjoy telling long involved stories, but your dad can't even tell a joke!

And then there's what you're like on the inside. Where do you get your personality? Do you like to sit quietly in a chair and read, lost for hours the way your mother does? Do you love the beach the way your cousins do? Or yearn to be a doctor like your dad? Are you more like your aunt than your mother? How so? Who shares what? Are there more people in your family who like to paint than who like to write? Who has the good sense of humor? Who is quick to anger? Do you have a temper, too? Has someone asked, "Who do you take after?" It's really a good question. Do you know the answer?

Knowing about your family can help you to learn a whole lot more about yourself. Knowing about your ancestors' place in their world can help you to understand your place in yours.

## IT'S NOT ALL MOM AND DAD

How you got to be you doesn't stop with just your immediate family. Maybe no one in your family now may be tall like you, but maybe your great-uncle was six feet tall. And his father before him might have been six feet five! Of course, if you are adopted, you may not look anything like the family you know and love. You may have your birth mother's flaming red hair or your birth father's love of math.

Your family genes stretch far back, further than anybody remembers. Think about it. Your mother had a mother, and her mother had a mother, and her mother had a mother, and her mother, too. Going back several generations, your great-grandfather's great-grandfather might have been a shoemaker in England. Your great-grandmother's

*Could this baby on her grandfather's knee be your great grand-mother?* ▼

*It's always good to gather four generations together for a photo.*

6

great-grandmother might have been making lasagna (a noodle and sauce dish) in Italy or borscht (a tasty beet soup) in Russia. All these people could be a part of your family tree! And it's exciting to discover how these blood relations were like you, and how they were different.

## THE GENES IN YOUR JEANS

The important part of the word genealogy, which means the study of family history, is gene. Genes are the materials in every cell of your body that give instructions to your body for creating the one and only special you. No one is exactly like you (only identical twins are the same). Genes are carried on tiny structures called chromosomes. Every cell in your body has 46 chromosomes that come in pairs of 23 each. Inside the chromosomes is your DNA (short for a word that's a real mouthful: deoxyribonucleic acid), and this DNA is what gives your body the messages to create you.

You received your chromosomes—and your genes—from your parents: some from your father and some from your mother. Before you were born, they blended together and created a blueprint for the person you would be. So, your parents got their genes from their parents (your mother from her mother and father, and your father from his mother and father). And those people, your grandparents, got their genes from your great-grandparents. I'm sure you can guess now where your great-grandparents got their genes. And aren't you getting excited about finally finding out just who all those people were and what they were like?

Genes dictate lots of things. Think of your extended family—your uncles, aunts, and grandparents. If they share the same big ears or deep voice, you can credit it to genes. But remember, not everyone will have the same family look, because your uncle may be part of your family "by marriage" not by blood, because he married your mother's sister. His genes come from a totally different family.

## WHY STUDY GENEALOGY?

Study genealogy and you will probably find yourself traveling to other times and other lands. You might discover that an ancestor on your father's side was a famous admiral. Maybe someone on your mother's side was a photographer who traveled all over the world! Discovering the occupations and abilities about your ancestors can open up whole new worlds for you. The more you know about your family and your past, the more you might discover about yourself. If a great-aunt was an important political speaker, maybe the power to lead is in your blood, too, and you can achieve much more than you ever thought you could! If a great-great-grandfather was a celebrated opera singer, maybe you should reconsider your shyness about joining the school chorus or try *a capella* singing!

Genealogy can help you discover your family's place in the world. And yours.

# Chapter 2
# GETTING STARTED

## YOUR FAMILY HISTORY

Did you ever hear someone say, "I know you like a book?" Well, imagine that your family history is a book. It's the story of how you got where you are, filled with photographs and stories of long-ago family members growing up, and maps of where they lived. It begins way back when, with your great-great-great-grandmother, and continues all the way down to you! Having a family scrapbook is a great way to know and understand your family. And knowing your family history is to really know yourself.

Your family history scrapbook will come, in time. For now, keep an eye out for a big scrapbook to buy, or put it on your gift "wish list." You'll want to set aside a page (or two or three) for each family member, starting with the oldest, say, your great-great-grandfather, and moving down to the youngest, which might be you. To fill up this "family story" book, you'll need to collect information on each person, including photographs and special keepsakes, which you can later paste into your family scrapbook. Imagine! Under a picture of your grandmother, for example, you might have information on when and where she was born, what school she went to, who she married, her likes and dislikes, and her famous apple pie recipe. Try to include other family "treasures," too, things that will remind you of her, such as a copy of her favorite joke, a report card, or a square cut from a dress she had when she was your age. All of these things, pasted into your scrapbook, will some day create a wonderful memory book to keep and display!

But before you can work on putting together your family scrapbook, you have to start gathering information—and have a place to put it!

# Starting off right

To start your genealogy research, you will need a few supplies right away:

- some small notebooks—you should carry one with you at all times to make notes whenever you run across some great information.
- sharpened pencils—be sure to keep a couple handy. Shorter stubs are less likely to break.
- a loose-leaf binder and paper—you need a place to collect and keep all the information you turn up. When you get information on someone, put his or her name at the top of a page. Write the information on the page, and keep the page in the binder. Each time you get new information, add it to the right person's page. Soon this loose-leaf binder will be your best friend: a genealogy workbook that will help you keep track of your family tree.

## THOSE FAMILY PHOTOS

Once you show an interest in genealogy, you can be sure that someone is going to drag out an old dusty album of photographs. Actually, putting names and then facts and stories to the faces you see there is a good part of the fun. Soon, you'll feel you really know them: the girl on the old merry-go-round, the serious young man in the sailor hat, the father proudly showing off the family car (with running boards). Then there are those baby pictures, confirmation or bar mitzvah photos, and school and graduation pictures, too. You're sure to find yourself in there somewhere. The pictures in the album may not mean much to you now, but they will.

The important thing, right at the start, is to take good care of any photographs you want to look at or borrow to copy for your genealogy projects. Try not to touch the picture part itself, only the edges. Depending on the age and kind of paper the pictures are printed on, even oil from your fingers could damage them. Most of the older photographs that you will find in family albums will be the only copy anyone has. If they are damaged or lost, they can't be replaced, so you'll need to make copies if you want to cut, pin up, or glue any pictures. And if you borrow any, be sure to return them in the same condition. You don't want to have a family feud on your hands!

*A tintype from the 1890's.*

## Fun facts

- Tintypes, the first "instant" photographs, were inexpensive and unbreakable. They were made out of metal!
- Stereoscopic pictures were two photos of the same thing placed side by side. With a stereoscopic viewer, you saw the picture in 3-D!

*A common stereoscope.*

11

# Chapter 3

# YOUR FAMILY TREE

A family tree, as we said, isn't a tree but a kind of map. Instead of showing miles, a family tree shows how family members are related to one another. It can go back over many years; from you to your great-grandparents and beyond. The family tree form is called that because of the way it shows family members "branching out" from one another, like tree branches are connected to each other and to the trunk of the tree.

## MAPPING YOUR FAMILY

Are you ready to begin drawing your family tree? Do you have enough information to begin? Yes, at least to start. You know who you are, and how you are related to your mother and your father (you are their child). And you know how you are related to your grandparents, your mother and father's parents. So, let's start you off with a really simple family tree.

1. Find a large piece of paper, make a circle near the bottom and inside write your full name (first, middle, and last). Under your name, put your birth date (month, day, and year).
2. Make two lines going upward and draw two more circles at the top, like balloons. In one, write in your mother's full name and her birth date. Write your father's full name in the other. Put in his birth date, too. (Ask for the correct spelling and birth dates.)

**3.** Make more lines going upward (more balloons): two from your mother's circle and two from your father's circle. Top each of them with two more circles. In these circles, write in your grandparents' full names—your mother's mother and father above her circle and your father's mother and father above his circle. Put in their birth dates.

That's a good start. Next, if you have brothers and sisters, and aunts and uncles, and cousins, you'll want to add them to your family tree, too. Your brothers and sisters are your siblings, which means that they are your parents' children, too. And your cousins are the children of your aunts and uncles. So they'll be listed on the family tree under their parents. This means you'll need a much bigger piece of paper, or some type of pedigree or genealogy form, to keep track of everybody!

## Family tree tips

List each person in your family tree, then try to find out:
- when the person was born. Where.
- what schools the person went to. Years graduated.
- where the person lived.
- what jobs the person held.
- if a person was in the military. What service, where and when.
- if a person emigrated. From where and when.
- if the person is dead. When. Where. How. Where buried.

How much of this or other information you will want to put into your family tree diagram is up to you. But don't miss out on gathering the information while you can, so you can record it in your loose-leaf binder and later in your family scrapbook.

## GROWING YOUR FAMILY TREE

Even if you start small, remember that big family trees grow from tiny roots. Here is a part of a family tree form. At the top would be the oldest relatives that you know, probably your grandparents. Vertical and horizontal lines map out your parents and their siblings, and you and your siblings, if you have them. Remember, you have two sets of grandparents—your mother's parents and your father's parents. That means you'll have eight great-grandparents. Your family tree will grow quickly once you start, so every time you learn about a relative, add his or her name to your family tree form, along with important vital statistics such as birth, marriage and death dates. When you hear or find new stories about a relative, write them all down in your loose-leaf notebook. By the time you're finished, you should have a huge family tree that you can frame and hang in your room and a notebook filled with lots of family facts.

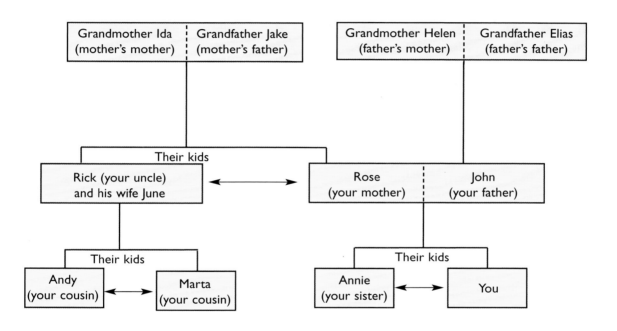

From this diagram it's easy to see how people in your family are related. Horizontal boxes side by side mean the people are siblings (brothers and sisters). Vertical lines tell us descent (who is the parent and who is the child). You can also see that your maternal grandmother and grandfather were married and had two kids.

With this kind of system, you can easily add more information. For example: Next to or beneath each name, you might write B (for birth) and D (for death) and put in the dates—at least the year, although the place is important, too. If the person is still living (such as you are, of course) put a small dash after the birth date. For example, if your birth year is 1995, you would write B1995–. Later on, after you've done some detective work, you'll have a lot more information to add.

If you want more information, write in M (for married) and the date. How would you show if someone was divorced? Since "D" stands for death, you can put a slash through the M and add the divorce date for ~~M~~ 1982–1991.

## BRINGING YOUR FAMILY TO LIFE

As you learn more about your family, you'll find yourself really getting to know them. You'll want to write down where family members were born, and when and where they got married (if they did). You will definitely want to add when, where, and how the person died (if they are no longer living), and where they are buried. People often make visits to the graves of family members on the departed relative's birthday or on the anniversary of their death. This is a good time for you to go, too. The person's full name and birth and death dates are etched on the cemetery gravestones. Be sure to bring one of your small notebooks and a pencil or two and take down the information. You may need it to order a death certificate or find an obituary.

Death certificates are official papers issued at the time of death. If your family doesn't have a death certificate for a deceased grandparent, you should be able to order a copy for a fee from the local courthouse where the person lived, or from the Office or Bureau of Vital Statistics. You'll need the full name and year and place of death, and a reason for requesting the certificate. Obituaries are much easier to find and often provide much more information.

An obituary is a short biography about the person who has died. Local newspapers print obituaries to tell their readers (often friends and neighbors of the deceased) that the person has passed away. Newspapers keep archives of everything they print. If you know the date a person died, you can search the archives of the local newspaper for that person's obituary. It is usually printed in an issue a day or two later. Libraries sometimes keep microfilm archives of old issues of local papers. An obituary can provide a lot of helpful information when you are researching your family tree.

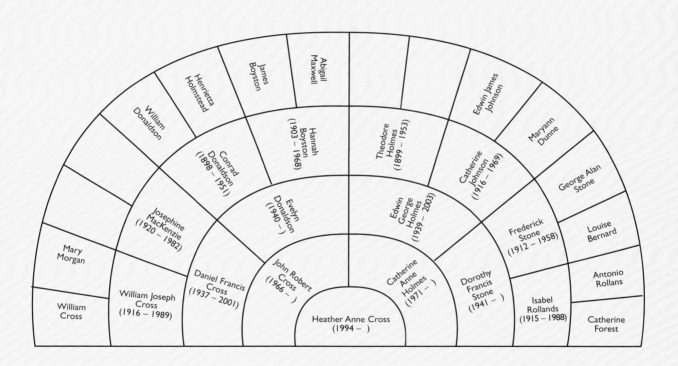

A fan-shaped pedigree chart such as this one is a good way to keep track of, and display, just your direct-line ancestors, rather than all family members. It is easy to see how several generations all come down to you.

# PEDIGREE CHART

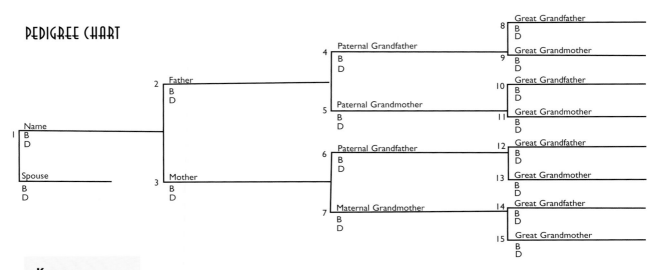

**Key**

**B**orn
**M**arried
**D**ied
**C**emetery/**C**hildren

This type of pedigree form gives you room under the name line for important family details: date and place of birth, death, marriage; where buried, children's names, etc.

It can be extended as far back in time as you have room on the paper. If each ancestor on the chart is numbered, it is easy to key file folders to the chart, then arrange the folders accordingly.

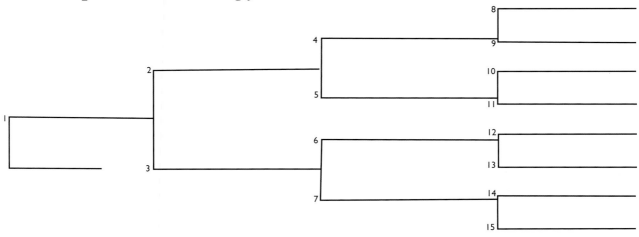

## Chapter 4
# DIGGING FOR YOUR ROOTS

*B*efore you get to know your ancestors, let's start with the person and the people you know best—you and your immediate family! The answers you find here will start you on your genealogical trail.

## HOW TO DO RESEARCH

Finding out facts about your family involves research. The first and easiest way to get some answers is simply by asking yourself some questions, or by interviewing your parents. This is called using primary sources, primary meaning "first." These are the people in your immediate family: your father and mother, yourself and your older siblings. Start by finding out the basic facts—names, dates, places. Later on, when you've figured out who everybody is, you can go back to people and collect family stories, called recording "oral history." In the meantime, if you do need to get some quieter relatives talking, asking a few of the questions on page 69 (taking oral histories) might help to draw them out.

## START WITH WHAT YOU KNOW

You may be surprised to discover just how much important information about your-self you already know, and how much you need to find out. You probably know what your name is and where you were born. But maybe you don't know your middle name (or names) or the exact time of your birth—a fun thing to know. So ask your parents to see and help you make a copy of your birth certificate. Certificates are official records used in keeping track of what happens in people's lives. There are certificates for birth, baptism, marriage, and death. Each of these certificates can offer a wealth of information about you, and about the people in your family tree.

## Watch for treasure

As you research and do your interviews, keep an eye and ear out for these great sources of information:

**1.** Marriage license—where and when a family member was married.

**2.** Diploma—where and when someone earned a degree.

**3.** Death certificate or newspaper obituary notice—where and when someone died (sometimes how or why they died). Also, where they are buried, and what family members survived him or her.

**4.** Family Bible—births, marriages and deaths may be recorded and the Bible handed down from generation to generation. A wonderful family heirloom.

**5.** Personal diaries and letters—names of family and friends (who could have important information), places the family might have lived (look at return address), important details of daily lives and wonderful stories of the times in which the people lived.

**6.** Internet—all manner of information: more is being added and made available daily.

## BEGIN AT THE BEGINNING

Birth records generally include the name of the child and the parents, and the exact date and even time of birth. The name of the hospital is there, too, and the signature of the doctor in charge. You might find some funny things, too, such as a footprint taken right after the baby was born, or a few strands of hair stuck to it.

Look at your birth certificate and you may notice that the name you've always used isn't exactly the one you were given at birth. If people call you Harry, your birth name may actually be Henry or Harold. Peggy is a common nickname for Margaret, but Peggy could actually be the name given on the birth certificate, not Margaret. Someone called Max might have been named Maximilian, after a long-ago Roman emperor, or Maxine!

As you search out old birth certificates, you might be surprised to find a person's last name isn't the same as on their birth certificate. It could be a simple spelling mistake, or that the person disliked the name so changed it. Sometimes, a name was simplified or changed when an immigrant moved to a new country with a different language and culture (Sandlovitz might have been shortened to Sands, while Roi (in French) was translated to King in English).

*Time out for a holiday photo with visiting cousins.*

## LET'S TALK

Now that you've found out some basic family facts, you're ready to learn about interviewing. But asking questions, even of people you know well, isn't always easy. You'll need to know what questions to ask and how to ask them to get the answers you want. Where do you start?

Think. Now that you have some information on family members, who do you think might be the most helpful? How about some of the oldest? Do you have several relatives who are about the same age, in their 60s or 70s, or maybe older?

Lucky you! These are the family members you want to talk to and interview as quickly as you can. They could be a great help to you in your genealogy search. Their stories of who their parents and grandparents were, where they came from, and how things were when they were kids are there waiting to be told.

But people are different. Some are willing to talk about just anything for hours, while others need to be put at ease before they will open up to you. During an interview, one person will answer questions with only a word or two, so you'll need to ask follow-up questions to get the information you're looking for. Another person will ramble on with a long involved story instead of telling you what you want to know. You need to take control the interview and bring the talkative ones back on track.

*It's nice ▲ to have the family dog in the picture.*

## SETTING UP AN INTERVIEW

To get ready to interview, before you sit down to questions, you'll need some way to catch and keep their responses, and whatever else they may say. A good way is to use a tape recorder (remember to use fresh batteries). That way, you'll have a record of any valuable information, and be able to listen to it again and again to refresh your memory. After the interview, you'll want to "transcribe" or copy the words onto paper to have easy access to it. If someone objects or is clearly uncomfortable being tape recorded, go back to that old standby of information gathering—a notebook and a few pencils or pens.

## ASKING QUESTIONS!

To make your researches easier and later organize the information in your workbook, it helps to have a form that can be filled out. Then you can be sure to ask the same questions of everyone you interview. For relatives who don't live nearby, the form can be sent in the mail (or by e-mail) with a note attached. Explain what you are doing and that you'd like each family member to fill out the form for you. Ask if they would "please" send back the filled-out form by a certain date (allowing two weeks or so is about right). That way the form is less likely to be set aside and forgotten, or mislaid. Copy this form, or make up one of your own:

1. **Full name** (first, middle, last)

2. **Date and place of birth**

3. **Father's name**

4. **Mother's maiden name**

5. **Current address**

6. **Past addresses** (when moved)

7. **Education** (when, where)

8. **Health problems**

9. **Employment**

10. **Married** (name, date, place)

11. **Children** (name, date, place born)

12. **Divorced** (name, date, place)

13. **Military service** (when, branch of service)

14. **Awards and honors received**

15. **Memberships** (club, church, organization)

16. **Pets**

17. **Special talents**

Is there anything else about yourself that you would like me to know?

Who else should receive a copy of this form (name, relationship, address)?

Asking the final questions above might get you some information you wouldn't have thought to ask about and leads to family members you don't know well. Add new names to your list of relatives to be interviewed or sent a copy of the form. It's a good idea, too, to leave space at the bottom of your form for any "Comments" or "Stories." If room is tight on the form, suggest that additional information be written on the back of the form or on a separate sheet. Note: Remember to ask each relative for a nice close-up photo (a head shot) that you can keep.

## HOW FAR BACK CAN YOU GO?

It's thrilling to have all that information coming in! As the forms are filled out or returned, use a three-hole punch along the left side and put the pages into your loose-leaf binder. Add only basic facts (such as birth date) to your working family tree. Later, you'll use a lot more of this helpful and interesting information in making up your family history scrapbook. For now, keep the forms all neat and safe in one handy place, your loose-leaf genealogy workbook.

## BE PREPARED!

Even when you are not planning to interview someone, keep a small notebook and a couple of sharp pencils or pens with you at all times. You never know when you might need it! At a family dinner, your father might start talking about the time his uncle won first prize in a yodeling contest. Or, you could be driving home with your mother when she starts telling you about how her grandfather won a lot of money in a lottery. Remember, when you record the information, write down who told you about it, and where and when you got the information (carry a small calendar so you can look up the date). Later, if you need to, you can go back to that person ("primary source") and ask for more information about a particular ancestor. Like the detectives on TV cop shows, whip out your notebook and jot things down. You can refer to them later, to jog your memory and your source's memory.

Genealogy work has its own language. Here is a list of vocabulary words that should help you in researching your family tree:

**Ancestor**—someone you are descended from—your parents' parents, their parents, and so on.

**Archives**—a collection of historical records and items: birth and death records, land deeds; back issues of old newspapers.

**Autobiography**—a life story, told by that person.

**Biography**—the life story of someone, told by someone else.

**Census**—an official count of residents (who they are, where they live) taken at certain times, such as every 10 years.

**Descendant**—someone who comes from you—your children, and their children.

**Emigrate**—to move from a country or a place to start a new life in a new country or place.

**Fraternal**—brothers born at same time (twins), but not from same egg (identical).

**Genealogy**—a "mapping" of family members, from the farthest back ancestor to the living members of the family.

**Generation**—family members on the same "step" of family history (great-grandparents, grandparents, parents).

**Genes**—biologically, what makes you who you are (DNA code).

**Head of Household**—the adult responsible for a family group.

**Immigrant**—a person who enters a country to stay and live permanently.

**Maiden name**—Surname of an unmarried woman, which may change at marriage.

**Maternal**—"from the mother." Relatives on your maternal side are directly related to your mother.

**Paternal**—"from the father." Relatives on your paternal side are directly related to your father.

**Pedigree**—a person's record, in chart form, of parental and ancestral information (Similar in meaning to genealogy).

**Relatives**—people who are directly related to you.

**Sibling**—a person's brother or sister.

**Spouse**—a person's husband or wife.

**Surname**—a person's last or "family" name.

*Loving hugs unite the generations everywhere in the world.*

➤

# Chapter 5

# GETTING ORGANIZED

Remember that loose-leaf binder we suggested you get? You'll definitely want to have one specific place to keep it and all that family information you've been gathering. A big binder that you keep at home (you won't want to be carrying it around with you) is something you'll always be able to find. It will be your genealogical workbook, and hold tons of detailed information. Your family tree diagram just maps out your family relationships, but the information stored in your loose-leaf binder can be used to put together a family scrapbook: along with pictures, quotations from letters, and other interesting things you've discovered about family members.

## YOUR GENEALOGICAL WORKBOOK

You can organize your loose-leaf genealogical workbook in different ways. The easiest way is to give family members their own page. Put the name of each family member at the top of a separate page. Right now, you probably know more about yourself than about any of your family members. So, start with your name, and set up the page in the binder so that when you open it, your page is on top. Next, put in a page for each of your siblings (sisters and brothers) if any, then your parents and their siblings (your aunts and uncles). (You will probably need to interview each of them to get information to fill in the pages.) After the pages for your aunts and uncles will come your grandparents' pages with their names at the top, and so on. This way, you can go back in time, from generation to generation, as far as your genealogical research takes you.

You will soon see, as you gather information and talk to and find out more about your relatives, that the information in your binder will grow and grow.

## MORE ORGANIZATION TIPS

Your loose-leaf binder is your best friend. It's here where you'll rewrite neatly your scribbled interview notes or copy down your taped interviews. Be sure to write down the date of the interview, and the name of the person interviewed. You may have more questions to ask, or need to update your notes.

A blackboard with chalk, white board with erasable marker or, better yet, a cork bulletin board with index cards and pushpins comes in handy, too. You can post "things to be done"—such as family members to follow up on, as you do your research.

Pick up a set of brightly colored pens to color code your notes, using red for your mother's side of the family and blue for your father's side, for example.

Use stick-on notes to draw your attention and remind yourself of something you need to do more work on. Different color note sheets can help here, too.

A number of folders with a cardboard box to hold them makes a handy filing system. You can use different color folders (or markings or labels) for each side of your family, or for different generations, or you can invent a system that works for you.

*Special occasion photos, like* 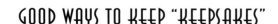 *50th wedding anniversaries, can help to fix the date of the picture.*

## GOOD WAYS TO KEEP "KEEPSAKES"

As you "grow" your family tree, you're going to run across items you'll want to keep. They won't fit in your binder and may even be too bulky for your scrapbook. Photo boxes, or plain old shoeboxes, make great catch-alls. They are perfect for envelopes of photos (remember to identify who's in the pictures), folded or rolled copies of birth and other certificates, expired passports and drivers' licenses. Letters from a homesick soldier, a child away at camp for the first time, or a stack of old love letters are wonderful family keepsakes. You'll want to hold onto military awards and medals, of course, but old school report cards are also fun to have. Note: If you need two or more boxes to hold everything, separate the contents and label or code the containers to make finding things easier.

## KEEP THINGS TOGETHER

If paperwork and other keepsakes are piling up, designate a section of your room as your Genealogical Research Center. You might even want to put up a sign that says so. Keep any audio or video tapes you've made here, along with your filled note-books (keep your current one with you at all times). Store your oversized or treasured photographs in sturdy flat boxes that will keep them safe, and odd-sized items neatly in photo or shoe boxes. Your loose-leaf binder, or binders if you are using more than one, should be where they are easy to reach and work with. And don't forget—every time you gather a new piece of information, be sure to bring it right to this special area. A bulletin board is a good idea, so that small scribbled notes can be

posted and won't become lost. It's a reminder, too, to follow-up or transfer the information later into your binder. Don't put it off too long, because that's how valuable information can get lost—and how a neat and tidy area can quickly morph into a messy one.

## "My Family" Box

Why not consider a file-sized box, with separators and manila folders, to keep things in place? (You'll want to decorate it appropriately, of course.)

**What You Need:**
- box about 12" by 12" by 9" deep
- cardboard separators
- stick-on labels
- manila folders (with tabs)
- copies of photos, clippings, to decorate box
- glue
- scissors
- markers
- shellac
- small brush

**What To Do:**
1. Cut cardboard to fit box (12" by 9½"), for use as separators.
2. Use markers to print labels: Maternal Side, Paternal Side, Maternal Grandparents, Paternal Grandparents, etc.
3. Dot glue the tabs and attach them to the sides of the separators. Change the positions of each label so each heading will be visible!
4. Cut around the copies of family photos. Be sure to include ones from both your maternal (mother) and paternal (father) side of the family. Dot glue on the back of the photographs and paste them all over your box.
5. Dip your brush into the shellac and carefully paint over your photos and your box. This will give it a protective covering and a nice shine.

On manila folders, use a marker that makes the words really stand out. Write the person's name, and put papers relating to that person in the folder. If there is too much, put the person's name on the folder, and then add "birth certificate," "diary pages," or "army records." Whatever the document, there's always a chance it could get misfiled. But if the folder is clearly and neatly labeled, it's a snap to know, when you come across it, where it should go, and re-file it.

## LABEL, LABEL, LABEL

You might want to invest in some labels to stick on the backs of photographs. Regular labels are made to stay on, and that is fine if the photographs are your own. If photographs are borrowed, use removeable labels to identify them, so you can return them in the same condition you received them. On the label, clearly identify the date, place, and person or persons in the photo (reading from left to right). Tip: Do this while you are looking at the photograph, and place the label on the photo after you write it all out. You are less likely to make a mistake in writing down the information, and there is less danger of damaging the photo from pressing too hard or having the ink bleed through to the photograph. Be sure ink is dry before "stacking" photos.

While we are talking about labels, don't forget to pick up some that will fit on whatever size audio tape cassettes you are using to do your interviewing. Once you have more than one or two cassettes, it will become increasingly hard to locate specific interviews when you want to find them.

## CARING FOR PHOTOGRAPHS

There are photographs and there are photographs. If you've just handed out a dozen copies of your latest class picture to relatives, it's no big deal if one or more become misplaced or lost, or are accidentally torn or damaged. But if your grandaunt lets you borrow her only picture of her mother,

*Turning sixteen has always been a reason to have a portrait taken.*

31

your great-grandmother, taken when she was a schoolgirl, so that you can make a copy, it's a different story. Lose it, and it's gone! Sticky fingerprints, ink from markers, spills, or creases from not handling it carefully can also destroy a cherished keepsake photo.

## Photo handling tips

- Hold all photos by the edges. Try not to touch the picture itself.
- Put photographs in clean envelopes or inside a folded sheet of paper to protect them.
- When mailing or carrying photographs, add a stiff piece of cardboard backing to keep the photograph flat (older photographs can be especially fragile and easily creased).
- Be careful writing on the backs of photographs. Marker ink can soak into older paper, and writing with pen or pencil can make impressions that show through on the picture side (write on regular or removeable labels and attach them instead).
- Don't use tape on the front (picture side) of photographs (if necessary, for example to stop a tear from causing more damage, attach tape to the back).
- Definitely, don't cut up any one-of-a-kind photos or use them in any projects. Make copies!

# FINDING YOUR PLACE

Papers and notepads and books-oh, my! At some point a bookmark—or several—might come in handy. Of course, you can use just about anything for a bookmark, but why not make special bookmarks, starring family members, for a cool way to mark your place in your genealogy research.

Where should you start? How about with you? Are you the baby of the family? The big sister? The pesky little brother? We all have roles to play, based on birth order and our position in the family (and many of us play those roles to the hilt). Show your place in the family. Search out a good photo of yourself and clip out of magazines some small pictures that say, "This is me!" If you're nuts about sports, decorate your bookmark with pictures of balls (soccer, baseball, football, tennis) or players in action. You're the "princess" of the family? Cut out a crown, or draw one, for your head. Some pasted-on "jewels" will also show your regal side. Small squares cut from blue jeans (if you're the rough-and-tumble sort) or bits of lace (for the more ladylike)—it's up to you.

*Birthdays are happy occasions for keepsake photos.*

*A tintype photo keeps family very near throughout the years.*

## Family Bookmarks

This easy, creative activity is designed to help you get to know your family members better, and keep you organized too. And, of course, they would make great "thank you" gifts to send to those special people in your family who helped with your research.

### What You Need:
- poster board
- scissors
- markers
- picture
- clippings, scraps, or small mementos
- glue

### What To Do:
**1.** Cut the poster board to a good bookmark size, say 3" wide by 8" long.
**2.** Arrange the photo (or photos) with whatever else you choose. Adjust their positions until you are happy with how it looks.
**3.** Glue each piece to the bookmark. Once the front side is dry, you can decorate the back if you wish—or glue or tape a long piece of colorful ribbon or yarn to it. Now make some bookmarks showing other family members. The more the merrier!

## Chapter 6
# SEARCHING ONLINE

Suppose you've gathered information on your immediate family by asking your parents questions about yourself and your family. You've started a family tree and filled out some forms. Interview tapes have been labeled and written out for your binder. You and your parents have searched through family papers and records. Now you need to dig deeper and farther back in time. A lot of the information you are looking for won't be first hand from your own knowledge, or even information your parents know. Where do you go from here? The answer could be as near as your home computer or as far as your local library.

Just as your parents and relatives are your primary sources of genealogy information, searching records are your secondary sources. They will help you dig deeper, and go farther and farther back into time.

When it comes to those secondary sources for researching your family tree, your computer is a great help. On-line, you can find information, listings, even copies of documents, but you have to know how to search, what to look for, and where to look.

If you go on the Internet often, you probably have a favorite search engine. Search engines are special Internet programs that search for key words. It brings up any document on the World Wide Web (the "www" in Internet addresses) in which that key word appears. Depending on what you enter and search for, you might get no "hits" at all, or maybe there will be ten, or even two hundred sites where that word or phrase appears. Google.com and yahoo.com, are two of the popular search engines on the Internet.

## STARTING THE "SEARCH"

Here is an example: Let's say your grandfather told you that his grandfather came to America in the early 1900s. You don't know the year, and you don't know how. First, you would go to your favorite search engine and type in his name. Put quotation marks around the name so the search engine will search for the first and last names together. Did you get any hits? Maybe not, or maybe you are surprised to see a list of several people with that name. Can you narrow the search? Check the details given: the year, the age of the person, where he came from or lived. If the names listed are clearly not your grandfather's grandfather, don't give up. Other search engines could have access to different information, and there are other places to search.

## FINDING VITAL RECORDS

Where did he live and work, and when and where did he die? Your next stop is to search websites that provide free Vital Records information (many websites charge a fee for use, but allow you to "try it out" first). Vital Records are official records of birth, death, marriage, and divorce organized by state or county in the United States. Some of this information is also picked up by genealogical sites, such as familysearch.com, or ancestry.com. There you type in your relative's name and any other details that might be helpful in the search. But have patience. Searches can take some time, especially if you have to check different states or locate appropriate websites in different countries.

As you do your searches, you may come up with many bits of information about your relative. You may find his Social Security Number (available on the Internet after a person has passed away), his wife's name, where they were married, where they lived, and even his occupation—all terrific helps. If you can, print off the information for your binder. If not, write the results of your searches onto that relative's loose-leaf page, date it, and copy down the full website address at the top. (The website address is the long string of letters, periods, and slashes showing in the address window when the site is open on screen.)

# CHECKING CENSUS RECORDS

Another "must" search for information on ancestors going back at least 70 years are census records. A census is a count of people who live in an area. These records are taken at certain times, generally every ten years, in countries around the world. Census takers go from door to door and fill in forms on every person living at that address. Sometimes, people are asked to fill out and send back census forms that they receive in the mail. So, if you search for and find a great-grandfather's name in the census records, you'll learn a lot of things about him, and about other family members living there at that time. Go to earlier and later census records, and you will be able to track changes in the family from census to census, such as new births (age 7 in 1830), and likely deaths (was 82 in 1830; in 1840 no longer living at that address), job changes, and much more.

In the United States, census records are available for every decade, or ten years, from 1790 to 1930. Information from some old census records may be found online. To actually see and examine a particular filled-out census form, you may need to go to a federal archive facility.

Offices in various parts of the country make these records available for genealogy research and other purposes.

Information available on census form:

- Road, street, number or name of house
- Name and surname of each person
- Relation to head of family
- Married, single, widowed
- Age last birthday
- Profession or occupation
- Employed, neither
- Where born

## LINKING UP

As you do your research on the computer, you'll often find phrases or words highlighted in another color or underlined. These are called "links." Click on these links and they will take you to other websites where you might find more information to speed you along in your search. If you are lucky enough to find yourself at a website with a whole lot of information on your family, don't lose it! Enter it as a "favorite" so the computer will make it available to you whenever you want to go back to it. It might be a good idea, too, to make a written note of it, just in case. Adding the website address to a loose-leaf or notebook page, or to a form that you have made up to organize your records, will keep it handy—in case you need to look up the site again, even if you are on a different computer.

## PAY-FOR-INFORMATION SITES

In doing only a few searches, you will notice that some genealogical sites ask you to "sign in" and some have fees for using the site. Should you pay for access to information? That depends on how far you have gotten with your searches, and how important it is for you to have access to information that you can't seem to find elsewhere. Check with your parents. They might have other leads to finding what you are looking for.

If you are just starting out, it is much more fun to see just how far you can get on your own. Later, if and when you've hit a dead end, or there are "holes" in your research that you're dying to fill, your parents may feel that paying a small fee would be worth it. If so, test out a likely website if you can before signing up for the service. Some sites will let you do a few searches to give you an idea of what kind of information and how much, is available. Maybe a few minutes work will fill that "hole" in your research, without you having to plunk down a good part of your allowance or hard-earned cash.

# THE BASICS OF SEARCHING

In case doing searches online is new to you, here are a few tips about how to go about it:

**1.** Connect search words in quotes; for example, "Clutters Boston" for a Clutter family who lived in Boston. The search engine will look for both "Clutters" and "Boston" together. That way you will avoid getting Closet "Clutters" or "Boston" Red Sox.

**2.** Don't bother with little words. Small, connecting words such as "the," "and," "or," are a waste of time. The search engine ignores them.

**3.** Be specific if you know details: your great-uncle was a member of "Knights of Columbus Baltimore 1900s." If you're not sure, search instead for "Men's Organizations Maryland 1900s" and check out the hits that come up.

Some Internet files can be very long, and would waste a lot of paper and printing ink if you printed them out. If you can, it's best to "copy" the information you want to keep to a Word file and save it that way. Otherwise, remember to carefully record all the information you find in your genealogy binder for safekeeping. Make a note of the website where you got the information, so you can return to it if you need to.

*Photos from those far away remind you to keep in touch.*

*Showing off new spring outfits is a time-honored tradition.*

39

# Chapter 7

# TRACKING YOUR ANCESTORS

## WHERE ARE YOUR ANCESTORS FROM?

Part of what makes genealogy so fascinating is that you aren't just tracing your family back through time, but through place as well. You may live in America now, but only Native Americans are original natives. Everyone else came from someplace else. That could mean that you have cousins in Ireland, China, South Africa, Peru, or somewhere else in the world. On the other hand, if you live in those countries now, your family may have moved there from a different country a long time ago. Records, if they still exist, could be hard to find, or written in a different language. No matter where you are, chances are that some family members immigrated to America in the past. So whether you have lost touch with your American cousins, or want to trace your family back to the "old country," here's one place to try.

## COMING TO AMERICA

Go to your computer and bring up your favorite search engine. Then type in the search phrase "Ellis Island." From 1892 to 1954, millions of people passed through the Ellis Island Immigration Center on their way to new lives in America. They sailed on ships into New York harbor from many different countries. Each person arriving on Ellis Island was given certain tests. The immigrants were examined by a doctor and given simple wooden puzzles to test their skill and intelligence. Imagine how difficult it was for people who often didn't speak the language to figure out what they were expected to do with these pieces of wood. But the immigrants came because once inside America, a whole new life awaited them.

Today, visitors come from everywhere to touch the names of ancestors etched into its "Wall of Honor." The Ellis Island website, ellisisland.org, can also help people find names on passenger lists. If your great-great-great grandfather didn't come through Ellis Island, do other searches under "immigration" (another incoming center was Angel Island in San Francisco Bay) and you just might be able to tell your grandfather something he doesn't know about his grandfather.

## America became their home

- Knute Rockne, Notre Dame's famed football coach, arrived in America from Norway, in 1893.
- Frank Capra, director of the Christmas favorite "It's a Wonderful Life" emigrated from Italy in 1903.
- Entertainer Bob Hope came through Ellis Island in 1908 from England.
- Bela Lugosi, famous for playing Dracula, emigrated from Hungary in 1921.
- Science fiction writer Isaac Asimov came to America from Russia in 1923.
- The Von Trapp family, made famous by "The Sound of Music," came to America from Germany in 1938.

Were your relatives among them? How would you go about finding out? First, of course, ask your parents or older relatives. Maybe someone in your family has an old passport or some immigration papers from another country. A passport is a document issued to allow people to travel from country to country. Inside the passport booklet, look for visa stamps, those special dated markings that tell when a family member passed from one country to another. Passports usually have a photograph of the family member, too. If your family often travels together, one of your parents' passports might include you, too. Some of your relatives may have emigrated before passports were known. However, they might have been issued immigration or travel documents, and these papers will provide information that you can record in your loose-leaf workbook and onto your family tree.

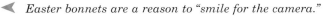 *Easter bonnets are a reason to "smile for the camera."*

If the document includes a photo of the traveler, you'll definitely want to copy it for that family scrapbook you are working on. Adding copies of interesting visa stamps will bring your ancestors' travels to life.

## WHAT'S IN A NAME?

Today more than 100 million Americans can claim an ancestor who arrived through Ellis Island. And millions of people throughout the world can claim ancestors who came to America and stayed! But finding them isn't always easy.

If you're looking for a relative with the last name of Schmidt, for example, you may not find him. His real name might have been Schmitter, or something similar. Why? Names may have been spelled incorrectly, or intentionally changed. An immigration official may have made a mistake in filling out a form, or simply misunderstood what an immigrant said. Newcomers themselves also changed their own names, wanting to "fit in." They worried that employers and others would find their foreign-sounding name hard to pronounce.

For that reason, many Asians, even today, take on new first names or nicknames, such as Tina or Harry, instead of using their birth names. Traditional Asian names are written with the surname first and the given name last: Chen (last name) Jen-Yu (first name) instead of Jen-Yu Chen. When looking up Asian names, here's a clue: the surname is almost always just one syllable, while the given name is longer.

Other ethnic groups had their own naming traditions. In Swedish tradition, a daughter of Lars who is named Christine, was called Christine Larsdatter. This was confusing to some people, so a new surname, like Olson, was selected.

Other immigrants Americanized their names: Finkelstein became Fink, the German name Schneider (meaning tailor) became Taylor, the Polish first name Wojciech changed to Albert, while the Russian Misha or Mikhail became Michael.

When doing searches, keep possible name changes, spellings, nicknames and abbreviations in mind. Frederick might be listed as Friedrich, Fred or Freddy; Richard as Ricardo or Rico; James might be given as Jimmy, or abbreviated to Jas. So, if searching for Mikhail Romanov doesn't work, for example, try Michael Romanov, Mike Romanov, or just M. Romanov. Some websites might offer alternate spellings of the name you entered, even for last names. Be sure to give these a look, too.

If, while you are doing name searches, you see a box that allows you to use something called Soundex, check it off. Soundex is a program that looks up names based on the sound of the consonants not on how the name is spelled. For example, Soundexing Clara would also bring up Klara and Claire. So, if you're unsure of the spelling of a name, use Soundex and see if the information you need comes up! Remember, part of genealogy is having hunches and making guesses, just like a detective!

A very long time ago, some people took their occupation as their surname. Henry Miller milled grains, while Tom Smith was a smithy, someone who shoed horses. If your name is Shepherd, it's possible that an ancestor may have herded sheep. Chances are your family isn't in that business anymore!

# WHEN NAMES CHANGE

Many American names have foreign origins. Michelle is a French name but, since crossing the ocean, it has stayed the same. Other names, however, have changed, and knowing this can help you find your ancestors a bit more easily. Here is a name game to give you some practice. See if you can match the list of the names on the left with their correct counterparts in the right-hand column. The answer is on the next page.

| | |
|---|---|
| Pablo | Ruth |
| Jacques | Anthony |
| Tamio | Beatrice |
| Maurice | Amy |
| Rivka | Paul |
| Aimee | Morris |
| Antonio | John |
| Bice | Thomas |

**Answer key:**

Pablo = Paul ● Jacques = John ● Tamio = Thomas ● Maurice = Morris ● Rivka = Ruth ● Aimee = Amy ● Antonio = Anthony ● Bice = Beatrice

## Fun fact

America has been called the "great melting pot." What does this mean? Think about what would happen if someone were to put crayons of all kinds together into a pot and heat it up. The wax would melt and the colors, shapes, and textures of all the crayons would blend together. So, calling America a melting pot means that all the different peoples came together and blended, creating a new mixture that is truly American!

## WHO YOU ARE IS A CLUE

Where to search on the Internet for genealogical information on your family tree depends on your ethnic background. Many African Americans today, for example, are descendants of slaves taken from their homes along the coastline between the Congo and Gambia Rivers in East Africa. Starting in 1619, these forced immigrants were uprooted, transported to the Americas and the Caribbean in ships, and sold as slaves. Most lost their proud African names to slave names, or took the plantation owner's last name as their own. That's why, in some small rural towns in the South, almost an entire population can have same last name. But, no matter where your ancestors come from, or who they were, there are archives available online to help you trace your ancestors back through several generations. One popular website, cyndislist.com, has links to a fascinating array of archives.

# FORGING CULTURAL LINKS ON THE GENEALOGY CHAIN

If you're looking for information on a missing family member, don't forget those important cultural ties. Just because people move to a new country doesn't mean they leave everything in the old culture behind. They usually arrange to live close by and get together often with people who speak the same language, eat the same foods, and enjoy the same things. Homesick for parts of the culture left behind, new immigrants stuck together and tried to recreate what was comfortable and familiar to them.

When large numbers of people were immigrating to America, little neighborhoods quickly sprang up—Chinatown, Germantown, Little Italy. You could find bagels in New York's Lower East Side, pasta in Little Italy, bratwurst in Germantown, dim sum and colorful silk clothing in Chinatown. This "coming together" of nationalities was repeated in large cities all across the country. All these cultural differences helped to make America as much of a Home Sweet Home as possible for a wonderfully diverse group of people, who simply recreated as much of their homeland as they could.

What parts of your ancestors' culture is still a part of your life? Is it your great Chinese grandmother's cold noodles and peanut sauce? Your great-great Italian grandmother's lasagna? The Greek songs your aunt sings at family gatherings? The folk dances the men in your family perform at celebrations? The piñata you break open at parties? What things in your life today are pieces of your cultural history?

Just as your mother's blue eyes might have been handed down to you, so are certain cultural traits. What did your great-grandmother teach your grandmother, who taught your mother, who taught you? These things are handed down like genes and sometimes changed. Your grandmother might have taught your mother to make her special Russian pudding with cream, but when your mother taught you, she might have used milk instead—or added raisins. How will you pass this down or change it for your children? These cultural family recipes are something you'll want to preserve by pasting them into your special family history scrapbook. You can paste your grandmother's recipe for blueberry bread into her section, and your uncle's recipe for Mexican refried beans into his.

Knowing about your ancestors' culture can help you find your ancestors, too. Look for leads to a Chinese ancestor in the Chinese community. If an Italian ancestor was famous for her pasta sauce, maybe an Italian community newspaper may have done a story on her. Whatever the nationality, local papers and community organizations are good sources of information. Maybe someone knew your grandmother when she lived in a different town. Or perhaps someone remembers the name of your grandmother's best friend. You can find wonderful clues where you never even expected to. All you have to do is ask relatives or ask people at cultural events you might attend with your family.

◀ *An old family photo might include your grandma, and her twin, as kids.*

# Chapter 8
# HERALDRY

## IT STARTED WITH THE KNIGHTS

Have you tried to research your family name on the Internet? If so, you might have found yourself at a website that talked about heraldry, and something called a coat of arms.

Coats of arms began about a thousand years ago (the twelfth century—that means the 1100s) in Europe. It was a time when knights wore full—and very heavy—suits of armor. At a distance, or with their head armor covering their faces, it was nearly impossible to identify friend from foe. During the noise of battle, knights couldn't call out loud enough to be heard and recognized. A quick and visual way was needed to identify who was who.

So knights had identifying marks put on their shields. They wore the same design on the loose cloth cape that covered their armor to protect them from the sun's heat. The markings on the "coat" of arms allowed a knight to be recognized, even if he was separated from his shield.

Gradually, people from noble or high-class families began to use coat of arms markings. The working poor often couldn't read or write, so these "picture names" helped them, too.

Soon the identifying marks became more complex. People added symbols of honors they had won, or to commemorate important family events and special occasions. Having a coat of arms became a mark of great pride. And the status from the coat of arms was something the whole family, or clan, could share.

With so many new coats of arms being worn, and new ones being made up, a procedure was set up to register them and keep track of the many symbols that appeared on them. Even today, who is entitled to wear what on a coat of arms is strictly regulated in some countries.

## Fun facts

- Lucky you, if you were the oldest son in the Middle Ages. You inherited your father's coat of arms intact. A younger son would only have a smaller picture to place in the middle of a shield.
- If you were a woman getting married, you would bring your family's coat of arms into your husband's, adding to the design.

# THE COAT OF ARMS

A coat of arms is made up of several different parts. The main sections are:

**1.** Crest—a small simple design that originally decorated a knight's helmet. The crest alone was never meant to represent family, but it's used today to personalize stationery or to stamp a special design into envelope sealing wax.

**2.** Shield—a half-oval shape. Early shields often held just a simple colored pattern; later ones were divided into quarters, showing designs representing the maternal and paternal family lines.

**3.** Supporters—a pair of animals on either side of the shield. These family protectors were chosen for their strength, intelligence, or cunning. Lions, tigers, or bears were popular supporters.

**4.** Motto—a short phrase or saying. Some families today have silly mottoes like "When the going gets tough, the tough go shopping." What would be your family motto?

Biking the World

## TRACING YOUR COAT OF ARMS

Do you have a coat of arms? If so, your family name may not be enough to find it. Individuals, and not families, were awarded coats of arms. So, even if your family name is not as common as Smith, you may find a choice of coats of arms given for your name.

How do you tell which one might be your family coat of arms? You would need to find out which coat of arms was granted to a particular ancestor. It may be possible to track a likely coat of arms based on where your ancestor lived. But that may not be easy. There could have been many people in that village with that same last name. And some coats of arm are listed only by country, rather than village.

If you really want to find out if an ancestor was ever awarded an actual coat of arms, search out and contact the College of Arms in your ancestor's country. You'll probably be asked for details on your genealogy and be charged a fee, but you may end up finding an official coat of arms connected to you through a family member.

## SOMETHING ALL MY OWN

It wouldn't be official, but that's no reason why you couldn't make up a coat of arms of your own. What could you put on it? Just about anything. You might want to display your country's flag, and the national flags of your ancestors. You could show your ethnic pride by including a drawing of the Swiss Alps or the Great Wall of China, the "boot" shape of Italy, or a kangaroo. Even showing a food, such as two crossed crusty loaves of French bread, can represent your nationality. Family events can be drawn onto the shield: a knight with a sword, the landing of the Mayflower, the broken chains of slavery. You might choose to show the blue ribbon you won in a horse show, a skateboard because skateboarding is your favorite sport, a chess piece, musical notes or the instrument you play, or anything else that means something to you.

# My Coat of Arms

Have you ever heard the expression "to come through with flying colors"? It means to hold a flag high in victory after a battle, clearly showing the winner's coat of arms. Luckily, you won't need to fight a battle. First, just create a coat of arms. Later you can make it larger, attach it to a stick, and proudly fly your own colors!

## What You Need:

- paper sheets
- markers, pencils, and paints
- tracing paper
- colored construction paper
- scissors
- glue

## What To Do:

**1.** Start with the shield. Select and trace one of the shapes given here, or draw one of your own, in the center of a sheet of paper. You can also enlarge it, or cut out a pattern, then cut a shield from heavy construction paper.

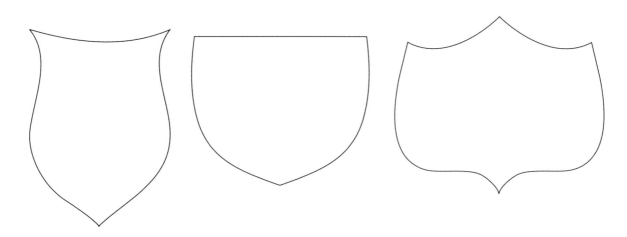

**2.** Draw lines to divide the shield in half, or into quarters. Use glue and construction paper or markers to add stripes of your favorite colors. Draw small pictures on your shield.

**3.** Draw a crest above the shield—a small and easy-to-recognize drawing to represent you, or your family.

**4.** If you wish, add a pair of supporters—one on each side of the shield, facing the center.

**5.** Think of a motto (short is best) and print it at the bottom of your coat of arms. It looks nicer on a ribbon, but you don't need one, just the motto.

Now you have a coat of arms. You can hang it on the outside of your door, or frame it to hang up in your room.

▲ *Childhood photos like this are always nice to look back on.*

*Even a simple snapshot can become a lovely family portrait.* ►

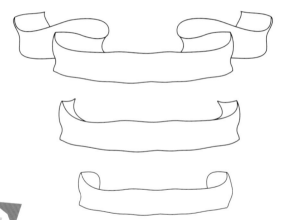

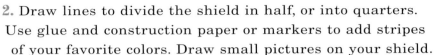

More information on heraldry and making your own coat of arms can be found at www.yourchildlearns.com/heraldry.htm.

52

# Chapter 9
# MAKING THE CONNECTIONS

Imagine that some relatives you've never met have come to visit. Suddenly one of them steps up to you and shakes your hand. "Hi, I'm Fred Jacobs, your third cousin, twice removed."

"Huh?" You know what a cousin is, but what's a third cousin? And "twice removed?" What's that mean? Family connections can be really complicated so in genealogy, it's important to be really precise. To start, here are some handy definitions:

- First cousin—a child of your aunt or uncle.
- Second cousin—a family member who shares great-grandparents with you, but not the same grandparents.
- Third and fourth cousins—third cousins share great-great-grandparents; fourth cousins share great-great-great grandparents, and... Well, you get the idea.

"Removed" means that the two people involved are not in the same generation. For example, you and your first cousins are in the same generation, probably both about the same age. A cousin is "once removed" if that cousin is in your parents' generation. It's like moving from the children's table to the adult table at big family dinners.

# FAMILY RELATIONSHIPS

Here is a chart to help you figure it out.

1. What is your relationship to the common ancestor? Find it in the row along the top of the grid.

2. What is the other person's relationship with that same common ancestor? Find it in the column down the left side.

3. Follow your row down and the other person's column across. The box where the column and the row meet in the grid tells you your relationship to that other person. For example, you are the grandchild (second column) of a common ancestor, your grandmother. You want to figure out who you are to another grandchild (second row) of that same ancestor. Match the two up on the grid! You are first cousins!

Note: In the chart opposite, G = Great.

Here's a little practice on the chart. Can you figure out these relationships?

1) You are a great-grandchild. Who are you to another great-grandchild?

2) You are a son. What relation is a great-granddaughter to you?

3) You are a great-grandchild. Who are you to a grandchild?

**Answer**

1) A great-grandchild and a great grandchild are second cousins.

2) A great-granddaughter and a son. The granddaughter is the son's grandniece.

3) A great-grandchild and a grandchild are first cousins once removed.

| Common Ancestor | You are | | | | | |
|---|---|---|---|---|---|---|
| Other person ↓ | son or daughter | grandchild | G-grandchild | G-G-grandchild | G-G-G-grandchild | G-G-G-G-grandchild |
| son/ daughter | brother or sister | nephew/ niece | grand nephew or grand niece | G-grand nephew/ niece | G-G-grand nephew/ niece | G-G-G-grand nephew/ niece |
| grandchild | nephew or niece | 1st cousin | 1st cousin once removed | 1st cousin twice removed | 1st cousin 3 times removed | 1st cousin 4 times removed |
| G-grandchild | grand nephew or grand niece | 1st cousin once removed | 2nd cousin | 2nd cousin once removed | 2nd cousin twice removed | 2nd cousin 3 times removed |
| G-G-grandchild | G-grand nephew/ niece | 1st cousin twice removed | 2nd cousin once removed | 3rd cousin | 3rd cousin once removed | 3rd cousin twice removed |
| G-G-G-grandchild | G-G-grand nephew/ niece | 1st cousin 3 times removed | 2nd cousin twice removed | 3rd cousin once removed | 4th cousin | 4th cousin once removed |
| G-G-G-G-grandchild | G-G-G-grand nephew/ niece | 1st cousin 4 times removed | 2nd cousin 3 times removed | 3rd cousin twice removed | 4th cousin once removed | 5th cousin |

No one expects you to memorize all this. Just keep the chart handy (put in a bookmark). Once you really get into family relationships, it's a reference tool that can't be beat.

## Chapter 10
# WINDOWS ON THE PAST

One good reason to look at the past is to try to predict the future. If many people in your family have had trouble with asthma, it could mean that you and future generations will too. Many diseases are passed down through the genes. This doesn't mean that just because some family members have heart disease, everyone will. Still, it is more likely to be a problem, so extra check-ups would be a good idea. And, with today's better health care and medicines, illnesses that were once a death sentence are now curable.

## TRACKING MEDICAL HISTORY

Diabetes, asthma, high cholesterol, heart disease: How can you find medical information of this kind about your family?

● A death certificate sometimes can give clues. Does it list the cause of death as heart disease or stroke?

- Relatives can sometimes provide answers. Your uncle may remember that your grandmother had terrible headaches or had to watch the sugar she ate, which would indicate diabetes.
- Obituaries can also give clues, too. If cause of death is not mentioned, a suggestion to send donations to an organization such as the Diabetes Foundation or American Heart Association would indicate what health problem that person had.

You should know that the names of many diseases have changed over time. If your great-grandmother tells you a granduncle had a terrible case of consumption, you may not have a clue what she's talking about. But you might if she called it what it is known as today: TB (for tuberculosis).

## MATCH THE ILLNESS

Let's play a match game. Here is a list of health problems of years past. They're still around today, but with different names. See if you can match the old names with what they're called today, then check out your answers on the next page.

| Years Past | | Today |
|---|---|---|
| Apoplexy | ___ | a. heart failure |
| Dropsy | ___ | b. typhus |
| Glandular fever | ___ | c. tonsillitis |
| Grippe | ___ | d. mononucleosis |
| Jail fever | ___ | e. pneumonia |
| Lockjaw | ___ | f. flu |
| Quincy | ___ | g. stroke |
| Lung fever | ___ | h. tetanus |

**Answer**

| | | |
|---|---|---|
| Apoplexy | _g_ | stroke |
| Dropsy | _a_ | heart failure |
| Glandular | _d_ | mononucleosis fever |
| Grippe | _f_ | flu |
| Jail fever | _b_ | typhus |
| Lockjaw | _h_ | tetanus |
| Quincy | _c_ | tonsillitis |
| Lung fever | _e_ | pneumonia |

# WORDS, LIKE FASHIONS, ALSO GO OUT OF DATE

When reading or hearing family stories, you may come across other words you don't recognize. Usually you can figure out the meaning of a word from the words surrounding it. Sometimes, it's a word you think you know, but it doesn't seem to mean what you think it does! You're at a total loss! Don't be afraid to ask questions! Sometimes the meanings of words change and some words can

mean several things. It helps to try to look up strange words in a dictionary. Even slang words can be found there. Learning slang from the past is also a part of the fun of discovering your family's world.

## Family Slang Dictionary

Do you use slang words when talking to friends? Well, believe it or not your parents, and their parents, did too. No wonder people of different generations don't always understand each other! Why not make a dictionary of slang words that were popular when your parents and grandparents were growing up?

### What You Need:
- small notebook
- pen or pencil

### What To Do:
**1.** Talk to your grandparents. Make up a list of words or phrases that they used to say. Write them (along with what they mean, and how they were used) in the little notebook. Some words might be "the cat's pajamas," or "groovy." Mark those pages as words your grandparents' used.

**2.** Now it's your parents' turn. Ask them what slang words they used to use. Write the words or phrases down on their pages along with the meanings.

**3.** Finally, add your own slang words to the notebook, and what you mean when you say them. Transfer the lists to the proper pages in your loose-leaf workbook, too, for safekeeping.

**4.** Now, look through the pages of your family slang dictionary with your parents and grandparents (and uncles and aunts, and cousins of all ages) when the family gets together. What a great way to learn to understand each other better! And someday, when future generations look at the book, they will know how to speak your "slanguage," too.

# Chapter 11
# THE GEOGRAPHY OF GENEALOGY

*W*here did your family come from? Where did they settle? Where did they move to after that? Maps can often point you in the right direction.

Old and new maps can help you track down information about your family. Actual birth, death, and property records are usually kept in state or county offices. If you have a general idea where a relative lived, a map of the area may confirm the name of the county and where records about the people who lived there may be kept. These archived records can provide all sorts of terrific information.

But don't rush off to find the latest, most complete map. Place names have been known to change over the years. Maybe a map dating back to when your relative was alive is more likely to be of help. It would show the old, original name of towns and their boundaries then. In early America, the boundary lines of townships and even states were flexible. You don't want to waste time researching a relative who, according to some record, lived in Connecticut, only to find out that the area was then a part of Rhode Island. State lines now are pretty much set, but county and town names or boundary lines are still changed or adjusted from time to time.

*Could you ever imagine your great, great grand-mother on a camel!*

What about world maps? Depending on where your ancestors are from, finding the proper map may even be more important. Over the years, countries have also changed names; for example, Ceylon to Sri Lanka (1972), Northern Rhodesia to Zambia (1964), and British Guiana to Guyana (1966). More recently, the countries that became part of the Union of Soviet Socialist Republics (USSR), or Russia, generations ago went back to their old names—or took on new ones—when the "Soviet bloc" broke up in 1989. And changes still go on today in various parts of the world.

Look for older maps in atlases, libraries, county or city offices, or online at historical map sites. If you can't find what you need, try looking online for information on specific place names. A search for "U.S. Place Names," for example, will bring you to a helpful site with free look-ups. Not only can you search and get information on just about every place name—you can click to see an aerial view of the site!

# THE GEOGRAPHY TRAIL

Here's your chance to really play detective. Look for clues, those details in the maps, that may bring your ancestors to life. If you know an ancestor lived somewhere near Phoenix, Arizona, look for any maps that will show you, in the greatest detail, the area where your ancestor lived. Look for locations within a county. Keep an eye out for maps that show the borders of neighboring areas. Courthouses or county offices in those areas might be good places to look for information about your relatives.

Some places are very difficult to find. It's not just that they may have changed their name. Some townships were simply too small to show up on a map. Others may have died out, becoming "ghost towns" that aren't on any modern map at all. That's where old maps are helpful. You can also find lists of things like abandoned post offices, which could offer important clues for you. If you know the neighborhood or street where an ancestor lived, you may find it! Try to find a map that was created around the time your ancestor was alive. That's likely to be the most accurate and helpful. You can find this kind of map at local libraries or museums. Ask the librarian or historical society for help.

# MAPS CAN TELL YOU

## 1. How your relatives lived

Maps can show you if an area was densely populated or rural, if there were many highways, or if it was mountainous. You can get an idea where your relatives were born, resided, attended school, worked, shopped, voted, traveled over land or water, raised families, and were laid to rest. Later maps of the

*Maybe some of your ancestors ▲ grew up on a farm too.*

same area might help you track down their children, and their children's children. Maybe you'll turn up some third, fourth, fifth, and sixth cousins you didn't know about.

## 2. What the land looked like

With certain types of maps, called "relief maps," you can see whether your relative lived in the mountains or on hilly terrain, or near small rivers or lakes. Relief maps may show conditions that would make moving or traveling to other areas difficult. Rivers that have bridges now, may not have had them when your family members lived nearby. Instead of trying to cross it, they may have traveled the river on boats because it was easier than making their way on land, through dense forests. Your ancestors may have even used the river to bring produce to market or go to school! Compare an old map to more modern ones, and you'll be able to see when and where new roads or bridges sprang up.

## 3. What your ancestors might have done for a living

If they lived near the ocean, maybe family members were fishermen. Turning up relatives in a mining town probably meant that they worked in the mines. People often worked where they lived, so consider each bit of information you uncover a valuable clue, and go from there. If you think an ancestor who lived in a heavily wooded area in Oregon in the early 1900s was a logger, and you haven't yet searched census records, why not try an online search for "Oregon loggers 1900s." Maybe you'll discover some interesting information on him.

## 4. What your ancestors did for fun

Maps can give tantalizing clues. Maybe your kin slid down grassy or snowy slopes on makeshift sleds, hiked or explored inviting caves in nearby hills, hunted in the woods, or swam in surrounding lakes. A special occasion may have meant a trip to town to catch the latest styles, or a reason to get together for a dress-up dance party. If your ancestors lived in the middle of the prairie, with no neighbors nearby, they still could have read, or made music and sung and laughed together. And at night, they might have sat outside, and pointed out pictures they imagined in the stars.

## WHAT'S IN A NAME?

Many place names are similar, or even the same (the U.S. has close to 85 places called Springfield). This can make your work harder. Even if a relative mentions that his grandmother lived in Tioga County, it doesn't mean it's Tioga County, New York. There's also a Tioga County bordering it, in Pennsylvania. New Jersey alone has four different villages called Washington. Which is the one where an ancestor lived?

When faced with place names, you'll need specifics or need to dig deeper. Use any clues you may find. Maybe one village was on a rocky hillside while another bordered a lake. If an ancestor wrote in her diary, "Went swimming again this morning. I'm so happy we live near a lake!" you can smile—you've probably found the correct Washington; but check out the other two, just in case. Pulling clues together and making connections is what makes you a good detective.

## Family Movement Map

So future generations can see who lived where, why not map your family's movements? When you're done, photos of the map can be tucked away for safekeeping in your big family scrapbook. Be sure to make extras. Family members will certainly be asking for copies of their own.

### What You Need:
- an appropriate map
- yarn or string
- clear removable tape or pushpins
- copies of photographs
- scissors

64

## What You Do:

1. Spread out the map and hang it against a wall.

2. Using clear tape or pushpins, affix a small photo (or photo copies) on the map where each family member lives (or lived).

3. Using a section of yarn, connect the children of a family to their parents. For example, if your great-grandparents lived in Utah, but their son moved with his family to Maine, attach a strip of yarn connecting the photo of the grandparents in Utah to the son and his family in Maine. If your family is more spread out, you can connect parents who live in Hong Kong with their five children: a son in Los Angeles, another in Sydney, Australia, and daughters in a suburb of Paris, one in Boston, and the youngest in Boulder, Colorado.

# Chapter 12

# FAMILY HISTORY STORIES

Have you heard the one about how your great-uncle Tom gobbled sixteen blueberry pies at a pie-eating contest and then went home and ate a full dinner? Does everyone still laugh about the how Grandma Ida Marie ran off and became a trapeze artist, then surprised everyone by becoming the toast of the town? Why do you think stories like these are repeated over and over? It's not just because they're such great stories. It's because they reveal as much about the person as a great photograph can.

Family stories can be about people doing everyday things, about their being part of great historical events, or just about places they've been and things they've seen. Such stories are just as much family heirlooms as a prized old pocket watch or a carefully preserved wedding dress.

## THE STORYTELLING TRADITION

Stories from the past can affect our lives even today. Here's one about an immigrant who arrived at Ellis Island about a hundred years ago. At the time, doctors at the center examined everyone. If they were sick, the doctor chalked an X on the back of their coat. Immigrants marked with the X would be held for a short time on the island to see if they got better. If they didn't get well, they were sent back. It was a terrible thing for people who had left everything, looking for freedom and better lives in America, to be turned away.

One day, a doctor listened to an immigrant's breathing sounds. He didn't like what he heard so he quickly chalked an X on the man's back. The man knew what that meant. In a panic, he looked out across the water at the land he was so desperate to reach. Suddenly, he turned and ran, then dove straight into the water, swimming for shore!

By the time he made it ashore, the police were waiting and easily took the exhausted man into custody. He was taken to court, but the judge hearing the story was more amazed than angry. "If you're healthy enough to swim that distance, you're certainly healthy enough to make it here," he said. Then he made it official—"You can stay."

The story is a true one—a family legend of a friend of mine. Every time someone was about to give up on something they truly wanted, she tells me, the story of the grandfather who swam to shore was retold. The message was: if your grandfather could overcome great odds, so can you! It made my friend proud! And it made her feel that, just like her grandfather, she could do anything if she set her mind to it.

Family stories knit generations together. They can encourage, console, or sometimes just make you laugh. And they can make you feel closer to your ancestors.

## MORE THAN A STORY

Family stories can also provide clues to finding out more information about your family. As part of a story, someone might mention the name of the town where a relative you've been searching for used to live. A story about great-grandma's prize quilt might lead you to a quilting organization with lists of present and past members online.

The collecting of family stories is sometimes called taking "oral histories," because they are verbal records of a time and a place. All this can help you in your genealogical research. You've

▲ *Clothing styles and city brownstones help to date and place a picture.*

read about World War II in your history books, but imagine how much more alive that dry information will be if you hear about it from someone who actually lived through it—someone related to you!

What will you do with these family stories? Besides helping you in your research, you may want to write out some of them and include them in your family scrapbook. For example, in her section, you might write out Grandma's story about how she met Grandpa. Or you can copy down all the stories and put them together in their own separate book. Or, if you taped the stories, you can make a new tape of all the best stories. Then make copies, or put the whole thing on CD, to give to family members.

## TAKING ORAL HISTORIES

There's an art to collecting family stories. Once you have the tools: pencils, notebook, and maybe a small tape recorder, the first thing you'll need to do is know how to listen. Give all your attention to the storyteller, and don't interrupt. Save your questions for the end. Don't rush the speaker, or criticize. How would you feel if you were telling a story and someone said, "Could you tell the story a little faster?" or "This part is boring, can we skip it and get to the good parts?" Instead, say things like, "This is fascinating!" or "I could listen forever!" with an interested look on your face. It's a sure way to get the storyteller to answer your follow-up questions and want to tell you more.

# MAKE UP A LIST OF QUESTIONS

Don't put someone on the spot by asking them to "Tell me a story about your life." Prepare a list of questions to help start things off. And don't forget a notebook or tape recorder to record their answers.

Here are a few starter or follow-up questions you may want to ask:

## Places

1. Where did you grow up?
2. What was your house like?
3. Where did you buy your clothes or shop for food?
4. What did you do for fun where you lived?
5. Did you travel? Where? What did you see?

## People

1. What were your parents like?
2. Do you remember your teachers?
3. Who did you admire most when you were growing up?
4. Who would you say played a part in changing your life?
5. Who was the first person you fell in love with and why?

## In Those Days

1. Can you tell me something about when you first moved here?
2. What kind of work did you and other family members do?
3. What was going on in the world that you remember most?
4. How did what happened affect you and the family?
5. How has life changed for you since then?

## Emotions

1. What story about yourself or your family makes you smile?
2. What story about yourself or your family makes you laugh?
3. What story about yourself or your family makes you cry?
4. What story about yourself or your family makes you wonder about things?
5. What story about yourself or your family makes you feel proud?

# The W's of Story Writing:

The first thing news reporters learn is to answer, in their stories, the five "W"s—Who, What, Where, When, and Why. Who is telling the story? What happened in the story? Where did the story take place? When did the story take place? Why is this story important? Tag on a "How" question and you can ask just about anything (now you're on your way to becoming a news reporter).

## WHAT'S YOUR STORY?

You're part of your family tree, too. So don't forget to write down your own stories. They will be memories that you can hand down to future generations. Keep them and any other family stories, in your loose-leaf workbook or put them in the family scrapbook.

◄ *Car models can help date photographs-early ones had running boards.*

# Chapter 13
# THE WAY THEY WERE

## Were the good old days really so good?

Grandparents, and their grandparents, might have mentioned or talked at length about how much better things were in "the old days." Their memories might have softened over time—because life in the "good old days" wasn't always easy. For example:

- Frontier women did laundry by putting it in washtubs and stamping on it with their feet, pounding it with rocks on a riverbank, or scrubbing it against a washboard.
- Until as late as 1860, pigs were free to roam urban American streets. This was encouraged because they would eat the garbage left strewn all over the roads.
- Federal child labor laws were passed in 1938. Before then, children often were made to work 12 to 15 hours a day in factories. If they got hurt or couldn't work, they were quickly replaced by others who needed the jobs. Before 1900, a third of all mill hands were children.

What about life today do you think could stand improvement? Imagine how things might be in the future. For example, do you hate having to take a daily vitamin? Some day, there might be a type of "vitamin pill" given to you at birth that would take care of all your vitamin needs for your entire life!

## WRITE A LETTER TO THE PAST

Pick one of your ancestors and write a letter to them. What would you say to your great-great-grandfather who came over from Poland? What would you tell him about yourself? What would you want to ask him? What do you think he would say to you?

## BE A GREAT-GREAT-GREAT FOR A DAY!

Recently, a few television stations ran several so-called "reality" shows where families, or groups of strangers who agreed to take part, lived together as pioneers did hundreds of years ago. They had no running water, no electricity. They wore the same kinds of clothes and used the same tools as the pioneers did, and grew and ate the same food as in "the old days." To make things even more realistic, some were given a list of rules to follow, based on those the pioneers lived under so long ago.

Even if you didn't see these shows, you can still imagine what life was like. Think about what you have now that they didn't. You can start with running water; and not only running water but hot and cold running water!

But back then...You open your eyes and try to wake up. There's no running water but you might splash your face from a basin of cold water (of course, in winter you would first have to break the film of ice covering it)! No indoor plumbing, so you know what a hassle it would be dealing with that! And forget taking a real bath or a shower.

Now, what was life like for your great-grandparents and grandparents? That's not as long ago as pioneer days, but what do you suppose they had at your age?

- Pen and ink or fountain pens, then ball points; no markers or highlighters or gel pens.
- Telegraph or dial-up telephones; definitely no wireless, or take-everywhere cell phones!

- Radio programs (think TV drama, sit-coms, concerts without a picture); no recorded music or call-in talk shows
- Wind-up, then thankfully, electric phonographs playing 78 rpm (revolutions per minute) records with one song on each side, then albums at 45 and 33 1/3rd rpm. No music-to-go, available 24/7.
- Silent movies, talkies, 3-D, stereo-sound, and wide-screen. Movie theater give-away nights and family car drive-ins. No DVDs to bring the theater experience right into your home.
- Propeller-driven planes, steam trains, automobiles with sideboards, trailers, but no vans or SUVs.

- Black-and-white TV, then color; no flat, wide, and hang-on-your-wall screens with news instantly "beamed in" from around the world.
- Manual, then electric typewriters; now, personal computers and printers, fax machines, digital cameras, even cell phones that take pictures, all unknown to your grandparents in "their day," are there for you today.

In the kitchen, your grandmother's mother probably had a wood- or oil-burning stove and an "ice-box" to keep things cold (the melting ice collected in a pan underneath and would overflow if she didn't empty it in time). For entertainment, books were always around, but forget computer games. Games were on boards and meant for two (chess, checkers) or a whole family to play together. Early TV had only a few channels, and programs were on for only a few hours a day. The shows were "live" so if someone made a mistake or something unexpected happened (think "Funniest Home Videos") everyone who was tuned in saw it! No hundred channels coming into your home by cable or bounced off satellites! No pictures sent back from cameras launched into outer space or "rovered" around on nearby planets.

Girls, you wouldn't be deciding what you wanted to be when you grow up. You were expected to marry and stay home, keeping house and taking care of your family while your husband went out to work. Your days would be spent canning, cooking, washing, ironing, and sewing. Of course, many of those things are still done today, but time-saving devices (washer/dryers, microwave ovens, sewing machines) have made things a lot easier. Now, people have the right to decide for themselves what they want to do with their lives and see how far they can go—whether it's to win gold medals at the Olympics, be the first one in the family to get a Ph.D. degree, or fly to Mars.

Yes, things have changed a lot over the years from your grandmother to you. Can you even imagine what things your grandchildren will see when you reach the age your grandmother is now? What will the world be like in your children's future?

## Genealogical timeline

Things are constantly changing, and it's hard to imagine what effect these changes had on your ancestors and older family members. Sometimes, to understand things, it helps to see them. Since your family stretches back through time, you can get a better picture of their life changes by making a genealogical timeline.

### What You Need:

- photographs, news clippings, historical items
- lightweight clothesline or twine
- small paper clips
- colored yarn or ribbon
- stick-on labels

## What to Do:

**1.** Gather some family photos, or make copies. You'll want pictures of your grandparents from babyhood to the present, of your mom and dad, and of yourself, too. Look for house photos: the one your great-grandparents lived in, the one your grandparents lived in and, finally, the house you live in now. If you want more, consider photos of family pets through the years, the cars your family owned, groups at special occasions, even favorite toys.

**2.** Put all the pictures in order chronologically, meaning the oldest ones first.

**3.** Tie a length of clothesline, twine, or ribbon so it stretches across a wall of your room. This is your basic timeline.

**4.** Divide the timeline into time periods by tying and hanging down some colored yarn or ribbon to represent time periods of ten, twenty-five, or fifty years. Tie them loosely so that space can be adjusted based on the number of photographs you want to hang.

**5.** To make the timeline's years easier to see, write the time periods (1920s, for example) on labels and attach them to the hanging markers.

**6.** Clip each photo from the pile onto the timeline, starting at the left: Your grandfather as a young boy. The year he was twenty-two. Your mom when she was five, and when she and your dad got married. Adjust the positions and time period markers as you go to fill the timeline with photographs.

**7.** If there's room, add historical information such as special dates, illustrations, and clippings from books. For example, if a relative fought in World War II, attach photographs or newspaper items about the war in that space on the timeline.

What did they do before these popular inventions? Ask your mom, dad, grandparents, and great-grandparents:

| | | | | | |
|---|---|---|---|---|---|
| ballpoint pen | 1938 | credit card | 1950 | roller blades | 1979 |
| Band-Aids | 1920 | crossword puzzle | 1913 | spiral notebook | 1924 |
| bar-code scanner | 1969 | hula hoop | 1958 | teabag | 1904 |
| | | jet engine | 1930 | 3-D movies | 1922 |
| bubble gum | 1928 | Post-it notes | 1974 | zipper | 1913 |

# Chapter 14
# FAMILY TRADITIONS

A tradition can be anything from going to Midnight Mass on Christmas Eve each year to always saying "bunny, bunny, bunny" for good luck when you wake up. What traditions have been handed down in your family?

Many families have a tradition of eating dinner together. It's a chance to talk over what happened during the day, or to air out problems. One friend took part in "family night." Her father would read something aloud and the family would discuss it and use it as a stepping-stone to more conversation. Another family I know had "game night." They would pull out a favorite board game, put out bowls of snacks, and sit around the table and play together. What do you think would be a great activity for your family to do every week? Go bowling? Cook dinner together?

If you do start a new family tradition, maybe it will still be going strong when your grandchildren are your age.

## CELEBRATION TIME!

What does your family celebrate? Christmas, Hanukkah, or Kwanza? A friend of mine picks up a small evergreen tree each year and decorates it with dreidels and Stars of David instead of Christmas balls. Or maybe your family celebrates Ramadan, Cinco de Mayo, or Asian New Year. The calendar is full of special days and opportunities for celebrating—and for starting new traditions.

The birthday cake was a new tradition a little over two hundred years ago. It started in Germany as a cake of sweetened bread dough. Birthday candles were lit so the smoke, on blowing them out, would carry your unspoken wish up to the gods.

So why not come up with your own family reason for celebrating, and schedule it every year on a certain date. It could be as simple as, every spring, planting marigolds in a small portion of your backyard to celebrate new life. The choices are as open as your imagination!

## TRADITIONAL FOODS

Certain foods are traditional for special holidays: hamentashen, cookies shaped like little 3-sided hats celebrate the Jewish holiday of Purim. Christmas cookies are flat shapes decorated with red and green sugar, while turkey and cranberry sauce is fine for Thanksgiving feasting. Countries around the world have traditional foods for holidays and family meals. If your ancestors lived in the South, chances are they ate more sweet potato pie, grits, and collard greens than their relatives in Boston, who tended toward Boston baked beans and Boston cream pie.

## HOME COOKING?

"It's just like mother used to make." How many times have you heard someone say that? Yes, holidays are good reasons for special fancy meals, and old-fashioned home cooking often deserves the highest praise any meal can get! It means food that's cooked with love and with care. And special recipes often have secret ingredients that are handed down from generation to generation. It's a great way to keep in contact with your ancestors. Make your great great-great grandmother's brownies the way she did, and you are recreating a part of your past!

Back when people didn't have cookbooks or the Internet to look for recipes, they wrote them out and handed them out, often on index cards, as gifts. My mother's recipe cards were often faded and worn from use. We looked forward to those family favorites. Why not make your own recipe box and stock it with your family's favorite recipes?

Collect every recipe you can find that has been handed down by family members (ask if they have more) and make a special family recipe box to hold them. Do some research and you may even find some recipes that an ancestor might have enjoyed. Then title them with zingy names such as Aunt Martha's Marvelous Munchy Candy Mounds, Uncle Bob's Spicy-Licious Barbeque Sauce, or Cousin Irma's Devilishly Delicious Devils' Food Cake.

## Recipe Box

When you're in a mood to cook, it's great to have your family's favorite recipes all in the same place. So now's the time to get started on this kitchen project.

### What To Do:

- photo storage or shoe box
- magazine clippings of anything to do with food. (Cut out pictures, and even lettering, to decorate your box with "Good Eating!" or "What's Cooking?")
- scissors
- white glue
- plastic dish
- soft brush
- tempura paint
- colored index cards to fit box

### What To Do:

1. First, paint your box a bright color. Be sure to let it dry completely!
2. Select pictures and lettering, and decide on a pattern.
3. Pour some glue into a plastic dish. Use a soft brush to apply the glue to the back of your paper cutouts and put them in place on the box.

**4.** Once the glue has dried, apply a thin layer of glue all over the box.

**5.** While the box is drying, write out or glue recipes on the cards—longer recipes both front and back, or on two or more cards stapled together.

**6.** Put the recipes in your box.

## Fun Facts

- Apples have been around for many years, but applesauce wasn't invented until 1390.
- The first potato chips (fried potatoes cut "thin") were made in 1853.
- It was at the 1904 World's Fair in St. Louis that ice cream and waffles were brought together-and the ice-cream cone was born.
- Believe it or not, none of your relatives tasted Jell-O® before 1910. That's when the quivering dessert was first invented.

## FAMILY SONGS

In the Appalachian Mountains, there is a tradition called "song catching." For years before the invention and popular use of tape recorders, people would "catch" songs. They were sung over and over until a younger person memorized them. In this way, their songs were passed down from generation to generation, in much the same way as oral histories were. Of course, as people took turns singing the songs, they sometimes changed them. A young woman with a nice soprano voice might have added some high trills, while an expert banjo player put in extra chords and harmonies. One singer probably sang a tune softly, while another sang out gleefully. It may have been the same song, but people sang it differently.

Historical events have also led to other kinds of songs. During World War II everybody, including your relatives, were probably singing along to the morale building "Boogie Woogie Bugle Boy from Company B," made famous by the Andrews Sisters. Another song, dating from the Revolutionary War, is still known today as "Yankee Doodle." The song was actually written by the British, making fun of the colonists as know-nothing bumpkins! Instead of getting upset, the colonists took the song as their own and sang it with pride. What songs do you suppose your ancestors sang and what did the songs mean to them? Ask your older family members to sing some traditional songs that they remember from their childhood. Maybe you can "catch them." Or make a whole tape of traditional songs.

## TAPE SOME FAVORITES

Get in tune with the songs that have been enjoyed by family members over the years. Does your Mom sing along to those "old" folk tunes her mother loved to sing, so you've learned the words, too? Does your Granddad suddenly stop talking to listen intently whenever he recognizes the great tenor voice of Pavarotti on a classical radio station? Maybe jazz, hip-hop, big band, rock-and-roll, or today's popular music is always playing in some room of your house, or through private earphones. If everybody marches to the beat of a different drummer, why not do some research and make up a "sampler" of favorites. Include something for everybody, from your Mom and Dad's special song, that they danced to at their wedding, to the tune that Grandma sings softly whenever she is sitting with her new grandchild. Set the sampler tape or CD playing at your next family barbecue or get-together, and you'll probably hear Grandpa Garcia, or Aunt Dorothy, or cousin Angelo say, "Listen, that's my favorite song." It's certainly something you'll want to keep, to remember everyone by for many years to come.

▲ *Bathing suits covered much more than they do today.*

## Chapter 15
# A FAMILY REUNION!

Now that you've gotten to know your whole family better, why not celebrate by helping them all get to know each other better, too? The best way to do this is with a family reunion. When's the last time you got together with your family? Thanksgiving dinner? New Year's Eve? When was the last time you saw ALL of your family—the aunts, cousins, nephews and second and third and even fourth cousins, too? A year ago at your Aunt Ray's wedding? Two years ago? Some families have yearly family gatherings where hundreds of members come together for picnics or parties.

Whether you make it a yearly event or a once-in-a lifetime celebration, having a family reunion is a great way for members to keep in touch. And what's more fun than a party? Although there's a lot you can do on your own, you're going to need the help of your parents for this.

First, what kind of party should you have? Give it some thought. A big picnic at the park? A barbecue in the backyard? Or will you need to rent a hall someplace? What is decided, once your parents sign on to the idea, will depend on the size of your family, the cost, when the reunion is scheduled, and what kind of things your family enjoys. Are you all beach-lovers? Or do you enjoy dressing up for formal occasions? Like jazz or classical music, or none at all? Does your family quickly line up for hotdogs and burgers from a grill, or prefer to sit down to a meal? Should you hire a DJ or live band, or can family members provide their own musical entertainment? These are all things to take into consideration.

## TIME TO SEND OUT INVITATIONS

You've got a go for the party? Good! Now, start by making up a list of those to be invited. Check it out with your parents, because you don't want to forget anyone. Some family members may live across the country, even halfway around the world. Some may have other things scheduled, so can't come. Still, they should be invited—and you may be pleasantly surprised to see them turn up or prepare something on their own to join in the family fun!

### Family Reunion Invitation

With many people to invite, it's a good idea to design and print up your own invitations. If you have a home computer, you might have a program that makes up cards so you can print them off on your own color laser printer! If not, it is perfectly fine to design a simple single-sheet invitation, to be taken and photocopied in black and white or in color.

**What You Need:**

- paper
- pens
- markers
- clippings
- access to photocopier
- envelopes to fit

*You're Invited*

**The First Annual Hobson Family Reunion!**

WHERE  The Riverdale Country Club
444 Madison Lane, Boston, Mass.

WHEN  1 TO 4 P.M., Saturday, June 4, 2005

Bring yourselves, bring your stories, bring photographs and other memorabilia to share!

RSVP TO (187) 242-6693

THE HOBSON FAMILY
1284 Dewey Road
Boston, MA 84210

**What To Do:**

1. First, decide what you want your invitation to look like. The cover could say something as simple as YOU'RE INVITED!
2. On a computer, you might scan and show a family photo; a single sheet can hold drawings or glued-on art.
3. Next, you want to give the occasion a name (The First Annual Hobson Family Reunion!), tell them where it will be (The Riverdale Country Club, 444 Madison Lane, Boston, Mass.), and when it will be (1 to 4 pm, Saturday, June 4, 2006).
4. Add a line suggesting what family members might bring, such as: Bring yourselves, your favorite stories, a family potluck with recipe. Bring special photographs and significant objects and other memorabilia to share.
5. Print the letters RSVP and your phone number. RSVP stands for the French "Repondez s'il vous plait" and asks that the person call and let you know if they will be coming or not.

Once the invitation is finished, you're ready to have as many cards or sheet invitations printed off as you need. Then all you have to do is address and stamp the envelopes, stuff them, and get them in the mail.

# A REAL FAMILY MEAL

Remember when you were collecting all those recipes for your recipe box and cook-book? Now is the time to ask family members who will be coming to make and bring their own family recipe to share. Check with them to see what, if anything, they will be able to bring. You will want to have a good selection of foods available, especially if certain family members have food allergies or need a special diet. Make up a list to see if you need another main dish, or salad or dessert, then check your family recipe box for something you would like to try—if you haven't already. If you're not an experienced cook, trying something new can be a challenge. Don't be afraid to ask your parents for help. After all, they are family, too!

## DECK THE HALLS!

To start things rolling, you might want to have a table set up where people can put the significant objects they brought with them. Your Great-aunt Ethel's first pair of roller skates, that comes with a key! The cloth doll your great-grandmother handed down to Aunt Takako. Your own first pair of baby shoes! As people arrive, they can put more and more interesting things on the table.

## AND HERE'S...THE FAMILY!

Bring out the results of your family research, and get ready for smiles:
- Your genealogical timeline—if you can't move it out of your room for the great day, you'll just have to clean up your room and invite everyone in.
- Your own family tree and genealogical loose-leaf binder—it's a good time for relatives to check over name spellings, dates, and facts. Keep a small notebook and pencil handy for any details to be changed or followed-up on.
- Your traditional and "sampler" tapes, and some albums with songs from the different decades (your parents probably have some put aside)—anybody want to sing along?
- Your oral history tape, along with written copies of favorite family stories— maybe they'll inspire a few more family members to tell stories of their own.
- Your family recipe box with favorite recipes–did anyone bring new old favorites?
- Your family scrapbook–by now you should have many pages in it, filled with photos, recipes, and facts, facts, facts.

## FAMILY PHOTO SPOT

You'll want to have a place where your reunion guests can enjoy looking over some family photos—and maybe add a few of their own. Maybe you can move your genealogical timeline from your room to the living room and leave room underneath for another line to hold photos brought by family members. If that doesn't work, put up a single line, or some shorter ones, to hang guests' photos. Attach a few pictures to start, and show what the lines are for, then leave a basket nearby with clips for your guests to use.

If there's no room for lines of photographs, set up a few cork bulletin boards. Keep pushpins handy for people to tack up any photos they brought. (If you place a pushpin off the top edge of a photo and another off the bottom edge, it can be hung without having to puncture the photograph itself.) Put out stick-on labels, pens and markers, and encourage your guests to label and identify people and places in the photos.

## LET THE FESTIVITIES BEGIN!

People coming to the reunion will bring their photos or tell stories about the people and places that mean something special to them, like the covered bridge where Grandpa proposed to Grandma! Big sister might bring her favorite Barbie, the one she got when she was six. Compare and contrast! How much have things changed. How have they stayed the same? Bring your treasures and memorabilia, too. It's show-and-tell time for everyone!

For "who's who" fun, post a variety of pictures on a bulletin board and, underneath, reveal who it is and when the photo was taken. Keep pictures of close family members together, so people can see who looks like whom. Be sure to have a group of "you must have been a beautiful baby" shots, with photos nearby of the same people as adults. See if everyone can match the baby pictures with the grown-ups they are today.

## WE'VE GOT GAMES!

Make sure you have plenty of things to do to keep the party rolling. One activity is to get everyone together for a "when I was a girl / when I was a boy" game. It's more fun when relatives of all ages (great-grandma to just-turned-teen) play. For this game, you need to prepare in advance a dozen or more slips of paper with a single question written on each. In turn, each person is asked to select a paper from the "hat," think back to when they were about 8 to 12 years old, and answer the question. Others playing the game can chime in with their answers and comments—but they still have to "select a paper" on their turn!

Here are a number of questions and requests to start you off. Add more of your own if you wish, but it's best to keep things general. You don't want to embarrass anyone.

- Who was really, really famous then and why?

- What was your favorite candy?

- What did you really love to wear?

- Sing the first two lines of your favorite song?

- Where did you like to go on summer vacations?

- What game did you like to play?

- What kind of pet did you have and why?

- What gift did you receive that was "special"?

- What movie did you go to see several times?

- Recite something that you learned in school.

- Who was President, and what was happening in the world?

- What TV or radio show did you always listen to?

- What was your favorite home-cooked meal?

- When you "went out" what was it you did?

- What happened to you that seems funny to you now, but maybe wasn't then?

## REMEMBER FAMILY PHOTOS!

Don't forget to have a couple of film or digital cameras so you or others can record this very special day. Check beforehand that the cameras are working and the film and batteries are fresh. If you have a video cam, play reporter and focus on as many family members as you can. Let each guest say a few words into the camera: Who they are. Where they are from. What family means to them. If there's no video cam, guests can still be photographed and asked to "say a few words" on audiotape. If you have your notebook handy, you might want to jot down a word or two to remind you to follow up on something. But don't try to write everything down, you won't have time. And you want to enjoy the family reunion, too!

The most important thing is, don't forget to take several photos of the whole entire clan! If you have a big family, now is a good time to gather outside, providing the weather is reasonable, and line up-shorter people, sitters and kneelers in front. (Ask if everyone can see the camera.) Maybe you can have a photographer come by, or a neighbor who is handy with a camera can take few shots—and a few more "just in case"—so nobody in the family will be left out of these very special photos.

# Chapter 16

# KEEPING IN TOUCH

Just because the reunion is over, doesn't mean the good times have to stop. There are lots of ways you can still keep in touch and share! Treasure your First Annual Family Reunion by gathering photos and preserving all those terrific memories for the next family get-together. Find the best photo of the whole family. Scan it onto thank-you cards, or have copies of the photo made to send to everyone. Photos can also be sent to those who didn't come—maybe next year, they'll be the first to arrive for the fun!

## START A FAMILY NEWSLETTER

In the meantime, a newsletter is a great way for a family to keep in touch and share news. You can take your list of all the people you invited to the reunion, including the ones who weren't able to come, and turn it into a newsletter mailing list. When would you send out your newsletter? Maybe once a year at holiday time? Midway between family reunions? Maybe even twice a year, six months apart? What will you call the newsletter? How about *The _____ Family Bugle?*

The most important details are: What is the newsletter going to say? How will you get the "news" for the newsletter?

Before you even think of that first issue, send a brief note to everyone telling them that you are starting a family newsletter. Ask that whenever they have news to report, or have family photos taken, they e-mail (if you have e-mail) or snail mail them to you! Tell them that you'd like to know things such as:

- Did anything special happen recently?

- How has the year been for you?

- What were the good things that happened?

- Did any bad things happen, that you want to tell us about?

- If you go to work, did anything interesting happen on the job?

- If you are in school, what are you studying?

- What movies did you see this year? Which ones did you especially like?

- What books did you read this year? What was your favorite and why?

- Did you watch any sports? Which teams do you root for?

Include questions on any other topics you'd like to hear about—most likely others in the family would also enjoy hearing. Then, gather up all the responses, put them in a folder, and refer to them when you write the text of your newsletter. Remember: try to include in the item as many answers as possible to: Who, What, Where, When, Why, and How. That's what the readers of your newsletter are going to want to know. Also, try to include as many different relatives in each newsletter as you can—so that they can look for mentions of themselves as well as catching up on other family members.

Next, you have to decide what your newsletter will look like. Will it be a hand-printed sheet that you photocopy, or a page or two printed out by computer on colored sheets of paper, or a file sent by e-mail? Do you want to include photographs? Do you want a "Good News" section? Do you want to share recipes? How about information on favorite travel spots? Maybe you want to add some original poems and stories, too. And don't forget items about the last family reunion, or reminders about the next family reunion you might be planning!

# LAUNCH A FAMILY WEBSITE

Whatever you can do with a newsletter, you can arrange to do on a website. With your family's permission and help, the right computer software, and some technical know-how, you might be able to get a website up and running yourself. Otherwise, there are books available to tell you what to do and how to do it, and websites that can help you set one up—or set it up for you. A website can be as creative and unique as you like, show photographs in full color, and even include short videos or animation. Since websites can be accessed from around the world, family members don't have to live right next door anymore, or down the block, or even in the next township over. People can live anywhere around the world and still be...family!

◀ *Lucky you, if a sign tells where a photo was taken.*

*And you ▶ thought great grandpa only used a cane as he got older!*

# Chapter 17

# BACK TO THE FUTURE

It's been fun, and through genealogy, you've gotten to know your whole family better, maybe going back to long before you were born. Now, what would you like family members still to come—your children, your children's children, and great- and grandnephews and nieces—to know about you? Why not put together a personal time capsule? You can leave them all a unique message that says, "Hello!" What better way is there to bring your whole family—past, present, and future members—together?

# A "My time" Capsule

The hardest part of a time capsule is deciding what to put inside. But whatever you do, don't forget to include copies of your family tree research. You'll be saving your descendants from having to do all that information gathering all over again.

## What You Need:

- a container (coffee can, cookie tin, small box, plastic bag or wrapping)
- markers
- items that say "my time"
- a safe place

What do you think your great-great grandkids would want to know about you and your time? What will you put in?

**1.** Photos: Put together a small photo album showing your family at work and play—how they live and dress. Label or caption each photo with the person's name and date, and where the photo was taken. Remember to include pictures of yourself, your friends, your room—after all, this is your capsule!

**2.** Clothing: What are the latest styles? Put in a pair of those squiggly laces you like for sneakers. Show you're a fan—include a baseball cap naming your favorite team.

**3.** Technology: You may not want to put in your prized MP3 player, but you can tuck in a photo and description of it and how much it cost. Cut out ads with prices for other "wish list" items—in the far future, they may not even be a memory.

**4.** Food: Avoid treating generations of ants to your favorite candy bar—a neatly flattened wrapper or two will do. What do you like to eat? Add a list. Maybe the finder of your time capsule will have the same taste in foods.

**5.** Newspapers: Today's headlines! Newspaper decays, so protect paper items in heavy plastic, or laminate clippings that mean something special to you and your family.

## MORE STUFF FOR YOUR TIME CAPSULE

Want to get closer to your family to come? Maybe some day you'll sit in a rocker and tell your grandkids stories about when you were their age. Maybe even your great-grandchildren. But your time capsule may not be found until after you're gone, and you're living it now. So, here's your chance. Write a letter to those future generations.

Here's an example:
> Dear great, great, great, great grandkids,
> My name is Elaine. It's 2003 and I'm eleven. George W. Bush is President. Living in Boston is lots of fun because there's so much to do: museums and shopping and movies and just hanging out and playing Frisbee in the Boston Commons. I intend to be an award-winning scientist when I grow up.

## TAKING THE GRAND TOUR

In the 1960s, Jacqueline Kennedy, the wife of President John F. Kennedy, gave TV viewers a historic guided tour of the White House. Why not treat your grandkids, or great-great grandkids, to a guided tour of the place you call home?

Do you have a video or regular camera? Buy, borrow, or rent one and produce your own tour. Start from the outside of your house and work your way in. Label your photos, or write or talk about what each room is used for—here's where I beat my brother at chess. Here's where my mother writes her novels. Point out interesting facts. This is the desk where I wrote my first short story! Here's where I go when I'm in a bad mood and want to be by myself. Make the tour as personal as you'd like—it's in the family, after all.

## DO NOT OPEN UNTIL...

Assemble everything into your time capsule. Identify it and mark it with a "Do not open until" date: 20 years from now, 30 years, maybe 50 years. Even New Year's Eve of the year 3000 (although you may not be around to see it)! On your genealogy page in your loose-leaf notebook, make a note about the time capsule (the date you made it up and where you put it) so that it is not forgotten and lost forever. Make sure that it is properly protected, and then put it away somewhere.

Where will you put your time capsule?

- In the backyard: If you bury it, draw yourself a map to remind yourself where it is. Protect the time capsule from water and other damage by wrapping it in strong plastic bags or sheeting.
- Hidden under a staircase, or behind a loose board in a wall: Out of sight, out of mind.
- In the attic: Put it out of the way, so it isn't accidentally tossed out the next time Mom or Dad has a cleaning fit up there.
- In your closet: You can keep an eye on it there, but snoopy siblings may get curious.

## A PEEK AT THE FUTURE

Just as you've discovered generations of your family going back a hundred or so years, there probably will be generations of your family going forward many years. Can you imagine that!

In *The Time Machine,* written by H. G. Wells, a man invents a machine to travel into the future. He remains in one place, sitting in the time machine in the basement of his house. Through his basement window, he can see a dummy in the window of a shop nearby. As he is "traveling," he watches the hem of the mannequin's dress get shorter, then longer, then shorter, then wider—as styles change through the years. Suddenly, the little shop window disappears—and he's there in the future!

Imagine your own home. Will it still be there in 20 years? Or 50 years? What will things be like in 100 years? Will houses be built on the ground, under ground, or stretch way up into the sky? Will there be speedy flyers hovering around, instead of streets and long highways filled with cars?

Imagine you are all grown up and married. What does your wife or husband look like? What kind of work do you do? What do your kids look like? Do people tell you that your children have your same crooked smile? Do your kids have a dog or a cat like you used to at their age? Did you just remember the date you put on your time capsule? Now imagine four and five generations of your family getting together someday at reunions—one that you started!

# AFTERWORD

## PLANT IT, IT'S YOUR FAMILY TREE

Part of what makes genealogy so much fun is that it keeps growing and changing before your very eyes. Everything you learn about your family adds to it. Your family is a vibrant and living thing, and what better way to symbolize it than with a living and growing tree?

Go to a local nursery and ask someone there to help you select a tiny seedling that will grow well for you. Get planting and growing instructions to take with you. When you get home, plant the tree right away. You may have a nice place selected in front of your house, or in your backyard. A very large pot on a porch or patio might do for a while, but a tree belongs in the ground. Its roots need room and nourishment in order to grow tall, and the branches and leaves of most trees will want to spread out. Care for your family tree and watch it grow from year to year. Every time you look at it, you'll be reminded of the wonderful living, growing thing each and everyone's family truly is.

# INDEX

ancestor, defined, 25
archives, defined, 25
autobiography, defined, 25
biography, defined, 25
birth certificates, 19—20, 21
bookmarks, 33—34
celebrations, 76—77
census/census records, 25, 37
certificates, 20
coat of arms, 47—52
cousins, 53, 54—55
cultural links, 45—46
death certificates, 16
descendant, defined, 25
Ellis Island, 40—41, 42
emigrate, defined, 25
family tree, 12—18
   growing, 14—16
   mapping out, 12—13
   pedigree charts, 17—18
   tips, 14
foods/cooking, 77—79, 83
fraternal, defined, 25
future, imagining, 94—95
games, 86—87
geneology
   defined, 25
   influence of, 5—6
   reasons for studying, 8

generations, 6—7, 26
genes, 7—8, 26
geography issues, 60—65
 good old days , 71
grandchildren, 54—55
grandparents, 6—7, 14—15, 53, 71
head of household, 26
heraldry, 47—52
immigrants, 26, 40—46
interviews, 21—24
keepsakes, 28
labels, 31
letter, to the past, 72
links, 38
maiden name, defined, 26
maps, 62—63, 64—65
maternal, defined, 26
medical history, 56—58
names
   of people, 42—44
   of places, 64—65
newsletters, 88—89
obituaries, 16—17
online searches, 35—39, 44
oral histories, 68—70
passports, 41—42
past, experiencing, 72—74
paternal, defined, 26
pedigree charts, 17—18, 26

photographs, 10—11, 31—32, 75,
   84—85, 87
questionnaire form, 22—24
relatives/relationships, 26,
   53—55
research, 19—26
   how to, 19
   interviews, 21—24
   obituaries for, 16—17
   online, 35—39, 44
   starting, 9—11, 19—20
   treasures, 20
reunions, 81—87
scrapbook, 9, 27
searching online, 35—39, 44
sibling, defined, 26
songs, 79—80
spouse, defined, 26
stories, 66—70
surname, defined, 26
time capsules, 91—94
timeline, 74—75
traditions, 76—80
trees, planting, 95
Vital Records, 36
vocabulary words, 25—26
websites, family, 90
word use research, 58—59
workbook organization, 27—34

S0-BCS-141

Denys Johnson-Davies has been called 'the pioneer translator of modern Arabic literature'. He has also made a name for himself as a writer of children's books, of which he has published more than fifty titles. He lives in Cairo, Egypt.

The book 'Memories in Translation' tells the story of how he became interested in Arabic and provides amusing anecdotes about the many Arab writers he has known; the book is available in both English and Arabic. Denys received the Sheikh Zayed Award for 2007 as the Personality of the Year in recognition of his contribution to making Arabic literature known outside the Arab world. Jerboa Books has published a volume of his short stories under the title 'Open Season in Beirut.'

For more than twenty years Elena Selivanova, a graduate of The Moscow Academy of Printing Arts, has been working with major Russian and foreign publishing houses. In publishing business she is a one-man-band: she works as an art director, designer and book illustrator. She is a constant participant of international exhibitions.

# The Traveller

Published in 2008 by JERBOA BOOKS

PO Box 333838 Dubai UAE

www.jerboabooks.com

ISBN 978-9948-431-63-3


Approved by the National Information Council UAE:

No 1539 27 December 2006


Text: © Denys Johnson-Davies

Illustrations: © Elena Selivanova

All rights reserved. No part of this publication may be reproduced,stored in or introduced into a retrieval system, or transmitted, in any form, or by any means (electronic, mechanical, photocopying, recording or otherwise) without the prior written permission of the copyright owners. Any person who does any unauthorised act in relation to this publication may be liable to criminal prosecution and civil claims for damages

# The Traveller

Denys Johnson-Davies

*Illustrations*
Elena Selivanova

This book would not have been possible
without the generous support of
Dubai Duty Free

ONCE A TRAVELLER WAS wandering through a vast desert in which nothing grew, not a tree or even a blade of grass. By chance he came across a deep pit. He looked inside it, hoping that maybe it contained some water. He was astonished to find that all it contained were several wretched creatures. They had slipped down its steep and slippery sides and fallen into the pit. They were a monkey, a snake, a tiger and also a man.

'I would be doing a good deed if I were to rescue this poor man who has fallen among these dangerous animals,' the traveller said to himself.

The traveller happened to have with him a long rope, so he let it down into the pit and called out to the man to take hold of it. But the monkey, being such a nimble animal, was the first to grasp the end of the rope and to climb out to safety.

So the traveller let down the rope a second time, only to find that the snake had twirled itself round it and had come out. When he let down the rope a third time, the traveller was alarmed to find that the tiger, with its great strength, had caught hold of the rope with his claws and had made its way up into the open air.

The traveller now found himself facing these three animals and was amazed to find them bowing down in front of him in thanks for the good deed he had done. At the same time they said to him:

'But do not help the man to come out of the pit because there is nothing so ungrateful as a man and especially this one.'

Then the monkey said to the traveller: 'My home is in a mountain close by the city. One day I hope I may have the chance to repay you in some way for your kindness.'

'And my home,' said the tiger, 'is also in a mountain near to the city. I, too, am always at your service for having rescued me from certain death in that terrible pit.'

'And I,' said the snake, 'have my home in the walls of that city. If by any chance you should pass by my way and be in need of any help, be sure that I am always ready to do what I can for you.'

The three animals then bowed down again to the traveller in thanks and went on their way in the direction of the city.

The traveller then remembered that the man was still in the pit.

Paying no heed to the animals' warning, he again let the rope down into the pit. It was only with much difficulty that he was able to pull the man out of the pit.

The man immediately kissed his hands in thanks and said:

'I am a jeweller from the nearby city where I have a shop. If you are ever in need of help, do not hesitate to call on me. I shall be delighted to repay you for having saved my life.'

The two men shook hands and the jeweller made his way to the city. The traveller continued on his journey.

Now it so happened that some weeks later the traveller passed by the city and found the monkey coming towards him.

The monkey immediately bowed down in front of him, saying : 'I wish I could give you a present to express my thanks to you but we monkeys own nothing in this world.'

'However, if you sit down here and rest a while I shall at least bring you something to refresh you after your journey.'

The monkey ran off and after a while brought back a variety of delicious fruits which they enjoyed together. The monkey left and the traveller continued on his way. As he approached the main gate to the city, the traveller was surprised to find the tiger appearing before him.

The tiger having bowed down in front of the traveller, said:

'How can I ever repay you for your kindness? I would like to bring you a present in gratitude for having rescued us from starvation in that pit. Just wait here and I shall see what I can find.'

The tiger bounded off and secretly entered the king's palace. With great stealth he made his way to the room where the King's daughter was still sleeping.

On a table by the bed the tiger saw a beautiful necklace. The tiger took it and brought it as a present to the traveller.

Not knowing that it had been stolen from the king's palace, the traveller accepted the necklace and thanked the tiger. He was amazed at the generosity of animals, how both the monkey and the tiger had insisted on repaying him for his kindness.

As the traveller had no use for a necklace, he called to mind the man he had saved from the pit and who had said that he was a jeweller. He went to see if he would buy the necklace.

The jeweller greeted the traveller in his shop. Directly he saw the necklace, he recognised it as one he himself had made for the king to give to his daughter.

Instead of asking the traveller how he had come by the necklace, the jeweller decided to go straight away to the palace. 'This is the chance of a lifetime,' he told himself. 'Let me go to the king and tell him that not only have I found the princess's necklace but I also know the man who stole it. The King will surely reward me handsomely.'

'Stay here while I arrange for you to be sent some food,' the jeweller told the traveller, and he hurried off to the palace.

The King immediately recognised the necklace as the one he had had made for the princess and which she reported had just been stolen from her room.

'Go to the jeweller's shop,' the King ordered his guards, where you will find a young man who is a stranger to this city. Seize him and bring him here immediately.'

Turning to the jeweller, the king thanked him for the return of the precious necklace, then added:

'But I am especially grateful to you for having found the scoundrel who was so shameless as to go into my daughter's room and steal the necklace from beside her as she slept. I shall reward you well for what you have done.'

In the meantime the traveller who was still in the jeweller's shop awaiting the man's return, was roughly seized by the king's guards and taken to the palace. There he was thrown down in front of the King's throne.

He tried to explain that the necklace had been given to him by a tiger, and this made the king even more angry against him.

'Do you take me for a fool?' the king shouted at the unfortunate man.

'Take him away and beat him, then put him in a cell by himself till tomorrow morning when I order that he be hanged in the main square of our city as a warning to others.'

The poor traveller was thrown into a a small dungeon from where he was taken out for regular beatings. During all this time he would call out:

'If only I had listened to the words of the monkey, the tiger and the snake and not taken that jeweller from the pit.'

It so happened that his words were heard by the snake who lived in a crevice in one of the city's walls. The snake immediately tried to think of some way of rescuing the traveller from the prison and so save him from being executed in the main square the following morning.

The snake immediately set out to the palace and quietly made its way to the room where the King's daughter lay sleeping. It then bit her on the arm and the poison entered her whole body. The girl called out in pain and right away the best doctors in the city were called to the bedside. Not one of them was able to do anything for her and she remained in a state between life and death, while the King shed bitter tears for his beloved daughter.

Next the snake went to one of its sisters who was a genie. It told the genie how the traveller had rescued it from the pit and how this man was now lying in prison.

So the sister snake who was a genie made itself invisible and entered the room of the girl without any of the doctors, or the king himself, noticing.

'Your cure,' she told the dying princess, 'lies in the hands of only one man. This man has been wrongfully imprisoned. Early tomorrow morning he will be put to death. Your only hope is for your father to have this man brought here at once.'

The sister snake then returned to the prison where the poor traveller was being held.

'You should have heeded brother's words,' it told him, 'and not rescued that ungrateful man from the pit. But I hope that the King will shortly order you to be taken to the palace where you will be asked to cure the princess of the poison that my brother has injected into her.'

'And how am I to do such a thing ?' asked the traveller. 'I am no doctor and have no knowledge of such poisons.'

The sister snake then showed the traveller some leaves that it had taken from a special tree.

'Take these leaves,' she told the man, 'and soak them in water, then have the princess drink the water when you are taken to the palace. This medicine will immediately allow the princess to arise from her bed in perfect health.'

The princess had whispered to her father that a mysterious voice had told her that she could be cured only by a foreigner to the city who now lay in prison. This person, who was innocent of any crime, should be brought in all haste to the palace as she felt that her strength was steadily being taken from her by the poison that was in her body.

So the King, who had despaired of his lovely daughter recovering, ordered the prisoner to be brought to the room where the princess lay.

Then the traveller asked for a glass of water and he soaked the leaves in it and gave the water to the princess.

The King and those with him were amazed to see the princess rise up from her bed, healthy and as though nothing had happened to her. The king then asked the traveller to tell him his story and how it was that the necklace had been stolen from the princess's bedroom.

The traveller told the King his history from the very beginning, from the time he had rescued the monkey and the tiger and the snake from the pit, and also the man who turned out to be the jeweller.

He recounted how each of the animals had in a different way shown its gratitude and how the tiger had stupidly stolen the necklace and had then given it to him as a present.

Only the man, the jeweller, had failed to show his gratitude. Instead he harmed him by telling the king that it was the traveller who had stolen the necklace and had then tried to sell it.

So the King ordered that the jeweller should be brought to the palace. The King then told him that he should have made sure of the man's guilt before reporting against him.

'This man had saved your life and you owed him a favour,' the king told the jeweller. 'If it had not been for his friend, the snake, this traveller would have been wrongly put to death tomorrow morning.'

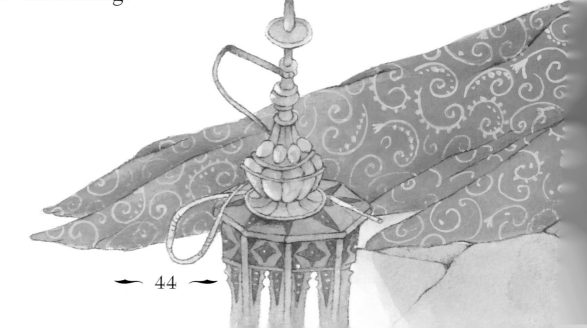

'All that you cared about was the reward that you would receive from me for having found the necklace.'

The king ordered that the jeweller be beaten for the bad way he had behaved towards the man who had rescued him from the pit.

'Truly,' said the king, 'animal is capable of showing more gratitude than man.'

S0-BNF-048

# Family Law

## PRACTICE AND PROCEDURE

## FIFTH EDITION

## VOLUME II: SUPPLEMENTARY MATERIALS

JoAnn Kurtz

emond ▪ Toronto, Canada ▪ 2018

Copyright © 2018 Emond Montgomery Publications Limited.

NOTICE & DISCLAIMER: All rights reserved. No part of this publication may be reproduced in any form by any means without the written consent of Emond Montgomery Publications. Emond Montgomery Publications and all persons involved in the creation of this publication disclaim any warranty as to the accuracy of this publication and shall not be responsible for any action taken in reliance on the publication, or for any errors or omissions contained in the publication. Nothing in this publication constitutes legal or other professional advice. If such advice is required, the services of the appropriate professional should be obtained.

We have attempted to request permission from, and to acknowledge in the text, all sources of material originally published elsewhere. If we have inadvertently overlooked an acknowledgment or failed to secure a permission, we offer our sincere apologies and undertake to rectify the omission in the next edition.

Emond Montgomery Publications Limited
60 Shaftesbury Avenue
Toronto ON  M4T 1A3
http://www.emond.ca/highered

Printed in Canada.

We acknowledge the financial support of the Government of Canada.  **Canadä**

Emond Montgomery Publications has no responsibility for the persistence or accuracy of URLs for external or third-party Internet websites referred to in this publication, and does not guarantee that any content on such websites is, or will remain, accurate or appropriate.

Vice president, publishing: Anthony Rezek
Publisher: Lindsay Sutherland
Director, development and production: Kelly Dickson
Developmental editor: Joanne Sutherland
Production editor: Natalie Berchem
Copy editor: Margaret Henderson
Typesetter: SPi Global
Text designer: Tara Agnerian
Permissions editor: Alison Lloyd-Baker
Proofreader: Ann Lau
Indexer: Paula Pike
Cover image: Pavel_Klimenko/Shutterstock

**Library and Archives Canada Cataloguing in Publication**

Kurtz, JoAnn, 1951-, author
    Family law : practice and procedure / JoAnn Kurtz.—Fifth edition.

(Working with the law)
Includes bibliographical references and indexes.
ISBN 978-1-77255-269-0 (v. 1 : softcover).—ISBN 978-1-77255-317-8 (v. 2 : softcover)

    1. Domestic relations—Ontario—Textbooks.    2. Textbooks.    I. Title.
I. Series: Working with the law

KEO213.K87 2018        346.71301'5        C2017-906819-9
KF505.ZB3K87 2018

# Contents

Child, Youth and Family Services Act, 2017 ............................... 1

Children's Law Reform Act ............................................... 123

Divorce Act ........................................................... 149

Family Law Act ........................................................ 165

Family Law Rules ...................................................... 195

Family Responsibility and Support Arrears Enforcement Act, 1996 ..... 267

Child Support Guidelines .............................................. 291

Formal Requirements of the Continuing Record
   Under the Family Law Rules ......................................... 315

Marriage Act .......................................................... 321

Civil Marriage Act .................................................... 327

Spousal Support Advisory Guidelines ................................... 331

# Child, Youth and Family Services Act, 2017

SO 2017, c14, Schedule 1

**Note: THIS ACT IS NOT YET IN FORCE. It comes into force on a day to be named by proclamation of the Lieutenant Governor.**

## PREAMBLE

The Government of Ontario acknowledges that children are individuals with rights to be respected and voices to be heard.

The Government of Ontario is committed to the following principles:

Services provided to children and families should be child-centred.

Children and families have better outcomes when services build on their strengths. Prevention services, early intervention services and community support services build on a family's strengths and are invaluable in reducing the need for more disruptive services and interventions.

Services provided to children and families should respect their diversity and the principle of inclusion, consistent with the *Human Rights Code* and the *Canadian Charter of Rights and Freedoms*.

Systemic racism and the barriers it creates for children and families receiving services must continue to be addressed. All children should have the opportunity to meet their full potential. Awareness of systemic biases and racism and the need to address these barriers should inform the delivery of all services for children and families.

Services to children and families should, wherever possible, help maintain connections to their communities.

In furtherance of these principles, the Government of Ontario acknowledges that the aim of the *Child, Youth and Family Services Act, 2017* is to be consistent with and build upon the principles expressed in the United Nations Convention on the Rights of the Child.

With respect to First Nations, Inuit and Métis children, the Government of Ontario acknowledges the following:

The Province of Ontario has unique and evolving relationships with First Nations, Inuit and Métis peoples.

First Nations, Inuit and Métis peoples are constitutionally recognized peoples in Canada, with their own laws, and distinct cultural, political and historical ties to the Province of Ontario.

Where a First Nations, Inuk or Métis child is otherwise eligible to receive a service under this Act, an inter-jurisdictional or intra-jurisdictional dispute should not prevent the timely provision of that service, in accordance with Jordan's Principle.

The United Nations Declaration on the Rights of Indigenous Peoples recognizes the importance of belonging to a community or nation, in accordance with the traditions and customs of the community or nation concerned.

Further, the Government of Ontario believes the following:

First Nations, Inuit and Métis children should be happy, healthy, resilient, grounded in their cultures and languages and thriving as individuals and as members of their families, communities and nations.

Honouring the connection between First Nations, Inuit and Métis children and their distinct political and cultural communities is essential to helping them thrive and fostering their well-being.

For these reasons, the Government of Ontario is committed, in the spirit of reconciliation, to working with First Nations, Inuit and Métis peoples to help ensure that wherever possible, they care for their children in accordance with their distinct cultures, heritages and traditions.

## PART I PURPOSES AND INTERPRETATION

### Purposes

**Paramount purpose and other purposes**

**Paramount purpose**

**1.** (1) The paramount purpose of this Act is to promote the best interests, protection and well-being of children.

**Other purposes**

(2) The additional purposes of this Act, so long as they are consistent with the best interests, protection and well-being of children, are to recognize the following:

1. While parents may need help in caring for their children, that help should give support to the autonomy and integrity of the family unit and, wherever possible, be provided on the basis of mutual consent.
2. The least disruptive course of action that is available and is appropriate in a particular case to help a child, including the provision of prevention services, early intervention services and community support services, should be considered.
3. Services to children and young persons should be provided in a manner that,
    i. respects a child's or young person's need for continuity of care and for stable relationships within a family and cultural environment,
    ii. takes into account physical, emotional, spiritual, mental and developmental needs and differences among children and young persons,
    iii. takes into account a child's or young person's race, ancestry, place of origin, colour, ethnic origin, citizenship, family diversity, disability, creed, sex, sexual orientation, gender identity and gender expression,
    iv. takes into account a child's or young person's cultural and linguistic needs,
    v. provides early assessment, planning and decision-making to achieve permanent plans for children and young persons in accordance with their best interests, and
    vi. includes the participation of a child or young person, the child's or young person's parents and relatives and the members of the child's or young person's extended family and community, where appropriate.
4. Services to children and young persons and their families should be provided in a manner that respects regional differences, wherever possible.
5. Services to children and young persons and their families should be provided in a manner that builds on the strengths of the families, wherever possible.
6. First Nations, Inuit and Métis peoples should be entitled to provide, wherever possible, their own child and family services, and all services to First Nations, Inuit and Métis children and young persons and their families should be provided in a manner that recognizes their cultures, heritages, traditions, connection to their communities, and the concept of the extended family.
7. Appropriate sharing of information, including personal information, in order to plan for and provide services is essential for creating successful outcomes for children and families.

### Interpretation

**Interpretation**

**Definitions**

**2.** (1) In this Act,

"agency" means a corporation; ("agence")

"band" has the same meaning as in the *Indian Act* (Canada); ("bande")

"Board" means the Child and Family Services Review Board continued under section 333; ("Commission")

"child" means a person younger than 18; ("enfant")

"child in care" means a child or young person who is receiving residential care from a service provider and includes,

(a) a child who is in the care of a foster parent, and
(b) a young person who is,

(i) detained in a place of temporary detention under the *Youth Criminal Justice Act* (Canada),

(ii) committed to a place of secure or open custody designated under subsection 24.1 (1) of the *Young Offenders Act* (Canada), whether in accordance with section 88 of the *Youth Criminal Justice Act* (Canada) or otherwise, or

(iii) held in a place of open custody under section 150 of this Act; ("enfant recevant des soins", "enfant qui reçoit des soins")

"court" means the Ontario Court of Justice or the Family Court of the Superior Court of Justice; ("tribunal")

"creed" includes religion; ("croyance")

"customary care" means the care and supervision of a First Nations, Inuk or Métis child by a person who is not the child's parent, according to the custom of the child's band or First Nations, Inuit or Métis community; ("soins conformes aux traditions")

"Director" means a Director appointed under subsection 53 (1); ("directeur")

"extended family" means persons to whom a child is related, including through a spousal relationship or adoption and, in the case of a First Nations, Inuk or Métis child, includes any member of,

    (a) a band of which the child is a member,

    (b) a band with which the child identifies,

    (c) a First Nations, Inuit or Métis community of which the child is a member, and

    (d) a First Nations, Inuit or Métis community with which the child identifies; ("famille élargie")

"First Nations, Inuit or Métis community" means a community listed by the Minister in a regulation made under section 68; ("communauté inuite, métisse ou de Premières Nations")

"foster care" means the provision of residential care to a child, by and in the home of a person who,

    (a) receives compensation for caring for the child, except under the *Ontario Works Act, 1997* or the *Ontario Disability Support Program Act, 1997*, and

    (b) is not the child's parent or a person with whom the child has been placed for adoption under Part VIII (Adoption and Adoption Licensing),

and "foster home" and "foster parent" have corresponding meanings; ("soins fournis par une famille d'accueil", "famille d'accueil", "parent de famille d'accueil")

"licence" means a licence issued under Part VIII (Adoption and Adoption Licensing) or Part IX (Residential Licensing); a reference to a licence in Part VIII is to a licence issued under that Part and a reference to a licence in Part IX is to a licence issued under that Part; ("permis")

"licensee" means the holder of a licence; ("titulaire de permis")

"local director" means a local director appointed under section 38; ("directeur local")

"mechanical restraints" means a device, material or equipment that reduces the ability of a person to move freely, and includes handcuffs, flex cuffs, leg irons, restraining belts, belly chains and linking chains; ("contentions mécaniques")

"Minister" means the Minister of Children and Youth Services or such other member of the Executive Council as may be designated under the *Executive Council Act* to administer this Act; ("ministre")

"Ministry" means the ministry of the Minister; ("ministère")

"old Act" means the *Child and Family Services Act*; ("ancienne loi")

"order" includes a refusal to make an order; ("arrêté, ordre et ordonnance")

"personal information" has the same meaning as in the *Freedom of Information and Protection of Privacy Act*; ("renseignements personnels")

"physical restraint" means a holding technique to restrict a person's ability to move freely but, for greater certainty, does not include,

    (a) restricting movement, physical redirection or physical prompting, if the restriction, redirection or prompting is brief, gentle and part of a behaviour teaching program, or

    (b) the use of helmets, protective mitts or other equipment to prevent a person from physically injuring or further physically injuring themself; ("contention physique")

"place of open custody" means a place or facility designated as a place of open custody under subsection 24.1 (1) of the *Young Offenders Act* (Canada), whether in accordance with section 88 of the *Youth Criminal Justice Act* (Canada) or otherwise; ("lieu de garde en milieu ouvert")

"place of open temporary detention" means a place of temporary detention in which the Minister has established an open detention program; ("lieu de détention provisoire en milieu ouvert")

"place of secure custody" means a place or facility designated for the secure containment or restraint of young persons under subsection 24.1 (1) of the *Young Offenders Act* (Canada), whether in accordance with section 88 of the *Youth Criminal Justice Act* (Canada) or otherwise; ("lieu de garde en milieu fermé")

"place of secure temporary detention" means a place of temporary detention in which the Minister has established a secure detention program; ("lieu de détention provisoire en milieu fermé")

"place of temporary detention" means a place or facility designated as a place of temporary detention under the *Youth Criminal Justice Act* (Canada); ("lieu de détention provisoire")

"prescribed" means prescribed by regulations; ("prescrit")

"program supervisor" means a program supervisor appointed under subsection 53 (2); ("superviseur de programme")

"provincial director" means,

    (a) a person, the group or class of persons or the body appointed or designated by the Lieutenant Governor in Council or the Lieutenant Governor in Council's delegate to perform any of the duties or functions of a provincial director under the *Youth Criminal Justice Act* (Canada), or

    (b) a person appointed under clause 146 (1) (a); ("directeur provincial")

"record" means a record of information in any form or in any medium, whether in written, printed, photographic or electronic form or otherwise, but does not include a computer program or other mechanism that can produce a record; ("dossier") "regulations" means the regulations made under this Act; ("règlements")

"relative" means, with respect to a child, a person who is the child's grandparent, great-uncle, great-aunt, uncle or aunt, including through a spousal relationship or adoption; ("membre de la parenté")

"residential care" means boarding, lodging and associated supervisory, sheltered or group care provided for a child away from the home of the child's parent, other than boarding, lodging or associated care for a child who has been placed in the lawful care and custody of a relative or member of the child's extended family or the child's community; ("soins en établissement")

"residential placement" means a place where residential care is provided; ("placement en établissement", "placé dans un établissement")

"service" includes,

(a) a service for a child with a developmental or physical disability or the child's family,

(b) a mental health service for a child or the child's family,

(c) a service related to residential care for a child,

(d) a service for a child who is or may be in need of protection or the child's family,

(e) a service related to adoption for a child, the child's family or others,

(f) counselling for a child or the child's family,

(g) a service for a child or the child's family that is in the nature of support or prevention and that is provided in the community,

(h) a service or program for or on behalf of a young person for the purposes of the *Youth Criminal Justice Act* (Canada) or the *Provincial Offences Act*, or

(i) a prescribed service; ("service")

"service provider" means,

(a) the Minister,

(b) a licensee,

(c) a person or entity, including a society, that provides a service funded under this Act, or

(d) a prescribed person or entity,

but does not include a foster parent; ("fournisseur de services")

"society" means an agency designated as a children's aid society under subsection 34 (1); ("société")

"treatment" has the same meaning as in subsection 2 (1) of the *Health Care Consent Act, 1996*; ("traitement")

"Tribunal" means the Licence Appeal Tribunal; ("Tribunal")

"young person" means,

(a) a person who is or, in the absence of evidence to the contrary, appears to be 12 or older but younger than 18 and who is charged with or found guilty of an offence under the *Youth Criminal Justice Act* (Canada) or the *Provincial Offences Act*, or

(b) if the context requires, any person who is charged under the *Youth Criminal Justice Act* (Canada) with having committed an offence while they were a young person or who is found guilty of an offence under the *Youth Criminal Justice Act* (Canada). ("adolescent")

### Interpretation, "parent"

(2) Unless this Act provides otherwise, a reference in this Act to a parent of a child is deemed to be a reference to,

(a) the person who has lawful custody of the child; or

(b) if more than one person has lawful custody of the child, all of the persons who have lawful custody of the child, excluding any person who is unavailable or unable to act, as the context requires.

### Member of child's or young person's community

(3) For the purposes of this Act, the following persons are members of a child's or young person's community:

1. A person who has ethnic, cultural or creedal ties in common with the child or young person or with a parent, sibling or relative of the child or young person.

2. A person who has a beneficial and meaningful relationship with the child or young person or with a parent, sibling or relative of the child or young person.

### Interpretation, child's or young person's bands and First Nations, Inuit or Métis communities

(4) In this Act, a reference to a child's or young person's bands and First Nations, Inuit or Métis communities includes all of the following:

1. Any band of which the child or young person is a member.

2. Any band with which the child or young person identifies.

3. Any First Nations, Inuit or Métis community of which the child or young person is a member.

4. Any First Nations, Inuit or Métis community with which the child or young person identifies.

### PART II    CHILDREN'S AND YOUNG PERSONS' RIGHTS

### Rights of Children and Young Persons Receiving Services

### Rights of children, young persons receiving services

**3.** Every child and young person receiving services under this Act has the following rights:

1. To express their own views freely and safely about matters that affect them.

2. To be engaged through an honest and respectful dialogue about how and why decisions affecting them are

made and to have their views given due weight, in accordance with their age and maturity.

3.  To be consulted on the nature of the services provided or to be provided to them, to participate in decisions about the services provided or to be provided to them and to be advised of the decisions made in respect of those services.

4.  To raise concerns or recommend changes with respect to the services provided or to be provided to them without interference or fear of coercion, discrimination or reprisal and to receive a response to their concerns or recommended changes.

5.  To be informed, in language suitable to their understanding, of their rights under this Part.

6.  To be informed, in language suitable to their understanding, of the existence and role of the Provincial Advocate for Children and Youth and of how the Provincial Advocate for Children and Youth may be contacted.

### Corporal punishment prohibited

**4.**  No service provider or foster parent shall inflict corporal punishment on a child or young person or permit corporal punishment to be inflicted on a child or young person in the course of the provision of a service to the child or young person.

### Detention restricted

**5.**  No service provider or foster parent shall detain a child or young person or permit a child or young person to be detained in locked premises in the course of the provision of a service to the child or young person, except as Part VI (Youth Justice) and Part VII (Extraordinary Measures) authorize.

### Physical restraint restricted

**6.**  No service provider or foster parent shall use or permit the use of physical restraint on a child or young person for whom the service provider or foster parent is providing services, except as the regulations authorize.

### Mechanical restraints restricted

**7.**  No service provider or foster parent shall use or permit the use of mechanical restraints on a child or young person for whom the service provider or foster parent is providing services, except as Part VI (Youth Justice), Part VII (Extraordinary Measures) and the regulations authorize.

### Rights of Children in Care
### Right to be heard in respect of decisions

**8.**  (1)  For greater certainty, the rights under section 3 of a child in care apply to decisions affecting them, including decisions with respect to,

(a)  the child's or young person's treatment, education or training or work programs;

(b)  the child's or young person's creed, community identity and cultural identity; and

(c)  the child's or young person's placement in or discharge from a residential placement or transfer to another residential placement.

### Views to be given due weight

(2)  The child's or young person's views with respect to the decisions described in subsection (1) shall be given due weight, in accordance with the child's or young person's age and maturity as required by paragraph 2 of section 3.

### Right to be informed re residential placement admission

**9.**  Upon admission to a residential placement, and at regular intervals thereafter, or, where intervals are prescribed, at the prescribed intervals thereafter, a child in care has a right to be informed, in language suitable to their understanding, of,

(a)  their rights under this Part;

(b)  the complaints procedures established under subsection 18 (1) and the further review available under section 19;

(c)  the review procedures available for children under sections 64, 65 and 66;

(d)  the review procedures available under section 152, in the case of a young person described in clause (b) of the definition of "child in care" in subsection 2 (1);

(e)  their responsibilities while in the placement; and

(f)  the rules governing day-to-day operation of the residential care, including disciplinary procedures.

### Rights of communication, etc.

**10.**  (1)  A child in care has a right,

(a)  to speak in private with, visit and receive visits from members of their family or extended family regularly, subject to subsection (2);

(b)  without unreasonable delay, to speak in private with and receive visits from,

(i)  their lawyer,

(ii)  another person representing the child or young person, including the Provincial Advocate for Children and Youth and members of the Provincial Advocate for Children and Youth's staff,

(iii)  the Ombudsman appointed under the *Ombudsman Act* and members of the Ombudsman's staff, and

(iv)  a member of the Legislative Assembly of Ontario or of the Parliament of Canada; and

(c)  to send and receive written communications that are not read, examined or censored by another person, subject to subsections (3) and (4).

### When child is in extended society care

(2)  A child in care who is in extended society care under an order made under paragraph 3 of subsection 101 (1) or clause 116 (1) (c) is not entitled as of right to speak with,

visit or receive visits from a member of their family or extended family, except under an order for access made under Part V (Child Protection) or an openness order or openness agreement made under Part VIII (Adoption and Adoption Licensing).

### Opening, etc., of written communications to child in care

(3) Subject to subsection (4), written communications to a child in care,

    (a) may be opened by the service provider or a member of the service provider's staff in the child's or young person's presence and may be inspected for articles prohibited by the service provider;

    (b) subject to clause (c), may be examined or read by the service provider or a member of the service provider's staff in the child's or young person's presence, where the service provider believes on reasonable grounds that the contents of the written communication may cause the child or young person physical or emotional harm;

    (c) shall not be examined or read by the service provider or a member of the service provider's staff if it is to or from a person described in subclause (1) (b) (i), (ii), (iii) or (iv); and

    (d) shall not be censored or withheld from the child or young person, except that articles prohibited by the service provider may be removed from the written communication and withheld from the child or young person.

### Opening, etc., of young person's written communications

(4) Written communications to and from a young person who is detained in a place of temporary detention or held in a place of secure custody or of open custody,

    (a) may be opened by the service provider or a member of the service provider's staff in the young person's presence and may be inspected for articles prohibited by the service provider;

    (b) may be examined or read by the service provider or a member of the service provider's staff and may be withheld from the recipient in whole or in part where the service provider or the member of their staff believes on reasonable grounds that the contents of the written communications,

        (i) may be prejudicial to the best interests of the young person, the public safety or the safety or security of the place of detention or custody, or

        (ii) may contain communications that are prohibited under the *Youth Criminal Justice Act* (Canada) or by court order;

    (c) shall not be examined or read under clause (b) if it is to or from the young person's lawyer; and

    (d) shall not be opened and inspected under clause (a) or examined or read under clause (b) if it is to or from a person described in subclause (1) (b) (ii), (iii) or (iv).

### Definition

(5) In this section,

"written communications" includes mail and electronic communication in any form.

### Conditions and limitations on visitors

**11.** (1) A service provider may impose such conditions and limitations on persons who are visiting a young person in a place of temporary detention, of open custody or of secure custody as are necessary to ensure the safety of staff or young persons in the facility.

### Suspending visits in emergencies

(2) Where a service provider has reasonable grounds to believe there are emergency circumstances within a facility that is a place of temporary detention, of open custody or of secure custody or within the community that may pose a risk to staff or young persons in the facility, the service provider may suspend visits until there are reasonable grounds to believe the emergency has been resolved and there is no longer a risk to staff or young persons in the facility.

### Limited exception

(3) Despite subsection (2), the service provider may not suspend visits from,

    (a) the Provincial Advocate for Children and Youth and members of the Provincial Advocate for Children and Youth's staff;

    (b) the Ombudsman appointed under the *Ombudsman Act* and members of the Ombudsman's staff; or

    (c) a member of the Legislative Assembly of Ontario or of the Parliament of Canada,

unless the provincial director determines that suspension is necessary to ensure public safety or the safety of staff or young persons in the facility.

### Personal liberties

**12.** A child in care has a right,

    (a) to have reasonable privacy and possession of their own personal property, subject to section 155; and

    (b) to receive instruction and participate in activities of their choice related to their creed, community identity and cultural identity, subject to section 14.

### Plan of care

**13.** (1) A child in care has a right to a plan of care designed to meet their particular needs, which shall be prepared within 30 days of the child's or young person's admission to the residential placement.

**Rights to care**

(2) A child in care has a right,

(a) to participate in the development of their individual plan of care and in any changes made to it;

(b) to have access to food that is of good quality and appropriate for the child or young person, including meals that are well balanced;

(c) to be provided with clothing that is of good quality and appropriate for the child or young person, given their size and activities and prevailing weather conditions;

(d) to receive medical and dental care, subject to section 14, at regular intervals and whenever required, in a community setting whenever possible;

(e) to receive an education that corresponds to their aptitudes and abilities, in a community setting whenever possible; and

(f) to participate in recreational, athletic and creative activities that are appropriate for their aptitudes and interests, in a community setting whenever possible.

**Parental consent, etc.**

**14.** Subject to subsection 94 (7) and sections 110 and 111 (custody during adjournment, interim and extended society care), the parent of a child in care retains any right that the parent may have,

(a) to direct the child's or young person's education and upbringing, in accordance with the child's or young person's creed, community identity and cultural identity; and

(b) to consent to treatment on behalf of an incapable child or young person, if the parent is the child's or young person's substitute decision-maker in accordance with section 20 of the *Health Care Consent Act, 1996.*

### Service Providers' Duties in respect of Children's and Young Persons' Rights

**Children's, young persons' rights to respectful services**

**15.** (1) Service providers shall respect the rights of children and young persons as set out in this Act.

**Children, young persons to be heard and represented**

(2) Service providers shall ensure that children and young persons and their parents have an opportunity to be heard and represented when decisions affecting their interests are made and to be heard when they have concerns about the services they are receiving.

**Exception**

(3) Subsection (2) does not apply to a child or young person or parent of a child or young person if there is good cause for not giving that person an opportunity to be heard or represented as described in that subsection.

**Criteria and safeguards re decisions**

(4) Service providers shall ensure that decisions affecting the interests and rights of children and young persons and their parents are made according to clear, consistent criteria and are subject to appropriate procedural safeguards.

**Information about Provincial Advocate for Children and Youth to be displayed and available**

(5) Service providers shall,

(a) prominently display at their premises, in a manner visible to persons receiving services, a notice advising of the existence and role of the Provincial Advocate for Children and Youth and of how the Provincial Advocate for Children and Youth may be contacted; and

(b) make available on request informational materials produced by the Provincial Advocate for Children and Youth.

**French language services**

**16.** Service providers shall, where appropriate, make services to children and young persons and their families available in the French language.

### Alternative Dispute Resolution

**Resolution of issues by prescribed method of alternative dispute resolution**

**17.** (1) If a child is or may be in need of protection under this Act, a society shall consider whether a prescribed method of alternative dispute resolution could assist in resolving any issue related to the child or a plan for the child's care.

**First Nations, Inuk or Métis child**

(2) If the issue referred to in subsection (1) relates to a First Nations, Inuk or Métis child, the society shall consult with a representative chosen by each of the child's bands and First Nations, Inuit or Métis communities to determine whether an alternative dispute resolution process established by the bands and communities or another prescribed alternative dispute resolution process could assist in resolving the issue.

**Children's Lawyer**

(3) If a society or a person, including a child, who is receiving child welfare services proposes that an alternative dispute resolution method or process referred to in subsection (1) or (2) be undertaken to assist in resolving an issue relating to a child or a plan for the child's care, the Children's Lawyer may provide legal representation to the child if, in the opinion of the Children's Lawyer, such legal representation is appropriate.

**Notice to band, community**

(4) If a society makes or receives a proposal that an alternative dispute resolution method or process referred to in

subsection (1) or (2) be undertaken under subsection (3) in a matter involving a First Nations, Inuk or Métis child, the society shall give notice of the proposal to a representative chosen by each of the child's bands and First Nations, Inuit or Métis communities.

### Complaints and Reviews
### Complaints procedure

**18.** (1) A service provider who provides residential care to children or young persons or who places children or young persons in residential placements shall establish a written procedure, in accordance with the regulations, for hearing and dealing with,

(a) complaints regarding alleged violations of the rights under this Part of children in care; and

(b) complaints by children in care or other persons affected by conditions or limitations imposed on visitors under subsection 11 (1) or suspensions of visits under subsection 11 (2).

### Provincial Advocate for Children and Youth

(2) The procedure established under subsection (1) must provide that the service provider shall tell the children in care that they may ask for the assistance of the Provincial Advocate for Children and Youth in,

(a) making a complaint under clause (1) (a) or (b); and

(b) requesting a further review under subsection 19 (1) of the complaint once the review by the service provider is completed.

### Review of complaint

(3) A service provider shall conduct a review or ensure that a review is conducted, in accordance with the procedure established under clause (1) (a) or (b), on the complaint of,

(a) a child in care or a group of children in care;

(b) the parent of a child in care who makes a complaint;

(c) another person representing the child in care who makes a complaint; or

(d) a person affected by a condition or limitation imposed on visitors under subsection 11 (1) or a suspension of visits under subsection 11 (2),

and shall seek to resolve the complaint.

### Response to complainants

(4) Upon completion of its review under subsection (3), the service provider shall inform each person who made the complaint, whether as an individual or as part of a group, of the results of the review.

### Further review

**19.** (1) Where a person referred to in subsection 18 (3) makes a complaint, whether as an individual or as part of a group, and is not satisfied with the results of the review conducted under that subsection and requests in writing that the Minister appoint a person to conduct a further review of the complaint, the Minister shall appoint a person who is not employed by the service provider to do so.

### Same

(2) A person appointed under subsection (1) shall review the complaint in accordance with the regulations and may do so by holding a hearing.

### Procedure

(3) The *Statutory Powers Procedure Act* does not apply to a hearing held under subsection (2).

### Powers of appointed person

(4) A person appointed under subsection (1) has, for the purposes of the review, all the powers of a program supervisor appointed under subsection 53 (2).

### Review and report within 30 days

(5) A person appointed under subsection (1) shall, within 30 days after the day of the appointment, complete the review, set out in a report the person's findings and recommendations, including the reasons for not holding a hearing if none was held, and provide copies of the report to,

(a) each person who made the complaint, whether as an individual or as part of a group;

(b) the service provider; and

(c) the Minister.

### Minister to advise persons affected of any decision

**20.** (1) Where the Minister decides to take any action with respect to a complaint after receiving a report under subsection 19 (5), the Minister shall advise the service provider and each person who made the complaint, whether as an individual or as part of a group, of the decision.

### Remedies preserved

(2) The Minister's decision referred to in subsection (1) does not affect any other remedy that may be available.

### Consent and Voluntary Services
### Consents and agreements

**21.** (1) In this section,

"capacity" means the capacity to understand and appreciate the nature of a consent or agreement and the consequences of giving, withholding or withdrawing the consent or making, not making or terminating the agreement; ("jouit de toutes ses facultés mentales")

"nearest relative", when used in reference to a person who is younger than 16, means the person with lawful custody of the person, and when used in reference to a person who is 16 or older, means the person who would be authorized to give or refuse consent to a treatment on the person's behalf under the *Health Care Consent Act, 1996* if the person were incapable with respect to the treatment under that Act. ("membre de la parenté le plus proche")

### Elements of valid consent or agreement, etc.

(2) A person's consent or withdrawal of a consent or participation in or termination of an agreement under this Act is valid if, at the time the consent is given or withdrawn or the agreement is made or terminated, the person,

(a) has capacity;

(b) is reasonably informed as to the nature and consequences of the consent or agreement, and of alternatives to it;

(c) gives or withdraws the consent or executes the agreement or notice of termination voluntarily, without coercion or undue influence; and

(d) has had a reasonable opportunity to obtain independent advice.

### Where person lacks capacity

(3) A person's nearest relative may give or withdraw a consent or participate in or terminate an agreement on the person's behalf if it has been determined on the basis of an assessment, not more than one year before the nearest relative acts on the person's behalf, that the person does not have capacity.

### Exceptions: ss. 180, 74 (2) (n)

(4) Subsection (3) does not apply to a consent under section 180 (consents to adoption) or to a parent's consent referred to in clause 74 (2) (n) (child in need of protection).

### Consent, etc., of minor

(5) A person's consent or withdrawal of a consent or participation in or termination of an agreement under this Act is not invalid by reason only that the person is younger than 18.

### Exception: Part X

(6) This section does not apply in respect of the collection, use or disclosure of personal information under Part X (Personal Information).

## Consent to service

### Consent to service: person 16 or older

22. (1) Subject to clause (2) (b) and subsection (3), a service provider may provide a service to a person who is 16 or older only with the person's consent, except where the court orders under this Act that the service be provided to the person.

### Consent to residential care: child younger than 16 or in society's care

(2) A service provider may provide residential care to a child,

(a) if the child is younger than 16, with the consent of the child's parent; and

(b) if the child is in a society's lawful custody, with the society's consent,

except where this Act provides otherwise.

### Exception—Part VI

(3) Subsections (1) and (2) do not apply where a service is provided to a young person under Part VI (Youth Justice).

### Discharge from residential placement

(4) A child who is placed in a residential placement with the consent referred to in subsection (1) or (2) may only be discharged from the placement,

(a) with the consent that would be required for a new residential placement;

(b) where the placement is made under the authority of an agreement made under subsection 75 (1) (temporary care agreements), in accordance with section 76 (notice of termination); or

(c) where the placement is made under the authority of an agreement made under subsection 77 (1) (agreements with 16 and 17 year olds), in accordance with subsection 77 (4) (notice of termination).

### Transfer to another placement

(5) A child who is placed in a residential placement with the consent referred to in subsection (1) or (2) shall not be transferred from one placement to another unless the consent that would be required for a new residential placement is given.

### Child's views and wishes

(6) Before a child is placed in or discharged from a residential placement or transferred from one residential placement to another with the consent referred to in subsection (2), the service provider shall,

(a) ensure that the child and the person whose consent is required under subsection (2) are made aware of and understand, as far as possible, the reasons for the placement, discharge or transfer; and

(b) take the child's views and wishes into account, given due weight in accordance with the child's age and maturity.

### Application of *Health Care Consent Act, 1996*

(7) If the service being provided is a treatment to which the *Health Care Consent Act, 1996* applies, the consent provisions of that Act apply instead of this section.

### Counselling service: child 12 or older

23. (1) A service provider may provide a counselling service to a child who is 12 or older with the child's consent, and no other person's consent is required, but if the child is younger than 16, the service provider shall discuss with the child at the earliest appropriate opportunity the desirability of involving the child's parent.

### Application of *Health Care Consent Act, 1996*

(2) If the counselling service being provided is a treatment to which the *Health Care Consent Act, 1996* applies, the consent provisions of that Act apply instead of subsection (1).

## PART III   FUNDING AND ACCOUNTABILITY

### Definition

**24.** In this Part,

"lead agency" means an entity designated as a lead agency under subsection 30 (1).

### Funding of Services and Lead Agencies

### Provision of services directly or by others

**25.** The Minister may,

(a) provide services;

(b) establish, operate and maintain premises for the provision of services;

(c) provide funding, pursuant to agreements, to persons, agencies, municipalities, organizations and other prescribed entities,

(i) for the provision or coordination of services by them,

(ii) for the acquisition, maintenance or operation of premises used for the provision or coordination of services,

(iii) for the establishment of advisory groups or committees with respect to services,

(iv) for research, evaluation, planning, development, co-ordination or redesign with respect to services,

(v) for any other prescribed purpose; and

(d) provide funding, pursuant to agreements, to lead agencies with respect to the performance of the functions referred to in subsection 30 (5).

### Services to persons older than 18

**26.** The Minister may provide services and provide funding pursuant to agreements for the provision of services to persons who are not children, and to their families, as if those persons were children.

### Minister's advisory committee

**27.** The Minister may appoint members to a Minister's advisory committee, established by order of the Lieutenant Governor in Council, to advise the Minister on child and family well-being.

### Security for payment of funds

**28.** The Minister may, as a condition of making a payment under this Part or the regulations, require the recipient of the funds to secure them by way of mortgage, lien, charge, caution, registration of agreement or in such other manner as the Minister determines.

### Conditions on transfer of assets

**29.** No service provider or lead agency shall transfer or assign any of its assets acquired with financial assistance from the Province of Ontario, except in accordance with the regulations or any term of an agreement with the Minister.

### Lead agencies

### Designation

**30.** (1) The Minister may designate an entity as a lead agency.

### Conditions of designation

(2) The Minister may impose conditions on a designation made under this section and may at any time amend or remove the conditions or impose new ones.

### Revocation of designation

(3) The Minister may revoke a designation made under this section.

### Categories of lead agencies

(4) The Minister may assign lead agencies to different lead agency categories established by the regulations.

### Functions of lead agencies

(5) Every lead agency shall perform the functions assigned to the lead agency's category by the regulations.

### List of lead agencies and categories

(6) The Minister shall maintain a list of lead agencies and their categories.

### Public availability

(7) The Minister shall make the list available to the public.

### Placements must comply with Act and regulations, etc.

**31.** No service provider shall place a child in a residential placement except in accordance with this Act, the regulations and the directives issued under this Act.

### Directives and Compliance Orders (Lead Agencies and Service Providers)

### Directives by Minister

### Non-application

**32.** (1) This section and section 33 do not apply in respect of,

(a) licensees under Part IX (Residential Licensing), when acting in their capacity as licensees under that Part; or

(b) societies, when performing their functions under subsection 35 (1).

### Directives

(2) The Minister may issue directives to service providers and lead agencies with respect to any prescribed matter.

### Binding

(3) Every service provider and lead agency shall comply with every directive issued to it under this section.

### General or particular

(4) A directive may be general or particular in its application.

## Law prevails

(5) For greater certainty, in the event of a conflict between a directive issued under this section and a provision of any applicable Act or rule of any applicable law, the provision or rule prevails.

## Public availability

(6) The Minister shall make every directive under this section available to the public.

## Non-application of Legislation Act, 2006

(7) Part III (Regulations) of the *Legislation Act, 2006* does not apply to a directive issued under this section.

## Compliance order

## Grounds

**33.** (1) A program supervisor may make an order under subsection (2) if the program supervisor believes on reasonable grounds that a service provider or lead agency has failed to comply with,

(a) this Act or the regulations;

(b) a directive issued under section 32;

(c) in the case of a service provider, an agreement referred to in clause 25 (c) or section 26; or

(d) in the case of a lead agency,

(i) an agreement referred to in clause 25 (d);

(ii) a condition imposed on the lead agency's designation under subsection 30 (2), or

(iii) subsection 30 (5) (functions of lead agencies).

## Order

(2) For the purposes of subsection (1), a program supervisor may issue an order to the service provider or lead agency that requires either or both of the following:

1. That the service provider or lead agency do anything, or refrain from doing anything, to achieve compliance within the time period specified in the order.

2. That the service provider or lead agency prepare, submit and implement, within the time period specified in the order, a plan for achieving compliance.

## Compliance required

(3) A service provider or lead agency served with an order under this section shall comply with the order within the time specified in it.

## Public availability

(4) The Minister,

(a) may make orders under this section available to the public; and

(b) shall make a summary of each order under this section available to the public in accordance with the regulations.

## Failure to comply

(5) If a service provider or lead agency fails to comply with an order made under this section within the time specified in it, the Minister may terminate all or part of the funding provided to the service provider or lead agency.

### Children's Aid Societies

## Children's aid society

## Designation

**34.** (1) The Minister may designate an agency as a children's aid society for a specified territorial jurisdiction and for any or all of the functions of a society set out in subsection 35 (1).

## Conditions on designation

(2) For any or all of the functions of a society set out in subsection 35 (1), the Minister may impose conditions on the designation and may at any time amend or remove the conditions or impose new ones.

## Amendment of designation

(3) The Minister may at any time amend a designation to provide that the society is no longer designated for a particular function or functions set out in subsection 35 (1) or to alter the society's territorial jurisdiction.

## Society deemed to be a local board

(4) A society is deemed to be a local board of each municipality in which it has jurisdiction for the purposes of the *Ontario Municipal Employees Retirement System Act, 2006* and the *Municipal Conflict of Interest Act.*

## Not Crown agents

(5) A society and its members, officers, employees and agents are not agents of the Crown in right of Ontario and shall not hold themselves out as such.

## No Crown liability

(6) No action or other proceeding shall be instituted against the Crown in right of Ontario for any act or omission of a society or its members, officers, employees or agents.

## Functions

**35.** (1) The functions of a children's aid society are to,

(a) investigate allegations or evidence that children may be in need of protection;

(b) protect children where necessary;

(c) provide guidance, counselling and other services to families for protecting children or for the prevention of circumstances requiring the protection of children;

(d) provide care for children assigned or committed to its care under this Act;

(e) supervise children assigned to its supervision under this Act;

(f) place children for adoption under Part VIII (Adoption and Adoption Licensing); and

(g) perform any other duties given to it by this Act or the regulations or any other Act.

**Prescribed standards, etc.**

(2) A society shall,

(a) provide the prescribed standard of services in its performance of its functions; and

(b) follow the prescribed procedures and practices.

**Governance matters**

**First Nations, Inuit or Métis representatives on board**

**36.** (1) A society that provides services to First Nations, Inuit or Métis children and families shall have the prescribed number of First Nations, Inuit or Métis representatives on its board of directors, appointed in the prescribed manner and for the prescribed terms.

**Employee may not sit on board**

(2) An employee of a society shall not be a member of the society's board.

**By-laws**

(3) The by-laws of a society shall include any provisions that are prescribed.

**No personal liability**

**37.** No action shall be instituted against a member of the board of directors or an officer or employee of a society for any act done in good faith in the execution or intended execution of the person's duty or for an alleged neglect or default in good faith in the execution of that duty.

**Appointment of local director**

**38.** Every society shall appoint a local director with the prescribed qualifications, powers and duties.

**Designation of places of safety**

**39.** For the purposes of Part V (Child Protection), a local director may designate a place as a place of safety and may designate a class of places as places of safety.

**Funding and Accountability Agreements**

**Funding**

**Payments by Minister**

**40.** (1) The Minister shall pay to every society, out of money appropriated for the purpose by the Legislature, an amount determined in accordance with the regulations.

**Manner of payment**

(2) An amount payable to a society under subsection (1), including advances on expenditures before they are incurred, shall be paid at the times and in the manner determined by the Minister.

**Accountability agreement**

**41.** (1) Every society shall enter into an accountability agreement with the Minister as a condition of receiving funding.

**Term**

(2) The term of an accountability agreement shall be for at least one of the Ministry's fiscal years but may be for a longer term specified by the Minister.

**Board approval**

(3) The society's board of directors shall approve the accountability agreement before the society enters into the agreement.

**Content**

(4) An accountability agreement must include a requirement that the society operate within its approved budget allocation and any other prescribed terms.

**If no agreement**

(5) If the Minister and a society cannot agree on the terms of an accountability agreement by a date determined by the Minister, the Minister may set the terms of the agreement.

**Directives and Compliance Orders (Societies)**

**Directives by Minister**

**42.** (1) The Minister may issue directives to societies, including directives with respect to financial and administrative matters and the performance of their functions under subsection 35 (1).

**Binding**

(2) A society shall comply with every directive issued to it under this section.

**General or particular**

(3) A directive may be general or particular in its application.

**Law prevails**

(4) For greater certainty, in the event of a conflict between a directive issued under this section and a provision of any applicable Act or rule of any applicable law, the provision or rule prevails.

**Public availability**

(5) The Minister shall make every directive under this section available to the public.

**Non-application of *Legislation Act, 2006***

(6) Part III (Regulations) of the *Legislation Act, 2006* does not apply to a directive issued under this section.

**Compliance order**

**Grounds**

**43.** (1) A Director may make an order under subsection (2) if the Director believes on reasonable grounds that a society has failed to comply with,

(a) this Act or the regulations;

(b) a condition imposed on the society's designation under subsection 34 (2);

(c) an accountability agreement entered into under section 41; or

(d) a directive issued under section 42.

### Order

(2) For the purposes of subsection (1), a Director may issue an order to the society that requires either or both of the following:

1. That the society do anything, or refrain from doing anything, to achieve compliance within the time period specified in the order.

2. That the society prepare, submit and implement, within the time period specified in the order, a plan for achieving compliance.

### Compliance required

(3) A society served with an order under this section shall comply with the order within the time specified in it.

### Public availability

(4) The Minister,

(a) may make orders under this section available to the public; and

(b) shall make a summary of each order under this section available to the public in accordance with the regulations.

### Minister's Powers

### Powers of Minister

### Grounds

**44.** (1) The Minister may exercise a power set out in subsection (3) if,

(a) a society has failed to comply with a compliance order made under section 43 within the time specified in it; or

(b) the Minister considers it to be in the public interest to do so.

### Public interest

(2) In considering the public interest under clause (1) (b), the Minister may consider any matter the Minister regards as relevant including,

(a) the quality of the financial and operational management of the society;

(b) the society's capabilities with respect to its corporate governance; and

(c) the quality of services provided by the society.

### Powers

(3) For the purposes of subsection (1), the Minister may do one or more of the following:

1. Order that the society cease a particular activity or take other corrective action within the time specified in the order.

2. Impose or amend conditions on the society's designation under subsection 34 (1).

3. Suspend, amend or revoke the designation of the society.

4. Appoint members of the society's board of directors if,

    i. there are vacancies on the board, or

    ii. there are no vacancies, but the appointment is for the purposes of designating that member as chair of the board under paragraph 7.

5. Remove members of the board and appoint others in their place.

6. Designate a chair of the board, if the office of chair is vacant.

7. Designate another chair of the board in place of the current chair.

8. Appoint a supervisor to operate and manage the affairs and activities of the society.

### Notice of proposal

(4) If the Minister proposes to act under subsection (3), the Minister shall give written notice of the proposal and reasons for it to the society.

### Immediate action

(5) Subsection (4) does not apply if,

(a) in the Minister's opinion, the society has, by its conduct, acquiesced to the Minister's proposal;

(b) the society has consented to the proposal; or

(c) there are not enough members on the board to form a quorum.

### Right to respond

(6) A society that receives notice under subsection (4) may make written submissions to the Minister within 14 days after receipt of the notice or within a different time period specified in the notice.

### Minister's decision

(7) After considering a written submission from the society or, if no submission is received, after the time period under subsection (6) has expired, the Minister may carry out the proposal and shall give written notice of the decision and reasons for it to the society.

### Decision final

(8) The Minister's decision is final.

### Provisional action

(9) Despite subsection (4), the Minister may provisionally exercise any of the powers set out in subsection (3) where, in the Minister's opinion, it is necessary to do so to avert an immediate threat to the public interest or to a person's health, safety or well-being.

### Notice

(10) The Minister shall give written notice of the provisional exercise of the power and reasons for it to the society.

### Decision final

(11) The Minister's decision to provisionally exercise the power is final.

### Appointments to board, etc.

### Members

**45.** (1) If the Minister appoints members of a society's board of directors under paragraph 4 or 5 of subsection 44 (3), the following rules apply:

1. The Minister shall ensure that the members do not constitute a majority of the number of members required to be on the board.
2. The members shall be appointed at the pleasure of the Minister for a period that does not exceed two years.
3. The members may serve as appointed members for no more than two consecutive years.
4. The members shall have the same rights and responsibilities as the members of the board that have been elected.

### Chair

(2) If the Minister designates a chair of the board of directors under paragraph 6 or 7 of subsection 44 (3), the following rules apply:

1. The chair may be designated from among the members of the board, including any members appointed by the Minister under paragraph 4 or 5 of subsection 44 (3).
2. The chair shall be designated at the pleasure of the Minister for a period that does not exceed two years.
3. The chair may serve as chair for no more than two consecutive years.
4. In the case of a designation under paragraph 7 of subsection 44 (3), the former chair may remain a member of the board.

### Appointment of supervisor

**46.** (1) This section applies if a supervisor is appointed to operate and manage the affairs and activities of a society under paragraph 8 of subsection 44 (3).

### Term of appointment

(2) The appointment of a supervisor is valid for a period not exceeding one year without the society's consent, but the Lieutenant Governor in Council may extend the period at any time.

### Powers and duties of supervisor

(3) Unless the appointment provides otherwise, the supervisor has the exclusive right to exercise all the powers and perform all the duties of the society and its members, directors, Executive Director and officers.

### Same

(4) The Minister may, in the appointment, specify the supervisor's powers and duties and the conditions governing them.

### Examples of powers and duties

(5) Without limiting the generality of subsection (4), the supervisor's powers and duties may include the following:

1. Carrying on the society's affairs and activities.
2. Entering into contracts on the society's behalf.
3. Arranging for bank accounts to be opened in the society's name.
4. Authorizing persons to sign financial and other documents on the society's behalf.
5. Hiring or dismissing employees of the society.
6. Making, amending or revoking the society's by-laws.
7. Executing and filing documents on the society's behalf, including applications under the *Corporations Act* and notices and returns under the *Corporations Information Act*.

> **Note:  On the first day that section 350 of Schedule 1 to the *Supporting Children, Youth and Families Act, 2017* and subsection 4 (1) of the *Not-for-Profit Corporations Act, 2010* are both in force, paragraph 7 of subsection 46 (5) of the Act is amended by striking out "the *Corporations Act*" and substituting "the *Not-for-Profit Corporations Act, 2010*". (See: 2017, c. 14, Sched. 3, s. 1)**

### Continued powers and duties of society, etc.

(6) If, under the appointment, the society or its members, directors, Executive Director or officers continue to have any powers or duties during the supervisor's appointment, any exercise of that power or performance of that duty by the society or its members, directors, Executive Director or officers during that time is valid only if approved by the supervisor in writing.

### Assistance

(7) The supervisor may apply to the Superior Court of Justice for an order directing a peace officer to assist the supervisor in occupying the premises of a society.

### Report to Minister

(8) The supervisor shall report to the Minister as the Minister requires.

### Minister's directions

(9) The Minister may issue directions to the supervisor with regard to any matter within the supervisor's jurisdiction, and the supervisor shall carry them out.

**No proceedings against Crown**

(10) No proceeding, other than a proceeding referred to in subsection (12), shall be commenced against the Crown or the Minister with respect to the appointment of the supervisor or any act of the supervisor done in good faith in the execution or intended execution of any duty or power under this Act or the regulations, or for an alleged neglect or default in the execution in good faith of that duty or power.

**No personal liability**

(11) No action or other proceeding shall be instituted against the supervisor for any act done in good faith in the execution or intended execution of any duty or power under this Act or the regulations, or for an alleged neglect or default in the execution in good faith of that duty or power.

**Crown liability**

(12) Despite subsections 5 (2) and (4) of the *Proceedings Against the Crown Act*, subsection (11) of this section does not relieve the Crown of liability to which the Crown would otherwise be subject in respect of a tort committed by a supervisor.

**Effect on board**

(13) On the appointment of a supervisor, the members of the society's board cease to hold office, unless the appointment provides otherwise.

**Same**

(14) During the term of the supervisor's appointment, the powers of any member of the board who continues to hold office are suspended, unless the appointment provides otherwise.

**No personal liability**

(15) No action or other proceeding shall be instituted against a member or former member of the board for anything done by the supervisor after the member's removal under subsection (13) or while the member's powers are suspended under subsection (14).

## Restructuring

### Amalgamation by societies

**Amalgamation proposal**

**47.** (1) Two or more societies that are proposing to amalgamate and continue as one society shall submit an amalgamation proposal to the Minister containing the information and in the form specified by the Minister.

**Minister approval of proposal**

(2) The Minister may amend the amalgamation proposal and may approve it in whole or in part.

**Amalgamation agreement**

(3) The societies shall not enter into an agreement to amalgamate under subsection 113 (2) of the *Corporations Act* until they have received the Minister's approval of the amalgamation

proposal under subsection (2). The amalgamation agreement must be consistent with the amalgamation proposal.

> **Note:** On the first day that section 350 of Schedule 1 to the *Supporting Children, Youth and Families Act, 2017* and subsection 4 (1) of the *Not-for-Profit Corporations Act, 2010* are both in force, subsection 47 (3) of the Act is amended by striking out "subsection 113 (2) of the *Corporations Act*" and substituting "subsection 110 (2) of the *Not-for-Profit Corporations Act, 2010*". (See: 2017, c. 14, Sched. 3, s. 2 (1))

**Minister approval of amalgamation application**

(4) The societies shall not apply to amalgamate under subsection 113 (4) of the *Corporations Act* until the application has first received the approval of the Minister.

> **Note:** On the first day that section 350 of Schedule 1 to the *Supporting Children, Youth and Families Act, 2017* and subsection 4 (1) of the *Not-for-Profit Corporations Act, 2010* are both in force, subsection 47 (4) of the Act is repealed and the following substituted: (See: 2017, c. 14, Sched. 3, s. 2 (2))

**Minister approval of articles of amalgamation**

(4) The societies shall not file articles of amalgamation under section 112 of the *Not-for-Profit Corporations Act, 2010* until the articles have first received the approval of the Minister. 2017, c. 14, Sched. 3, s. 2 (2).

**Minister's directions**

(5) The Minister may, at any time, issue directions to the societies with regard to the proposed amalgamation, including requiring that a society provide information or documents to the Minister, and the society shall comply with the directions.

**Restructuring by Minister's order**

**48.** (1) If the Minister considers it to be in the public interest, including to enhance the efficiency, effectiveness and consistency of services, the Minister may order a society to do any of the following on or after the date set out in the order:

1. To amalgamate with one or more other societies.
2. To transfer all or any part of its operations to one or more other societies.
3. To cease operating, to dissolve or to wind up its operations.
4. To do anything or refrain from doing anything in order for the society to achieve anything under paragraphs 1 to 3.

## Minister's directions

(2) The Minister may, in the order, include directions to provide the following to the Minister within the time set out in the order:

1. A plan to implement the order, including with respect to the transfer of assets, liabilities, rights and obligations, and of employees.
2. A timeline according to which the order will be implemented.
3. A proposed budget for implementation of the order.
4. Information about the status of the implementation of the order.
5. In the case of an order made under paragraph 1 of subsection (1), an amalgamation agreement for the Minister's approval.
6. Information with respect to any other matter specified by the Minister.

## Notice of proposed order

(3) If the Minister proposes to make an order under subsection (1), the Minister shall give written notice of the proposed order and any directions contained in the order, and reasons for them, to each affected society.

## Notice to employees and bargaining agents

(4) Each society that receives a notice under subsection (3) shall give a copy of the notice to affected employees and their bargaining agents.

## Right to respond re directions

(5) A society may make written submissions to the Minister within 30 days after receipt of the notice or within a different time period specified in the notice. The written submissions may be with respect to any directions contained in the order, but not with respect to the order itself.

## Minister's decision re directions

(6) After considering a written submission from the society or, if no submission is received, after the time period under subsection (5) has expired, the Minister may confirm, revoke or amend the directions contained in the order.

## Notice of order

(7) The Minister shall give a copy of the order to each affected society.

## Duty of society

(8) Each society that receives an order under subsection (7) shall,

(a) give notice of the order to affected employees and their bargaining agents and to other persons or entities whose contracts are affected by the order; and

(b) make the order available to the public.

## Additional changes

(9) The Minister may, at any time, revoke or amend an order made under this section, including any directions contained in the order. If the Minister does so, subsections (3) to (8) apply with necessary modifications.

## Compliance

(10) A society that is the subject of an order under this section shall comply with it.

## Corporate powers

(11) A society that is the subject of an order under this section is deemed to have the necessary powers to comply with the order, despite any of the following:

1. Any Act or regulation.
2. Any other instrument related to the corporate governance of a society, including the *Corporations Act* or any letters patent, supplementary letters patent or by-laws.

> **Note: On the first day that section 350 of Schedule 1 to the *Supporting Children, Youth and Families Act, 2017* and subsection 4 (1) of the *Not-for-Profit Corporations Act, 2010* are both in force, paragraph 2 of subsection 48 (11) of the Act is amended by striking out "the *Corporations Act* or any letters patent, supplementary letters patent or by-laws" at the end and substituting "the *Not-for-Profit Corporations Act, 2010* or any articles or by-laws". (See: 2017, c. 14, Sched. 3, s. 3 (1))**

## Non-application of *Legislation Act, 2006*

(12) Part III (Regulations) of the *Legislation Act, 2006* does not apply to an order made under this section.

## Minister approval of amalgamation agreement

(13) When a society provides an amalgamation agreement to the Minister in accordance with directions given under paragraph 5 of subsection (2), the Minister may amend the agreement and may approve it in whole or in part.

## Minister approval of amalgamation application

(14) A society shall not apply to amalgamate under subsection 113 (4) of the *Corporations Act* until the application has first received the approval of the Minister.

> **Note: On the first day that section 350 of Schedule 1 to the *Supporting Children, Youth and Families Act, 2017* and subsection 4 (1) of the *Not-for-Profit Corporations Act, 2010* are both in force, subsection 48 (14) of the Act is repealed and the following substituted: (See: 2017, c. 14, Sched. 3, s. 3 (2))**

### Minister approval of articles of amalgamation

(14) A society shall not file articles of amalgamation under section 112 of the *Not-for-Profit Corporations Act, 2010* until the articles have first received the approval of the Minister. 2017, c. 14, Sched. 3, s. 3 (2).

### Appointment of supervisor for restructuring

**49.** (1) The Minister may appoint a supervisor to implement or facilitate the implementation of an order made under section 48 if,

(a) an affected society has failed to comply with the order; or

(b) in the Minister's opinion, there is undue delay, lack of progress or disagreement between or among affected parties that is preventing or is likely to prevent an affected society from complying with the order.

### Application of other provisions

(2) If the Minister proposes to appoint a supervisor under subsection (1), subsections 44 (4) to (8) and subsections 46 (2) to (15) apply with necessary modifications.

### Board compliance

(3) The members of an affected society's board of directors shall comply with decisions of a supervisor appointed under subsection (1) to facilitate the implementation of an order made under section 48 with regard to matters within the supervisor's jurisdiction.

### Conflict with *Corporations Act*, etc.

**50.** In the event of a conflict between sections 44 to 49 and any of the following, sections 44 to 49 prevail:

1. The *Corporations Act* or regulations made under that Act.

2. A society's letters patent, supplementary letters patent or by-laws.

> **Note: On the first day that section 350 of Schedule 1 to the *Supporting Children, Youth and Families Act, 2017* and subsection 4 (1) of the *Not-for-Profit Corporations Act, 2010* are both in force, section 50 of the Act is repealed and the following substituted: (See: 2017, c. 14, Sched. 3, s. 4)**

### Conflict with society's articles or by-laws

**50.** In the event of a conflict between sections 44 to 49 and a society's articles or by-laws, sections 44 to 49 prevail. 2017, c. 14, Sched. 3, s. 4.

### Transfer of property held for charitable purpose

**51.** (1) If an order made under section 48 directs a society to transfer to a transferee property that it holds for a charitable purpose, all gifts, trusts, bequests, devises and grants of property that form part of the property being transferred are deemed to be gifts, trusts, bequests, devises and grants of property to the transferee.

### Specified purpose

(2) If a will, deed or other document by which a gift, trust, bequest, devise or grant mentioned in subsection (1) is made indicates that the property being transferred is to be used for a specified purpose, the transferee shall use it for the specified purpose.

### Application

(3) Subsections (1) and (2) apply whether the will, deed or document by which the gift, trust, bequest, devise or grant is made, is made before or after this section comes into force.

### No compensation

**52.** (1) Despite any other Act, no person or entity, including a society, is entitled to any compensation for any loss or damages arising from any direct or indirect action that the Minister or a supervisor appointed under section 44 or 49 takes under this Act, including making an order under section 48.

### Same, transfer of property

(2) Despite any other Act, no person or entity, including a society, is entitled to compensation for any loss or damages, including loss of use, loss of revenue and loss of profit, arising from the transfer of property under an order made under section 48.

### No expropriation

(3) Nothing in this Part and nothing done or not done in accordance with this Part constitutes an expropriation or injurious affection for the purposes of the *Expropriations Act* or otherwise at law.

## Appointments and Delegations
### Directors and program supervisors
### Appointment of Director

**53.** (1) The Minister may appoint any person as a Director to perform any or all of the duties and functions and exercise any or all of the powers of a Director under this Act and the regulations.

### Appointment of program supervisor

(2) The Minister may appoint any person as a program supervisor to perform any or all of the duties and functions and exercise any or all of the powers of a program supervisor under this Act and the regulations.

### Limitations, etc., on appointments

(3) The Minister may set out in an appointment made under this section any conditions or limitations to which it is subject.

### Remuneration and expenses

(4) The remuneration and expenses of a person appointed under this section who is not a public servant employed under Part III of the *Public Service of Ontario Act, 2006* shall be fixed by the Minister and shall be paid out of money appropriated for the purpose by the Legislature.

### Duties of Director with respect to societies

**54.** (1) A Director shall exercise the powers and perform the duties of a society in any area in which no society is functioning.

### Powers of local director

(2) In exercising the powers and performing the duties of a society under subsection (1), a Director has all the powers of a local director.

### Delegation by Minister

**55.** (1) Where, under this Act, a power is given to or a duty is imposed on the Minister, a Director, a program supervisor or an employee in the Ministry, the Minister may delegate that power or duty to any other person or class of persons.

### Conditions, etc.

(2) The delegation must be made in writing and is subject to such limitations, conditions and requirements as are set out in it.

### Deeds and contracts

(3) Section 6 of the *Executive Council Act* does not apply to a deed or contract that is executed under a delegation made under this section.

### Reports and Information
### Reports and information to Minister

**56.** Every service provider and lead agency shall,

(a) make the prescribed reports and provide the prescribed information, including personal information, to the Minister, in the prescribed form and at the prescribed intervals; and

(b) make a report and provide information, including personal information, to the Minister whenever the Minister requests it.

### Reports and information to prescribed entities

**57.** Every service provider and lead agency shall provide the prescribed reports and the prescribed information to the prescribed entities in the prescribed manner.

### Information available to the public

**58.** Every service provider and lead agency shall make the prescribed information available to the public in the prescribed manner.

### Program Supervisor Inspections
### Inspection by program supervisor without a warrant

**59.** (1) For the purpose of determining compliance with this Act, the regulations and the directives issued under this Act, a program supervisor may, at any reasonable time and without a warrant or notice, enter the following premises in order to conduct an inspection:

1. Premises where a service is provided under this Act.
2. Premises where a lead agency's function referred to in subsection 30 (5) is performed.

3. Business premises of a service provider.
4. Business premises of a lead agency.

### Limitation, dwelling

(2) The power to enter and inspect a premises described in subsection (1) shall not be exercised to enter and inspect any room or place actually being used as a dwelling, except with the consent of the occupier.

### Identification

(3) A program supervisor conducting an inspection shall, upon request, produce proper identification.

### Application of other provisions

(4) Sections 276 (powers on inspection) and 279 (admissibility of certain documents) apply with necessary modifications with respect to an inspection conducted under this section.

### Inspection by program supervisor with a warrant

**60.** (1) A program supervisor may, without notice, apply to a justice for a warrant under this section.

### Issuance of warrant

(2) A justice may issue a warrant authorizing a program supervisor named in the warrant to enter the premises specified in the warrant and to exercise any of the powers mentioned in subsection 276 (1), if the justice is satisfied on information under oath or affirmation,

(a) that the premises is a premises described in subsection 59 (1);

(b) in the case of a premises that is not used as a dwelling,

(i) that the program supervisor has been prevented from exercising a right of entry to the premises under section 59 or a power under subsection 276 (1), or

(ii) that there are reasonable grounds to believe that the program supervisor will be prevented from exercising a right of entry to the premises under section 58 or a power under subsection 276 (1); and

(c) in the case of a premises that is used as a dwelling,

(i) that,

(A) the program supervisor believes on reasonable grounds that a service being provided, or the manner of providing it, is causing harm or is likely to cause harm to a person's health, safety or well-being as a result of non-compliance with this Act, the regulations or the directives issued under this Act, and

(B) it is necessary for the program supervisor to exercise the powers mentioned in subsection 276 (1) in order to inspect the service or the manner of providing it, or

(ii) that a ground exists that is prescribed for the purposes of this subclause.

### Expert help

(3)  The warrant may authorize persons who have special, expert or professional knowledge to accompany and assist the program supervisor in the execution of the warrant.

### Expiry of warrant

(4)  A warrant issued under this section shall name a date on which it expires, which shall be no later than 30 days after the warrant is issued.

### Extension of time

(5)  A justice may extend the date on which a warrant issued under this section expires for an additional period of no more than 30 days, upon application without notice by the program supervisor named in the warrant.

### Use of force

(6)  A program supervisor named in a warrant issued under this section may use whatever force is necessary to execute the warrant and may call upon a peace officer for assistance in executing the warrant.

### Time of execution

(7)  A warrant issued under this section may be executed between 8 a.m. and 8 p.m. only, unless the warrant specifies otherwise.

### Other matters

(8)  Subsections 276 (2) to (7) and section 279 apply with necessary modifications with respect to the exercise of powers referred to in subsection (2) under a warrant issued under this section.

### Definition

(9)  In this section,
"justice" means a provincial judge or a justice of the peace.

### Inspection report

**61.** (1)  After completing an inspection, a program supervisor shall prepare an inspection report and give a copy of the report to,

    (a)  a Director;

    (b)  the service provider or lead agency; and

    (c)  any other prescribed person.

### All non-compliance to be documented

(2)  If a program supervisor finds that a service provider or lead agency has not complied with a requirement of this Act, the regulations or a directive issued under this Act, the program supervisor shall document the non-compliance in the inspection report.

### Review by Residential Placement Advisory Committee

### Definitions

**62.**  In sections 63 to 66,

"advisory committee" means a residential placement advisory committee established under subsection 63 (1); ("comité consultatif")

"institution" means,

    (a)  a children's residence, other than a maternity home, operated by the Minister or under the authority of a licence issued under Part IX (Residential Licensing) in which residential care can be provided to 10 or more children at a time, or

    (b)  a building, group of buildings or part of a building, designated by a Director, in which residential care can be provided to 10 or more children at a time; ("foyer")

"residential placement" does not include,

    (a)  a placement made under the *Youth Criminal Justice Act* (Canada) or under Part VI (Youth Justice),

    (b)  commitment to a secure treatment program under Part VII (Extraordinary Measures), or

    (c)  a placement with a person who is neither a service provider nor a foster parent; ("placement en établissement")

"special need" means a need that is related to or caused by a developmental disability or a behavioural, emotional, physical, mental or other disability. ("besoin particulier")

### Residential placement advisory committees

**63.** (1)  The Minister may establish residential placement advisory committees and shall specify the territorial jurisdiction of each advisory committee.

### Composition

(2)  Each residential placement advisory committee shall consist of persons whom the Minister considers appropriate, which may include,

    (a)  persons engaged in providing services;

    (b)  other persons who have demonstrated an informed concern for the welfare of children;

    (c)  one representative of the Ministry; and

    (d)  if the Minister wishes, a representative of a band or First Nations, Inuit or Métis community.

### Payments to members, hiring of staff

(3)  The Minister may pay allowances and reasonable travelling expenses to the members of an advisory committee, and may authorize an advisory committee to hire support staff.

### Duties of advisory committee

(4)  An advisory committee has a duty to advise, inform and assist parents, children and service providers with respect to the availability and appropriateness of residential care and alternatives to residential care, to conduct reviews under section 64 and to name persons for the purpose of subsection 75 (11) (contact with child under temporary care agreement), and has such further duties as are prescribed.

### Reports to Minister

(5) An advisory committee shall make a report of its activities to the Minister annually and at any other time requested by the Minister.

## Review by advisory committee

### Mandatory review

**64.** (1) An advisory committee shall review,

(a) every residential placement in an institution of a child who resides within the advisory committee's jurisdiction, if the residential placement is intended to last or actually lasts 90 days or more,

(i) as soon as possible, but no later than 45 days after the day on which the child is placed in the institution,

(ii) unless the residential placement is reviewed under subclause (i), within 12 months of the establishment of the advisory committee or within such longer period as the Minister allows, and

(iii) while the residential placement continues, at least once during each nine-month period after the review under subclause (i) or (ii);

(b) every residential placement of a child who objects to the residential placement and resides within the advisory committee's jurisdiction,

(i) within the week immediately following the day that is 14 days after the child is placed, and

(ii) while the residential placement continues, at least once during each nine-month period after the review under subclause (i); and

(c) an existing or proposed residential placement of a child that the Minister refers to the advisory committee, within 30 days of the referral.

### Discretionary review

(2) An advisory committee may at any time review or re-review, on a person's request or on its own initiative, an existing or proposed residential placement of a child who resides within the advisory committee's jurisdiction.

### Review to be informal, etc.

(3) An advisory committee shall conduct a review under this section in an informal manner and in the absence of the public, and in the course of the review may,

(a) interview the child, members of the child's family and any representatives of the child and family;

(b) interview persons engaged in providing services and other persons who may have an interest in the matter or may have information that would assist the advisory committee;

(c) examine documents and reports that are presented to the committee; and

(d) examine records relating to the child and members of the child's family that are disclosed to the committee.

### Service providers to assist advisory committee

(4) At an advisory committee's request, a service provider shall assist and co-operate with the advisory committee in its conduct of a review.

### Matters to be considered

(5) In conducting a review, an advisory committee shall,

(a) consider whether the child has a special need;

(b) consider the child's views and wishes, given due weight in accordance with the child's age and maturity;

(c) consider what programs are available for the child in the residential placement or proposed residential placement, and whether a program available to the child is likely to benefit the child;

(d) consider whether the residential placement or proposed residential placement is appropriate for the child in the circumstances;

(e) if it considers that a less restrictive alternative to the residential placement would be more appropriate for the child in the circumstances, specify that alternative;

(f) consider the importance of continuity in the child's care and the possible effect on the child of disruption of that continuity; and

(g) in the case of a First Nations, Inuk or Métis child, also consider the importance, in recognition of the uniqueness of First Nations, Inuit and Métis cultures, heritages and traditions, of preserving the child's cultural identity and connection to community.

## Advisory committee's recommendations

### Persons to be advised

**65.** (1) An advisory committee that conducts a review shall advise the following persons of its recommendations as soon as the review has been completed:

1. The service provider.
2. Any representative of the child.
3. The child's parent or, where the child is in a society's lawful custody, the society.
4. The child, in language suitable to the child's understanding.
5. In the case of a First Nations, Inuk or Métis child, the persons described in paragraphs 1, 2, 3 and 4 and a representative chosen by each of the child's bands and First Nations, Inuit or Métis communities.

### Child to be advised of right to review by Board of residential placement

(2) An advisory committee that conducts a review shall advise the child of the child's right to a further review under section 66.

### Report to Minister

(3) An advisory committee that conducts a review shall, within 30 days of completing the review, make a report of its findings and recommendations to the Minister.

### Recommendation for less restrictive service

(4) Where an advisory committee considers that the provision of a less restrictive service to a child would be more appropriate for the child than the residential placement, the advisory committee shall recommend in its report under subsection (3) that the less restrictive service be provided to the child.

## Review by Board

### Child may request review

**66.** (1) A child who is in a residential placement to which the child objects may apply to the Board for a determination of where the child should remain or be placed, if the residential placement has been reviewed by an advisory committee under section 64 and,

(a) the child is dissatisfied with the advisory committee's recommendations; or

(b) the advisory committee's recommendations are not followed.

### Board to conduct review

(2) The Board shall conduct a review with respect to an application made under subsection (1) and may do so by holding a hearing.

### Notice to child of hearing

(3) The Board shall advise the child whether it intends to hold a hearing or not within 10 days of receiving the child's application.

### Parties

(4) The parties to a hearing under this section are,

(a) the child;

(b) the child's parent or, where the child is in a society's lawful custody, the society;

(c) in the case of a First Nations, Inuk or Métis child, the persons described in clauses (a) and (b) and a representative chosen by each of the child's bands and First Nations, Inuit or Métis communities; and

(d) any other persons that the Board specifies.

### Time for determination

(5) The Board shall complete its review and make a determination within 30 days of receiving a child's application, unless,

(a) the Board holds a hearing with respect to the application; and

(b) the parties consent to a longer period for the Board's determination.

### Board's order

(6) After conducting a review under subsection (2), the Board may,

(a) order that the child be transferred to another residential placement, if the Board is satisfied that the other residential placement is available;

(b) order that the child be discharged from the residential placement; or

(c) confirm the existing residential placement.

## Offences

### Offences

**67.** (1) A person or entity is guilty of an offence if the person or entity,

(a) contravenes section 56 (reports and information);

(b) contravenes section 57 (reports and information to prescribed entities);

(c) contravenes section 58 (information available to public);

(d) knowingly provides false information in a statement, report or return required to be provided under this Part or the regulations.

### Penalty

(2) A person or entity convicted of an offence under subsection (1) is liable to a fine of not more than $5,000.

### Offence—obstruction of program supervisor

(3) A person is guilty of an offence if the person hinders, obstructs or interferes with a program supervisor conducting an inspection under this Part, or otherwise impedes a program supervisor in exercising the powers or performing the duties of a program supervisor under this Part.

### Penalty

(4) A person convicted of an offence under subsection (3) is liable to a fine of not more than $5,000.

### Limitation

(5) A proceeding in respect of an offence under subsection (1) or (3) shall not be commenced more than two years after the day on which evidence of the offence first came to the knowledge of the Director or program supervisor.

### Directors, officers and employees

(6) If a corporation commits an offence under this section, a director, officer or employee of the corporation who authorized, permitted or concurred in the commission of the offence is also guilty of the offence.

## PART IV   FIRST NATIONS, INUIT AND MÉTIS CHILD AND FAMILY SERVICES

### Regulations listing First Nations, Inuit and Métis communities

**68.** (1) The Minister may make regulations establishing lists of First Nations, Inuit and Métis communities for the purposes of this Act.

### More than one community

(2) A regulation made under subsection (1) may list one or more communities as a First Nations, Inuit or Métis community.

## Consent of representatives

(3) Before making a regulation under subsection (1), the Minister must obtain the consent of the community's representatives.

## Agreements with bands and First Nations, Inuit or Métis communities

69. The Minister may, for the provision of services,

(a) make agreements with bands and First Nations, Inuit or Métis communities and with any other parties whom the bands or communities choose to involve; and

(b) provide funding to the persons or entities referred to in clause (a) pursuant to such agreements.

## Designation of child and family service authority

70. (1) A band or First Nations, Inuit or Métis community may designate a body as a First Nations, Inuit or Métis child and family service authority.

## Agreements, etc.

(2) Where a band or First Nations, Inuit or Métis community has designated a First Nations, Inuit or Métis child and family service authority, the Minister,

(a) shall, at the band's or community's request, enter into negotiations for the provision of services by the child and family service authority;

(b) may enter into agreements with the child and family service authority and, if the band or community agrees, any other person, for the provision of services; and

(c) may designate the child and family service authority, with its consent, as a society under subsection 34 (1).

## Subsidy for customary care

71. If a band or First Nations, Inuit or Métis community declares that a First Nations, Inuk or Métis child is being cared for under customary care, a society or entity may grant a subsidy to the person caring for the child.

## Consultation with bands and First Nations, Inuit or Métis communities

72. A society, person or entity that provides services or exercises powers under this Act with respect to First Nations, Inuit or Métis children or young persons shall regularly consult with their bands and First Nations, Inuit or Métis communities about the provision of the services or the exercise of the powers and about matters affecting the children or young persons, including,

(a) bringing children to a place of safety and the placement of children in residential care;

(b) the provision of family support services;

(c) the preparation of plans for the care of children;

(d) status reviews under Part V (Child Protection);

(e) temporary care agreements under Part V (Child Protection);

(f) society agreements with 16 and 17 year olds under Part V (Child Protection);

(g) adoption placements;

(h) the establishment of emergency houses; and

(i) any other matter that is prescribed.

## Consultation in specified cases

73. A society, person or entity that proposes to provide a prescribed service to a First Nations, Inuk or Métis child or young person, or to exercise a prescribed power under this Act in relation to such a child or young person, shall consult with a representative chosen by each of the child's or young person's bands and First Nations, Inuit or Métis communities in accordance with the regulations.

## PART V   CHILD PROTECTION
### Interpretation

### Interpretation
### Definitions

74. (1) In this Part,

"child protection worker" means a Director, a local director or a person who meets the prescribed requirements and who is authorized by a Director or local director for the purposes of section 81 (commencing child protection proceedings) and for other prescribed purposes; ("préposé à la protection de l'enfance")

"extra-provincial child protection order" means a temporary or final order made by a court of another province or a territory of Canada, or of a prescribed jurisdiction outside Canada if it meets prescribed conditions, pursuant to child welfare legislation of that province, territory or other jurisdiction, placing a child into the care and custody of a child welfare authority or other person named in the order; ("ordonnance extraprovinciale de protection d'un enfant")

"parent", when used in reference to a child, means each of the following persons, but does not include a foster parent:

1. A parent of the child under section 6, 8, 9, 10, 11 or 13 of the *Children's Law Reform Act*.

2. In the case of a child conceived through sexual intercourse, an individual described in one of paragraphs 1 to 5 of subsection 7 (2) of the *Children's Law Reform Act*, unless it is proved on a balance of probabilities that the sperm used to conceive the child did not come from the individual.

3. An individual who has been found or recognized by a court of competent jurisdiction outside Ontario to be a parent of the child.

4. In the case of an adopted child, a parent of the child as provided for under section 217 or 218.

5. An individual who has lawful custody of the child.

6. An individual who, during the 12 months before intervention under this Part, has demonstrated a settled intention to treat the child as a child of the individual's family, or has acknowledged parentage of the child and provided for the child's support.

7. An individual who, under a written agreement or a court order, is required to provide for the child, has custody of the child or has a right of access to the child.

8. An individual who acknowledged parentage of the child by filing a statutory declaration under section 12 of the *Children's Law Reform Act* as it read before the day subsection 1 (1) of the *All Families Are Equal Act (Parentage and Related Registrations Statute Law Amendment), 2016* came into force; ("parent")

"place of safety" means a foster home, a hospital, a person's home that satisfies the requirements of subsection (4) or a place or one of a class of places designated as a place of safety by a Director or local director under section 39, but does not include a place of temporary detention, of open custody or of secure custody; ("lieu sûr")

## Child in need of protection

(2) A child is in need of protection where,

(a) the child has suffered physical harm, inflicted by the person having charge of the child or caused by or resulting from that person's,

(i) failure to adequately care for, provide for, supervise or protect the child, or

(ii) pattern of neglect in caring for, providing for, supervising or protecting the child;

(b) there is a risk that the child is likely to suffer physical harm inflicted by the person having charge of the child or caused by or resulting from that person's,

(i) failure to adequately care for, provide for, supervise or protect the child, or

(ii) pattern of neglect in caring for, providing for, supervising or protecting the child;

(c) the child has been sexually abused or sexually exploited, by the person having charge of the child or by another person where the person having charge of the child knows or should know of the possibility of sexual abuse or sexual exploitation and fails to protect the child;

(d) there is a risk that the child is likely to be sexually abused or sexually exploited as described in clause (c);

(e) the child requires treatment to cure, prevent or alleviate physical harm or suffering and the child's parent or the person having charge of the child does not provide the treatment or access to the treatment, or, where the child is incapable of consenting to the treatment under the *Health Care Consent Act, 1996* and the parent is a substitute decision-maker for the child, the parent refuses or is unavailable or unable to consent to the treatment on the child's behalf;

(f) the child has suffered emotional harm, demonstrated by serious,

(i) anxiety,

(ii) depression,

(iii) withdrawal,

(iv) self-destructive or aggressive behaviour, or

(v) delayed development,

and there are reasonable grounds to believe that the emotional harm suffered by the child results from the actions, failure to act or pattern of neglect on the part of the child's parent or the person having charge of the child;

(g) the child has suffered emotional harm of the kind described in subclause (f) (i), (ii), (iii), (iv) or (v) and the child's parent or the person having charge of the child does not provide services or treatment or access to services or treatment, or, where the child is incapable of consenting to treatment under the *Health Care Consent Act, 1996*, refuses or is unavailable or unable to consent to the treatment to remedy or alleviate the harm;

(h) there is a risk that the child is likely to suffer emotional harm of the kind described in subclause (f) (i), (ii), (iii), (iv) or (v) resulting from the actions, failure to act or pattern of neglect on the part of the child's parent or the person having charge of the child;

(i) there is a risk that the child is likely to suffer emotional harm of the kind described in subclause (f) (i), (ii), (iii), (iv) or (v) and that the child's parent or the person having charge of the child does not provide services or treatment or access to services or treatment, or, where the child is incapable of consenting to treatment under the *Health Care Consent Act, 1996*, refuses or is unavailable or unable to consent to treatment to prevent the harm;

(j) the child suffers from a mental, emotional or developmental condition that, if not remedied, could seriously impair the child's development and the child's parent or the person having charge of the child does not provide treatment or access to treatment, or where the child is incapable of consenting to treatment under the *Health Care Consent Act, 1996*, refuses or is unavailable or unable to consent to the treatment to remedy or alleviate the condition;

(k) the child's parent has died or is unavailable to exercise custodial rights over the child and has not made adequate provision for the child's care and custody, or the child is in a residential placement and the parent refuses or is unable or unwilling to resume the child's care and custody;

(l) the child is younger than 12 and has killed or seriously injured another person or caused serious damage to another person's property, services or treatment are necessary to prevent a recurrence and the child's parent or the person having charge of the child does not provide services or treatment or access to services or treatment, or, where the child is incapable of consenting to treatment under the *Health Care Consent Act, 1996*, refuses or is unavailable or unable to consent to treatment;

(m) the child is younger than 12 and has on more than one occasion injured another person or caused loss or damage to another person's property, with the encouragement of the person having charge of the child or because of that person's failure or inability to supervise the child adequately;

(n) the child's parent is unable to care for the child and the child is brought before the court with the parent's consent and, where the child is 12 or older, with the child's consent, for the matter to be dealt with under this Part; or

(o) the child is 16 or 17 and a prescribed circumstance or condition exists.

## Best interests of child

(3) Where a person is directed in this Part to make an order or determination in the best interests of a child, the person shall,

(a) consider the child's views and wishes, given due weight in accordance with the child's age and maturity, unless they cannot be ascertained;

(b) in the case of a First Nations, Inuk or Métis child, consider the importance, in recognition of the uniqueness of First Nations, Inuit and Métis cultures, heritages and traditions, of preserving the child's cultural identity and connection to community, in addition to the considerations under clauses (a) and (c); and

(c) consider any other circumstance of the case that the person considers relevant, including,

(i) the child's physical, mental and emotional needs, and the appropriate care or treatment to meet those needs,

(ii) the child's physical, mental and emotional level of development,

(iii) the child's race, ancestry, place of origin, colour, ethnic origin, citizenship, family diversity, disability, creed, sex, sexual orientation, gender identity and gender expression,

(iv) the child's cultural and linguistic heritage,

(v) the importance for the child's development of a positive relationship with a parent and a secure place as a member of a family,

(vi) the child's relationships and emotional ties to a parent, sibling, relative, other member of the child's extended family or member of the child's community,

(vii) the importance of continuity in the child's care and the possible effect on the child of disruption of that continuity,

(viii) the merits of a plan for the child's care proposed by a society, including a proposal that the child be placed for adoption or adopted, compared with the merits of the child remaining with or returning to a parent,

(ix) the effects on the child of delay in the disposition of the case,

(x) the risk that the child may suffer harm through being removed from, kept away from, returned to or allowed to remain in the care of a parent, and

(xi) the degree of risk, if any, that justified the finding that the child is in need of protection.

## Place of safety

(4) For the purposes of the definition of "place of safety" in subsection (1), a person's home is a place of safety for a child if,

(a) the person is a relative of the child or a member of the child's extended family or community; and

(b) a society or, in the case of a First Nations, Inuk or Métis child, a society or a child and family service authority, has conducted an assessment of the person's home in accordance with the prescribed procedures and is satisfied that the person is willing and able to provide a safe home environment for the child.

## Definition, child and family service authority

(5) In subsection (4),

"child and family service authority" means a First Nations, Inuit or Métis child and family service authority designated under section 70.

### Voluntary Agreements
## Temporary care agreement

**75.** (1) A person who is temporarily unable to care adequately for a child in the person's custody, and the society having jurisdiction where the person resides, may make a written agreement for the society's care and custody of the child.

## Older child to be party to agreement

(2) No temporary care agreement shall be made in respect of a child who is 12 or older unless the child is a party to the agreement.

## Exception: developmental disability

(3) Subsection (2) does not apply where it has been determined on the basis of an assessment not more than one year before the agreement is made, that the child does not have capacity to participate in the agreement because of a developmental disability.

## Duty of society

(4) A society shall not make a temporary care agreement unless the society,

(a) has determined that an appropriate residential placement that is likely to benefit the child is available; and

(b) is satisfied that no course of action less disruptive to the child, such as care in the child's own home, is able to adequately protect the child.

## Term of agreement limited

(5)  No temporary care agreement shall be made for a term exceeding six months, but the parties to a temporary care agreement may, with a Director's written approval, agree to extend it for a further period or periods if the total term of the agreement, as extended, does not exceed 12 months.

## Time limit

(6)  No temporary care agreement shall be made or extended so as to result in a child being in a society's care and custody, for a period exceeding,

(a)  12 months, if the child is younger than 6 on the day the agreement is entered into or extended; or

(b)  24 months, if the child is 6 or older on the day the agreement is entered into or extended.

## Calculating time in care

(7)  The time during which a child has been in a society's care and custody pursuant to the following shall be counted in calculating the period referred to in subsection (6):

1.  An interim society care order made under paragraph 2 of subsection 101 (1).
2.  A temporary care agreement under subsection (1) of this section.
3.  A temporary order made under clause 94 (2) (d).

## Previous periods to be counted

(8)  The period referred to in subsection (6) shall include any previous periods that the child was in a society's care and custody as described in subsection (7) other than periods that precede a continuous period of five or more years that the child was not in a society's care and custody.

## Authority to consent to medical treatment may be transferred

(9)  A temporary care agreement may provide that, where the child is found incapable of consenting to treatment under the *Health Care Consent Act, 1996*, the society is entitled to act in the place of a parent in providing consent to treatment on the child's behalf.

## Contents of temporary care agreement

(10)  A temporary care agreement shall include the following:

1.  A statement by all the parties to the agreement that the child's care and custody are transferred to the society.
2.  A statement by all the parties to the agreement that the child's placement is voluntary.
3.  A statement, by the person referred to in subsection (1), that the person is temporarily unable to care for the child adequately and has discussed with the society alternatives to residential placement of the child.
4.  An undertaking by the person referred to in subsection (1) to maintain contact with the child and be involved in the child's care.

5.  If it is not possible for the person referred to in subsection (1) to maintain contact with the child and be involved in the child's care, the person's designation of another person who is willing to do so.
6.  The name of the individual who is the primary contact between the society and the person referred to in subsection (1).
7.  Such other provisions as are prescribed.

## Designation by advisory committee

(11)  Where the person referred to in subsection (1) does not give an undertaking under paragraph 4 of subsection (10) or designate another person under paragraph 5 of subsection (10), a residential placement advisory committee established under subsection 63 (1) that has jurisdiction may, in consultation with the society, name a suitable person who is willing to maintain contact with the child and be involved in the child's care.

## Variation of agreement

(12)  The parties to a temporary care agreement may vary the agreement from time to time in a manner that is consistent with this Part and the regulations made under it.

## Agreement expires at 18

(13)  No temporary care agreement shall continue beyond the 18th birthday of the person who is its subject.

## Notice of termination of agreement

**76.**  (1)  A party to a temporary care agreement may terminate the agreement at any time by giving every other party written notice that the party wishes to terminate the agreement.

## When notice takes effect

(2)  Where notice is given under subsection (1), the agreement terminates on the expiry of five days, or such longer period not exceeding 21 days as the agreement specifies, after the day on which every other party has actually received the notice.

## Society response to notice of termination

(3)  Where notice of a wish to terminate a temporary care agreement is given by or to a society under subsection (1), the society shall as soon as possible, and in any event before the agreement terminates under subsection (2),

(a)  cause the child to be returned to the person who made the agreement, or to a person who has obtained an order for the child's custody since the agreement was made;

(b)  where the society is of the opinion that the child would be in need of protection if returned to the person referred to in clause (a), bring the child before the court under this Part to determine whether the child would be in need of protection in that case; or

(c)  where the child is 16 or 17 and the criteria set out in clauses 77 (1) (a), (b), (c) and (d) are met, make a written agreement with the child under subsection 77 (1).

**Expiry of agreement**

(4) Where a temporary care agreement expires or is about to expire and is not extended, the society shall, before the agreement expires or as soon as practicable thereafter, but in any event within 21 days after the agreement expires,

(a) cause the child to be returned to the person who made the agreement, or to a person who has obtained an order for the child's custody since the agreement was made;

(b) where the society is of the opinion that the child would be in need of protection if returned to the person referred to in clause (a), bring the child before the court under this Part to determine whether the child would be in need of protection in that case; or

(c) where the child is 16 or 17 and the criteria set out in clauses 77 (1) (a), (b), (c) and (d) are met, make a written agreement with the child under subsection 77 (1).

**Society agreements with 16 and 17 year olds**

77. (1) The society and a child who is 16 or 17 may make a written agreement for services and supports to be provided for the child where,

(a) the society has jurisdiction where the child resides;

(b) the society has determined that the child is or may be in need of protection;

(c) the society is satisfied that no course of action less disruptive to the child, such as care in the child's own home or with a relative, neighbour or other member of the child's community or extended family, is able to adequately protect the child; and

(d) the child wants to enter into the agreement.

**Term of agreement**

(2) The agreement may be for a period not exceeding 12 months, but may be renewed if the total term of the agreement, as extended, does not exceed 24 months.

**Previous or current involvement with society not a bar to agreement**

(3) A child may enter into an agreement under this section regardless of any previous or current involvement with a society, and without regard to any time during which the child has been in a society's care pursuant to an agreement made under section 75 (1) or pursuant to an order made under clause 94 (2) (d) or paragraph 2 or 3 of subsection 101 (1).

**Notice of termination of agreement**

(4) A party to an agreement made under this section may terminate the agreement at any time by giving every other party written notice that the party wishes to terminate the agreement.

**Agreement expires at 18**

(5) No agreement made under this section shall continue beyond the 18th birthday of the person who is its subject.

**Current agreements and orders must be terminated first**

(6) Despite subsection (3), an agreement may not come into force under this section until any temporary care agreement under section 75 or order for the care or supervision of a child under this Part is terminated.

**Representation by Children's Lawyer**

(7) The Children's Lawyer may provide legal representation to the child entering into an agreement under this section if, in the opinion of the Children's Lawyer, such legal representation is appropriate.

### Legal Representation

**Legal representation of child**

78. (1) A child may have legal representation at any stage in a proceeding under this Part.

**Court to consider issue**

(2) Where a child does not have legal representation in a proceeding under this Part, the court,

(a) shall, as soon as practicable after the commencement of the proceeding; and

(b) may, at any later stage in the proceeding,

determine whether legal representation is desirable to protect the child's interests.

**Direction for legal representation**

(3) Where the court determines that legal representation is desirable to protect a child's interests, the court shall direct that legal representation be provided for the child.

**Criteria**

(4) Where,

(a) the court is of the opinion that there is a difference of views between the child and a parent or a society, and the society proposes that the child be removed from a person's care or be placed in interim or extended society care under paragraph 2 or 3 of subsection 101 (1);

(b) the child is in the society's care and,

(i) no parent appears before the court, or

(ii) it is alleged that the child is in need of protection within the meaning of clause 74 (2) (a), (c), (f), (g) or (j); or

(c) the child is not permitted to be present at the hearing,

legal representation is deemed to be desirable to protect the child's interests, unless the court is satisfied, taking into account the child's views and wishes, given due weight in accordance with the child's age and maturity, that the child's interests are otherwise adequately protected.

**Where parent a minor**

(5) Where a child's parent is younger than 18, the Children's Lawyer shall represent the parent in a proceeding under this Part unless the court orders otherwise.

## Parties and Notice

### Parties

**79.** (1) The following are parties to a proceeding under this Part:

1. The applicant.
2. The society having jurisdiction in the matter.
3. The child's parent.
4. In the case of a First Nations, Inuk or Métis child, the persons described in paragraphs 1, 2 and 3 and a representative chosen by each of the child's bands and First Nations, Inuit or Métis communities.

### Director to be added

(2) At any stage in a proceeding under this Part, the court shall add a Director as a party on the Director's motion.

### Right to participate

(3) Any person, including a foster parent, who has cared for the child continuously during the six months immediately before the hearing,

    (a) is entitled to the same notice of the proceeding as a party;

    (b) may be present at the hearing;

    (c) may be represented by a lawyer; and

    (d) may make submissions to the court,

but shall take no further part in the hearing without leave of the court.

### Child 12 or older

(4) A child 12 or older who is the subject of a proceeding under this Part is entitled to receive notice of the proceeding and to be present at the hearing, unless the court is satisfied that being present at the hearing would cause the child emotional harm and orders that the child not receive notice of the proceeding and not be permitted to be present at the hearing.

### Child younger than 12

(5) A child younger than 12 who is the subject of a proceeding under this Part is not entitled to receive notice of the proceeding or to be present at the hearing unless the court is satisfied that the child,

    (a) is capable of understanding the hearing; and

    (b) will not suffer emotional harm by being present at the hearing,

and orders that the child receive notice of the proceeding and be permitted to be present at the hearing.

### Child's participation

(6) A child who is the applicant under subsection 113 (4) or 115 (4) (status review), receives notice of a proceeding under this Part or has legal representation in a proceeding is entitled to participate in the proceeding and to appeal under section 121 as if the child were a party.

### Dispensing with notice

(7) Where the court is satisfied that the time required for notice to a person might endanger the child's health or safety, the court may dispense with notice to that person.

## Customary Care

### Customary care

**80.** A society shall make all reasonable efforts to pursue a plan for customary care for a First Nations, Inuk or Métis child if the child,

    (a) is in need of protection;

    (b) cannot remain in or be returned to the care and custody of the person who had charge of the child immediately before intervention under this Part or, where there is an order for the child's custody that is enforceable in Ontario, of the person entitled to custody under the order; and

    (c) is a member of or identifies with a band, or is a member of or identifies with a First Nations, Inuit or Métis community.

## Commencing Child Protection Proceedings

### Warrants, orders, etc.

### Application

**81.** (1) A society may apply to the court to determine whether a child is in need of protection.

### Warrant to bring child to place of safety

(2) A justice of the peace may issue a warrant authorizing a child protection worker to bring a child to a place of safety if the justice of the peace is satisfied on the basis of a child protection worker's sworn information that there are reasonable and probable grounds to believe that,

    (a) the child is younger than 16;

    (b) the child is in need of protection; and

    (c) a less restrictive course of action is not available or will not protect the child adequately.

### When warrant may not be refused

(3) A justice of the peace shall not refuse to issue a warrant under subsection (2) by reason only that the child protection worker may bring the child to a place of safety under subsection (7).

### Order to produce child or bring child to place of safety

(4) Where the court is satisfied, on a person's application upon notice to a society, that there are reasonable and probable grounds to believe that,

    (a) a child is in need of protection, the matter has been reported to the society, the society has not made an application under subsection (1), and no child protection worker has sought a warrant under subsection (2) or brought the child to a place of safety under subsection (7); and

(b) the child cannot be protected adequately otherwise than by being brought before the court,

the court may order,

(c) that the person having charge of the child produce the child before the court at the time and place named in the order for a hearing under subsection 90 (1) to determine whether the child is in need of protection; or

(d) where the court is satisfied that an order under clause (c) would not protect the child adequately, that a child protection worker employed by the society bring the child to a place of safety.

### Child's name, location not required

(5) It is not necessary, in an application under subsection (1), a warrant under subsection (2) or an order made under subsection (4), to describe the child by name or to specify the premises where the child is located.

### Authority to enter, etc.

(6) A child protection worker authorized to bring a child to a place of safety by a warrant issued under subsection (2) or an order made under clause (4) (d) may at any time enter any premises specified in the warrant or order, by force if necessary, and may search for and remove the child.

### Bring child to place of safety without warrant

(7) A child protection worker who believes on reasonable and probable grounds that,

(a) a child is in need of protection;

(b) the child is younger than 16; and

(c) there would be a substantial risk to the child's health or safety during the time necessary to bring the matter on for a hearing under subsection 90 (1) or obtain a warrant under subsection (2),

may without a warrant bring the child to a place of safety.

### Police assistance

(8) A child protection worker acting under this section may call for the assistance of a peace officer.

### Consent to examine child

(9) A child protection worker acting under subsection (7) or under a warrant issued under subsection (2) or an order made under clause (4) (d) may authorize the child's medical examination where a parent's consent would otherwise be required.

### Right of entry, etc.

(10) A child protection worker who believes on reasonable and probable grounds that a child referred to in subsection (7) is on any premises may without a warrant enter the premises, by force, if necessary, and search for and remove the child.

### Regulations re power of entry

(11) A child protection worker authorized to enter premises under subsection (6) or (10) shall exercise the power of entry in accordance with the regulations.

### Peace officer has powers of child protection worker

(12) Subsections (2), (6), (7), (10) and (11) apply to a peace officer as if the peace officer were a child protection worker.

### Protection from personal liability

(13) No action shall be instituted against a peace officer or child protection worker for any act done in good faith in the execution or intended execution of that person's duty under this section or for an alleged neglect or default in the execution in good faith of that duty.

### Exception, 16 and 17 year olds brought to place of safety with consent

**82.** (1) A child protection worker may bring a child who is 16 or 17 and who is subject to a temporary or final supervision order to a place of safety if the child consents.

### Temporary or final supervision order

(2) In this section,

"temporary or final supervision order" means an order under clause 94 (2) (b) or (c), paragraph 1 or 4 of subsection 101 (1), subsection 112 (8) or 115 (10) or clause 116 (1) (a).

### Special Cases of Bringing Children to a Place of Safety

### Bringing children who are removed from or leave care to place of safety

### With warrant

**83.** (1) A justice of the peace may issue a warrant authorizing a child protection worker to bring a child to a place of safety if the justice of the peace is satisfied on the basis of a child protection worker's sworn information that,

(a) the child is actually or apparently younger than 16, and,

(i) has left or been removed from a society's lawful care and custody without its consent, or

(ii) is the subject of an extra-provincial child protection order and has left or been removed from the lawful care and custody of the child welfare authority or other person named in the order; and

(b) there are reasonable and probable grounds to believe that there is no course of action available other than bringing the child to a place of safety that would adequately protect the child.

### When warrant may not be refused

(2) A justice of the peace shall not refuse to issue a warrant to a person under subsection (1) by reason only that the person may bring the child to a place of safety under subsection (4).

### No need to specify premises

(3) It is not necessary in a warrant under subsection (1) to specify the premises where the child is located.

**Without warrant**

(4) A peace officer or child protection worker may without a warrant bring the child to a place of safety if the peace officer or child protection worker believes on reasonable and probable grounds that,

(a) the child is actually or apparently younger than 16, and,

(i) has left or been removed from a society's lawful care and custody without its consent, or

(ii) is the subject of an extra-provincial child protection order and has left or been removed from the lawful care and custody of the child welfare authority or other person named in the order; and

(b) there would be a substantial risk to the child's health or safety during the time necessary to obtain a warrant under subsection (1).

**Bringing child younger than 12 home or to place of safety**

**84.** (1) A peace officer who believes on reasonable and probable grounds that a child actually or apparently younger than 12 has committed an act in respect of which a person 12 or older could be found guilty of an offence may bring the child to a place of safety without a warrant and on doing so,

(a) shall return the child to the child's parent or other person having charge of the child as soon as practicable; or

(b) where it is not possible to return the child to the parent or other person within a reasonable time, shall bring the child to a place of safety until the child can be returned to the parent or other person.

**Notice to parent, etc.**

(2) The person in charge of a place of safety in which a child is detained under subsection (1) shall make reasonable efforts to notify the child's parent or other person having charge of the child of the child's detention so that the child may be returned to the parent or other person.

**Where child not returned to parent, etc., within 12 hours**

(3) Where a child brought to a place of safety under subsection (1) cannot be returned to the child's parent or other person having charge of the child within 12 hours of being brought to the place of safety, the child is deemed to have been brought to a place of safety under subsection 81 (7) and not under subsection (1).

**Children who withdraw from parent's care**
**Warrant to bring child to a place of safety**

**85.** (1) A justice of the peace may issue a warrant authorizing a peace officer or child protection worker to bring a child to a place of safety if the justice of the peace is satisfied on the basis of the sworn information of a person that,

(a) the child is younger than 16;

(b) the child has withdrawn from the person's care and control without the person's consent; and

(c) the person believes on reasonable and probable grounds that the child's health or safety may be at risk if the child is not brought to a place of safety.

**Child to be returned or brought to a place of safety**

(2) A person acting under a warrant issued under subsection (1) shall return the child to the person with care and control of the child as soon as practicable and where it is not possible to return the child to that person within a reasonable time, bring the child to a place of safety.

**Notice to person with care, custody or control**

(3) The person in charge of a place of safety to which a child is brought under subsection (2) shall make reasonable efforts to notify the person with care and control of the child that the child is in the place of safety so that the child may be returned to that person.

**Where child not returned within 12 hours**

(4) Where a child brought to a place of safety under subsection (2) cannot be returned to the person with care and control of the child within 12 hours of being brought to the place of safety, the child is deemed to have been brought to a place of safety under subsection 81 (2) and not under subsection (1).

**Where custody enforcement proceedings more appropriate**

(5) A justice of the peace shall not issue a warrant under subsection (1) in respect of a child who has withdrawn from the care and control of a person where a proceeding under section 36 of the *Children's Law Reform Act* would be more appropriate.

**No need to specify premises**

(6) It is not necessary in a warrant under subsection (1) to specify the premises where the child is located.

**Child protection proceedings**

(7) Where a peace officer or child protection worker believes on reasonable and probable grounds that a child brought to a place of safety under this section is in need of protection and there may be a substantial risk to the health or safety of the child if the child were returned to the person with care and control of the child,

(a) the peace officer or child protection worker may bring the child to a place of safety under subsection 81 (7); or

(b) where the child has been brought to a place of safety under subsection (4), the child is deemed to have been brought there under subsection 81 (7).

**Authority to enter, etc.**

**86.** (1) A person authorized to bring a child to a place of safety by a warrant issued under subsection 83 (1) or 85 (1) may at any time enter any premises specified in the warrant, by force, if necessary, and may search for and remove the child

### Right of entry, etc.

(2)  A person authorized under subsection 83 (4) or 84 (1) who believes on reasonable and probable grounds that a child referred to in the relevant subsection is on any premises may without a warrant enter the premises, by force, if necessary, and search for and remove the child.

### Regulations re power of entry

(3)  A person authorized to enter premises under this section shall exercise the power of entry in accordance with the regulations.

### Police assistance

(4)  A child protection worker acting under section 83 or 85 may call for the assistance of a peace officer.

### Consent to examine child

(5)  Where subsection 84 (3) or 85 (4) applies to a child brought to a place of safety, a child protection worker may authorize the child's medical examination where a parent's consent would be otherwise required.

### Protection from personal liability

(6)  No action shall be instituted against a peace officer or child protection worker for any act done in good faith in the execution or intended execution of that person's duty under this section or section 83, 84 or 85 or for an alleged neglect or default in the execution in good faith of that duty.

**Hearings and Orders**

### Rules re hearings

### Definition

**87.**  (1)  In this section,
"media" means the press, radio and television media.

### Application

(2)  This section applies to hearings held under this Part, except hearings under section 134 (child abuse register).

> **Note:  On a day to be named by proclamation of the Lieutenant Governor, subsection 87 (2) of the Act is repealed and the following substituted: (See: 2017, c. 14, Sched. 3, s. 5)**

### Application

(2)  This section applies to hearings held under this Part. 2017, c. 14, Sched. 3, s. 5.

### Hearings separate from criminal proceedings

(3)  A hearing shall be held separately from hearings in criminal proceedings.

### Hearings private unless court orders otherwise

(4)  A hearing shall be held in the absence of the public, subject to subsection (5), unless the court orders that the hearing be held in public after considering,

(a)  the wishes and interests of the parties; and

(b)  whether the presence of the public would cause emotional harm to a child who is a witness at or a participant in the hearing or is the subject of the proceeding.

### Media representatives may attend

(5)  Media representatives chosen in accordance with subsection (6) may be present at a hearing that is held in the absence of the public, unless the court makes an order excluding them under subsection (7).

### Selection of media representatives

(6)  The media representatives who may be present at a hearing that is held in the absence of the public shall be chosen as follows:

1.  The media representatives in attendance shall choose not more than two persons from among themselves.
2.  Where the media representatives in attendance are unable to agree on a choice of persons, the court may choose not more than two media representatives who may be present at the hearing.
3.  The court may permit additional media representatives to be present at the hearing.

### Order excluding media representatives or prohibiting publication

(7)  Where the court is of the opinion that the presence of the media representative or representatives or the publication of the report, as the case may be, would cause emotional harm to a child who is a witness at or a participant in the hearing or is the subject of the proceeding, the court may make an order,

(a)  excluding a particular media representative from all or part of a hearing;

(b)  excluding all media representatives from all or a part of a hearing; or

(c)  prohibiting the publication of a report of the hearing or a specified part of the hearing.

### Prohibition re identifying child

(8)  No person shall publish or make public information that has the effect of identifying a child who is a witness at or a participant in a hearing or the subject of a proceeding, or the child's parent or foster parent or a member of the child's family.

### Prohibition re identifying person charged

(9)  The court may make an order prohibiting the publication of information that has the effect of identifying a person charged with an offence under this Part.

### Transcript

(10)  No person except a party or a party's lawyer shall be given a copy of a transcript of the hearing, unless the court orders otherwise.

## Time in place of safety limited

**88.** As soon as practicable, but in any event within five days after a child is brought to a place of safety under section 81, subclause 83 (1) (a) (ii) or subsection 136 (5),

(a) the matter shall be brought before a court for a hearing under subsection 90 (1) (child protection hearing);

(b) the child shall be returned to the person who last had charge of the child or, where there is an order for the child's custody that is enforceable in Ontario, to the person entitled to custody under the order;

(c) if the child is the subject of an extra-provincial child protection order, the child shall be returned to the child welfare authority or other person named in the order;

(d) a temporary care agreement shall be made under subsection 75 (1); or

(e) an agreement shall be made under section 77 (agreements with 16 and 17 year olds).

## Time in place of safety limited, 16 or 17 year old

**89.** As soon as practicable, but in any event within five days after a child who is 16 or 17 is brought to a place of safety with the child's consent under section 82,

(a) the matter shall be brought before a court for a hearing under subsection 90 (1); or

(b) the child shall be returned to the person entitled to custody of the child under an order made under this Part.

## Child protection hearing

**90.** (1) Where an application is made under subsection 81 (1) or a matter is brought before the court to determine whether the child is in need of protection, the court shall hold a hearing to determine the issue and make an order under section 101.

## Child's name, age, etc.

(2) As soon as practicable, and in any event before determining whether a child is in need of protection, the court shall determine,

(a) the child's name and age;

(b) whether the child is a First Nations, Inuk or Métis child and, if so, the child's bands and First Nations, Inuit or Métis communities; and

(c) where the child was brought to a place of safety before the hearing, the location of the place from which the child was removed.

## Territorial jurisdiction

**91.** (1) In this section,
"territorial jurisdiction" means a society's territorial jurisdiction under subsection 34 (1).

## Place of hearing

(2) A hearing under this Part with respect to a child shall be held in the territorial jurisdiction in which the child ordinarily resides, except that,

(a) where the child is brought to a place of safety before the hearing, the hearing shall be held in the territorial jurisdiction in which the place from which the child was removed is located;

(b) where the child is in interim society care under an order made under paragraph 2 or 4 of subsection 101 (1) or extended society care under an order made under paragraph 3 of subsection 101 (1) or clause 116 (1) (c), the hearing shall be held in the society's territorial jurisdiction; and

(c) where the child is the subject of an order for society supervision under paragraph 1 of subsection 101 (1) or clause 116 (1) (a), the hearing may be held in the society's territorial jurisdiction or in the territorial jurisdiction in which the parent or other person with whom the child is placed resides.

## Transfer of proceeding

(3) Where the court is satisfied at any stage of a proceeding under this Part that there is a preponderance of convenience in favour of conducting it in another territorial jurisdiction, the court may order that the proceeding be transferred to that other territorial jurisdiction and be continued as if it had been commenced there.

## Orders affecting society

(4) The court shall not make an order placing a child in the care or under the supervision of a society unless the place where the court sits is within the society's territorial jurisdiction.

## Power of court

**92.** The court may, on its own initiative, summon a person to attend before it, testify and produce any document or thing, and may enforce obedience to the summons as if it had been made in a proceeding under the *Family Law Act*.

## Evidence

## Past conduct toward children

**93.** (1) Despite anything in the *Evidence Act*, in any proceeding under this Part,

(a) the court may consider the past conduct of a person toward any child if that person is caring for or has access to or may care for or have access to a child who is the subject of the proceeding; and

(b) any oral or written statement or report that the court considers relevant to the proceeding, including a transcript, exhibit or finding or the reasons for a decision in an earlier civil or criminal proceeding, is admissible into evidence.

### Evidence re disposition and finding

(2)  In a hearing under subsection 90 (1), evidence relating only to the disposition of the matter shall not be considered in determining if the child is in need of protection.

### Adjournments

**94.**  (1)  The court shall not adjourn a hearing for more than 30 days,

(a)  unless all the parties present and the person who will be caring for the child during the adjournment consent; or

(b)  if the court is aware that a party who is not present at the hearing objects to the longer adjournment.

### Custody during adjournment

(2)  Where a hearing is adjourned, the court shall make a temporary order for care and custody providing that the child,

(a)  remain in or be returned to the care and custody of the person who had charge of the child immediately before intervention under this Part;

(b)  remain in or be returned to the care and custody of the person referred to in clause (a), subject to the society's supervision and on such reasonable terms and conditions as the court considers appropriate;

(c)  be placed in the care and custody of a person other than the person referred to in clause (a), with the consent of that other person, subject to the society's supervision and on such reasonable terms and conditions as the court considers appropriate; or

(d)  remain or be placed in the care and custody of the society, but not be placed in a place of temporary detention, of open or of secure custody.

### Where child is subject to extra-provincial order

(3)  Where a court makes an order under clause (2) (d) in the case of a child who is the subject of an extra-provincial child protection order the society may, during the period of the adjournment, return the child to the care and custody of the child welfare authority or other person named in the order.

### Criteria

(4)  The court shall not make an order under clause (2) (c) or (d) unless the court is satisfied that there are reasonable grounds to believe that there is a risk that the child is likely to suffer harm and that the child cannot be protected adequately by an order under clause (2) (a) or (b).

### Placement with relative, etc.

(5)  Before making a temporary order for care and custody under clause (2) (d), the court shall consider whether it is in the child's best interests to make an order under clause (2) (c) to place the child in the care and custody of a person who is a relative of the child or a member of the child's extended family or community.

### Terms and conditions in order

(6)  A temporary order for care and custody of a child under clause (2) (b) or (c) may impose,

(a)  reasonable terms and conditions relating to the child's care and supervision;

(b)  reasonable terms and conditions on the child's parent, the person who will have care and custody of the child under the order, the child and any other person, other than a foster parent, who is putting forward a plan or who would participate in a plan for care and custody of or access to the child; and

(c)  reasonable terms and conditions on the society that will supervise the placement, but shall not require the society to provide financial assistance or to purchase any goods or services.

### Application of s. 107

(7)  Where the court makes an order under clause (2) (d), section 110 (child in interim society care) applies with necessary modifications.

### Access

(8)  An order made under clause (2) (c) or (d) may contain provisions regarding any person's right of access to the child on such terms and conditions as the court considers appropriate.

### Power to vary

(9)  The court may at any time vary or terminate an order made under subsection (2).

### Evidence on adjournments

(10)  For the purpose of this section, the court may admit and act on evidence that the court considers credible and trustworthy in the circumstances.

### Child's views and wishes

(11)  Before making an order under subsection (2), the court shall take into consideration the child's views and wishes, given due weight in accordance with the child's age and maturity, unless they cannot be ascertained.

### Use of prescribed methods of alternative dispute resolution

**95.**  At any time during a proceeding under this Part, the court may, in the best interests of the child and with the consent of the parties, adjourn the proceeding to permit the parties to attempt through a prescribed method of alternative dispute resolution to resolve any dispute between them with respect to any matter that is relevant to the proceeding.

### Delay: court to fix date

**96.**  Where an application is made under subsection 81 (1) or a matter is brought before the court to determine whether a child is in need of protection and the determination has not been made within three months after the commencement of the proceeding, the court,

(a) shall by order fix a date for the hearing of the application, and the date may be the earliest date that is compatible with the just disposition of the application; and

(b) may give such directions and make such orders with respect to the proceeding as are just.

## Reasons, etc.

**97.** (1) Where the court makes an order under this Part, the court shall give,

(a) a statement of any terms or conditions imposed on the order;

(b) a statement of every plan for the child's care proposed to the court;

(c) a statement of the plan for the child's care that the court is applying in its decision; and

(d) reasons for its decision, including,

(i) a brief statement of the evidence on which the court bases its decision, and

(ii) where the order has the effect of removing or keeping the child from the care of the person who had charge of the child immediately before intervention under this Part, a statement of the reasons why the child cannot be adequately protected while in the person's care.

## No requirement to identify person or place

(2) Clause (1) (b) does not require the court to identify a person with whom or a place where it is proposed that a child be placed for care and supervision.

## Assessments

## Order for assessment

**98.** (1) In the course of a proceeding under this Part, the court may order that one or more of the following persons undergo an assessment within a specified time by a person appointed in accordance with subsections (3) and (4):

1. The child.
2. A parent of the child.
3. Any other person, other than a foster parent, who is putting forward or would participate in a plan for the care and custody of or access to the child.

## Criteria for ordering assessment

(2) An assessment may be ordered if the court is satisfied that,

(a) an assessment of one or more of the persons specified in subsection (1) is necessary for the court to make a determination under this Part; and

(b) the evidence sought from an assessment is not otherwise available to the court.

## Assessor selected by parties

(3) An order under subsection (1) shall specify a time within which the parties to the proceeding may select a person to perform the assessment and submit the name of the selected person to the court.

## Appointment of person selected by parties

(4) The court shall appoint the person selected by the parties to perform the assessment if the court is satisfied that the person meets the following criteria:

1. The person is qualified to perform medical, emotional, developmental, psychological, educational or social assessments.
2. The person has consented to perform the assessment.

## Appointment of a person not selected by parties

(5) If the court is of the opinion that the person selected by the parties under subsection (3) does not meet the criteria set out in subsection (4), the court shall select and appoint another person who does meet the criteria.

## Regulations

(6) An order under subsection (1) and the assessment required by that order shall comply with such requirements as may be prescribed.

## Report

(7) The person performing an assessment under subsection (1) shall make a written report of the assessment to the court within the time specified in the order, which shall not be more than 30 days, unless the court is of the opinion that a longer assessment period is necessary.

## Copies of report

(8) At least seven days before the court considers the report at a hearing, the court or, where the assessment was requested by a party, that party, shall provide a copy of the report to,

(a) the person assessed, subject to subsections (9) and (10);

(b) the child's lawyer or agent;

(c) a parent appearing at the hearing, or the parent's lawyer;

(d) the society caring for or supervising the child;

(e) a Director, where the Director requests a copy;

(f) in the case of a First Nations, Inuk or Métis child, the persons described in clauses (a) (b) (c), (d) and (e) and a representative chosen by each of the child's bands and First Nations, Inuit or Métis communities; and

(g) any other person who, in the opinion of the court, should receive a copy of the report for the purposes of the case.

## Child younger than 12

(9) Where the person assessed is a child younger than 12, the child shall not receive a copy of the report unless the court considers it desirable that the child receive a copy of the report.

## Child 12 or older

(10) Where the person assessed is a child 12 or older, the child shall receive a copy of the report, except that where

the court is satisfied that disclosure of all or part of the report to the child would cause the child emotional harm, the court may withhold all or part of the report from the child.

### Conflict

(11) Subsections (9) and (10) prevail despite anything in the *Personal Health Information Protection Act, 2004*.

### Assessment is evidence

(12) The report of an assessment ordered under subsection (1) is evidence and is part of the court record of the proceeding.

### Inference from refusal

(13) The court may draw any inference it considers reasonable from a person's refusal to undergo an assessment ordered under subsection (1).

### Report inadmissible

(14) The report of an assessment ordered under subsection (1) is not admissible into evidence in any other proceeding except,

(a) a proceeding under this Part, including an appeal under section 121;

(b) a proceeding referred to in section 137;

(c) a proceeding under Part VIII (Adoption and Adoption Licensing) respecting an application to make, vary or terminate an openness order; or

(d) a proceeding under the *Coroners Act*,

without the consent of the person or persons assessed.

### Consent order: special requirements

**99.** Where a child is brought before the court on consent as described in clause 74 (2) (n), the court shall, before making an order under section 101 or 102 that would remove the child from the parent's care and custody,

(a) ask whether,

(i) the society has offered the parent and child services that would enable the child to remain with the parent, and

(ii) the parent and, where the child is 12 or older, the child, has consulted independent legal counsel in connection with the consent; and

(b) be satisfied that,

(i) the parent and, where the child is 12 or older, the child, understands the nature and consequences of the consent,

(ii) every consent is voluntary, and

(iii) the parent and, where the child is 12 or older, the child, consents to the order being sought.

### Society's plan for child

**100.** The court shall, before making an order under section 101, 102, 114 or 116, obtain and consider a plan for the child's care prepared in writing by the society and including,

(a) a description of the services to be provided to remedy the condition or situation on the basis of which the child was found to be in need of protection;

(b) a statement of the criteria by which the society will determine when its care or supervision is no longer required;

(c) an estimate of the time required to achieve the purpose of the society's intervention;

(d) where the society proposes to remove or has removed the child from a person's care,

(i) an explanation of why the child cannot be adequately protected while in the person's care, and a description of any past efforts to do so, and

(ii) a statement of what efforts, if any, are planned to maintain the child's contact with the person;

(e) where the society proposes to remove or has removed the child from a person's care permanently, a description of the arrangements made or being made for the child's long-term stable placement; and

(f) a description of the arrangements made or being made to recognize the importance of the child's culture and to preserve the child's heritage, traditions and cultural identity.

### Order where child in need of protection

**101.** (1) Where the court finds that a child is in need of protection and is satisfied that intervention through a court order is necessary to protect the child in the future, the court shall make one of the following orders or an order under section 102, in the child's best interests:

### Supervision order

1. That the child be placed in the care and custody of a parent or another person, subject to the supervision of the society, for a specified period of at least three months and not more than 12 months.

### Interim society care

2. That the child be placed in interim society care and custody for a specified period not exceeding 12 months.

### Extended society care

3. That the child be placed in extended society care until the order is terminated under section 116 or expires under section 123.

### Consecutive orders of interim society care and supervision

4. That the child be placed in interim society care and custody under paragraph 2 for a specified period and then be returned to a parent or another person under paragraph 1, for a period or periods not exceeding a total of 12 months.

## Court to inquire

(2) In determining which order to make under subsection (1) or section 102, the court shall ask the parties what efforts the society or another person or entity has made to assist the child before intervention under this Part.

## Less disruptive alternatives preferred

(3) The court shall not make an order removing the child from the care of the person who had charge of the child immediately before intervention under this Part unless the court is satisfied that alternatives that are less disruptive to the child, including non-residential care and the assistance referred to in subsection (2), would be inadequate to protect the child.

## Community placement to be considered

(4) Where the court decides that it is necessary to remove the child from the care of the person who had charge of the child immediately before intervention under this Part, the court shall, before making an order under paragraph 2 or 3 of subsection (1), consider whether it is possible to place the child with a relative, neighbour or other member of the child's community or extended family under paragraph 1 of subsection (1) with the consent of the relative or other person.

## First Nations, Inuk or Métis child

(5) Where the child referred to in subsection (4) is a First Nations, Inuk or Métis child, unless there is a substantial reason for placing the child elsewhere, the court shall place the child with a member of the child's extended family if it is possible or, if it is not possible,

(a) in the case of a First Nations child, another First Nations family;

(b) in the case of an Inuk child, another Inuit family; or

(c) in the case of a Métis child, another Métis family.

## Further hearing with notice for orders for interim or extended society care

(6) When the court has dispensed with notice to a person under subsection 79 (7), the court shall not make an order for interim society care under paragraph 2 of subsection (1) for a period exceeding 30 days or an order for extended society care under paragraph 3 of subsection (1) until a further hearing under subsection 90 (1) has been held upon notice to that person.

## Terms and conditions of supervision order

(7) If the court makes a supervision order under paragraph 1 of subsection (1), the court may impose,

(a) reasonable terms and conditions relating to the child's care and supervision;

(b) reasonable terms and conditions on,

(i) the child's parent,

(ii) the person who will have care and custody of the child under the order,

(iii) the child, and

(iv) any other person, other than a foster parent, who is putting forward or would participate in a plan for the care and custody of or access to the child; and

(c) reasonable terms and conditions on the society that will supervise the placement, but shall not require the society to provide financial assistance or purchase any goods or services.

## Order for child to remain or return to person who had charge before intervention

(8) Where the court finds that a child is in need of protection but is not satisfied that a court order is necessary to protect the child in the future, the court shall order that the child remain with or be returned to the person who had charge of the child immediately before intervention under this Part.

## No order where child not subject to parental control

(9) Where the court finds that a child who was not subject to parental control immediately before intervention under this Part by virtue of having withdrawn from parental control or who withdraws from parental control after intervention under this Part is in need of protection, but is not satisfied that a court order is necessary to protect the child in the future, the court shall make no order in respect of the child.

## Custody order

102. (1) Subject to subsection (6), if a court finds that an order under this section instead of an order under subsection 101 (1) would be in a child's best interests, the court may make an order granting custody of the child to one or more persons, other than a foster parent of the child, with the consent of the person or persons.

## Deemed to be order under s. 28 *Children's Law Reform Act*

(2) An order made under subsection (1) and any access order under section 104 that is made at the same time as the order under subsection (1) is deemed to be made under section 28 of the *Children's Law Reform Act* and the court,

(a) may make any order under subsection (1) that the court may make under section 28 of that Act; and

(b) may give any directions that it may give under section 34 of that Act.

## Restraining order

(3) When making an order under subsection (1), the court may, without a separate application, make a restraining order in accordance with section 35 of the *Children's Law Reform Act*.

## Deemed to be final order under s. 35 *Children's Law Reform Act*

(4) An order under subsection (3) is deemed to be a final order made under section 35 of the *Children's Law Reform Act*, and shall be treated for all purposes as if it had been made under that section.

### Appeal under s. 121

(5) Despite subsections (2) and (4), an order under subsection (1) or (3) and any access order under section 104 that is made at the same time as an order under subsection (1) are orders under this Part for the purposes of appealing from the orders under section 121.

### Conflict of laws

(6) No order shall be made under this section if,

(a) an order granting custody of the child has been made under the *Divorce Act* (Canada); or

(b) in the case of an order that would be made by the Ontario Court of Justice, the order would conflict with an order made by a superior court.

### Application of s. 101 (3)

(7) Subsection 101 (3) applies for the purposes of this section.

### Effect of custody proceedings

**103.** If, under this Part, a proceeding is commenced or an order for the care, custody or supervision of a child is made, any proceeding respecting custody of or access to the same child under the *Children's Law Reform Act* is stayed except by leave of the court in the proceeding under that Act.

### Access

### Access order

**104.** (1) The court may, in the child's best interests,

(a) when making an order under this Part; or

(b) upon an application under subsection (2),

make, vary or terminate an order respecting a person's access to the child or the child's access to a person, and may impose such terms and conditions on the order as the court considers appropriate.

### Who may apply

(2) Where a child is in a society's care and custody or supervision, the following may apply to the court at any time for an order under subsection (1):

1. The child.
2. Any other person, including a sibling of the child and, in the case of a First Nations, Inuk or Métis child, a representative chosen by each of the child's bands and First Nations, Inuit or Métis communities.
3. The society.

### Notice

(3) An applicant referred to in paragraph 2 of subsection (2) shall give notice of the application to the society.

### Society to give notice of application

(4) A society making or receiving an application under subsection (2) shall give notice of the application to,

(a) the child, subject to subsections 79 (4) and (5) (notice to child);

(b) the child's parent;

(c) the person caring for the child at the time of the application; and

(d) in the case of a First Nations, Inuk or Métis child, the persons described in clauses (a), (b) and (c) and a representative chosen by each of the child's bands and First Nations, Inuit or Métis communities.

### Child older than 16

(5) No order respecting access to a person 16 or older shall be made under subsection (1) without the person's consent.

### Six-month period

(6) No application shall be made under subsection (2) by a person other than a society within six months of,

(a) the making of an order under section 101;

(b) the disposition of a previous application by the same person under subsection (2);

(c) the disposition of an application under section 113 or 115; or

(d) the final disposition or abandonment of an appeal from an order referred to in clause (a), (b) or (c),

whichever is later.

### No application where child placed for adoption

(7) No person or society shall make an application under subsection (2) where the child,

(a) is in extended society care under an order made under paragraph 3 of subsection 101 (1) or clause 116 (1) (c);

(b) has been placed in a person's home by the society or by a Director for the purpose of adoption under Part VIII (Adoption and Adoption Licensing); and

(c) still resides in that person's home.

### Access: where child removed from person in charge

**105.** (1) Where an order is made under paragraph 1 or 2 of subsection 101 (1) removing a child from the person who had charge of the child immediately before intervention under this Part, the court shall make an order for access by the person unless the court is satisfied that continued contact with the person would not be in the child's best interests.

### Access after custody order under s. 102

(2) If a custody order is made under section 102 removing a child from the person who had charge of the child immediately before intervention under this Part, the court shall make an order for access by the person unless the court is satisfied that continued contact will not be in the child's best interests.

### Access after supervision order or custody order under s. 116 (1)

(3) If an order is made for supervision under clause 116 (1) (a) or for custody under clause 116 (1) (b), the court shall make an order for access by every person who had access before the application for the order was made under section 115,

unless the court is satisfied that continued contact will not be in the child's best interests.

### Existing access order terminated if order made for extended society care

(4) Where the court makes an order that a child be in extended society care under paragraph 3 of subsection 101 (1) or clause 116 (1) (c), any order for access made under this Part with respect to the child is terminated.

### When court may order access to child in extended society care

(5) A court shall not make or vary an access order under section 104 with respect to a child who is in extended society care under an order made under paragraph 3 of subsection 101 (1) or clause 116 (1) (c) unless the court is satisfied that the order or variation would be in the child's best interests.

### Additional considerations for best interests test

(6) The court shall consider, as part of its determination of whether an order or variation would be in the child's best interests under subsection (5),

(a) whether the relationship between the person and the child is beneficial and meaningful to the child; and

(b) if the court considers it relevant, whether the ordered access will impair the child's future opportunities for adoption.

### Court to specify access holders and access recipients

(7) Where a court makes or varies an access order under section 104 with respect to a child who is in extended society care under an order made under paragraph 3 of subsection 101 (1) or clause 116 (1) (c), the court shall specify,

(a) every person who has been granted a right of access; and

(b) every person with respect to whom access has been granted.

### When court to terminate access to child in extended society care

(8) The court shall terminate an access order with respect to a child who is in extended society care under an order made under paragraph 3 of subsection 101 (1) or clause 116 (1) (c) if the order is no longer in the best interests of the child as determined under subsection (6).

### Society may permit contact or communication

(9) If a society believes that contact or communication between a person and a child who is in extended society care under an order made under paragraph 3 of subsection 101 (1) or clause 116 (1) (c) is in the best interests of the child and no openness order under Part VIII (Adoption and Adoption Licensing) or access order is in effect with respect to the person and the child, the society may permit contact or communication between the person and the child.

### Review of access order made concurrently with custody order

**106.** No order for access under section 104 is subject to review under this Act if it is made at the same time as a custody order under section 102, but it may be the subject of an application under section 21 of the *Children's Law Reform Act* and the provisions of that Act apply as if the order had been made under that Act.

### Restriction on access order

**107.** If a society has applied to a court for an order under this Act respecting access to a child by a parent of the child and the court makes the order, the court shall specify in the order the supervision to which the access is subject if, at the time of making the order, the parent has been charged with or convicted of an offence under the *Criminal Code* (Canada) involving an act of violence against the child or the other parent of the child, unless the court considers it appropriate not to make the access subject to such supervision.

### Payment Orders
### Order for payment by parent

**108.** (1) Where the court places a child in the care of,

(a) a society; or

(b) a person other than the child's parent, subject to a society's supervision,

the court may order a parent or a parent's estate to pay the society a specified amount at specified intervals for each day the child is in the society's care or supervision.

### Criteria

(2) In making an order under subsection (1), the court shall consider those of the following circumstances of the case that the court considers relevant:

1. The assets and means of the child and of the parent or the parent's estate.
2. The child's capacity to provide for their own support.
3. The capacity of the parent or the parent's estate to provide support.
4. The child's and the parent's age and physical and mental health.
5. The child's mental, emotional and physical needs.
6. Any legal obligation of the parent or the parent's estate to provide support for another person.
7. The child's aptitude for and reasonable prospects of obtaining an education.
8. Any legal right of the child to support from another source, other than out of public money.

### Order ends at 18

(3) No order made under subsection (1) shall extend beyond the day on which the child turns 18.

## Power to vary

(4) The court may vary, suspend or terminate an order made under subsection (1) where the court is satisfied that the circumstances of the child or parent have changed.

## Collection by municipality

(5) The council of a municipality may enter into an agreement with the board of directors of a society providing for the collection by the municipality, on the society's behalf, of the amounts ordered to be paid by a parent under subsection (1).

## Enforcement

(6) An order made against a parent under subsection (1) may be enforced as if it were an order for support made under Part III of the *Family Law Act*.

### Interim and Extended Society Care

## Placement of children

**109.** (1) This section applies where a child is in interim society care under an order made under paragraph 2 of subsection 101 (1) or extended society care under an order made under paragraph 3 of subsection 101 (1) or clause 116 (1) (c).

## Placement

(2) The society having care of a child shall choose a residential placement for the child that,

(a) represents the least restrictive alternative for the child;

(b) where possible, respects the child's race, ancestry, place of origin, colour, ethnic origin, citizenship, family diversity, creed, sex, sexual orientation, gender identity and gender expression;

(c) where possible, respects the child's cultural and linguistic heritage;

(d) in the case of a First Nations, Inuk or Métis child, is with, if possible, a member of the child's extended family or, if that is not possible,

(i) in the case of a First Nations child, another First Nations family,

(ii) in the case of an Inuk child, another Inuit family, or

(iii) in the case of a Métis child, another Métis family; and

(e) takes into account the child's views and wishes, given due weight in accordance with the child's age and maturity, and the views and wishes of any parent who is entitled to access to the child.

## Education

(3) The society having care of a child shall ensure that the child receives an education that corresponds to the child's aptitudes and abilities.

## Placement outside or removal from Ontario

(4) The society having care of a child shall not place the child outside Ontario or permit a person to remove the child from Ontario permanently unless a Director is satisfied that extraordinary circumstances justify the placement or removal.

## Rights of child, parent and foster parent

(5) The society having care of a child shall ensure that,

(a) the child is afforded all the rights referred to in Part II (Children's and Young Persons' Rights); and

(b) the wishes of any parent who is entitled to access to the child and, where the child is in extended society care under an order made under paragraph 3 of subsection 101 (1) or clause 116 (1) (c), of any foster parent with whom the child has lived continuously for two years are taken into account in the society's major decisions concerning the child.

## Change of placement

(6) The society having care of a child may remove the child from a foster home or other residential placement where, in the opinion of a Director or local director, it is in the child's best interests to do so.

## Notice of proposed removal

(7) If a child is in extended society care under an order made under paragraph 3 of subsection 101 (1) or clause 116 (1) (c) and has lived continuously with a foster parent for two years and a society proposes to remove the child from the foster parent under subsection (6), the society shall,

(a) give the foster parent at least 10 days notice in writing of the proposed removal and of the foster parent's right to apply for a review under subsection (8); and

(b) in the case of a First Nations, Inuk or Métis child, give the notice required by clause (a), and

(i) give at least 10 days notice in writing of the proposed removal to a representative chosen by each of the child's bands and First Nations, Inuit or Métis communities, and

(ii) after the notice is given under subclause (i), consult with representatives chosen by the bands and communities relating to the plan of care for the child.

## Application for review

(8) A foster parent who receives a notice under clause (7) (a) may, within 10 days after receiving the notice, apply to the Board in accordance with the regulations for a review of the proposed removal.

## Board hearing

(9) Upon receipt of an application by a foster parent for a review of a proposed removal, the Board shall hold a hearing under this section.

### First Nations, Inuk or Métis child

(10)  Upon receipt of an application for review of a proposed removal of a First Nations, Inuk or Métis child, the Board shall also give notice of receipt of the application and of the date of the hearing to a representative chosen by each of the child's bands and First Nations, Inuit or Métis communities.

### Practices and procedures

(11)  The *Statutory Powers Procedure Act* applies to a hearing under this section and the Board shall comply with such additional practices and procedures as may be prescribed.

### Composition of Board

(12)  At a hearing under this section, the Board shall be composed of members with the prescribed qualifications and prescribed experience.

### Parties

(13)  The following persons are parties to a hearing under this section:

1. The applicant.
2. The society.
3. If the child is a First Nations, Inuk or Métis child, the persons described in paragraphs 1 and 2 and a representative chosen by each of the child's bands and First Nations, Inuit or Métis communities.
4. Any person that the Board adds under subsection (14).

### Additional parties

(14)  The Board may add a person as a party to a review if, in the Board's opinion, it is necessary to do so in order to decide all the issues in the review.

### Board decision

(15)  The Board shall, in accordance with its determination of which action is in the best interests of the child, confirm the proposal to remove the child or direct the society not to carry out the proposed removal, and shall give written reasons for its decision.

### No removal before decision

(16)  Subject to subsection (17), the society shall not carry out the proposed removal of the child unless,

(a)  the time for applying for a review of the proposed removal under subsection (8) has expired and an application is not made; or

(b)  if an application for a review of the proposed removal is made under subsection (8), the Board has confirmed the proposed removal under subsection (15).

### Where child at risk

(17)  A society may remove the child from the foster home before the expiry of the time for applying for a review under subsection (8) or at any time after the application for a review is made if, in the opinion of a local director, there is a risk that the child is likely to suffer harm during the time necessary for a review by the Board.

### Review of certain placements

(18)  Sections 63, 64, 65 and 66 (review by residential placement advisory committee, further review by the Board) apply with necessary modifications to a residential placement made by a society under this section.

### Definition

(19)  In this section,
"residential placement" has the same meaning as in section 62.

### Child in interim society care

**110.** (1)  Where a child is in interim society care under an order made under paragraph 2 of subsection 101 (1), the society has the rights and responsibilities of a parent for the purpose of the child's care, custody and control.

### Consent to treatment—society or parent may act

(2)  Where a child is in interim society care under an order made under paragraph 2 of subsection 101 (1), and the child is found incapable of consenting to treatment under the *Health Care Consent Act, 1996*, the society may act in the place of a parent in providing consent to treatment on behalf of the child, unless the court orders that the parent shall retain the authority under that Act to give or refuse consent to treatment on behalf of the incapable child.

### Exception

(3)  The court shall not make an order under subsection (2) where failure to consent to necessary treatment was a ground for finding that the child was in need of protection.

### Court may authorize society to act re consent to treatment

(4)  Where a parent referred to in an order made under subsection (2) refuses or is unavailable or unable to consent to treatment for the incapable child and the court is satisfied that the treatment would be in the child's best interests, the court may authorize the society to act in the place of a parent in providing consent to the treatment on the child's behalf.

### Consent to child's marriage

(5)  Where a child is in interim society care under an order made under paragraph 2 of subsection 101 (1), the child's parent retains any right that the parent may have under the *Marriage Act* to give or refuse consent to the child's marriage.

### Child in extended society care

**111.** (1)  Where a child is in extended society care under an order made under paragraph 3 of subsection 101 (1) or clause 116 (1) (c), the Crown has the rights and responsibilities of a parent for the purpose of the child's care, custody and control, and the Crown's powers, duties and obligations in respect of the child, except those assigned to a Director by this Act or the regulations, shall be exercised and performed by the society caring for the child.

### Consent to treatment—society may act

(2)  Where a child is in extended society care under an order made under paragraph 3 of subsection 101 (1) or clause 116 (1) (c), and the child is found incapable of consenting to treatment under the *Health Care Consent Act, 1996*, the society may act in the place of a parent in providing consent to treatment on behalf of the child.

### Society's obligation to pursue family relationship for child in extended society care

**112.** Where a child is in extended society care under an order made under paragraph 3 of subsection 101 (1) or clause 116 (1) (c), the society shall make all reasonable efforts to assist the child to develop a positive, secure and enduring relationship within a family through one of the following:

1. An adoption.
2. A custody order under subsection 116 (1).
3. In the case of a First Nations, Inuk or Métis child,

    i. a plan for customary care,
    ii. an adoption, or
    iii. a custody order under subsection 116 (1).

### Review

### Status review

**113.** (1)  This section applies where a child is the subject of an order made under paragraph 1 or 4 of subsection 101 (1) for society supervision or under paragraph 2 of subsection 101 (1) for interim society care.

### Society to seek status review

(2)  The society having care, custody or supervision of a child,

(a)  may apply to the court at any time for a review of the child's status;

(b)  shall apply to the court for a review of the child's status before the order expires, unless the expiry is by reason of section 123; and

(c)  shall apply to the court for a review of the child's status within five days after removing the child, if the society has removed the child from the care of a person with whom the child was placed under an order for society supervision.

### Application of subs. (2) (a) and (c)

(3)  If a child is the subject of an order for society supervision, clauses (2) (a) and (c) also apply to the society that has jurisdiction in the county or district in which the parent or other person with whom the child is placed resides.

### Others may seek status review

(4)  An application for review of a child's status may be made on notice to the society by,

(a)  the child, if the child is at least 12;

(b)  a parent of the child;

(c)  the person with whom the child was placed under an order for society supervision; or

(d)  in the case of a First Nations, Inuk or Métis child, a person described in clause (a), (b) or (c) or a representative chosen by each of the child's bands and First Nations, Inuit or Métis communities.

### Notice

(5)  A society making an application under subsection (2) or receiving notice of an application under subsection (4) shall give notice of the application to,

(a)  the child, except as otherwise provided under subsection 79 (4) or (5);

(b)  the child's parent;

(c)  the person with whom the child was placed under an order for society supervision;

(d)  any foster parent who has cared for the child continuously during the six months immediately before the application; and

(e)  in the case of a First Nations, Inuk or Métis child, the persons described in clauses (a), (b), (c) and (d) and a representative chosen by each of the child's bands and First Nations, Inuit or Métis communities.

### Six-month period

(6)  No application shall be made under subsection (4) within six months after the latest of,

(a)  the day the original order was made under subsection 101 (1);

(b)  the day the last application by a person under subsection (4) was disposed of; or

(c)  the day any appeal from an order referred to in clause (a) or the disposition referred to in clause (b) was finally disposed of or abandoned.

### Exception

(7)  Subsection (6) does not apply if the court is satisfied that a major element of the plan for the child's care that the court applied in its decision is not being carried out.

### Interim care and custody

(8)  If an application is made under this section, the child shall remain in the care and custody of the person or society having charge of the child until the application is disposed of, unless the court is satisfied that the child's best interests require a change in the child's care and custody.

### Court may vary, etc.

**114.** Where an application for review of a child's status is made under section 113, the court may, in the child's best interests,

(a)  vary or terminate the original order made under subsection 101 (1), including a term or condition or a provision for access that is part of the order;

(b) order that the original order terminate on a specified future date;

(c) make a further order or orders under section 101; or

(d) make an order under section 102.

### Status review for children in, or formerly in, extended society care

**115.** (1) This section applies where a child is in extended society care under an order made under paragraph 3 of subsection 101 (1) or clause 116 (1) (c), or is subject to an order for society supervision made under clause 116 (1) (a) or for custody made under clause 116 (1) (b).

### Society to seek status review

(2) The society that has or had care, custody or supervision of the child,

(a) may apply to the court at any time, subject to subsection (9), for a review of the child's status;

(b) shall apply to the court for a review of the child's status before the order expires if the order is for society supervision, unless the expiry is by reason of section 123; and

(c) shall apply to the court for a review of the child's status within five days after removing the child, if the society has removed the child,

(i) from the care of a person with whom the child was placed under an order for society supervision described in clause 116 (1) (a), or

(ii) from the custody of a person who had custody of the child under a custody order described in clause 116 (1) (b).

### Application of subs. (2) (a) and (c)

(3) Clauses (2) (a) and (c) also apply to the society that has jurisdiction in the county or district,

(a) in which the parent or other person with whom the child is placed resides, if the child is the subject of an order for society supervision under clause 116 (1) (a); or

(b) in which the person who has custody resides, if the child is the subject of a custody order under clause 116 (1) (b).

### Others may seek status review

(4) An application for review of a child's status under this section may be made on notice to the society by,

(a) the child, if the child is at least 12;

(b) a parent of the child;

(c) the person with whom the child was placed under an order for society supervision described in clause 116 (1) (a);

(d) the person to whom custody of the child was granted, if the child is subject to an order for custody described in clause 116 (1) (b);

(e) a foster parent, if the child has lived continuously with the foster parent for at least two years immediately before the application; or

(f) in the case of a First Nations, Inuk or Métis child, a person described in clause (a), (b), (c), (d) or (e) or a representative chosen by each of the child's bands and First Nations, Inuit or Métis communities.

### When leave to apply required

(5) Despite clause (4) (b), a parent of a child shall not make an application under subsection (4) without leave of the court if the child has, immediately before the application, received continuous care for at least two years from the same foster parent or from the same person under a custody order.

### Notice

(6) A society making an application under subsection (2) or receiving notice of an application under subsection (4) shall give notice of the application to,

(a) the child, except as otherwise provided under subsection 79 (4) or (5);

(b) the child's parent, if the child is younger than 16;

(c) the person with whom the child was placed, if the child is subject to an order for society supervision described in clause 116 (1) (a);

(d) the person to whom custody of the child was granted, if the child is subject to an order for custody described in clause 116 (1) (b);

(e) any foster parent who has cared for the child continuously during the six months immediately before the application; and

(f) in the case of a First Nations, Inuk or Métis child, the persons described in clause (a), (b), (c), (d) or (e) and a representative chosen by each of the child's bands and First Nations, Inuit or Métis communities.

### Six-month period

(7) No application shall be made under subsection (4) within six months after the latest of,

(a) the day the order was made under subsection 101 (1) or 116 (1), whichever is applicable;

(b) the day the last application by a person under subsection (4) was disposed of; or

(c) the day any appeal from an order referred to in clause (a) or a disposition referred to in clause (b) was finally disposed of or abandoned.

### Exception

(8) Subsection (7) does not apply if,

(a) the child is the subject of,

(i) an order for society supervision made under clause 116 (1) (a),

(ii) an order for custody made under clause 116 (1) (b), or

(iii) an order for extended society care made under paragraph 3 of subsection 101 (1) or clause 116 (1) (c) and an order for access under section 104; and

(b) the court is satisfied that a major element of the plan for the child's care that the court applied in its decision is not being carried out.

### No review if child placed for adoption

(9) No person or society shall make an application under this section with respect to a child who is in extended society care under an order made under paragraph 3 of subsection 101 (1) or clause 116 (1) (c) who has been placed in a person's home by the society or by a Director for the purposes of adoption under Part VIII (Adoption and Adoption Licensing), if the child still resides in the person's home.

### Interim care and custody

(10) If an application is made under this section, the child shall remain in the care and custody of the person or society having charge of the child until the application is disposed of, unless the court is satisfied that the child's best interests require a change in the child's care and custody.

### Court order

**116.** (1) If an application for review of a child's status is made under section 115, the court may, in the child's best interests,

(a) order that the child be placed in the care and custody of a parent or another person, subject to the supervision of the society, for a specified period of at least three months and not more than 12 months;

(b) order that custody be granted to one or more persons, including a foster parent, with the consent of the person or persons;

(c) order that the child be placed in extended society care until the order is terminated under this section or expires under section 123; or

(d) terminate or vary any order made under section 101 or this section.

### Variation, termination or new order

(2) When making an order under subsection (1), the court may, subject to section 105, vary or terminate an order for access or make a further order under section 104.

### Termination of extended society care order

(3) Any previous order for extended society care made under paragraph 3 of subsection 101 (1) or clause (1) (c) is terminated if an order described in clause (1) (a) or (b) is made in respect of a child.

### Terms and conditions of supervision order

(4) If the court makes a supervision order described in clause (1) (a), the court may impose,

(a) reasonable terms and conditions relating to the child's care and supervision;

(b) reasonable terms and conditions on,

(i) the child's parent,

(ii) the person who will have care and custody of the child under the order,

(iii) the child, and

(iv) any other person, other than a foster parent, who is putting forward a plan or who would participate in a plan for care and custody of or access to the child; and

(c) reasonable terms and conditions on the society that will supervise the placement, but shall not require the society to provide financial assistance or purchase any goods or services.

### Access

(5) Section 105 applies with necessary modifications if the court makes an order described in clause (1) (a), (b) or (c).

### Custody proceeding

(6) Where an order is made under this section or a proceeding is commenced under this Part, any proceeding respecting custody of or access to the same child under the *Children's Law Reform Act* is stayed except by leave of the court in the proceeding under that Act.

### Rights and responsibilities

(7) A person to whom custody of a child is granted by an order under this section has the rights and responsibilities of a parent in respect of the child and must exercise those rights and responsibilities in the best interests of the child.

### Director's annual review of children in extended society care

**117.** (1) A Director or a person authorized by a Director shall, at least once during each calendar year, review the status of every child,

(a) who is in extended society care under an order made under paragraph 3 of subsection 101 (1) or clause 116 (1) (c);

(b) who was in extended society care under an order described in clause (a) throughout the immediately preceding 24 months; and

(c) whose status has not been reviewed under this section or under section 116 during that time.

### Direction to society

(2) After a review under subsection (1), the Director may direct the society to make an application for review of the child's status under subsection 115 (2) or give any other direction that, in the Director's opinion, is in the child's best interests.

### Investigation by judge

**118.** (1) The Minister may appoint a judge of the Court of Ontario to investigate a matter relating to a child in a society's care or the proper administration of this Part, and a judge who is appointed shall conduct the investigation and make a written report to the Minister.

### Application of *Public Inquiries Act, 2009*

(2) Section 33 of the *Public Inquiries Act, 2009* applies to an investigation by a judge under subsection (1).

### Complaint to society

**119.** (1) A person may make a complaint to a society relating to a service sought or received by that person from the society in accordance with the regulations.

### Complaint review procedure

(2) Where a society receives a complaint under subsection (1), it shall deal with the complaint in accordance with the complaint review procedure established by regulation, subject to subsection 120 (2).

### Public availability

(3) A society shall make information relating to the complaint review procedure available to the public and to any person upon request.

### Society's decision

(4) Subject to subsection (5), the decision of a society made upon completion of the complaint review procedure is final.

### Application for review by Board

(5) If a complaint relates to one of the following matters, the complainant may apply to the Board in accordance with the regulations for a review of the decision made by the society upon completion of the complaint review procedure:

1. A matter described in subsection 120 (4).
2. Any other prescribed matter.

### Review by Board

(6) Upon receipt of an application under subsection (5), the Board shall give the society notice of the application and conduct a review of the society's decision.

### Composition of Board

(7) The Board shall be composed of members with the prescribed qualifications and prescribed experience.

### Hearing optional

(8) The Board may hold a hearing and, if a hearing is held, the Board shall comply with the prescribed practices and procedures.

### Non-application

(9) The *Statutory Powers Procedure Act* does not apply to a hearing under this section.

### Board decision

(10) Upon completing its review of a decision by a society in relation to a complaint, the Board may,

(a) in the case of a matter described in subsection 120 (4), make any order described in subsection 120 (7), as appropriate;

(b) redirect the matter to the society for further review;

(c) confirm the society's decision; or

(d) make such other order as may be prescribed.

### No review if matter within purview of court

(11) A society shall not conduct a review of a complaint under this section if the subject of the complaint,

(a) is an issue that has been decided by the court or is before the court; or

(b) is subject to another decision-making process under this Act or the *Labour Relations Act, 1995*.

### Complaint to Board

**120.** (1) If a complaint in respect of a service sought or received from a society relates to a matter described in subsection (4), the person who sought or received the service may,

(a) decide not to make the complaint to the society under section 119 and make the complaint directly to the Board under this section; or

(b) where the person first makes the complaint to the society under section 119, submit the complaint to the Board before the society's complaint review procedure is completed.

### Notice to society

(2) If a person submits a complaint to the Board under clause (1) (b) after having brought the complaint to the society under section 119, the Board shall give the society notice of that fact and the society may terminate or stay its review, as it considers appropriate.

### Complaint to Board

(3) A complaint to the Board under this section shall be made in accordance with the regulations.

### Matters for Board review

(4) The following matters may be reviewed by the Board under this section:

1. Allegations that the society has refused to proceed with a complaint made by the complainant under subsection 119 (1) as required under subsection 119 (2).
2. Allegations that the society has failed to respond to the complainant's complaint within the timeframe required by regulation.
3. Allegations that the society has failed to comply with the complaint review procedure or with any other procedural requirements under this Act relating to the review of complaints.
4. Allegations that the society has failed to comply with subsection 15 (2).
5. Allegations that the society has failed to provide the complainant with reasons for a decision that affects the complainant's interests.
6. Such other matters as may be prescribed.

### Review by Board

(5) Upon receipt of a complaint under this section, the Board shall conduct a review of the matter.

### Application

(6) Subsections 119 (7), (8) and (9) apply with necessary modification to a review of a complaint made under this section.

### Board decision

(7) After reviewing the complaint, the Board may,

(a) order the society to proceed with the complaint made by the complainant in accordance with the complaint review procedure established by regulation;

(b) order the society to provide a response to the complainant within a period specified by the Board;

(c) order the society to comply with the complaint review procedure established by regulation or with any other requirements under this Act;

(d) order the society to provide written reasons for a decision to a complainant;

(e) dismiss the complaint; or

(f) make such other order as may be prescribed.

### No review if matter within purview of court

(8) The Board shall not conduct a review of a complaint under this section if the subject of the complaint,

(a) is an issue that has been decided by the court or is before the court; or

(b) is subject to another decision-making process under this Act or the *Labour Relations Act, 1995*.

### Appeals

### Appeal

**121.** (1) An appeal from a court's order under this Part may be made to the Superior Court of Justice by,

(a) the child, if the child is entitled to participate in the proceeding under subsection 79 (6) (child's participation);

(b) any parent of the child;

(c) the person who had charge of the child immediately before intervention under this Part;

(d) a Director or local director; or

(e) in the case of a First Nations, Inuk or Métis child, a person described in clause (a), (b), (c) or (d) or a representative chosen by each of the child's bands and First Nations, Inuit or Métis communities.

### Exception

(2) Subsection (1) does not apply to an order for an assessment under section 98.

### Care and custody pending appeal

(3) Where a decision regarding the care and custody of a child is appealed under subsection (1), execution of the decision shall be stayed for the 10 days immediately following service of the notice of appeal on the court that made the decision, and where the child is in the society's care and custody at the time the decision is made, the child shall remain in the care and custody of the society until,

(a) the 10-day period of the stay has expired; or

(b) an order is made under subsection (4),

whichever is earlier.

### Temporary order

(4) The Superior Court of Justice may, in the child's best interests, make a temporary order for the child's care and custody pending final disposition of the appeal, and the court may, on any party's motion before the final disposition of the appeal, vary or terminate the order or make a further order.

### No extension where child placed for adoption

(5) No extension of the time for an appeal shall be granted where the child has been placed for adoption under Part VIII (Adoption and Adoption Licensing).

### Further evidence

(6) The court may receive further evidence relating to events after the appealed decision.

### Place of hearing

(7) An appeal under this section shall be heard in the county or district in which the order appealed from was made.

### Application of s. 87

(8) Section 87 (rules re hearings) applies with necessary modifications to an appeal under this section.

### Expiry of Orders

### Time limit

**122.** (1) Subject to subsections (4) and (5), the court shall not make an order for interim society care under paragraph 2 of subsection 101 (1) that results in a child being in the care and custody of a society for a period exceeding,

(a) 12 months, if the child is younger than 6 on the day the court makes the order; or

(b) 24 months, if the child is 6 or older on the day the court makes the order.

### Calculation of time limit

(2) The time during which a child has been in a society's care and custody pursuant to the following shall be counted in calculating the period referred to in subsection (1):

1. An agreement made under subsection 75 (1) (temporary care agreement).

2. A temporary order made under clause 94 (2) (d) (custody during adjournment).

### Previous periods to be counted

(3) The period referred to in subsection (1) shall include any previous periods that the child was in a society's care and custody under an interim society care order made under

paragraph 2 of subsection 101 (1) or as described in subsection (2) other than periods that precede a continuous period of five or more years that the child was not in a society's care and custody.

### Deemed extension of time limit

(4) Where the period referred to in subsection (1) or (5) expires and,

(a) an appeal of an order made under subsection 101 (1) has been commenced and is not yet finally disposed of; or

(b) the court has adjourned a hearing under section 114 (status review),

the period is deemed to be extended until the appeal has been finally disposed of and any new hearing ordered on appeal has been completed or an order has been made under section 114, as the case may be.

### Six-month extension

(5) Subject to paragraphs 2 and 4 of subsection 101 (1), the court may by order extend the period permitted under subsection (1) by a period not to exceed six months if it is in the child's best interests to do so.

### Expiry of orders

**123.** An order under this Part expires when the child who is the subject of the order,

(a) turns 18; or

(b) marries,

whichever comes first.

### Continued Care and Support
### Continued care and support

**124.** A society or prescribed entity shall enter into an agreement to provide care and support to a person in accordance with the regulations in each of the following circumstances:

1. A custody order under clause 116 (1) (b) or an order for extended society care under paragraph 3 of subsection 101 (1) or clause 116 (1) (c) was made in relation to that person as a child and the order expires under section 123.

2. The person entered into an agreement with the society under section 77 and the agreement expires on the person's 18th birthday.

3. The person is 18 or older and was eligible for the prescribed support services.

4. In the case of a First Nations, Inuk or Métis person who is 18 or older, paragraph 1, 2 or 3 applies or the person was being cared for under customary care immediately before their 18th birthday and the person who was caring for them was receiving a subsidy from the society or an entity under section 71.

### Duty to Report
### Duty to report child in need of protection

**125.** (1) Despite the provisions of any other Act, if a person, including a person who performs professional or official duties with respect to children, has reasonable grounds to suspect one of the following, the person shall immediately report the suspicion and the information on which it is based to a society:

1. The child has suffered physical harm inflicted by the person having charge of the child or caused by or resulting from that person's,
   i. failure to adequately care for, provide for, supervise or protect the child, or
   ii. pattern of neglect in caring for, providing for, supervising or protecting the child.

2. There is a risk that the child is likely to suffer physical harm inflicted by the person having charge of the child or caused by or resulting from that person's,
   i. failure to adequately care for, provide for, supervise or protect the child, or
   ii. pattern of neglect in caring for, providing for, supervising or protecting the child.

3. The child has been sexually abused or sexually exploited by the person having charge of the child or by another person where the person having charge of the child knows or should know of the possibility of sexual abuse or sexual exploitation and fails to protect the child.

4. There is a risk that the child is likely to be sexually abused or sexually exploited as described in paragraph 3.

5. The child requires treatment to cure, prevent or alleviate physical harm or suffering and the child's parent or the person having charge of the child does not provide the treatment or access to the treatment, or, where the child is incapable of consenting to the treatment under the *Health Care Consent Act, 1996*, refuses or is unavailable or unable to consent to, the treatment on the child's behalf.

6. The child has suffered emotional harm, demonstrated by serious,
   i. anxiety,
   ii. depression,
   iii. withdrawal,
   iv. self-destructive or aggressive behaviour, or
   v. delayed development,

and there are reasonable grounds to believe that the emotional harm suffered by the child results from the actions, failure to act or pattern of neglect on the part of the child's parent or the person having charge of the child.

7. The child has suffered emotional harm of the kind described in subparagraph 6 i, ii, iii, iv or v and the child's parent or the person having charge of the child does not provide services or treatment or access to services or treatment, or, where the child is incapable of consenting to treatment under the *Health Care Consent Act, 1996*, refuses or is unavailable or unable to consent to, treatment to remedy or alleviate the harm.

8. There is a risk that the child is likely to suffer emotional harm of the kind described in subparagraph 6 i, ii, iii, iv or v resulting from the actions, failure to act or pattern of neglect on the part of the child's parent or the person having charge of the child.

9. There is a risk that the child is likely to suffer emotional harm of the kind described in subparagraph 6 i, ii, iii, iv or v and the child's parent or the person having charge of the child does not provide services or treatment or access to services or treatment, or, where the child is incapable of consenting to treatment under the *Health Care Consent Act, 1996*, refuses or is unavailable or unable to consent to, treatment to prevent the harm.

10. The child suffers from a mental, emotional or developmental condition that, if not remedied, could seriously impair the child's development and the child's parent or the person having charge of the child does not provide the treatment or access to the treatment, or where the child is incapable of consenting to the treatment under the *Health Care Consent Act, 1996*, refuses or is unavailable or unable to consent to, treatment to remedy or alleviate the condition.

11. The child's parent has died or is unavailable to exercise custodial rights over the child and has not made adequate provision for the child's care and custody, or the child is in a residential placement and the parent refuses or is unable or unwilling to resume the child's care and custody.

12. The child is younger than 12 and has killed or seriously injured another person or caused serious damage to another person's property, services or treatment are necessary to prevent a recurrence and the child's parent or the person having charge of the child does not provide services or treatment or access to services or treatment, or, where the child is incapable of consenting to treatment under the *Health Care Consent Act, 1996*, refuses or is unavailable or unable to consent to treatment.

13. The child is younger than 12 and has on more than one occasion injured another person or caused loss or damage to another person's property, with the encouragement of the person having charge of the child or because of that person's failure or inability to supervise the child adequately.

## Ongoing duty to report

(2) A person who has additional reasonable grounds to suspect one of the matters set out in subsection (1) shall make a further report under subsection (1) even if the person has made previous reports with respect to the same child.

## Person must report directly

(3) A person who has a duty to report a matter under subsection (1) or (2) shall make the report directly to the society and shall not rely on any other person to report on the person's behalf.

## Duty to report does not apply to older children

(4) Subsections (1) and (2) do not apply in respect of a child who is 16 or 17, but a person may make a report under subsection (1) or (2) in respect of a child who is 16 or 17 if either a circumstance or condition described in paragraphs 1 to 11 of subsection (1) or a prescribed circumstance or condition exists.

## Offence

(5) A person referred to in subsection (6) is guilty of an offence if,

(a) the person contravenes subsection (1) or (2) by not reporting a suspicion; and

(b) the information on which it was based was obtained in the course of the person's professional or official duties.

## Professionals and officials

(6) Subsection (5) applies to every person who performs professional or official duties with respect to children including,

(a) a health care professional, including a physician, nurse, dentist, pharmacist and psychologist;

(b) a teacher, person appointed to a position designated by a board of education as requiring an early childhood educator, school principal, social worker, family counsellor, youth and recreation worker, and operator or employee of a child care centre or home child care agency or provider of licensed child care within the meaning of the *Child Care and Early Years Act, 2014*;

(c) a religious official;

(d) a mediator and an arbitrator;

(e) a peace officer and a coroner;

(f) a lawyer; and

(g) a service provider and an employee of a service provider.

## Volunteer excluded

(7) In clause (6) (b), "youth and recreation worker" does not include a volunteer.

## Director, officer or employee of corporation

(8) A director, officer or employee of a corporation who authorizes, permits or concurs in the commission of an offence under subsection (5) by an employee of the corporation is guilty of an offence.

### Penalty

(9) A person convicted of an offence under subsection (5) or (8) is liable to a fine of not more than $5,000.

### Section overrides privilege; protection from liability

(10) This section applies although the information reported may be confidential or privileged, and no action for making the report shall be instituted against a person who acts in accordance with this section unless the person acts maliciously or without reasonable grounds for the suspicion.

### Solicitor-client privilege

(11) Nothing in this section abrogates any privilege that may exist between a lawyer and the lawyer's client.

### Conflict

(12) This section prevails despite anything in the *Personal Health Information Protection Act, 2004*.

### Society to assess and verify report of child in need of protection

**126.** (1) A society that receives a report under section 125 that a child, including a child in the society's care or supervision, is or may be in need of protection shall as soon as possible carry out an assessment as prescribed and verify the reported information, or ensure that the information is assessed and verified by another society.

### Protection from liability

(2) No action or other proceeding for damages shall be instituted against an officer or employee of a society, acting in good faith, for an act done in the execution or intended execution of the duty imposed on the society by subsection (1) or for an alleged neglect or default of that duty.

### Society to report abuse of child in its care and custody

**127.** (1) A society that obtains information that a child in its care and custody is or may be suffering or may have suffered abuse shall report the information to a Director as soon as possible.

### Definition

(2) In this section and in sections 129 and 133,

"to suffer abuse", when used in reference to a child, means to be in need of protection within the meaning of clause 74 (2) (a), (c), (e), (f), (g) or (j).

> **Note:** On a day to be named by proclamation of the Lieutenant Governor, subsection 127 (2) of the Act is repealed and the following substituted: (See: 2017, c. 14, Sched. 3, s. 6)

### Definition

(2) In this section and section 129,

"to suffer abuse", when used in reference to a child, means to be in need of protection within the meaning of clause 74 (2) (a), (c), (e), (f), (g) or (j). 2017, c. 14, Sched. 3, s. 6.

### Duty to report child's death

**128.** A person or society that obtains information that a child has died shall report the information to a coroner if,

(a) a court made an order under this Act denying access to the child by a parent of the child or making the access subject to supervision;

(b) on the application of a society, a court varied the order to grant the access or to make it no longer subject to supervision; and

(c) the child subsequently died as a result of a criminal act committed by a parent or family member who had custody or charge of the child at the time of the act.

### Review Teams

### Review team

**129.** (1) In this section,

"review team" means a team established by a society under subsection (2).

### Composition

(2) Every society shall establish a review team that includes,

(a) persons who are professionally qualified to perform medical, psychological, developmental, educational or social assessments; and

(b) at least one legally qualified medical practitioner.

### Chair

(3) The members of a review team shall choose a chair from among themselves.

### Duty of team

(4) Whenever a society refers the case of a child who may be suffering or may have suffered abuse to its review team, the review team or a panel of at least three of its members, designated by the chair, shall,

(a) review the case; and

(b) recommend to the society how the child may be protected.

### Disclosure to team permitted

(5) Despite the provisions of any other Act, a person may disclose to a review team or to any of its members information reasonably required for a review under subsection (4).

### Section overrides privilege; protection from liability

(6) Subsection (5) applies although the information disclosed may be confidential or privileged and no action for disclosing the information shall be instituted against a person who acts in accordance with subsection (5), unless the person acts maliciously or without reasonable grounds.

### Where child not to be returned without review or hearing

(7) Where a society with a review team has information that a child placed in its care under subsection 94 (2)

(custody during adjournment) or subsection 101 (1) (order where child in need of protection) may have suffered abuse, the society shall not return the child to the care of the person who had charge of the child at the time of the possible abuse unless,

> (a) the society has,
>> (i) referred the case to its review team, and
>> (ii) obtained and considered the review team's recommendations; or
>
> (b) the court has terminated the order placing the child in the society's care.

### Court-Ordered Access to Records

## Production of records

### Definition

**130.** (1) In this section and sections 131 and 132,

"record of personal health information" has the same meaning as in the *Mental Health Act.*

### Motion or application for production of record

(2) A Director or a society may at any time make a motion or an application for an order under subsection (3) or (4) for the production of a record or part of a record.

### Order on motion

(3) Where the court is satisfied that a record or part of a record that is the subject of a motion referred to in subsection (2) contains information that may be relevant to a proceeding under this Part and that the person in possession or control of the record has refused to permit a Director or the society to inspect it, the court may order that the person in possession or control of the record produce it or a specified part of it for inspection and copying by the Director, by the society or by the court.

### Order on application

(4) Where the court is satisfied that a record or part of a record that is the subject of an application referred to in subsection (2) may be relevant to assessing compliance with one of the following and that the person in possession or control of the record has refused to permit a Director or the society to inspect it, the court may order that the person in possession or control of the record produce it or a specified part of it for inspection and copying by the Director, by the society or by the court:

1. An order under clause 94 (2) (b) or (c) that is subject to supervision.
2. An order under clause 94 (2) (c) or (d) with respect to access.
3. A supervision order under paragraph 1 or 4 of subsection 101 (1).
4. An access order under section 104.
5. An order with respect to access or supervision on an application under section 113 or 115.
6. A custody order under section 116.
7. A restraining order under section 137.

### Court may examine record

(5) In considering whether to make an order under subsection (3) or (4), the court may examine the record.

### Information confidential

(6) No person who obtains information by means of an order made under subsection (3) or (4) shall disclose the information except,

> (a) as specified in the order; and
> (b) in testimony in a proceeding under this Part.

### Conflict

(7) Subsection (6) prevails despite anything in the *Personal Health Information Protection Act, 2004.*

### Solicitor-client privilege

(8) Subject to subsection (9), this section applies despite any other Act, but nothing in this section abrogates any privilege that may exist between a lawyer and the lawyer's client.

### Application of Mental Health Act

(9) Where a motion or an application under subsection (2) concerns a record of personal health information, subsection 35 (6) (attending physician's statement, hearing) of the *Mental Health Act* applies and the court shall give equal consideration to,

> (a) the matters to be considered under subsection 35 (7) of that Act; and
> (b) the need to protect the child.

### Application of s. 294

(10) Where a motion or an application under subsection (2) concerns a record that is a record of a mental disorder within the meaning of section 294, that section applies and the court shall give equal consideration to,

> (a) the matters to be considered under subsection 294 (6); and
> (b) the need to protect the child.

### Warrant for access to record

**131.** (1) The court or a justice of the peace may issue a warrant for access to a record or a specified part of it if the court or justice of the peace is satisfied on the basis of information on oath from a Director or a person designated by a society that there are reasonable grounds to believe that the record or part of the record is relevant to investigate an allegation that a child is or may be in need of protection.

### Authority conferred by warrant

(2) The warrant authorizes the Director or the person designated by the society to,

> (a) inspect the record specified in the warrant during normal business hours or during the hours specified in the warrant;

(b) make copies from the record in any manner that does not damage the record; and

(c) remove the record for the purpose of making copies.

### Return of record

(3) A person who removes a record under clause (2) (c) shall promptly return it after copying it.

### Admissibility of copies

(4) A copy of a record that is the subject of a warrant under this section and that is certified as being a true copy of the original by the person who made the copy is admissible in evidence to the same extent as and has the same evidentiary value as the record.

### Duration of warrant

(5) The warrant is valid for seven days.

### Execution

(6) The Director or the person designated by the society may call on a peace officer for assistance in executing the warrant.

### Solicitor-client privilege

(7) This section applies despite any other Act, but nothing in this section abrogates any privilege that may exist between a lawyer and the lawyer's client.

### Application of *Mental Health Act*

(8) If a warrant issued under this section concerns a record of personal health information and the warrant is challenged under subsection 35 (6) (attending physician's statement, hearing) of the *Mental Health Act*, equal consideration shall be given to,

(a) the matters set out in subsection 35 (7) of that Act; and

(b) the need to protect the child.

### Application of s. 294

(9) If a warrant issued under this section concerns a record of a mental disorder within the meaning of section 294 and the warrant is challenged under section 294, equal consideration shall be given to,

(a) the matters set out in subsection 294 (6); and

(b) the need to protect the child.

### Telewarrant

**132.** (1) Where a Director or a person designated by a society believes that there are reasonable grounds for the issuance of a warrant under section 131 and that it would be impracticable to appear personally before the court or a justice of the peace to make application for a warrant in accordance with section 131, the Director or person designated by the society may submit an information on oath by telephone or other means of telecommunication to a justice designated for the purpose by the Chief Justice of the Ontario Court of Justice.

### Same

(2) The information shall,

(a) include a statement of the grounds to believe that the record or part of the record is relevant to investigate an allegation that a child is or may be in need of protection; and

(b) set out the circumstances that make it impracticable for the Director or person designated by the society to appear personally before a court or justice of the peace.

### Warrant to be issued

(3) The justice may issue a warrant for access to the record or the specified part of it if the justice is satisfied that the application discloses,

(a) reasonable grounds to believe that the record or the part of a record is relevant to investigate an allegation that a child is or may be in need of protection; and

(b) reasonable grounds to dispense with personal appearance for the purpose of an application under section 131.

### Validity of warrant

(4) A warrant issued under this section is not subject to challenge by reason only that there were not reasonable grounds to dispense with personal appearance for the purpose of an application under section 131.

### Application of provisions

(5) Subsections 131 (2) to (9) apply with necessary modifications with respect to a warrant issued under this section.

### Definition

(6) In this section,

"justice" means justice of the peace, a judge of the Ontario Court of Justice or a judge of the Family Court of the Superior Court of Justice.

### Child Abuse Register

### Register

**133.** (1) In this section and in section 134,

"Director" means the person appointed under subsection (2); ("directeur")

"register" means the register maintained under subsection (5); ("registre")

"registered person" means a person identified in the register, but does not include,

(a) a person who reports to a society under subsection 125 (1) or (2) and is not the subject of the report, or

(b) the child who is the subject of a report. ("personne inscrite")

### Director

(2) The Minister may appoint an employee in the Ministry as Director for the purposes of this section.

### Duty of society

(3) A society that receives a report under section 125 that a child, including a child in the society's care, is or may be suffering or may have suffered abuse shall verify the reported information as soon as possible, or ensure that the information is verified by another society, in the manner determined by the Director, and if the information is verified, the society that verified it shall report it to the Director in the prescribed form as soon as possible.

### Protection from liability

(4) No action or other proceeding for damages shall be instituted against an officer or employee of a society, acting in good faith, for an act done in the execution or intended execution of the duty imposed on the society by subsection (3) or for an alleged neglect or default of that duty.

### Child abuse register

(5) The Director shall maintain a register in the prescribed manner for the purpose of recording information reported to the Director under subsection (3), but the register shall not contain information that has the effect of identifying a person who reports to a society under subsection 125 (1) or (2) and is not the subject of the report.

### Register confidential

(6) Despite Part X (Personal Information) and any other Act, no person shall inspect, remove or alter or permit the inspection, removal or alteration of information in the register, or disclose or permit the disclosure of information that the person obtained from the register, except as this section authorizes.

### Coroner's inquest, etc.

(7) The following persons may inspect, remove and disclose information in the register in accordance with that person's authority:

1. A coroner, or a legally qualified medical practitioner or peace officer authorized in writing by a coroner, acting in connection with an investigation or inquest under the *Coroners Act*.
2. The Children's Lawyer or the Children's Lawyer's authorized agent.

### Minister or Director may permit access to register

(8) The Minister or the Director may permit the following persons to inspect and remove information in the register and to disclose the information to a person referred to in subsection (7) or to another person referred to in this subsection, subject to such terms and conditions as the Director may impose:

1. A person who is employed,
   i.   in the Ministry,
   ii.  by a society, or
   iii. by a child welfare authority outside Ontario.

2. A person who is providing or proposes to provide counselling or treatment to a registered person.

### Minister or Director may disclose information

(9) The Minister or the Director may disclose information in the register to a person referred to in subsection (7) or (8).

### Research

(10) A person who is engaged in research may, with the Director's written approval, inspect and use the information in the register, but shall not,

(a) use or communicate the information for any purpose except research, academic pursuits or the compilation of statistical data; or

(b) communicate any information that may have the effect of identifying a person named in the register.

### Access by child or registered person

(11) A child, a registered person or the child's or registered person's lawyer or agent may inspect only the information in the register that refers to the child or registered person.

### Physician

(12) A legally qualified medical practitioner may, with the Director's written approval, inspect the information in the register that is specified by the Director.

### Amendment of register

(13) The Director or an employee in the Ministry acting under the Director's authority,

(a) shall remove a name from or otherwise amend the register where the regulations require the removal or amendment; and

(b) may amend the register to correct an error.

### Register inadmissible: exceptions

(14) The register shall not be admitted into evidence in a proceeding except,

(a) to prove compliance or non-compliance with this section;

(b) in a hearing or appeal under section 134;

(c) in a proceeding under the *Coroners Act*; or

(d) in a proceeding referred to in section 138.

> **Note: On a day to be named by proclamation of the Lieutenant Governor, section 133 of the Act is repealed. (See: 2017, c. 14, Sched. 3, s. 7)**

### Hearing re registered person
### Definition

**134.** (1) In this section,

"hearing" means a hearing held under clause (4) (b).

### Notice to registered person

(2) Where an entry is made in the register, the Director shall as soon as possible give written notice to each registered person referred to in the entry indicating that,

(a) the person is identified in the register;

(b) the person or the person's lawyer or agent is entitled to inspect the information in the register that refers to or identifies the person; and

(c) the person is entitled to request that the Director remove the person's name from or otherwise amend the register.

### Request to amend register

(3) A registered person who receives notice under subsection (2) may request that the Director remove the person's name from or otherwise amend the register.

### Director's response

(4) On receiving a request under subsection (3), the Director may,

(a) grant the request; or

(b) hold a hearing, on 10 days written notice to the parties, to determine whether to grant or refuse the request.

### Delegation

(5) The Director may authorize another person to hold a hearing and exercise the Director's powers and duties under subsection (8).

### Procedure

(6) The *Statutory Powers Procedure Act* applies to a hearing and a hearing shall be conducted in accordance with the prescribed practices and procedures.

### Hearing

(7) The parties to a hearing are,

(a) the registered person;

(b) the society that verified the information referring to or identifying the registered person; and

(c) any other person specified by the Director.

### Director's decision

(8) Where the Director determines, after holding a hearing, that the information in the register with respect to a registered person is in error or should not be in the register, the Director shall remove the registered person's name from or otherwise amend the register, and may order that the society's records be amended to reflect the Director's decision.

### Appeal to Divisional Court

(9) A party to a hearing may appeal the Director's decision to the Divisional Court.

### Hearing private

(10) A hearing or appeal under this section shall be held in the absence of the public and no media representative shall be permitted to attend.

### Publication

(11) No person shall publish or make public information that has the effect of identifying a witness at or a participant in a hearing, or a party to a hearing other than a society.

### Record inadmissible: exception

(12) The record of a hearing or appeal under this section shall not be admitted into evidence in any other proceeding except a proceeding under clause 142 (1) (c) (confidentiality of child abuse register) or clause 142 (1) (d) (amendment of society's records).

> **Note: On a day to be named by proclamation of the Lieutenant Governor, section 134 of the Act is repealed. (See: 2017, c. 14, Sched. 3, s. 7)**

### Powers of Director
### Director's power to transfer

**135.** (1) A Director may direct, in the best interests of a child in the care or supervision of a society, that the child,

(a) be transferred to the care or supervision of another society; or

(b) be transferred from one placement to another placement designated by the Director.

### Criteria

(2) In determining whether to direct a transfer under clause (1) (b), the Director shall take into account,

(a) the length of time the child has spent in the existing placement;

(b) the views of the foster parents; and

(c) the views and wishes of the child, given due weight in accordance with the child's age and maturity.

### Offences, Restraining Orders, Recovery on Child's Behalf and Injunctions
### Abuse, failure to provide for reasonable care, etc.
### Definition

**136.** (1) In this section,

"abuse" means a state or condition of being physically harmed, sexually abused or sexually exploited.

### Child abuse

(2) No person having charge of a child shall,

(a) inflict abuse on the child; or

(b) by failing to care and provide for or supervise and protect the child adequately,

(i) permit the child to suffer abuse, or

(ii) permit the child to suffer from a mental, emotional or developmental condition that, if not remedied, could seriously impair the child's development.

### Leaving child unattended

(3)  No person having charge of a child younger than 16 shall leave the child without making provision for the child's supervision and care that is reasonable in the circumstances.

### Allowing child to loiter, etc.

(4)  No parent of a child younger than 16 shall permit the child to,

(a)  loiter in a public place between the hours of midnight and 6 a.m.; or

(b)  be in a place of public entertainment between the hours of midnight and 6 a.m., unless the parent accompanies the child or authorizes a specified individual 18 or older to accompany the child.

### Police may bring child home or to place of safety

(5)  Where a child who is actually or apparently younger than 16 is in a place to which the public has access between the hours of midnight and 6 a.m. and is not accompanied by a person described in clause (4) (b), a peace officer may bring the child to a place of safety without a warrant and proceed as if the child had been brought to a place of safety under subsection 84 (1).

### Child protection hearing

(6)  The court may, in connection with a case arising under subsection (2), (3) or (4), proceed under this Part as if an application had been made under subsection 81 (1) (child protection proceeding) in respect of the child.

### Restraining order

137. (1)  Instead of making an order under subsection 101 (1) or section 116 or in addition to making a temporary order under subsection 94 (2) or an order under subsection 101 (1) or section 116, the court may make one or more of the following orders in the child's best interests:

1.  An order restraining or prohibiting a person's access to or contact with the child, and may include in the order such directions as the court considers appropriate for implementing the order and protecting the child.

2.  An order restraining or prohibiting a person's contact with the person who has lawful custody of the child following a temporary order made under subsection 94 (2) or an order made under subsection 101 (1) or clause 116 (1) (a) or (b).

### Notice

(2)  An order shall not be made under subsection (1) unless notice of the proceeding has been served personally on the person to be named in the order.

### Duration of the order

(3)  An order made under subsection (1) shall continue in force for such period as the court considers in the best interests of the child and,

(a)  if the order is made in addition to a temporary order made under subsection 94 (2) or an order made under

subsection 101 (1) or clause 116 (1) (a), (b) or (c), the order may provide that it continues in force, unless it is varied, extended or terminated by the court, as long as the temporary order made under subsection 94 (2) or the order made under subsection 101 (1) or clause 116 (1) (a), (b) or (c), as the case may be, remains in force; or

(b)  if the order is made instead of an order under subsection 101 (1) or clause 116 (1) (a), (b) or (c) or if the order is made in addition to an order under clause 116 (1) (d), the order may provide that it continues in force until it is varied or terminated by the court.

### Application for extension, variation or termination

(4)  An application for the extension, variation or termination of an order made under subsection (1) may be made by,

(a)  the person who is the subject of the order;

(b)  the child;

(c)  the person having charge of the child;

(d)  a society;

(e)  a Director; or

(f)  in the case of a First Nations, Inuk or Métis child, a person described in clause (a), (b), (c), (d) or (e) or a representative chosen by each of the child's bands and First Nations, Inuit or Métis communities.

### Order for extension, variation or termination

(5)  Where an application is made under subsection (4), the court may, in the child's best interests,

(a)  extend the order for such period as the court considers to be in the best interests of the child, in the case of an order described in clause (3) (a); or

(b)  vary or terminate the order.

### Child in society's care not to be returned while order in force

(6)  Where a society has care of a child and an order made under subsection (1) prohibiting a person's access to the child is in force, the society shall not return the child to the care of,

(a)  the person named in the order; or

(b)  a person who may permit that person to have access to the child.

### Legal claim for recovery because of abuse

138. (1)  In this section,

"to suffer abuse", when used in reference to a child, means to be in need of protection within the meaning of clause 74 (2) (a), (c), (e), (f), (g) or (j).

### Recovery on child's behalf

(2)  When the Children's Lawyer is of the opinion that a child has a cause of action or other claim because the child has suffered abuse and considers it to be in the child's best interests, the Children's Lawyer may institute and conduct proceedings on the child's behalf for the recovery of damages or other compensation.

### Society may apply

(3) Where a child is in a society's care and custody, subsection (2) also applies to the society with necessary modifications.

### Prohibition

**139.** No person shall place a child in the care and custody of a society, and no society shall take a child into its care and custody, except in accordance with this Part.

### Offences re interfering, etc. with child in society supervision or care

**140.** If a child is the subject of an order for society supervision, interim society care or extended society care made under paragraph 1, 2 or 3 of subsection 101 (1) or clause 116 (1) (a) or (c), no person shall,

(a) induce or attempt to induce the child to leave the care of the person with whom the child is placed by the court or by the society, as the case may be;

(b) detain or harbour the child after the person or society referred to in clause (a) requires that the child be returned;

(c) interfere with the child or remove or attempt to remove the child from any place; or

(d) for the purpose of interfering with the child, visit or communicate with the person referred to in clause (a).

### Offences re false information, obstruction, etc.

**141.** No person shall,

(a) knowingly give false information in an application under this Part; or

(b) obstruct, interfere with or attempt to obstruct or interfere with a child protection worker or a peace officer who is acting under section 81, 83, 84, 85 or 86.

### Other offences

**142.** (1) A person who contravenes,

(a) an order for access made under subsection 104 (1);

(b) subsection 130 (6) (disclosure of information);

(c) subsection 133 (6) or (10) (confidentiality of child abuse register);

> **Note: On a day to be named by proclamation of the Lieutenant Governor, clause 142 (1) (c) of the Act is repealed. (See: 2017, c. 14, Sched. 3, s. 8 (1))**

(d) an order made under subsection 134 (8) (amendment of society's records);

> **Note: On a day to be named by proclamation of the Lieutenant Governor, clause 142 (1) (d) of the Act is repealed. (See: 2017, c. 14, Sched. 3, s. 8 (1))**

(e) subsection 136 (3) or (4) (leaving child unattended, etc.);

(f) a restraining order made under subsection 137 (1);

(g) section 139 (unauthorized placement);

(h) any provision of section 140 (interference with child, etc.); or

(i) clause 141 (a) or (b) (false information, obstruction, etc.),

and a director, officer or employee of a corporation who authorizes, permits or concurs in such a contravention by the corporation is guilty of an offence and on conviction is liable to a fine of not more than $5,000 or to imprisonment for a term of not more than one year, or to both.

### Offence of child abuse

(2) A person who contravenes subsection 136 (2) (child abuse), and a director, officer or employee of a corporation who authorizes, permits or concurs in such a contravention by the corporation is guilty of an offence and on conviction is liable to a fine of not more than $5,000 or to imprisonment for a term of not more than two years, or to both.

### Offences re publication

(3) A person who contravenes subsection 87 (8) or 134 (11) (publication of identifying information) or an order prohibiting publication made under clause 87 (7) (c) or subsection 87 (9), and a director, officer or employee of a corporation who authorizes, permits or concurs in such a contravention by the corporation, is guilty of an offence and on conviction is liable to a fine of not more than $10,000 or to imprisonment for a term of not more than three years, or to both.

> **Note: On a day to be named by proclamation of the Lieutenant Governor, subsection 142 (3) of the Act is amended by striking out "or 134 (11)". (See: 2017, c. 14, Sched. 3, s. 8 (2))**

### Injunction

**143.** (1) The Superior Court of Justice may grant an injunction to restrain a person from contravening section 140, on the society's application.

### Variation, etc.

(2) The court may vary or terminate an order made under subsection (1), on any person's application.

## PART VI    YOUTH JUSTICE

### Definitions

**144.** In this Part,

"bailiff" means a bailiff appointed under clause 146 (1) (c); ("huissier")

"Board" means the Custody Review Board continued under subsection 151 (1); ("Commission")

"probation officer" means,

(a) a person appointed or designated by the Lieutenant Governor in Council or their delegate to perform any of the duties or functions of a youth worker under the *Youth Criminal Justice Act* (Canada), or

(b) a probation officer appointed under clause 146 (1) (b); ("agent de probation")

### Programs and Officers

## Programs

### Secure and open temporary detention programs

**145.** (1) The Minister may establish the following in places of temporary detention:

1. Secure temporary detention programs, in which restrictions are continuously imposed on the liberty of young persons by physical barriers, close staff supervision or limited access to the community.

2. Open temporary detention programs, in which restrictions that are less stringent than in a secure temporary detention program are imposed on the liberty of young persons.

### Secure custody programs

(2) The Minister may establish secure custody programs in places of secure custody.

### Open custody programs

(3) The Minister may establish open custody programs in places of open custody.

### Where locking up permitted

(4) A place of secure custody and a place of secure temporary detention may be locked for the detention of young persons.

### Appointments by Minister

**146.** (1) The Minister may appoint any person or class of persons as,

(a) a provincial director, to perform any or all of the duties and functions of a provincial director,

(i) under the *Youth Criminal Justice Act* (Canada), and

(ii) under this Act and the regulations;

(b) a probation officer, to perform any or all of the duties and functions,

(i) of a youth worker under the *Youth Criminal Justice Act* (Canada),

(ii) of a probation officer for purposes related to young persons under the *Provincial Offences Act*, and

(iii) of a probation officer under this Act and the regulations; and

(c) a bailiff, to perform any or all of the duties and functions of a bailiff under the regulations.

### Conditions or limitations on appointments

(2) The Minister may set out in an appointment made under subsection (1) any conditions or limitations to which it is subject.

### Probation officer and bailiff have powers of peace officer

(3) While performing their duties and functions, a probation officer appointed under clause (1) (b) and a bailiff appointed under clause (1) (c) have the powers of a peace officer.

### Designation of peace officers

(4) The Minister may designate in writing,

(a) a person who is an employee in the Ministry or is employed in a place of open custody, of secure custody or of temporary detention to be a peace officer while performing the person's duties and functions; or

(b) a class of persons, from among the persons described in clause (a), to be peace officers while performing their duties and functions.

### Conditions or limitations on designations

(5) The Minister may set out in a designation made under subsection (4) any conditions or limitations to which it is subject.

### Remuneration and expenses

(6) The remuneration and expenses of a person appointed under subsection (1) who is not a public servant employed under Part III of the *Public Service of Ontario Act, 2006* shall be fixed by the Minister and shall be paid out of legislative appropriations.

### Reports and information

**147.** A person in charge of a place of temporary detention, of open custody or of secure custody, a bailiff and a probation officer,

(a) shall make the prescribed reports and provide the prescribed information to the Minister, in the prescribed form and at the prescribed intervals; and

(b) shall make a report and provide information to the Minister whenever the Minister requests it.

### Temporary Detention

## Open and secure temporary detention

### Open temporary detention unless provincial director determines otherwise

**148.** (1) A young person who is detained under the *Youth Criminal Justice Act* (Canada) in a place of temporary detention shall be detained in a place of open temporary detention unless a provincial director determines under subsection (2) that the young person is to be detained in a place of secure temporary detention.

**Where secure temporary detention available**

(2) A provincial director may detain a young person in a place of secure temporary detention if the provincial director is satisfied that it is necessary on one of the following grounds:

1. The young person is charged with an offence for which an adult would be liable to imprisonment for five years or more and,

    i. the offence includes causing or attempting to cause serious bodily harm to another person,

    ii. the young person has, at any time, failed to appear in court when required to do so under the *Youth Criminal Justice Act* (Canada) or escaped or attempted to escape from lawful detention, or

    iii. the young person has, within the 12 months immediately preceding the offence on which the current charge is based, been convicted of an offence for which an adult would be liable to imprisonment for five years or more.

2. The young person is detained in a place of temporary detention and leaves or attempts to leave without the consent of the person in charge or is charged with having escaped or attempting to escape from lawful custody or being unlawfully at large under the *Criminal Code* (Canada).

3. The provincial director is satisfied, having regard to all the circumstances, including any substantial likelihood the young person will commit a criminal offence or interfere with the administration of justice if placed in a place of open temporary detention, that it is necessary to detain the young person in a place of secure temporary detention,

    i. to ensure the young person's attendance at court,

    ii. for the protection and safety of the public, or

    iii. for the safety or security within a place of temporary detention.

**Until return to secure custody**

(3) Despite subsection (1), a young person who is apprehended because they have left or have not returned to a place of secure custody may be detained in a place of secure temporary detention until they are returned to the first-named place of custody.

**Until determination**

(4) Despite subsection (1), a young person who is detained under the *Youth Criminal Justice Act* (Canada) in a place of temporary detention may be detained in a place of secure temporary detention for a period not exceeding 24 hours while a provincial director makes a determination in respect of the young person under subsection (2).

**Review of secure temporary detention**

(5) A young person who is being detained in a place of secure temporary detention and who is brought before a youth justice court for a review of an order for detention made under the *Youth Criminal Justice Act* (Canada) or the *Criminal Code* (Canada) may request that the youth justice court review the level of their detention.

**Powers of youth justice court**

(6) The youth justice court conducting a review of an order for detention may confirm the provincial director's decision under subsection (2) or may direct that the young person be transferred to a place of open temporary detention.

**Application for return to secure temporary detention**

(7) A provincial director may apply to a youth justice court for a review of an order directing that a young person be transferred to a place of open temporary detention under subsection (6) on the basis that it is necessary that the young person be returned to a place of secure temporary detention because of either of the following:

1. A material change in the circumstances.

2. Any other grounds that the provincial director considers appropriate.

**Powers of youth justice court**

(8) The youth justice court conducting a review of an order transferring a young person to a place of open temporary detention may confirm the court's decision under subsection (6) or may direct that the young person be transferred to a place of secure temporary detention.

## Custody

### Detention under *Provincial Offences Act*
**Pre-trial detention**

**149.** (1) Where a young person is ordered to be detained in custody under subsection 150 (4) (order for detention) or 151 (2) (further orders) of the *Provincial Offences Act*, the young person shall be detained in a place of temporary detention.

**Open custody for provincial offences**

(2) Where a young person is sentenced to a term of imprisonment under the *Provincial Offences Act*,

    (a) the term of imprisonment shall be served in a place of open custody, subject to subsections (3) and (4);

    (b) section 91 (reintegration leave) of the *Youth Criminal Justice Act* (Canada) applies with necessary modifications; and

    (c) sections 28 (remission) and 28.1 (determinations of remission) and Part III (Ontario Parole and Earned Release Board) of the *Ministry of Correctional Services Act* apply with necessary modifications.

### Transfer to place of secure custody

(3) Where a young person is placed in open custody under clause (2) (a), the provincial director may transfer the young person to a place of secure custody if, in the opinion of the provincial director, the transfer is necessary for the safety of the young person or the safety of others in the place of open custody.

### Concurrent terms

(4) Where a young person is committed to custody under the *Youth Criminal Justice Act* (Canada) and is sentenced concurrently to a term of imprisonment under the *Provincial Offences Act*, the term of imprisonment under the *Provincial Offences Act* shall be served in the same place as the sentence under the *Youth Criminal Justice Act* (Canada).

### Young persons in open custody

150. Where a young person is sentenced to a term of imprisonment for breach of probation under clause 75 (d) of the *Provincial Offences Act,* to be served in open custody as set out in section 103 of that Act,

(a) the young person shall be held in a place of open custody specified by a provincial director; and

(b) the provisions of section 91 (reintegration leave) of the *Youth Criminal Justice Act* (Canada) apply with necessary modifications.

## Custody Review Board

### Custody Review Board

151. (1) The Custody Review Board is continued under the name Custody Review Board in English and Commission de révision des placements sous garde in French and shall have the powers and duties given to it by this Part and the regulations.

### Members

(2) The Board shall be composed of the prescribed number of members who shall be appointed by the Lieutenant Governor in Council.

### Chair and vice-chairs

(3) The Lieutenant Governor in Council may appoint a member of the Board as chair and may appoint one or more other members as vice-chairs.

### Quorum

(4) The prescribed number of members of the Board are a quorum.

### Remuneration

(5) The chair and vice-chairs and the other members of the Board shall be paid the remuneration determined by the Lieutenant Governor in Council and are entitled to their reasonable and necessary travelling and living expenses while attending meetings or otherwise engaged in the work of the Board.

### Duties of Board

(6) The Board shall conduct reviews under section 152 and perform such other duties as are assigned to it by the regulations.

### Application to Board

152. (1) A young person may apply to the Board for a review of,

(a) the particular place where the young person is held or to which the young person has been transferred;

(b) a provincial director's refusal to authorize the young person's reintegration leave under section 91 of the *Youth Criminal Justice Act* (Canada); or

(c) the young person's transfer from a place of open custody to a place of secure custody under subsection 24.2 (9) of the *Young Offenders Act* (Canada) in accordance with section 88 of the *Youth Criminal Justice Act* (Canada).

### 30 day time limit

(2) An application under subsection (1) must be made within 30 days of the decision, placement or transfer, as the case may be.

### Duty of Board to conduct review

(3) The Board shall conduct a review with respect to an application made under subsection (1) and may do so by holding a hearing.

### Advise whether hearing to be held

(4) The Board shall advise the young person whether it intends to hold a hearing or not within 10 days of receiving the young person's application.

### Procedure

(5) The *Statutory Powers Procedure Act* does not apply to a hearing held under subsection (3).

### Time period for review

(6) The Board shall complete its review and make a determination within 30 days of receiving a young person's application, unless,

(a) the Board holds a hearing with respect to the application; and

(b) the young person and the provincial director whose decision is being reviewed consent to a longer period for the Board's determination.

### Board's recommendations

(7) After conducting a review under subsection (3), the Board may,

(a) recommend to the provincial director,

(i) where the Board is of the opinion that the place where the young person is held or to which the young person has been transferred is not appropriate to meet the young person's needs, that the young person be transferred to another place,

(ii) that the young person's reintegration leave be authorized under section 91 of the *Youth Criminal Justice Act* (Canada), or

(iii) where the young person has been transferred as described in clause (1) (c), that the young person be returned to a place of open custody; or

(b) confirm the decision, placement or transfer.

### Apprehension of Young Persons who are Absent from Custody without Permission

#### Apprehension

#### Apprehension of young person absent from place of temporary detention

**153.** (1) A peace officer, the person in charge of a place of temporary detention or that person's delegate, who believes on reasonable and probable grounds that a young person detained under the *Youth Criminal Justice Act* (Canada) or the *Provincial Offences Act* in a place of temporary detention has left the place without the consent of the person in charge and fails or refuses to return there may apprehend the young person with or without a warrant and take the young person or arrange for the young person to be taken to a place of temporary detention.

#### Apprehension of young person absent from place of open custody

(2) A peace officer, the person in charge of a place of open custody or that person's delegate, who believes on reasonable and probable grounds that a young person held in a place of open custody as described in section 150,

(a) has left the place without the consent of the person in charge and fails or refuses to return there; or

(b) fails or refuses to return to the place of open custody upon completion of a period of reintegration leave under clause 150 (b),

may apprehend the young person with or without a warrant and take the young person or arrange for the young person to be taken to a place of open custody or a place of temporary detention.

#### Young person to be returned within 48 hours

(3) A young person who is apprehended under this section shall be returned to the place from which the young person is absent within 48 hours after being apprehended unless the provincial director detains the young person in secure temporary detention under paragraph 2 of subsection 148 (2).

#### Warrant to apprehend young person

(4) A justice of the peace who is satisfied on the basis of a sworn information that there are reasonable and probable grounds to believe that a young person held in a place of temporary detention or open custody,

(a) has left the place without the consent of the person in charge and fails or refuses to return there; or

(b) fails or refuses to return to a place of open custody upon completion of a period of reintegration leave under clause 150 (b),

may issue a warrant authorizing a peace officer, the person in charge of the place of temporary detention or open custody or that person's delegate to apprehend the young person.

#### Authority to enter, etc.

(5) Where a person authorized to apprehend a young person under subsection (1) or (2) believes on reasonable and probable grounds that a young person referred to in the relevant subsection is on any premises, the person may with or without a warrant enter the premises, by force, if necessary, and search for and remove the young person.

#### Regulations regarding exercise of power of entry

(6) A person authorized to enter premises under subsection (5) shall exercise the power of entry in accordance with the regulations.

### Inspections and Investigations

#### Inspections and investigations

**154.** (1) The Minister may designate any person to conduct such inspections or investigations as the Minister may require in connection with the administration of this Part.

#### Dismissal for cause for obstruction of inspection

(2) Any person employed in the Ministry who obstructs an inspection or investigation or withholds, destroys, conceals or refuses to furnish any information or thing required for purposes of an inspection or investigation may be dismissed for cause from employment.

### Searches

#### Permissible searches

**155.** (1) The person in charge of a place of open custody, of secure custody or of temporary detention may authorize a search, to be carried out in accordance with the regulations, of the following:

1. The place of open custody, of secure custody or of temporary detention.
2. The person of any young person or any other person on the premises of the place of open custody, of secure custody or of temporary detention.
3. The property of any young person or any other person on the premises of the place of open custody, of secure custody or of temporary detention.
4. Any vehicle entering or on the premises of the place of open custody, of secure custody or of temporary detention.

#### Contraband

(2) Any contraband found during a search may be seized and disposed of in accordance with the regulations.

### Meaning of contraband

(3) For the purposes of subsection (2),

"contraband" means,

(a) anything that a young person is not authorized to have,

(b) anything that a young person is authorized to have but in a place where they are not authorized to have it, and

(c) anything that a young person is authorized to have but that is being used for a purpose for which they are not authorized to use it.

### Mechanical Restraints

### Mechanical restraints

### Limits on use

**156.** (1) The person in charge of a place of secure custody or of secure temporary detention shall ensure that no young person who is detained in the place of secure custody or of secure temporary detention is,

(a) restrained by the use of mechanical restraints, other than in accordance with this section and the regulations;

(b) restrained by the use of mechanical restraints as a means of punishment.

### Conditions for use

(2) The person in charge of a place of secure custody or of secure temporary detention may authorize the use of mechanical restraints on a young person who is detained in the place of secure custody or of secure temporary detention only if all of the following are satisfied:

1. There is an imminent risk, if mechanical restraints were not used, that:

    i. the young person or another person would suffer physical injury,

    ii the young person would escape the place of secure custody or of secure temporary detention, or

    iii. the young person would cause significant property damage.

2. Alternatives to the use of mechanical restraints would not be, or have not been, effective to reduce or eliminate the risk referred to in paragraph 1.

3. The use of the mechanical restraints is reasonably necessary to reduce or eliminate the risk referred to in paragraph 1.

### Exception for transportation

(3) Despite subsection (2), mechanical restraints may be used on a young person who is detained in a place of secure custody or of secure temporary detention where it is reasonably necessary for the transportation of the young person to another place of custody or detention, or to or from court or the community.

### PART VII    EXTRAORDINARY MEASURES

### Definitions

**157.** In this Part,

"administrator" means the person in charge of a secure treatment program; ("administrateur")

"intrusive procedure" means,

(a) the use of mechanical restraints,

(b) an aversive stimulation technique, or

(c) any other procedure that is prescribed as an intrusive procedure; ("technique d'ingérence")

"mental disorder" means a substantial disorder of emotional processes, thought or cognition which grossly impairs a person's capacity to make reasoned judgments; ("trouble mental")

"psychotropic drug" means a drug or combination of drugs prescribed as a psychotropic drug; ("psychotrope")

"secure de-escalation room" means a locked room approved under subsection 173 (1) for use for the de-escalation of situations and behaviour involving children or young persons; ("pièce de désescalade sous clé")

"secure treatment program" means a program established or approved by the Minister under subsection 158 (1). ("programme de traitement en milieu fermé")

### Secure Treatment Programs

### Secure treatment programs

### Minister may establish or approve programs

**158.** (1) The Minister may,

(a) establish, operate and maintain; or

(b) approve,

programs for the treatment of children with mental disorders, in which continuous restrictions are imposed on the liberty of the children.

### Terms and conditions

(2) The Minister may impose terms and conditions on an approval given under subsection (1) and may vary or amend the terms and conditions or impose new terms and conditions at any time.

### Admission of children

(3) No child shall be admitted to a secure treatment program except by a court order under section 164 (commitment to secure treatment program) or under section 171 (emergency admission).

### Locking up permitted

**159.** The premises of a secure treatment program may be locked for the detention of children.

### Mechanical restraints permitted

**160.** (1) Subject to subsection (3), an administrator may use and permit the use of mechanical restraints on a child as a means of controlling the child's behaviour.

**Consent not required**

(2) An administrator is not required to obtain the consent of or on behalf of the child before using mechanical restraints under this section.

**Limitations**

(3) An administrator shall ensure that mechanical restraints are not used on a child in a secure treatment program except,

(a) in accordance with this Part, the policies established under subsection (4) and the regulations; and

(b) in an emergency situation under the common law duty of a caregiver to restrain or confine a person when immediate action is necessary to prevent serious bodily harm to the person or others.

**Policy**

(4) A service provider that is approved to provide a secure treatment program shall,

(a) establish a policy on the use of mechanical restraints that complies with this Act and the regulations; and

(b) ensure that the administrator and the employees of the program comply with the policy.

### Commitment to Secure Treatment
### Application for order for child's commitment

**161.** (1) Any one of the following persons may, with the administrator's written consent, apply to the court for an order for the child's commitment to a secure treatment program:

1. Where the child is younger than 16,

    i. the child's parent,

    ii. a person other than an administrator who is caring for the child, if the child's parent consents to the application, or

    iii. a society that has custody of the child under an order made under Part V (Child Protection).

2. Where the child is 16 or older,

    i. the child,

    ii. the child's parent, if the child consents to the application,

    iii. a society that has custody of the child under an order made under Part V (Child Protection), if the child consents to the application, or

    iv. a physician.

**Time for hearing**

(2) Where an application is made under subsection (1), the court shall deal with the matter within 10 days of the making of an order under subsection (6) (legal representation) or, where no such order is made, within 10 days of the making of the application.

**Adjournments**

(3) The court may adjourn the hearing of an application but shall not adjourn it for more than 30 days unless the applicant and the child consent to the longer adjournment.

**Interim order**

(4) Where a hearing is adjourned, the court may make a temporary order for the child's commitment to a secure treatment program if the court is satisfied that the child meets the criteria for commitment set out in clauses 164 (1) (a) to (f) and, where the child is younger than 12, the Minister consents to the child's admission.

**Evidence on adjournments**

(5) For the purpose of subsection (4), the court may admit and act on evidence that the court considers credible and trustworthy in the circumstances.

**Legal representation of child**

(6) Where an application is made under subsection (1) in respect of a child who does not have legal representation, the court shall, as soon as practicable and in any event before the hearing of the application, direct that legal representation be provided for the child.

**Hearing private**

(7) A hearing under this section shall be held in the absence of the public and no media representative shall be permitted to attend.

**Child entitled to be present**

(8) The child who is the subject of an application under subsection (1) is entitled to be present at the hearing unless,

(a) the court is satisfied that being present at the hearing would cause the child emotional harm; or

(b) the child, after obtaining legal advice, consents in writing to the holding of the hearing without the child's presence.

**Court may require child's presence**

(9) The court may require a child who has consented to the holding of the hearing without the child being present under clause (8) (b) to be present at all or part of the hearing.

**Oral evidence**

**162.** (1) Where an application is made under subsection 161 (1), the court shall deal with the matter by holding a hearing and shall hear oral evidence unless the child, after obtaining legal advice, consents in writing to the making of an order under subsection 164 (1) without the hearing of oral evidence, and the consent is filed with the court.

**Court may hear oral evidence despite consent**

(2) The court may hear oral evidence although the child has given a consent under subsection (1).

## Time limitation

(3) A child's consent under subsection (1) is not effective for more than the period referred to in subsection 165 (1) (period of commitment).

## Assessment

**163.** (1) The court may, at any time after an application is made under subsection 161 (1), order that the child attend within a specified time for an assessment before a specified person who is qualified, in the court's opinion, to perform an assessment to assist the court to determine whether the child should be committed to a secure treatment program and has consented to perform the assessment.

## Report

(2) The person performing an assessment under subsection (1) shall make a written report of the assessment to the court within the time specified in the order, which shall not be more than 30 days unless the court is of the opinion that a longer assessment period is necessary.

## Who may not perform assessment

(3) The court shall not order an assessment to be performed by a person who provides services in the secure treatment program to which the application relates.

## Copies of report

(4) The court shall provide a copy of the report to,

(a) the applicant;

(b) the child, subject to subsection (6);

(c) the child's lawyer;

(d) a parent appearing at the hearing;

(e) a society that has custody of the child under an order made under Part V (Child Protection);

(f) the administrator; and

(g) in the case of a First Nations, Inuk or Métis child, the persons described in clauses (a), (b), (c), (d), (e) and (f) and a representative chosen by each of the child's bands and First Nations, Inuit or Métis communities.

## Same

(5) The court may cause a copy of the report to be given to a parent who does not attend the hearing but is, in the court's opinion, actively interested in the proceedings.

## Court may withhold report from child

(6) The court may withhold all or part of the report from the child where the court is satisfied that disclosure of all or part of the report to the child would cause the child emotional harm.

## Commitment to secure treatment: criteria

**164.** (1) The court may order that a child be committed to a secure treatment program only where the court is satisfied that,

(a) the child has a mental disorder;

(b) the child has, as a result of the mental disorder, within the 45 days immediately preceding,

(i) the application under subsection 161 (1),

(ii) the child's detention or custody under the *Youth Criminal Justice Act* (Canada) or under the *Provincial Offences Act*, or

(iii) the child's admission to a psychiatric facility under the *Mental Health Act* as an involuntary patient,

caused or attempted to cause serious bodily harm to themself or another person;

(c) the child has,

(i) within the 12 months immediately preceding the application, but on another occasion than that referred to in clause (b), caused, attempted to cause or by words or conduct made a substantial threat to cause serious bodily harm to themself or another person, or

(ii) in committing the act or attempt referred to in clause (b), caused or attempted to cause a person's death;

(d) the secure treatment program would be effective to prevent the child from causing or attempting to cause serious bodily harm to themself or another person;

(e) treatment appropriate for the child's mental disorder is available at the place of secure treatment to which the application relates; and

(f) no less restrictive method of providing treatment appropriate for the child's mental disorder is appropriate in the circumstances.

## Where child younger than 12

(2) Where the child is younger than 12, the court shall not make an order under subsection (1) unless the Minister consents to the child's commitment.

## Additional requirement where applicant is physician

(3) Where the applicant is a physician, the court shall not make an order under subsection (1) unless the court is satisfied that the applicant believes the criteria set out in that subsection are met.

## Period of commitment

**165.** (1) The court shall specify in an order under subsection 164 (1) the period not exceeding 180 days for which the child shall be committed to the secure treatment program.

## Where society is applicant

(2) Where a child is committed to a secure treatment program on a society's application and the period specified in the court's order is greater than 60 days, the child shall be released on a day 60 days after the child's admission to the secure treatment program unless before that day,

(a) the child's parent consents to the child's commitment for a longer period; or

(b) the child is made the subject of an order for interim society care under paragraph 2 of subsection 101 (1) or for extended society care under paragraph 3 of subsection 101 (1) or clause 116 (1) (c), but in no case shall the child be committed to the secure treatment program for longer than the period specified under subsection (1).

### How time is calculated

(3)  In the calculation of a child's period of commitment, time spent in the secure treatment program before an order has been made under section 164 (commitment) or pending an application under section 167 (extension) shall be counted.

### Where order expires after 18th birthday

(4)  A person who is the subject of an order made under subsection 164 (1) or 167 (5) may be kept in the secure treatment program after turning 18, until the order expires.

### Reasons, plans, etc.

**166.** (1)  Where the court makes an order under subsection 164 (1) or 167 (5), the court shall give,

    (a)  reasons for its decision;

    (b)  a statement of the plan, if any, for the child's care on release from the secure treatment program; and

    (c)  a statement of the less restrictive alternatives considered by the court, and the reasons for rejecting them.

### Plan for care on release

(2)  Where no plan for the child's care on release from the secure treatment program is available at the time of the order, the administrator shall, within 90 days of the date of the order, prepare such a plan and file it with the court.

## Extension of Period of Commitment

### Extension

**167.** (1)  Where a child is the subject of an order made under subsection 164 (1) (commitment) or subsection (5),

    (a)  a person referred to in subsection 161 (1), with the administrator's written consent; or

    (b)  the administrator, with a parent's written consent or, where the child is in a society's lawful custody, the society's consent,

may, before the expiry of the period of commitment, apply for an order extending the child's commitment to the secure treatment program.

### Same

(2)  Where a person is kept in the secure treatment program under subsection 165 (4) after turning 18,

    (a)  the person, with the written consent of the administrator;

    (b)  the person's parent, with the written consent of the person and the administrator;

    (c)  a physician, with the written consent of the administrator and the person; or

    (d)  the administrator, with the written consent of the person,

may, before the expiry of the period of commitment, apply for one further order extending the person's commitment to the secure treatment program.

### Person may be kept in program while application pending

(3)  Where an application is made under subsection (1) or (2), the person may be kept in the secure treatment program until the application is disposed of.

### ss. 161 (3), (6-9), 162, 163 apply

(4)  Subsections 161 (3), (6), (7), (8) and (9) (hearing) and sections 162 (waive oral evidence) and 163 (assessment) apply with necessary modifications to an application made under subsection (1) or (2).

### Criteria for extension

(5)  The court may make an order extending a child's commitment to a secure treatment program only where the court is satisfied that,

    (a)  the child has a mental disorder;

    (b)  the secure treatment program would be effective to prevent the child from causing or attempting to cause serious bodily harm to themself or another person;

    (c)  no less restrictive method of providing treatment appropriate for the child's mental disorder is appropriate in the circumstances;

    (d)  the child is receiving the treatment proposed at the time of the original order under subsection 164 (1), or other appropriate treatment; and

    (e)  there is an appropriate plan for the child's care on release from the secure treatment program.

### Period of extension

(6)  The court shall specify in an order under subsection (5) the period not exceeding 180 days for which the child shall be committed to the secure treatment program.

## Release by Administrator

### Release

### Unconditional release by administrator

**168.** (1)  The administrator may release a child from a secure treatment program unconditionally where the administrator,

    (a)  has given the person with lawful custody of the child reasonable notice of the intention to release the child; and

    (b)  is satisfied that,

        (i)  the child no longer requires the secure treatment program, and

        (ii)  there is an appropriate plan for the child's care on release from the secure treatment program.

### Conditional release

(2)  The administrator may release a child from a secure treatment program temporarily for medical or compassionate reasons, or for a trial placement in an open setting, for

such period and on such terms and conditions as the administrator determines.

### Administrator may release despite court order

(3) Subsections (1) and (2) apply despite an order made under subsection 164 (1) (commitment) or 167 (5) (extension).

## Review of Commitment

### Review of commitment

**169.** (1) Any one of the following persons may apply to the court for an order terminating an order made under subsection 164 (1) (commitment) or 167 (5) (extension):

1. The child, where the child is 12 or older.
2. The child's parent.
3. The society having care, custody or supervision of the child.

### ss. 161 (3), (6-9), 162, 163 apply

(2) Subsections 161 (3), (6), (7), (8) and (9) (hearing) and sections 162 (waive oral evidence) and 163 (assessment) apply with necessary modifications to an application made under subsection (1).

### Termination of order

(3) The court shall make an order terminating a child's commitment unless the court is satisfied that,

(a) the child has a mental disorder;

(b) the secure treatment program would continue to be effective to prevent the child from causing or attempting to cause serious bodily harm to themself or another person;

(c) no less restrictive method of providing treatment appropriate for the child's mental disorder is appropriate in the circumstances; and

(d) the child is receiving the treatment proposed at the time of the most recent order under subsection 164 (1) or 167 (5), or other appropriate treatment.

### Same

(4) In making an order under subsection (3), the court shall consider whether there is an appropriate plan for the child's care on release from the secure treatment program.

### ss. 167 (3-6), 168, 169 apply

**170.** Subsections 167 (3), (4), (5) and (6) and sections 168 and 169 apply with necessary modifications to a person who is 18 or older and committed to a secure treatment program as if the person were a child.

## Emergency Admission

### Emergency admission

**171.** (1) Any one of the following persons may apply to the administrator for the emergency admission of a child to a secure treatment program:

1. Where the child is younger than 16,
    i. the child's parent,

ii. a person who is caring for the child with a parent's consent,

iii. a child protection worker who brought the child to a place of safety under section 81, or

iv. a society that has custody of the child under an order made under Part V (Child Protection).

2. Where the child is 16 or older,
    i. the child,
    ii. the child's parent, if the child consents to the application,
    iii. a society that has custody of the child under an order made under Part V (Child Protection), if the child consents to the application, or
    iv. a physician.

### Criteria for admission

(2) The administrator may admit a child to the secure treatment program on an application under subsection (1) for a period not to exceed 30 days where the administrator believes on reasonable grounds that,

(a) the child has a mental disorder;

(b) the child has, as a result of the mental disorder, caused, attempted to cause or by words or conduct made a substantial threat to cause serious bodily harm to themself or another person;

(c) the secure treatment program would be effective to prevent the child from causing or attempting to cause serious bodily harm to themself or another person;

(d) treatment appropriate for the child's mental disorder is available at the place of secure treatment to which the application relates; and

(e) no less restrictive method of providing treatment appropriate for the child's mental disorder is appropriate in the circumstances.

### Admission on consent

(3) The administrator may admit the child under subsection (2) although the criterion set out in clause (2) (b) is not met, where,

(a) the other criteria set out in subsection (2) are met;

(b) the child, after obtaining legal advice, consents to the admission; and

(c) if the child is younger than 16, the child's parent or, where the child is in a society's lawful custody, the society consents to the child's admission.

### Where child younger than 12

(4) Where the child is younger than 12, the administrator shall not admit the child under subsection (2) unless the Minister consents to the child's admission.

### Additional requirement where applicant is physician

(5) Where the applicant is a physician, the administrator shall not admit the child under subsection (2) unless the

administrator is satisfied that the applicant believes the criteria set out in that subsection are met.

### Notices required

(6) The administrator shall ensure that within 24 hours after a child is admitted to a secure treatment program under subsection (2),

(a) the child is given written notice of the child's right to a review under subsection (9); and

(b) the Provincial Advocate for Children and Youth and the Children's Lawyer are given notice of the admission.

### Mandatory advice

(7) The Provincial Advocate for Children and Youth shall ensure that as soon as possible after the notice is received a person who is not employed to provide services in the secure treatment program explains to the child the child's right to a review in language suitable to the child's understanding.

### Children's Lawyer to ensure child represented

(8) The Children's Lawyer shall represent the child at the earliest possible opportunity and in any event within five days after receiving a notice under subsection (6) unless the Children's Lawyer is satisfied that another person will provide legal representation for the child within that time.

### Application for review

(9) Where a child is admitted to a secure treatment program under this section, any person, including the child, may apply to the Board for an order releasing the child from the secure treatment program.

### Child may be kept in program while application pending

(10) Where an application is made under subsection (9), the child may be kept in the secure treatment program until the application is disposed of.

### Procedure

(11) Subsections 161 (7), (8) and (9) (hearing) and section 162 (waive oral evidence) apply with necessary modifications to an application made under subsection (9).

### Time for review

(12) Where an application is made under subsection (9), the Board shall dispose of the matter within five days of the making of the application.

### Order

(13) The Board shall make an order releasing the child from the secure treatment program unless the Board is satisfied that the child meets the criteria for emergency admission set out in clauses (2) (a) to (e).

## Police Assistance
### Powers of peace officers, period of commitment
### Police may take child for secure treatment

**172.** (1) A peace officer may take a child to a place where there is a secure treatment program,

(a) for emergency admission, at the request of an applicant referred to in subsection 171 (1); or

(b) where an order for the child's commitment to the secure treatment program has been made under section 164.

### Apprehension of child who leaves

(2) Where a child who has been admitted to a secure treatment program leaves the facility in which the secure treatment program is located without the consent of the administrator, a peace officer may apprehend the child with or without a warrant and return the child to the facility.

### Period of commitment

(3) Where a child is returned to a facility under subsection (2), the time that the child was absent from the facility shall not be taken into account in calculating the period of commitment.

## Secure De-escalation
### Director's approval

**173.** (1) A Director may approve a locked room that complies with the prescribed standards and is located in premises where a service is provided, for use for the de-escalation of situations and behaviour involving children or young persons, on such terms and conditions as the Director determines.

### Withdrawal of approval

(2) Where a Director is of the opinion that a secure de-escalation room is unnecessary or is being used in a manner that contravenes this Part or the regulations, the Director may withdraw the approval given under subsection (1) and shall give the affected service provider notice of the decision, with reasons.

### Secure de-escalation

**174.** (1) No service provider or foster parent shall place in a locked room a child or young person who is in the service provider's or foster parent's care or permit the child or young person to be placed in a locked room, except in accordance with this section and the regulations.

### Secure treatment, secure custody and secure temporary detention

(2) Subsection (1) does not prohibit the routine locking at night of rooms in the premises of secure treatment programs or in places of secure custody and places of secure temporary detention under Part VI (Youth Justice).

## Criteria for use of a secure de-escalation room

(3)  A child or young person may be placed in a secure de-escalation room where,

(a)  in the service provider's opinion,

(i)  the child's or young person's conduct indicates that the child or young person is likely, in the immediate future, to cause serious property damage or to cause another person serious bodily harm, and

(ii)  no less restrictive method of restraining the child or young person is practicable; and

(b)  where the child is younger than 12, a Director gives permission for the child to be placed in a secure de-escalation room because of exceptional circumstances.

## One-hour limit

(4)  A child or young person who is placed in a secure de-escalation room shall be released within one hour unless the person in charge of the premises approves the child's or young person's longer stay in a secure de-escalation room in writing and records the reasons for not restraining the child or young person by a less restrictive method.

## Continuous observation

(5)  Subject to subsection (9), the service provider shall ensure that a child or young person who is placed in a secure de-escalation room is continuously observed by a responsible person.

## Review

(6)  Where a child or young person is kept in a secure de-escalation room for more than one hour, the person in charge of the premises shall review the child's or young person's placement in a secure de-escalation room at prescribed intervals.

## Release

(7)  A child or young person who is placed in a secure de-escalation room shall be released as soon as the person in charge is satisfied that the child or young person is not likely to cause serious property damage or serious bodily harm in the immediate future.

## Maximum periods

(8)  Subject to subsection (9), in no event shall a child or young person be kept in a secure de-escalation room for a period or periods that exceed an aggregate of eight hours in a given 24-hour period or an aggregate of 24 hours in a given week.

## Exception

(9)  A service provider is not required to comply with subsections (5) and (8) with respect to a young person who is 16 or older and who is held in a place of secure custody or of secure temporary detention, but a service provider shall comply with the following standards and procedures and with any additional standards and procedures that may be prescribed:

1.  The young person must be observed every 15 minutes by a responsible person and these observations must be recorded in the young person's case record.

2.  The service provider must determine whether, given the needs of the young person, the young person should be observed at regular intervals that are more frequent than every 15 minutes, and, if that determination is made, the young person must be observed by a responsible person at the more frequent intervals determined by the service provider and these observations must be recorded in the young person's case record.

3.  The young person must not be kept in a secure de-escalation room for a continuous period in excess of 24 hours or for a period or periods that exceed an aggregate of 24 hours in a seven-day period.

4.  Despite paragraph 3, the service provider may extend a young person's placement in a secure de-escalation room for a continuous period beyond 24 hours or for an aggregate of more than 24 hours in a given seven-day period, if the provincial director approves the extension.

5.  The provincial director may approve the extension of the placement of a young person in a secure de-escalation room beyond 24 continuous hours or beyond an aggregate of 24 hours in a given seven-day period if the provincial director has reasonable and probable grounds to believe that the young person's continued placement in a secure de-escalation room is necessary for the safety of staff or young persons in the facility.

## Review of use of secure de-escalation

**175.**  A person in charge of premises containing a secure de-escalation room shall review,

(a)  the need for the secure de-escalation room; and

(b)  the prescribed matters,

every three months or, in the case of secure custody or secure temporary detention, every six months from the date on which the secure de-escalation room is approved under subsection 173 (1), shall make a written report of each review to a Director and shall make such additional reports as are prescribed.

### Psychotropic Drugs
### Consent required for use of psychotropic drugs

**176.**  A service provider shall not administer or permit the administration of a psychotropic drug to a child or young person in the service provider's care without a consent in accordance with the *Health Care Consent Act, 1996.*

### Professional Advisory Board

**Professional Advisory Board**

**177.** (1) The Minister may establish a Professional Advisory Board, composed of physicians and other professionals who,

(a) have special knowledge in the use of intrusive procedures and psychotropic drugs;

(b) have demonstrated an informed concern for the welfare and interests of children; and

(c) are not employed in the Ministry.

**Chair**

(2) The Minister shall appoint one of the members of the Professional Advisory Board as its chair.

**Duties of Board**

(3) The Professional Advisory Board shall, at the Minister's request,

(a) advise the Minister on prescribing procedures as intrusive procedures;

(b) investigate and review the use of intrusive procedures and psychotropic drugs and make recommendations to the Minister; and

(c) review the practices and procedures of service providers with respect to,

(i) secure de-escalation,

(ii) intrusive procedures, and

(iii) psychotropic drugs,

and make recommendations to the Minister.

**Request for review**

**178.** Any person may request that the Minister refer the matter of the use of a secure de-escalation room or an intrusive procedure in respect of a child or young person, or the administration of a psychotropic drug to a child or young person, to the Professional Advisory Board for investigation and review.

### PART VIII    ADOPTION AND ADOPTION LICENSING
### Interpretation

**Interpretation**

**179.** (1) In this Part,

"birth parent" means a person who satisfies the prescribed criteria; ("parent de naissance")

"birth relative" means,

(a) in respect of a child who has not been adopted, a relative of the child, and

(b) in respect of a child who has been adopted, a person who would have been a relative of the child if the child had not been adopted; ("membre de la parenté de naissance")

"birth sibling" means, in respect of a person, a child of the same birth parent as the person, and includes a child adopted by the birth parent and a person whom the birth parent has demonstrated a settled intention to treat as a child of their family; ("frère ou sœur de naissance")

"openness agreement" means an agreement referred to in section 212; ("accord de communication")

"openness order" means an order made by a court in accordance with this Act for the purposes of facilitating communication or maintaining a relationship between the child and,

(a) a birth parent, birth sibling or birth relative of the child,

(b) a person with whom the child has a significant relationship or emotional tie, including a foster parent of the child or a member of the child's extended family or community, or

(c) in the case of a First Nations, Inuk or Métis child,

(i) a person described in clause (a) or (b), or

(ii) a member of the child's bands and First Nations, Inuit or Métis communities who may not have had a significant relationship or emotional tie with the child in the past but will help the child to develop or maintain a connection with the child's First Nations, Inuit or Métis cultures, heritages and traditions and to preserve the child's cultural identity and connection to community; ("ordonnance de communication")

"spouse" has the same meaning as in Parts I and II of the *Human Rights Code*. ("conjoint")

**Best interests of child**

(2) Where a person is directed in this Part to make an order or determination in the best interests of a child, the person shall,

(a) consider the child's views and wishes, given due weight in accordance with the child's age and maturity, unless they cannot be ascertained;

(b) in the case of a First Nations, Inuk or Métis child, consider the importance, in recognition of the uniqueness of First Nations, Inuit and Métis cultures, heritages and traditions, of preserving the child's cultural identity and connection to community, in addition to the considerations under clauses (a) and (c); and

(c) consider any other circumstance of the case that the person considers relevant, including,

(i) the child's physical, mental and emotional needs, and the appropriate care or treatment to meet those needs,

(ii) the child's physical, mental and emotional level of development,

(iii) the child's race, ancestry, place of origin, colour, ethnic origin, citizenship, family diversity, disability, creed, sex, sexual orientation, gender identity and gender expression,

(iv) the child's cultural and linguistic heritage,

(v) the importance for the child's development of a positive relationship with a parent and a secure place as a member of a family,

(vi) the child's relationships and emotional ties to a parent, sibling, relative, other member of the child's extended family or member of the child's community,

(vii) the importance of continuity in the child's care and the possible effect on the child of disruption of that continuity, and

(viii) the effects on the child of delay in the disposition of the case.

### Consent to Adoption

**Consents**

**180.** (1) In this section,

"parent", when used in reference to a child, means each of the following persons, but does not include a licensee or a foster parent:

1. A parent of the child under section 6, 8, 9, 10, 11 or 13 of the *Children's Law Reform Act*.

2. In the case of a child conceived through sexual intercourse, an individual described in one of paragraphs 1 to 5 of subsection 7 (2) of the *Children's Law Reform Act*, unless it is proved on a balance of probabilities that the sperm used to conceive the child did not come from the individual.

3. An individual who has been found or recognized by a court of competent jurisdiction outside Ontario to be a parent of the child.

4. In the case of an adopted child, a parent of the child as provided for under section 217 or 218 of this Act.

5. An individual who has lawful custody of the child.

6. An individual who, during the 12 months before the child is placed for adoption under this Part, has demonstrated a settled intention to treat the child as a child of the individual's family, or has acknowledged parentage of the child and provided for the child's support.

7. An individual who, under a written agreement or a court order, is required to provide for the child, has custody of the child or has a right of access to the child.

8. An individual who acknowledged parentage of the child by filing a statutory declaration under section 12 of the *Children's Law Reform Act* as it read before the day subsection 1 (1) of the *All Families Are Equal Act (Parentage and Related Registrations Statute Law Amendment), 2016* came into force.

**Consent of parent, etc.**

(2) An order for the adoption of a child who is younger than 16, or is 16 or older but has not withdrawn from parental control, shall not be made without,

(a) the written consent of every parent; or

(b) where the child is in extended society care under an order made under paragraph 3 of subsection 101 (1) or clause 116 (1) (c), the written consent of a Director.

**Same**

(3) A consent under clause (2) (a) shall not be given before the child is seven days old.

**Same**

(4) Where a child is being placed for adoption by a society or licensee, a consent under clause (2) (a) shall not be given until,

(a) the society or licensee has advised the parent of the parent's right,

(i) to withdraw the consent under subsection (8), and

(ii) to be informed, on their request, whether an adoption order has been made in respect of the child;

(b) the society or licensee has advised the parent of such other matters as may be prescribed; and

(c) the society or licensee has given the parent an opportunity to seek counselling and independent legal advice with respect to the consent.

**Custody of child**

(5) Where,

(a) a child is being placed for adoption by a society or licensee;

(b) every consent required under subsection (2) has been given and has not been withdrawn under subsection (8); and

(c) the 21-day period referred to in subsection (8) has expired,

the rights and responsibilities of the child's parents with respect to the child's custody, care and control are transferred to the society or licensee, until the consent is withdrawn under subsection 182 (1) (late withdrawal with leave of court) or an order is made for the child's adoption under section 199.

**Consent of person to be adopted**

(6) An order for the adoption of a person who is seven or older shall not be made without the person's written consent.

**Same**

(7) A consent under subsection (6) shall not be given until the person has had an opportunity to obtain counselling and independent legal advice with respect to the consent.

### Withdrawal of consent

(8) A person who gives a consent under subsection (2) or (6) may withdraw it in writing within 21 days after the consent is given and where that person had custody of the child immediately before giving the consent, the child shall be returned to that person as soon as the consent is withdrawn.

### Dispensing with person's consent

(9) The court may dispense with a person's consent required under subsection (6) where the court is satisfied that,

(a) obtaining the consent would cause the person emotional harm; or

(b) the person is not able to consent because of a developmental disability.

### Consent of applicant's spouse

(10) An adoption order shall not be made on the application of a person who is a spouse without the written consent of the other spouse.

### Consents by minors: role of Children's Lawyer

(11) Where a person who gives a consent under clause (2) (a) is younger than 18, the consent is not valid unless the Children's Lawyer is satisfied that the consent is fully informed and reflects the person's true wishes.

### Affidavits of execution

(12) An affidavit of execution in the prescribed form shall be attached to a consent and a withdrawal of a consent under this section.

### Form of foreign consents

(13) A consent required under this section that is given outside Ontario and whose form does not comply with the requirements of subsection (12) and the regulations is not invalid for that reason alone, if its form complies with the laws of the jurisdiction where it is given.

### Dispensing with consent

**181.** The court may dispense with a consent required under section 180 for the adoption of a child, except the consent of the child or of a Director, where the court is satisfied that,

(a) it is in the child's best interests to do so; and

(b) the person whose consent is required has received notice of the proposed adoption and of the application to dispense with consent, or a reasonable effort to give the notice has been made.

### Late withdrawal of consent

**182.** (1) The court may permit a person who gave a consent to the adoption of a child under section 180 to withdraw the consent after the 21-day period referred to in subsection 180 (8) where the court is satisfied that it is in the child's best interests to do so, and where that person had custody of the child immediately before giving the consent, the child shall be returned to that person as soon as the consent is withdrawn.

### Exception: child placed for adoption

(2) Subsection (1) does not apply where the child has been placed with a person for adoption and remains in that person's care.

## Placement for Adoption
### Only societies and licensees may place children, etc.

**183.** (1) No person except a society or licensee shall,

(a) place a child with another person for adoption; or

(b) take, send or attempt to take or send a child who is a resident of Ontario out of Ontario to be placed for adoption.

### Only societies and certain licensees may bring children into Ontario

(2) No person except a society or a licensee whose licence contains a term permitting the licensee to act under this subsection shall bring a child who is not a resident of Ontario into Ontario to be placed for adoption.

### Director's approval of proposed placement

(3) No licensee except a licensee exempted under subsection (6) shall do the following without first obtaining a Director's approval of the proposed placement under section 188:

1. Place a child who is a resident of Canada with another person for adoption.

2. Take, send or attempt to take or send a child who is a resident of Ontario out of Ontario to be placed for adoption.

### Placement of child from outside Canada

(4) No licensee described in subsection (2) shall bring a child who is not a resident of Canada into Ontario to be placed for adoption without,

(a) first obtaining a Director's approval of the person with whom the child is to be placed as eligible and suitable to adopt under section 189; and

(b) after the approval referred to in clause (a) is obtained, obtaining a Director's approval of the proposed placement under section 190.

### Director's approval required

(5) No person shall receive a child for adoption, except from a society or from a licensee exempted under subsection (6), without first receiving a Director's approval of the placement under subsection 188 (3) or 190 (2), as the case may be.

### Designation of licensee

(6) A Director may designate a licensee that is an agency as exempt from the requirements of subsection (3).

### Placements to be registered

(7) A society or licensee who places a child with another person for adoption shall register the placement in the prescribed manner within 30 days after placing the child.

### Same: Director

(8) A Director who becomes aware of any placement for adoption of a child that has not been registered under subsection (7) shall promptly register the placement in the prescribed manner.

### Exception: family adoptions within Canada, etc.

(9) Subsections (1), (2), (3), (5), (7) and (8) do not apply to,

(a) the placement for adoption of a child with the child's relative, the child's parent or a spouse of the child's parent, if the child to be placed is a resident of Canada and the placement is within Ontario; or

(b) the taking or sending of a child out of Ontario for adoption by the child's relative, the child's parent or a spouse of the child's parent, if the placement is within Canada.

### Limitation on placement by society

**184.** A society shall not place a child who is in extended society care under an order made under paragraph 3 of subsection 101 (1) or clause 116 (1) (c) for adoption until,

(a) the time for commencing an appeal of the order has expired; or

(b) any appeal of the order has been finally disposed of or abandoned.

### Adoption planning

**185.** (1) Nothing in this Act prohibits a society from planning for the adoption of a child who is in extended society care under an order made under paragraph 3 of subsection 101 (1) or clause 116 (1) (c) and in respect of whom there is an access order in effect under Part V (Child Protection).

### Openness

(2) Where a society begins planning for the adoption of a child who is in extended society care under an order made under paragraph 3 of subsection 101 (1) or clause 116 (1) (c), the society shall consider the benefits of an openness order or openness agreement in respect of the child.

### First Nations, Inuk or Métis child

**186.** (1) If a society intends to begin planning for the adoption of a First Nations, Inuk or Métis child, the society shall give written notice of its intention to a representative chosen by each of the child's bands and First Nations, Inuit or Métis communities.

### Care plan proposed by band or community

(2) If a representative chosen by each of the child's bands or First Nations, Inuit or Métis communities receives notice under subsection (1), each band and community may, within 60 days of the representative receiving the notice,

(a) prepare its own plan for the care of the child; and

(b) submit its plan to the society.

### Condition for placement

(3) A society shall not place a First Nations, Inuk or Métis child with another person for adoption until,

(a) at least 60 days after notice is given to a representative chosen by each of the bands and First Nations, Inuit or Métis communities have elapsed; or

(b) if a band or First Nations, Inuit or Métis community has submitted a plan for the care of the child, the society has considered the plan.

### First Nations, Inuk or Métis child, openness, etc.

**187.** (1) Where a society begins planning for the adoption of a First Nations, Inuk or Métis child, the society shall consider the importance of developing or maintaining the child's connection to the child's bands and First Nations, Inuit or Métis communities.

### Openness agreement or openness order

(2) For the purposes of subsection (1), the society shall include consideration of the benefits of,

(a) an openness agreement in respect of the child and a member of the child's bands and First Nations, Inuit or Métis communities; or

(b) where the child is in extended society care under an order made under paragraph 3 of subsection 101 (1) or clause 116 (1) (c), an openness order in respect of the child and a representative of the child's bands and First Nations, Inuit or Métis communities.

### Child from inside Canada: proposed placement

**188.** (1) A licensee who intends to act as described in subsection 183 (3) shall notify a Director of the proposed placement and at the same time provide the Director with a report of an adoption homestudy of the person with whom placement is proposed.

### Who may make homestudy

(2) The report of the adoption homestudy shall be prepared by a person who, in the opinion of the Director or a local director, is qualified to make an adoption homestudy.

### Review by Director

(3) The Director shall review the report of the adoption homestudy promptly and,

(a) approve the proposed placement;

(b) approve the proposed placement subject to any conditions the Director considers appropriate, including supervision by,

(i) a specified society, licensee or person, or

(ii) in the case of a placement outside Ontario, a specified child welfare authority recognized in the jurisdiction of the placement or a prescribed person; or

(c) refuse to approve the proposed placement.

**Notice**

(4) The Director shall promptly give notice of the approval, the approval subject to conditions or the refusal, as the case may be,

(a) to the person with whom the placement is proposed; and

(b) to the licensee.

**Right to hearing**

(5) When a Director gives notice of a refusal or an approval subject to conditions, the person with whom placement is proposed and the licensee are entitled to a hearing before the Board.

**Application of other provisions**

(6) Sections 233 (hearings), 234 (review of conditions), 266 (parties) and 267 (appeal) apply to the hearing with necessary modifications and for that purpose references to the Tribunal are deemed to be references to the Board.

**Extension of time**

(7) If the Board is satisfied that there are reasonable grounds for the person with whom placement is proposed or the licensee to apply for an extension of the time fixed for requiring the hearing and for the Board to grant relief, it may,

(a) extend the time either before or after the expiration of the time; and

(b) give the directions that it considers proper as a result of extending the time.

**Recording of evidence**

(8) The evidence taken before the Board at the hearing shall be recorded.

**Placement outside Canada**

(9) A Director shall not approve the proposed placement of a child outside Canada unless the Director is satisfied that a prescribed special circumstance justifies the placement.

**Child from outside Canada: homestudy**

**189.** (1) A licensee who intends to bring a child who is not a resident of Canada into Ontario to be placed for adoption shall provide the Director with a report of an adoption homestudy of the person with whom placement is proposed to assess the person's eligibility and suitability to adopt.

**Who may make homestudy**

(2) The report of the adoption homestudy shall be prepared by a person who, in the opinion of the Director or a local director, is qualified to make an adoption homestudy.

**Review by Director**

(3) The Director shall review the report of the adoption homestudy promptly and,

(a) approve the person unconditionally as eligible and suitable to adopt;

(b) approve the person subject to any conditions the Director considers appropriate; or

(c) refuse to approve the person.

**Notice**

(4) The Director shall promptly give notice of the approval, the approval subject to conditions or the refusal, as the case may be,

(a) to the person who is the subject of the homestudy; and

(b) to the licensee.

**Right to hearing**

(5) When a Director gives notice of a refusal or an approval subject to conditions, the person who is the subject of the homestudy is entitled to a hearing before the Board.

**Application of other provisions**

(6) The following provisions apply to the hearing:

1. Sections 233 (hearings), 234 (review of conditions), 266 (parties) and 267 (appeal), with necessary modifications and for that purpose references to the Tribunal are deemed to be references to the Board.

2. Subsections 188 (7) (extension of time) and (8) (recording of evidence).

**Child from outside Canada: review of proposed placement**

**190.** (1) If a person has been approved or approved subject to conditions as eligible and suitable to adopt under section 189 and a licensee proposes to place a child with the person for adoption, the licensee shall request that a Director review the proposed placement.

**Review by Director**

(2) The Director shall promptly review the proposed placement and,

(a) approve the proposed placement unconditionally;

(b) approve the proposed placement subject to any conditions the Director considers appropriate, including supervision by a specified society, licensee or person; or

(c) refuse to approve the proposed placement.

**Notice**

(3) The Director shall promptly give notice of the approval, the approval subject to conditions or the refusal, as the case may be,

(a) to the person with whom the placement is proposed; and

(b) to the licensee.

**Right to hearing**

(4) When a Director gives notice of a refusal or an approval subject to conditions, the person with whom the placement is proposed and the licensee are entitled to a hearing before the Board.

### Application of other provisions

(5) The following provisions apply to the hearing:

1. Sections 233 (hearings), 234 (review of conditions), 266 (parties) and 267 (appeal), with necessary modifications and for that purpose references to the Tribunal are deemed to be references to the Board.
2. Subsections 188 (7) (extension of time) and (8) (recording of evidence).

### Access orders terminate

**191.** (1) When a child is placed for adoption by a society or licensee, every order respecting access to the child is terminated, including an access order made under Part V (Child Protection) in respect of a child who is in extended society care under an order made under paragraph 3 of subsection 101 (1) or clause 116 (1) (c).

### No interference, etc., with child in placement

(2) Where a child has been placed for adoption by a society or licensee and no adoption order has been made, no person shall,

(a) interfere with the child; or

(b) for the purpose of interfering with the child, visit or communicate with the child or with the person with whom the child has been placed.

### Decision to Refuse to Place Child or to Remove Child after Placement

### Decision of society or licensee

**192.** (1) This section applies if,

(a) a society decides to refuse an application to adopt a particular child made by a foster parent or other person; or

(b) a society or licensee decides to remove a child who has been placed with a person for adoption.

### Notice of decision

(2) The society or licensee who makes a decision referred to in subsection (1) shall,

(a) give at least 10 days notice in writing of the decision to the person who applied to adopt the child or with whom the child had been placed for adoption;

(b) include in the notice under clause (a) notice of the person's right to apply for a review of the decision under subsection (3); and

(c) in the case of a First Nations, Inuk or Métis child, give the notice required by clauses (a) and (b) and,

(i) give at least 10 days notice in writing of the decision to a representative chosen by each of the child's bands and First Nations, Inuit or Métis communities, and

(ii) after the notice is given, consult with the band or community representatives relating to the planning for the care of the child.

### Application for review

(3) A person who receives notice of a decision under subsection (2) may, within 10 days after receiving the notice, apply to the Board in accordance with the regulations for a review of the decision subject to subsection (4).

### Where no review

(4) If a society receives an application to adopt a child and, at the time of the application, the child had been placed for adoption with another person, the applicant is not entitled to a review of the society's decision to refuse the application.

### Board hearing

(5) Upon receipt of an application under subsection (3) for a review of a decision, the Board shall hold a hearing under this section.

### First Nations, Inuk or Métis child

(6) Upon receipt of an application for review of a decision relating to a First Nations, Inuk or Métis child, the Board shall give notice of the application and of the date of the hearing to a representative chosen by each of the child's bands and First Nations, Inuit or Métis communities.

### Practices and procedures

(7) The *Statutory Powers Procedure Act* applies to a hearing under this section and the Board shall comply with such additional practices and procedures as may be prescribed.

### Composition of Board

(8) At a hearing under subsection (5), the Board shall be composed of members with the prescribed qualifications and prescribed experience.

### Parties

(9) The following persons are parties to a hearing under this section:

1. The applicant.
2. The society or licensee.
3. In the case of a First Nations, Inuk or Métis child, the persons described in paragraphs 1 and 2 and a representative chosen by each of the child's bands and First Nations, Inuit or Métis communities.
4. Any person that the Board adds under subsection (10).

### Additional parties

(10) The Board may add a person as a party to a review if, in the Board's opinion, it is necessary to do so in order to decide all the issues in the review.

### Board decision

(11) The Board shall, in accordance with its determination of which action is in the best interests of the child, confirm or rescind the decision under review and shall give written reasons for its decision.

## Subsequent placement

(12)  After a society or licensee has made a decision referred to in subsection (1) in relation to a child, the society shall not place the child for adoption with a person other than the person who has a right to apply for a review under subsection (3) unless,

(a)  the time for applying for a review of the decision under subsection (3) has expired and an application is not made; or

(b)  if an application for a review of the decision is made under subsection (3), the Board has confirmed the decision.

## No removal before Board decision

(13)  Subject to subsection (14), if a society or licensee has decided to remove a child from the care of a person with whom the child was placed for adoption, the society or licensee, as the case may be, shall not carry out the proposed removal of the child unless,

(a)  the time for applying for a review of the decision under subsection (3) has expired and an application is not made; or

(b)  if an application for a review of the decision is made under subsection (3), the Board has confirmed the decision.

## Where child at risk

(14)  A society or licensee may carry out a decision to remove a child from the care of a person with whom the child was placed for adoption before the expiry of the time for applying for a review under subsection (3) or at any time after the application for a review is made if, in the opinion of a Director or local director, there is a risk that the child is likely to suffer harm during the time necessary for a review by the Board.

## Notice to Director

**193.**  (1)  Where a child has been placed for adoption under this Part, no order for the child's adoption has been made and,

(a)  the person with whom the child is placed asks the society or licensee that placed the child to remove the child; or

(b)  the society or licensee proposes to remove the child from the person with whom the child was placed,

the society or licensee shall notify a Director.

## Same

(2)  Where no order for a child's adoption has been made and a year has expired since,

(a)  the earlier of the child's placement for adoption or the giving of the most recent consent under clause 180 (2) (a); or

(b)  the most recent review under subsection (3) of this section,

whichever is later, the society or licensee shall notify a Director, unless the child is in extended society care under an order made under paragraph 3 of subsection 101 (1) or clause 116 (1) (c).

## Director to review

(3)  A Director who receives a notice under subsection (1) or (2) shall conduct a review in accordance with the regulations.

### Openness Orders
## No access order in effect
## Application for openness order

**194.**  (1)  If a child who is in extended society care under an order made under paragraph 3 of subsection 101 (1) or clause 116 (1) (c) is the subject of a plan for adoption, and no access order is in effect under Part V (Child Protection), the society having care and custody of the child may apply to the court for an openness order in respect of the child at any time before an order for adoption of the child is made under section 199.

## Notice of application

(2)  A society making an application under this section shall give notice of the application to,

(a)  the child;

(b)  every person who will be permitted to communicate with or have a relationship with the child if the order is made;

(c)  any person with whom the society has placed or plans to place the child for adoption; and

(d)  any society that will supervise or participate in the arrangement under the openness order.

## Method of giving notice to a child

(3)  Notice to a child under subsection (2) shall be given by leaving a copy with,

(a)  the Children's Lawyer;

(b)  the child's lawyer, if any; and

(c)  the child if they are 12 or older.

## Openness order

(4)  The court may make an openness order under this section in respect of a child if the court is satisfied that,

(a)  the openness order is in the best interests of the child;

(b)  the openness order will permit the continuation of a relationship with a person that is beneficial and meaningful to the child; and

(c)  the following entities and persons have consented to the order:

(i)  the society,

(ii)  the person who will be permitted to communicate with or have a relationship with the child if the order is made,

(iii) the person with whom the society has placed or plans to place the child for adoption, and

(iv) the child if they are 12 or older.

### Termination of openness order if extended society care order terminates

(5) Any openness order made under this section in respect of a child terminates if the child ceases to be in extended society care under an order made under paragraph 3 of subsection 101 (1) or clause 116 (1) (c) by reason of an order made under subsection 116 (1).

### Access order in effect
### Notice of intent to place for adoption

**195.** (1) This section applies where,

(a) a society intends to place a child who is in extended society care under an order made under paragraph 3 of subsection 101 (1) or clause 116 (1) (c) for adoption; and

(b) an order under Part V (Child Protection) is in effect respecting a person's access to the child or the child's access to another person.

### Notice

(2) In the circumstances described in subsection (1), the society shall give notice to the following persons:

1. Every person who has been granted a right of access under the access order.
2. Every person with respect to whom access has been granted under the access order.

### Contents of notice

(3) The society shall include in the notice the following information:

1. Notice that the society intends to place the child for adoption.
2. Notice that the access order terminates upon placement for adoption.
3. In the case of notice to a person described in paragraph 1 of subsection (2), the fact that the person has a right to apply for an openness order within 30 days after notice is received.
4. In the case of notice to a person described in paragraph 2 of subsection (2), the fact that the person described in paragraph 1 of subsection (2) has the right to apply for an openness order within 30 days after notice is received.

### Method of giving notice

(4) Notice may be given by,

(a) if the person is not a child, leaving a copy,

(i) with the person,

(ii) if the person appears to be mentally incapable in respect of an issue in the notice, with the person and with the guardian of the person's property or, if none, with the Public Guardian and Trustee, or

(iii) with a lawyer who accepts the notice in writing on a copy of the document; or

(b) if the person is a child, leaving a copy,

(i) with the Children's Lawyer,

(ii) with the child's lawyer, if any, and

(iii) with the child, if they are 12 or older.

### Alternate method

(5) On application without notice by a society, the court may order that notice under subsection (2) be given by another method chosen by the court if the society,

(a) provides detailed evidence showing,

(i) what steps have been taken to locate the person to whom the notice is to be given, and

(ii) if the person has been located, what steps have been taken to give the notice to the person; and

(b) shows that the method of giving notice could reasonably be expected to bring the notice to the person's attention.

### Notice not required

(6) On application without notice by a society, the court may order that the society is not required to give notice under subsection (2) if,

(a) reasonable efforts to locate the person to whom the notice is to be given have not been or would not be successful; and

(b) there is no method of giving notice that could reasonably be expected to bring the notice to the person's attention.

### Access order in effect
### Application for openness order

**196.** (1) A person described in paragraph 1 of subsection 195 (2) may, within 30 days after notice is received, apply to the court for an openness order.

### Notice of application

(2) A person making an application for an openness order under this section shall give notice of the application to,

(a) the society having care and custody of the child;

(b) if someone other than the child is bringing the application, the child; and

(c) if the child is bringing the application, the person who will be permitted to communicate with or have a relationship with the child if the order is made.

### Method of giving notice to child

(3) Notice to a child under subsection (2) shall be given by leaving a copy with,

(a) the Children's Lawyer;

(b) the child's lawyer, if any; and

(c) the child if they are 12 or older.

### Limitation on placement

(4) A society shall not place the child for adoption before the time for applying for an openness order under subsection (1) has expired unless every person who is entitled to do so has made an application for an openness order under this section.

### Information before placement

(5) Where an application for an openness order under this section has been made, a society shall, before placing the child for adoption, advise the person with whom it plans to place the child of the following:

1. The fact that such an application has been made.
2. The relationship of the applicant to the child or, if the child is the applicant, the relationship of the child to the person with whom the child will be permitted to communicate or have a relationship if the order is made.
3. The details of the openness arrangement requested.

### Outcome of application

(6) Where an application for an openness order under this section has been made, a society shall advise the person with whom the society has placed or plans to place the child for adoption or, after an adoption order is made, the adoptive parent, of the outcome of the application.

### Openness order

(7) The court may make an openness order under this section in respect of a child if it is satisfied that,

(a) the openness order is in the best interests of the child;

(b) the openness order will permit the continuation of a relationship with a person that is beneficial and meaningful to the child; and

(c) the child has consented to the order, if they are 12 or older.

### Same

(8) In deciding whether to make an openness order under this section, the court shall consider the ability of the person with whom the society has placed or plans to place the child for adoption or, after the adoption order is made, the adoptive parent, to comply with the arrangement under the openness order.

### Consent of society required

(9) The court shall not, under this section, direct a society to supervise or participate in the arrangement under an openness order without the consent of the society.

### Termination of openness order if extended society care order terminates

(10) Any openness order made under this section in respect of a child terminates if the extended society care order made under paragraph 3 of subsection 101 (1) or clause 116 (1) (c) to which the child was subject terminates by reason of an order made under subsection 116 (1).

### Temporary orders

(11) The court may make such temporary order relating to openness under this section as the court considers to be in the child's best interests.

### Openness order—band and First Nations, Inuit or Métis community

**197.** (1) This section applies where a society intends to place a First Nations, Inuk or Métis child who is in extended society care under an order made under paragraph 3 of subsection 101 (1) or clause 116 (1) (c) for adoption.

### Notice

(2) In the circumstances described in subsection (1), the society shall give notice to the following persons:

1. A representative chosen by each of the child's bands and First Nations, Inuit or Métis communities.
2. The child.

### Contents of notice

(3) The society shall include in the notice the following information:

1. Notice that the society intends to place the child for adoption.
2. The fact that the person has a right to apply for an openness order within 30 days after notice is received.
3. The fact that the society has a right to apply for an openness order within 30 days after notice is given.

### Method of giving notice, etc.

(4) Where notice is required under subsection (2),

(a) notice shall be given by,

(i) if the person is not a child, leaving a copy with the person or with a lawyer who accepts the notice in writing on a copy of the document, or

(ii) if the person is a child, leaving a copy,

(A) with the Children's Lawyer,

(B) with the child's lawyer, if any, and

(C) with the child, if they are 12 or older; and

(b) subsections 195 (5) and (6) apply with necessary modifications.

### Application for openness order

(5) A person described in paragraph 1 or 2 of subsection (2) may, within 30 days after notice is received, apply to the court for an openness order.

### Same, society

(6) The society may, within 30 days after notice is given, apply to the court for an openness order.

### Notice of application

(7) A person or society making an application for an openness order under this section shall give notice of the application to every other person or society who could have made such an application.

## Method of giving notice to a child

(8) Notice to a child under subsection (7) shall be given by leaving a copy with,

  (a) the Children's Lawyer;
  (b) the child's lawyer, if any; and
  (c) the child if they are 12 or older.

## Openness order

(9) The court may make an openness order under this section in respect of a child if it is satisfied that,

  (a) the openness order is in the best interests of the child;
  (b) the openness order will help the child to develop or maintain a connection with the child's First Nations, Inuit or Métis cultures, heritages and traditions and to preserve the child's cultural identity and connection to community;
  (c) the child has consented to the order, if they are 12 or older.

## Application of other provisions

(10) Subsections 196 (4) to (6) and (8) to (11) apply with necessary modifications for the purposes of this section.

## Application to vary or terminate openness order before adoption

**198.** (1) A society or a person with whom a child has been placed for adoption may apply to the court for an order to vary or terminate an openness order made under section 194, 196 or 197.

## Time for making application

(2) An application under this section shall not be made after an order for the adoption of the child is made under section 199.

## Notice of application

(3) A society or person making an application under this section shall give notice of the application to,

  (a) the child;
  (b) every person who is permitted to communicate with or have a relationship with the child under the openness order;
  (c) any person with whom the society has placed or plans to place the child for adoption, if the application under this section is made by the society; and
  (d) any society that supervises or participates in the arrangement under the openness order that is the subject of the application.

## Method of giving notice to a child

(4) Notice to a child under subsection (3) shall be given by leaving a copy with,

  (a) the Children's Lawyer;
  (b) the child's lawyer, if any; and
  (c) the child if they are 12 or older.

## Order to vary openness order before adoption

(5) The court shall not make an order to vary an openness order under this section unless the court is satisfied that,

  (a) a material change in circumstances has occurred;
  (b) the proposed order is in the child's best interests; and
  (c) either,

   (i) the proposed order would continue a relationship that is beneficial and meaningful to the child, or
   (ii) in the case of an openness order made under section 197, the proposed order would help the child to develop or maintain a connection with the child's First Nations, Inuit or Métis cultures, heritages and traditions and to preserve the child's cultural identity and connection to community.

## Order to terminate openness order before adoption

(6) The court shall not terminate an openness order under this section unless the court is satisfied that,

  (a) a material change in circumstances has occurred;
  (b) termination of the order is in the child's best interests; and
  (c) in the case of an openness order made under section 194 or 196, the relationship that is the subject of the order is no longer beneficial and meaningful to the child.

## Consent of society required

(7) The court shall not, under this section, direct a society to supervise or participate in the arrangement under an openness order without the consent of the society.

## Alternative dispute resolution

(8) At any time during a proceeding under this section, the court may, in the best interests of the child and with the consent of the parties, adjourn the proceedings to permit the parties to attempt through a prescribed method of alternative dispute resolution to resolve any dispute between them with respect to any matter that is relevant to the proceeding.

## Temporary orders

(9) The court may make such temporary order relating to openness under this section as the court considers to be in the child's best interests.

## Adoption Orders

## Orders for adoption

## Adoption of child

**199.** (1) The court may make an order for the adoption of a child who is younger than 16, or is 16 or older but has not withdrawn from parental control, and,

  (a) has been placed for adoption by a society or licensee; or
  (b) has been placed for adoption by a person other than a society or licensee and has resided with the applicant for at least two years,

in the child's best interests, on the application of the person with whom the child is placed.

### Family adoption

(2) The court may make an order for the adoption of a child, in the child's best interests, on the application of,

    (a) a relative of the child;

    (b) the child's parent; or

    (c) the spouse of the child's parent.

### Adoption of adult, etc.

(3) The court may make an order for the adoption of,

    (a) a person 18 or older; or

    (b) a child who is 16 or older and has withdrawn from parental control,

on another person's application.

### Who may apply

(4) An application under this section may only be made,

    (a) by one individual; or

    (b) jointly, by two individuals who are spouses of one another.

### Residency requirement

(5) The court shall not make an order under this section for the adoption of, or on the application of, a person who is not a resident of Ontario.

### Where applicant a minor

**200.** The court shall not make an order under section 199 on the application of a person who is younger than 18 unless the court is satisfied that special circumstances justify making the order.

### Where order not to be made

**201.** Where the court has made an order,

    (a) dispensing with a consent under section 181; or

    (b) refusing to permit the late withdrawal of a consent under subsection 182 (1),

the court shall not make an order under section 199 until the later of,

    (c) the time for commencing an appeal of the order has expired; or

    (d) any appeal of the order has been finally disposed of or abandoned.

### Director's statement

**202.** (1) Where an application is made for an order for the adoption of a child under subsection 199 (1), a Director shall, before the hearing, file a written statement with the court indicating,

    (a) that the child has resided with the applicant for at least six months or, in the case of an application under clause 199 (1) (b), for at least two years and, in the Director's opinion, it would be in the child's best interests to make the order;

    (b) in the case of an application under clause 199 (1) (a), that for specified reasons it would be in the child's best interests, in the Director's opinion, to make the order although the child has resided with the applicant for less than six months; or

    (c) that the child has resided with the applicant for at least six months or, in the case of an application under clause 199 (1) (b), for at least two years and, in the Director's opinion, it would not be in the child's best interests to make the order.

### Additional circumstances

(2) The written statement shall refer to any additional circumstances that the Director wishes to bring to the court's attention.

### Local director may make statement

(3) Where a child was placed by a society and has resided with the applicant for at least six months, the written statement may be made and filed by the local director.

### Amendment of statement, etc.

(4) The Director or local director, as the case may be, may amend the written statement at any time and may attend at the hearing and make submissions.

### Where recommendation negative

(5) Where the written statement indicates that, in the Director's or local director's opinion, it would not be in the child's best interests to make the order, a copy of the statement shall be filed with the court and served on the applicant at least 30 days before the hearing.

### Report of child's adjustment

(6) The written statement shall be based on a report of the child's adjustment in the applicant's home, prepared by,

    (a) the society that placed the child or has jurisdiction where the child is placed; or

    (b) a person approved by the Director or local director.

### Family adoptions

(7) Where an application is made for an order for the adoption of a child under subsection 199 (2),

    (a) subsections (1), (2), (4), (5) and (6) apply to the application, if the child was not a resident of Canada before being placed for adoption; and

    (b) the court may order that subsections (1), (2), (4), (5) and (6) apply to the application, if the child was a resident of Canada before being placed for adoption.

### Place of hearing

**203.** (1) An application for an adoption order shall be heard and dealt with in the county or district in which,

    (a) the applicant; or

    (b) the person to be adopted,

resides at the time the application is filed.

## Transfer of proceeding

(2) Where the court is satisfied at any stage of an application for an adoption order that there is a preponderance of convenience in favour of conducting it in another county or district, the court may order that it be transferred to that other county or district and be continued as if it had been commenced there.

## Rules re applications

## Hearing in private

**204.** (1) An application for an adoption order shall be heard and dealt with in the absence of the public.

## Court files private

(2) No person shall have access to the court file concerning an application for an adoption order, except,

(a) the court and authorized court employees;

(b) the parties and the persons representing them under the authority of the *Law Society Act*; and

(c) a Director and a local director.

## Stale applications

(3) Where an application for an adoption order is not heard within 12 months of the day on which the applicant signed it,

(a) the court shall not hear the application unless the court is satisfied that it is just to do so; and

(b) the applicant may make another application.

## No right to notice

(4) A person is not entitled to receive notice of an application under section 199 if,

(a) the person has given a consent under clause 180 (2) (a) and has not withdrawn it;

(b) the person's consent has been dispensed with under section 181; or

(c) the person is a parent of a child who is in extended society care under an order made under paragraph 3 of subsection 101 (1) or clause 116 (1) (c) who is placed for adoption.

## Power of court

**205.** (1) The court may, on its own initiative, summon a person to attend before it, testify and produce any document or thing, and may enforce obedience to the summons as if it had been made in a proceeding under the *Family Law Act*.

## Duty of court

(2) The court shall not make an order for the adoption of a child under subsection 199 (1) or (2) unless the court is satisfied that,

(a) every person who has given a consent under section 180 understands the nature and effect of the adoption order; and

(b) every applicant understands and appreciates the special role of an adoptive parent.

## Participation of child

(3) Where an application is made for an order for the adoption of a child under subsection 199 (1) or (2), the court,

(a) shall inquire into the child's capacity to understand and appreciate the nature of the application;

(b) shall take the child's views and wishes into account and give them due weight in accordance with the child's age and maturity; and

(c) where it is practical to do so, shall hear the child.

## Participation of adult, etc.

(4) Where an application is made for an order for the adoption of a person under subsection 199 (3), the court shall consider the person's views and wishes and, on request, hear the person.

## Change of name

**206.** (1) Where the court makes an order under section 199, the court may, at the request of the applicant or applicants and, where the person adopted is 12 or older, with the person's written consent,

(a) change the person's surname to a surname that the person could have been given if the person had been born to the applicant or applicants; and

(b) change the person's given name.

> **Note: On a day to be named by proclamation of the Lieutenant Governor, subsection 206 (1) of the Act is repealed and the following substituted: (See: 2017, c. 14, Sched. 3, s. 9)**

## Change of name

(1) Subject to subsection (1.1), when the court makes an order under section 199, the court may, at the request of the applicant or applicants,

(a) change the person's surname to any surname that the person could have been given if the person had been born in Ontario to the applicant or applicants at the time of the order;

(b) change the person's forename;

(c) change the person's surname as described in clause (a) and change the person's forename;

(d) change the person's single name to a single name that is determined in accordance with the traditional culture of the person or the applicant or applicants if the Registrar General under the *Vital Statistics Act* approves the single name;

(e) change the person's single name to a name with at least one forename and a surname as described in clause (a); or

(f) change the person's forename and surname to a single name that is determined in accordance with the traditional culture of the person or the applicant or applicants if the Registrar General under the *Vital Statistics Act* approves the single name. 2017, c. 14, Sched. 3, s. 9.

### Same

(1.1) A court shall not make a change described in subsection (1) unless,

(a) doing so is in the best interests of the child, if the person adopted is a child; and

(b) the person adopted consents, if the person is 12 or older. 2017, c. 14, Sched. 3, s. 9.

### When child's consent not required

(2) A child's consent to a change of name under subsection (1) is not required where the child's consent was dispensed with under subsection 180 (9).

### Varying or terminating openness orders after adoption

**207.** (1) Any of the following persons may apply to the court to vary or terminate an openness order made under section 194, 196 or 197 after an order for adoption has been made under section 199:

1. An adoptive parent.
2. The adopted child.
3. A person who is permitted to communicate or have a relationship with the child under the openness order.
4. Any society that supervises or participates in the arrangement under the openness order that is the subject of the application.

### Leave

(2) Despite paragraphs 2 and 3 of subsection (1), the child and a person who is permitted to communicate or have a relationship with the child under an openness order shall not make an application under subsection (1) without leave of the court.

### Jurisdiction

(3) An application under subsection (1) shall be made in the county or district,

(a) in which the child resides, if the child resides in Ontario; or

(b) in which the adoption order for the child was made if the child does not reside in Ontario, unless the court is satisfied that the preponderance of convenience favours having the matter dealt with by the court in another county or district.

### Notice

(4) A person making an application under subsection (1) shall give notice of the application to every other person who could have made an application under that subsection with respect to the order.

### Method of giving notice to a child

(5) Notice to a child under subsection (4) shall be given by leaving a copy with,

(a) the Children's Lawyer;

(b) the child's lawyer, if any; and

(c) the child if they are 12 or older.

### Order to vary openness order

(6) The court shall not make an order to vary an openness order under this section unless the court is satisfied that,

(a) a material change in circumstances has occurred;

(b) the proposed order is in the child's best interests; and

(c) either,

(i) the proposed order would continue a relationship that is beneficial and meaningful to the child, or

(ii) in the case of an openness order made under section 197, the proposed order would help the child to develop or maintain a connection with the child's First Nations, Inuit or Métis cultures, heritages and traditions and to preserve the child's cultural identity and connection to community.

### Order to terminate openness order

(7) The court shall not terminate an openness order under this section unless the court is satisfied that,

(a) a material change in circumstances has occurred;

(b) termination of the order is in the child's best interests; and

(c) in the case of an openness order made under section 194 or 196, the relationship that is the subject of the order is no longer beneficial and meaningful to the child.

### Consent of society required

(8) The court shall not, under this section, direct a society to supervise or participate in the arrangement under an openness order without the consent of the society.

### Alternative dispute resolution

(9) At any time during a proceeding under this section, the court may, in the best interests of the child and with the consent of the parties, adjourn the proceedings to permit the parties to attempt through a prescribed method of alternative dispute resolution to resolve any dispute between them with respect to a matter relevant to the proceeding.

### Appeal of order to vary or terminate openness order

**208.** (1) An appeal from a court's order under section 198 or 207 may be made to the Superior Court of Justice by,

(a) any person who was entitled to apply for the order to vary or terminate the openness order; or

(b) any person who was entitled to notice of the application to vary or terminate the openness order.

### Temporary order

(2) Pending final disposition of the appeal, the Superior Court of Justice may on any party's motion make a temporary order in the child's best interests that varies or suspends an openness order.

### No time extension

(3) No extension of the time for an appeal shall be granted.

### Further evidence

(4)  The court may receive further evidence relating to events after the appealed decision.

### Place of hearing

(5)  An appeal under this section shall be heard in the county or district in which the order appealed from was made.

### Application of s. 204

**209.**  Subsections 204 (1) and (2) apply with necessary modifications to proceedings under sections 194, 196, 197, 198, 207 and 208.

### Child may participate

**210.**  A child is entitled to participate in the proceeding under section 194, 196, 197, 198, 207 or 208 as if they were a party.

### Legal representation of child

**211.**  (1)  A child may have legal representation at any stage in a proceeding under section 194, 196, 197, 198, 207 or 208 and subsection 78 (2) applies with necessary modifications to such a proceeding.

### Children's Lawyer

(2)  The Children's Lawyer may provide legal representation to a child under this Part if, in the opinion of the Children's Lawyer, such representation is appropriate.

### Court may refer matter to Children's Lawyer

(3)  Where the court determines that legal representation is desirable, the court may refer the matter to the Children's Lawyer.

## Openness Agreements
### Who may enter into openness agreement

**212.**  (1)  For the purposes of facilitating communication or maintaining relationships, an openness agreement may be made by an adoptive parent of a child or by a person with whom a society or licensee has placed or plans to place a child for adoption and any of the following persons:

1.  A birth parent, birth relative or birth sibling of the child.
2.  A foster parent of the child or another person who cared for the child or in whose custody the child was placed at any time.
3.  A member of the child's extended family or community with whom the child has a significant relationship or emotional tie.
4.  An adoptive parent of a birth sibling of the child or a person with whom a society or licensee has placed or plans to place a birth sibling of the child for adoption.
5.  In the case of a First Nations, Inuk or Métis child,
    i.  a person described in paragraph 1, 2, 3 or 4, or
    ii.  a member of the child's bands and First Nations, Inuit or Métis communities who may not have had a significant relationship or emotional tie with the child in the past but will help the child to develop or maintain a connection with the child's First Nations, Inuit or Métis cultures, heritages and traditions and to preserve the child's cultural identity and connection to community.

### When agreement may be made

(2)  An openness agreement may be made at any time before or after an adoption order is made.

### Agreement may include dispute resolution process

(3)  An openness agreement may include a process to resolve disputes arising under the agreement or with respect to matters associated with it.

### Child's views and wishes of child

(4)  Before an openness agreement is made, the child's views and wishes shall be taken into account and given due weight in accordance with the child's age and maturity.

## Interim Orders
### Interim order

**213.**  (1)  Where an application is made for an order for the adoption of a child under subsection 199 (1) or (2), the court, after considering the statement made under subsection 202 (1), may postpone the determination of the matter and make an interim order in the child's best interests placing the child in the applicant's care and custody for a specified period not exceeding one year.

### Terms and conditions

(2)  The court may make an order under subsection (1) subject to any terms and conditions that the court considers appropriate respecting,

(a)  the child's maintenance and education;

(b)  supervision of the child; and

(c)  any other matter the court considers advisable in the child's best interests.

### Not an adoption order

(3)  An order under subsection (1) is not an adoption order.

### Consents required

(4)  Sections 180 and 181 (consents to adoption) apply to an order under subsection (1) with necessary modifications.

### Departure from Ontario

(5)  Where an applicant takes up residence outside Ontario after obtaining an order under subsection (1), the court may nevertheless make an adoption order under subsection 199 (1) or (2) where the statement made under subsection 202 (1) indicates that, in the Director's or local director's opinion, it would be in the child's best interests to make the order.

### Successive adoption orders

**214.** An adoption order under subsection 199 (1) or (2) or an interim custody order under subsection 213 (1) may be made in respect of a person who is the subject of an earlier adoption order.

## Appeals

### Appeals

### Appeal: adoption order

**215.** (1) An appeal from a court's order under section 199 may be made to the Superior Court of Justice by,

(a) the applicant for the adoption order; and

(b) the Director or local director who made the statement under subsection 202 (1).

### Same: dispensing with consent

(2) An appeal from a court's order under section 181 dispensing with a consent may be made to the Superior Court of Justice by,

(a) the persons referred to in subsection (1) of this section; and

(b) the person whose consent was dispensed with.

### Same: late withdrawal of consent

(3) An appeal from a court's order under subsection 182 (1) permitting the late withdrawal of a consent may be made to the Superior Court of Justice by,

(a) the persons referred to in subsection (1) of this section; and

(b) the person who gave the consent.

### No extension of time for appeal

(4) No extension of the time for an appeal shall be granted.

### Place of hearing

(5) An appeal under this section shall be heard in the county or district in which the order appealed from was made.

### Hearing in private

(6) An appeal under this section shall be heard in the absence of the public.

## Effect of Adoption Order

### Order final

**216.** (1) An adoption order under section 199 is final and irrevocable, subject only to section 215 (appeals), and shall not be questioned or reviewed in any court by way of injunction, declaratory judgment, *certiorari*, *mandamus*, prohibition, *habeas corpus* or application for judicial review.

### Validity of adoption order not affected by openness order or agreement

(2) Compliance or non-compliance with the terms of an openness order or openness agreement relating to a child does not affect the validity of an order made under section 199 for the adoption of the child.

### Status of adopted child

**217.** (1) In this section,

"adopted child" means a person who was adopted in Ontario.

### Same

(2) For all purposes of law, as of the date of the making of an adoption order,

(a) the adopted child becomes the child of the adoptive parent and the adoptive parent becomes the parent of the adopted child; and

(b) the adopted child ceases to be the child of the person who was the adopted child's parent before the adoption order was made and that person ceases to be the parent of the adopted child, except where the person is the spouse of the adoptive parent.

### How relationships determined

(3) The relationship to one another of all persons, including the adopted child, the adoptive parent, the kindred of the adoptive parent, the parent before the adoption order was made and the kindred of that former parent shall for all purposes be determined in accordance with subsection (2).

### Reference in will or other document

(4) In any will or other document made at any time before or after the day this subsection comes into force and whether the maker of the will or document is alive on that day or not, a reference to a person or group or class of persons described in terms of relationship by blood or marriage to another person is deemed to refer to or include, as the case may be, a person who comes within the description as a result of an adoption, unless the contrary is expressed.

### Application of section

(5) This section applies and is deemed always to have applied with respect to any adoption made under any Act that is in force, but not so as to affect,

(a) any interest in property or right of the adopted child that has indefeasibly vested before the date of the making of an adoption order; and

(b) any interest in property or right that has indefeasibly vested before the day this subsection comes into force.

### Exception

(6) Subsections (2) and (3) do not apply for the purposes of the laws relating to incest and the prohibited degrees of marriage to remove a person from a relationship that would have existed but for those subsections.

### Effect of foreign adoption

**218.** An adoption effected according to the law of another jurisdiction, before or after the day this section comes into force, has the same effect in Ontario as an adoption under this Part.

### No order for access by birth parent, etc.

**219.** Where an order for the adoption of a child has been made under this Part, no court shall make an order under this Part for access to the child by,

(a) a birth parent; or

(b) a member of a birth parent's family.

## Maintenance of Relationships

### Maintenance of relationships

**220.** (1) A society shall make all reasonable efforts to assist a child to maintain relationships with persons that are beneficial and meaningful to the child in the following circumstances:

1. The child was placed for adoption by the society and the society has decided not to finalize the adoption of the child by the person with whom the child was placed.

2. A child returns to the care of a society after an adoption order was made.

### Openness order or agreement or access order

(2) For the purposes of subsection (1), in addition to what is permitted under subsection 105 (9), a society shall,

(a) facilitate contact or communication provided for under an existing openness order or openness agreement in respect of the child and the persons who are subject to or parties to the openness order or openness agreement, as the case may be; and

(b) consider whether to apply for an order for access under Part V (Child Protection) in respect of the child and the persons.

### Existing openness order continues in force

(3) For greater certainty, in a circumstance described in paragraph 1 or 2 of subsection (1), an existing openness order continues to be in force until it is varied or terminated.

## Records, Confidentiality and Disclosure

### Parent to be informed on request

**221.** At the request of a person whose consent to an adoption was required under clause 180 (2) (a) or clause 137 (2) (a) of the old Act and was given or was dispensed with, any society or the licensee that placed the child for adoption shall inform the person whether an order has been made for the child's adoption.

### Court papers

**222.** (1) In this section,

"court" includes the Superior Court of Justice.

### Requirement to seal documents

(2) Subject to subsections (3) and 224 (2), the documents used on an application for an adoption order under this Part or Part VII (Adoption) of the old Act shall be sealed up together with a certified copy of the original order and filed in the court office by the appropriate court officer, and shall not be opened for inspection except by court order.

### Transmission of order

(3) Within 30 days after an adoption order is made under this Part, the proper officer of the court shall cause a sufficient number of certified copies of it to be made, under the seal of the proper certifying authority, and shall provide,

(a) the original order to the adoptive parent;

(b) one certified copy to the Registrar General under the *Vital Statistics Act*, or, if the adopted child was born outside Ontario, two certified copies;

(c) if the adopted child is registered or entitled to be registered under the *Indian Act* (Canada), one certified copy to the Registrar under that Act; and

(d) one certified copy to such other persons as may be prescribed.

### Other court files

(4) Unless the court orders otherwise, only the court may examine identifying information that comes from the records of any of the following persons that is contained in any court file respecting the judicial review of a decision made by any of them:

1. A designated custodian under section 223.

2. A person who, by virtue of a regulation made under paragraph 18 of subsection 346 (1), reviews or hears appeals of decisions concerning the disclosure of information under section 224 or 225.

3. A person referred to in subsection 224 (1) or 225 (1).

### Same

(5) No person shall, without the court's permission, disclose identifying information described in subsection (4) that the person obtained from the court file.

### Definition

(6) In subsections (4) and (5),

"identifying information" means information whose disclosure, alone or in combination with other information, will in the circumstances reveal the identity of the person to whom it relates.

### Designation of custodians of information

**223.** (1) The Lieutenant Governor in Council may, by regulation, designate one or more persons to act as custodians of information that relates to adoptions and may impose such conditions and restrictions with respect to the designation as the Lieutenant Governor in Council considers appropriate.

### Powers and duties

(2) A designated custodian may exercise such powers and shall perform such duties as may be prescribed with respect to the information provided to the custodian under this Act.

### Same, disclosure of information

(3) A designated custodian may exercise such other powers and shall perform such other duties as may be prescribed for a purpose relating to the disclosure of information that relates to adoptions, including performing searches upon request for such persons, and in such circumstances, as may be prescribed.

### Agreements

(4) The Minister may enter into agreements with designated custodians concerning their powers and duties under this section and the agreements may provide for payments to be made to the designated custodians.

### Disclosure to designated custodian

**224.** (1) The Minister, the Registrar General under the *Vital Statistics Act*, a society, a licensee and such other persons as may be prescribed shall give a designated custodian under section 223 such information that relates to adoptions as may be prescribed in such circumstances as may be prescribed.

### Same, adoption orders

(2) A court shall give a designated custodian a certified copy of an adoption order made under this Part together with such other documents as may be prescribed in such circumstances as may be prescribed.

### Disclosure to others
### By the Minister

**225.** (1) The Minister shall give such information that relates to adoptions as may be prescribed to such persons as may be prescribed in such circumstances as may be prescribed.

### By a society

(2) A society shall give such information that relates to adoptions as may be prescribed to such persons as may be prescribed in such circumstances as may be prescribed.

### By a licensee

(3) A licensee shall give such information that relates to adoptions as may be prescribed to such persons as may be prescribed in such circumstances as may be prescribed.

### By a custodian

(4) A designated custodian under section 223 shall give such information that relates to adoptions as may be prescribed to such persons as may be prescribed in such circumstances as may be prescribed.

### Scope of application

**226.** Sections 224 and 225 apply with respect to information that relates to an adoption regardless of when the adoption order was made.

### Confidentiality of Adoption Records
### Confidentiality of adoption information

**227.** (1) Despite any other Act, after an adoption order is made, no person shall inspect, remove, alter or disclose information that relates to the adoption and is kept by the Ministry, a society, a licensee or a designated custodian under section 223 and no person shall permit it to be inspected, removed, altered or disclosed unless the inspection, removal, alteration or disclosure is,

(a) necessary for the maintenance or updating of the information by the Ministry, society, licensee or designated custodian or their staff; or

(b) authorized by this Act or the regulations.

### Powers of courts and tribunals

(2) Subsection (1) does not affect the power of a court or tribunal to compel a witness to testify or to compel the production of a document.

### Application

(3) This section applies regardless of when the adoption order was made.

### Privacy

(4) The *Freedom of Information and Protection of Privacy Act* does not apply to information that relates to an adoption.

### Injunction
### Injunction

**228.** (1) The Superior Court of Justice may grant an injunction to restrain a person from contravening subsection 191 (2), on the society's or licensee's application.

### Variation, etc.

(2) The Court may vary or terminate an order made under subsection (1), on any person's application.

### Licensing—Requirement for Licence; Issuance and Renewal
### Licences
### Licence required

**229.** (1) No person other than a society shall place a child for adoption, except under the authority of a licence issued by a Director.

### Issuing licence

(2) Subject to section 231, a person who applies for a licence in accordance with this Part and the regulations and pays the prescribed fee is entitled to be issued a licence by a Director, subject to any conditions imposed by the Director.

### To individual or non-profit agency only

(3) Despite subsection (2), a licence shall only be issued to an individual or a non-profit agency.

### Renewal of licence

(4) Subject to section 232, a licensee who applies for renewal of the licence in accordance with this Part and the regulations and pays the prescribed fee is entitled to have the licence renewed by a Director, subject to any conditions imposed by the Director.

### Provisional licence or renewal

(5) Where an applicant for a licence or renewal of a licence does not meet all the requirements for the issuing or renewal of the licence and requires time to meet them, a Director may, subject to such conditions as the Director may impose, issue a provisional licence for the period that the Director considers necessary to give the applicant time to meet the requirements.

### Not transferable

(6) A licence is not transferable.

### Definition

(7) In this section,

"non-profit agency" means a corporation without share capital that has objects of a charitable nature and,

(a) to which Part III of the *Corporations Act* applies, or

> **Note: On the first day that section 350 of Schedule 1 to the *Supporting Children, Youth and Families Act, 2017* and subsection 4 (1) of the *Not-for-Profit Corporations Act, 2010* are both in force, clause (a) of the definition of "non-profit agency" in subsection 229 (7) of the Act is amended by striking out "Part III of the *Corporations Act*" and substituting "the *Not-for-Profit Corporations Act, 2010* or a predecessor of that Act". (See: 2017, c. 14, Sched. 3, s. 10)**

(b) that is incorporated by or under a general or special Act of the Parliament of Canada.

### Conditions of licence

**230.** (1) On issuing or renewing a licence or at any other time, a Director may impose on the licence the conditions that the Director considers appropriate.

### Amending conditions

(2) A Director may, at any time, amend the conditions imposed on the licence.

### Notice

(3) The Director shall notify the licensee in writing of the imposition or amendment of the conditions.

### Contents of notice

(4) The notice shall set out the reasons for imposing or amending the conditions and shall state that the licensee is entitled to a hearing by the Tribunal if they request one in accordance with subsection 234 (1).

### Conditions take effect upon notice

(5) The imposition or amendment of conditions takes effect immediately upon the licensee's receipt of the notice and is not stayed by a request for a hearing by the Tribunal.

### Licensee must comply

(6) Every licensee shall comply with the conditions to which the licence is subject.

## Licensing—Refusal and Revocation

### Grounds for refusal

**231.** A Director may propose to refuse to issue a licence where, in the Director's opinion,

(a) the applicant or an employee of the applicant, or, where the applicant is a corporation, an officer or director of the corporation is not competent to place children for adoption in a responsible manner in accordance with this Act and the regulations;

(b) the past conduct of any person mentioned in clause (a) affords reasonable grounds for belief that the placement of children for adoption will not be carried on in a responsible manner in accordance with this Act and the regulations; or

(c) a ground exists that is prescribed as a ground for refusing to issue a licence.

### Grounds for revocation, refusal to renew

**232.** A Director may propose to revoke or refuse to renew a licence where, in the Director's opinion,

(a) the licensee or an employee of the licensee, or where the licensee is a corporation, an officer or director of the corporation has contravened or has knowingly permitted a person under their control or direction or associated with them to contravene,

    (i) this Act or the regulations,

    (ii) any other applicable law, or

    (iii) a condition of the licence;

(b) the placement of children for adoption is carried on in a manner that is prejudicial to the children's health, safety or welfare;

(c) a person has made a false statement in the application for the licence or for its renewal, or in a report or document required to be furnished by this Act or the regulations or any other applicable law;

(d) a change has occurred in the employees, officers or directors of the licensee that would, if the licensee were applying for the licence in the first instance, afford grounds under clause 231 (b) for refusing to issue the licence; or

(e) a ground exists that is prescribed as a ground for revoking or refusing to renew a licence.

## Licensing—Hearing by Tribunal

### Hearings arising out of s. 231 or 232

### Notice of proposal

**233.** (1) Where a Director proposes to refuse to issue a licence under section 231 or to revoke or refuse to renew a licence under section 232, the Director shall notify the applicant or licensee of the proposal in writing.

### Request for hearing

(2) A notice under subsection (1) shall set out the reasons for the proposal and shall state that the applicant or licensee

is entitled to a hearing by the Tribunal if they deliver a written request for a hearing to the Director and to the Tribunal within 10 days after the notice is given.

### Powers of Director where no hearing requested

(3) Where an applicant or licensee does not request a hearing under subsection (2), the Director may carry out the proposal.

### Powers of Tribunal where hearing requested

(4) Where an applicant or licensee requests a hearing under subsection (2), the Tribunal shall appoint a time for and hold a hearing and may, on hearing the matter,

(a) order the Director to carry out the proposal; or

(b) order the Director to take such other action as the Tribunal considers appropriate, in accordance with this Part and the regulations.

### Discretion of Tribunal

(5) In making an order under subsection (4), the Tribunal may substitute its opinion for that of the Director.

### Review of conditions by Tribunal

**234.** (1) A licensee who is dissatisfied with the conditions imposed by a Director under subsection 229 (2), (4) or (5) or section 230 is entitled to a hearing by the Tribunal if the licensee delivers a written request for a hearing to the Director and to the Tribunal within 15 days after receiving the licence.

### Powers of Tribunal

(2) Where a licensee requests a hearing under subsection (1), the Tribunal shall appoint a time for and hold a hearing and may, on hearing the matter,

(a) confirm any or all of the conditions;

(b) strike out any or all of the conditions; or

(c) impose such other conditions as the Tribunal considers appropriate.

### Continuation of licence pending renewal

**235.** Subject to section 236, where a licensee has applied for renewal of a licence and paid the prescribed fee within the prescribed time or, if no time is prescribed, before the licence expires, the licence is deemed to continue,

(a) until the renewal is granted; or

(b) where the licensee is served with notice that the Director proposes to revoke the licence or to refuse to grant the renewal, until the time for requiring a hearing has expired and, where a hearing is required, until the Tribunal has made its decision.

### Suspension of licence

**236.** (1) A Director may, by giving written notice to a licensee, suspend the licence where, in the Director's opinion, the manner in which children are placed for adoption by the licensee is an immediate threat to the health, safety or welfare of the children.

### Suspension takes effect upon notice

(2) A suspension takes effect immediately upon the licensee's receipt of the notice and is not stayed by a request for a hearing by the Tribunal.

### s. 233 (2)-(4) apply

(3) Where a notice is given under subsection (1), subsections 233 (2), (3) and (4) apply with necessary modifications.

### Application of other provisions

**237.** Sections 266 and 267 apply with necessary modifications to proceedings before the Tribunal under this Part and to appeals of its orders.

## Licensing—Delivery of Licence and Records
### Licence and record to be delivered

**238.** If a licence is revoked or renewal of it refused, or if a licensee ceases to place children for adoption, the licensee shall,

(a) promptly deliver the licence to the Minister; and

(b) deliver all the records in the licensee's possession or control that relate to the children to whom services were being provided to a prescribed person or entity within the prescribed time.

## Licensing—Injunctions
### Injunction

**239.** (1) A Director may apply to the Superior Court of Justice for an order enjoining a licensee from placing children for adoption while the licence is suspended under section 236.

### Variance or discharge

(2) A licensee may apply to the court for an order varying or discharging an order made under subsection (1).

## Offences
### No payments for adoption

**240.** No person, whether before or after a child's birth, shall give, receive or agree to give or receive a payment or reward of any kind in connection with,

(a) the child's adoption or placement for adoption;

(b) a consent under section 180 to the child's adoption; or

(c) negotiations or arrangements with a view to the child's adoption,

except for,

(d) the prescribed expenses of a licensee, or such greater expenses as are approved by a Director;

(e) proper legal fees and disbursements; and

(f) a subsidy paid by a society or by the Minister to an adoptive parent or to a person with whom a child is placed for adoption.

### Offences

**241.** (1) A person who contravenes subsection 183 (1), (2), (3) or (4) (placement for adoption) and a director, officer or employee of a corporation who authorizes, permits or concurs in such a contravention by the corporation is guilty of an offence, whether an order is subsequently made for the child's adoption or not, and on conviction is liable to a fine of not more than $5,000 or to imprisonment for a term of not more than two years, or to both.

### Same

(2) A person who contravenes subsection 183 (5) (receiving child) is guilty of an offence and on conviction is liable to a fine of not more than $5,000 or to imprisonment for a term of not more than two years, or to both.

### Same

(3) A person who contravenes subsection 191 (2) (interference with child) is guilty of an offence and on conviction is liable to a fine of not more than $5,000 or to imprisonment for a term of not more than one year, or to both.

### Same

(4) A person who contravenes section 240 and a director, officer or employee of a corporation who authorizes, permits or concurs in such a contravention by the corporation is guilty of an offence and on conviction is liable to a fine of not more than $25,000 or to imprisonment for a term of not more than three years, or to both.

### Limitation

(5) A proceeding under subsection (1), (2) or (4) shall not be commenced more than two years after the day on which the offence was, or is alleged to have been, committed.

### Offences—licensing

**242.** (1) A person is guilty of an offence if the person,

(a) knowingly provides false information in an application for a licence or renewal of a licence under this Part or in a statement, report or return required to be provided in respect of a licensing matter under this Part or the regulations; or

(b) fails to comply with an order or direction made by a court in relation to a licensing matter under this Part.

### Directors, officers and employees

(2) It is an offence for a director, officer or employee of a corporation to authorize, permit or concur in the commission by the corporation of an offence described in subsection (1).

### Penalty

(3) Every person convicted of an offence under this section is liable to a fine of not more than $5,000.

## PART IX    RESIDENTIAL LICENSING

### Definitions

**243.** In this Part,

"children's residence" means any of the following residences where children live and receive residential care:

1. A parent model residence having five or more children not of common parentage.
2. A staff model residence having three or more children not of common parentage, including an institution that is supervised or operated by a society or a place of temporary detention, of secure custody or of open custody.
3. Any other prescribed residence.

A children's residence does not include the following:

4. A house licensed under the *Private Hospitals Act*.
5. A child care centre as defined in the *Child Care and Early Years Act, 2014*.
6. A recreational camp under the *Health Protection and Promotion Act*.
7. A home for special care under the *Homes for Special Care Act*.
8. A school or private school as defined in the *Education Act*.
9. A hostel intended for short term accommodation.
10. A hospital that receives financial aid from the Government of Ontario.
11. A group home or similar facility that receives financial assistance from the Minister of Community Safety and Correctional Services but receives no financial assistance from the Minister under this Act.
12. Any other prescribed place; ("foyer pour enfants")

"directive" means a directive issued by the Minister under section 252; ("directive")

"parent model residence" means a building, group of buildings or part of a building where not more than two adult persons live and provide care for children on a continuous basis; ("foyer de type familial")

"placing agency" means a person or entity, including a society, that places a child in residential care or in foster care and includes a licensee; ("agence de placement")

"staff model residence" means a building, group of buildings or part of a building where adult persons are employed to provide care for children on the basis of scheduled periods of duty. ("foyer avec rotation de personnel")

### Protective Measures

### Licence required

**244.** No person shall do any of the following except under the authority of a licence:

1. Operate a children's residence.

2. Provide residential care, directly or indirectly, in places that are not children's residences,

    i. for three or more children not of common parentage, or

    ii. in such circumstances as may be prescribed.

### Prohibition—past offence

**245.** No person shall operate a children's residence or provide residential care under the authority of a licence if they have been convicted of a prescribed offence.

### Prohibition—holding out as licensed

**246.** No person shall represent or hold out expressly or by implication that they are licensed to operate a children's residence or to provide residential care unless the person is licensed to do so.

### Placements must comply with Act and regulations, etc.

**247.** No licensee shall place a child in a children's residence or other place where residential care is provided except in accordance with this Act, the regulations and the directives.

### Duty to keep licence

**248.** (1) A licensee shall keep a copy of the licence at the following premises and shall ensure that the licence is available for public inspection:

1. In the case of a children's residence, at the residence.
2. In the case of any other place where residential care is provided under the authority of a licence, at the business premises of the licensee or other prescribed premises.

### Duty to post information

(2) A licensee shall post any prescribed information in a conspicuous place at the children's residence or other place where residential care is provided under the authority of a licence.

### Duty to provide licence and other information

**249.** (1) Before a child is placed in a children's residence or other place where residential care is provided under the authority of a licence, the licensee shall give the following to the placing agency, where the placing agency is not the licensee, or to the person placing the child:

1. A copy of the licence to operate the children's residence or to provide residential care, as the case may be.
2. Any other prescribed information.

### Record of compliance

(2) The licensee shall make and keep a record of its compliance with subsection (1),

    (a) in the case of a children's residence, at the residence; or

    (b) in the case of any other place where residential care is provided under the authority of a licence, at the business premises of the licensee or other prescribed premises.

### Report certain matters to a Director

**250.** (1) If, in the course of employment, it comes to the attention of a prescribed person that there are reasonable grounds to suspect that there is an immediate threat to the health, safety or welfare of any child placed in a children's residence or other place where residential care is provided under the authority of a licence, the person shall immediately report the suspicion and the information on which it is based to a Director.

### Inspection

(2) If a suspicion is reported to a Director under subsection (1), the Director shall have an inspector conduct an inspection or make inquiries for the purpose of determining compliance with this Act, the regulations and the directives.

### Solicitor-client privilege

(3) Nothing in this section abrogates any privilege that may exist between a lawyer and the lawyer's client.

### Duty to report

(4) Nothing in this section affects the duty to report a suspicion under section 125.

### Director may exempt

**251.** A Director may, in the prescribed circumstances, exempt the following from any provision of this Part, the regulations under this Part or a directive for the time period and on the conditions specified by the Director:

1. A place or class of places where residential care is provided under the authority of a licence.
2. A person or class of persons who provide, or are applying to provide, residential care under the authority of a licence.

### Directives by Minister

**252.** (1) The Minister may issue directives to licensees with respect to any prescribed matter.

### Binding

(2) A licensee shall comply with every directive issued to it under this section.

### General or particular

(3) A directive may be general or particular in its application.

### Law prevails

(4) For greater certainty, in the event of a conflict between a directive issued under this section and a provision of any applicable Act or rule of any applicable law, the provision or rule prevails.

### Public availability

(5) The Minister shall make every directive under this section available to the public.

### Non-application of *Legislation Act, 2006*

(6) Part III (Regulations) of the *Legislation Act, 2006* does not apply to a directive issued under this section.

### Publication of information by Minister

**253.** (1) The Minister may publish the following information with respect to licences and applications for licences:

1. The name of the licensee and prescribed contact information.
2. The name of the children's residence or other place where residential care is provided.
3. The conditions, if any, imposed on the licence under section 255.
4. The term of the licence specified under section 256.
5. The class, if any, assigned to the licence under section 258.
6. The maximum number of children for whom residential care may be provided by the licensee, set out in the licence under section 259.
7. Information about the programs and services to be provided under the authority of the licence.
8. A summary of each proposal to refuse to issue a licence under section 261, or under section 195 of the old Act, or to revoke or refuse to renew a licence under section 262, or under section 196 of the old Act, unless the refusal or revocation was not carried out.
9. A summary of each notice of a suspension under section 264, or under section 200 of the old Act.
10. The amount that the licensee shall charge for the provision of residential care under section 268.
11. A summary of each inspection report prepared under section 278.
12. Any other prescribed licensing information.

### Not in force

(2) The authority under subsection (1) includes the authority to publish information with respect to licences that are no longer in force.

### Manner

(3) The Minister may publish the information in any manner or format the Minister considers appropriate.

### Licences

### Issuance and renewal of licence

### Application

**254.** (1) An application for a licence or the renewal of a licence to operate a children's residence or to provide residential care shall be made by submitting to a Director,

(a) an application in a form approved by the Minister;

(b) an attestation, to be completed by the applicant in a form approved by the Minister, confirming that the applicant is not prohibited from operating a children's residence or from providing residential care under the authority of a licence under section 245;

(c) any other information or documentation that may be specified by the Minister; and

(d) payment of the prescribed fee.

### Additional requirements

(2) An applicant for a licence or the renewal of a licence shall comply with any other prescribed requirements and the directives that relate to the application process, unless the applicant withdraws the application.

### Director's duty to issue or renew

(3) A Director shall issue or renew a licence if the applicant applied in accordance with subsections (1) and (2) unless,

(a) the Director proposes to refuse to do so in accordance with section 261 or 262; or

(b) the applicant is under 18 years old, is a partnership or is an association of persons.

### Not transferable

(4) A licence is not transferable.

### Conditions of licence

**255.** (1) On issuing or renewing a licence or at any other time, a Director may impose on the licence the conditions that the Director considers appropriate.

### Amending conditions

(2) A Director may, at any time, amend the conditions imposed on the licence.

### Notice

(3) The Director shall notify the licensee in writing of the imposition or amendment of the conditions.

### Contents of notice

(4) The notice shall set out the reasons for imposing or amending the conditions and shall state that the licensee is entitled to a hearing by the Tribunal if they request one in accordance with subsection 265 (2).

### Conditions take effect upon notice

(5) The imposition or amendment of conditions takes effect immediately upon the licensee's receipt of the notice and is not stayed by a request for a hearing by the Tribunal.

### Licensee must comply

(6) Every licensee shall comply with the conditions to which the licence is subject.

### Term of licence

**256.** (1) A licence shall be issued or renewed,

(a) for a term specified by the Director in accordance with the regulations; or

(b) if there are no regulations governing the term, for a term specified by the Director that does not exceed one year.

**Expiry at end of term**

(2)  A licence expires at the end of its term, unless it is deemed to continue under section 257.

**Revocation for cause**

(3)  Nothing in this section prevents a licence from being revoked or suspended.

**Continuation of licence pending renewal**

**257.**  Subject to a suspension under section 264, if a licensee has applied for renewal of a licence and paid the prescribed fee before the licence expires, the licence is deemed to continue,

(a)  until the renewal is granted; or

(b)  if the licensee is given notice that the Director proposes to revoke or refuse to renew the licence under section 262, until the time for requiring a hearing by the Tribunal has expired and, if a hearing is required, until the Tribunal has made its decision.

**Class of licence**

**258.**  A Director may assign a class to a licence in accordance with the regulations,

(a)  when issuing or renewing a licence; or

(b)  at any other time, if authorized by the regulations.

**Maximum number of children**

**259.**  (1)  On issuing or renewing a licence, a Director may set out in the licence the maximum number of children for whom residential care may be provided by the licensee in the children's residence or other place where residential care is provided.

**Changing maximum number**

(2)  A Director may at any time, but with notice to the licensee that is reasonable in the circumstances, change the maximum number of children set out in the licence.

**Licensee must comply**

(3)  A licensee shall not admit to the children's residence or other place where residential care is provided more children than the maximum number set out in the licence, unless the admission is approved by a Director for a specified period of time.

**Appeals of class or maximum number**

**260.**  If authorized by the regulations, a licensee may, in accordance with the regulations,

(a)  require a review by the Tribunal of,

(i)  the class assigned to a licence under section 258, or

(ii)  the maximum number of children set out in a licence under section 259; and

(b)  appeal the Tribunal's decision to the Divisional Court.

**Refusals and revocations**

**Proposal to refuse to issue**

**261.**  A Director may propose to refuse to issue a licence if, in the Director's opinion,

(a)  the applicant or an employee of the applicant, or where the applicant is a corporation, an officer or director of the corporation is not competent to operate a children's residence or to provide residential care, as the case may be, in a responsible manner in accordance with this Act, the regulations or any other applicable law;

(b)  the past conduct of any person mentioned in clause (a) affords reasonable grounds to believe that the operation of the children's residence or the provision of residential care will not be carried on in a responsible manner in accordance with this Act, the regulations or any other applicable law;

(c)  the premises in which the applicant proposes to operate the children's residence or to provide residential care do not comply with the requirements of this Part, the regulations or any other applicable law;

(d)  any person has made a false statement in the application for the licence, or in any report, document or other information required to be furnished by this Act or the regulations or any other applicable law;

(e)  a licence held by the applicant has been revoked or the renewal of such a licence has been refused and there has been no material change in the applicant's circumstances; or

(f)  a ground exists that is prescribed as a ground for refusing to issue a licence.

**Proposal to revoke or refuse to renew**

**262.**  A Director may propose to revoke or refuse to renew a licence if, in the Director's opinion,

(a)  the licensee or an employee of the licensee, or where the licensee is a corporation, an officer or director of the corporation has contravened or has knowingly permitted a person under their control or direction or associated with them to contravene,

(i)  this Act or the regulations,

(ii)  any other applicable law, or

(iii)  a condition of the licence;

(b)  the conduct of any person mentioned in clause (a) affords reasonable grounds to believe,

(i)  that the person is not competent to operate a children's residence or to provide residential care in a responsible manner in accordance with this Act, the regulations or any other applicable law, or

(ii)  that the children's residence or other place where residential care is provided is not being or will not be operated in accordance with this Act, the regulations or any other applicable law;

(c) the premises where the children's residence is located or the residential care is provided do not comply with the requirements of this Part, the regulations or any other applicable law;

(d) the operation of the children's residence or the provision of residential care is carried on in a manner that is prejudicial to the children's health, safety or welfare;

(e) any person has made a false statement in the application for the licence or for its renewal, or in a report or document required to be furnished by this Act or the regulations or any other applicable law;

(f) a change has occurred in the employees, officers or directors of the licensee that would, if the licensee were applying for the licence in the first instance, afford grounds under clause 261 (b) for refusing to issue the licence; or

(g) a ground exists that is prescribed as a ground for refusing to renew or for revoking a licence.

### Notice of proposal

**263.** (1) The Director shall notify the applicant or licensee, as the case may be, in writing if the Director proposes to,

(a) refuse to issue a licence under section 261; or

(b) revoke or refuse to renew a licence under section 262.

### Contents of notice

(2) The notice of proposal shall set out the reasons for the proposed action and shall state that the applicant or licensee is entitled to a hearing by the Tribunal if they request one in accordance with subsection 265 (2).

### Suspension

**264.** (1) A Director may suspend a licence if, in the Director's opinion, the manner in which the children's residence is operated or residential care is provided is an immediate threat to the health, safety or welfare of the children.

### Notice

(2) The Director shall notify the licensee in writing of the suspension.

### Contents of notice

(3) The notice shall set out the reasons for the suspension and shall state that the licensee is entitled to a hearing by the Tribunal if they request one in accordance with subsection 265 (2).

### Suspension takes effect upon notice

(4) A suspension takes effect immediately upon the licensee's receipt of the notice and is not stayed by a request for a hearing by the Tribunal.

### No application

(5) No person whose licence is suspended may apply to a Director for a licence during the suspension.

## Hearings by Tribunal

### Hearings by Tribunal

**265.** (1) An applicant or licensee to whom any of the following notices is given by a Director may request a hearing by the Tribunal in accordance with subsection (2):

1. A notice of proposal to refuse to issue a licence under section 261.
2. A notice of proposal to revoke or refuse to renew a licence under section 262.
3. A notice to impose or amend conditions on a licence under section 255.
4. A notice to suspend a licence under section 264.

### Request for hearing

(2) The applicant or licensee may request a hearing by giving a written request to the Director who gave the notice referred to in subsection (1), and to the Tribunal,

(a) in the case of a notice to impose or amend conditions on a licence, within 15 days after the person is given the notice; or

(b) in the case of all other notices, within 10 days after the person is given the notice.

### If hearing regarding proposal is not requested

(3) If an applicant or licensee to whom a notice of proposal to refuse to issue a licence or to revoke or refuse to renew a licence is given does not request a hearing in accordance with subsection (2), the Director may carry out the proposal.

### Hearing

(4) If an applicant or licensee requests a hearing in accordance with subsection (2), the Tribunal shall appoint a time for and hold a hearing.

### Powers of tribunal

(5) After holding the hearing, the Tribunal may by order,

(a) in the case of a proposal to refuse to issue a licence or to revoke or refuse to renew a licence,

(i) direct the Director to carry out the proposal, or

(ii) direct the Director to take such other action as the Tribunal considers appropriate, in accordance with this Part and the regulations;

(b) in the case of the imposition or amendment of conditions on a licence,

(i) confirm any or all of the conditions,

(ii) strike out any or all of the conditions, or

(iii) impose such other conditions as the Tribunal considers appropriate; or

(c) in the case of the suspension of a licence,

(i) confirm the suspension, or

(ii) direct the Director to take such other action as the Tribunal considers appropriate, in accordance with this Part and the regulations.

**Discretion of tribunal**

(6) In making an order under clause (5) (a) or (c), the Tribunal may substitute its opinion for that of the Director.

**Rules for proceedings**

**Parties**

**266.** (1) The following persons are parties to a proceeding under this Part:

1. The applicant or licensee requiring the hearing.
2. The Director.
3. Any other person specified by the Tribunal.

**Members with prior involvement**

(2) A member of the Tribunal who has taken part, before a hearing, in any investigation or consideration of its subject matter that relates to the applicant or licensee shall not take part in the hearing.

**Discussion of subject matter of hearing**

(3) A member of the Tribunal who takes part in a hearing shall not communicate with any person, except another member, a lawyer who is not the lawyer of any party, or an employee of the Tribunal, about the subject matter of the hearing, unless all parties are notified and given an opportunity to participate.

**When Tribunal seeks independent legal advice**

(4) The Tribunal may seek independent legal advice about the subject matter of a hearing and, if it does so, shall disclose the nature of the advice to the parties to enable them to respond.

**Examination of documentary evidence**

(5) A party to a proceeding under this Part shall be given an opportunity, before the hearing, to examine any written or documentary evidence that will be produced and any report whose contents will be given in evidence at the hearing.

**Only members at entire hearing to participate in decision**

(6) No member of the Tribunal shall participate in a decision of the Tribunal under this Part unless the member was present throughout the hearing and heard the evidence and arguments of the parties.

**All members at hearing to participate in decision**

(7) Unless the parties consent, the Tribunal shall not make a decision under this Part unless all the members who were present at the hearing participate in the decision.

**Final decision of Tribunal within 90 days**

(8) Despite section 21 of the *Statutory Powers Procedure Act*, the Tribunal shall make a final decision and notify the parties of it within 90 days after the day the Tribunal receives the applicant's or licensee's request for a hearing under subsection 265 (2) of this Act.

**Appeals**

**Appeal from Tribunal**

**267.** (1) Any party to a hearing before the Tribunal under this Part may appeal from the Tribunal's decision to the Divisional Court.

**Record to be filed in the court**

(2) If notice of an appeal is served under this section, the Tribunal shall promptly file with the court the record of the proceeding in which the decision appealed from was made.

**Minister entitled to be heard**

(3) The Minister, represented by a lawyer or otherwise, is entitled to be heard on the argument of an appeal under this section.

**Amount Charged by Licensee**

**Amount**

**268.** (1) A licensee shall charge the amount set out in or determined in accordance with the regulations for the provision of residential care under the authority of a licence.

**Exemption**

(2) A regulation may exempt a licensee or class of licensees from subsection (1) and may prescribe conditions and circumstances for any such exemption.

**Licensee Ceasing to Operate, etc.**

**Licence and records to be delivered**

**269.** If a licence is revoked or renewal of it refused, or if a licensee ceases to operate a children's residence or to provide residential care, the licensee shall,

(a) promptly deliver the licence to the Minister; and

(b) deliver all the records in the licensee's possession or control that relate to the children to whom services were being provided to a prescribed person or entity within the prescribed time.

**Notice to placing agency or other person; removal of children**

**270.** If a licence is revoked or suspended or renewal of it refused, or if a licensee ceases to operate a children's residence or to provide residential care,

(a) the licensee shall promptly notify, in writing, every placing agency or person who has a child placed in the children's residence or other place where residential care is provided of the revocation, suspension, refusal or cessation; and

(b) the placing agency or person who placed a child shall arrange for the child's removal from the residence or other place as soon as is practicable, having regard to the child's best interests, and the Minister may assist in finding an alternative placement for the child.

### Occupation by Minister and Injunctions
### Order for Minister's occupation

**271.** (1) If a Director's notice of proposal to revoke or refuse to renew a licence under clause 263 (1) (b) or notice of suspension under subsection 264 (2) has been given to a licensee and the matter has not yet been finally disposed of, the Minister may apply without notice to the Superior Court of Justice for an order,

    (a) authorizing the Minister or a person appointed by the Minister, pending the outcome of the proceeding and until alternative accommodation may be found for the children who are being cared for, to,

        (i) occupy and operate the children's residence or the other premises where residential care is provided, or

        (ii) provide the residential care, directly or indirectly; and

    (b) directing a peace officer to assist the Minister or a person appointed by the Minister as may be necessary in occupying the premises under subclause (a) (i).

### Where court may make order

(2) The court may make an order referred to in subsection (1) where it is satisfied that the health, safety or welfare of the children being cared for require it.

### Interim management

(3) If an order described in subclause (1) (a) (i) has been made, the Minister or the person appointed by the Minister may, despite sections 25 and 39 of the *Expropriations Act*, immediately occupy and operate or arrange for the occupation and operation of the premises for a period not exceeding six months.

### Injunction

**272.** (1) A Director may apply to the Superior Court of Justice for an order enjoining any person from,

    (a) contravening section 244 (licence required); or

    (b) operating a children's residence or providing residential care while the licence is suspended under section 264.

### Variance or discharge

(2) Any person may apply to the court for an order varying or discharging an order made under subsection (1).

### Residential Licensing Inspections
### Appointment of inspectors

**273.** (1) The Minister may appoint inspectors for the purposes of this Part.

### Director is an inspector

(2) A Director is, by virtue of their office, an inspector.

### Powers and duties

(3) An inspector shall have the powers and duties set out in this Part and such other powers and duties as may be prescribed.

### Restrictions

(4) The Minister may restrict an inspector's powers of entry and inspection to specified premises.

### Certificate of appointment

(5) The Minister shall issue to every inspector a certificate of appointment which the inspector shall produce, on request, when exercising the powers or performing the duties of an inspector.

### Purpose of inspection

**274.** An inspector shall conduct inspections for the purpose of determining compliance with this Act, the regulations and the directives.

### Inspections without warrant

**275.** An inspector may, at any reasonable time and without a warrant or notice, enter and inspect,

    (a) the business premises of a licensee;

    (b) the premises of a children's residence;

    (c) a premises, other than a children's residence, where residential care is provided under the authority of a licence; or

    (d) a premises where the inspector suspects on reasonable grounds that residential care is provided without the authority of a licence, where a licence is required under this Part.

### Powers on inspection

**276.** (1) An inspector conducting an inspection may,

    (a) examine the services provided;

    (b) examine a record or other thing that is relevant to the inspection;

    (c) demand the production for inspection of a record or other thing that is relevant to the inspection, including a record or other thing that is not kept on the premises;

    (d) on issuing a written receipt, remove for review or copying a record or other thing that is relevant to the inspection;

    (e) in order to produce a record in readable form, use data storage, information processing or retrieval devices or systems that are normally used in carrying on business at the premises;

    (f) photograph, film or make any other kind of recording that is relevant to the inspection, including of a child or other person at the premises, but only in a manner that does not intercept any private communications and that is in keeping with reasonable expectations of privacy;

    (g) question a person, including a child, on matters relevant to the inspection;

    (h) call upon experts for assistance in carrying out the inspection; and

    (i) exercise any other prescribed power.

### Demand

(2) A demand that a record or other thing be produced for inspection may be made orally or in writing and must indicate,

(a) the nature of the record or thing required; and

(b) when the record or thing is to be produced.

### Obligation to produce and assist

(3) If an inspector demands that a record or other thing be produced for inspection, the person having custody of the record or other thing shall produce it for the inspector within the time provided for in the demand, and shall, on the inspector's demand,

(a) provide whatever assistance is reasonably necessary to produce the record or thing in readable form, including using a data storage, processing or retrieval device or system; and

(b) provide whatever assistance is reasonably necessary to interpret the record or thing for the inspector.

### Child's right to refuse

(4) Despite clause (1) (g), a child may refuse to be questioned by an inspector.

### Child's right to meet with inspector

(5) An inspector shall meet privately with a child who is receiving residential care in the place being inspected, if the child requests such a meeting.

### Power to exclude persons

(6) An inspector who questions a person under clause (1) (g) may exclude from questioning any person except a lawyer for the person being questioned.

### Return of things

(7) A record or other thing that has been removed for review or copying,

(a) shall be made available to the person from whom it was removed on request and at a time and place that are convenient for the person and the inspector; and

(b) shall be returned to the person within a reasonable time.

### Warrant

**277.** (1) An inspector may, without notice, apply to a justice for a warrant under this section.

### Issuance of warrant

(2) A justice may issue a warrant authorizing an inspector named in the warrant to enter the premises specified in the warrant, and to exercise any of the powers mentioned in subsection 276 (1), if the justice is satisfied on information under oath or affirmation,

(a) that the premises,

(i) is the business premises of a licensee,

(ii) is a children's residence,

(iii) is a place, other than a children's residence, where residential care is provided under the authority of a licence, or

(iv) is a place where the inspector suspects on reasonable grounds that residential care is provided without the authority of a licence, where a licence is required under this Part; and

(b) that,

(i) the inspector has been prevented from exercising a right of entry to the premises under section 275 or a power under subsection 276 (1), or

(ii) there are reasonable grounds to believe that the inspector will be prevented from exercising a right of entry to the premises under section 275 or a power under subsection 276 (1).

### Dwellings

(3) The power to enter a premises described in clause (2) (a) with a warrant shall not be exercised to enter a premises that is used as a dwelling, except if,

(a) the justice is informed that the warrant is being sought to authorize entry into a dwelling; and

(b) the justice authorizes the entry into the dwelling.

### Expert help

(4) The warrant may authorize persons who have special, expert or professional knowledge to accompany and assist the inspector in the execution of the warrant.

### Expiry of warrant

(5) A warrant issued under this section shall name a date on which it expires, which shall be no later than 30 days after the warrant is issued.

### Extension of time

(6) A justice may extend the date on which a warrant issued under this section expires for an additional period of no more than 30 days, upon application without notice by the inspector named in the warrant.

### Use of force

(7) An inspector named in a warrant issued under this section may use whatever force is necessary to execute the warrant and may call upon a peace officer for assistance in executing the warrant.

### Time of execution

(8) A warrant issued under this section may be executed between 8 a.m. and 8 p.m. only, unless the warrant specifies otherwise.

### Other matters

(9) Subsections 276 (2) to (7) apply, with necessary modifications, with respect to the exercise of powers referred to in subsection (2) under a warrant issued under this section.

### Definition

(10)  In this section,

"justice" means a provincial judge or a justice of the peace.

### Inspection report

**278.** (1)  After completing an inspection, an inspector shall prepare an inspection report and give a copy of the report to,

(a)  a Director;

(b)  the licensee; and

(c)  any other prescribed person.

### All non-compliance to be documented

(2)  If an inspector finds that a licensee has not complied with a requirement of this Act, the regulations or a directive, the inspector shall document the non-compliance in the inspection report.

### Admissibility of certain documents

**279.**  A copy made under subsection 276 (1) that purports to be certified by the inspector as being a true copy of the original is admissible in evidence in any proceeding to the same extent as, and has the same evidentiary value as, the original.

## Offences

### Offences

**280.** (1)  A person is guilty of an offence if the person,

(a)  contravenes subsection 244 (1) (licence required);

(b)  contravenes section 245 (prohibition—past offence);

(c)  contravenes section 246 (prohibition—holding out as licensed);

(d)  contravenes subsection 259 (3) (licensee must comply with maximum number of children);

(e)  contravenes clause 269 (b) (records to be delivered);

(f)  causes a child to be cared for in a children's residence operated by a person who is not licensed, or in another place where residential care is provided by a person who is required to be but is not licensed to provide residential care;

(g)  is a child's parent or a person under a legal duty to provide for the child and permits the child to be cared for in a children's residence or other place referred to in clause (f);

(h)  fails to comply with an order or direction made by a court under this Part;

(i)  contravenes any other provision of this Act or the regulations prescribed for the purposes of this subsection.

### Penalty

(2)  A person convicted of an offence under subsection (1) is liable to,

(a)  a fine of not more than $1,000 for each day on which the offence continues or imprisonment for a term of not more than one year or both, in the case of an individual; or

(b)  a fine of not more than $1,000 for each day on which the offence continues, if the person is not an individual.

### Offence—obstruction of inspector, false information, etc.

(3)  A person is guilty of an offence if the person,

(a)  hinders, obstructs, or interferes with an inspector conducting an inspection under this Part, or otherwise impedes an inspector in exercising the powers or performing the duties of an inspector under this Part.

(b)  knowingly provides false information in an application under this Part or in a statement, report or return required to be provided under this Part or the regulations; or

(c)  contravenes any other provision of this Act or the regulations prescribed for the purposes of this subsection.

### Penalty

(4)  A person convicted of an offence under subsection (3) is liable to a fine of not more than $5,000.

### Limitation

(5)  A proceeding in respect of an offence under subsection (1) or (3) shall not be commenced more than two years after the day on which evidence of the offence first came to the knowledge of the Director or inspector.

### Directors, officers and employees

(6)  If a corporation commits an offence under this section, a director, officer or employee of the corporation who authorized, permitted or concurred in the commission of the offence is also guilty of the offence.

## PART X    PERSONAL INFORMATION
### Definitions

### Definitions

**281.**  In this Part,

"Assistant Commissioner" means an Assistant Commissioner appointed under the *Freedom of Information and Protection of Privacy Act*; ("commissaire adjoint")

"capable" means able to understand the information that is relevant to deciding whether to consent to the collection, use or disclosure of personal information and able to appreciate the reasonably foreseeable consequences of giving, withholding or withdrawing the consent and "capacity" has a corresponding meaning; ("capable")

"Commissioner" means the Information and Privacy Commissioner appointed under the *Freedom of Information and Protection of Privacy Act*; ("commissaire")

"incapable" means not capable, and "incapacity" has a corresponding meaning; ("incapable")

"information practices" means the policy or policies respecting the collection, use, modification, disclosure, retention or disposal of personal information and the administrative, technical and physical safeguards and practices that the service provider maintains with respect to the information; ("pratiques relatives aux renseignements")

"proceeding" includes a proceeding held in, before or under the rules of a court, a tribunal, a commission, a justice of the peace, a coroner, a committee of a College within the meaning of the *Regulated Health Professions Act, 1991*, a committee of the Ontario College of Social Workers and Social Service Workers under the *Social Work and Social Service Work Act, 1998*, an arbitrator or a mediator; ("instance")

"service" means a service or program that is provided or funded under this Act or provided under the authority of a licence; ("service")

"service provider" includes a lead agency designated under section 30; ("fournisseur de services")

"substitute decision-maker" means a person who is authorized under this Part to consent, withhold or withdraw consent on behalf of an individual to the collection, use or disclosure of personal information about the individual. ("mandataire spécial")

### Confidentiality provisions prevail

**282.** Subsections 87 (8), (9) and (10) and 134 (11) prevail over this Part.

> Note: On a day to be named by proclamation of the Lieutenant Governor, section 282 of the Act is amended by striking out "and 134 (11)". (See: 2017, c. 14, Sched. 3, s. 11)

### Minister's Powers to Collect, Use and Disclose Personal Information

### Collection, use and disclosure of personal information by the Minister

### Collection of personal information

**283.** (1) The Minister may collect personal information, directly or indirectly, for purposes related to the following matters, and may use it for those purposes:

1. Administering this Act and the regulations.
2. Determining compliance with this Act and the regulations.
3. Planning, managing or delivering services that the Ministry provides or funds, in whole or in part, allocating resources to any of them, evaluating or monitoring any of them or detecting, monitoring and preventing fraud or any unauthorized receipt of services or benefits related to any of them.
4. Conducting risk management and error management activities in respect of the services that the Ministry provides or funds, in whole or in part.
5. Conducting activities to improve or maintain the quality of the services that the Ministry provides or funds, in whole or in part.

6. Conducting research and analysis that relate to children and their families, including longitudinal studies, by or on behalf of the Ministry that relate to,
   i. a service,
   ii. the transition of children and their families between and out of services, including the resulting outcomes, or
   iii. programs that support the learning, development, health and well-being of children and their families, including programs provided or funded in whole or in part by the Ministry or any other ministry of the Government of Ontario.

### Personal information required by Minister

(2) The Minister may require any of the following persons to disclose to the Minister such personal information as is reasonably necessary for the purposes described in subsection (1):

1. A service provider.
2. Any other prescribed person who has information that is relevant to any of the purposes described in subsection (1).

### Information other than personal information

(3) The Minister shall not collect, use or disclose personal information if other information will serve the purpose of the collection, use or disclosure.

### Personal information limited to what is reasonably necessary

(4) The Minister shall not collect, use or disclose more personal information than is reasonably necessary to meet the purpose of the collection, use or disclosure.

### Sharing with other ministers

(5) The Minister and other ministers of the Crown in right of Ontario who may be prescribed may disclose personal information to and indirectly collect personal information from each other for the purposes set out in paragraphs 3 and 6 of subsection (1).

### Deemed compliance

(6) For the purpose of clause 42 (1) (e) of the *Freedom of Information and Protection of Privacy Act*, clause 32 (e) of the *Municipal Freedom of Information and Protection of Privacy Act* or clause 43 (1) (h) of the *Personal Health Information Protection Act, 2004*, a disclosure of personal information by an institution or a health information custodian, within the meaning of those Acts, under subsection (2) or (5) is deemed to be for the purposes of complying with this Act.

### Personal information for research

(7) The collection, use or disclosure of personal information to conduct research and analysis described in paragraph 6 of subsection (1) is subject to any requirements and restrictions that may be prescribed.

### Notice required by s. 39 (2) of FIPPA

(8) If the Minister collects personal information indirectly under subsection (1), the notice required by subsection 39 (2) of the *Freedom of Information and Protection of Privacy Act* may be given by,

    (a) a public notice posted on a government of Ontario website; or

    (b) any other method that may be prescribed.

### Information requested by Minister
### Collection of information by service providers

**284.** (1) The Minister may request that a service provider collect information, including personal information, directly from the individuals to whom it provides a service as is reasonably necessary for a prescribed purpose that is consistent with a purpose described in subsection 283 (1) and, upon being so requested, a service provider shall collect the information directly from the individuals.

### Disclosure to Minister

(2) A service provider shall disclose the information collected under subsection (1) to the Minister within the time period and in the form and manner specified by the Minister.

### Notice required by s. 39 (2) of FIPPA

(3) If the Minister collects personal information indirectly under subsection (1), the notice required by subsection 39 (2) of the *Freedom of Information and Protection of Privacy Act* may be given by,

    (a) a public notice posted on a government of Ontario website; or

    (b) any other method that may be prescribed.

### Notice to and by service providers

(4) The Minister shall advise a service provider that collected personal information under subsection (1) of the notice referred to in subsection (3) and the service provider shall advise the individual to whom it provides a service of the information set out in the notice in the form and manner specified by the Minister.

### Collection, Use and Disclosure of Personal Information by Service Providers
### Application of Part

**285.** (1) Subject to subsections (2), (3), (4), (5) and (7), sections 286 to 332 apply to the collection, use and disclosure of personal information by a service provider.

### Exceptions—where other Acts apply to an institution

(2) Sections 286 to 292 and 306 to 332 do not apply to an institution within the meaning of the *Freedom of Information and Protection of Privacy Act* or the *Municipal Freedom of Information and Protection of Privacy Act*.

### Exceptions—where other Acts apply to a health information custodian

(3) Sections 286 to 292 and 295 to 332 do not apply to a health information custodian within the meaning of the *Personal Health Information Protection Act, 2004* in respect of the collection, use or disclosure of personal health information.

### Exceptions—adoption matters

(4) Sections 286 to 332 do not apply to,

    (a) the use or disclosure under section 227 by a licensee or a society of information that relates to an adoption; or

    (b) the collection, use or disclosure of information given to a designated custodian under section 224 or to another person under section 225.

### Exceptions—other matters

(5) Sections 286 to 332 do not apply to,

    (a) records in the register maintained under subsection 133 (5);

    (b) records to which subsection 130 (6) or (8) apply;

    (c) reports for which an order was made under subsection 163 (6).

> **Note: On a day to be named by proclamation of the Lieutenant Governor, subsection 285 (5) of the Act is repealed and the following substituted: (See: 2017, c. 14, Sched. 3, s. 12)**

### Exceptions—other matters

(5) Sections 286 to 332 do not apply to,

    (a) records to which subsection 130 (6) or (8) apply; or

    (b) reports for which an order was made under subsection 163 (6). 2017, c. 14, Sched. 3, s. 12.

### Service provider's records

(6) Except if this Act or its regulations provide otherwise, this Part applies to any record in the custody or under the control of a service provider regardless of whether it was recorded before or after this Part comes into force.

### Where disclosure is prohibited under federal law

(7) For greater certainty, nothing in this Part permits or requires the disclosure of information whose disclosure is prohibited under the *Criminal Code* (Canada), the *Youth Criminal Justice Act* (Canada) or any other law of Canada.

### Collection, use and disclosure of personal information—requirement for consent

**286.** A service provider shall not collect personal information about an individual for the purpose of providing a service or use or disclose that information unless,

    (a) the service provider has the individual's consent under this Act and the collection, use or disclosure, to the best of the service provider's knowledge, is necessary for a lawful purpose; or

(b) the collection, use or disclosure without the individual's consent is permitted or required by this Act.

## Collection, use and disclosure of information other than personal information

**287.** (1) A service provider shall not collect personal information for the purposes of providing a service or use or disclose that personal information if other information will serve the purpose of the collection, use or disclosure.

## Collection, use and disclosure of personal information limited to what is reasonably necessary

(2) For the purposes of providing a service, a service provider shall not collect, use or disclose more personal information than is reasonably necessary to provide the service.

## Exception

(3) This section does not apply to personal information that a service provider is required by law to collect, use or disclose.

## Indirect collection of personal information
### With consent

**288.** (1) A service provider may collect personal information indirectly for the purpose of providing a service if the individual to whom the information relates consents to the collection being made indirectly.

### Without consent

(2) A service provider may collect personal information indirectly for the purpose of providing a service and without the consent of the individual to whom the information relates if,

(a) the information to be collected is reasonably necessary to provide a service or to assess, reduce or eliminate a risk of serious harm to a person or group of persons and it is not reasonably possible to collect personal information directly from the individual,

(i) that can reasonably be relied on as accurate and complete, or

(ii) in a timely manner;

(b) the information is to be collected by a society from another society or from a child welfare authority outside of Ontario and the information is reasonably necessary to assess, reduce or eliminate a risk of harm to a child;

(c) the information is to be collected by a society and the information is reasonably necessary for a prescribed purpose related to a society's functions under subsection 35 (1);

(d) the indirect collection of information is authorized by the Commissioner; or

(e) subject to the requirements and restrictions, if any, that are prescribed, the indirect collection of information is permitted or required by law or by a treaty, agreement or arrangement made under an Act or an Act of Canada.

## Direct collection without consent

**289.** A service provider may collect personal information directly from the individual to whom the information relates, even if the individual is not capable, if,

(a) the collection is reasonably necessary for the provision of a service and it is not reasonably possible to obtain consent in a timely manner;

(b) the collection is reasonably necessary to assess, reduce or eliminate a risk of serious harm to a person or group of persons; or

(c) the service provider is a society and the information is reasonably necessary to assess, reduce or eliminate a risk of harm to a child.

## Notice to individual re use or disclosure of information

**290.** Where a service provider collects personal information directly from an individual, the service provider shall give the individual notice that the information may be used or disclosed in accordance with this Part.

## Permitted use

**291.** (1) A service provider may use personal information collected for the purpose of providing a service,

(a) for the purpose for which the information was collected or created and for all the functions reasonably necessary for carrying out that purpose, including providing the information to an officer, employee, consultant or agent of the service provider, but not if the information was collected with the consent of the individual or under clause 288 (2) (a) and the individual expressly instructs otherwise;

(b) if the service provider believes on reasonable grounds that the use is reasonably necessary to assess, reduce or eliminate a risk of serious harm to a person or group of persons;

(c) for a purpose for which this Act, another Act or an Act of Canada permits or requires a person to disclose it to the service provider;

(d) for planning, managing or delivering services that the service provider provides or funds, in whole or in part, allocating resources to any of them, evaluating or monitoring any of them or detecting, monitoring or preventing fraud or any unauthorized receipt of services or benefits related to any of them;

(e) for the purpose of risk management and error management activities;

(f) for the purpose of activities to improve or maintain the quality of a service;

(g) for the purpose of disposing of the information or modifying the information in order to conceal the identity of the individual;

(h) for the purpose of seeking the individual's consent, or the consent of the individual's substitute-decision maker, when the personal information used by the service provider for this purpose is limited to the name and contact information of the individual and the name and contact information of the substitute decision-maker, where applicable;

(i) for the purpose of a proceeding or contemplated proceeding in which the service provider or an officer, employee, agent or former officer, employee or agent of the service provider is, or is expected to be, a party or witness, if the information relates to or is a matter in issue in the proceeding or contemplated proceeding;

(j) for research conducted by the service provider, subject to the requirements and restrictions, if any, that may be prescribed; or

(k) subject to the requirements and restrictions, if any, that are prescribed, if permitted or required by law or by a treaty, agreement or arrangement made under an Act or an Act of Canada.

### Exception

(2) Despite clause (1) (a), where the individual to whom the personal information relates expressly instructs otherwise,

(a) a society may nonetheless use that personal information,

(i) if it is reasonably necessary to assess, reduce or eliminate a risk of harm to a child, or

(ii) for a prescribed purpose related to a society's functions under subsection 35 (1); and

(b) a service provider may nonetheless use that personal information if it is reasonably necessary to assess, reduce or eliminate a risk of serious harm to a person or group of persons.

### Disclosure without consent

**292.** (1) A service provider may, without the consent of the individual, disclose personal information about an individual that has been collected for the purpose of providing a service,

(a) to a law enforcement agency in Canada to aid an investigation undertaken with a view to a law enforcement proceeding or to allow the agency to determine whether to undertake such an investigation;

(b) to a proposed litigation guardian or legal representative of the individual for the purpose of having the person appointed as such;

(c) to a litigation guardian or legal representative who is authorized under the Rules of Civil Procedure, or by a court order, to commence, defend or continue a proceeding on behalf of the individual or to represent the individual in a proceeding;

(d) for the purpose of contacting a relative, member of the extended family, friend or potential substitute decision-maker of the individual, if the individual is injured, incapacitated or otherwise not capable;

(e) for the purpose of contacting a relative, member of the extended family or friend of the individual if the individual is deceased;

(f) subject to section 294, for the purpose of complying with,

(i) a summons, order or similar requirement issued in a proceeding by a person having jurisdiction to compel the production of information, or

(ii) a procedural rule that relates to the production of information in a proceeding;

(g) if the service provider believes on reasonable grounds that the disclosure is necessary to assess, reduce or eliminate a risk of serious harm to a person or group of persons; or

(h) if permitted or required by law or by a treaty, agreement or arrangement made under an Act or an Act of Canada, subject to the requirements and restrictions, if any, that are prescribed.

### To assess, etc. risk of harm to a child

(2) A society may disclose to another society or to a child welfare authority outside Ontario personal information that has been collected for the purpose of providing a service if the information is reasonably necessary to assess, reduce or eliminate a risk of harm to a child.

### For a prescribed purpose related to society's functions

(3) A society may disclose personal information that has been collected for the purpose of providing a service if the information is reasonably necessary for a prescribed purpose related to a society's functions under subsection 35 (1).

### Definition

(4) In this section,

"law enforcement" has the same meaning as in subsection 2 (1) of the *Freedom of Information and Protection of Privacy Act*.

### Disclosure for planning and managing services, etc.
### Disclosure to prescribed entity

**293.** (1) A service provider may disclose personal information collected by the service provider under the authority of this Act to a prescribed entity for the purposes of analysis or compiling statistical information with respect to the management of, evaluation or monitoring of services, the allocation of resources to or planning for those services, including their delivery, if the prescribed entity meets the requirements under subsection (5).

### Disclosure to other person or entity

(2) A service provider may, subject to the prescribed requirements and restrictions, disclose personal information collected by the service provider under the authority of this Act to a person or entity that is not a prescribed entity for the purposes described in subsection (1) and a person or entity to whom a service provider discloses personal information under this subsection shall comply with any prescribed requirements and restrictions with respect to the use, security, disclosure, return or disposal of the information.

### Minister may require disclosure

(3) The Minister may require a service provider to disclose information, including personal information, to a prescribed entity, if the prescribed entity meets the requirements under subsection (5), or to a person or entity that is not a prescribed entity, for the purposes described in subsection (1) and a person or entity, including a prescribed entity, to whom a service provider discloses information under this subsection shall comply with any prescribed requirements and restrictions with respect to the use, security, disclosure, return or disposal of the information.

### Exception

(4) Subsections (1), (2) and (3) do not apply to prescribed information in prescribed circumstances.

### Requirements for prescribed entity

(5) A service provider may disclose personal information to a prescribed entity under subsection (1) or (3) if,

(a) the prescribed entity has in place practices and procedures to protect the privacy of the individuals whose personal information it receives and to maintain the confidentiality of the information; and

(b) the Commissioner has approved the practices and procedures.

### Exception

(6) Despite clause (5) (b), a service provider may disclose personal information to a prescribed entity under subsection (1) or (3) before the first anniversary of the day this section comes into force even if the Commissioner has not approved its practices and procedures.

### Review of practices and procedures by Commissioner

(7) The Commissioner shall review the practices and procedures of each prescribed entity every three years after they were first approved and advise the service provider whether the prescribed entity continues to meet the requirements of subsection (5).

### Prescribed entity or other person or entity may collect personal information

(8) A prescribed entity or a person or entity that is not a prescribed entity is authorized to collect the personal information that a service provider may disclose to it under subsection (1), (2) or (3).

### Use and disclosure of personal information by prescribed entity, other person or entity

(9) Subject to the exceptions and additional requirements, if any, that are prescribed, a prescribed entity or a person or entity that is not a prescribed entity that receives personal information under subsection (1), (2) or (3) shall not use the information except for the purposes for which it received the information and shall not disclose the information except as required by law.

### Deemed compliance

(10) For the purpose of clause 42 (1) (e) of the *Freedom of Information and Protection of Privacy Act*, clause 32 (e) of the *Municipal Freedom of Information and Protection of Privacy Act* or clause 43 (1) (h) of the *Personal Health Information Protection Act, 2004*, a disclosure of personal information by an institution or a health information custodian, within the meaning of those Acts, under this section is deemed to be for the purposes of complying with this Act.

## Records of mental disorders
### Definitions

**294.** (1) In this section,

"court" includes the Divisional Court; ("tribunal")

"record of a mental disorder" means a record or a part of a record made about an individual concerning a substantial disorder of the individual's emotional processes, thought or cognition which grossly impairs the individual's capacity to make reasoned judgments. ("dossier relatif à un trouble mental")

### Disclosure pursuant to summons, etc.

(2) A service provider shall disclose, transmit or permit the examination of a record of a mental disorder pursuant to a summons, order, direction, notice or similar requirement in respect of a matter in issue or that may be in issue in a court or other body unless a physician states in writing that the physician believes that to do so,

(a) is likely to detrimentally affect the treatment or recovery of the individual to whom the record relates; or

(b) is likely to result in,

(i) injury to the mental condition of another individual, or

(ii) bodily harm to another individual.

### Court or body to determine whether to disclose

(3) Where the disclosure, transmittal or examination of a record of a mental disorder is required by a court or body before which a matter is in issue, the court or body shall determine whether the record referred to in the physician's statement should be disclosed, transmitted or examined.

### Hearing

(4) Before making a determination under subsection (3), the court or body shall give notice to the physician and, if the

court or body holds a hearing to determine whether the record should be disclosed, transmitted or examined, it shall be held in the absence of the public.

### Matters to be considered

(5) In making a determination under subsection (3), the court or body shall consider whether or not the disclosure, transmittal or examination of the record of a mental disorder referred to in the physician's statement is likely to have a result described in clause (2) (a) or (b) and, for that purpose, the court or body may examine the record.

### Order

(6) The court or body shall not order that the record of a mental disorder referred to in the physician's statement be disclosed, transmitted or examined if the court or body is satisfied that a result described in clause (2) (a) or (b) is likely, unless satisfied that to do so is essential in the interests of justice.

### Conflict

(7) Subsections (2) to (6) apply despite anything in the *Personal Health Information Protection Act, 2004*.

### Return of record to service provider

(8) Where a record of a mental disorder is ordered to be disclosed, transmitted or examined under this section, the clerk of the court or body in which it is admitted in evidence or, if not so admitted, the person to whom the record is transmitted, shall return the record to the service provider as soon as possible after the determination of the matter in issue in respect of which the record was required.

## Consent

### Elements of consent for collection, use and disclosure of personal information

**295.** (1) If this Act or any other Act requires the consent of an individual to the collection, use or disclosure of personal information by a service provider, the consent,

(a) must be a consent of the individual;

(b) must be knowledgeable;

(c) must relate to the information; and

(d) must not be obtained through deception or coercion.

### Implied consent for collection and use

(2) A consent to the collection and use of personal information may be implied if the collection is made directly from the individual to whom the information relates and is collected for the purpose of providing a service.

### Consent may be written or oral

(3) A consent may be written or oral, but an oral consent may be relied on only if the service provider that obtains the consent makes a written record that sets out the following information:

1. The name of the individual who gave the consent.
2. The information to which the consent relates.
3. The manner in which the notice of purposes required by subsection (5) was provided to the individual.

### Knowledgeable consent

(4) A consent to the collection, use or disclosure of personal information is knowledgeable if it is reasonable in the circumstances to believe that the individual to whom the information relates knows,

(a) the purposes of the collection, use or disclosure; and

(b) that the individual may give, withhold or withdraw consent.

### Notice of purposes

(5) Unless it is not reasonable in the circumstances, an individual is deemed to know the purposes of the collection, use or disclosure of personal information about the individual if the service provider,

(a) posts a notice describing the purposes where it is likely to come to the individual's attention;

(b) makes such a notice readily available to the individual;

(c) gives the individual a copy of such notice; or

(d) otherwise communicates the content of such notice to the individual.

### Transition

(6) A consent that an individual gives, before the day that subsection (1) comes into force, to a collection, use or disclosure of personal information is a valid consent if it meets the requirements of this section for consent.

### Withdrawal of consent

**296.** A consent may be withdrawn by the individual who gave the consent by providing notice to the service provider, but the withdrawal of the consent shall not have retroactive effect.

### Conditional consent

**297.** If an individual places a condition on their consent to the collection, use or disclosure of personal information, the condition is not effective to the extent that it purports to prohibit or restrict the making of any record of personal information by a service provider that is required by law or by established standards of professional or institutional practice.

### Presumption of consent's validity

**298.** A service provider that has obtained an individual's consent to the collection, use or disclosure of personal information about the individual or who has received a copy of a document purporting to be a record of the individual's consent, may presume that the consent fulfils the requirements of this Act and that the individual has not withdrawn it, unless it is not reasonable to do so.

### Capacity and Substitute Decision-Making
### Presumption of capacity

**299.** An individual is presumed to be capable, and a service provider may rely on this presumption unless the service provider has reasonable grounds to believe that the individual is not capable.

### Differing capacity
### Re different information

**300.** (1) An individual may be capable with respect to some parts of personal information, but incapable with respect to other parts.

### At different times

(2) An individual may be capable at one time, but incapable at another time.

### Substitute decision-maker

**301.** (1) An individual who is capable may give, withhold or withdraw consent or may, if the individual is 16 or older, authorize in writing another individual who is 16 or older and capable to be the individual's substitute decision-maker.

### For child younger than 16

(2) If the individual is a child younger than 16, the child's parent or a society or other person who is authorized to give, withhold or withdraw consent in the place of the parent may be the child's substitute decision-maker unless the information relates to,

(a) treatment about which the child has made a decision in accordance with the *Health Care Consent Act, 1996*; or

(b) counselling to which the child has consented on their own under this Act or the old Act.

### Capable child prevails over substitute decision-maker

(3) If the individual is a child younger than 16 who is capable and if there is a person who is authorized to act as the substitute decision-maker of the child under subsection (2), a decision of the child to give, withhold or withdraw the consent prevails over a conflicting decision by the substitute decision-maker.

### Person authorized under *PHIPA* may be substitute decision-maker

(4) Where an individual is not capable of consenting to the collection, use or disclosure of personal information, a person who would be authorized to consent to the collection, use or disclosure of personal health information on the individual's behalf under the *Personal Health Information Protection Act, 2004* may be the individual's substitute decision-maker.

### Factors to consider for consent

**302.** (1) A person who consents under this Part on behalf of or in the place of an individual to a collection, use or disclosure of personal information by a service provider, who withholds or withdraws such a consent or who provides an express instruction under clause 291 (1) (a) shall take into consideration,

(a) the wishes, values and beliefs that,

(i) if the individual is capable, the person knows the individual holds and believes the individual would want reflected in decisions made concerning the individual's personal information, or

(ii) if the individual is incapable or deceased, the person knows the individual held when capable or alive and believes the individual would have wanted reflected in decisions made concerning the individual's personal information;

(b) whether the benefits that the person expects from the collection, use or disclosure of the information outweigh the risk of negative consequences occurring as a result of the collection, use or disclosure;

(c) whether the purpose for which the collection, use or disclosure is sought can be accomplished without the collection, use or disclosure; and

(d) whether the collection, use or disclosure is necessary to satisfy any legal obligation.

### Determination of compliance

(2) If a substitute decision-maker, on behalf of an incapable individual, gives, withholds or withdraws a consent to a collection, use or disclosure of personal information about the individual by a service provider or provides an express instruction under clause 291 (1) (a) and if the service provider is of the opinion that the substitute decision-maker has not complied with subsection (1), the service provider may apply to a body prescribed for the purposes of this section for a determination as to whether the substitute decision-maker complied with that subsection.

### Deemed application concerning capacity

(3) An application to a body prescribed under subsection (2) is deemed to include an application to a prescribed body under subsection 304 (3) with respect to the individual's capacity, unless the individual's capacity has been determined by a prescribed body under section 304 within the previous six months.

### Parties

(4) The parties to the application are:

1. The service provider.
2. The incapable individual.
3. The substitute decision-maker.
4. Any other person whom the prescribed body specifies.

### Power of prescribed body

(5) In determining whether the substitute decision-maker complied with subsection (1), the prescribed body may substitute its opinion for that of the substitute decision-maker.

### Directions

(6) If the prescribed body determines that the substitute decision-maker did not comply with subsection (1), it may give the substitute decision-maker directions and, in doing so, shall take into consideration the matters set out in clauses (1) (a) to (d).

### Time for compliance

(7) The prescribed body shall specify the time within which the substitute decision-maker must comply with its directions.

### Deemed not authorized

(8) If the substitute decision-maker does not comply with the directions of the prescribed body within the time specified by the prescribed body, the substitute decision-maker is deemed not to meet the requirements of subsection 301 (4).

### Public Guardian and Trustee

(9) If the substitute decision-maker who is given directions is the Public Guardian and Trustee, the substitute decision-maker is required to comply with the directions and subsection (7) does not apply to the substitute decision-maker.

### Procedure

(10) A body prescribed for the purposes of this section shall comply with the prescribed requirements and restrictions in conducting the review.

### Additional authority of substitute decision-maker

**303.** (1) If this Part permits or requires an individual to make a request, give an instruction or take a step and a substitute decision-maker is authorized to consent or withhold or withdraw consent on behalf of the individual to the collection, use or disclosure of personal information about the individual, the substitute decision-maker may also make the request, give the instruction or take the step on behalf of the individual.

### References to individual read as substitute decision-maker

(2) If a substitute decision-maker makes a request, gives an instruction or takes a step under subsection (1) on behalf of an individual, references in this Part to the individual with respect to the request made, the instruction given or the step taken by the substitute decision-maker shall be read as references to the substitute decision-maker, and not to the individual.

### Determination of incapacity

**304.** (1) A service provider that determines that an individual is incapable shall do so in accordance with the requirements and restrictions, if any, that are prescribed.

### Information about determination

(2) If it is reasonable in the circumstances, a service provider shall provide, to an individual determined to be incapable, information about the consequences of the determination of incapacity, including the information, if any, that is prescribed.

### Review of determination

(3) When a service provider determines that an individual is incapable, the individual or a prescribed person may apply to a body prescribed for the purposes of this section for a review of the determination.

### Review body

(4) A body prescribed for the purposes of this section shall comply with the prescribed requirements and restrictions in conducting the review.

### Parties

(5) The parties to an application made under subsection (3) are,

 (a) the individual or prescribed person who applied for the review of the determination;

 (b) the service provider who made the determination of incapacity; and

 (c) any other persons whom the prescribed body specifies.

### Powers of review body

(6) A body prescribed for the purposes of this section may confirm the determination of incapacity or may determine that the individual is capable.

### Restriction on repeated applications

(7) If a determination that an individual is incapable is confirmed on the final disposition of an application under this section, the individual shall not make a new application under this section for a determination with respect to the same or a similar issue within six months after the final disposition of the earlier application, unless the body prescribed for the purposes of this section gives leave in advance.

### Grounds for leave

(8) The prescribed body may give leave for the new application to be made if it is satisfied that there has been a material change in circumstances that justifies reconsideration of the individual's capacity.

### Appointment of representative

**305.** (1) An individual who is 16 or older and who is determined to be incapable may apply to a body prescribed for the purposes of this section for appointment of a representative to consent on the individual's behalf to a collection, use or disclosure of personal information by a service provider.

### Application by proposed representative

(2) If an individual is incapable, another individual who is 16 or older may apply to a body prescribed for the purposes of this section to be appointed as a representative to consent on behalf of the incapable individual to a collection, use or disclosure of personal information.

### Deemed application concerning capacity

(3) An application to a prescribed body under subsection (1) or (2) is deemed to include an application to a prescribed body under subsection 304 (3) with respect to the individual's capacity, unless the individual's capacity has been determined by a prescribed body under section 304 within the previous six months.

### Exception

(4) Subsections (1) and (2) do not apply if the individual to whom the personal information relates has a guardian of the person, a guardian of property, an attorney for personal care or an attorney for property, who has authority to give or refuse consent to the collection, use or disclosure.

### Parties

(5) The parties to the application are:

1. The individual to whom the personal information relates.
2. The proposed representative named in the application.
3. Every person who is described in paragraph 4, 5, 6 or 7 of subsection 26 (1) of the *Personal Health Information Protection Act, 2004*.
4. All other persons whom the prescribed body specifies.

### Appointment

(6) In an appointment under this section, the prescribed body may authorize the representative to consent, on behalf of the individual to whom the personal information relates, to,

(a) a particular collection, use or disclosure at a particular time;

(b) a collection, use or disclosure of the type specified by the prescribed body in circumstances specified by the prescribed body, if the individual is determined to be incapable at the time the consent is sought; or

(c) any collection, use or disclosure at any time, if the individual is determined to be incapable at the time the consent is sought.

### Criteria for appointment

(7) The prescribed body may make an appointment under this section if it is satisfied that the following requirements are met:

1. The individual to whom the personal information relates does not object to the appointment.
2. The representative consents to the appointment, is at least 16 and is capable.

3. The appointment is in the best interests of the individual to whom the personal information relates.

### Powers of prescribed body

(8) Unless the individual to whom the personal information relates objects, the prescribed body may,

(a) appoint as representative a different individual than the one named in the application;

(b) limit the duration of the appointment;

(c) impose any other condition on the appointment; or

(d) on any person's application, remove, vary or suspend a condition imposed on the appointment or impose an additional condition on the appointment.

### Termination

(9) A body prescribed for the purposes of this section may, on any person's application, terminate an appointment made under this section if,

(a) the individual to whom the personal information relates or the representative requests the termination;

(b) the representative is no longer capable;

(c) the appointment is no longer in the best interests of the individual to whom the personal information relates; or

(d) the individual to whom the personal information relates has a guardian of the person, a guardian of property, an attorney for personal care or an attorney for property, who has authority to give or refuse consent to the types of collections, uses and disclosures for which the appointment was made and in the circumstances to which the appointment applies.

### Procedure

(10) A body prescribed for the purposes of this section shall comply with the prescribed requirements and restrictions in conducting the review.

## Integrity and Protection of Personal Information
### Steps to ensure accuracy, etc. of personal information
### Personal information used by service provider

**306.** (1) A service provider that uses personal information for the purpose of providing a service shall take reasonable steps to ensure that the information is as accurate, complete and up-to-date as is necessary for the purposes for which it uses the information.

### Personal information disclosed by service provider

(2) A service provider that discloses personal information that has been collected for the purpose of providing a service shall,

(a) take reasonable steps to ensure that the information is as accurate, complete and up-to-date as is necessary for the purposes of the disclosure that are known to the service provider at the time of the disclosure; or

(b) clearly set out for the recipient of the disclosure the limitations, if any, on the accuracy, completeness or up-to-date character of the information.

### Record of disclosed personal information

(3) A service provider that discloses personal information that has been collected for the purpose of providing a service shall record the disclosures made under the prescribed provisions in the prescribed manner.

### Steps to ensure collection of personal information is authorized

**307.** A service provider shall take reasonable steps to ensure that personal information is not collected without authority.

### Steps to ensure security of personal information

**308.** (1) A service provider shall take reasonable steps to ensure that personal information that has been collected for the purpose of providing a service and that is in the service provider's custody or control is protected against theft, loss and unauthorized use or disclosure and to ensure that the records containing the information are protected against unauthorized copying, modification or disposal.

### Notice of theft, loss, etc. to individual

(2) Subject to any prescribed exceptions and additional requirements, if personal information that has been collected for the purpose of providing a service and that is in a service provider's custody or control is stolen or lost or if it is used or disclosed without authority, the service provider shall,

(a) notify the individual to whom the information relates at the first reasonable opportunity of the theft, loss or unauthorized use or disclosure; and

(b) include in the notice a statement that the individual is entitled to make a complaint to the Commissioner under section 316.

### Notice to Commissioner and Minister

(3) If the circumstances surrounding the theft, loss or unauthorized use or disclosure meet the prescribed requirements, the service provider shall notify the Commissioner and the Minister of the theft, loss or unauthorized use or disclosure.

### Handling of records

**309.** (1) A service provider,

(a) shall take reasonable steps to ensure that the records of personal information collected for the purpose of providing a service that are in its custody or control are retained, transferred and disposed of in a secure manner; and

(b) shall comply with any prescribed requirements in respect of the retention, transfer and disposal of those records.

### Retention of records subject to access request

(2) Despite subsection (1), a service provider that has custody or control of personal information that is subject to a request for access under section 312 shall retain the information for as long as necessary to allow the individual to exhaust any recourse under this Act that they may have with respect to the request.

### Disclosure to successor

**310.** (1) A service provider may disclose personal information about an individual to a potential successor of the service provider, for the purpose of allowing the potential successor to assess and evaluate the operations of the service provider, if the potential successor first enters into an agreement with the service provider to keep the information confidential and secure and not to retain any of the information longer than is necessary for the purpose of the assessment or evaluation.

### Transfer to successor

(2) A service provider may transfer records of personal information about an individual to the service provider's successor if the service provider makes reasonable efforts to give notice to the individual before transferring the records or, if that is not reasonably possible, as soon as possible after transferring the records.

### Definitions

(3) In this section,
"potential successor" and "successor" mean a potential successor or a successor that is a service provider or that will be a service provider if it becomes a successor.

### Written public statement by service provider

**311.** (1) A service provider shall, in a manner that is practical in the circumstances, make available to the public a written statement in plain, easy-to-understand language that,

(a) provides a general description of the service provider's information practices;

(b) describes how to contact the service provider;

(c) describes how an individual may obtain access to or request correction of a record of personal information about the individual that is in the custody or control of the service provider; and

(d) describes how to make a complaint to the service provider and to the Commissioner under this Part.

### Use or disclosure contrary to service provider's information practices

(2) If a service provider uses or discloses personal information about an individual, without the individual's consent, in a manner that is outside the scope of the service provider's description of its information practices under clause (1) (a), the service provider shall,

(a) inform the individual of the uses and disclosures at the first reasonable opportunity, unless the individual does not have a right of access under section 312 to a record of the information;

(b) make a note of the uses and disclosures; and

(c) keep the note as part of the record of personal information about the individual that it has in its custody or under its control or in a form that is linked to that record.

### Individual's Access to Personal Information

### Individual's right of access

**312.** (1) An individual has a right of access to a record of personal information about the individual that is in a service provider's custody or control and that relates to the provision of a service to the individual unless,

(a) the record or the information in the record is subject to a legal privilege that restricts its disclosure to the individual;

(b) another Act, an Act of Canada or a court order prohibits its disclosure to the individual;

(c) the information in the record was collected or created primarily in anticipation of or for use in a proceeding, and the proceeding, together with all appeals or processes resulting from it, has not been concluded; or

(d) granting the access could reasonably be expected to,

　(i) result in a risk of serious harm to the individual or another individual,

　(ii) lead to the identification of an individual who was required by law to provide information in the record to the service provider, or

　(iii) lead to the identification of an individual who provided information in the record to the service provider explicitly or implicitly in confidence if the service provider considers it appropriate in the circumstances that the identity of the individual be kept confidential.

### Right of access to part of record not restricted

(2) Despite subsection (1), an individual has a right of access to that part of a record of personal information about the individual that can reasonably be severed from the part of the record to which the individual does not have a right of access under any of clauses (1) (a) to (d).

### Right of access to part of record not dedicated to provision of service

(3) Despite subsection (1), if a record is not a record dedicated primarily to the provision of a service to the individual requesting access, the individual has a right of access only to the personal information about the individual in the record that can reasonably be severed from the record.

### Consultation regarding harm

(4) Before deciding to refuse to grant an individual access to a record of personal information under subclause (1) (d) (i),

a service provider may consult with a member of the College of Physicians and Surgeons of Ontario, a member of the College of Psychologists of Ontario or a member of the Ontario College of Social Workers and Social Service Workers.

### Informal access

(5) Nothing in this Part prevents a service provider from granting an individual access to a record of personal information to which the individual has a right of access, if the individual makes an oral request for access or does not make a request for access under section 313.

### Service provider may communicate with individual

(6) Nothing in this Part prevents a service provider from communicating with an individual or the individual's substitute decision-maker with respect to a record of personal information to which the individual has a right of access.

### Request for access

**313.** (1) An individual may exercise a right of access to a record of personal information by making a written request for access to the service provider that has custody or control of the information.

### Details required

(2) The request must contain sufficient detail to enable the service provider to identify and locate the record with reasonable efforts.

### Service provider must assist individual making request

(3) If the request does not contain sufficient detail to enable the service provider to identify and locate the record with reasonable efforts, the service provider shall offer assistance to the person requesting access in reformulating the request to comply with subsection (2).

### Response of service provider

**314.** (1) A service provider that receives a request from an individual for access to a record of personal information shall,

(a) make the record available to the individual for examination and, at the request of the individual, provide a copy of the record to the individual and if reasonably practical, an explanation of the purpose and nature of the record and any term, code or abbreviation used in the record;

(b) give a written notice to the individual stating that, after a reasonable search, the service provider has concluded that the record does not exist, cannot be found, or is not a record to which this Part applies;

(c) if the service provider refuses the request, in whole or in part, under any provision of this Part other than clause 312 (1) (c) or (d), give a written notice to the individual stating that the service provider is refusing the request, in whole or in part, providing a reason for the refusal and stating that the individual is entitled to make a complaint about the refusal to the Commissioner under section 316; or

(d) subject to subsection (2), if the service provider refuses the request, in whole or in part, under clause 312 (1) (c) or (d), give a written notice to the individual stating that the individual is entitled to make a complaint about the refusal to the Commissioner under section 316 and that the service provider is refusing,

(i) the request, in whole or in part, while citing which of clauses 312 (1) (c) and (d) apply,

(ii) the request, in whole or in part, under one or both of clauses 312 (1) (c) and (d), while not citing which of those provisions apply, or

(iii) to confirm or deny the existence of any record subject to clauses 312 (1) (c) and (d).

## Exception

(2) A service provider shall not act under subclause (1) (d) (i) where doing so would reasonably be expected in the circumstances known to the person making the decision on behalf of the service provider to reveal to the individual, directly or indirectly, information to which the individual does not have a right of access.

## Time for response

(3) As soon as possible, but no later than 30 days after receiving the request, the service provider shall, by written notice to the individual, give the response required by subsection (1) or extend the deadline for responding by not more than 90 days if,

(a) responding to the request within 30 days would unreasonably interfere with the operations of the service provider because the information consists of numerous pieces of information or locating the information would necessitate a lengthy search; or

(b) the time required to undertake an assessment under subsection 312 (1) necessary to respond to the request within 30 days after receiving it would make it not reasonably practical to respond within that time.

## Extension of time—notice and response

(4) A service provider that extends the time limit under subsection (3) shall,

(a) give the individual written notice of the extension setting out the length of the extension and the reason for it; and

(b) respond as required by subsection (1) as soon as possible but no later than the expiry of the time limit as extended.

## Expedited access

(5) Despite subsections (3) and (4), if the individual provides the service provider with evidence satisfactory to the service provider that the individual requires access to the requested record of personal information within a specified time period, the service provider shall respond within that time period if the service provider is reasonably able to do so.

## Frivolous or vexatious requests

(6) A service provider that believes on reasonable grounds that a request for access to a record of personal information is frivolous or vexatious or is made in bad faith may refuse to grant the individual access to the requested record and, in that case, shall provide the individual with a notice that sets out the reasons for the refusal and that states that the individual is entitled to make a complaint about the refusal to the Commissioner under section 316.

## Deemed refusal

(7) A service provider that does not respond to a request for access within the time required is deemed to have refused the request.

## Right to complain

(8) If the service provider refuses or is deemed to have refused the request, in whole or in part,

(a) the individual is entitled to make a complaint about the refusal to the Commissioner under section 316; and

(b) in the complaint, the burden of proof in respect of the refusal lies on the service provider.

## Identity of individual

(9) A service provider shall not make a record of personal information or a part of it available to an individual or provide a copy of it to an individual under clause (1) (a) without first taking reasonable steps to be satisfied as to the individual's identity.

## No fee for access

(10) A service provider shall not charge a fee for providing access to a record under this section, except in the prescribed circumstances.

**Corrections to Records**

## Correction to record

### Interpretation

**315.** (1) In this section, a reference to a correction to a record or to correct a record includes the addition of, or adding, information to make the record complete.

### Written request

(2) If a service provider has granted an individual access to a record of personal information and if the individual believes that the record is inaccurate or incomplete, the individual may request in writing that the service provider correct the record.

## Informal request

(3)  If the individual makes an oral request that the service provider correct the record, nothing in this section prevents the service provider from making the requested correction.

## Time for response

(4)  As soon as possible, but no later than 30 days after receiving a request for a correction under subsection (2), the service provider shall, by written notice to the individual, grant or refuse the individual's request or extend the deadline for responding by not more than 90 days if,

(a)  responding to the request within 30 days would unreasonably interfere with the operations of the service provider; or

(b)  the time required to undertake the consultations necessary to respond to the request within 30 days would make it not reasonably practical to respond within that time.

## Extension of time

(5)  A service provider that extends the time limit under subsection (4) shall by written notice to the individual,

(a)  set out the length of the extension and the reason for it; and

(b)  grant or refuse the individual's request as soon as possible in the circumstances but no later than the expiry of the time limit as extended.

## Frivolous or vexatious requests

(6)  A service provider that believes on reasonable grounds that a request for a correction is frivolous or vexatious or is made in bad faith may refuse to grant the request and, in that case, shall provide the individual with a notice that sets out the reasons for the refusal and that states that the individual is entitled to make a complaint about the refusal to the Commissioner under section 316.

## Deemed refusal

(7)  A service provider that does not respond to a request for a correction within the time required is deemed to have refused the request.

## Right to complain

(8)  If the service provider refuses or is deemed to have refused the request, in whole or in part,

(a)  the individual is entitled to make a complaint about the refusal to the Commissioner under section 316; and

(b)  in the complaint, the burden of proof in respect of the refusal lies on the service provider.

## Duty to correct

(9)  The service provider shall grant a request for a correction if the individual demonstrates, to the service provider's satisfaction, that the record is inaccurate or incomplete and gives the service provider the information necessary to enable the service provider to correct the record.

## Exceptions

(10)  Despite subsection (9), a service provider is not required to correct a record of personal information if,

(a)  it consists of a record that was not originally created by the service provider and the service provider does not have sufficient knowledge, expertise or authority to correct the record; or

(b)  it consists of a professional opinion or observation that was made in good faith about the individual.

## Manner of making the correction

(11)  Upon granting a request for a correction, the service provider shall,

(a)  make the requested correction,

(i)  by recording the correct information in the record or, if that is not possible, by ensuring that there is a practical system in place to inform a person who accesses the record that the information in the record is incorrect or incomplete and to direct the person to the correct information, and

(ii)  by striking out the incorrect information in a manner that does not obliterate the record or, if that is not possible, by labelling the information as incorrect, severing the incorrect information from the record, storing it separately from the record and maintaining a link in the record that enables a person to trace the incorrect information;

(b)  give notice to the individual of what has been done under clause (a); and

(c)  at the request of the individual, give written notice of the requested correction, to the extent reasonably possible, to the persons to whom the service provider has disclosed the information with respect to which the individual requested the correction of the record, unless the correction cannot reasonably be expected to have an effect on the ongoing provision of services.

## Notice of refusal

(12)  A notice of refusal under subsection (4) or (5) must give the reasons for the refusal and inform the individual that the individual is entitled to,

(a)  prepare a concise statement of disagreement that sets out the correction that the service provider has refused to make;

(b)  require that the service provider attach the statement of disagreement as part of the records that it holds of the individual's personal information and disclose the statement of disagreement whenever the service provider discloses information to which the statement relates;

(c) require that the service provider make all reasonable efforts to disclose the statement of disagreement to any person who would have been notified under clause (11) (c) if the service provider had granted the requested correction; and

(d) make a complaint about the refusal to the Commissioner under section 316.

### Rights of individual

(13) If a service provider refuses a request for a correction, in whole or in part, or is deemed to have refused the request, the individual is entitled to take any of the actions described in subsection (12).

### Service provider's duty

(14) If the individual takes an action described in clause (12) (b) or (c), the service provider shall comply with the requirements described in the applicable clause.

### No fee for correction

(15) A service provider shall not charge a fee for correcting a record under this section, or for complying with subsection (14).

### Complaints, Reviews and Inspections
### Complaint to Commissioner

**316.** (1) A person who has reasonable grounds to believe that another person has contravened or is about to contravene a provision of this Part or the regulations made for the purposes of this Part may make a complaint to the Commissioner.

### Time for complaint

(2) A complaint made under subsection (1) must be in writing and must be filed within,

(a) one year after the subject-matter of the complaint first came to the attention of the complainant or should reasonably have come to the attention of the complainant, whichever is the shorter; or

(b) whatever longer period of time that the Commissioner permits if the Commissioner is satisfied that it does not result in prejudice to any person.

### Same, refusal of request

(3) A complaint that an individual makes under clause 314 (1) (c) or (d), subsection 314 (8), 315 (6) or (8) or clause 315 (12) (d) must be in writing and must be filed within six months after the service provider refused or is deemed to have refused the individual's request.

### Response of Commissioner

**317.** (1) Upon receiving a complaint made under this Part, the Commissioner may inform the person about whom the complaint is made of the nature of the complaint and,

(a) inquire as to what means, other than the complaint, that the complainant is using or has used to resolve the subject-matter of the complaint;

(b) require the complainant to try to effect a settlement, within the time period that the Commissioner specifies, with the person about which the complaint is made; or

(c) authorize a mediator to review the complaint and to try to effect a settlement, within the time period that the Commissioner specifies, between the complainant and the person about which the complaint is made.

### Dealings without prejudice

(2) If the Commissioner takes an action described in clause (1) (b) or (c) but no settlement is effected within the time period specified,

(a) none of the dealings between the parties to the attempted settlement shall prejudice the rights and duties of the parties under this Part;

(b) none of the information disclosed in the course of trying to effect a settlement shall prejudice the rights and duties of the parties under this Part; and

(c) none of the information disclosed in the course of trying to effect a settlement and that is subject to mediation privilege shall be used or disclosed outside the attempted settlement, including in a review of a complaint under this section or in an inspection under section 320, unless all parties expressly consent.

### Commissioner's review

(3) If the Commissioner does not take an action described in clause (1) (b) or (c) or if the Commissioner takes an action described in one of those clauses but no settlement is effected within the time period specified, the Commissioner may review the subject-matter of a complaint made under this Part if satisfied that there are reasonable grounds to do so.

### No review

(4) The Commissioner may decide not to review the subject-matter of the complaint for whatever reason the Commissioner considers proper, including if satisfied that,

(a) the person about which the complaint is made has responded adequately to the complaint;

(b) the complaint has been or could be more appropriately dealt with, initially or completely, by means of a procedure, other than a complaint under this Part;

(c) the length of time that has elapsed between the date when the subject-matter of the complaint arose and the date the complaint was made is such that a review under this section would likely result in undue prejudice to any person;

(d) the complainant does not have a sufficient personal interest in the subject-matter of the complaint; or

(e) the complaint is frivolous or vexatious or is made in bad faith.

### Notice

(5) Upon deciding not to review the subject-matter of a complaint, the Commissioner shall give notice of the decision to the complainant and shall specify in the notice the reason for the decision.

### Same

(6) Upon deciding to review the subject-matter of a complaint, the Commissioner shall give notice of the decision to the person about whom the complaint is made.

### Commissioner's self-initiated review

**318.** (1) The Commissioner may, on the Commissioner's own initiative, conduct a review of any matter if the Commissioner has reasonable grounds to believe that a person has contravened or is about to contravene a provision of this Part or the regulations and that the subject-matter of the review relates to the contravention.

### Notice

(2) Upon deciding to conduct a review under this section, the Commissioner shall give notice of the decision to every person whose activities are being reviewed.

### Conduct of Commissioner's review

**319.** (1) In conducting a review under section 317 or 318, the Commissioner may make the rules of procedure that the Commissioner considers necessary and the *Statutory Powers Procedure Act* does not apply to the review.

### Evidence

(2) In conducting a review under section 317 or 318, the Commissioner may receive and accept any evidence and other information that the Commissioner sees fit, whether on oath or by affidavit or otherwise and whether or not it is or would be admissible in a court of law.

### Inspection powers

**320.** (1) In conducting a review under section 317 or 318, the Commissioner may, without a warrant or court order, enter and inspect any premises in accordance with this section if,

(a) the Commissioner has reasonable grounds to believe that,

(i) the person about whom the complaint was made or the person whose activities are being reviewed is using the premises for a purpose related to the subject-matter of the complaint or the review, as the case may be, and

(ii) the premises contains books, records or other documents relevant to the subject-matter of the complaint or the review, as the case may be; and

(b) the Commissioner is conducting the inspection for the purpose of determining whether the person has contravened or is about to contravene a provision of this Part or the regulations.

### Review powers

(2) In conducting a review under section 317 or 318, the Commissioner may,

(a) demand the production of any books, records or other documents relevant to the subject-matter of the review or copies of extracts from the books, records or other documents;

(b) inquire into all information, records, information practices of a service provider and other matters that are relevant to the subject-matter of the review;

(c) demand the production for inspection of anything described in clause (b);

(d) use any data storage, processing or retrieval device or system belonging to the person being investigated in order to produce a record in readable form of any books, records or other documents relevant to the subject-matter of the review; or

(e) on the premises that the Commissioner has entered, review or copy any books, records or documents that a person produces to the Commissioner, if the Commissioner pays the reasonable cost recovery fee that the service provider or person being reviewed may charge.

### Entry to dwellings

(3) The Commissioner shall not, without the consent of the occupier, exercise a power to enter a place that is being used as a dwelling, except under the authority of a search warrant issued under subsection (4).

### Search warrants

(4) Where a justice of the peace is satisfied by evidence upon oath or affirmation that there is reasonable ground to believe it is necessary to enter a place that is being used as a dwelling to investigate a complaint that is the subject of a review under section 317 or 318, the justice of the peace may issue a warrant authorizing the entry by a person named in the warrant.

### Time and manner for entry

(5) The Commissioner shall exercise the power to enter premises under this section only during reasonable hours for the premises and only in such a manner so as not to interfere with services that are being provided to any person on the premises at the time of entry.

### No obstruction

(6) No person shall obstruct the Commissioner who is exercising powers under this section or provide the Commissioner with false or misleading information.

### Written demand

(7) A demand for books, records or documents or copies of extracts from them under subsection (2) must be in writing and must include a statement of the nature of the things that are required to be produced.

### Obligation to assist

(8) If the Commissioner makes a demand for any thing under subsection (2), the person having custody of the thing shall produce it to the Commissioner and, at the request of the Commissioner, shall provide whatever assistance is reasonably necessary, including using any data storage, processing or retrieval device or system to produce a record in readable form, if the demand is for a document.

### Removal of documents

(9) If a person produces books, records and other documents to the Commissioner, other than those needed for the current provision of services to any person, the Commissioner may, on issuing a written receipt, remove them and may review or copy any of them if the Commissioner is not able to review and copy them on the premises that the Commissioner has entered.

### Return of documents

(10) The Commissioner shall carry out any reviewing or copying of documents with reasonable dispatch, and shall promptly after the reviewing or copying return the documents to the person who produced them.

### Admissibility of copies

(11) A copy certified by the Commissioner as a copy is admissible in evidence to the same extent, and has the same evidentiary value, as the thing copied.

### Answers under oath

(12) In conducting a review under section 317 or 318, the Commissioner may, by summons, in the same manner and to the same extent as a superior court of record, require the appearance of any person before the Commissioner and compel them to give oral or written evidence on oath or affirmation.

### Inspection of record without consent

(13) Despite subsections (2) and (12), the Commissioner shall not inspect a record of, require evidence of, or inquire into, personal information without the consent of the individual to whom it relates, unless,

(a) the Commissioner first determines that it is reasonably necessary to do so, subject to any conditions or restrictions that the Commissioner specifies, which shall include a time limitation, in order to carry out the review and that the public interest in carrying out the review justifies dispensing with obtaining the individual's consent in the circumstances; and

(b) the Commissioner provides a statement to the person who has custody or control of the record to be inspected, or the evidence or information to be inquired into, setting out the Commissioner's determination under clause (a) together with brief written reasons and any restrictions and conditions that the Commissioner has specified.

### Limitation on delegation

(14) Despite subsection 327 (1), the power to make a determination under clause (13) (a) and to approve the brief written reasons under clause (13) (b) may not be delegated except to an Assistant Commissioner.

### Document privileged

(15) A document or thing produced by a person in the course of a review is privileged in the same manner as if the review were a proceeding in a court.

### Protection

(16) Except on the trial of a person for perjury in respect of the person's sworn testimony, no statement made or answer given by that or any other person in the course of a review by the Commissioner is admissible in evidence in any court or at any inquiry or in any other proceedings, and no evidence in respect of proceedings before the Commissioner shall be given against any person.

### Protection under federal Act

(17) The Commissioner shall inform a person giving a statement or answer in the course of a review by the Commissioner of the person's right to object to answer any question under section 5 of the *Canada Evidence Act*.

### Representations

(18) The Commissioner shall give the person who made the complaint, the person about whom the complaint is made and any other affected person an opportunity to make representations to the Commissioner.

### Representative

(19) A person who is given an opportunity to make representations to the Commissioner may be represented by a lawyer or another person.

### Access to representations

(20) The Commissioner may permit a person to be present during the representations that another person makes to the Commissioner or to have access to them unless doing so would reveal,

(a) the substance of a record of personal information, for which a service provider claims to be entitled to refuse a request for access made under section 313; or

(b) personal information to which an individual is not entitled to request access under section 313.

### Proof of appointment

(21) If the Commissioner or an Assistant Commissioner has delegated their powers under this section to an officer or employee of the Commissioner, the officer or employee who exercises the powers shall, upon request, produce the certificate of delegation signed by the Commissioner or Assistant Commissioner, as the case may be.

### Powers of Commissioner

**321.** (1) After conducting a review under section 317 or 318, the Commissioner may,

(a) if the review relates to a complaint into a request by an individual under subsection 313 (1) for access to a record of personal information, make an order directing the service provider about whom the complaint was made to grant the individual access to the requested record;

(b) if the review relates to a complaint into a request by an individual under subsection 315 (2) for correction of a record of personal information, make an order directing the service provider about whom a complaint was made to make the requested correction;

(c) make an order directing any person whose activities the Commissioner reviewed to perform a duty imposed by this Part or the regulations;

(d) make an order directing any person whose activities the Commissioner reviewed to cease collecting, using or disclosing personal information if the Commissioner determines that the person is collecting, using or disclosing the information, as the case may be, or is about to do so in contravention of this Part or the regulations or an agreement entered into under this Part;

(e) make an order directing any person whose activities the Commissioner reviewed to dispose of records of personal information that the Commissioner determines the person collected, used or disclosed in contravention of this Part or the regulations or an agreement entered into under this Part but only if the disposal of the records is not reasonably expected to adversely affect the provision of services to an individual;

(f) make an order directing any service provider whose activities the Commissioner reviewed to change, cease or not implement any information practices specified by the Commissioner, if the Commissioner determines that the information practices contravene this Part or the regulations;

(g) make an order directing any service provider whose activities the Commissioner reviewed to implement information practices specified by the Commissioner, if the Commissioner determines that the information practices are reasonably necessary in order to achieve compliance with this Part and the regulations;

(h) make an order directing any person who is an agent or employee of a service provider, whose activities the Commissioner reviewed and that an order made under any of clauses (a) to (g) directs to take any action or to refrain from taking any action, to take the action or to refrain from taking the action if the Commissioner considers that it is necessary to make the order against the agent or employee to ensure that the service provider will comply with the order made against the service provider; or

(i) make comments and recommendations on the privacy implications of any matter that is the subject of the review.

### Terms of order

(2) An order that the Commissioner makes under subsection (1) may contain the terms that the Commissioner considers appropriate.

### Copy of order, etc.

(3) Upon making comments, recommendations or an order under subsection (1), the Commissioner shall provide a copy of them, including reasons for any order made, to,

(a) the complainant and the person about whom the complaint was made, if the Commissioner made the comments, recommendations or order after conducting a review under section 317 of a complaint;

(b) the person whose activities the Commissioner reviewed, if the Commissioner made the comments, recommendations or order after conducting a review under section 318;

(c) all other persons to whom the order is directed;

(d) the body or bodies that are legally entitled to regulate or review the activities of a service provider directed in the order or to whom the comments or recommendations relate; and

(e) any other person whom the Commissioner considers appropriate.

### No order

(4) If, after conducting a review under section 317 or 318, the Commissioner does not make an order under subsection (1), the Commissioner shall give the complainant, if any, and the person whose activities the Commissioner reviewed a notice that sets out the Commissioner's reasons for not making an order.

### Appeal of order

**322.** (1) A person affected by an order of the Commissioner made under any of clauses 321 (1) (c) to (h) may appeal the order to the Divisional Court on a question of law in accordance with the rules of court by filing a notice of appeal within 30 days after receiving the copy of the order.

### Certificate of Commissioner

(2) In an appeal under this section, the Commissioner shall certify to the Divisional Court,

(a) the order and a statement of the Commissioner's reasons for making the order;

(b) the record of all hearings that the Commissioner has held in conducting the review on which the order is based;

(c) all written representations that the Commissioner received before making the order; and

(d) all other material that the Commissioner considers is relevant to the appeal.

### Confidentiality of information

(3) In an appeal under this section, the court may take precautions to avoid the disclosure by the court or any person of any personal information about an individual, including, where appropriate, receiving representations without notice, conducting hearings in private or sealing the court files.

### Court order

(4) On hearing an appeal under this section, the court may, by order,

(a) direct the Commissioner to make the decisions and to do the acts that the Commissioner is authorized to do under this Part and that the court considers proper; and

(b) if necessary, vary or set aside the Commissioner's order.

### Compliance by Commissioner

(5) The Commissioner shall comply with the court's order.

### Enforcement of order

323. An order made by the Commissioner under this Part that has become final as a result of there being no further right of appeal may be filed with the Superior Court of Justice and on filing becomes and is enforceable as a judgment or order of the Superior Court of Justice to the same effect.

### Further order of Commissioner

324. (1) After conducting a review under section 317 or 318 and making an order under subsection 321 (1), the Commissioner may rescind or vary the order or may make a further order under that subsection if new facts relating to the subject-matter of the review come to the Commissioner's attention or if there is a material change in the circumstances relating to the subject-matter of the review.

### Circumstances

(2) The Commissioner may exercise the powers described in subsection (1) even if the order that the Commissioner rescinds or varies has been filed with the Superior Court of Justice under section 323.

### Copy of order, etc.

(3) Upon making a further order under subsection (1), the Commissioner shall provide a copy of it to the persons described in clauses 321 (3) (a) to (e) and shall include with the copy a notice setting out,

(a) the Commissioner's reasons for making the order; and

(b) if the order was made under any of clauses 321 (1) (c) to (h), a statement that the persons affected by the order have the right to appeal described in subsection (4).

### Appeal

(4) A person affected by an order that the Commissioner rescinds, varies or makes under any of clauses 321 (1) (c) to (h) may appeal the order to the Divisional Court on a question of law in accordance with the rules of court by filing a notice of appeal within 30 days after receiving the copy of the order and subsections 322 (2) to (5) apply to the appeal.

### Damages for breach of privacy

325. (1) If the Commissioner has made an order under this Part that has become final as the result of there being no further right of appeal, a person affected by the order may commence a proceeding in the Superior Court of Justice for damages for actual harm that the person has suffered as a result of a contravention of this Part or the regulations.

### Same

(2) If a person has been convicted of an offence under this Part and the conviction has become final as a result of there being no further right of appeal, a person affected by the conduct that gave rise to the offence may commence a proceeding in the Superior Court of Justice for damages for actual harm that the person has suffered as a result of the conduct.

### Damages for mental anguish

(3) If, in a proceeding described in subsection (1) or (2), the Superior Court of Justice determines that the harm suffered by the plaintiff was caused by a contravention or offence, as the case may be, that the defendants engaged in wilfully or recklessly, the court may include in its award of damages an award for mental anguish.

### General powers of Commissioner

326. The Commissioner may,

(a) engage in or commission research into matters affecting the carrying out of the purposes of this Part;

(b) conduct public education programs and provide information concerning this Part and the Commissioner's role and activities;

(c) receive representations from the public concerning the operation of this Part;

(d) on the request of a service provider, offer comments on the service provider's actual or proposed information practices;

(e) assist in investigations and similar procedures conducted by a person who performs similar functions to the Commissioner under the laws of Canada, except that in providing assistance, the Commissioner shall not use or disclose information collected by or for the Commissioner under this Part; and

(f) in appropriate circumstances, authorize the collection of personal information about an individual in a manner other than directly from the individual.

### Delegation by Commissioner

**327.** (1) The Commissioner may in writing delegate any of the Commissioner's powers, duties or functions under this Part, including the power to make orders, to an Assistant Commissioner or to an officer or employee of the Commissioner.

### Subdelegation by Assistant Commissioner

(2) An Assistant Commissioner may in writing delegate any of the powers, duties or functions delegated to the Assistant Commissioner under subsection (1) to any other officers or employees of the Commissioner, subject to the conditions and restrictions that the Assistant Commissioner specifies in the delegation.

### Limitations re personal information

**328.** (1) The Commissioner and any person acting under the Commissioner's authority may collect, use or retain personal information in the course of carrying out any functions under this Part solely if no other information will serve the purpose of the collection, use or retention of the personal information and in no other circumstances.

### Extent of information

(2) The Commissioner and any person acting under the Commissioner's authority shall not in the course of carrying out any functions under this Part collect, use or retain more personal information than is reasonably necessary to enable the Commissioner to perform the Commissioner's functions relating to this Part or for a proceeding under it.

### Confidentiality

(3) The Commissioner and any person acting under the Commissioner's authority shall not disclose any information that comes to their knowledge in the course of exercising their functions under this Part unless,

(a) the disclosure is required for the purpose of exercising those functions;

(b) the information relates to a service provider, the disclosure is made to a body that is legally entitled to regulate or review the activities of the service provider and the Commissioner or an Assistant Commissioner is of the opinion that the disclosure is justified;

(c) the Commissioner obtained the information under subsection 320 (12) and the disclosure is required in a prosecution for an offence under section 131 of the *Criminal Code* (Canada) in respect of sworn testimony; or

(d) the disclosure is made to the Attorney General, the information relates to the commission of an offence against an Act or an Act of Canada and the Commissioner is of the view that there is evidence of such an offence.

### Same

(4) Despite anything in subsection (3), the Commissioner and any person acting under the Commissioner's authority shall not disclose the identity of a person, other than a complainant under subsection 316 (1), who has provided information to the Commissioner and who has requested the Commissioner to keep the person's identity confidential, unless the disclosure is necessary to comply with section 125 (duty to report child in need of protection).

### Information in review or proceeding

(5) The Commissioner in a review under section 317 or 318 and a court, tribunal or other person, including the Commissioner, in a proceeding mentioned in section 325 or this section shall take every reasonable precaution, including, when appropriate, receiving representations without notice and conducting hearings that are closed to the public, to avoid the disclosure of any information for which a service provider is entitled to refuse a request for access made under section 313.

### Not compellable witness

(6) The Commissioner and any person acting under the Commissioner's authority shall not be required to give evidence in a court or in a proceeding of a judicial nature concerning anything coming to their knowledge in the exercise of their functions under this Part that they are prohibited from disclosing under subsection (3) or (4).

### Immunity

**329.** No action or other proceeding for damages may be instituted against the Commissioner or any person acting under the Commissioner's authority for,

(a) anything done, reported or said in good faith and in the exercise or intended exercise of any of their powers or duties under this Part; or

(b) any alleged neglect or default in the exercise in good faith of any of their powers or duties under this Part.

## Prohibitions, Immunity and Offences

### Non-retaliation

**330.** No one shall dismiss, suspend, demote, discipline, harass or otherwise disadvantage a person by reason that,

(a) the person, acting in good faith and on the basis of reasonable belief, has disclosed to the Commissioner that any other person has contravened or is about to contravene a provision of this Part or the regulations;

(b) the person, acting in good faith and on the basis of reasonable belief, has done or stated an intention of doing anything that is required to be done in order to avoid having any person contravene a provision of this Part or the regulations;

(c) the person, acting in good faith and on the basis of reasonable belief, has refused to do or stated an intention of refusing to do anything that is in contravention of a provision of this Part or the regulations; or

(d) any person believes that the person will do anything described in clause (a), (b) or (c).

## Immunity

**331.** (1) No action or other proceeding for damages may be instituted against a service provider or any other person for,

(a) anything done, reported or said, in good faith and reasonably in the circumstances, in the exercise or intended exercise of any of their powers or duties under this Part; or

(b) any alleged neglect or default that was reasonable in the circumstances in the exercise in good faith of any of their powers or duties under this Part.

## Crown liability

(2) Despite subsections 5 (2) and (4) of the *Proceedings Against the Crown Act*, subsection (1) of this section does not relieve the Crown of liability in respect of a tort committed by a person mentioned in subsection (1) to which it would otherwise be subject.

## Substitute decision-maker

(3) A person who, on behalf of or in the place of an individual, gives, withholds or withdraws consent to a collection, use or disclosure of personal information about the individual, or makes a request, gives an instruction or takes a step is not liable for damages for doing so if the person acts reasonably in the circumstances, in good faith and in accordance with this Part and the regulations.

## Reliance on assertion

(4) Unless it is not reasonable to do so in the circumstances, a person is entitled to rely on the accuracy of an assertion made by another person, in connection with a collection, use or disclosure of, or access to, the information under this Part, to the effect that the other person,

(a) is a person who is authorized to request access to a record of personal information under subsection 313 (1); or

(b) is a person who is authorized under subsection 301 (1), (2) or (4) to consent to the collection, use or disclosure of personal information about another individual.

## Offences

**332.** (1) A person is guilty of an offence if the person,

(a) wilfully collects, uses or discloses personal information in contravention of this Part or the regulations made for the purposes of this Part;

(b) makes a request under this Act, under false pretences, for access to or correction of a record of personal information;

(c) in connection with the collection, use or disclosure of personal information or access to a record of personal information, makes an assertion, knowing that it is untrue, to the effect that the person,

(i) is a person who is authorized to consent to the collection, use or disclosure of personal information about another individual, or

(ii) is a person entitled to access to a record of personal information under section 312;

(d) disposes of a record of personal information in the custody or under the control of a service provider with an intent to evade a request for access to the record that the service provider has received under subsection 313 (1);

(e) wilfully disposes of a record of personal information in contravention of section 309;

(f) wilfully fails to comply with clause 308 (2) (a);

(g) wilfully obstructs the Commissioner or a person known to be acting under the authority of the Commissioner in the performance of their functions in relation to this Part;

(h) wilfully makes a false statement to mislead or attempt to mislead the Commissioner or a person known to be acting under the authority of the Commissioner in the performance of their functions in relation to this Part;

(i) wilfully fails to comply with an order made by the Commissioner or a person known to be acting under the authority of the Commissioner in relation to this Part; or

(j) contravenes section 330.

## Penalty

(2) A person who is guilty of an offence under subsection (1) is liable, on conviction, to a fine of not more than $5,000.

## Officers, etc.

(3) If a corporation commits an offence under this Part, every officer, member, employee or agent of the corporation who authorized the offence, or who had the authority to prevent the offence from being committed but knowingly refrained from doing so, is a party to and guilty of the offence and is liable, on conviction, to the penalty for the offence, whether or not the corporation has been prosecuted or convicted.

**No prosecution**

(4) No person is liable to prosecution for an offence under this or any other Act by reason of complying with a requirement of the Commissioner in relation to this Part.

**Consent of Attorney General**

(5) A prosecution for an offence under subsection (1) shall not be commenced without the consent of the Attorney General.

**Presiding judge**

(6) The Crown may, by notice to the clerk of the Ontario Court of Justice, require that a provincial judge preside over a proceeding in respect of an offence under subsection (1).

**Protection of information**

(7) In a prosecution for an offence under subsection (1) or where documents or materials are filed with a court under sections 158 to 160 of the *Provincial Offences Act* in relation to an investigation into an offence under this Part, the court may, at any time, take precautions to avoid the disclosure by the court or any person of any personal information, including, where appropriate,

(a) removing the identifying information of any person whose personal information is referred to in any documents or materials;

(b) receiving representations without notice;

(c) conducting hearings or parts of hearings in private; or

(d) sealing all or part of the court files.

**No limitation**

(8) Section 76 of the *Provincial Offences Act* does not apply to a prosecution under this Part.

## PART XI    MISCELLANEOUS MATTERS

**Child and Family Services Review Board**

**333.** (1) The Child and Family Services Review Board is continued under the name Child and Family Services Review Board in English and Commission de révision des services à l'enfance et à la famille in French.

**Composition and duties**

(2) The Board is composed of the prescribed number of members appointed by the Lieutenant Governor in Council and has the powers and duties given to it by this Act and the regulations.

**Chair and vice-chairs**

(3) The Lieutenant Governor in Council may appoint a member of the Board as chair and may appoint one or more other members as vice-chairs.

**Quorum**

(4) The prescribed number of members of the Board are a quorum.

**Remuneration**

(5) The chair and vice-chairs and the other members of the Board shall be paid the remuneration determined by the Lieutenant Governor in Council and are entitled to their reasonable and necessary travelling and living expenses while attending meetings or otherwise engaged in the work of the Board.

**Police record checks**

**334.** The Lieutenant Governor in Council may, by regulation, require the following persons to provide a police record check concerning the person to any other person or body in accordance with the regulations:

1. A person who provides or receives services under this Act.

2. A person residing, employed or volunteering in premises where services are provided or received under this Act.

3. Such other persons who may be prescribed.

**Society may request police record checks from police, etc.**

**335.** A society may, in prescribed circumstances or for a prescribed purpose, ask the Ontario Provincial Police, a municipal police force or a prescribed entity for police record checks or other prescribed information.

**Review of Act**

**336.** (1) The Minister shall periodically conduct a review of this Act or those provisions of it specified by the Minister.

**Beginning of review**

(2) The Minister shall inform the public when a review under this section begins and what provisions of this Act are included in the review.

**Consultation with children and young persons**

(3) The Minister shall consult with children and young persons when conducting a review under this section.

**Written report**

(4) The Minister shall prepare a written report, in plain language, respecting the review, including the matters described in sections 337 and 338, and shall make that report available to the public.

**Period for review**

(5) The first review shall be completed and the report made available to the public within five years after the day this section comes into force.

### Subsequent reviews

(6) Each subsequent review shall be completed and the report made available to the public within five years after the day the report on the previous review has been made available to the public.

### Review to address rights of children and young persons

**337.** Every review of this Act shall address the rights of children and young persons in Part II.

### Review to address First Nations, Inuit and Métis issues

**338.** Every review of this Act shall address the following matters:

1. The additional purpose of the Act described in paragraph 6 of subsection 1 (2), with a view to evaluating the progress that has been made in working with First Nations, Inuit and Métis peoples to achieve that purpose.
2. The provisions imposing obligations on societies when providing services to a First Nations, Inuk or Métis person or in respect of First Nations, Inuit or Métis children, with a view to ensuring compliance by societies with those provisions.

## PART XII    REGULATIONS

### General

### Lieutenant Governor in Council regulations

**339.** (1) The Lieutenant Governor in Council may make regulations for the purposes of this Act,

1. prescribing and governing a dispute resolution mechanism, in accordance with Jordan's Principle, to resolve inter-jurisdictional and intra-jurisdictional disputes in respect of services provided under this Act;
2. prescribing additional services that are services under this Act;
3. prescribing additional powers and duties of Directors and program supervisors;
4. prescribing additional persons and entities who are service providers;
5. governing the use of physical restraint under this Act, including prescribing standards and procedures for its use, requiring service providers to develop policies governing its use and prescribing provisions that must be or may not be included in those policies;
6. governing the use of mechanical restraints under this Act, including prescribing standards and procedures for their use;
7. prescribing and governing an internal procedure by which complaints, other than complaints under section 18 or 119, may be made to service providers,

and prescribing and governing an external review by a specified entity of specified classes of such complaints;

8. exempting a service provider, lead agency or service, or any class of them, from any provision or requirement of this Act or the regulations for a specified period or periods;
9. defining any word or expression used in this Act that is not already defined in this Act and further defining any word or expression used in this Act that is already defined in this Act;
10. prescribing or otherwise providing for anything required or permitted by this Act to be prescribed or otherwise provided for in the regulations, including governing anything required or permitted to be done in accordance with the regulations, which is not already provided for in this Part, except as otherwise provided in paragraph 1 of subsection 347 (2);
11. governing transitional matters that may arise due to the enactment of this Act or the repeal of the old Act.

### Conflicts

(2) If there is a conflict between a regulation made under paragraph 11 of subsection (1) and any provision of this Act or the regulations, the regulation made under paragraph 11 of subsection (1) prevails.

### Minister's regulations

(3) The Minister may make regulations for the purposes of this Act,

1. prescribing performance standards and performance measures for the provision of services to children in care, including prescribing a process for determining what the performance standards and performance measures should be, and implementing the performance standards and performance measures that are prescribed;
2. governing the determination of the bands and First Nations, Inuit or Métis communities with which a First Nations, Inuit or Métis child identifies;
3. governing how service providers, in making decisions in respect of any child, are to take into account the child's race, ancestry, place of origin, colour, ethnic origin, citizenship, family diversity, disability, creed, sex, sexual orientation, gender identity and gender expression in order to give effect to the purpose set out in subparagraph 3 iii of subsection 1 (2);
4. governing how service providers, in making decisions in respect of any child, are to take into account the child's cultural and linguistic needs in order to give effect to the purpose set out in subparagraph 3 iv of subsection 1 (2);

5. governing how service providers, in making decisions in respect of any child, are to take into account regional differences in order to give effect to the purpose set out in paragraph 4 of subsection 1 (2);

6. governing how service providers, in the case of a First Nations, Inuk or Métis child, are to take into account the child's cultures, heritages, traditions, connection to community and the concept of the extended family, in order to give effect to the purpose set out in paragraph 6 of subsection 1 (2);

7. prescribing persons who may represent children and their parents in order to assist service providers in taking into account all the characteristics and needs of a child, and all the other factors referred to in subparagraphs 3 iii and iv and paragraphs 4 and 6 of subsection 1 (2) for the purposes set out in those subparagraphs and paragraphs, and respecting how such persons shall be selected or appointed and governing their roles and duties as representatives;

8. prescribing procedures and conditions of eligibility for the admission of children and other persons to and their discharge from places where services are provided;

9. governing the residential placement of children and prescribing procedures for placements, discharge, assessments and case management;

10. requiring that residential placements with or by service providers be made in accordance with written agreements, and prescribing their form and contents;

11. prescribing the qualifications, powers and duties of persons employed in providing services;

12. prescribing classes of persons employed or to be employed in providing services who must undertake training, prescribing that training and prescribing the circumstances under which that training must be undertaken;

13. requiring and prescribing medical and other related or ancillary services for the care and treatment of children and other persons in places where services are provided;

14. permitting notices, orders or other documents that are required under this Act to be provided in writing to be provided in electronic or other form instead, subject to the conditions or restrictions that are specified;

15. governing how notices, orders and other documents or things are to be given or served under this Act, including providing rules for when they are deemed to be received;

16. prescribing forms and providing for their use;

17. modifying any provision or requirement of this Act or the regulations to accommodate persons with disabilities within the meaning of the *Accessibility for Ontarians with Disabilities Act, 2005.*

## Regulations: Part II (Children's and Young Persons' Rights)

**340.** The Lieutenant Governor in Council may make regulations for the purposes of Part II,

1. governing how the rights of children and young persons in this Act are to be respected and promoted by service providers;

2. prescribing intervals for the purpose of section 9;

3. governing internal complaints procedures to be established under section 18;

4. establishing procedures for reviews under section 19;

5. prescribing an alternative dispute resolution method for the purpose of subsection 17 (1) and an alternative dispute resolution process other than the one established by the bands and communities referred to in subsection 17 (2) for the purpose of that subsection.

## Regulations: Part III (Funding and Accountability)
### Minister's regulations

**341.** (1) The Minister may make regulations for the purposes of Part III,

1. prescribing entities to whom funding may be provided for the purposes of clause 25 (c);

2. prescribing other purposes for which funding may be provided under clause 25 (c);

3. prescribing the information to be contained in or excluded from a summary of an order made available to the public under clause 33 (4) (b) or 43 (4) (b);

4. prescribing standards of services and procedures and practices to be followed by societies for the purposes of subsection 35 (2);

5. governing the management and operation of societies;

6. prescribing a system for determining the amounts of payments under subsection 40 (1);

7. prescribing terms that shall or may be included in accountability agreements for the purposes of subsection 41 (4);

8. governing the provision of services;

9. governing the accommodation, facilities and equipment to be provided,

   i. in buildings in which services are provided, and
   ii. in the course of the provision of services;

10. governing the establishment, management, operation, location, construction, alteration and renovation of buildings in which services are provided;

11. prescribing the accounts and records to be kept by societies, the claims, returns and reports to be made and budgets to be submitted to the Minister and the methods, time and manner in which they shall be made or submitted;

12. requiring service providers to keep records, and prescribing the form and content of those records;

13. providing for the recovery, by an agency or by the Minister, from the person or persons in whose charge a child is or has been or from the estate of that person or persons of amounts paid by the agency for the child's care and maintenance, and prescribing the circumstances and the manner in which such a recovery may be made;

14. providing for the recovery of payments made to societies under Part III and the regulations;

15. governing the construction, alteration, renovation, extension, furnishing and equipping of homes operated or supervised by societies, other than children's residences as defined in Part IX (Residential Licensing), where residential care is provided to children;

16. prescribing reports to be made and information to be provided under section 56, their form and the intervals at which they are to be made or provided;

17. prescribing entities and the reports and information to be provided to them and the manner in which they are to be provided for the purpose of section 57;

18. prescribing information and the manner of making it public for the purpose of section 58;

19. prescribing other persons to whom a program supervisor shall give an inspection report for the purposes of clause 61 (1) (c);

20. prescribing rules to determine whether a child resides within an advisory committee's jurisdiction;

21. prescribing practices, procedures and further duties for advisory committees.

### Standards of service, etc.

(2) A regulation made under paragraph 4 of subsection (1),

(a) may exempt one or more societies from anything that is prescribed under that paragraph;

(b) may prescribe standards of services that only apply to one or more societies provided for in the regulations;

(c) may prescribe procedures and practices that are only required to be followed by one or more societies provided for in the regulations.

### Amounts of payments to societies

(3) A regulation made under paragraph 6 of subsection (1) is, if it so provides, effective with reference to a period before it is filed.

### Lieutenant Governor in Council regulations

(4) The Lieutenant Governor in Council may make regulations for the purposes of Part III,

1. governing the transfer and assignment of assets of service providers and lead agencies for the purposes of section 29;

2. establishing and respecting categories of lead agencies for the purposes of subsection 30 (4);

3. prescribing the functions of each lead agency category for the purposes of subsection 30 (5);

4. prescribing matters about which the Minister may issue directives for the purposes of subsection 32 (2);

5. prescribing other duties of a society for the purposes of clause 35 (1) (g);

6. respecting the composition of boards of directors of societies, including prescribing qualifications or eligibility criteria for board members, and requiring board members to undertake training programs and prescribing those programs;

7. prescribing the number of First Nations, Inuit or Métis representatives on the boards of directors of societies, the manner of their appointment and their terms, for the purpose of subsection 36 (1);

8. prescribing provisions to be included in the by-laws of societies for the purpose of subsection 36 (3);

9. providing for an executive committee of the board of directors of a society, its composition, quorum, powers and duties;

10. prescribing fees that may be charged for services and the conditions under which a fee may be charged;

11. respecting matters that relate to or arise as a result of an amalgamation under section 47 or a Minister's order under section 48, including rules governing court orders made with respect to a society;

12. prescribing grounds for the purposes of subclause 60 (2) (c) (ii).

### Restructuring

(5) A regulation made under paragraph 11 of subsection (4) prevails over the *Corporations Act* or regulations made under that Act to the extent of any conflict.

> **Note:** On the first day that section 350 of Schedule 1 to the *Supporting Children, Youth and Families Act, 2017* and subsection 4 (1) of the *Not-for-Profit Corporations Act, 2010* are both in force, subsection 341 (5) of the Act is amended by striking out "the *Corporations Act*" and substituting "the *Not-for-Profit Corporations Act, 2010*". (See: 2017, c. 14, Sched. 3, s. 13)

### Regulations: Part IV (First Nations, Inuit and Métis Child and Family Services)

#### Lieutenant Governor in Council regulations

**342.** (1) The Lieutenant Governor in Council may make regulations for the purposes of Part IV,

1. modifying or excluding the application of any provision or requirement of this Act or the regulations to a First Nations, Inuit or Métis child and family service authority, a band or First Nations, Inuit or Métis community or specified persons or classes of persons, including persons caring for children under customary care, and providing for other provisions or requirements to apply instead of or in addition to the provisions or requirements of this Act and the regulations.

#### Minister's regulations

(2) The Minister may make regulations for the purposes of Part IV,

1. governing the process for establishing lists of First Nations, Inuit or Métis communities in a regulation made under subsection 68 (1), including procedures that a community must follow and requirements that a community must meet;
2. prescribing matters requiring consultation between societies, persons or entities and bands or First Nations, Inuit or Métis communities for the purposes of clause 72 (i);
3. governing consultations with bands and First Nations, Inuit or Métis communities under sections 72 and 73 and prescribing the procedures and practices to be followed by societies, persons and entities and the duties of societies, persons and entities during the consultations;
4. prescribing services and powers for the purposes of section 73.

### Regulations: Part V (Child Protection)

#### Lieutenant Governor in Council regulations

**343.** (1) The Lieutenant Governor in Council may make regulations for the purposes of Part V,

1. prescribing jurisdictions outside Canada whose court orders may be recognized as extra-provincial child protection orders, and conditions for such recognition;
2. prescribing additional circumstances and conditions that constitute a 16 or 17 year old being in need of protection for the purpose of clause 74 (2) (o);
3. governing the exercise of the powers of entry set out in subsections 81 (6) and (10) and 86 (1) and (2);
4. prescribing methods of alternative dispute resolution for the purpose of section 95;

5. assigning to a Director any powers, duties or obligations of the Crown with respect to children who are in extended society care under an order made under paragraph 3 of subsection 101 (1) or clause 116 (1) (c);
6. prescribing additional criteria for when an assessment may be ordered under section 98, and governing the scope of an assessment and the form of an assessment report under that section;
7. respecting applications for a review by the Board under subsection 109 (8);
8. prescribing additional practices and procedures for the purposes of subsection 109 (11);
9. prescribing the qualifications or experience a member of the Board is required to have in order to conduct reviews under subsection 109 (9), 119 (6) or 120 (5);
10. respecting the making of complaints to a society under subsection 119 (1) or to the Board under subsection 119 (5) or 120 (3);
11. prescribing matters for the purposes of paragraph 2 of subsection 119 (5) and paragraph 6 of subsection 120 (4);
12. prescribing additional orders that may be made by the Board for the purposes of clauses 119 (10) (d) and 120 (7) (f);
13. prescribing practices and procedures for the purposes of hearings conducted by the Board under subsection 119 (8) or during a review of a complaint under section 120;
14. respecting the format of warrants under sections 131 and 132 and the procedures to be followed in applying for, issuing, receiving and filing warrants of different formats;
15. prescribing manners of applying for a warrant under section 132, including a manner other than submitting an information on oath, setting out the circumstances under which those manners may be used and providing for any additional requirements that must be met if those manners are used;
16. respecting the manner in which the register referred to in subsection 133 (5) is to be kept;

**Note: On a day to be named by proclamation of the Lieutenant Governor, paragraph 16 of subsection 343 (1) of the Act is repealed. (See: 2017, c. 14, Sched. 3, s. 14)**

17. requiring the removal of a name from the register referred to in subsection 133 (5), or the amendment of the register, under specified circumstances, and specifying those circumstances;

**Note: On a day to be named by proclamation of the Lieutenant Governor, paragraph 17 of subsection 343 (1) of the Act is repealed. (See: 2017, c. 14, Sched. 3, s. 14)**

18. prescribing practices and procedures for hearings held under clause 134 (4) (b).

**Note: On a day to be named by proclamation of the Lieutenant Governor, paragraph 18 of subsection 343 (1) of the Act is repealed. (See: 2017, c. 14, Sched. 3, s. 14)**

### Minister's regulations

(2) The Minister may make regulations for the purposes of Part V,

1. prescribing requirements and purposes for the purpose of the definition of child protection worker;
2. respecting the procedures to be followed by a society or a child and family service authority for the purposes of subsection 74 (4);
3. prescribing additional provisions to be included in a temporary care agreement for the purpose of paragraph 7 of subsection 75 (10);
4. prescribing the manner of varying a temporary care agreement under subsection 75 (12);
5. prescribing duties and obligations of societies and rights and responsibilities of children in respect of agreements made under section 77 (agreements with 16 and 17 year olds), including prescribing the services and supports that may be provided under them, prescribing additional circumstances for making such agreements and provisions to be contained in them and governing their variation and termination;
6. prescribing the complaint review procedure that societies are required to follow for the purpose of subsection 119 (2);
7. governing agreements entered into under section 124, including prescribing entities required to enter into the agreements, the expiry, renewal and termination of the agreements, the provisions to be included in the agreements, the care and support to be provided to persons under the agreements, the terms and conditions on which the care and support is to be provided and any exceptions to the requirement that an agreement be entered into or that care and support be provided under section 124;
8. prescribing support services for the purposes of paragraph 3 of subsection 124 (1);

9. prescribing circumstances and conditions for the purposes of subsection 125 (4);
10. respecting assessments to be made under subsection 126 (1).

### Regulations: Part VI (Youth Justice)

**344.** The Lieutenant Governor in Council may make regulations for the purposes of Part VI,

1. governing the establishment, operation, maintenance, management and use of places of temporary detention, of open custody and of secure custody;
2. governing the establishment and operation of and the accommodation, equipment and services to be provided in any premises established, operated, maintained or designated for the purposes of the *Youth Criminal Justice Act* (Canada);
3. prescribing additional duties and functions of,
    i. probation officers, and
    ii. provincial directors;
4. prescribing the duties and functions of bailiffs;
5. prescribing the qualifications of probation officers;
6. prescribing additional duties and functions of persons in charge of places of temporary detention, of open custody and of secure custody;
7. prescribing reports to be made and information to be furnished under section 147, their form and the intervals at which they are to be made or furnished;
8. governing the conduct, discipline, rights and privileges of young persons in places of temporary detention, of open custody or of secure custody;
9. prescribing procedures for the admission of young persons to and their discharge from places of temporary detention, of open custody or of secure custody or premises in which a service is provided;
10. prescribing the number of members of the Board and the number of members that is a quorum;
11. prescribing additional powers, duties and procedures of the Board;
12. governing the exercise of the power of entry given under subsection 153 (5);
13. governing searches under subsection 155 (1);
14. prescribing procedures for the seizure and disposition of contraband found during a search;
15. respecting any matter considered necessary or advisable to carry out effectively the intent and purpose of Part VI.

### Regulations: Part VII (Extraordinary Measures)

**345.** The Lieutenant Governor in Council may make regulations for the purposes of Part VII,

1. prescribing procedures for the admission of persons to and their discharge from secure treatment programs;

2. prescribing standards for secure treatment programs;

3. governing policies on the use of mechanical restraints required by section 160, including prescribing provisions that must be or may not be included;

4. prescribing standards for secure de-escalation rooms;

5. prescribing procedures to be followed when a child or young person is placed in or released from a secure de-escalation room;

6. prescribing the frequency of reviews under subsection 174 (6);

7. prescribing additional standards and procedures with which a service provider must comply under subsection 174 (9);

8. prescribing matters to be reviewed and prescribing additional reports under section 175;

9. prescribing procedures as intrusive procedures;

10. prescribing drugs, combinations of drugs or classes of drugs as psychotropic drugs.

## Regulations: Part VIII (Adoption and Adoption Licensing)

**346.** (1) The Lieutenant Governor in Council may make regulations for the purposes of Part VIII,

1. designating a person or body to exercise powers and perform duties with respect to adoption;

2. governing the person or body designated under paragraph 1, including prescribing the powers and duties of the person or body;

3. prescribing criteria for the purposes of the definition of "birth parent" in subsection 179 (1);

4. prescribing matters for the purposes of clause 180 (4) (b);

5. prescribing special circumstances for the purposes of subsection 188 (9) (placement outside Canada);

6. governing applications for review under subsection 192 (3);

7. prescribing additional practices and procedures for the purposes of subsection 192 (7);

8. prescribing the qualifications or experience a member of the Board is required to have for the purpose of subsection 192 (8);

9. governing procedures to be followed by a Director in making a review under subsection 193 (3), what types of decisions and directions the Director is authorized to make after conducting a review, and any consequences following as a result of a decision or direction;

10. prescribing an alternative dispute resolution method for the purposes of subsections 198 (8) and 207 (9);

11. governing the placement of children for adoption;

12. prescribing rules and standards governing the placement of children for adoption by licensees;

13. governing openness orders under Part VIII;

14. prescribing persons for the purposes of clause 222 (3) (d);

15. prescribing the powers and duties of a designated custodian under section 223 and governing the fees that the designated custodian may charge in connection with the exercise of its powers and the performance of its duties;

16. governing the disclosure of information under section 224 to a designated custodian;

17. governing the disclosure of information under section 225 by the Minister, a society, a licensee or a designated custodian;

18. establishing and governing a mechanism for the review or appeal of a decision made by the Minister, a society, a licensee or a designated custodian concerning the disclosure of information under section 224 or 225;

19. governing the fees that a society, licensee or designated custodian may charge for the disclosure of information under section 224 or 225;

20. governing the inspection, removal or alteration of information related to an adoption for the purposes of clause 227 (1) (b);

21. exempting a licensee or class of licensees from any or all provisions or requirements of Part VIII or the regulations under it, either indefinitely or for a specified period;

22. governing the issuing, renewal and expiry of licences and prescribing fees payable by an applicant for a licence or its renewal;

23. prescribing grounds for which the issuance of a licence may be refused for the purposes of clause 231 (c);

24. prescribing grounds for which a licence may be revoked or the renewal of a licence may be refused for the purposes of clause 232 (e);

25. prescribing expenses that may be charged under clause 240 (d) and the conditions under which such expenses may be charged.

### Functions of Central Authority

(2) In subsection (3),

"Central Authority" means the Central Authority designated under clause 24 (a) of the *Intercountry Adoption Act, 1998*; ("Autorité centrale")

"Convention" means the Convention on Protection of Children and Co-operation in respect of Intercountry Adoption, set out in the Schedule to the *Intercountry Adoption Act, 1998*. ("Convention")

**Same**

(3) The Lieutenant Governor in Council may make regulations assigning functions of the Central Authority under Part VIII to public authorities, accredited bodies or persons in accordance with Article 22 of the Convention.

**Minister's regulations**

(4) The Minister may make regulations for the purposes of Part VIII,

1. prescribing the form of an affidavit of execution for the purposes of subsection 180 (12);
2. prescribing the manner in which placements are to be registered under subsection 183 (7);
3. prescribing persons for the purposes of subclause 188 (3) (b) (ii);
4. prescribing persons and entities and timing requirements for the purposes of clause 238 (b);
5. prescribing the accounts and records to be kept by licensees;
6. requiring licensees and applicants for a licence or renewal of a licence to provide information, returns and reports, and respecting the manner in which the information, returns and reports must be provided;
7. providing for the inspection of the records of licensees;
8. governing the qualifications of persons employed by licensees;
9. requiring licensees to be bonded or to submit letters of credit in the prescribed form and terms and with the prescribed collateral security, prescribing the form, terms and collateral security and providing for the forfeiture of bonds and letters of credit and the disposition of the proceeds.

## Regulations: Part IX (Residential Licensing)

### Lieutenant Governor in Council regulations

**347.** (1) The Lieutenant Governor in Council may make regulations for the purposes of Part IX,

1. prescribing other residences for the purposes of paragraph 3 of the definition of "children's residence" in section 243;
2. prescribing other places for the purposes of paragraph 12 of the definition of "children's residence" in section 243;
3. prescribing circumstances in which a licence is required to provide residential care for the purposes of subparagraph 2 ii of section 244;
4. prescribing circumstances for the purposes of section 251;
5. prescribing matters about which the Minister may issue directives for the purposes of subsection 252 (1);

6. governing reviews and appeals under section 260;
7. governing the issuance, renewal and expiry of licences and prescribing fees payable by an applicant for a licence or its renewal;
8. prescribing grounds for which the issuance of a licence may be refused for the purposes of clause 261 (f);
9. prescribing grounds for which a licence may be revoked or the renewal of a licence may be refused for the purposes of clause 262 (g);
10. prescribing other powers and duties of an inspector for the purposes of subsection 273 (3);
11. prescribing other powers of an inspector for the purposes of clause 276 (1) (i);
12. prescribing provisions of Part IX or the regulations for the purposes of clause 280 (1) (i);
13. prescribing provisions of Part IX or the regulations for the purposes of clause 280 (3) (c).

### Minister's regulations

(2) The Minister may make regulations for the purposes of Part IX,

1. prescribing or otherwise providing for anything required or permitted by Part IX, except anything referred to in subsection (1) of this section, to be prescribed or otherwise provided for in the regulations, including governing anything required or permitted to be done in accordance with the regulations;
2. specifying and governing classes of licence that may be assigned for the purposes of section 258;
3. governing the amount or method of determining the amount that a licensee may charge for the provision of residential care under the authority of a licence for the purposes of section 268, including governing reviews and variation of the amount or method and circumstances in which a licensee may charge a different amount than the amount that could otherwise be charged;
4. governing the management and operation of, and the accommodation, facilities, equipment and services to be provided in, children's residences and other places where residential care is provided under the authority of a licence;
5. specifying and governing performance standards and performance measures with respect to the provision of services in children's residences or other places where residential care is provided under the authority of a licence, including standards with respect to quality of care and responsiveness to cultural needs;
6. prescribing the accounts and records to be kept by licensees;

7. prescribing the qualifications, powers and duties of persons supervising children in children's residences or other places where residential care is provided under the authority of a licence;

8. prescribing screening measures to be conducted for licensees, applicants for a licence or renewal of a licence and other persons providing residential care to children in children's residences or other places where residential care is provided under the authority of a licence;

9. governing procedures for the admission to and discharge of children from children's residences or other places where residential care is provided under the authority of a licence;

10. requiring licensees and applicants for a licence or renewal of a licence to provide information, returns and reports, and respecting the manner in which the information, returns and reports must be provided.

## Regulations: Part X (Personal Information)

**348.** The Lieutenant Governor in Council may make regulations for the purposes of Part X,

1. prescribing persons for the purpose of paragraph 2 of subsection 283 (2);

2. prescribing other ministers with whom the Minister may share information for the purposes of subsection 283 (5);

3. prescribing requirements and restrictions in relation to research and analysis for the purposes of subsection 283 (7);

4. prescribing and governing methods of giving notice under clauses 283 (8) (b) and 284 (3) (b);

5. prescribing the purposes for the collection under section 284;

6. prescribing purposes related to a society's functions for the purposes of clause 288 (2) (c), subclause 291 (2) (a) (ii) and subsection 292 (3);

7. specifying requirements that an express instruction mentioned in clause 291 (1) (a) must meet;

8. prescribing requirements and restrictions for the purposes of clauses 288 (2) (e), 291 (1) (j) and (k) and 292 (1) (h) and subsections 293 (2) and (3), 302 (10), 304 (1) and (4) and 305 (10);

9. prescribing entities for the purpose of section 293;

10. prescribing information and circumstances for the purposes of subsection 293 (4);

11. prescribing exceptions and additional requirements for the purposes of subsection 293 (9);

12. prescribing a body for the purposes of sections 302, 304 and 305;

13. prescribing information for the purpose of subsection 304 (2);

14. prescribing persons for the purpose of subsection 304 (3);

15. prescribing provisions and prescribing and governing the manner of recording disclosures for the purpose of subsection 306 (3);

16. prescribing exceptions and additional requirements for the purposes of subsection 308 (2);

17. prescribing requirements for the purposes of subsection 308 (3) and clause 309 (1) (b);

18. prescribing circumstances for the purposes of subsection 314 (10) and governing the fees that may be charged in those circumstances;

19. permitting notices, statements or any other things, that under this Part are required to be provided in writing, to be provided in electronic or other form instead, subject to the conditions or restrictions that are specified by the regulations made under this section;

20. requiring service providers to provide information to the Commissioner and specifying the type of information to be provided and the time at which and manner in which it is to be provided.

## Regulations: Part XI (Miscellaneous Matters)

**349.** The Lieutenant Governor in Council may make regulations for the purposes of Part XI,

1. prescribing the number of members of the Board and the number of members that is a quorum;

2. prescribing additional powers, duties and procedures of the Board;

3. respecting police record checks for the purposes of section 334, including,

   i. requiring different classes of persons to provide different types of police record checks or different types of information as part of a check,

   ii. prescribing procedures and practices to be followed when a police record check is required,

   iii. prescribing other persons for the purposes of paragraph 3 of section 334, and

   iv. requiring police record checks to be obtained from jurisdictions outside Ontario in specified circumstances;

4. respecting police record checks for the purposes of section 335, including,

   i. prescribing other entities from whom a society may request police record checks or other information,

ii.  prescribing other information that may be requested,

iii.  prescribing circumstances in which and purposes for which the request may be made, and

iv.  prescribing procedures and practices to be followed when a police record check or other information is requested.

## PART XIII   REPEAL, COMMENCEMENT AND SHORT TITLE

**350.** Omitted (amends, repeals or revokes other legislation).

**351.** Omitted (provides for coming into force of provisions of this Act).

**352.** Omitted (enacts short title of this Act).

# Children's Law Reform Act

RSO 1990, c C.12

PART I
## PARENTAGE
### INTERPRETATION AND APPLICATION

| | | |
|---|---|---|
| 1. | Definitions and interpretation, Part I | 125 |
| 2. | Rules of construction | 126 |
| 3. | Application. | 126 |

### RULES OF PARENTAGE

| | | |
|---|---|---|
| 4. | Person is child of parents | 126 |
| 5. | Provision of reproductive material, embryo not determinative | 126 |
| 6. | Birth parent | 126 |
| 7. | Other biological parent, if sexual intercourse | 126 |
| 8. | Birth parent's spouse, if assisted reproduction or insemination by sperm donor. | 127 |
| 9 | Parents under pre-conception parentage agreements | 127 |
| 10. | Surrogacy, up to four intended parents. | 127 |
| 11. | Surrogacy, more than four intended parents. | 128 |
| 12. | Posthumous conception. | 128 |
| 13. | Declaration of parentage, general. | 129 |
| 14. | Reopening on new evidence. | 129 |
| 15. | Effect of declaration | 129 |

### EXTRA-PROVINCIAL DECLARATORY ORDERS

| | | |
|---|---|---|
| 16. | Extra-provincial declaratory orders. | 129 |

### OTHER MATTERS

| | | |
|---|---|---|
| 17. | Other Matters | 130 |
| 17.1 | Admissibility in evidence of acknowledgment against interest | 130 |
| 17.2 | Blood, DNA tests | 130 |
| 17.3 | Confidentiality | 130 |
| 17.4 | Court statement. | 130 |
| 17.5 | Certified copies of documents filed with the Registrar General | 130 |
| 17.6 | Duties of Registrar General. | 130 |

PART III
## CUSTODY, ACCESS AND GUARDIANSHIP
### INTERPRETATION

| | | |
|---|---|---|
| 18. | Definitions, Part III | 130 |
| 19. | Purposes, Part III. | 131 |

### Custody and Access

20.    Entitlement to custody . . . . . . . . . . . . . . . . . . . . . . . . . . . . . . . . . . . . . . . . . . . . . . . . . . . . . . . . . . . . . . . 131
21.    Application for custody or access . . . . . . . . . . . . . . . . . . . . . . . . . . . . . . . . . . . . . . . . . . . . . . . . . . . . . . 131
21.1   Police records checks, non-parents . . . . . . . . . . . . . . . . . . . . . . . . . . . . . . . . . . . . . . . . . . . . . . . . . . . . 131
21.2   CAS records search, non-parents . . . . . . . . . . . . . . . . . . . . . . . . . . . . . . . . . . . . . . . . . . . . . . . . . . . . . . 132
21.3   Other proceedings . . . . . . . . . . . . . . . . . . . . . . . . . . . . . . . . . . . . . . . . . . . . . . . . . . . . . . . . . . . . . . . . . 132
22.    Jurisdiction . . . . . . . . . . . . . . . . . . . . . . . . . . . . . . . . . . . . . . . . . . . . . . . . . . . . . . . . . . . . . . . . . . . . . . 133
23.    Serious harm to child . . . . . . . . . . . . . . . . . . . . . . . . . . . . . . . . . . . . . . . . . . . . . . . . . . . . . . . . . . . . . . . 133
24.    Merits of application for custody or access . . . . . . . . . . . . . . . . . . . . . . . . . . . . . . . . . . . . . . . . . . . . . . 133
25.    Declining jurisdiction . . . . . . . . . . . . . . . . . . . . . . . . . . . . . . . . . . . . . . . . . . . . . . . . . . . . . . . . . . . . . . . 134
26.    Delay . . . . . . . . . . . . . . . . . . . . . . . . . . . . . . . . . . . . . . . . . . . . . . . . . . . . . . . . . . . . . . . . . . . . . . . . . . . 134
27.    Effect of divorce proceedings . . . . . . . . . . . . . . . . . . . . . . . . . . . . . . . . . . . . . . . . . . . . . . . . . . . . . . . . 134

### Custody and Access—Orders

28     Powers of court . . . . . . . . . . . . . . . . . . . . . . . . . . . . . . . . . . . . . . . . . . . . . . . . . . . . . . . . . . . . . . . . . . . . 134
29.    Order varying an order . . . . . . . . . . . . . . . . . . . . . . . . . . . . . . . . . . . . . . . . . . . . . . . . . . . . . . . . . . . . . . 135

### Custody and Access—assistance to Court

30.    Assessment of needs of child . . . . . . . . . . . . . . . . . . . . . . . . . . . . . . . . . . . . . . . . . . . . . . . . . . . . . . . . . 135
31.    Further evidence from outside Ontario . . . . . . . . . . . . . . . . . . . . . . . . . . . . . . . . . . . . . . . . . . . . . . . . . . 136
32.    Request from outside Ontario for further evidence . . . . . . . . . . . . . . . . . . . . . . . . . . . . . . . . . . . . . . . . 136

### Custody and Access—Enforcement

33.    Supervision of custody or access . . . . . . . . . . . . . . . . . . . . . . . . . . . . . . . . . . . . . . . . . . . . . . . . . . . . . . 136
34.    Restraining order . . . . . . . . . . . . . . . . . . . . . . . . . . . . . . . . . . . . . . . . . . . . . . . . . . . . . . . . . . . . . . . . . . 136
35.    Order where child unlawfully withheld . . . . . . . . . . . . . . . . . . . . . . . . . . . . . . . . . . . . . . . . . . . . . . . . . . 137
36.    Court orders, removal and return of children . . . . . . . . . . . . . . . . . . . . . . . . . . . . . . . . . . . . . . . . . . . . . 137
37.    Contempt of orders of Ontario Court of Justice . . . . . . . . . . . . . . . . . . . . . . . . . . . . . . . . . . . . . . . . . . . 138
38.    Information as to address . . . . . . . . . . . . . . . . . . . . . . . . . . . . . . . . . . . . . . . . . . . . . . . . . . . . . . . . . . . . 138

### Custody and Access—Extra-Provincial Matters

39.    Interim powers of court . . . . . . . . . . . . . . . . . . . . . . . . . . . . . . . . . . . . . . . . . . . . . . . . . . . . . . . . . . . . . . 138
40.    Enforcement of extra-provincial orders . . . . . . . . . . . . . . . . . . . . . . . . . . . . . . . . . . . . . . . . . . . . . . . . . 138
41.    Superseding order, material change in circumstances . . . . . . . . . . . . . . . . . . . . . . . . . . . . . . . . . . . . . . . 139
42.    Superseding order, serious harm . . . . . . . . . . . . . . . . . . . . . . . . . . . . . . . . . . . . . . . . . . . . . . . . . . . . . . . 139
43.    True copy of extra-provincial order . . . . . . . . . . . . . . . . . . . . . . . . . . . . . . . . . . . . . . . . . . . . . . . . . . . . . 139
44.    Court may take notice of foreign law . . . . . . . . . . . . . . . . . . . . . . . . . . . . . . . . . . . . . . . . . . . . . . . . . . . . 139
45.    Convention on Civil Aspects of International Child Abduction . . . . . . . . . . . . . . . . . . . . . . . . . . . . . . . . . 139

### Guardianship

46.    Appointment of guardian . . . . . . . . . . . . . . . . . . . . . . . . . . . . . . . . . . . . . . . . . . . . . . . . . . . . . . . . . . . . 145
47.    Parents and joint guardians . . . . . . . . . . . . . . . . . . . . . . . . . . . . . . . . . . . . . . . . . . . . . . . . . . . . . . . . . . . 145
48.    Criteria . . . . . . . . . . . . . . . . . . . . . . . . . . . . . . . . . . . . . . . . . . . . . . . . . . . . . . . . . . . . . . . . . . . . . . . . . . 145
49.    Effect of appointment . . . . . . . . . . . . . . . . . . . . . . . . . . . . . . . . . . . . . . . . . . . . . . . . . . . . . . . . . . . . . . . 145
50.    Payment of debt due to child if no guardian . . . . . . . . . . . . . . . . . . . . . . . . . . . . . . . . . . . . . . . . . . . . . . . 145
51.    Accounts . . . . . . . . . . . . . . . . . . . . . . . . . . . . . . . . . . . . . . . . . . . . . . . . . . . . . . . . . . . . . . . . . . . . . . . . . 145
52.    Transfer of property to child . . . . . . . . . . . . . . . . . . . . . . . . . . . . . . . . . . . . . . . . . . . . . . . . . . . . . . . . . . 145
53.    Management fees and expenses . . . . . . . . . . . . . . . . . . . . . . . . . . . . . . . . . . . . . . . . . . . . . . . . . . . . . . . . 145
54.    Bond by guardian . . . . . . . . . . . . . . . . . . . . . . . . . . . . . . . . . . . . . . . . . . . . . . . . . . . . . . . . . . . . . . . . . . . 146
55.    Where child has support obligation . . . . . . . . . . . . . . . . . . . . . . . . . . . . . . . . . . . . . . . . . . . . . . . . . . . . . 146

56.   Removal and resignation of guardian . . . . . . . . . . . . . . . . . . . . . . . . . . . . . . . . . . . . . . . . . . . . . . . . . 146
57.   Notice to Estate Registrar for Ontario. . . . . . . . . . . . . . . . . . . . . . . . . . . . . . . . . . . . . . . . . . . . . . . . . 146

### DISPOSITION OF PROPERTY

58.   Court order re property of child. . . . . . . . . . . . . . . . . . . . . . . . . . . . . . . . . . . . . . . . . . . . . . . . . . . . . . 146
59.   Order for maintenance where power of appointment in favour of children . . . . . . . . . . . . . . . . . . . . . . 146

### TESTAMENTARY CUSTODY AND GUARDIANSHIP

60.   Appointments by will. . . . . . . . . . . . . . . . . . . . . . . . . . . . . . . . . . . . . . . . . . . . . . . . . . . . . . . . . . . . . . 146

### PROCEDURE

61.   Procedure, general . . . . . . . . . . . . . . . . . . . . . . . . . . . . . . . . . . . . . . . . . . . . . . . . . . . . . . . . . . . . . . . . 147
62.   Application or response by minor. . . . . . . . . . . . . . . . . . . . . . . . . . . . . . . . . . . . . . . . . . . . . . . . . . . . . 147
63.   Child entitled to be heard. . . . . . . . . . . . . . . . . . . . . . . . . . . . . . . . . . . . . . . . . . . . . . . . . . . . . . . . . . . 147
64.   Where child is sixteen or more years old. . . . . . . . . . . . . . . . . . . . . . . . . . . . . . . . . . . . . . . . . . . . . . . . 148
65.   All proceedings in one court . . . . . . . . . . . . . . . . . . . . . . . . . . . . . . . . . . . . . . . . . . . . . . . . . . . . . . . . . 148
66.   Consent and domestic contracts . . . . . . . . . . . . . . . . . . . . . . . . . . . . . . . . . . . . . . . . . . . . . . . . . . . . . . 148
67.   Part subject to contracts . . . . . . . . . . . . . . . . . . . . . . . . . . . . . . . . . . . . . . . . . . . . . . . . . . . . . . . . . . . . 148
68.   Jurisdiction of Superior Court of Justice . . . . . . . . . . . . . . . . . . . . . . . . . . . . . . . . . . . . . . . . . . . . . . . . 148
69.   Confidentiality . . . . . . . . . . . . . . . . . . . . . . . . . . . . . . . . . . . . . . . . . . . . . . . . . . . . . . . . . . . . . . . . . . . . 148
70.   Where to apply for interim orders and variations. . . . . . . . . . . . . . . . . . . . . . . . . . . . . . . . . . . . . . . . . . 148
71.   Interim order. . . . . . . . . . . . . . . . . . . . . . . . . . . . . . . . . . . . . . . . . . . . . . . . . . . . . . . . . . . . . . . . . . . . . 148
72.   Appeal from Ontario Court of Justice. . . . . . . . . . . . . . . . . . . . . . . . . . . . . . . . . . . . . . . . . . . . . . . . . . 148
73.   Order effective pending appeal . . . . . . . . . . . . . . . . . . . . . . . . . . . . . . . . . . . . . . . . . . . . . . . . . . . . . . . 148
74.   Rule of construction, guardianship of person and property . . . . . . . . . . . . . . . . . . . . . . . . . . . . . . . . . . 148

### PART I   PARENTAGE
#### Interpretation and Application
**Definitions and interpretation, Part I**
**Definitions**

**1.** (1)  In this Part,

"assisted reproduction" means a method of conceiving other than by sexual intercourse;

"birth" means birth as defined in the *Vital Statistics Act* and includes a still-birth as defined in that Act;

"birth parent" means, in relation to a child, the person who gives birth to the child;

"court" means the Family Court or the Superior Court of Justice;

"embryo" means embryo as defined in the *Assisted Human Reproduction Act* (Canada);

"insemination by a sperm donor" means an attempt to conceive a child through sexual intercourse in the circumstances described in subsection 7(4);

"reproductive material" means all or any part of a sperm, ovum or other human cell or a human gene;

"spouse" means the person to whom a person is married or with whom the person is living in a conjugal relationship outside marriage;

"surrogate" means a person who agrees to carry a child conceived through assisted reproduction if, at the time of conception, the person intends to relinquish entitlement to parentage of the child, once born, to one or more persons.

**If marriage is void**

(2)  For the purposes of the definition of "spouse" in subsection (1), two persons who, in good faith, go through a form of marriage with each other that is void but who live in a conjugal relationship are deemed to be married during the time they live in a conjugal relationship, and the marriage is deemed to be terminated when they cease to do so.

**Interpretation, conception through assisted reproduction**

(3)  For the purposes of this Part, a child conceived through assisted reproduction is deemed to have been con-

ceived on the day the reproductive material or embryo used in the assisted reproduction is implanted in the birth parent.

## Rules of construction

### Relationship by blood or marriage

**2.** (1) For the purposes of construing any Act, regulation or, subject to subsection (3), instrument, unless a contrary intention appears, a reference to a person or group or class of persons described in terms of relationship by blood or marriage to another person,

(a) includes a person who comes within that description by reason of the relationship of parent and child set out in this Part; and

(b) in respect of a child conceived through assisted reproduction or through insemination by a sperm donor, does not include,

(i) a person who provided reproductive material or an embryo for use in the conception if that person is not a parent of the child, or

(ii) a person related to a person referred to in subclause (i).

### Application to Acts, statutory instruments

(2) Subsection (1) applies to an Act, regulation or other instrument made under an Act, regardless of when it was enacted or made.

### Application to other instruments

(3) In the case of an instrument that is not made under an Act,

(a) subsection (1) applies to the instrument if it was made on or after the day subsection 1(1) of the *All Families Are Equal Act (Parentage and Related Registrations Statute Law Amendment), 2016* came into force;

(b) subsection (1) as it read immediately before the day subsection 1(1) of the *All Families Are Equal Act (Parentage and Related Registrations Statute Law Amendment), 2016* came into force continues to apply to an instrument made before that day, if it was made on or after March 31, 1978.

### References assuming two parents

(4) If, under this Part, a child has more than two parents, a reference in any Act or regulation to the parents of the child that is not intended to exclude a parent shall, unless a contrary intention appears, be read as a reference to all of the child's parents, even if the terminology used assumes that a child would have no more than two parents.

### References to "le père ou la mère", "le père et la mère", etc.

(5) For the purposes of construing the French version of any Act or regulation, unless a contrary intention appears, the terms "père" and "mère" used together, conjunctively or disjunctively, in relation to a child, shall be construed as referring to a parent or parents of the child as set out in this Part.

### Application

**3.** This Part governs the determination of parentage for all purposes of the law of Ontario.

## Rules of Parentage

### Person is child of parents

**4.** (1) A person is the child of his or her parents.

### Determining parent of a child

(2) A parent of a child is,

(a) a person who is a parent of the child under sections 6 to 13, except in the case of an adopted child;

(b) in the case of an adopted child, a parent of the child as provided for under section 158 or 159 of the *Child and Family Services Act*.

### Kindred relationships

(3) The relationship of parent and child set out in subsections (1) and (2) shall be followed in determining the kindred relationships that flow from it.

### For all purposes of Ontario law

(4) For greater certainty, this section applies for all purposes of the law of Ontario.

### Provision of reproductive material, embryo not determinative

**5.** A person who provides reproductive material or an embryo for use in the conception of a child through assisted reproduction is not, and shall not be recognized in law to be, a parent of the child unless he or she is a parent of the child under this Part.

### Birth parent

**6.** (1) The birth parent of a child is, and shall be recognized in law to be, a parent of the child.

### Exception, surrogacy

(2) Subsection (1) is subject to the relinquishment of an entitlement to parentage by a surrogate under section 10, or to a declaration by a court to that effect under section 10 or 11.

### Other biological parent, if sexual intercourse

**7.** (1) The person whose sperm resulted in the conception of a child conceived through sexual intercourse is, and shall be recognized in law to be, a parent of the child.

### Presumption

(2) Unless the contrary is proven on a balance of probabilities, there is a presumption in respect of a child conceived through sexual intercourse that a person is, and shall be recognized in law to be, the parent referred to in subsection (1) if any of the following circumstances applies:

1. The person was the birth parent's spouse at the time of the child's birth.

2. The person was married to the child's birth parent by a marriage that was terminated by death or judgment

of nullity within 300 days before the child's birth or by divorce where the judgment of divorce was granted within 300 days before the child's birth.

3. The person was living in a conjugal relationship with the child's birth parent before the child's birth and the child is born within 300 days after they cease to live in a conjugal relationship.

4. The person has certified the child's birth, as a parent of the child, under the *Vital Statistics Act* or a similar Act in another jurisdiction in Canada.

5. The person has been found or recognized by a court of competent jurisdiction outside Ontario to be a parent of the child.

### Conflicting presumptions

(3) If circumstances exist that give rise to a presumption by more than one person under subsection (2), no presumption shall be made under that subsection.

### Non-application, insemination by a sperm donor

(4) This section is deemed not to apply to a person whose sperm is used to conceive a child through sexual intercourse if, before the child is conceived, the person and the intended birth parent agree in writing that the person does not intend to be a parent of the child.

### Same, sperm donor not a parent

(5) A person to whom subsection (4) applies is not, and shall not be recognized in law to be, a parent of a child conceived in the circumstances set out in that subsection.

### Birth parent's spouse, if assisted reproduction or insemination by sperm donor
### Assisted reproduction

**8.** (1) If the birth parent of a child conceived through assisted reproduction had a spouse at the time of the child's conception, the spouse is, and shall be recognized in law to be, a parent of the child.

### Insemination by a sperm donor

(2) If the birth parent of a child conceived through insemination by a sperm donor had a spouse at the time of the child's conception, the spouse is, and shall be recognized in law to be, a parent of the child.

### Non-application, lack of consent

(3) This section does not apply if, before the child's conception,

(a) the spouse did not consent to be a parent of the child; or

(b) the spouse consented to be a parent of the child but withdrew the consent.

### Non-application, surrogacy or posthumous conception

(4) This section does not apply if the birth parent is a surrogate or if the child is conceived after the death of a person declared under section 12 to be his or her parent.

### Parents under pre-conception parentage agreements
### Definition

**9.** (1) In this section,

"pre-conception parentage agreement" means a written agreement between two or more parties in which they agree to be, together, the parents of a child yet to be conceived.

### Application

(2) This section applies with respect to a pre-conception parentage agreement only if,

(a) there are no more than four parties to the agreement;

(b) the intended birth parent is not a surrogate, and is a party to the agreement;

(c) if the child is to be conceived through sexual intercourse but not through insemination by a sperm donor, the person whose sperm is to be used for the purpose of conception is a party to the agreement; and

(d) if the child is to be conceived through assisted reproduction or through insemination by a sperm donor, the spouse, if any, of the person who intends to be the birth parent is a party to the agreement, subject to subsection (3).

### If spouse intends to not be a parent

(3) Clause (2)(d) does not apply if, before the child is conceived, the birth parent's spouse provides written confirmation that he or she does not consent to be a parent of the child and does not withdraw the confirmation.

### Recognition of parentage

(4) On the birth of a child contemplated by a pre-conception parentage agreement, together with every party to a pre-conception parentage agreement who is a parent of the child under section 6 (birth parent), 7 (other biological parent) or 8 (birth parent's spouse), the other parties to the agreement are, and shall be recognized in law to be, parents of the child.

### Surrogacy, up to four intended parents
### Definitions

**10.** (1) In this section and in section 11,

"intended parent" means a party to a surrogacy agreement, other than the surrogate;

"surrogacy agreement" means a written agreement between a surrogate and one or more persons respecting a child to be carried by the surrogate, in which,

(a) the surrogate agrees to not be a parent of the child, and

(b) each of the other parties to the agreement agrees to be a parent of the child.

### Application

(2) This section applies only if the following conditions are met:

1. The surrogate and one or more persons enter into a surrogacy agreement before the child to be carried by the surrogate is conceived.

2. The surrogate and the intended parent or parents each received independent legal advice before entering into the agreement.

3. Of the parties to the agreement, there are no more than four intended parents.

4. The child is conceived through assisted reproduction.

### Recognition of parentage

(3) Subject to subsection (4), on the surrogate providing to the intended parent or parents consent in writing relinquishing the surrogate's entitlement to parentage of the child,

(a) the child becomes the child of each intended parent and each intended parent becomes, and shall be recognized in law to be, a parent of the child; and

(b) the child ceases to be the child of the surrogate and the surrogate ceases to be a parent of the child.

### Limitation

(4) The consent referred to in subsection (3) must not be provided before the child is seven days old.

### Parental rights and responsibilities

(5) Unless the surrogacy agreement provides otherwise, the surrogate and the intended parent or parents share the rights and responsibilities of a parent in respect of the child from the time of the child's birth until the child is seven days old, but any provision of the surrogacy agreement respecting parental rights and responsibilities after that period is of no effect.

### Failure to give consent

(6) Any party to a surrogacy agreement may apply to the court for a declaration of parentage with respect to the child if the consent referred to in subsection (3) is not provided by the surrogate because,

(a) the surrogate is deceased or otherwise incapable of providing the consent;

(b) the surrogate cannot be located after reasonable efforts have been made to do so; or

(c) the surrogate refuses to provide the consent.

### Declaration

(7) If an application is made under subsection (6), the court may,

(a) grant the declaration that is sought; or

(b) make any other declaration respecting the parentage of a child born to the surrogate as the court sees fit.

### Child's best interests

(8) The paramount consideration by the court in making a declaration under subsection (7) shall be the best interests of the child.

### Effect of surrogacy agreement

(9) A surrogacy agreement is unenforceable in law, but may be used as evidence of,

(a) an intended parent's intention to be a parent of a child contemplated by the agreement; and

(b) a surrogate's intention to not be a parent of a child contemplated by the agreement.

### Surrogacy, more than four intended parents

11. (1) If the conditions set out in subsection 10(2) are met other than the condition set out in paragraph 3 of that subsection, any party to the surrogacy agreement may apply to the court for a declaration of parentage respecting a child contemplated by the agreement.

### Time limit

(2) An application under subsection (1) may not be made,

(a) until the child is born; and

(b) unless the court orders otherwise, after the first anniversary of the child's birth.

### Parental rights and responsibilities

(3) Unless the surrogacy agreement provides otherwise, the surrogate and the intended parents share the rights and responsibilities of a parent in respect of the child from the time of the child's birth until the court makes a declaration of parentage respecting the child.

### Declaration

(4) If an application is made under subsection (1), the court may make any declaration that the court may make under section 10 and, for the purpose, subsections 10(8) and (9) apply with necessary modifications.

### Post-birth consent of surrogate

(5) A declaration naming one or more intended parents as a parent of the child and determining that the surrogate is not a parent of the child shall not be made under subsection (4) unless, after the child's birth, the surrogate provides to the intended parents consent in writing relinquishing the surrogate's entitlement to parentage of the child.

### Waiver

(6) Despite subsection (5), the court may waive the consent if any of the circumstances set out in subsection 10(6) apply.

### Posthumous conception

12. (1) A person who, at the time of a deceased person's death, was his or her spouse, may apply to the court for a declaration that the deceased person is a parent of a child conceived after his or her death through assisted reproduction.

### Time limit

(2) An application under subsection (1) may not be made,

(a) until the child is born; and

(b) unless the court orders otherwise, later than 90 days after the child's birth.

### Declaration

(3) he court may grant the declaration if the following conditions are met:

1. The deceased person consented in writing to be, together with the applicant, the parents of a child conceived posthumously through assisted reproduction, and did not withdraw the consent before his or her death.
2. If the child was born to a surrogate, the applicant is a parent of the child under section 10, and there is no other parent of the child.

### Declaration of parentage, general

**13.** (1) At any time after a child is born, any person having an interest may apply to the court for a declaration that a person is or is not a parent of the child.

### Exception, adopted child

(2) Subsection (1) does not apply if the child is adopted.

### Declaration

(3) If the court finds on the balance of probabilities that a person is or is not a parent of a child, the court may make a declaration to that effect.

### Restriction

(4) Despite subsection (3), the court shall not make any of the following declarations of parentage respecting a child under that subsection unless the conditions set out in subsection (5) are met:

1. A declaration of parentage that results in the child having more than two parents.
2. A declaration of parentage that results in the child having as a parent one other person, in addition to his or her birth parent, if that person is not a parent of the child under section 7, 8 or 9.

### Conditions

(5) The following conditions apply for the purposes of subsection (4):

1. The application for the declaration is made on or before the first anniversary of the child's birth, unless the court orders otherwise.
2. Every other person who is a parent of the child is a party to the application.
3. There is evidence that, before the child was conceived, every parent of the child and every person in respect of whom a declaration of parentage respecting that child is sought under the application intended to be, together, parents of the child.
4. The declaration is in the best interests of the child.

### Reopening on new evidence

**14.** (1) If a declaration is made by the court under this Part and evidence becomes available that was not available at the hearing of the application, the court may, on application, set aside or vary the order and make any other orders or give any directions that the court considers necessary.

### No effect on rights, property interests

(2) Setting aside an order under subsection (1) does not affect rights and duties that were exercised or performed, or interests in property that were distributed, before the order was set aside.

### Effect of declaration

**15.** (1) A declaration made under this Part shall be recognized for all purposes.

### Deemed effective from birth

(2) A declaration made under this Part is deemed to have been effective from the child's birth.

### Extra-Provincial Declaratory Orders

### Extra-provincial declaratory orders

**16.** (1) In this section,

"extra-provincial declaratory order" means an order, or part of an order, that makes a declaration of parentage similar to a declaration that may be made under section 13, if it is made by a court or tribunal outside Ontario that has jurisdiction to make such an order.

### Recognition of Canadian orders

(2) Subject to subsection (3), a court shall recognize an extra-provincial declaratory order made in another jurisdiction in Canada.

### Exception

(3) A court may decline to recognize an extra-provincial declaratory order made in another jurisdiction in Canada if,

(a) evidence becomes available that was not available during the proceeding that led to the making of the extra-provincial declaratory order; or

(b) the court is satisfied that the extra-provincial declaratory order was obtained by fraud or duress.

### Recognition of non-Canadian orders

(4) Subject to subsection (5), a court shall recognize an extra-provincial declaratory order that was made in a jurisdiction outside Canada if,

(a) the child or at least one parent of the child was habitually resident in the jurisdiction of the court or tribunal that made the extra-provincial declaratory order at the time the proceeding that led to its making was commenced or at the time the extra-provincial declaratory order was made; or

(b) the child or at least one parent of the child had a real and substantial connection with the jurisdiction of the court or tribunal that made the extra-provincial declaratory order at the time the proceeding that led to its making was commenced or at the time the extra-provincial declaratory order was made.

### Exception

(5) A court may decline to recognize an extra-provincial declaratory order made in a jurisdiction outside Canada,

(a) in the circumstances described in clause (3)(a) or (b); or

(b) if the extra-provincial declaratory order is contrary to public policy in Ontario.

### Effect of recognition of order

(6) An extra-provincial declaratory order that is recognized by the court shall be deemed to be an order of the court under section 13, and shall be treated for all purposes as if it were an order made under that section.

## Other Matters

### Corresponding change of surname

**17.** (1) Any person declared under section 10, 11 or 13 to be a parent of a child may apply to the court for an order that the child's surname be changed to any surname that the child could have been given under subsection 10(3) or (3.1) of the *Vital Statistics Act* if the child had been born at the time of the declaration.

### Same

(2) An application under subsection (1) to change a child's surname may be made at the same time as an application for a declaration under section 10, 11 or 13.

### Best interests of the child

(3) An order under subsection (1) changing a child's surname may be made only if it is in the best interests of the child.

### Admissibility in evidence of acknowledgment against interest

**17.1** A written acknowledgment of parentage that is admitted in evidence in any proceeding against the interest of the person making the acknowledgment is proof, in the absence of evidence to the contrary, of the fact.

### Blood, DNA tests

**17.2** (1) On the application of a party in a proceeding in which the court is called on to determine a child's parentage, the court may give the party leave to obtain a blood test, DNA test or any other test the court considers appropriate of a person named in the order granting leave, and to submit the results in evidence.

### Conditions

(2) The court may impose conditions, as it thinks proper, on an order under subsection (1).

### Consent to procedure

(3) The *Health Care Consent Act, 1996* applies to the test as if it were treatment under that Act.

### Inference from refusal

(4) If a person named in an order under subsection (1) refuses to submit to the test, the court may draw such inferences as it thinks appropriate.

### Exception

(5) Subsection (4) does not apply if the refusal is the decision of a substitute decision-maker as defined in section 9 of the *Health Care Consent Act, 1996.*

### Confidentiality

**17.3** Section 70 applies with necessary modifications if a proceeding includes an application under this Part.

### Court statement

**17.4** On the making of a declaratory order under this Part that a person is or is not a parent of a child, the clerk of the court shall file with the Registrar General a statement, in the form provided by the Ministry of the Attorney General, respecting the order.

### Certified copies of documents filed with the Registrar General
### Court statement

**17.5** (1) On application and payment of the required fee under the *Vital Statistics Act*, any person may obtain from the Registrar General a certified copy of a statement filed under section 17.4.

### Statutory declaration of parentage

(2) On application and payment of the required fee under the *Vital Statistics Act*, any person who has an interest, provides substantially accurate particulars and satisfies the Registrar General as to the reason for requiring it may obtain from the Registrar General a certified copy of a statutory declaration filed under section 12 of this Act as it read before the day subsection 1(1) of the *All Families Are Equal Act (Parentage and Related Registrations Statute Law Amendment), 2016* came into force.

### Certified copy as evidence

(3) A certified copy obtained under this section that is signed by the Registrar General or Deputy Registrar General, or on which the signature of either is reproduced by any method, is admissible in any court in Ontario as proof, in the absence of evidence to the contrary, of the filing and contents of the statement.

### Duties of Registrar General

**17.6** Nothing in this Act shall be construed as requiring the Registrar General to amend a registration showing parentage other than in recognition of an order made under this Part and in accordance with the requirements of the *Vital Statistics Act.*

## PART II

**3.–17.** Repealed.

## PART III  CUSTODY, ACCESS AND GUARDIANSHIP
### Interpretation

### Definitions, Part III

**18.** (1) In this Part,

"court" means the Ontario Court of Justice, the Family Court or the Superior Court of Justice;

"extra-provincial order" means an order, or that part of an order, of an extra-provincial tribunal that grants to a person custody of or access to a child;

"extra-provincial tribunal" means a court or tribunal outside Ontario that has jurisdiction to grant to a person custody of or access to a child;

"separation agreement" means an agreement that is a valid separation agreement under Part IV of the *Family Law Act*.

### Child

(2)  A reference in this Part to a child is a reference to the child while a minor.

### Purposes, Part III

**19.**  The purposes of this Part are,

(a)  to ensure that applications to the courts in respect of custody of, incidents of custody of, access to and guardianship for children will be determined on the basis of the best interests of the children;

(b)  to recognize that the concurrent exercise of jurisdiction by judicial tribunals of more than one province, territory or state in respect of the custody of the same child ought to be avoided, and to make provision so that the courts of Ontario will, unless there are exceptional circumstances, refrain from exercising or decline jurisdiction in cases where it is more appropriate for the matter to be determined by a tribunal having jurisdiction in another place with which the child has a closer connection;

(c)  to discourage the abduction of children as an alternative to the determination of custody rights by due process; and

(d)  to provide for the more effective enforcement of custody and access orders and for the recognition and enforcement of custody and access orders made outside Ontario.

### Custody and Access

### Entitlement to custody

**20.**  (1)  Except as otherwise provided in this Part, a child's parents are equally entitled to custody of the child.

### Rights and responsibilities

(2)  A person entitled to custody of a child has the rights and responsibilities of a parent in respect of the person of the child and must exercise those rights and responsibilities in the best interests of the child.

### Authority to act

(3)  Where more than one person is entitled to custody of a child, any one of them may exercise the rights and accept the responsibilities of a parent on behalf of them in respect of the child.

### Where parents separate

(4)  Where the parents of a child live separate and apart and the child lives with one of them with the consent, implied consent or acquiescence of the other of them, the right of the other to exercise the entitlement of custody and the incidents of custody, but not the entitlement to access, is suspended until a separation agreement or order otherwise provides.

### Access

(5)  The entitlement to access to a child includes the right to visit with and be visited by the child and the same right as a parent to make inquiries and to be given information as to the health, education and welfare of the child.

### Marriage of child

(6)  The entitlement to custody of or access to a child terminates on the marriage of the child.

### Entitlement subject to agreement or order

(7)  Any entitlement to custody or access or incidents of custody under this section is subject to alteration by an order of the court or by separation agreement.

### Application for custody or access

**21.**  (1)  A parent of a child or any other person, including a grandparent, may apply to a court for an order respecting custody of or access to the child or determining any aspect of the incidents of custody of the child.

### Affidavit

(2)  An application under subsection (1) for custody of or access to a child shall be accompanied by an affidavit, in the form prescribed for the purpose by the rules of court, of the person applying for custody or access, containing,

(a)  the person's proposed plan for the child's care and upbringing;

(b)  information respecting the person's current or previous involvement in any family proceedings, including proceedings under Part III of the *Child and Family Services Act* (child protection), or in any criminal proceedings; and

(c)  any other information known to the person that is relevant to the factors to be considered by the court under subsections 24(2), (3) and (4) in determining the best interests of the child.

### Police records checks, non-parents

**21.1**  (1)  Every person who applies under section 21 for custody of a child and who is not a parent of the child shall file with the court the results of a recent police records check respecting the person in accordance with the rules of court.

### Admissibility

(2)  The results obtained by the court under subsection (1) and any information, statement or document derived from the information contained in the results are admissible in evidence in the application, if the court considers it to be relevant.

### Use of evidence

(3)  Subject to subsection 24(3), evidence that is determined by the court to be admissible under subsection (2) shall be considered in determining the best interests of the child under section 24.

### Regulations

(4) The Lieutenant Governor in Council may make regulations defining "police records check" for the purposes of subsection (1).

## CAS records search, non-parents

### Definition

**21.2.** (1) In this section,

"society" means an approved agency designated as a children's aid society under the *Child and Family Services Act*.

### Request for report

(2) Every person who applies under section 21 for custody of a child and who is not a parent of the child shall submit a request, in the form provided by the Ministry of the Attorney General, to every society or other body or person prescribed by the regulations, for a report as to,

(a) whether a society has records relating to the person applying for custody; and

(b) if there are records and the records indicate that one or more files relating to the person have been opened, the date on which each file was opened and, if the file was closed, the date on which the file was closed.

### Request to be filed

(3) A copy of each request made under subsection (2) shall be filed with the court.

### Report required

(4) Within 30 days of receiving a request under subsection (2), a society or other body or person shall provide the court in which the application was filed with a report, in the form provided by the Ministry of the Attorney General, containing the information required under that subsection, and shall provide a copy of the report to the requesting party.

### Duty of clerk

(5) Subject to subsection (6), if the report indicates that there are records relating to the requesting party, the clerk of the court shall, 20 days after all of the reports that were requested by the party have been received by the court,

(a) give a copy of the report to every other party and to counsel, if any, representing the child; and

(b) file the report in the court file.

### Exception

(6) The court may, on motion by the requesting party, order,

(a) that the time period referred to in subsection (5) be lengthened; or

(b) that all or part of the report be sealed in the court file and not disclosed if,

(i) the court determines that some or all of the information contained in the report is not relevant to the application, or

(ii) the party withdraws the application.

### Admissibility

(7) A report that is filed under subsection (5) and any information, statement or document derived from the information contained in the report is admissible in evidence in the application, if the court considers it to be relevant.

### Use of evidence

(8) Subject to subsection 24(3), evidence that is determined by the court to be admissible under subsection (7) shall be considered in determining the best interests of the child under section 24.

### Interpretation

(9) Nothing done under this section constitutes publication of information or making information public for the purposes of subsection 45(8) of the *Child and Family Services Act* or an order under clause 70(1)(b).

### Regulations

(10) The Lieutenant Governor in Council may make regulations for the purposes of subsection (2),

(a) specifying one or more societies or other bodies or persons to whom a request must be submitted;

(b) governing the manner and scope of the search required to be undertaken in response to a request;

(c) specifying classes of files that shall be excluded from the report.

## Other proceedings

### Application by non-parent

**21.3.** (1) Where an application for custody of a child is made by a person who is not a parent of the child, the clerk of the court shall provide to the court and to the parties information in writing respecting any current or previous family proceedings involving the child or any person who is a party to the application and who is not a parent of the child.

### Same

(2) Where an application for custody of a child is made by a person who is not a parent of the child, the court may require the clerk of the court to provide to the court and to the parties information in writing respecting any current or previous criminal proceedings involving any person who is a party to the application and who is not a parent of the child.

### Same

(3) Written information provided under subsection (1) or (2) shall also be provided to counsel, if any, representing the child who is the subject of the application.

### Admissibility

(4) Written information that is provided to the court under subsection (1) or (2) and any information, statement or document derived from that information is admissible in evidence in the application, if the court considers it to be relevant.

## Use of evidence

(5) Subject to subsection 24(3), evidence that is determined by the court to be admissible under subsection (4) shall be considered in determining the best interests of the child under section 24.

## Interpretation

(6) Nothing done under this section constitutes publication of information or making information public for the purposes of subsection 45(8) of the *Child and Family Services Act* or an order under clause 70(1)(b).

## Regulations

(7) The Attorney General may make regulations for the purposes of this section,

(a) defining "family proceeding" and "criminal proceeding";

(b) prescribing the scope, content and form of the written information that shall or may be provided under this section;

(c) providing for a process for removing from the written information provided under subsection (1) or (2) information respecting a proceeding that does not involve the child who is the subject of the application or a person who is a party and is not a parent of the child, as the case may be.

## Jurisdiction

**22.** (1) A court shall only exercise its jurisdiction to make an order for custody of or access to a child where,

(a) the child is habitually resident in Ontario at the commencement of the application for the order;

(b) although the child is not habitually resident in Ontario, the court is satisfied,

(i) that the child is physically present in Ontario at the commencement of the application for the order,

(ii) that substantial evidence concerning the best interests of the child is available in Ontario,

(iii) that no application for custody of or access to the child is pending before an extra-provincial tribunal in another place where the child is habitually resident,

(iv) that no extra-provincial order in respect of custody of or access to the child has been recognized by a court in Ontario,

(v) that the child has a real and substantial connection with Ontario, and

(vi) that, on the balance of convenience, it is appropriate for jurisdiction to be exercised in Ontario.

## Habitual residence

(2) A child is habitually resident in the place where he or she resided,

(a) with both parents;

(b) where the parents are living separate and apart, with one parent under a separation agreement or with the

consent, implied consent or acquiescence of the other or under a court order; or

(c) with a person other than a parent on a permanent basis for a significant period of time,

whichever last occurred.

## Abduction

(3) The removal or withholding of a child without the consent of the person having custody of the child does not alter the habitual residence of the child unless there has been acquiescence or undue delay in commencing due process by the person from whom the child is removed or withheld.

## Serious harm to child

**23.** Despite sections 22 and 41, a court may exercise its jurisdiction to make or to vary an order in respect of the custody of or access to a child where,

(a) the child is physically present in Ontario; and

(b) the court is satisfied that the child would, on the balance of probabilities, suffer serious harm if,

(i) the child remains in the custody of the person legally entitled to custody of the child,

(ii) the child is returned to the custody of the person legally entitled to custody of the child, or

(iii) the child is removed from Ontario.

## Merits of application for custody or access

**24.** (1) The merits of an application under this Part in respect of custody of or access to a child shall be determined on the basis of the best interests of the child, in accordance with subsections (2), (3) and (4).

## Best interests of child

(2) The court shall consider all the child's needs and circumstances, including,

(a) the love, affection and emotional ties between the child and,

(i) each person, including a parent or grandparent, entitled to or claiming custody of or access to the child,

(ii) other members of the child's family who reside with the child, and

(iii) persons involved in the child's care and upbringing;

(b) the child's views and preferences, if they can reasonably be ascertained;

(c) the length of time the child has lived in a stable home environment;

(d) the ability and willingness of each person applying for custody of the child to provide the child with guidance and education, the necessaries of life and any special needs of the child;

(e) the plan proposed by each person applying for custody of or access to the child for the child's care and upbringing;

(f) the permanence and stability of the family unit with which it is proposed that the child will live;

(g) the ability of each person applying for custody of or access to the child to act as a parent; and

(h) any familial relationship between the child and each person who is a party to the application.

## Past conduct

(3) A person's past conduct shall be considered only,

(a) in accordance with subsection (4); or

(b) if the court is satisfied that the conduct is otherwise relevant to the person's ability to act as a parent.

## Violence and abuse

(4) In assessing a person's ability to act as a parent, the court shall consider whether the person has at any time committed violence or abuse against,

(a) his or her spouse;

(b) a parent of the child to whom the application relates;

(c) a member of the person's household; or

(d) any child.

## Same

(5) For the purposes of subsection (4), anything done in self-defence or to protect another person shall not be considered violence or abuse.

## Declining jurisdiction

**25.** A court having jurisdiction under this Part in respect of custody or access may decline to exercise its jurisdiction where it is of the opinion that it is more appropriate for jurisdiction to be exercised outside Ontario.

## Delay

**26.** (1) Where an application under this Part in respect of custody of or access to a child has not been heard within six months after the commencement of the proceedings, the clerk of the court shall list the application for the court and give notice to the parties of the date and time when and the place where the court will fix a date for the hearing of the application.

## Exception

(1.1) Subsection (1) does not apply to an application under this Part that relates to the custody of or access to a child if the child is the subject of an application or order under Part III of the *Child and Family Services Act*, unless the application under this Part relates to,

(a) an order in respect of the child that was made under subsection 57.1(1) of the *Child and Family Services Act*;

(b) an order referred to in subsection 57.1(3) of the *Child and Family Services Act* that was made at the same time as an order under subsection 57.1(1) of that Act; or

(c) an access order in respect of the child under section 58 of the *Child and Family Services Act* that was made at the same time as an order under subsection 57.1(1) of that Act.

## Directions

(2) At a hearing of a matter listed by the clerk in accordance with subsection (1), the court by order may fix a date for the hearing of the application and may give such directions in respect of the proceedings and make such order in respect of the costs of the proceedings as the court considers appropriate.

## Early date

(3) Where the court fixes a date under subsection (2), the court shall fix the earliest date that, in the opinion of the court, is compatible with a just disposition of the application.

## Effect of divorce proceedings

**27.** Where an action for divorce is commenced under the *Divorce Act* (Canada), any application under this Part in respect of custody of or access to a child that has not been determined is stayed except by leave of the court.

### Custody and Access—Orders

## Powers of court

**28.** (1) The court to which an application is made under section 21,

(a) by order may grant the custody of or access to the child to one or more persons;

(b) by order may determine any aspect of the incidents of the right to custody or access; and

(c) may make such additional order as the court considers necessary and proper in the circumstances, including an order,

(i) limiting the duration, frequency, manner or location of contact or communication between any of the parties, or between a party and the child,

(ii) prohibiting a party or other person from engaging in specified conduct in the presence of the child or at any time when the person is responsible for the care of the child,

(iii) prohibiting a party from changing the child's residence, school or day care facility without the consent of another party or an order of the court,

(iv) prohibiting a party from removing the child from Ontario without the consent of another party or an order of the court,

(v) requiring the delivery, to the court or to a person or body specified by the court, of the child's passport, the child's health card within the meaning of the *Health Insurance Act* or any other document relating to the child that the court may specify,

(vi) requiring a party to give information or to consent to the release of information respecting the health, education and welfare of the child to another party or other person specified by the court, or

(vii) requiring a party to facilitate communication by the child with another party or other person specified by the court in a manner that is appropriate for the child.

## Exception

(2) If an application is made under section 21 with respect to a child who is the subject of an order made under section 57.1 of the *Child and Family Services Act*, the court shall treat the application as if it were an application to vary an order made under this section.

## Same

(3) If an order for access to a child was made under Part III of the *Child and Family Services Act* at the same time as an order for custody of the child was made under section 57.1 of that Act, the court shall treat an application under section 21 relating to access to the child as if it were an application to vary an order made under this section.

## Order varying an order

**29.** (1) A court shall not make an order under this Part that varies an order in respect of custody or access made by a court in Ontario unless there has been a material change in circumstances that affects or is likely to affect the best interests of the child.

### Custody and Access—Assistance to Court

## Assessment of needs of child

**30.** (1) The court before which an application is brought in respect of custody of or access to a child, by order, may appoint a person who has technical or professional skill to assess and report to the court on the needs of the child and the ability and willingness of the parties or any of them to satisfy the needs of the child.

## When order may be made

(2) An order may be made under subsection (1) on or before the hearing of the application in respect of custody of or access to the child and with or without a request by a party to the application.

## Agreement by parties

(3) The court shall, if possible, appoint a person agreed upon by the parties, but if the parties do not agree the court shall choose and appoint the person.

## Consent to act

(4) The court shall not appoint a person under subsection (1) unless the person has consented to make the assessment and to report to the court within the period of time specified by the court.

## Attendance for assessment

(5) In an order under subsection (1), the court may require the parties, the child and any other person who has been given notice of the proposed order, or any of them, to attend for assessment by the person appointed by the order.

## Refusal to attend

(6) Where a person ordered under this section to attend for assessment refuses to attend or to undergo the assessment, the court may draw such inferences in respect of the ability and willingness of any person to satisfy the needs of the child as the court considers appropriate.

## Report

(7) The person appointed under subsection (1) shall file his or her report with the clerk of the court.

## Copies of report

(8) The clerk of the court shall give a copy of the report to each of the parties and to counsel, if any, representing the child.

## Admissibility of report

(9) The report mentioned in subsection (7) is admissible in evidence in the application.

## Assessor may be witness

(10) Any of the parties, and counsel, if any, representing the child, may require the person appointed under subsection (1) to attend as a witness at the hearing of the application.

## Directions

(11) Upon motion, the court by order may give such directions in respect of the assessment as the court considers appropriate.

## Fees and expenses

(12) The court shall require the parties to pay the fees and expenses of the person appointed under subsection (1).

## Idem, proportions or amounts

(13) The court shall specify in the order the proportions or amounts of the fees and expenses that the court requires each party to pay.

## Idem, serious financial hardship

(14) The court may relieve a party from responsibility for payment of any of the fees and expenses of the person appointed under subsection (1) where the court is satisfied that payment would cause serious financial hardship to the party.

## Other expert evidence

(15) The appointment of a person under subsection (1) does not prevent the parties or counsel representing the child from submitting other expert evidence as to the needs of the child and the ability and willingness of the parties or any of them to satisfy the needs of the child.

## Mediation

**31.** (1) Upon an application for custody of or access to a child, the court, at the request of the parties, by order may appoint a person selected by the parties to mediate any matter specified in the order.

## Consent to act

(2) The court shall not appoint a person under subsection (1) unless the person,

(a) has consented to act as mediator; and

(b) has agreed to file a report with the court within the period of time specified by the court.

### Duty of mediator

(3) It is the duty of a mediator to confer with the parties and endeavour to obtain an agreement in respect of the matter.

### Form of report

(4) Before entering into mediation on the matter, the parties shall decide whether,

(a) the mediator is to file a full report on the mediation, including anything that the mediator considers relevant to the matter in mediation; or

(b) the mediator is to file a report that either sets out the agreement reached by the parties or states only that the parties did not reach agreement on the matter.

### Filing of report

(5) The mediator shall file his or her report with the clerk of the court in the form decided upon by the parties under subsection (4).

### Copies of report

(6) The clerk of the court shall give a copy of the report to each of the parties and to counsel, if any, representing the child.

### Admissions made in the course of mediation

(7) Where the parties have decided that the mediator's report is to be in the form described in clause (4)(b), evidence of anything said or of any admission or communication made in the course of the mediation is not admissible in any proceeding except with the consent of all parties to the proceeding in which the order was made under subsection (1).

### Fees and expenses

(8) The court shall require the parties to pay the fees and expenses of the mediator.

### Idem, proportions or amounts

(9) The court shall specify in the order the proportions or amounts of the fees and expenses that the court requires each party to pay.

### Idem, serious financial hardship

(10) The court may relieve a party from responsibility for payment of any of the fees and expenses of the mediator where the court is satisfied that payment would cause serious financial hardship to the party.

### Further evidence from outside Ontario

**32.** (1) Where a court is of the opinion that it is necessary to receive further evidence from a place outside Ontario before making a decision, the court may send to the Attorney General, Minister of Justice or similar officer of the place outside Ontario such supporting material as may be necessary together with a request,

(a) that the Attorney General, Minister of Justice or similar officer take such action as may be necessary in order to require a named person to attend before the proper tribunal in that place and produce or give evidence in respect of the subject-matter of the application; and

(b) that the Attorney General, Minister of Justice or similar officer or the tribunal send to the court a certified copy of the evidence produced or given before the tribunal.

### Cost of obtaining evidence

(2) A court that acts under subsection (1) may assess the cost of so acting against one or more of the parties to the application or may deal with such cost as costs in the cause.

### Request from outside Ontario for further evidence

**33.** (1) Where the Attorney General receives from an extra-provincial tribunal a request similar to that referred to in section 32 and such supporting material as may be necessary, it is the duty of the Attorney General to refer the request and the material to the proper court.

### Obtaining evidence

(2) A court to which a request is referred by the Attorney General under subsection (1) shall require the person named in the request to attend before the court and produce or give evidence in accordance with the request.

## Custody and Access—Enforcement

### Supervision of custody or access

**34.** (1) Where an order is made for custody of or access to a child, a court may give such directions as it considers appropriate for the supervision of the custody or access by a person, a children's aid society or other body.

### Consent to act

(2) A court shall not direct a person, a children's aid society or other body to supervise custody or access as mentioned in subsection (1) unless the person, society or body has consented to act as supervisor.

### Restraining order

**35.** (1) On application, the court may make an interim or final restraining order against any person if the applicant has reasonable grounds to fear for his or her own safety or for the safety of any child in his or her lawful custody.

### Provisions of order

(2) A restraining order made under subsection (1) shall be in the form prescribed by the rules of court and may contain one or more of the following provisions, as the court considers appropriate:

1. Restraining the respondent, in whole or in part, from directly or indirectly contacting or communicating with the applicant or any child in the applicant's lawful custody.
2. Restraining the respondent from coming within a specified distance of one or more locations.
3. Specifying one or more exceptions to the provisions described in paragraphs 1 and 2.
4. Any other provision that the court considers appropriate.

### Transition

(3) This section, as it read on October 14, 2009, continues to apply to,

(a) any prosecution or other proceeding begun under this section before October 15, 2009; and

(b) any order made under this section that was in force on October 14, 2009.

### Order where child unlawfully withheld

**36.** (1) Where a court is satisfied upon application by a person in whose favour an order has been made for custody of or access to a child that there are reasonable and probable grounds for believing that any person is unlawfully withholding the child from the applicant, the court by order may authorize the applicant or someone on his or her behalf to apprehend the child for the purpose of giving effect to the rights of the applicant to custody or access, as the case may be.

### Order to locate and take child

(2) Where a court is satisfied upon application that there are reasonable and probable grounds for believing,

(a) that any person is unlawfully withholding a child from a person entitled to custody of or access to the child;

(b) that a person who is prohibited by court order or separation agreement from removing a child from Ontario proposes to remove the child or have the child removed from Ontario; or

(c) that a person who is entitled to access to a child proposes to remove the child or to have the child removed from Ontario and that the child is not likely to return, the court by order may direct a police force, having jurisdiction in any area where it appears to the court that the child may be, to locate, apprehend and deliver the child to the person named in the order.

### Application without notice

(3) An order may be made under subsection (2) upon an application without notice where the court is satisfied that it is necessary that action be taken without delay.

### Duty to act

(4) The police force directed to act by an order under subsection (2) shall do all things reasonably able to be done to locate, apprehend and deliver the child in accordance with the order.

### Entry and search

(5) For the purpose of locating and apprehending a child in accordance with an order under subsection (2), a member of a police force may enter and search any place where he or she has reasonable and probable grounds for believing that the child may be with such assistance and such force as are reasonable in the circumstances.

### Time

(6) An entry or a search referred to in subsection (5) shall be made only between 6 a.m. and 9 p.m. standard time unless the court, in the order, authorizes entry and search at another time.

### Expiration of order

(7) An order made under subsection (2) shall name a date on which it expires, which shall be a date not later than six months after it is made unless the court is satisfied that a longer period of time is necessary in the circumstances.

### When application may be made

(8) An application under subsection (1) or (2) may be made in an application for custody or access or at any other time.

## Court orders, removal and return of children

### To prevent unlawful removal of child

**37.** (1) Where a court, upon application, is satisfied upon reasonable and probable grounds that a person prohibited by court order or separation agreement from removing a child from Ontario proposes to remove the child from Ontario, the court in order to prevent the removal of the child from Ontario may make an order under subsection (3).

### To ensure return of child

(2) Where a court, upon application, is satisfied upon reasonable and probable grounds that a person entitled to access to a child proposes to remove the child from Ontario and is not likely to return the child to Ontario, the court in order to secure the prompt, safe return of the child to Ontario may make an order under subsection (3).

### Order by court

(3) An order mentioned in subsection (1) or (2) may require a person to do any one or more of the following:

1. Transfer specific property to a named trustee to be held subject to the terms and conditions specified in the order.

2. Where payments have been ordered for the support of the child, make the payments to a specified trustee subject to the terms and conditions specified in the order.

3. Post a bond, with or without sureties, payable to the applicant in such amount as the court considers appropriate.

4. Deliver the person's passport, the child's passport and any other travel documents of either of them that the court may specify to the court or to an individual or body specified by the court.

### Idem, Ontario Court of Justice

(4) The Ontario Court of Justice shall not make an order under paragraph 1 of subsection (3).

### Terms and conditions

(5) In an order under paragraph 1 of subsection (3), the court may specify terms and conditions for the return or the disposition of the property as the court considers appropriate.

### Safekeeping

(6) A court or an individual or body specified by the court in an order under paragraph 4 of subsection (3) shall hold a passport or travel document delivered in accordance with the order in safekeeping in accordance with any directions set out in the order.

### Directions

(7) In an order under subsection (3), a court may give such directions in respect of the safekeeping of the property, payments, passports or travel documents as the court considers appropriate.

### Contempt of orders of Ontario Court of Justice

**38.** (1) In addition to its powers in respect of contempt, the Ontario Court of Justice may punish by fine or imprisonment, or both, any wilful contempt of or resistance to its process or orders under this Act, other than orders under section 35, but the fine shall not in any case exceed $5,000 nor shall the imprisonment exceed ninety days.

### Conditions of imprisonment

(2) An order for imprisonment under subsection (1) may be made conditional upon default in the performance of a condition set out in the order and may provide for the imprisonment to be served intermittently.

### Transition

(3) This section, as it read on October 14, 2009, continues to apply to orders referred to in clause 35 (3)(b).

### Information as to address

**39.** (1) Where, upon application to a court, it appears to the court that,

(a) for the purpose of bringing an application in respect of custody or access under this Part; or

(b) for the purpose of the enforcement of an order for custody or access,

the proposed applicant or person in whose favour the order is made has need to learn or confirm the whereabouts of the proposed respondent or person against whom the order referred to in clause (b) is made, the court may order any person or public body to provide the court with such particulars of the address of the proposed respondent or person against whom the order referred to in clause (b) is made as are contained in the records in the custody of the person or body, and the person or body shall give the court such particulars as are contained in the records and the court may then give the particulars to such person or persons as the court considers appropriate.

### Exception

(2) A court shall not make an order on an application under subsection (1) where it appears to the court that the purpose of the application is to enable the applicant to identify or to obtain particulars as to the identity of a person who has custody of a child, rather than to learn or confirm the whereabouts of the proposed respondent or the enforcement of an order for custody or access.

### Compliance with order

(3) The giving of information in accordance with an order under subsection (1) shall be deemed for all purposes not to be a contravention of any Act or regulation or any common law rule of confidentiality.

### Section binds Crown

(4) This section binds the Crown in right of Ontario.

### Custody and Access—Extra-provincial Matters
### Interim powers of court

**40.** Upon application, a court,

(a) that is satisfied that a child has been wrongfully removed to or is being wrongfully retained in Ontario; or

(b) that may not exercise jurisdiction under section 22 or that has declined jurisdiction under section 25 or 42, may do any one or more of the following:

1. Make such interim order in respect of the custody or access as the court considers is in the best interests of the child.

2. Stay the application subject to,

    i. the condition that a party to the application promptly commence a similar proceeding before an extra-provincial tribunal, or

    ii. such other conditions as the court considers appropriate.

3. Order a party to return the child to such place as the court considers appropriate and, in the discretion of the court, order payment of the cost of the reasonable travel and other expenses of the child and any parties to or witnesses at the hearing of the application.

### Enforcement of extra-provincial orders

**41.** (1) Upon application by any person in whose favour an order for the custody of or access to a child has been made by an extra-provincial tribunal, a court shall recognize the order unless the court is satisfied,

(a) that the respondent was not given reasonable notice of the commencement of the proceeding in which the order was made;

(b) that the respondent was not given an opportunity to be heard by the extra-provincial tribunal before the order was made;

(c) that the law of the place in which the order was made did not require the extra-provincial tribunal to have regard for the best interests of the child;

(d) that the order of the extra-provincial tribunal is contrary to public policy in Ontario; or

(e) that, in accordance with section 22, the extra-provincial tribunal would not have jurisdiction if it were a court in Ontario.

### Effect of recognition of order

(2) An order made by an extra-provincial tribunal that is recognized by a court shall be deemed to be an order of the court and enforceable as such.

### Conflicting orders

(3) A court presented with conflicting orders made by extra-provincial tribunals for the custody of or access to a child that, but for the conflict, would be recognized and enforced by the court under subsection (1) shall recognize and enforce the order that appears to the court to be most in accord with the best interests of the child.

### Further orders

(4) A court that has recognized an extra-provincial order may make such further orders under this Part as the court considers necessary to give effect to the order.

### Superseding order, material change in circumstances

**42.** (1) Upon application, a court by order may supersede an extra-provincial order in respect of custody of or access to a child where the court is satisfied that there has been a material change in circumstances that affects or is likely to affect the best interests of the child and,

(a) the child is habitually resident in Ontario at the commencement of the application for the order; or

(b) although the child is not habitually resident in Ontario, the court is satisfied,

(i) that the child is physically present in Ontario at the commencement of the application for the order,

(ii) that the child no longer has a real and substantial connection with the place where the extra-provincial order was made,

(iii) that substantial evidence concerning the best interests of the child is available in Ontario,

(iv) that the child has a real and substantial connection with Ontario, and

(v) that, on the balance of convenience, it is appropriate for jurisdiction to be exercised in Ontario.

### Declining jurisdiction

(2) A court may decline to exercise its jurisdiction under this section where it is of the opinion that it is more appropriate for jurisdiction to be exercised outside Ontario.

### Superseding order, serious harm

**43.** Upon application, a court by order may supersede an extra-provincial order in respect of custody of or access to a child if the court is satisfied that the child would, on the balance of probability, suffer serious harm if,

(a) the child remains in the custody of the person legally entitled to custody of the child;

(b) the child is returned to the custody of the person entitled to custody of the child; or

(c) the child is removed from Ontario.

### True copy of extra-provincial order

**44.** A copy of an extra-provincial order certified as a true copy by a judge, other presiding officer or registrar of the tribunal that made the order or by a person charged with keeping the orders of the tribunal is proof, in the absence of evidence to the contrary, of the making of the order, the content of the order and the appointment and signature of the judge, presiding officer, registrar or other person.

### Court may take notice of foreign law

**45.** For the purposes of an application under this Part, a court may take notice, without requiring formal proof, of the law of a jurisdiction outside Ontario and of a decision of an extra-provincial tribunal.

## Convention on Civil Aspects of International Child Abduction

### Definition

**46.** (1) In this section,

"convention" means the Convention on the Civil Aspects of International Child Abduction, set out in the Schedule to this section.

### Convention in force

(2) On, from and after the 1st day of December, 1983, except as provided in subsection (3), the convention is in force in Ontario and the provisions thereof are law in Ontario.

### Crown, legal costs under convention

(3) The Crown is not bound to assume any costs resulting under the convention from the participation of legal counsel or advisers or from court proceedings except in accordance with the *Legal Aid Services Act*, 1998.

### Central Authority

(4) The Ministry of the Attorney General shall be the Central Authority for Ontario for the purpose of the convention.

### Application to court

(5) An application may be made to a court in pursuance of a right or an obligation under the convention.

### Request to ratify convention

(6) The Attorney General shall request the Government of Canada to submit a declaration to the Ministry of Foreign Affairs of the Kingdom of the Netherlands, declaring that the convention extends to Ontario.

### Regulations

(7) The Lieutenant Governor in Council may make such regulations as the Lieutenant Governor in Council considers necessary to carry out the intent and purpose of this section.

### Conflict

(8) Where there is a conflict between this section and any other enactment, this section prevails.

## SCHEDULE
### Convention on the Civil Aspects of International Child Abduction

The States signatory to the present Convention,

Firmly convinced that the interests of children are of paramount importance in matters relating to their custody,

Desiring to protect children internationally from the harmful effects of their wrongful removal or retention and to establish procedures to ensure their prompt return to the State of their habitual residence, as well as to secure protection for rights of access,

Have resolved to conclude a Convention to this effect and have agreed upon the following provisions:

### Chapter I—Scope of the Convention
#### Article 1

The objects of the present Convention are:

(a) to secure the prompt return of children wrongfully removed to or retained in any Contracting State; and

(b) to ensure that rights of custody and of access under the law of one Contracting State are effectively respected in the other Contracting States.

#### Article 2

Contracting States shall take all appropriate measures to secure within their territories the implementation of the objects of the Convention. For this purpose they shall use the most expeditious procedures available.

#### Article 3

The removal or the retention of a child is to be considered wrongful where:

(a) it is in breach of rights of custody attributed to a person, an institution or any other body, either jointly or alone, under the law of the State in which the child was habitually resident immediately before the removal or retention; and

(b) at the time of removal or retention those rights were actually exercised, either jointly or alone, or would have been so exercised but for the removal or retention.

The rights of custody mentioned in sub-paragraph (a) above, may arise in particular by operation of law or by reason of a judicial or administrative decision, or by reason of an agreement having legal effect under the law of that State.

#### Article 4

The Convention shall apply to any child who was habitually resident in a Contracting State immediately before any breach of custody or access rights. The Convention shall cease to apply when the child attains the age of 16 years.

#### Article 5

For the purposes of this Convention:

(a) "rights of custody" shall include rights relating to the care of the person of the child and, in particular, the right to determine the child's place of residence;

(b) "rights of access" shall include the right to take a child for a limited period of time to a place other than the child's habitual residence.

### Chapter II—Central Authorities
#### Article 6

A Contracting State shall designate a Central Authority to discharge the duties which are imposed by the Convention upon such authorities.

Federal States, States with more than one system of law or States having autonomous territorial organizations shall be free to appoint more than one Central Authority and to specify the territorial extent of their powers. Where a State has appointed more than one Central Authority, it shall designate the Central Authority to which applications may be addressed for transmission to the appropriate Central Authority within that State.

#### Article 7

Central Authorities shall co-operate with each other and promote co-operation amongst the competent authorities in their respective States to secure the prompt return of children and to achieve the other objects of this Convention.

In particular, either directly or through any intermediary, they shall take all appropriate measures:

(a) to discover the whereabouts of a child who has been wrongfully removed or retained;

(b) to prevent further harm to the child or prejudice to interested parties by taking or causing to be taken provisional measures;

(c) to secure the voluntary return of the child or to bring about an amicable resolution of the issues;

(d) to exchange, where desirable, information relating to the social background of the child;

(e) to provide information of a general character as to the law of their State in connection with the application of the Convention;

(f) to initiate or facilitate the institution of judicial or administrative proceedings with a view to obtaining the return of the child and, in a proper case, to make arrangements for organizing or securing the effective exercise of rights of access;

(g) where the circumstances so require, to provide or facilitate the provision of legal aid and advice, including the participation of legal counsel and advisers;

(h) to provide such administrative arrangements as may be necessary and appropriate to secure the safe return of the child;

(i) to keep each other informed with respect to the operation of this Convention and, as far as possible, to eliminate any obstacles to its application.

## Chapter III—Return of Children

### Article 8

Any person, institution or other body claiming that a child has been removed or retained in breach of custody rights may apply either to the Central Authority of the child's habitual residence or to the Central Authority of any other Contracting State for assistance in securing the return of the child.

The application shall contain:

(a) information concerning the identity of the applicant, of the child and of the person alleged to have removed or retained the child;

(b) where available, the date of birth of the child;

(c) the grounds on which the applicant's claim for return of the child is based;

(d) all available information relating to the whereabouts of the child and the identity of the person with whom the child is presumed to be.

The application may be accompanied or supplemented by:

(e) an authenticated copy of any relevant decision or agreement;

(f) a certificate or an affidavit emanating from a Central Authority, or other competent authority of the State of the child's habitual residence, or from a qualified person, concerning the relevant law of that State;

(g) any other relevant document.

### Article 9

If the Central Authority which receives an application referred to in Article 8 has reason to believe that the child is in another Contracting State, it shall directly and without delay transmit the application to the Central Authority of that Contracting State and inform the requesting Central Authority, or the applicant, as the case may be.

### Article 10

The Central Authority of the State where the child is shall take or cause to be taken all appropriate measures in order to obtain the voluntary return of the child.

### Article 11

The judicial or administrative authorities of Contracting States shall act expeditiously in proceedings for the return of children.

If the judicial or administrative authority concerned has not reached a decision within six weeks from the date of commencement of the proceedings, the applicant or the Central Authority

of the requested State, on its own initiative or if asked by the Central Authority of the requesting State, shall have the right to request a statement of the reasons for the delay. If a reply is received by the Central Authority of the requested State, that Authority shall transmit the reply to the Central Authority of the requesting State, or to the applicant, as the case may be.

### Article 12

Where a child has been wrongfully removed or retained in terms of Article 3 and, at the date of commencement of the proceedings before the judicial or administrative authority of the Contracting State where the child is, a period of less than one year has elapsed from the date of the wrongful removal or retention, the authority concerned shall order the return of the child forthwith.

The judicial or administrative authority, even where the proceedings have been commenced after the expiration of the period of one year referred to in the preceding paragraph, shall also order the return of the child, unless it is demonstrated that the child is now settled in its new environment.

Where the judicial or administrative authority in the requested State has reason to believe that the child has been taken to another State, it may stay the proceedings or dismiss the application for the return of the child.

### Article 13

Despite the provisions of the preceding Article, the judicial or administrative authority of the requested State is not bound to order the return of the child if the person, institution or other body which opposes its return establishes that:

(a) the person, institution or other body having the care of the person of the child was not actually exercising the custody rights at the time of removal or retention, or had consented to or subsequently acquiesced in the removal or retention; or

(b) there is a grave risk that his or her return would expose the child to physical or psychological harm or otherwise place the child in an intolerable situation.

The judicial or administrative authority may also refuse to order the return of the child if it finds that the child objects to being returned and has attained an age and degree of maturity at which it is appropriate to take account of its views.

In considering the circumstances referred to in this Article, the judicial and administrative authorities shall take into account the information relating to the social background of the child provided by the Central Authority or other competent authority of the child's habitual residence.

### Article 14

In ascertaining whether there has been a wrongful removal or retention within the meaning of Article 3, the judicial or administrative authorities of the requested State may take notice directly of the law of, and of judicial or administrative decisions, formally recognized or not in the State of the habitual residence of the child, without recourse to the specific procedures for the proof of that law or for the recognition of foreign decisions which would otherwise be applicable.

## Article 15

The judicial or administrative authorities of a Contracting State may, prior to the making of an order for the return of the child, request that the applicant obtain from the authorities of the State of the habitual residence of the child a decision or other determination that the removal or retention was wrongful within the meaning of Article 3 of the Convention, where such a decision or determination may be obtained in that State. The Central Authorities of the Contracting States shall so far as practicable assist applicants to obtain such a decision or determination.

## Article 16

After receiving notice of a wrongful removal or retention of a child in the sense of Article 3, the judicial or administrative authorities of the Contracting State to which the child has been removed or in which it has been retained shall not decide on the merits of rights of custody until it has been determined that the child is not to be returned under this Convention or unless an application under this Convention is not lodged within a reasonable time following receipt of the notice.

## Article 17

The sole fact that a decision relating to custody has been given in or is entitled to recognition in the requested State shall not be a ground for refusing to return a child under this Convention, but the judicial or administrative authorities of the requested State may take account of the reasons for that decision in applying this Convention.

## Article 18

The provisions of this Chapter do not limit the power of a judicial or administrative authority to order the return of the child at any time.

## Article 19

A decision under this Convention concerning the return of the child shall not be taken to be a determination on the merits of any custody issue.

## Article 20

The return of the child under the provisions of Article 12 may be refused if this would not be permitted by the fundamental principles of the requested State relating to the protection of human rights and fundamental freedoms.

## Chapter IV—Rights of Access

## Article 21

An application to make arrangements for organizing or securing the effective exercise of rights of access may be presented to the Central Authorities of the Contracting States in the same way as an application for the return of a child.

The Central Authorities are bound by the obligations of co-operation which are set forth in Article 7 to promote the peaceful enjoyment of access rights and the fulfilment of any conditions to which the exercise of those rights may be subject. The Central Authorities shall take steps to remove, as far as possible, all obstacles to the exercise of such rights.

The Central Authorities, either directly or through intermediaries, may initiate or assist in the institution of proceedings with a view to organizing or protecting these rights and securing respect for the conditions to which the exercise of these rights may be subject.

## Chapter V—General Provisions

## Article 22

No security, bond or deposit, however described, shall be required to guarantee the payment of costs and expenses in the judicial or administrative proceedings falling within the scope of this Convention.

## Article 23

No legalization or similar formality may be required in the context of this Convention.

## Article 24

Any application, communication or other document sent to the Central Authority of the requested State shall be in the original language, and shall be accompanied by a translation into the official language or one of the official languages of the requested State or, where that is not feasible, a translation into French or English.

However, a Contracting State may, by making a reservation in accordance with Article 42, object to the use of either French or English, but not both, in any application, communication or other document sent to its Central Authority.

## Article 25

Nationals of the Contracting States and persons who are habitually resident within those States shall be entitled in matters concerned with the application of this Convention to legal aid and advice in any other Contracting State on the same conditions as if they themselves were nationals of and habitually resident in that State.

## Article 26

Each Central Authority shall bear its own costs in applying this Convention.

Central Authorities and other public services of Contracting States shall not impose any charges in relation to applications submitted under this Convention. In particular, they may not require any payment from the applicant towards the costs and expenses of the proceedings or, where applicable, those arising from the participation of legal counsel or advisers. However, they may require the payment of the expenses incurred or to be incurred in implementing the return of the child.

However, a Contracting State may, by making a reservation in accordance with Article 42, declare that it shall not be bound to assume any costs referred to in the preceding paragraph resulting from the participation of legal counsel or advisers or from court proceedings, except insofar as those costs may be covered by its system of legal aid and advice.

Upon ordering the return of a child or issuing an order concerning rights of access under this Convention, the judicial or administrative authorities may, where appropriate, direct the person who removed or retained the child, or who prevented the exercise of rights of access, to pay necessary expenses incurred by or on behalf of the applicant, including travel expenses, any costs incurred or payments made for locating the child, the costs of legal representation of the applicant, and those of returning the child.

### Article 27

When it is manifest that the requirements of this Convention are not fulfilled or that the application is otherwise not well founded, a Central Authority is not bound to accept the application. In that case, the Central Authority shall forthwith inform the applicant or the Central Authority through which the application was submitted, as the case may be, of its reasons.

### Article 28

A Central Authority may require that the application be accompanied by a written authorization empowering it to act on behalf of the applicant, or to designate a representative so to act.

### Article 29

This Convention shall not preclude any person, institution or body who claims that there has been a breach of custody or access rights within the meaning of Article 3 or 21 from applying directly to the judicial or administrative authorities of a Contracting State, whether or not under the provisions of this Convention.

### Article 30

Any application submitted to the Central Authorities or directly to the judicial or administrative authorities of a Contracting State in accordance with the terms of this Convention, together with documents and any other information appended thereto or provided by a Central Authority, shall be admissible in the courts or administrative authorities of the Contracting States.

### Article 31

In relation to a State which in matters of custody of children has two or more systems of law applicable in different territorial units:

  (a) any reference to habitual residence in that State shall be construed as referring to habitual residence in a territorial unit of that State;

  (b) any reference to the law of the State of habitual residence shall be construed as referring to the law of the territorial unit in that State where the child habitually resides.

### Article 32

In relation to a State which in matters of custody of children has two or more systems of law applicable to different categories of persons, any reference to the law of that State shall be construed as referring to the legal system specified by the law of that State.

### Article 33

A State within which different territorial units have their own rules of law in respect of custody of children shall not be bound to apply this Convention where a State with a unified system of law would not be bound to do so.

### Article 34

This Convention shall take priority in matters within its scope over the Convention of 5 October 1961 concerning the powers of authorities and the law applicable in respect of the protection of minors, as between Parties to both Conventions. Otherwise the present Convention shall not restrict the application of an international instrument in force between the State of origin and the State addressed or other law of the State addressed for the purposes of obtaining the return of a child who has been wrongfully removed or retained or of organizing access rights.

### Article 35

This Convention shall apply as between Contracting States only to wrongful removals or retentions occurring after its entry into force in those States.

Where a declaration has been made under Article 39 or 40, the reference in the preceding paragraph to a Contracting State shall be taken to refer to the territorial unit or units in relation to which this Convention applies.

### Article 36

Nothing in this Convention shall prevent two or more Contracting States, in order to limit the restrictions to which the return of the child may be subject, from agreeing among themselves to derogate from any provisions of this Convention which may imply such a restriction.

### Chapter VI—Final Clauses

### Article 37

The Convention shall be open for signature by the States which were Members of the Hague Conference on Private International Law at the time of its Fourteenth Session.

It shall be ratified, accepted or approved and the instruments of ratification, acceptance or approval shall be deposited with the Ministry of Foreign Affairs of the Kingdom of the Netherlands.

### Article 38

Any other State may accede to the Convention.

The instrument of accession shall be deposited with the Ministry of Foreign Affairs of the Kingdom of the Netherlands.

The Convention shall enter into force for a State acceding to it on the first day of the third calendar month after the deposit of its instrument of accession.

The accession will have effect only as regards the relations between the acceding State and such Contracting States as will have declared their acceptance of the accession. Such a declaration will also have to be made by any Member State ratifying, accepting or approving the Convention after an accession. Such declaration shall be deposited at the Ministry of Foreign Affairs of the Kingdom of the Netherlands; this Ministry shall forward, through diplomatic channels, a certified copy to each of the Contracting States.

The Convention will enter into force as between the acceding State and the State that has declared its acceptance of the accession on the first day of the third calendar month after the deposit of the declaration of acceptance.

## Article 39

Any State may, at the time of signature, ratification, acceptance, approval or accession, declare that the Convention shall extend to all the territories for the international relations of which it is responsible, or to one or more of them. Such a declaration shall take effect at the time the Convention enters into force for that State.

Such declaration, as well as any subsequent extension, shall be notified to the Ministry of Foreign Affairs of the Kingdom of the Netherlands.

## Article 40

If a Contracting State has two or more territorial units in which different systems of law are applicable in relation to matters dealt with in this Convention, it may at the time of signature, ratification, acceptance, approval or accession declare that this Convention shall extend to all its territorial units or only to one or more of them and may modify this declaration by submitting another declaration at any time.

Any such declaration shall be notified to the Ministry of Foreign Affairs of the Kingdom of the Netherlands and shall state expressly the territorial units to which the Convention applies.

## Article 41

Where a Contracting State has a system of government under which executive, judicial and legislative powers are distributed between central and other authorities within that State, its signature or ratification, acceptance or approval of, or accession to this Convention, or its making of any declaration in terms of Article 40 shall carry no implication as to the internal distribution of powers within that State.

## Article 42

Any State may, not later than the time of ratification, acceptance, approval or accession, or at the time of making a declaration in terms of Article 39 or 40, make one or both of the reservations provided for in Article 24 and Article 26, third paragraph. No other reservation shall be permitted.

Any State may at any time withdraw a reservation it has made. The withdrawal shall be notified to the Ministry of Foreign Affairs of the Kingdom of the Netherlands.

The reservation shall cease to have effect on the first day of the third calendar month after the notification referred to in the preceding paragraph.

## Article 43

The Convention shall enter into force on the first day of the third calendar month after the deposit of the third instrument of ratification, acceptance, approval or accession referred to in Articles 37 and 38.

Thereafter the Convention shall enter into force:

1. for each State ratifying, accepting, approving or acceding to it subsequently, on the first day of the third calendar month after the deposit of its instrument of ratification, acceptance, approval or accession;
2. for any territory or territorial unit to which the Convention has been extended in conformity with Article 39 or 40, on the first day of the third calendar month after the notification referred to in that Article.

## Article 44

The Convention shall remain in force for five years from the date of its entry into force in accordance with the first paragraph of Article 43 even for States which subsequently have ratified, accepted, approved it or acceded to it. If there has been no denunciation, it shall be renewed tacitly every five years.

Any denunciation shall be notified to the Ministry of Foreign Affairs of the Kingdom of the Netherlands at least six months before the expiry of the five year period. It may be limited to certain of the territories or territorial units to which the Convention applies.

The denunciation shall have effect only as regards the State which has notified it. The Convention shall remain in force for the other Contracting States.

## Article 45

The Ministry of Foreign Affairs of the Kingdom of the Netherlands shall notify the States Members of the Conference, and the States which have acceded in accordance with Article 38, of the following:

1. the signatures and ratifications, acceptances and approvals referred to in Article 37;
2. the accessions referred to in Article 38;
3. the date on which the Convention enters into force in accordance with Article 43;
4. the extensions referred to in Article 39;
5. the declarations referred to in Articles 38 and 40;

6. the reservations referred to in Article 24 and Article 26, third paragraph, and the withdrawals referred to in Article 42;

7. the denunciations referred to in Article 44.

Done at The Hague, on the 25th day of October, 1980.

## Guardianship

### Appointment of guardian

**47.** (1) Upon application by a child's parent or by any other person, on notice to the Children's Lawyer, a court may appoint a guardian of the child's property.

### Responsibility of guardian

(2) A guardian of the property of a child has charge of and is responsible for the care and management of the property of the child.

### Parents and joint guardians

### Parents as guardians

**48.** (1) As between themselves and subject to any court order or any agreement between them, the parents of a child are equally entitled to be appointed by a court as guardians of the property of the child.

### Parent and other person

(2) As between a parent of a child and a person who is not a parent of the child, the parent has a preferential entitlement to be appointed by a court as a guardian of the property of the child.

### More than one guardian

(3) A court may appoint more than one guardian of the property of a child.

### Guardians jointly responsible

(4) Where more than one guardian is appointed of the property of a child, the guardians are jointly responsible for the care and management of the property of the child.

### Criteria

**49.** In deciding an application for the appointment of a guardian of the property of a child, the court shall consider all the circumstances, including,

(a) the ability of the applicant to manage the property of the child;

(b) the merits of the plan proposed by the applicant for the care and management of the property of the child; and

(c) the views and preferences of the child, where such views and preferences can reasonably be ascertained.

### Effect of appointment

**50.** The appointment of a guardian by a court under this Part has effect in all parts of Ontario.

### Payment of debt due to child if no guardian

**51.** (1) If no guardian of a child's property has been appointed, a person who is under a duty to pay money or deliver personal property to the child discharges that duty, to the extent of the amount paid or the value of the personal property delivered, subject to subsection (1.1), by paying money or delivering personal property to,

(a) the child, if the child has a legal obligation to support another person;

(b) a parent with whom the child resides; or

(c) a person who has lawful custody of the child.

### Same

(1.1) The total of the amount of money paid and the value of personal property delivered under subsection (1) shall not exceed the prescribed amount or, if no amount is prescribed, $10,000.

### Money payable under judgment

(2) Subsection (1) does not apply in respect of money payable under a judgment or order of a court.

### Receipt for payment

(3) A receipt or discharge for money or personal property not in excess of the amount or value set out in subsection (1) received for a child by a parent with whom the child resides or a person who has lawful custody of the child has the same validity as if a court had appointed the parent or the person as a guardian of the property of the child.

### Responsibility for money or property

(4) A parent with whom a child resides or a person who has lawful custody of a child who receives and holds money or personal property referred to in subsection (1) has the responsibility of a guardian for the care and management of the money or personal property.

### Regulations

(5) The Lieutenant Governor in Council may, by regulation, prescribe an amount for the purpose of subsection (1.1).

### Accounts

**52.** A guardian of the property of a child may be required to account or may voluntarily pass the accounts in respect of the care and management of the property of the child in the same manner as a trustee under a will may be required to account or may pass the accounts in respect of the trusteeship.

### Transfer of property to child

**53.** A guardian of the property of a child shall transfer to the child all property of the child in the care of the guardian when the child attains the age of eighteen years.

### Management fees and expenses

**54.** A guardian of the property of a child is entitled to payment of a reasonable amount for fees for and expenses of management of the property of the child.

### Bond by guardian

**55.** (1) A court that appoints a guardian of the property of a child shall require the guardian to post a bond, with or without sureties, payable to the child in such amount as the court considers appropriate in respect of the care and management of the property of the child.

### Where parent appointed guardian

(2) Subsection (1) does not apply where the court appoints a parent of a child as guardian of the property of the child and the court is of the opinion that it is appropriate not to require the parent to post a bond.

### Where child has support obligation

**56.** Upon application by a child who has a legal obligation to support another person, the court that appointed a guardian of the property of the child or a co-ordinate court by order shall end the guardianship for the child.

### Removal and resignation of guardian
### Removal

**57.** (1) A guardian of the property of a child may be removed by a court for the same reasons for which a trustee may be removed.

### Resignation

(2) A guardian of the property of a child, with the permission of a court, may resign as guardian upon such conditions as the court considers appropriate.

### Notice to Estate Registrar for Ontario

**58.** A notice of every application to a court for appointment of a guardian of the property of a child shall be transmitted by the clerk of the court to the Estate Registrar for Ontario.

## Disposition of Property
### Court order re property of child

**59.** (1) Upon application by a child's parent or by any other person, on notice to the Children's Lawyer, the Superior Court of Justice by order may require or approve, or both,

    (a) the disposition or encumbrance of all or part of the interest of the child in land;

    (b) the sale of the interest of the child in personal property; or

    (c) the payment of all or part of any money belonging to the child or of the income from any property belonging to the child, or both.

### Criteria

(2) An order shall be made under subsection (1) only where the Court is of the opinion that the disposition, encumbrance, sale or payment is necessary or proper for the support or education of the child or will substantially benefit the child.

### Conditions

(3) An order under subsection (1) may be made subject to such conditions as the Court considers appropriate.

### Limitation

(4) The Court shall not require or approve a disposition or encumbrance of the interest of a child in land contrary to a term of the instrument by which the child acquired the interest.

### Execution of documents

(5) The Court, where it makes an order under subsection (1), may order that the child or another person named in the order execute any documents necessary to carry out the disposition, encumbrance, sale or payment.

### Directions

(6) The Court by order may give such directions as it considers necessary for the carrying out of an order made under subsection (1).

### Validity of documents

(7) Every document executed in accordance with an order under this section is as effectual as if the child by whom it was executed was eighteen years of age or, if executed by another person in accordance with the order, as if the child had executed it and had been eighteen years of age at the time.

### Liability

(8) No person incurs or shall be deemed to incur liability by making a payment in accordance with an order under clause (1)(c).

### Order for maintenance where power of appointment in favour of children

**60.** (1) Upon application by or with the consent of a person who has an estate for life in property with power to devise or appoint the property to one or more of his or her children, the Superior Court of Justice may order that such part of the proceeds of the property as the Court considers proper be used for the support, education or benefit of one or more of the children.

### Idem

(2) An order may be made under subsection (1) whether or not,

    (a) there is a gift over in the event that there are no children to take under the power; or

    (b) any person could dispose of the property in the event that there are no children to take under the power.

## Testamentary Custody and Guardianship
### Appointments by will

### Custody

**61.** (1) A person entitled to custody of a child may appoint by will one or more persons to have custody of the child after the death of the appointor.

### Guardianship

(2) A guardian of the property of a child may appoint by will one or more persons to be guardians of the property of the child after the death of the appointor.

### Appointment by minor

(3) An unmarried parent who is a minor may make an appointment mentioned in subsection (1) or (2) by a written appointment signed by the parent.

### Limitation

(4) An appointment under subsection (1), (2) or (3) is effective only,

(a) if the appointor is the only person entitled to custody of the child or who is the guardian of the property of the child, as the case requires, on the day immediately before the appointment is to take effect; or

(b) if the appointor and any other person entitled to custody of the child or who is the guardian of the property of the child, as the case requires, die at the same time or in circumstances that render it uncertain which survived the other.

### Where more than one appointment

(5) Where two or more persons are appointed to have custody of or to be guardians of the property of a child by appointors who die as mentioned in clause (4)(b), only the appointments of the persons appointed by both or all of the appointors are effective.

### Consent of appointee

(6) No appointment under subsection (1), (2) or (3) is effective without the consent of the person appointed.

### Expiration of appointment

(7) An appointment under subsection (1), (2) or (3) for custody of a child or guardianship of the property of a child expires ninety days after the appointment becomes effective or, where the appointee applies under this Part for custody of the child or guardianship of the property of the child within the ninety-day period, when the application is disposed of.

### Application or order under ss. 21, 47

(8) An appointment under this section does not apply to prevent an application for or the making of an order under section 21 or 47.

### Application

(9) This section applies in respect of,

(a) any will made on or after the 1st day of October, 1982; and

(b) any will made before the 1st day of October, 1982, if the testator is living on that day.

## Procedure

### Procedure, general

### Joinder of proceedings

**62.** (1) An application under this Part may be made in the same proceeding and in the same manner as an application under the Family Law Act, or in another proceeding.

### Nature of order

(2) An application under this Part may be an original application or for the variance of an order previously given or to supersede an order of an extra-provincial tribunal.

### Parties

(3) The parties to an application under this Part in respect of a child shall include,

(a) the child' parents;

(b) a person who has demonstrated a settled intention to treat the child as a child of his or her family;

(c) a person who had the actual care and upbringing of the child immediately before the application; and

(d) any other person whose presence as a party is necessary to determine the matters in issue.

### Combining of applications

(4) Where, in an application under this Part, it appears to the court that it is necessary or desirable in the best interests of the child to have other matters first or simultaneously determined, the court may direct that the application stand over until such other proceedings are brought or determined as the court considers appropriate, subject to section 26.

### Where identity of father not known

(5) Where there is no presumption of paternity and the identity of the father is not known or is not reasonably capable of being ascertained, the court may order substituted service or may dispense with service of documents upon the father in the proceeding.

### Application or response by minor

**63.** (1) A minor who is a parent may make an application under this Part without a next friend and may respond without a litigation guardian.

### Consent by minor

(2) A consent in respect of a matter provided for by this Part is not invalid by reason only that the person giving the consent is a minor.

### Child entitled to be heard

**64.** (1) In considering an application under this Part, a court where possible shall take into consideration the views and preferences of the child to the extent that the child is able to express them.

### Interview by court

(2) The court may interview the child to determine the views and preferences of the child.

### Recording

(3) The interview shall be recorded.

### Counsel

(4) The child is entitled to be advised by and to have his or her counsel, if any, present during the interview.

### Where child is sixteen or more years old

**65.** Nothing in this Part abrogates the right of a child of sixteen or more years of age to withdraw from parental control.

### All proceedings in one court

**66.** Except as otherwise provided, where an application is made to a court under this Part, no person who is a party to the proceeding shall make an application under this Part to any other court in respect of a matter in issue in the proceeding, but the court may order that the proceeding be transferred to a court having other jurisdiction where, in the opinion of the court, the court having other jurisdiction is more appropriate to determine the matters in issue that should be determined at the same time.

### Consent and domestic contracts

### Consent orders

**67.** (1) Upon the consent of the parties in an application under this Part, the court may make any order that the court is otherwise empowered to make by this Part, subject to the duty of the court to have regard to the best interests of the child.

### Incorporation of contract in order

(2) Any matter provided for in this Part and in a domestic contract as defined in the *Family Law Act* may be incorporated in an order made under this Part.

### Part subject to contracts

**68.** Where a domestic contract as defined in the *Family Law Act* makes provision in respect of a matter that is provided for in this Part, the contract prevails except as otherwise provided in Part IV of the *Family Law Act*.

### Jurisdiction of Superior Court of Justice

**69.** This Part does not deprive the Superior Court of Justice of its parens patriae jurisdiction.

### Confidentiality

**70.** (1) Where a proceeding includes an application under this Part, the court shall consider whether it is appropriate to order,

(a) that access to all or part of the court file be limited to,

(i) the court and authorized court employees,

(ii) the parties and their counsel,

(iii) counsel, if any, representing the child who is the subject of the application, and

(iv) any other person that the court may specify; or

(b) that no person shall publish or make public information that has the effect of identifying any person referred to in any document relating to the application that appears in the court file.

### Considerations

(2) In determining whether to make an order under subsection (1), the court shall consider,

(a) the nature and sensitivity of the information contained in the documents relating to the application under this Part that appear in the court file; and

(b) whether not making the order could cause physical, mental or emotional harm to any person referred to in those documents.

### Order on application

(3) Any interested person may make an application for an order under subsection (1).

### Varying or discharging order

(4) The court may vary or discharge an order made under subsection (1).

### Where to apply for interim orders and variations
### Place of application for interim order

**71.** (1) An application for an interim order shall be made to the court in which the original proceeding was taken.

### Place of application to vary order

(2) An application under this Part to vary an order may be made to the court in which the original proceeding was taken or to a co-ordinate court in another part of Ontario.

### Interim order

**72.** In a proceeding under this Part, the court may make such interim order as the court considers appropriate.

### Appeal from Ontario Court of Justice

**73.** An appeal from an order of the Ontario Court of Justice under this Part lies to the Superior Court of Justice.

### Order effective pending appeal

**74.** An order under this Part is effective even if an appeal is taken from the order, unless the court that made the order or the court to which the appeal is taken orders otherwise.

### Rule of construction, guardianship of person and property

**75.** (1) For the purposes of construing any instrument, Act or regulation, unless the contrary intention appears, a reference to a guardian with respect to the person of a child shall be construed to refer to custody of the child and a reference to a guardian with respect to property of a child shall be construed to refer to guardianship of the property of the child.

### Application

(2) Subsection (1) applies to any instrument, any Act of the Legislature or any regulation, order or by-law made under an Act of the Legislature enacted or made before, on or after the 1st day of October, 1982.

**76.** Repealed.

**77.** Repealed.

**78.** Repealed.

**79.–83.** Repealed.

**84.** Omitted (provides for amendments to this Act).

**85.** Omitted (provides for coming into force of provisions of this Act).

# Divorce Act

RSC 1985, c 3 (2d Supp)

### Short Title
1. Short title ........................................................................... 150

### Interpretation
2. Definitions .......................................................................... 150

### Jurisdiction
3. Jurisdiction in divorce proceedings ................................................. 151
4. Jurisdiction in corollary relief proceedings......................................... 151
5. Jurisdiction in variation proceedings ............................................... 152
6. Transfer of divorce proceeding where custody application ............................ 152
7. Exercise of jurisdiction by judge.................................................... 152

### Divorce
8. Divorce ............................................................................. 152
9. Duty of legal adviser................................................................ 153
10. Duty of court—reconciliation ....................................................... 153
11. Duty of court—bars ................................................................. 153
12. Effective date generally............................................................ 154
13. Legal effect throughout Canada ..................................................... 154
14. Marriage dissolved ................................................................. 154

### Corollary Relief

#### Interpretation
15. Definition of "spouse".............................................................. 154

#### Child Support Orders
16. Child support order ................................................................ 154

#### Spousal Support Orders
17. Spousal support order............................................................... 155

#### Priority
18. Priority to child support .......................................................... 155

#### Custody Orders
19. Order for custody................................................................... 156

#### Variation, Rescission or Suspension of Orders
20. Order for variation, rescission or suspension....................................... 156
21. Variation order by affidavit, etc. ................................................. 158

PROVISIONAL ORDERS 158

22. Definitions ........................................................................ 158
23. Transmission ..................................................................... 158
24. Definition of "court" ............................................................ 159
25. Assignment of order ............................................................. 160

APPEALS

26. Appeal to appellate court ....................................................... 160

GENERAL

27. Definition of "spouse" ........................................................... 160
28. Recognition of foreign divorce .................................................. 161
29. Provincial laws of evidence ..................................................... 161
30. Proof of signature or office ..................................................... 161
31. Definition of "competent authority" ............................................ 161
32. Agreements with provinces ...................................................... 162
33. Regulations ...................................................................... 162
34. Guidelines ....................................................................... 162
35. Fees ............................................................................. 163
36. Review and report ............................................................... 163

## SHORT TITLE

**Short title**

1. This Act may be cited as the *Divorce Act*.

## INTERPRETATION

**Definitions**

2. (1) In this Act,

"age of majority," in respect of a child, means the age of majority as determined by the laws of the province where the child ordinarily resides, or, if the child ordinarily resides outside of Canada, eighteen years of age;

"appellate court," in respect of an appeal from a court, means the court exercising appellate jurisdiction with respect to that appeal;

"applicable guidelines" means

(a) where both spouses or former spouses are ordinarily resident in the same province at the time an application for a child support order or a variation order in respect of a child support order is made, or the amount of a child support order is to be recalculated pursuant to section 25.1, and that province has been designated by an order made under subsection (5), the laws of the province specified in the order, and

(b) in any other case, the Federal Child Support Guidelines;

"child of the marriage" means a child of two spouses or former spouses who, at the material time,

(a) is under the age of majority and who has not withdrawn from their charge, or

(b) is the age of majority or over and under their charge but unable, by reason of illness, disability or other cause, to withdraw from their charge or to obtain the necessaries of life;

"child support order" means an order made under subsection 15.1(1);

"corollary relief proceeding" means a proceeding in a court in which either or both former spouses seek a child support order, a spousal support order or a custody order;

"court," in respect of a province, means

(a) for the Province of Ontario, the Superior Court of Justice,

(a.1) for the Province of Newfoundland and Labrador, the Trial Division of the Supreme Court of the Province,

(b) for the Province of Quebec, the Superior Court,

(c) for the Provinces of Nova Scotia, British Columbia and Prince Edward Island, the Supreme Court of the Province,

(d) for the Province of New Brunswick, Manitoba, Saskatchewan or Alberta, the Court of Queen's Bench for the Province, and

(e) for Yukon or the Northwest Territories, the Supreme Court, and in Nunavut, the Nunavut Court of Justice,

and includes such other court in the province the judges of which are appointed by the Governor General as is designated by the Lieutenant Governor in Council of the province as a court for the purposes of this Act;

"custody" includes care, upbringing and any other incident of custody;

"custody order" means an order made under subsection 16(1);

"divorce proceeding" means a proceeding in a court in which either or both spouses seek a divorce alone or together with a child support order, a spousal support order or a custody order;

"Federal Child Support Guidelines" means the guidelines made under section 26.1;

"provincial child support service" means any service, agency or body designated in an agreement with a province under subsection 25.1(1);

"spousal support order" means an order made under subsection 15.2(1);

"spouse" means either of a man or woman who are married to each other;

"support order" means a child support order or a spousal support order;

"variation order" means an order made under subsection 17(1);

"variation proceeding" means a proceeding in a court in which either or both former spouses seek a variation order.

### Child of the marriage

(2)  For the purposes of the definition "child of the marriage" in subsection (1), a child of two spouses or former spouses includes

    (a)  any child for whom they both stand in the place of parents; and

    (b)  any child of whom one is the parent and for whom the other stands in the place of a parent.

### Term not restrictive

(3)  The use of the term "application" to describe a proceeding under this Act in a court shall not be construed as limiting the name under which and the form and manner in which that proceeding may be taken in that court, and the name, manner and form of the proceeding in that court shall be such as is provided for by the rules regulating the practice and procedure in that court.

### Idem

(4)  The use in section 21.1 of the terms "affidavit" and "pleadings" to describe documents shall not be construed as limiting the name that may be used to refer to those documents in a court and the form of those documents, and the name and form of the documents shall be such as is provided for by the rules regulating the practice and procedure in that court.

### Provincial child support guidelines

(5)  The Governor in Council may, by order, designate a province for the purposes of the definition "applicable guidelines" in subsection (1) if the laws of the province establish comprehensive guidelines for the determination of child support that deal with the matters referred to in section 26.1. The order shall specify the laws of the province that constitute the guidelines of the province.

### Amendments included

(6)  The guidelines of a province referred to in subsection (5) include any amendments made to them from time to time.

## JURISDICTION

### Jurisdiction in divorce proceedings

**3.** (1)  A court in a province has jurisdiction to hear and determine a divorce proceeding if either spouse has been ordinarily resident in the province for at least one year immediately preceding the commencement of the proceeding.

### Jurisdiction where two proceedings commenced on different days

(2)  Where divorce proceedings between the same spouses are pending in two courts that would otherwise have jurisdiction under subsection (1) and were commenced on different days and the proceeding that was commenced first is not discontinued within thirty days after it was commenced, the court in which a divorce proceeding was commenced first has exclusive jurisdiction to hear and determine any divorce proceeding then pending between the spouses and the second divorce proceeding shall be deemed to be discontinued.

### Jurisdiction where two proceedings commenced on same day

(3)  Where divorce proceedings between the same spouses are pending in two courts that would otherwise have jurisdiction under subsection (1) and were commenced on the same day and neither proceeding is discontinued within thirty days after it was commenced, the Federal Court has exclusive jurisdiction to hear and determine any divorce proceeding then pending between the spouses and the divorce proceedings in those courts shall be transferred to the Federal Court on the direction of that Court.

### Jurisdiction in corollary relief proceedings

**4.** (1)  A court in a province has jurisdiction to hear and determine a corollary relief proceeding if

    (a)  either former spouse is ordinarily resident in the province at the commencement of the proceeding; or

    (b)  both former spouses accept the jurisdiction of the court.

### Jurisdiction where two proceedings commenced on different days

(2)  Where corollary relief proceedings between the same former spouses and in respect of the same matter are pending in two courts that would otherwise have jurisdiction under subsection (1) and were commenced on different days and the proceeding that was commenced first is not discontinued within thirty days after it was commenced, the court in which a corollary relief proceeding was commenced first has exclusive jurisdiction to hear and determine any corollary relief proceeding then pending between the former spouses in respect of that matter and the second corollary relief proceeding shall be deemed to be discontinued.

### Jurisdiction where two proceedings commenced on same day

(3) Where proceedings between the same former spouses and in respect of the same matter are pending in two courts that would otherwise have jurisdiction under subsection (1) and were commenced on the same day and neither proceeding is discontinued within thirty days after it was commenced, the Federal Court has exclusive jurisdiction to hear and determine any corollary relief proceeding then pending between the former spouses in respect of that matter and the corollary relief proceedings in those courts shall be transferred to the Federal Court on the direction of that Court.

### Jurisdiction in variation proceedings

**5.** (1) A court in a province has jurisdiction to hear and determine a variation proceeding if

(a) either former spouse is ordinarily resident in the province at the commencement of the proceeding; or

(b) both former spouses accept the jurisdiction of the court.

### Jurisdiction where two proceedings commenced on different days

(2) Where variation proceedings between the same former spouses and in respect of the same matter are pending in two courts that would otherwise have jurisdiction under subsection (1) and were commenced on different days and the proceeding that was commenced first is not discontinued within thirty days after it was commenced, the court in which a variation proceeding was commenced first has exclusive jurisdiction to hear and determine any variation proceeding then pending between the former spouses in respect of that matter and the second variation proceeding shall be deemed to be discontinued.

### Jurisdiction where two proceedings commenced on same day

(3) Where variation proceedings between the same former spouses and in respect of the same matter are pending in two courts that would otherwise have jurisdiction under subsection (1) and were commenced on the same day and neither proceeding is discontinued within thirty days after it was commenced, the Federal Court has exclusive jurisdiction to hear and determine any variation proceeding then pending between the former spouses in respect of that matter and the variation proceedings in those courts shall be transferred to the Federal Court on the direction of that Court.

### Transfer of divorce proceeding where custody application

**6.** (1) Where an application for an order under section 16 is made in a divorce proceeding to a court in a province and is opposed and the child of the marriage in respect of whom the order is sought is most substantially connected with another province, the court may, on application by a spouse or on its own motion, transfer the divorce proceeding to a court in that other province.

### Transfer of corollary relief proceeding where custody application

(2) Where an application for an order under section 16 is made in a corollary relief proceeding to a court in a province and is opposed and the child of the marriage in respect of whom the order is sought is most substantially connected with another province, the court may, on application by a former spouse or on its own motion, transfer the corollary relief proceeding to a court in that other province.

### Transfer of variation proceeding where custody application

(3) Where an application for a variation order in respect of a custody order is made in a variation proceeding to a court in a province and is opposed and the child of the marriage in respect of whom the variation order is sought is most substantially connected with another province, the court may, on application by a former spouse or on its own motion, transfer the variation proceeding to a court in that other province.

### Exclusive jurisdiction

(4) Notwithstanding sections 3 to 5, a court in a province to which a proceeding is transferred under this section has exclusive jurisdiction to hear and determine the proceeding.

### Exercise of jurisdiction by judge

**7.** The jurisdiction conferred on a court by this Act to grant a divorce shall be exercised only by a judge of the court without a jury.

## DIVORCE

### Divorce

**8.** (1) A court of competent jurisdiction may, on application by either or both spouses, grant a divorce to the spouse or spouses on the ground that there has been a breakdown of their marriage.

### Breakdown of marriage

(2) Breakdown of a marriage is established only if

(a) the spouses have lived separate and apart for at least one year immediately preceding the determination of the divorce proceeding and were living separate and apart at the commencement of the proceeding; or

(b) the spouse against whom the divorce proceeding is brought has, since celebration of the marriage,

(i) committed adultery, or

(ii) treated the other spouse with physical or mental cruelty of such a kind as to render intolerable the continued cohabitation of the spouses.

### Calculation of period of separation

(3) For the purposes of paragraph (2)(a),

(a) spouses shall be deemed to have lived separate and apart for any period during which they lived apart and either of them had the intention to live separate and apart from the other; and

(b) a period during which spouses have lived separate and apart shall not be considered to have been interrupted or terminated

(i) by reason only that either spouse has become incapable of forming or having an intention to continue to live separate and apart or of continuing to live separate and apart of the spouse's own volition, if it appears to the court that the separation would probably have continued if the spouse had not become so incapable, or

(ii) by reason only that the spouses have resumed cohabitation during a period of, or periods totalling, not more than ninety days with reconciliation as its primary purpose.

## Duty of legal adviser

**9.** (1) It is the duty of every barrister, solicitor, lawyer or advocate who undertakes to act on behalf of a spouse in a divorce proceeding

(a) to draw to the attention of the spouse the provisions of this Act that have as their object the reconciliation of spouses, and

(b) to discuss with the spouse the possibility of the reconciliation of the spouses and to inform the spouse of the marriage counselling or guidance facilities known to him or her that might be able to assist the spouses to achieve a reconciliation,

unless the circumstances of the case are of such a nature that it would clearly not be appropriate to do so.

## Idem

(2) It is the duty of every barrister, solicitor, lawyer or advocate who undertakes to act on behalf of a spouse in a divorce proceeding to discuss with the spouse the advisability of negotiating the matters that may be the subject of a support order or a custody order and to inform the spouse of the mediation facilities known to him or her that might be able to assist the spouses in negotiating those matters.

## Certification

(3) Every document presented to a court by a barrister, solicitor, lawyer or advocate that formally commences a divorce proceeding shall contain a statement by him or her certifying that he or she has complied with this section.

## Duty of court—reconciliation

**10.** (1) In a divorce proceeding, it is the duty of the court, before considering the evidence, to satisfy itself that there is no possibility of the reconciliation of the spouses, unless the circumstances of the case are of such a nature that it would clearly not be appropriate to do so.

## Adjournment

(2) Where at any stage in a divorce proceeding it appears to the court from the nature of the case, the evidence or the attitude of either or both spouses that there is a possibility of the reconciliation of the spouses, the court shall

(a) adjourn the proceeding to afford the spouses an opportunity to achieve a reconciliation; and

(b) with the consent of the spouses or in the discretion of the court, nominate

(i) a person with experience or training in marriage counselling or guidance, or

(ii) in special circumstances, some other suitable person,

to assist the spouses to achieve a reconciliation.

## Resumption

(3) Where fourteen days have elapsed from the date of any adjournment under subsection (2), the court shall resume the proceeding on the application of either or both spouses.

## Nominee not competent or compellable

(4) No person nominated by a court under this section to assist spouses to achieve a reconciliation is competent or compellable in any legal proceedings to disclose any admission or communication made to that person in his or her capacity as a nominee of the court for that purpose.

## Evidence not admissible

(5) Evidence of anything said or of any admission or communication made in the course of assisting spouses to achieve a reconciliation is not admissible in any legal proceedings.

## Duty of court—bars

**11.** (1) In a divorce proceeding, it is the duty of the court

(a) to satisfy itself that there has been no collusion in relation to the application for a divorce and to dismiss the application if it finds that there was collusion in presenting it;

(b) to satisfy itself that reasonable arrangements have been made for the support of any children of the marriage, having regard to the applicable guidelines, and, if such arrangements have not been made, to stay the granting of the divorce until such arrangements are made; and

(c) where a divorce is sought in circumstances described in paragraph 8(2)(b), to satisfy itself that there has been no condonation or connivance on the part of the spouse bringing the proceeding, and to dismiss the application for a divorce if that spouse has condoned or connived at the act or conduct complained of unless, in the opinion of the court, the public interest would be better served by granting the divorce.

## Revival

(2) Any act or conduct that has been condoned is not capable of being revived so as to constitute a circumstance described in paragraph 8(2)(b).

## Condonation

(3) For the purposes of this section, a continuation or resumption of cohabitation during a period of, or periods totalling, not more than ninety days with reconciliation as its primary purpose shall not be considered to constitute condonation.

## Definition of "collusion"

(4) In this section, "collusion" means an agreement or conspiracy to which an applicant for a divorce is either directly or indirectly a party for the purpose of subverting the administration of justice, and includes any agreement, understanding or arrangement to fabricate or suppress evidence or to deceive the court, but does not include an agreement to the extent that it provides for separation between the parties, financial support, division of property or the custody of any child of the marriage.

## Effective date generally

**12.** (1) Subject to this section, a divorce takes effect on the thirty-first day after the day on which the judgment granting the divorce is rendered.

## Special circumstances

(2) Where, on or after rendering a judgment granting a divorce,

(a) the court is of the opinion that by reason of special circumstances the divorce should take effect earlier than the thirty-first day after the day on which the judgment is rendered, and

(b) the spouses agree and undertake that no appeal from the judgment will be taken, or any appeal from the judgment that was taken has been abandoned,

the court may order that the divorce takes effect at such earlier time as it considers appropriate.

## Effective date where appeal

(3) A divorce in respect of which an appeal is pending at the end of the period referred to in subsection (1), unless voided on appeal, takes effect on the expiration of the time fixed by law for instituting an appeal from the decision on that appeal or any subsequent appeal, if no appeal has been instituted within that time.

## Certain extensions to be counted

(4) For the purposes of subsection (3), the time fixed by law for instituting an appeal from a decision on an appeal includes any extension thereof fixed pursuant to law before the expiration of that time or fixed thereafter on an application instituted before the expiration of that time.

## No late extensions of time for appeal

(5) Notwithstanding any other law, the time fixed by law for instituting an appeal from a decision referred to in subsection (3) may not be extended after the expiration of that time, except on an application instituted before the expiration of that time.

## Effective date where decision of Supreme Court of Canada

(6) A divorce in respect of which an appeal has been taken to the Supreme Court of Canada, unless voided on the appeal, takes effect on the day on which the judgment on the appeal is rendered.

## Certificate of divorce

(7) Where a divorce takes effect in accordance with this section, a judge or officer of the court that rendered the judgment granting the divorce or, where that judgment has been appealed, of the appellate court that rendered the judgment on the final appeal, shall, on request, issue to any person a certificate that a divorce granted under this Act dissolved the marriage of the specified persons effective as of a specified date.

## Conclusive proof

(8) A certificate referred to in subsection (7), or a certified copy thereof, is conclusive proof of the facts so certified without proof of the signature or authority of the person appearing to have signed the certificate.

## Legal effect throughout Canada

**13.** On taking effect, a divorce granted under this Act has legal effect throughout Canada.

## Marriage dissolved

**14.** On taking effect, a divorce granted under this Act dissolves the marriage of the spouses.

## COROLLARY RELIEF

### Interpretation

## Definition of "spouse"

**15.** In sections 15.1 to 16, "spouse" has the meaning assigned by subsection 2(1), and includes a former spouse.

### Child Support Orders

## Child support order

**15.1** (1) A court of competent jurisdiction may, on application by either or both spouses, make an order requiring a spouse to pay for the support of any or all children of the marriage.

## Interim order

(2) Where an application is made under subsection (1), the court may, on application by either or both spouses, make an interim order requiring a spouse to pay for the support of any or all children of the marriage, pending the determination of the application under subsection (1).

## Guidelines apply

(3) A court making an order under subsection (1) or an interim order under subsection (2) shall do so in accordance with the applicable guidelines.

### Terms and conditions

(4) The court may make an order under subsection (1) or an interim order under subsection (2) for a definite or indefinite period or until a specified event occurs, and may impose terms, conditions or restrictions in connection with the order or interim order as it thinks fit and just.

### Court may take agreement, etc., into account

(5) Notwithstanding subsection (3), a court may award an amount that is different from the amount that would be determined in accordance with the applicable guidelines if the court is satisfied

(a) that special provisions in an order, a judgment or a written agreement respecting the financial obligations of the spouses, or the division or transfer of their property, directly or indirectly benefit a child, or that special provisions have otherwise been made for the benefit of a child; and

(b) that the application of the applicable guidelines would result in an amount of child support that is inequitable given those special provisions.

### Reasons

(6) Where the court awards, pursuant to subsection (5), an amount that is different from the amount that would be determined in accordance with the applicable guidelines, the court shall record its reasons for having done so.

### Consent orders

(7) Notwithstanding subsection (3), a court may award an amount that is different from the amount that would be determined in accordance with the applicable guidelines on the consent of both spouses if it is satisfied that reasonable arrangements have been made for the support of the child to whom the order relates.

### Reasonable arrangements

(8) For the purposes of subsection (7), in determining whether reasonable arrangements have been made for the support of a child, the court shall have regard to the applicable guidelines. However, the court shall not consider the arrangements to be unreasonable solely because the amount of support agreed to is not the same as the amount that would otherwise have been determined in accordance with the applicable guidelines.

## Spousal Support Orders

### Spousal support order

**15.2** (1) A court of competent jurisdiction may, on application by either or both spouses, make an order requiring a spouse to secure or pay, or to secure and pay, such lump sum or periodic sums, or such lump sum and periodic sums, as the court thinks reasonable for the support of the other spouse.

### Interim order

(2) Where an application is made under subsection (1), the court may, on application by either or both spouses, make an interim order requiring a spouse to secure or pay, or to secure and pay, such lump sum or periodic sums, or such lump sum and periodic sums, as the court thinks reasonable for the support of the other spouse, pending the determination of the application under subsection (1).

### Terms and conditions

(3) The court may make an order under subsection (1) or an interim order under subsection (2) for a definite or indefinite period or until a specified event occurs, and may impose terms, conditions or restrictions in connection with the order as it thinks fit and just.

### Factors

(4) In making an order under subsection (1) or an interim order under subsection (2), the court shall take into consideration the condition, means, needs and other circumstances of each spouse, including

(a) the length of time the spouses cohabited;

(b) the functions performed by each spouse during cohabitation; and

(c) any order, agreement or arrangement relating to support of either spouse.

### Spousal misconduct

(5) In making an order under subsection (1) or an interim order under subsection (2), the court shall not take into consideration any misconduct of a spouse in relation to the marriage.

### Objectives of spousal support order

(6) An order made under subsection (1) or an interim order under subsection (2) that provides for the support of a spouse should

(a) recognize any economic advantages or disadvantages to the spouses arising from the marriage or its breakdown;

(b) apportion between the spouses any financial consequences arising from the care of any child of the marriage over and above any obligation for the support of any child of the marriage;

(c) relieve any economic hardship of the spouses arising from the breakdown of the marriage; and

(d) in so far as practicable, promote the economic self-sufficiency of each spouse within a reasonable period of time.

## Priority

### Priority to child support

**15.3** (1) Where a court is considering an application for a child support order and an application for a spousal support order, the court shall give priority to child support in determining the applications.

### Reasons

(2) Where, as a result of giving priority to child support, the court is unable to make a spousal support order or the court makes a spousal support order in an amount that is less than it otherwise would have been, the court shall record its reasons for having done so.

### Consequences of reduction or termination of child support order

(3) Where, as a result of giving priority to child support, a spousal support order was not made, or the amount of a spousal support order is less than it otherwise would have been, any subsequent reduction or termination of that child support constitutes a change of circumstances for the purposes of applying for a spousal support order, or a variation order in respect of the spousal support order, as the case may be.

## Custody Orders

### Order for custody

**16.** (1) A court of competent jurisdiction may, on application by either or both spouses or by any other person, make an order respecting the custody of or the access to, or the custody of and access to, any or all children of the marriage.

### Interim order for custody

(2) Where an application is made under subsection (1), the court may, on application by either or both spouses or by any other person, make an interim order respecting the custody of or the access to, or the custody of and access to, any or all children of the marriage pending determination of the application under subsection (1).

### Application by other person

(3) A person, other than a spouse, may not make an application under subsection (1) or (2) without leave of the court.

### Joint custody or access

(4) The court may make an order under this section granting custody of, or access to, any or all children of the marriage to any one or more persons.

### Access

(5) Unless the court orders otherwise, a spouse who is granted access to a child of the marriage has the right to make inquiries, and to be given information, as to the health, education and welfare of the child.

### Terms and conditions

(6) The court may make an order under this section for a definite or indefinite period or until the happening of a specified event and may impose such other terms, conditions or restrictions in connection therewith as it thinks fit and just.

### Order respecting change of residence

(7) Without limiting the generality of subsection (6), the court may include in an order under this section a term requiring any person who has custody of a child of the marriage and who intends to change the place of residence of that child to notify, at least thirty days before the change or within such other period before the change as the court may specify, any person who is granted access to that child of the change, the time at which the change will be made and the new place of residence of the child.

### Factors

(8) In making an order under this section, the court shall take into consideration only the best interests of the child of the marriage as determined by reference to the condition, means, needs and other circumstances of the child.

### Past conduct

(9) In making an order under this section, the court shall not take into consideration the past conduct of any person unless the conduct is relevant to the ability of that person to act as a parent of a child.

### Maximum contact

(10) In making an order under this section, the court shall give effect to the principle that a child of the marriage should have as much contact with each spouse as is consistent with the best interests of the child and, for that purpose, shall take into consideration the willingness of the person for whom custody is sought to facilitate such contact.

## Variation, Rescission or Suspension of Orders

### Order for variation, rescission or suspension

**17.** (1) A court of competent jurisdiction may make an order varying, rescinding or suspending, prospectively or retroactively,

    (a) a support order or any provision thereof on application by either or both former spouses; or

    (b) a custody order or any provision thereof on application by either or both former spouses or by any other person.

### Application by other person

(2) A person, other than a former spouse, may not make an application under paragraph (1)(b) without leave of the court.

### Terms and conditions

(3) The court may include in a variation order any provision that under this Act could have been included in the order in respect of which the variation order is sought.

### Factors for child support order

(4) Before the court makes a variation order in respect of a child support order, the court shall satisfy itself that a change

of circumstances as provided for in the applicable guidelines has occurred since the making of the child support order or the last variation order made in respect of that order.

### Factors for spousal support order

(4.1)  Before the court makes a variation order in respect of a spousal support order, the court shall satisfy itself that a change in the condition, means, needs or other circumstances of either former spouse has occurred since the making of the spousal support order or the last variation order made in respect of that order, and, in making the variation order, the court shall take that change into consideration.

### Factors for custody order

(5)  Before the court makes a variation order in respect of a custody order, the court shall satisfy itself that there has been a change in the condition, means, needs or other circumstances of the child of the marriage occurring since the making of the custody order or the last variation order made in respect of that order, as the case may be, and, in making the variation order, the court shall take into consideration only the best interests of the child as determined by reference to that change.

### Variation order

(5.1)  For the purposes of subsection (5), a former spouse's terminal illness or critical condition shall be considered a change of circumstances of the child of the marriage, and the court shall make a variation order in respect of access that is in the best interests of the child.

### Conduct

(6)  In making a variation order, the court shall not take into consideration any conduct that under this Act could not have been considered in making the order in respect of which the variation order is sought.

### Guidelines apply

(6.1)  A court making a variation order in respect of a child support order shall do so in accordance with the applicable guidelines.

### Court may take agreement, etc., into account

(6.2)  Notwithstanding subsection (6.1), in making a variation order in respect of a child support order, a court may award an amount that is different from the amount that would be determined in accordance with the applicable guidelines if the court is satisfied

(a)  that special provisions in an order, a judgment or a written agreement respecting the financial obligations of the spouses, or the division or transfer of their property, directly or indirectly benefit a child, or that special provisions have otherwise been made for the benefit of a child; and

(b)  that the application of the applicable guidelines would result in an amount of child support that is inequitable given those special provisions.

### Reasons

(6.3)  Where the court awards, pursuant to subsection (6.2), an amount that is different from the amount that would be determined in accordance with the applicable guidelines, the court shall record its reasons for having done so.

### Consent orders

(6.4)  Notwithstanding subsection (6.1), a court may award an amount that is different from the amount that would be determined in accordance with the applicable guidelines on the consent of both spouses if it is satisfied that reasonable arrangements have been made for the support of the child to whom the order relates.

### Reasonable arrangements

(6.5)  For the purposes of subsection (6.4), in determining whether reasonable arrangements have been made for the support of a child, the court shall have regard to the applicable guidelines. However, the court shall not consider the arrangements to be unreasonable solely because the amount of support agreed to is not the same as the amount that would otherwise have been determined in accordance with the applicable guidelines.

### Objectives of variation order varying spousal support order

(7)  A variation order varying a spousal support order should

(a)  recognize any economic advantages or disadvantages to the former spouses arising from the marriage or its breakdown;

(b)  apportion between the former spouses any financial consequences arising from the care of any child of the marriage over and above any obligation for the support of any child of the marriage;

(c)  relieve any economic hardship of the former spouses arising from the breakdown of the marriage; and

(d)  in so far as practicable, promote the economic self-sufficiency of each former spouse within a reasonable period of time.

(8)  Repealed.

### Maximum contact

(9)  In making a variation order varying a custody order, the court shall give effect to the principle that a child of the marriage should have as much contact with each former spouse as is consistent with the best interests of the child and, for that purpose, where the variation order would grant custody of the child to a person who does not currently have custody, the court shall take into consideration the willingness of that person to facilitate such contact.

### Limitation

(10)  Notwithstanding subsection (1), where a spousal support order provides for support for a definite period or until

a specified event occurs, a court may not, on an application instituted after the expiration of that period or the occurrence of the event, make a variation order for the purpose of resuming that support unless the court is satisfied that

(a) a variation order is necessary to relieve economic hardship arising from a change described in subsection (4.1) that is related to the marriage; and

(b) the changed circumstances, had they existed at the time of the making of the spousal support order or the last variation order made in respect of that order, as the case may be, would likely have resulted in a different order.

### Copy of order

(11) Where a court makes a variation order in respect of a support order or a custody order made by another court, it shall send a copy of the variation order, certified by a judge or officer of the court, to that other court.

### Variation order by affidavit, etc.

**17.1** Where both former spouses are ordinarily resident in different provinces, a court of competent jurisdiction may, in accordance with any applicable rules of the court, make a variation order pursuant to subsection 17(1) on the basis of the submissions of the former spouses, whether presented orally before the court or by means of affidavits or any means of telecommunication, if both former spouses consent thereto.

### Provisional Orders

### Definitions

**18.** (1) In this section and section 19,

"Attorney General," in respect of a province, means

(a) for Yukon, the member of the Executive Council of Yukon designated by the Commissioner of Yukon,

(b) for the Northwest Territories, the member of the Executive Council of the Northwest Territories designated by the Commissioner of the Northwest Territories,

(b.1) for Nunavut, the member of the Executive Council of Nunavut designated by the Commissioner of Nunavut, and

(c) for the other provinces, the Attorney General of the province,

and includes any person authorized in writing by the member or Attorney General to act for the member or Attorney General in the performance of a function under this section or section 19;

"provisional order" means an order made pursuant to subsection (2).

### Provisional order

(2) Notwithstanding paragraph 5(1)(a) and subsection 17(1), where an application is made to a court in a province for a variation order in respect of a support order and

(a) the respondent in the application is ordinarily resident in another province and has not accepted the jurisdiction of the court, or both former spouses have not consented to the application of section 17.1 in respect of the matter, and

(b) in the circumstances of the case, the court is satisfied that the issues can be adequately determined by proceeding under this section and section 19,

the court shall make a variation order with or without notice to and in the absence of the respondent, but such order is provisional only and has no legal effect until it is confirmed in a proceeding under section 19 and, where so confirmed, it has legal effect in accordance with the terms of the order confirming it.

### Transmission

(3) Where a court in a province makes a provisional order, it shall send to the Attorney General for the province

(a) three copies of the provisional order certified by a judge or officer of the court;

(b) a certified or sworn document setting out or summarizing the evidence given to the court; and

(c) a statement giving any available information respecting the identification, location, income and assets of the respondent.

### Idem

(4) On receipt of the documents referred to in subsection (3), the Attorney General shall send the documents to the Attorney General for the province in which the respondent is ordinarily resident.

### Further evidence

(5) Where, during a proceeding under section 19, a court in a province remits the matter back for further evidence to the court that made the provisional order, the court that made the order shall, after giving notice to the applicant, receive further evidence.

### Transmission

(6) Where evidence is received under subsection (5), the court that received the evidence shall forward to the court that remitted the matter back a certified or sworn document setting out or summarizing the evidence, together with such recommendations as the court that received the evidence considers appropriate.

### Transmission

**19.** (1) On receipt of any documents sent pursuant to subsection 18(4), the Attorney General for the province in which the respondent is ordinarily resident shall send the documents to a court in the province.

### Procedure

(2) Subject to subsection (3), where documents have been sent to a court pursuant to subsection (1), the court shall serve

on the respondent a copy of the documents and a notice of a hearing respecting confirmation of the provisional order and shall proceed with the hearing, in the absence of the applicant, taking into consideration the certified or sworn document setting out or summarizing the evidence given to the court that made the provisional order.

### Return to Attorney General

(3) Where documents have been sent to a court pursuant to subsection (1) and the respondent apparently is outside the province and is not likely to return, the court shall send the documents to the Attorney General for that province, together with any available information respecting the location and circumstances of the respondent.

### Idem

(4) On receipt of any documents and information sent pursuant to subsection (3), the Attorney General shall send the documents and information to the Attorney General for the province of the court that made the provisional order.

### Right of respondent

(5) In a proceeding under this section, the respondent may raise any matter that might have been raised before the court that made the provisional order.

### Further evidence

(6) Where, in a proceeding under this section, the respondent satisfies the court that for the purpose of taking further evidence or for any other purpose it is necessary to remit the matter back to the court that made the provisional order, the court may so remit the matter and adjourn the proceeding for that purpose.

### Order of confirmation or refusal

(7) Subject to subsection (7.1), at the conclusion of a proceeding under this section, the court shall make an order

   (a) confirming the provisional order without variation;
   (b) confirming the provisional order with variation; or
   (c) refusing confirmation of the provisional order.

### Guidelines apply

(7.1) A court making an order under subsection (7) in respect of a child support order shall do so in accordance with the applicable guidelines.

### Further evidence

(8) The court, before making an order confirming the provisional order with variation or an order refusing confirmation of the provisional order, shall decide whether to remit the matter back for further evidence to the court that made the provisional order.

### Interim order for support of children

(9) Where a court remits a matter pursuant to this section in relation to a child support order, the court may, pending the making of an order under subsection (7), make an interim order in accordance with the applicable guidelines requiring a spouse to pay for the support of any or all children of the marriage.

### Interim order for support of spouse

(9.1) Where a court remits a matter pursuant to this section in relation to a spousal support order, the court may make an interim order requiring a spouse to secure or pay, or to secure and pay, such lump sum or periodic sums, or such lump sum and periodic sums, as the court thinks reasonable for the support of the other spouse, pending the making of an order under subsection (7).

### Terms and conditions

(10) The court may make an order under subsection (9) or (9.1) for a definite or indefinite period or until a specified event occurs, and may impose terms, conditions or restrictions in connection with the order as it thinks fit and just.

### Provisions applicable

(11) Subsections 17(4), (4.1) and (6) to (7) apply, with such modifications as the circumstances require, in respect of an order made under subsection (9) or (9.1) as if it were a variation order referred to in those subsections.

### Report and filing

(12) On making an order under subsection (7), the court in a province shall

   (a) send a copy of the order, certified by a judge or officer of the court, to the Attorney General for that province, to the court that made the provisional order and, where that court is not the court that made the support order in respect of which the provisional order was made, to the court that made the support order;
   (b) where an order is made confirming the provisional order with or without variation, file the order in the court; and
   (c) where an order is made confirming the provisional order with variation or refusing confirmation of the provisional order, give written reasons to the Attorney General for that province and to the court that made the provisional order.

### Definition of "court"

**20.** (1) In this section, "court," in respect of a province, has the meaning assigned by subsection 2(1) and includes such other court having jurisdiction in the province as is designated by the Lieutenant Governor in Council of the province as a court for the purposes of this section.

### Legal effect throughout Canada

(2) Subject to subsection 18(2), an order made under any of sections 15.1 to 17 or subsection 19(7), (9) or (9.1) has legal effect throughout Canada.

### Enforcement

(3)  An order that has legal effect throughout Canada pursuant to subsection (2) may be

(a)  registered in any court in a province and enforced in like manner as an order of that court; or

(b)  enforced in a province in any other manner provided for by the laws of that province, including its laws respecting reciprocal enforcement between the province and a jurisdiction outside Canada.

### Variation of orders

(4)  Notwithstanding subsection (3), a court may only vary an order that has legal effect throughout Canada pursuant to subsection (2) in accordance with this Act.

### Assignment of order

**20.1**  (1)  A support order may be assigned to

(a)  any minister of the Crown for Canada designated by the Governor in Council;

(b)  any minister of the Crown for a province, or any agency in a province, designated by the Lieutenant Governor in Council of the province;

(c)  any member of the Legislative Assembly of Yukon, or any agency in Yukon, designated by the Commissioner of Yukon;

(d)  any member of the Legislative Assembly of the Northwest Territories, or any agency in the Northwest Territories, designated by the Commissioner of the Northwest Territories; or

(e)  any member of the Legislative Assembly of Nunavut, or any agency in Nunavut, designated by the Commissioner of Nunavut.

### Rights

(2)  A minister, member or agency referred to in subsection (1) to whom an order is assigned is entitled to the payments due under the order, and has the same right to be notified of, and to participate in, proceedings under this Act to vary, rescind, suspend or enforce the order as the person who would otherwise be entitled to the payments.

## APPEALS

### Appeal to appellate court

**21.**  (1)  Subject to subsections (2) and (3), an appeal lies to the appellate court from any judgment or order, whether final or interim, rendered or made by a court under this Act.

### Restriction on divorce appeals

(2)  No appeal lies from a judgment granting a divorce on or after the day on which the divorce takes effect.

### Restriction on order appeals

(3)  No appeal lies from an order made under this Act more than thirty days after the day on which the order was made.

### Extension

(4)  An appellate court or a judge thereof may, on special grounds, either before or after the expiration of the time fixed by subsection (3) for instituting an appeal, by order extend that time.

### Powers of appellate court

(5)  The appellate court may

(a)  dismiss the appeal; or

(b)  allow the appeal and

(i)  render the judgment or make the order that ought to have been rendered or made, including such order or such further or other order as it deems just, or

(ii)  order a new hearing where it deems it necessary to do so to correct a substantial wrong or miscarriage of justice.

### Procedure on appeals

(6)  Except as otherwise provided by this Act or the rules or regulations, an appeal under this section shall be asserted, heard and decided according to the ordinary procedure governing appeals to the appellate court from the court rendering the judgment or making the order being appealed.

## GENERAL

### Definition of "spouse"

**21.1**  (1)  In this section, "spouse" has the meaning assigned by subsection 2(1) and includes a former spouse.

### Affidavit re removal of barriers to religious remarriage

(2)  In any proceedings under this Act, a spouse (in this section referred to as the "deponent") may serve on the other spouse and file with the court an affidavit indicating

(a)  that the other spouse is the spouse of the deponent;

(b)  the date and place of the marriage, and the official character of the person who solemnized the marriage;

(c)  the nature of any barriers to the remarriage of the deponent within the deponent's religion the removal of which is within the other spouse's control;

(d)  where there are any barriers to the remarriage of the other spouse within the other spouse's religion the removal of which is within the deponent's control, that the deponent

(i)  has removed those barriers, and the date and circumstances of that removal, or

(ii)  has signified a willingness to remove those barriers, and the date and circumstances of that signification;

(e)  that the deponent has, in writing, requested the other spouse to remove all of the barriers to the remarriage of the deponent within the deponent's religion the removal of which is within the other spouse's control;

(f) the date of the request described in paragraph (e); and

(g) that the other spouse, despite the request described in paragraph (e), has failed to remove all of the barriers referred to in that paragraph.

### Powers of court where barriers not removed

(3) Where a spouse who has been served with an affidavit under subsection (2) does not

(a) within fifteen days after that affidavit is filed with the court or within such longer period as the court allows, serve on the deponent and file with the court an affidavit indicating that all of the barriers referred to in paragraph (2)(e) have been removed, and

(b) satisfy the court, in any additional manner that the court may require, that all of the barriers referred to in paragraph (2)(e) have been removed,

the court may, subject to any terms that the court considers appropriate,

(c) dismiss any application filed by that spouse under this Act, and

(d) strike out any other pleadings and affidavits filed by that spouse under this Act.

### Special case

(4) Without limiting the generality of the court's discretion under subsection (3), the court may refuse to exercise its powers under paragraphs (3)(c) and (d) where a spouse who has been served with an affidavit under subsection (2)

(a) within fifteen days after that affidavit is filed with the court or within such longer period as the court allows, serves on the deponent and files with the court an affidavit indicating genuine grounds of a religious or conscientious nature for refusing to remove the barriers referred to in paragraph (2)(e); and

(b) satisfies the court, in any additional manner that the court may require, that the spouse has genuine grounds of a religious or conscientious nature for refusing to remove the barriers referred to in paragraph (2)(e).

### Affidavits

(5) For the purposes of this section, an affidavit filed with the court by a spouse must, in order to be valid, indicate the date on which it was served on the other spouse.

### Where section does not apply

(6) This section does not apply where the power to remove the barrier to religious remarriage lies with a religious body or official.

### Recognition of foreign divorce

**22.** (1) A divorce granted, on or after the coming into force of this Act, pursuant to a law of a country or subdivision of a country other than Canada by a tribunal or other authority having jurisdiction to do so shall be recognized for all purposes of determining the marital status in Canada of any person, if either former spouse was ordinarily resident in that country or subdivision for at least one year immediately preceding the commencement of proceedings for the divorce.

### Idem

(2) A divorce granted, after July 1, 1968, pursuant to a law of a country or subdivision of a country other than Canada by a tribunal or other authority having jurisdiction to do so, on the basis of the domicile of the wife in that country or subdivision determined as if she were unmarried and, if she was a minor, as if she had attained the age of majority, shall be recognized for all purposes of determining the marital status in Canada of any person.

### Other recognition rules preserved

(3) Nothing in this section abrogates or derogates from any other rule of law respecting the recognition of divorces granted otherwise than under this Act.

### Provincial laws of evidence

**23.** (1) Subject to this or any other Act of Parliament, the laws of evidence of the province in which any proceedings under this Act are taken, including the laws of proof of service of any document, apply to such proceedings.

### Presumption

(2) For the purposes of this section, where any proceedings are transferred to the Federal Court under subsection 3(3) or 5(3), the proceedings shall be deemed to have been taken in the province specified in the direction of the Court to be the province with which both spouses or former spouses, as the case may be, are or have been most substantially connected.

### Proof of signature or office

**24.** A document offered in a proceeding under this Act that purports to be certified or sworn by a judge or an officer of a court shall, unless the contrary is proved, be proof of the appointment, signature or authority of the judge or officer and, in the case of a document purporting to be sworn, of the appointment, signature or authority of the person before whom the document purports to be sworn.

### Definition of "competent authority"

**25.** (1) In this section, "competent authority," in respect of a court, or appellate court, in a province means the body, person or group of persons ordinarily competent under the laws of that province to make rules regulating the practice and procedure in that court.

### Rules

(2) Subject to subsection (3), the competent authority may make rules applicable to any proceedings under this Act in a court, or appellate court, in a province, including, without limiting the generality of the foregoing, rules

(a) regulating the practice and procedure in the court, including the addition of persons as parties to the proceedings;

(b) respecting the conduct and disposition of any proceedings under this Act without an oral hearing;

(b.1) respecting the application of section 17.1 in respect of proceedings for a variation order;

(c) regulating the sittings of the court;

(d) respecting the fixing and awarding of costs;

(e) prescribing and regulating the duties of officers of the court;

(f) respecting the transfer of proceedings under this Act to or from the court; and

(g) prescribing and regulating any other matter considered expedient to attain the ends of justice and carry into effect the purposes and provisions of this Act.

### Exercise of power

(3) The power to make rules for a court or appellate court conferred by subsection (2) on a competent authority shall be exercised in the like manner and subject to the like terms and conditions, if any, as the power to make rules for that court conferred on that authority by the laws of the province.

### Not statutory instruments

(4) Rules made pursuant to this section by a competent authority that is not a judicial or quasi-judicial body shall be deemed not to be statutory instruments within the meaning and for the purposes of the Statutory Instruments Act.

### Agreements with provinces

**25.1** (1) With the approval of the Governor in Council, the Minister of Justice may, on behalf of the Government of Canada, enter into an agreement with a province authorizing a provincial child support service designated in the agreement to

(a) assist courts in the province in the determination of the amount of child support; and

(b) recalculate, at regular intervals, in accordance with the applicable guidelines, the amount of child support orders on the basis of updated income information.

### Effect of recalculation

(2) Subject to subsection (5), the amount of a child support order as recalculated pursuant to this section shall for all purposes be deemed to be the amount payable under the child support order.

### Liability

(3) The former spouse against whom a child support order was made becomes liable to pay the amount as recalculated pursuant to this section thirty-one days after both former spouses to whom the order relates are notified of the recalculation in the manner provided for in the agreement authorizing the recalculation.

### Right to vary

(4) Where either or both former spouses to whom a child support order relates do not agree with the amount of the order as recalculated pursuant to this section, either former spouse may, within thirty days after both former spouses are notified of the recalculation in the manner provided for in the agreement authorizing the recalculation, apply to a court of competent jurisdiction for an order under subsection 17(1).

### Effect of application

(5) Where an application is made under subsection (4), the operation of subsection (3) is suspended pending the determination of the application, and the child support order continues in effect.

### Withdrawal of application

(6) Where an application made under subsection (4) is withdrawn before the determination of the application, the former spouse against whom the order was made becomes liable to pay the amount as recalculated pursuant to this section on the day on which the former spouse would have become liable had the application not been made.

### Regulations

**26.** (1) The Governor in Council may make regulations for carrying the purposes and provisions of this Act into effect and, without limiting the generality of the foregoing, may make regulations

(a) respecting the establishment and operation of a central registry of divorce proceedings in Canada; and

(b) providing for uniformity in the rules made pursuant to section 25.

### Regulations prevail

(2) Any regulations made pursuant to subsection (1) to provide for uniformity in the rules prevail over those rules.

### Guidelines

**26.1** (1) The Governor in Council may establish guidelines respecting the making of orders for child support, including, but without limiting the generality of the foregoing, guidelines

(a) respecting the way in which the amount of an order for child support is to be determined;

(b) respecting the circumstances in which discretion may be exercised in the making of an order for child support;

(c) authorizing a court to require that the amount payable under an order for child support be paid in periodic payments, in a lump sum or in a lump sum and periodic payments;

(d) authorizing a court to require that the amount payable under an order for child support be paid or secured, or paid and secured, in the manner specified in the order;

(e) respecting the circumstances that give rise to the making of a variation order in respect of a child support order;

(f) respecting the determination of income for the purposes of the application of the guidelines;

(g) authorizing a court to impute income for the purposes of the application of the guidelines; and

(h) respecting the production of income information and providing for sanctions when that information is not provided.

### Principle

(2) The guidelines shall be based on the principle that spouses have a joint financial obligation to maintain the children of the marriage in accordance with their relative abilities to contribute to the performance of that obligation.

### Definition of "order for child support"

(3) In subsection (1), "order for child support" means

(a) an order or interim order made under section 15.1;

(b) a variation order in respect of a child support order; or

(c) an order or an interim order made under section 19.

### Fees

**27.** (1) The Governor in Council may, by order, authorize the Minister of Justice to prescribe a fee to be paid by any person to whom a service is provided under this Act or the regulations.

### Agreements

(2) The Minister of Justice may, with the approval of the Governor in Council, enter into an agreement with the government of any province respecting the collection and remittance of any fees prescribed pursuant to subsection (1).

### Review and report

**28.** The Minister of Justice shall undertake a comprehensive review of the provisions and operation of the Federal Child Support Guidelines and the determination of child support under this Act and shall cause a report on the review to be laid before each House of Parliament within five years after the coming into force of this section. ...

# Family Law Act

RSO 1990, c F.3

| 1. | Preamble | 167 |
|----|----------|-----|
| 2. | Definitions | 167 |
| 3. | Procedural and other miscellaneous matters | 167 |
| 4. | Mediation | 168 |

## PART I
### FAMILY PROPERTY

| 5. | Definitions | 169 |
|----|-------------|-----|
| 6. | Equalization of net family properties | 169 |
| 7. | Election | 170 |
| 8. | Application to court | 172 |
| 9. | Statement of property | 172 |
| 10. | Powers of court | 172 |
| 11. | Determination of questions of title between spouses | 172 |
| 12. | Interest in a pension plan | 173 |
| 13. | Operating business or farm | 173 |
| 14. | Orders for preservation | 174 |
| 15. | Variation and realization of security | 174 |
| 16. | Order regarding conduct | 174 |
| 17. | Presumptions | 174 |
| 18. | Conflict of laws | 174 |
| 19. | Application of Part | 174 |

## PART II
### MATRIMONIAL HOME

| 20. | Definitions | 174 |
|-----|-------------|-----|
| 21. | Matrimonial home | 174 |
| 22. | Possession of matrimonial home | 174 |
| 23. | Designation of matrimonial home | 174 |
| 24. | Alienation of matrimonial home | 175 |
| 25. | Right of redemption and to notice | 175 |
| 26. | Powers of court respecting alienation | 176 |
| 27. | Order for possession of matrimonial home | 176 |
| 28. | Variation | 177 |
| 29. | Order regarding conduct | 177 |
| 30. | Spouse without interest in matrimonial home | 177 |
| 31. | Registration of order | 177 |
| 32. | Application of Part | 177 |

PART III
**SUPPORT OBLIGATIONS**

33.    Definitions . . . . . . . . . . . . . . . . . . . . . . . . . . . . . . . . . . . . . . . . . . . . . . . . . . . . . . . . . . . . . 177
34.    Obligation of spouses for support. . . . . . . . . . . . . . . . . . . . . . . . . . . . . . . . . . . . . . . . . . 177
35.    Obligation of parent to support child . . . . . . . . . . . . . . . . . . . . . . . . . . . . . . . . . . . . . . 178
36.    Obligation of child to support parent . . . . . . . . . . . . . . . . . . . . . . . . . . . . . . . . . . . . . . 178
37.    Order for support. . . . . . . . . . . . . . . . . . . . . . . . . . . . . . . . . . . . . . . . . . . . . . . . . . . . . . . 178
38.    Powers of court. . . . . . . . . . . . . . . . . . . . . . . . . . . . . . . . . . . . . . . . . . . . . . . . . . . . . . . . . 179
39.    Domestic contract, etc., may be filed with court . . . . . . . . . . . . . . . . . . . . . . . . . . . . 180
40.    Effect of divorce proceeding . . . . . . . . . . . . . . . . . . . . . . . . . . . . . . . . . . . . . . . . . . . . . 180
41.    Application for variation . . . . . . . . . . . . . . . . . . . . . . . . . . . . . . . . . . . . . . . . . . . . . . . . 181
42.    Indexing existing orders . . . . . . . . . . . . . . . . . . . . . . . . . . . . . . . . . . . . . . . . . . . . . . . . 181
43.    Priority to child support . . . . . . . . . . . . . . . . . . . . . . . . . . . . . . . . . . . . . . . . . . . . . . . . 182
44.    Administrative calculation of child support. . . . . . . . . . . . . . . . . . . . . . . . . . . . . . . . 182
45.    Administrative recalculation of child support. . . . . . . . . . . . . . . . . . . . . . . . . . . . . . 183
46.    Restraining orders. . . . . . . . . . . . . . . . . . . . . . . . . . . . . . . . . . . . . . . . . . . . . . . . . . . . . . 184
47.    Financial statement. . . . . . . . . . . . . . . . . . . . . . . . . . . . . . . . . . . . . . . . . . . . . . . . . . . . . 184
48.    Obtaining information. . . . . . . . . . . . . . . . . . . . . . . . . . . . . . . . . . . . . . . . . . . . . . . . . . . 184
49.    Arrest of absconding debtor . . . . . . . . . . . . . . . . . . . . . . . . . . . . . . . . . . . . . . . . . . . . . 185
50.    Provisional orders . . . . . . . . . . . . . . . . . . . . . . . . . . . . . . . . . . . . . . . . . . . . . . . . . . . . . 185
51.    Necessities of life . . . . . . . . . . . . . . . . . . . . . . . . . . . . . . . . . . . . . . . . . . . . . . . . . . . . . . 186
52.    Restraining order. . . . . . . . . . . . . . . . . . . . . . . . . . . . . . . . . . . . . . . . . . . . . . . . . . . . . . . 186
53.    Application for custody. . . . . . . . . . . . . . . . . . . . . . . . . . . . . . . . . . . . . . . . . . . . . . . . . . 186
54.    Order regarding conduct . . . . . . . . . . . . . . . . . . . . . . . . . . . . . . . . . . . . . . . . . . . . . . . . 186
55.    Appeal from Ontario Court of Justice. . . . . . . . . . . . . . . . . . . . . . . . . . . . . . . . . . . . . . 186
56.    Contempt of orders of Ontario Court of Justice . . . . . . . . . . . . . . . . . . . . . . . . . . . . . 186

PART IV
**DOMESTIC CONTRACTS**

57.    Definitions . . . . . . . . . . . . . . . . . . . . . . . . . . . . . . . . . . . . . . . . . . . . . . . . . . . . . . . . . . . . . 186
58.    Marriage contracts . . . . . . . . . . . . . . . . . . . . . . . . . . . . . . . . . . . . . . . . . . . . . . . . . . . . . . 187
59.    Cohabitation agreements. . . . . . . . . . . . . . . . . . . . . . . . . . . . . . . . . . . . . . . . . . . . . . . . . 187
60.    Separation agreements. . . . . . . . . . . . . . . . . . . . . . . . . . . . . . . . . . . . . . . . . . . . . . . . . . . 187
61.    Form and capacity. . . . . . . . . . . . . . . . . . . . . . . . . . . . . . . . . . . . . . . . . . . . . . . . . . . . . . . 187
62.    Provisions that may be set aside or disregarded . . . . . . . . . . . . . . . . . . . . . . . . . . . . 187
63.    Provisions re pension plan . . . . . . . . . . . . . . . . . . . . . . . . . . . . . . . . . . . . . . . . . . . . . . . 188
64.    Rights of donors of gifts . . . . . . . . . . . . . . . . . . . . . . . . . . . . . . . . . . . . . . . . . . . . . . . . . 188
65.    Contracts made outside Ontario . . . . . . . . . . . . . . . . . . . . . . . . . . . . . . . . . . . . . . . . . . 188
66.    Paternity agreements. . . . . . . . . . . . . . . . . . . . . . . . . . . . . . . . . . . . . . . . . . . . . . . . . . . . 189
67.    Family arbitrations, agreements and awards. . . . . . . . . . . . . . . . . . . . . . . . . . . . . . . . 189
68.    Other third-party decision-making processes in family matters. . . . . . . . . . . . . . . 189
69.    Contracting out . . . . . . . . . . . . . . . . . . . . . . . . . . . . . . . . . . . . . . . . . . . . . . . . . . . . . . . . . 189
70.    No agreement in advance of dispute . . . . . . . . . . . . . . . . . . . . . . . . . . . . . . . . . . . . . . 189
71.    Award re pension plan. . . . . . . . . . . . . . . . . . . . . . . . . . . . . . . . . . . . . . . . . . . . . . . . . . . 189
72.    Conditions for enforceability. . . . . . . . . . . . . . . . . . . . . . . . . . . . . . . . . . . . . . . . . . . . . 190
73.    Secondary arbitration . . . . . . . . . . . . . . . . . . . . . . . . . . . . . . . . . . . . . . . . . . . . . . . . . . . 190
74.    Enforcement . . . . . . . . . . . . . . . . . . . . . . . . . . . . . . . . . . . . . . . . . . . . . . . . . . . . . . . . . . . . 190
75.    Application of Act to existing contracts. . . . . . . . . . . . . . . . . . . . . . . . . . . . . . . . . . . . . 191

PART V
## DEPENDANTS' CLAIM FOR DAMAGES
76.     Right of dependants to sue in tort...................................................191
77.     Offer to settle for global sum......................................................191
78.     Assessment of damages, insurance..................................................191

PART VI
## AMENDMENTS TO THE COMMON LAW
79.     Unity of legal personality abolished................................................191
80.     Actions between parent and child ..................................................191
81.     Recovery for prenatal injuries .....................................................191
82.     Domicile of minor .................................................................191
83.     General ............................................................................192
84.     Transition .........................................................................194

### Preamble

Whereas it is desirable to encourage and strengthen the role of the family; and whereas for that purpose it is necessary to recognize the equal position of spouses as individuals within marriage and to recognize marriage as a form of partnership; and whereas in support of such recognition it is necessary to provide in law for the orderly and equitable settlement of the affairs of the spouses upon the breakdown of the partnership, and to provide for other mutual obligations in family relationships, including the equitable sharing by parents of responsibility for their children;

Therefore, Her Majesty, by and with the advice and consent of the Legislative Assembly of the Province of Ontario, enacts as follows:

### Definitions

**1.** (1) In this Act,

"child" includes a person whom a parent has demonstrated a settled intention to treat as a child of his or her family, except under an arrangement where the child is placed for valuable consideration in a foster home by a person having lawful custody;

"child support guidelines" means the guidelines established by the regulations made under subsections 69(2) and (3);

"cohabit" means to live together in a conjugal relationship, whether within or outside marriage;

"court" means the Ontario Court of Justice, the Family Court of the Superior Court of Justice or the Superior Court of Justice;

"domestic contract" means a domestic contract as defined in Part IV (Domestic Contracts);

"parent" includes a person who has demonstrated a settled intention to treat a child as a child of his or her family, except under an arrangement where the child is placed for valuable consideration in a foster home by a person having lawful custody;

"paternity agreement" means a paternity agreement as defined in Part IV (Domestic Contracts);

"regulations" means the regulations made under this Act;

"spouse" means either of two persons who,

(a) are married to each other, or

(b) have together entered into a marriage that is voidable or void, in good faith on the part of a person relying on this clause to assert any right.

### Polygamous marriages

(2) In the definition of "spouse," a reference to marriage includes a marriage that is actually or potentially polygamous, if it was celebrated in a jurisdiction whose system of law recognizes it as valid.

### Procedural and other miscellaneous matters
### Staying application

**2.** (1) If, in an application under this Act, it appears to the court that for the appropriate determination of the spouses' affairs it is necessary or desirable to have other matters determined first or simultaneously, the court may stay the application until another proceeding is brought or determined as the court considers appropriate.

### All proceedings in one court

(2)  Except as this Act provides otherwise, no person who is a party to an application under this Act shall make another application under this Act to another court, but the court may order that the proceeding be transferred to a court having other jurisdiction where, in the first court's opinion, the other court is more appropriate to determine the matters in issue that should be determined at the same time.

### Applications in Superior Court of Justice

(3)  In the Superior Court of Justice, an application under this Act may be made by action or application.

### Statement re removal of barriers to remarriage

(4)  A party to an application under section 7 (net family property), 10 (questions of title between spouses), 33 (support), 34 (powers of court) or 37 (variation) may serve on the other party and file with the court a statement, verified by oath or statutory declaration, indicating that,

(a)  the author of the statement has removed all barriers that are within his or her control and that would prevent the other spouse's remarriage within that spouse's faith; and

(b)  the other party has not done so, despite a request.

### Idem

(5)  Within ten days after service of the statement, or within such longer period as the court allows, the party served with a statement under subsection (4) shall serve on the other party and file with the court a statement, verified by oath or statutory declaration, indicating that the author of the statement has removed all barriers that are within his or her control and that would prevent the other spouse's remarriage within that spouse's faith.

### Dismissal, etc.

(6)  When a party fails to comply with subsection (5),

(a)  if the party is an applicant, the proceeding may be dismissed;

(b)  if the party is a respondent, the defence may be struck out.

### Exception

(7)  Subsections (5) and (6) do not apply to a party who does not claim costs or other relief in the proceeding.

### Extension of times

(8)  The court may, on motion, extend a time prescribed by this Act if it is satisfied that,

(a)  there are apparent grounds for relief;

(b)  relief is unavailable because of delay that has been incurred in good faith; and

(c)  no person will suffer substantial prejudice by reason of the delay.

### Incorporation of contract in order

(9)  A provision of a domestic contract in respect of a matter that is dealt with in this Act may be incorporated in an order made under this Act.

### Act subject to contracts

(10)  A domestic contract dealing with a matter that is also dealt with in this Act prevails unless this Act provides otherwise.

### Registration of orders

(11)  An order made under this Act that affects real property does not affect the acquisition of an interest in the real property by a person acting in good faith without notice of the order, unless the order is registered in the proper land registry office.

### Mediation

3. (1)  In an application under this Act, the court may, on motion, appoint a person whom the parties have selected to mediate any matter that the court specifies.

### Consent to act

(2)  The court shall appoint only a person who,

(a)  has consented to act as mediator; and

(b)  has agreed to file a report with the court within the period of time specified by the court.

### Duty of mediator

(3)  The mediator shall confer with the parties, and with the children if the mediator considers it appropriate to do so, and shall endeavour to obtain an agreement between the parties.

### Full or limited report

(4)  Before entering into mediation, the parties shall decide whether,

(a)  the mediator is to file a full report on the mediation, including anything that he or she considers relevant; or

(b)  the mediator is to file a limited report that sets out only the agreement reached by the parties or states only that the parties did not reach agreement.

### Filing and copies of report

(5)  The mediator shall file with the clerk or registrar of the court a full or limited report, as the parties have decided, and shall give a copy to each of the parties.

### Admissions, etc., in the course of mediation

(6)  If the parties have decided that the mediator is to file a limited report, no evidence of anything said or of any admission or communication made in the course of the mediation is admissible in any proceeding, except with the consent of all parties to the proceeding in which the mediator was appointed.

### Fees and expenses

(7)  The court shall require the parties to pay the mediator's fees and expenses and shall specify in the order the pro-

portions or amounts of the fees and expenses that each party is required to pay.

### Idem, serious financial hardship

(8) The court may require one party to pay all the mediator's fees and expenses if the court is satisfied that payment would cause the other party or parties serious financial hardship.

## PART I FAMILY PROPERTY

### Definitions

**4.** (1) In this Part,

"court" means a court as defined in subsection 1(1), but does not include the Ontario Court of Justice;

"matrimonial home" means a matrimonial home under section 18 and includes property that is a matrimonial home under that section at the valuation date;

"net family property" means the value of all the property, except property described in subsection (2), that a spouse owns on the valuation date, after deducting,

    (a) the spouse's debts and other liabilities, and

    (b) the value of property, other than a matrimonial home, that the spouse owned on the date of the marriage, after deducting the spouse's debts and other liabilities, other than debts or liabilities related directly to the acquisition or significant improvement of a matrimonial home, calculated as of the date of the marriage;

"property" means any interest, present or future, vested or contingent, in real or personal property and includes,

    (a) property over which a spouse has, alone or in conjunction with another person, a power of appointment exercisable in favour of himself or herself,

    (b) property disposed of by a spouse but over which the spouse has, alone or in conjunction with another person, a power to revoke the disposition or a power to consume or dispose of the property, and

    (c) in the case of a spouse's rights under a pension plan, the imputed value, for family law purposes, of the spouse's interest in the plan, as determined in accordance with section 10.1, for the period beginning with the date of the marriage and ending on the valuation date;

"valuation date" means the earliest of the following dates:

1. The date the spouses separate and there is no reasonable prospect that they will resume cohabitation.
2. The date a divorce is granted.
3. The date the marriage is declared a nullity.
4. The date one of the spouses commences an application based on subsection 5(3) (improvident depletion) that is subsequently granted.
5. The date before the date on which one of the spouses dies leaving the other spouse surviving.

### Net family property, liabilities

(1.1) The liabilities referred to in clauses (a) and (b) of the definition of "net family property" in subsection (1) include any applicable contingent tax liabilities in respect of the property.

### Excluded property

(2) The value of the following property that a spouse owns on the valuation date does not form part of the spouse's net family property:

1. Property, other than a matrimonial home, that was acquired by gift or inheritance from a third person after the date of the marriage.
2. Income from property referred to in paragraph 1, if the donor or testator has expressly stated that it is to be excluded from the spouse's net family property.
3. Damages or a right to damages for personal injuries, nervous shock, mental distress or loss of guidance, care and companionship, or the part of a settlement that represents those damages.
4. Proceeds or a right to proceeds of a policy of life insurance, as defined under the *Insurance Act*, that are payable on the death of the life insured.
5. Property, other than a matrimonial home, into which property referred to in paragraphs 1 to 4 can be traced.
6. Property that the spouses have agreed by a domestic contract is not to be included in the spouse's net family property.
7. Unadjusted pensionable earnings under the *Canada Pension Plan*.

### Onus of proof re deductions and exclusions

(3) The onus of proving a deduction under the definition of "net family property" or an exclusion under subsection (2) is on the person claiming it.

### Close of business

(4) When this section requires that a value be calculated as of a given date, it shall be calculated as of close of business on that date.

### Net family property not to be less than zero

(5) If a spouse's net family property as calculated under subsections (1), (2) and (4) is less than zero, it shall be deemed to be equal to zero.

### Equalization of net family properties
### Divorce, etc.

**5.** (1) When a divorce is granted or a marriage is declared a nullity, or when the spouses are separated and there is no reasonable prospect that they will resume cohabitation, the spouse whose net family property is the lesser of the two net family properties is entitled to one-half the difference between them.

### Death of spouse

(2) When a spouse dies, if the net family property of the deceased spouse exceeds the net family property of the

surviving spouse, the surviving spouse is entitled to one-half the difference between them.

### Improvident depletion of spouse's net family property

(3) When spouses are cohabiting, if there is a serious danger that one spouse may improvidently deplete his or her net family property, the other spouse may on an application under section 7 have the difference between the net family properties divided as if the spouses were separated and there were no reasonable prospect that they would resume cohabitation.

### No further division

(4) After the court has made an order for division based on subsection (3), neither spouse may make a further application under section 7 in respect of their marriage.

### Idem

(5) Subsection (4) applies even though the spouses continue to cohabit, unless a domestic contract between the spouses provides otherwise.

### Variation of share

(6) The court may award a spouse an amount that is more or less than half the difference between the net family properties if the court is of the opinion that equalizing the net family properties would be unconscionable, having regard to,

(a) a spouse's failure to disclose to the other spouse debts or other liabilities existing at the date of the marriage;

(b) the fact that debts or other liabilities claimed in reduction of a spouse's net family property were incurred recklessly or in bad faith;

(c) the part of a spouse's net family property that consists of gifts made by the other spouse;

(d) a spouse's intentional or reckless depletion of his or her net family property;

(e) the fact that the amount a spouse would otherwise receive under subsection (1), (2) or (3) is disproportionately large in relation to a period of cohabitation that is less than five years;

(f) the fact that one spouse has incurred a disproportionately larger amount of debts or other liabilities than the other spouse for the support of the family;

(g) a written agreement between the spouses that is not a domestic contract; or

(h) any other circumstance relating to the acquisition, disposition, preservation, maintenance or improvement of property.

### Purpose

(7) The purpose of this section is to recognize that child care, household management and financial provision are the joint responsibilities of the spouses and that inherent in the marital relationship there is equal contribution, whether financial or otherwise, by the spouses to the assumption of these responsibilities, entitling each spouse to the equalization of the net family properties, subject only to the equitable considerations set out in subsection (6).

### Election

### Spouse's will

6. (1) When a spouse dies leaving a will, the surviving spouse shall elect to take under the will or to receive the entitlement under section 5.

### Spouse's intestacy

(2) When a spouse dies intestate, the surviving spouse shall elect to receive the entitlement under Part II of the *Succession Law Reform Act* or to receive the entitlement under section 5.

### Spouse's partial intestacy

(3) When a spouse dies testate as to some property and intestate as to other property, the surviving spouse shall elect to take under the will and to receive the entitlement under Part II of the *Succession Law Reform Act*, or to receive the entitlement under section 5.

### Property outside estate

(4) A surviving spouse who elects to take under the will or to receive the entitlement under Part II of the *Succession Law Reform Act*, or both in the case of a partial intestacy, shall also receive the other property to which he or she is entitled because of the first spouse's death.

### Gifts by will

(5) The surviving spouse shall receive the gifts made to him or her in the deceased spouse's will in addition to the entitlement under section 5 if the will expressly provides for that result.

### Amounts to be credited

(6) The rules in subsection (7) apply if a surviving spouse elects or has elected to receive an entitlement under section 5 and is,

(a) the beneficiary of a policy of life insurance, as defined in the *Insurance Act*, that was taken out on the life of the deceased spouse and owned by the deceased spouse or was taken out on the lives of a group of which he or she was a member;

(b) the beneficiary of a lump sum payment provided under a pension or similar plan on the death of the deceased spouse; or

(c) the recipient of property or a portion of property to which the surviving spouse becomes entitled by right of survivorship or otherwise on the death of the deceased spouse.

### Same

(7) The following rules apply in the circumstances described in subsection (6):

1. The amount of every payment and the value of every property or portion of property described in that subsection, less any contingent tax liability in respect of the payment, property or portion of property, shall be credited against the surviving spouse's entitlement under section 5.

2. If the total amount of the credit under paragraph 1 exceeds the entitlement under section 5, the deceased

spouse's personal representative may recover the excess amount from the surviving spouse.

3. Paragraphs 1 and 2 do not apply in respect of a payment, property or portion of property if,

    i. the deceased spouse provided in a written designation, will or other written instrument, as the case may be, that the surviving spouse shall receive the payment, property or portion of property in addition to the entitlement under section 5, or

    ii. in the case of property or a portion of property referred to in clause (6)(c), if the surviving spouse's entitlement to the property or portion of property was established by or on behalf of a third person, either the deceased spouse or the third person provided in a will or other written instrument that the surviving spouse shall receive the property or portion of property in addition to the entitlement under section 5.

### Effect of election to receive entitlement under s. 5

(8) When a surviving spouse elects to receive the entitlement under section 5, the gifts made to him or her in the deceased spouse's will are revoked and the will shall be interpreted as if the surviving spouse had died before the other, unless the will expressly provides that the gifts are in addition to the entitlement under section 5.

### Idem

(9) When a surviving spouse elects to receive the entitlement under section 5, the spouse shall be deemed to have disclaimed the entitlement under Part II of the *Succession Law Reform Act*.

### Manner of making election

(10) The surviving spouse's election shall be in the form prescribed by the regulations and shall be filed in the office of the Estate Registrar for Ontario within six months after the first spouse's death.

### Deemed election

(11) If the surviving spouse does not file the election within that time, he or she shall be deemed to have elected to take under the will or to receive the entitlement under the *Succession Law Reform Act*, or both, as the case may be, unless the court, on application, orders otherwise.

### Priority of spouse's entitlement

(12) The spouse's entitlement under section 5 has priority over,

    (a) the gifts made in the deceased spouse's will, if any, subject to subsection (13);

    (b) a person's right to a share of the estate under Part II (Intestate Succession) of the *Succession Law Reform Act*;

    (c) an order made against the estate under Part V (Support of Dependants) of the *Succession Law Reform Act*, except an order in favour of a child of the deceased spouse.

### Exception

(13) The spouse's entitlement under section 5 does not have priority over a gift by will made in accordance with a contract that the deceased spouse entered into in good faith and for valuable consideration, except to the extent that the value of the gift, in the court's opinion, exceeds the consideration.

### Distribution within six months of death restricted

(14) No distribution shall be made in the administration of a deceased spouse's estate within six months of the spouse's death, unless,

    (a) the surviving spouse gives written consent to the distribution; or

    (b) the court authorizes the distribution.

### Idem, notice of application

(15) No distribution shall be made in the administration of a deceased spouse's death after the personal representative has received notice of an application under this Part, unless,

    (a) the applicant gives written consent to the distribution; or

    (b) the court authorizes the distribution.

### Extension of limitation period

(16) If the court extends the time for a spouse's application based on subsection 5(2), any property of the deceased spouse that is distributed before the date of the order and without notice of the application shall not be brought into the calculation of the deceased spouse's net family property.

### Exception

(17) Subsections (14) and (15) do not prohibit reasonable advances to dependants of the deceased spouse for their support.

### Definition

(18) In subsection (17),

"dependant" has the same meaning as in Part V of the *Succession Law Reform Act*.

### Liability of personal representative

(19) If the personal representative makes a distribution that contravenes subsection (14) or (15), the court makes an order against the estate under this Part and the undistributed portion of the estate is not sufficient to satisfy the order, the personal representative is personally liable to the applicant for the amount that was distributed or the amount that is required to satisfy the order, whichever is less.

### Order suspending administration

(20) On motion by the surviving spouse, the court may make an order suspending the administration of the deceased spouse's estate for the time and to the extent that the court decides.

## Application to court

**7.** (1) The court may, on the application of a spouse, former spouse or deceased spouse's personal representative, determine any matter respecting the spouses' entitlement under section 5.

## Personal action; estates

(2) Entitlement under subsections 5(1), (2) and (3) is personal as between the spouses but,

(a) an application based on subsection 5(1) or (3) and commenced before a spouse's death may be continued by or against the deceased spouse's estate; and

(b) an application based on subsection 5(2) may be made by or against a deceased spouse's estate.

## Limitation

(3) An application based on subsection 5(1) or (2) shall not be brought after the earliest of,

(a) two years after the day the marriage is terminated by divorce or judgment of nullity;

(b) six years after the day the spouses separate and there is no reasonable prospect that they will resume cohabitation;

(c) six months after the first spouse's death.

## Statement of property

**8.** In an application under section 7, each party shall serve on the other and file with the court, in the manner and form prescribed by the rules of the court, a statement verified by oath or statutory declaration disclosing particulars of,

(a) the party's property and debts and other liabilities,

(i) as of the date of the marriage,

(ii) as of the valuation date, and

(iii) as of the date of the statement;

(b) the deductions that the party claims under the definition of "net family property";

(c) the exclusions that the party claims under subsection 4(2); and

(d) all property that the party disposed of during the two years immediately preceding the making of the statement, or during the marriage, whichever period is shorter.

## Powers of court

**9.** (1) In an application under section 7, the court may order,

(a) that one spouse pay to the other spouse the amount to which the court finds that spouse to be entitled under this Part;

(b) that security, including a charge on property, be given for the performance of an obligation imposed by the order;

(c) that, if necessary to avoid hardship, an amount referred to in clause (a) be paid in instalments during a period not exceeding ten years or that payment of all or part of the amount be delayed for a period not exceeding ten years; and

(d) that, if appropriate to satisfy an obligation imposed by the order,

(i) property be transferred to or in trust for or vested in a spouse, whether absolutely, for life or for a term of years, or

(ii) any property be partitioned or sold.

## Financial information, inspections

(2) The court may, at the time of making an order for instalment or delayed payments or on motion at a later time, order that the spouse who has the obligation to make payments shall,

(a) furnish the other spouse with specified financial information, which may include periodic financial statements; and

(b) permit inspections of specified property of the spouse by or on behalf of the other spouse, as the court directs.

## Variation

(3) If the court is satisfied that there has been a material change in the circumstances of the spouse who has the obligation to make instalment or delayed payments, the court may, on motion, vary the order, but shall not vary the amount to which the court found the spouse to be entitled under this Part.

## Ten-year period

(4) Subsections (3) and 2(8) (extension of times) do not permit the postponement of payment beyond the ten-year period mentioned in clause (1)(c).

## Determination of questions of title between spouses

**10.** (1) A person may apply to the court for the determination of a question between that person and his or her spouse or former spouse as to the ownership or right to possession of particular property, other than a question arising out of an equalization of net family properties under section 5, and the court may,

(a) declare the ownership or right to possession;

(b) if the property has been disposed of, order payment in compensation for the interest of either party;

(c) order that the property be partitioned or sold for the purpose of realizing the interests in it; and

(d) order that either or both spouses give security, including a charge on property, for the performance of an obligation imposed by the order,

and may make ancillary orders or give ancillary directions.

## Estates

(2) An application based on subsection (1) may be made by or continued against the estate of a deceased spouse.

## Interest in a pension plan
### Imputed value for family law purposes

**10.1** (1) The imputed value, for family law purposes, of a spouse's interest in a pension plan to which the *Pension Benefits Act* applies is determined in accordance with section 67.2 of that Act.

> **Note: On a day to be named by proclamation of the Lieutenant Governor, subsection 10.1(1) of the Act is amended by striking out "section 67.2" and substituting "section 67.2 or, in the case of a spouse's interest in a variable benefit account, section 67.7."**
>
> **Same**
>
> (1.1) The imputed value, for family law purposes, of a spouse's interest in a pension plan to which the *Pooled Registered Pension Plans Act, 2015* applies is determined in accordance with section 17 of that Act.
>
> **See: 2017, c. 8, Sched. 27, s. 21 (1).**

### Same

(2) The imputed value, for family law purposes, of a spouse's interest in any other pension plan is determined, where reasonably possible, in accordance with section 67.2 of the *Pension Benefits Act* with necessary modifications.

> **Note: On a day to be named by proclamation of the Lieutenant Governor, subsection 10.1 (2) of the Act is amended by striking out "section 67.2" and substituting "section 67.2 or, in the case of a spouse's interest in a variable benefit account, section 67.7."**
>
> **See: 2017, c. 8, Sched. 27, s. 21(1).**

### Order for immediate transfer of a lump sum

(3) An order made under section 9 or 10 may provide for the immediate transfer of a lump sum out of a pension plan but, except as permitted under subsection (5), not for any other division of a spouse's interest in the plan.

### Same

(4) In determining whether to order the immediate transfer of a lump sum out of a pension plan and in determining the amount to be transferred, the court may consider the following matters and such other matters as the court considers appropriate:

1. The nature of the assets available to each spouse at the time of the hearing.
2. The proportion of a spouse's net family property that consists of the imputed value, for family law purposes, of his or her interest in the pension plan.
3. The liquidity of the lump sum in the hands of the spouse to whom it would be transferred.

4. Any contingent tax liabilities in respect of the lump sum that would be transferred.
5. The resources available to each spouse to meet his or her needs in retirement and the desirability of maintaining those resources.

### Order for division of pension payments

(5) If payment of the first instalment of a spouse's pension under a pension plan is due on or before the valuation date, an order made under section 9 or 10 may provide for the division of pension payments but not for any other division of the spouse's interest in the plan.

### Same

(6) Subsections 9(2) and (4) do not apply with respect to an order made under section 9 or 10 that provides for the division of pension payments.

### Restrictions re certain pension plans

(7) If the *Pension Benefits Act* applies to the pension plan, the restrictions under sections 67.3 and 67.4 of that Act apply with respect to the division of the spouse's interest in the plan by an order under section 9 or 10.

> **Note: On a day to be named by proclamation of the Lieutenant Governor, subsection 10.1(7) of the Act is amended by adding "or under sections 67.8 and 67.9 of that Act in relation to variable benefits" after "of that Act."**
>
> **Same**
>
> (7.1) If the *Pooled Registered Pension Plans Act, 2015* applies to the pension plan, the restrictions under sections 19 and 20 of that Act apply with respect to the division of the spouse's interest in the plan by an order under section 9 or 10 of this Act.
>
> **See: 2017, c. 8, Sched. 27, s. 21(2).**

### Transition, valuation date

(8) This section applies whether the valuation date is before, on or after the date on which this section comes into force.

### Transition, previous orders

(9) This section does not apply to an order made before the date on which this section comes into force that requires one spouse to pay to the other spouse the amount to which that spouse is entitled under section 5.

### Operating business or farm

**11.** (1) An order made under section 9 or 10 shall not be made so as to require or result in the sale of an operating business or farm or so as to seriously impair its operation, unless there is no reasonable alternative method of satisfying the award.

**Idem**

(2) To comply with subsection (1), the court may,

(a) order that one spouse pay to the other a share of the profits from the business or farm; and

(b) if the business or farm is incorporated, order that one spouse transfer or have the corporation issue to the other shares in the corporation.

**Orders for preservation**

**12.** In an application under section 7 or 10, if the court considers it necessary for the protection of the other spouse's interests under this Part, the court may make an interim or final order,

(a) restraining the depletion of a spouse's property; and

(b) for the possession, delivering up, safekeeping and preservation of the property.

**Variation and realization of security**

**13.** If the court has ordered security or charged a property with security for the performance of an obligation under this Part, the court may, on motion,

(a) vary or discharge the order; or

(b) on notice to all persons having an interest in the property, direct its sale for the purpose of realizing the security or charge.

**Order regarding conduct**

**13.1** In making any order under this Part, the court may also make an interim order prohibiting, in whole or in part, a party from directly or indirectly contacting or communicating with another party, if the court determines that the order is necessary to ensure that an application under this Part is dealt with justly.

**Presumptions**

**14.** The rule of law applying a presumption of a resulting trust shall be applied in questions of the ownership of property between spouses, as if they were not married, except that,

(a) the fact that property is held in the name of spouses as joint tenants is proof, in the absence of evidence to the contrary, that the spouses are intended to own the property as joint tenants; and

(b) money on deposit in the name of both spouses shall be deemed to be in the name of the spouses as joint tenants for the purposes of clause (a).

**Conflict of laws**

**15.** The property rights of spouses arising out of the marital relationship are governed by the internal law of the place where both spouses had their last common habitual residence or, if there is no place where the spouses had a common habitual residence, by the law of Ontario.

**Application of Part**

**16.** (1) This Part applies to property owned by spouses,

(a) whether they were married before or after the 1st day of March, 1986; and

(b) whether the property was acquired before or after that day.

**Application of s. 14**

(2) Section 14 applies whether the event giving rise to the presumption occurred before or after the 1st day of March, 1986.

## PART II MATRIMONIAL HOME

**Definitions**

**17.** In this Part,

"court" means a court as defined in subsection 1(1) but does not include the Ontario Court of Justice;

"property" means real or personal property.

**Matrimonial home**

**18.** (1) Every property in which a person has an interest and that is or, if the spouses have separated, was at the time of separation ordinarily occupied by the person and his or her spouse as their family residence is their matrimonial home.

**Ownership of shares**

(2) The ownership of a share or shares, or of an interest in a share or shares, of a corporation entitling the owner to occupy a housing unit owned by the corporation shall be deemed to be an interest in the unit for the purposes of subsection (1).

**Residence on farmland, etc.**

(3) If property that includes a matrimonial home is normally used for a purpose other than residential, the matrimonial home is only the part of the property that may reasonably be regarded as necessary to the use and enjoyment of the residence.

**Possession of matrimonial home**

**19.** (1) Both spouses have an equal right to possession of a matrimonial home.

**Idem**

(2) When only one of the spouses has an interest in a matrimonial home, the other spouse's right of possession,

(a) is personal as against the first spouse; and

(b) ends when they cease to be spouses, unless a separation agreement or court order provides otherwise.

**Designation of matrimonial home**

**20.** (1) One or both spouses may designate property owned by one or both of them as a matrimonial home, in the form prescribed by the regulations made.

### Contiguous property

(2) The designation may include property that is described in the designation and is contiguous to the matrimonial home.

### Registration

(3) The designation may be registered in the proper land registry office.

### Effect of designation by both spouses

(4) On the registration of a designation made by both spouses, any other property that is a matrimonial home under section 18 but is not designated by both spouses ceases to be a matrimonial home.

### Effect of designation by one spouse

(5) On the registration of a designation made by one spouse only, any other property that is a matrimonial home under section 18 remains a matrimonial home.

### Cancellation of designation

(6) The designation of a matrimonial home is cancelled, and the property ceases to be a matrimonial home, on the registration or deposit of,

(a) a cancellation, executed by the person or persons who made the original designation, in the form prescribed by the regulations;

(b) a decree absolute of divorce or judgment of nullity;

(c) an order under clause 23(e) cancelling the designation; or

(d) proof of death of one of the spouses.

### Revival of other matrimonial homes

(7) When a designation of a matrimonial home made by both spouses is cancelled, section 18 applies again in respect of other property that is a matrimonial home.

### Alienation of matrimonial home

**21.** (1) No spouse shall dispose of or encumber an interest in a matrimonial home unless,

(a) the other spouse joins in the instrument or consents to the transaction;

(b) the other spouse has released all rights under this Part by a separation agreement;

(c) a court order has authorized the transaction or has released the property from the application of this Part; or

(d) the property is not designated by both spouses as a matrimonial home and a designation of another property as a matrimonial home, made by both spouses, is registered and not cancelled.

### Setting aside transaction

(2) If a spouse disposes of or encumbers an interest in a matrimonial home in contravention of subsection (1), the transaction may be set aside on an application under

section 23, unless the person holding the interest or encumbrance at the time of the application acquired it for value, in good faith and without notice, at the time of acquiring it or making an agreement to acquire it, that the property was a matrimonial home.

### Proof that property not a matrimonial home

(3) For the purpose of subsection (2), a statement by the person making the disposition or encumbrance,

(a) verifying that he or she is not, or was not, a spouse at the time of the disposition or encumbrance;

(b) verifying that the person is a spouse who is not separated from his or her spouse and that the property is not ordinarily occupied by the spouses as their family residence;

(c) verifying that the person is a spouse who is separated from his or her spouse and that the property was not ordinarily occupied by the spouses, at the time of their separation, as their family residence;

(d) where the property is not designated by both spouses as a matrimonial home, verifying that a designation of another property as a matrimonial home, made by both spouses, is registered and not cancelled; or

(e) verifying that the other spouse has released all rights under this Part by a separation agreement,

shall, unless the person to whom the disposition or encumbrance is made had notice to the contrary, be deemed to be sufficient proof that the property is not a matrimonial home.

### Idem, attorney's personal knowledge

(4) The statement shall be deemed to be sufficient proof that the property is not a matrimonial home if it is made by the attorney of the person making the disposition or encumbrance, on the basis of the attorney's personal knowledge.

### Liens arising by operation of law

(5) This section does not apply to the acquisition of an interest in property by operation of law or to the acquisition of a lien under section 48 of the *Legal Aid Services Act, 1998*.

### Right of redemption and to notice

**22.** (1) When a person proceeds to realize upon a lien, encumbrance or execution or exercises a forfeiture against property that is a matrimonial home, the spouse who has a right of possession under section 19 has the same right of redemption or relief against forfeiture as the other spouse and is entitled to the same notice respecting the claim and its enforcement or realization.

### Service of notice

(2) A notice to which a spouse is entitled under subsection (1) shall be deemed to be sufficiently given if served or given personally or by registered mail addressed to the spouse at his or her usual or last known address or, if none, the ad-

dress of the matrimonial home, and, if notice is served or given by mail, the service shall be deemed to have been made on the fifth day after the day of mailing.

### Idem: power of sale

(3) When a person exercises a power of sale against property that is a matrimonial home, sections 33 and 34 of the *Mortgages Act* apply and subsection (2) does not apply.

### Payments by spouse

(4) If a spouse makes a payment in exercise of the right conferred by subsection (1), the payment shall be applied in satisfaction of the claim giving rise to the lien, encumbrance, execution or forfeiture.

### Realization may continue in spouse's absence

(5) Despite any other Act, when a person who proceeds to realize upon a lien, encumbrance or execution or exercises a forfeiture does not have sufficient particulars of a spouse for the purpose and there is no response to a notice given under subsection (2) or under section 33 of the *Mortgages Act*, the realization or exercise of forfeiture may continue in the absence and without regard to the interest of the spouse and the spouse's rights under this section end on the completion of the realization or forfeiture.

### Powers of court respecting alienation

**23.** The court may, on the application of a spouse or person having an interest in property, by order,

    (a) determine whether or not the property is a matrimonial home and, if so, its extent;

    (b) authorize the disposition or encumbrance of the matrimonial home if the court finds that the spouse whose consent is required,

        (i) cannot be found or is not available,

        (ii) is not capable of giving or withholding consent, or

        (iii) is unreasonably withholding consent,

subject to any conditions, including provision of other comparable accommodation or payment in place of it, that the court considers appropriate;

    (c) dispense with a notice required to be given under section 22;

    (d) direct the setting aside of a transaction disposing of or encumbering an interest in the matrimonial home contrary to subsection 21(1) and the revesting of the interest or any part of it on the conditions that the court considers appropriate; and

    (e) cancel a designation made under section 20 if the property is not a matrimonial home.

### Order for possession of matrimonial home

**24.** (1) Regardless of the ownership of a matrimonial home and its contents, and despite section 19 (spouse's right of possession), the court may on application, by order,

    (a) provide for the delivering up, safekeeping and preservation of the matrimonial home and its contents;

    (b) direct that one spouse be given exclusive possession of the matrimonial home or part of it for the period that the court directs and release other property that is a matrimonial home from the application of this Part;

    (c) direct a spouse to whom exclusive possession of the matrimonial home is given to make periodic payments to the other spouse;

    (d) direct that the contents of the matrimonial home, or any part of them,

        (i) remain in the home for the use of the spouse given possession, or

        (ii) be removed from the home for the use of a spouse or child;

    (e) order a spouse to pay for all or part of the repair and maintenance of the matrimonial home and of other liabilities arising in respect of it, or to make periodic payments to the other spouse for those purposes;

    (f) authorize the disposition or encumbrance of a spouse's interest in the matrimonial home, subject to the other spouse's right of exclusive possession as ordered; and

    (g) where a false statement is made under subsection 21(3), direct,

        (i) the person who made the false statement, or

        (ii) a person who knew at the time he or she acquired an interest in the property that the statement was false and afterwards conveyed the interest,

to substitute other real property for the matrimonial home, or direct the person to set aside money or security to stand in place of it, subject to any conditions that the court considers appropriate.

### Temporary or interim order

(2) The court may, on motion, make a temporary or interim order under clause (1)(a), (b), (c), (d) or (e).

### Order for exclusive possession: criteria

(3) In determining whether to make an order for exclusive possession, the court shall consider,

    (a) the best interests of the children affected;

    (b) any existing orders under Part I (Family Property) and any existing support orders or other enforceable support obligations;

    (c) the financial position of both spouses;

    (d) any written agreement between the parties;

    (e) the availability of other suitable and affordable accommodation; and

    (f) any violence committed by a spouse against the other spouse or the children.

### Best interests of child

(4) In determining the best interests of a child, the court shall consider,

(a) the possible disruptive effects on the child of a move to other accommodation; and

(b) the child's views and preferences, if they can reasonably be ascertained.

### Offence

(5) A person who contravenes an order for exclusive possession is guilty of an offence and upon conviction is liable,

(a) in the case of a first offence, to a fine of not more than $5,000 or to imprisonment for a term of not more than three months, or to both; and

(b) in the case of a second or subsequent offence, to a fine of not more than $10,000 or to imprisonment for a term of not more than two years, or to both.

### Arrest without warrant

(6) A police officer may arrest without warrant a person the police officer believes on reasonable and probable grounds to have contravened an order for exclusive possession.

### Existing orders

(7) Subsections (5) and (6) also apply in respect of contraventions, committed on or after the 1st day of March, 1986, of orders for exclusive possession made under Part III of the *Family Law Reform Act*, being chapter 152 of the Revised Statutes of Ontario, 1980.

### Variation

### Possessory order

**25.** (1) On the application of a person named in an order made under clause 24(1)(a), (b), (c), (d) or (e) or his or her personal representative, if the court is satisfied that there has been a material change in circumstances, the court may discharge, vary or suspend the order.

### Conditions

(2) On the motion of a person who is subject to conditions imposed in an order made under clause 23(b) or (d) or 24(1)(g), or his or her personal representative, if the court is satisfied that the conditions are no longer appropriate, the court may discharge, vary or suspend them.

### Existing orders

(3) Subsections (1) and (2) also apply to orders made under the corresponding provisions of Part III of the *Family Law Reform Act*, being chapter 152 of the Revised Statutes of Ontario, 1980.

### Order regarding conduct

**25.1** In making any order under this Part, the court may also make an interim order prohibiting, in whole or in part, a party from directly or indirectly contacting or communicating with another party, if the court determines that the order is necessary to ensure that an application under this Part is dealt with justly.

### Spouse without interest in matrimonial home

### Joint tenancy with third person

**26.** (1) If a spouse dies owning an interest in a matrimonial home as a joint tenant with a third person and not with the other spouse, the joint tenancy shall be deemed to have been severed immediately before the time of death.

### Sixty-day period after spouse's death

(2) Despite clauses 19(2)(a) and (b) (termination of spouse's right of possession), a spouse who has no interest in a matrimonial home but is occupying it at the time of the other spouse's death, whether under an order for exclusive possession or otherwise, is entitled to retain possession against the spouse's estate, rent free, for sixty days after the spouse's death.

### Registration of order

**27.** Orders made under this Part or under Part III of the *Family Law Reform Act*, being chapter 152 of the Revised Statutes of Ontario, 1980 are registrable against land under the *Registry Act* and the *Land Titles Act*.

### Application of Part

**28.** (1) This Part applies to matrimonial homes that are situated in Ontario.

### Idem

(2) This Part applies,

(a) whether the spouses were married before or after the 1st day of March, 1986; and

(b) whether the matrimonial home was acquired before or after that day.

### PART III  SUPPORT OBLIGATIONS

### Definitions

**29.** In this Part,

"dependant" means a person to whom another has an obligation to provide support under this Part;

"spouse" means a spouse as defined in subsection 1(1), and in addition includes either of two persons who are not married to each other and have cohabited,

(a) continuously for a period of not less than three years, or

(b) in a relationship of some permanence, if they are the parents of a child as set out in section 4 of the *Children's Law Reform Act.*

### Obligation of spouses for support

**30.** Every spouse has an obligation to provide support for himself or herself and for the other spouse, in accordance with need, to the extent that he or she is capable of doing so.

## Obligation of parent to support child

**31.** (1) Every parent has an obligation to provide support for his or her unmarried child who is a minor or is enrolled in a full time program of education, to the extent that the parent is capable of doing so.

## Idem

(2) The obligation under subsection (1) does not extend to a child who is sixteen years of age or older and has withdrawn from parental control.

## Obligation of child to support parent

**32.** Every child who is not a minor has an obligation to provide support, in accordance with need, for his or her parent who has cared for or provided support for the child, to the extent that the child is capable of doing so.

## Order for support

**33.** (1) A court may, on application, order a person to provide support for his or her dependants and determine the amount of support.

## Applicants

(2) An application for an order for the support of a dependant may be made by the dependant or the dependant's parent.

## Same

(2.1) The *Limitations Act, 2002* applies to an application made by the dependant's parent or by an agency referred to in subsection (3) as if it were made by the dependant himself or herself.

## Same

(3) An application for an order for the support of a dependant who is the respondent's spouse or child may also be made by one of the following agencies,

(a) the Ministry of Community and Social Services in the name of the Minister;

(b) a municipality, excluding a lower-tier municipality in a regional municipality;

(c) a district social services administration board under the *District Social Services Administration Boards Act*;

(d) Repealed.

(e) a delivery agent under the *Ontario Works Act, 1997*, if the agency is providing or has provided a benefit under the *Family Benefits Act*, assistance under the *General Welfare Assistance Act* or the *Ontario Works Act, 1997* or income support under the *Ontario Disability Support Program Act, 1997* in respect of the dependant's support, or if an application for such a benefit or assistance has been made to the agency by or on behalf of the dependant.

## Setting aside domestic contract

(4) The court may set aside a provision for support or a waiver of the right to support in a domestic contract and may determine and order support in an application under subsection (1) although the contract contains an express provision excluding the application of this section,

(a) if the provision for support or the waiver of the right to support results in unconscionable circumstances;

(b) if the provision for support is in favour of or the waiver is by or on behalf of a dependant who qualifies for an allowance for support out of public money; or

(c) if there is default in the payment of support under the contract at the time the application is made.

## Adding party

(5) In an application the court may, on a respondent's motion, add as a party another person who may have an obligation to provide support to the same dependant.

## Idem

(6) In an action in the Superior Court of Justice, the defendant may add as a third party another person who may have an obligation to provide support to the same dependant.

## Purposes of order for support of child

(7) An order for the support of a child should,

(a) recognize that each parent has an obligation to provide support for the child;

(b) apportion the obligation according to the child support guidelines.

## Purposes of order for support of spouse

(8) An order for the support of a spouse should,

(a) recognize the spouse's contribution to the relationship and the economic consequences of the relationship for the spouse;

(b) share the economic burden of child support equitably;

(c) make fair provision to assist the spouse to become able to contribute to his or her own support; and

(d) relieve financial hardship, if this has not been done by orders under Parts I (Family Property) and II (Matrimonial Home).

## Determination of amount for support of spouses, parents

(9) In determining the amount and duration, if any, of support for a spouse or parent in relation to need, the court shall consider all the circumstances of the parties, including,

(a) the dependant's and respondent's current assets and means;

(b) the assets and means that the dependant and respondent are likely to have in the future;

(c) the dependant's capacity to contribute to his or her own support;

(d) the respondent's capacity to provide support;

(e) the dependant's and respondent's age and physical and mental health;

(f) the dependant's needs, in determining which the court shall have regard to the accustomed standard of living while the parties resided together;

(g) the measures available for the dependant to become able to provide for his or her own support and the length of time and cost involved to enable the dependant to take those measures;

(h) any legal obligation of the respondent or dependant to provide support for another person;

(i) the desirability of the dependant or respondent remaining at home to care for a child;

(j) a contribution by the dependant to the realization of the respondent's career potential;

(k) Repealed.

(l) if the dependant is a spouse,

(i) the length of time the dependant and respondent cohabited,

(ii) the effect on the spouse's earning capacity of the responsibilities assumed during cohabitation,

(iii) whether the spouse has undertaken the care of a child who is of the age of eighteen years or over and unable by reason of illness, disability or other cause to withdraw from the charge of his or her parents,

(iv) whether the spouse has undertaken to assist in the continuation of a program of education for a child eighteen years of age or over who is unable for that reason to withdraw from the charge of his or her parents,

(v) any housekeeping, child care or other domestic service performed by the spouse for the family, as if the spouse were devoting the time spent in performing that service in remunerative employment and were contributing the earnings to the family's support,

(v.1) Repealed.

(vi) the effect on the spouse's earnings and career development of the responsibility of caring for a child; and

(m) any other legal right of the dependant to support, other than out of public money.

## Conduct

(10) The obligation to provide support for a spouse exists without regard to the conduct of either spouse, but the court may in determining the amount of support have regard to a course of conduct that is so unconscionable as to constitute an obvious and gross repudiation of the relationship.

## Application of child support guidelines

(11) A court making an order for the support of a child shall do so in accordance with the child support guidelines.

## Exception: special provisions

(12) Despite subsection (11), a court may award an amount that is different from the amount that would be determined in accordance with the child support guidelines if the court is satisfied,

(a) that special provisions in an order or a written agreement respecting the financial obligations of the parents, or the division or transfer of their property, directly or indirectly benefit a child, or that special provisions have otherwise been made for the benefit of a child; and

(b) that the application of the child support guidelines would result in an amount of child support that is inequitable given those special provisions.

## Reasons

(13) Where the court awards, under subsection (12), an amount that is different from the amount that would be determined in accordance with the child support guidelines, the court shall record its reasons for doing so.

## Exception: consent orders

(14) Despite subsection (11), a court may award an amount that is different from the amount that would be determined in accordance with the child support guidelines on the consent of both parents if the court is satisfied that,

(a) reasonable arrangements have been made for the support of the child to whom the order relates; and

(b) where support for the child is payable out of public money, the arrangements do not provide for an amount less than the amount that would be determined in accordance with the child support guidelines.

## Reasonable arrangements

(15) For the purposes of clause (14)(a), in determining whether reasonable arrangements have been made for the support of a child,

(a) the court shall have regard to the child support guidelines; and

(b) the court shall not consider the arrangements to be unreasonable solely because the amount of support agreed to is not the same as the amount that would otherwise have been determined in accordance with the child support guidelines.

## Powers of court

**34.** (1) In an application under section 33, the court may make an interim or final order,

(a) requiring that an amount be paid periodically, whether annually or otherwise and whether for an indefinite or limited period, or until the happening of a specified event;

(b) requiring that a lump sum be paid or held in trust;

(c) requiring that property be transferred to or in trust for or vested in the dependant, whether absolutely, for life or for a term of years;

(d) respecting any matter authorized to be ordered under clause 24(1)(a), (b), (c), (d) or (e) (matrimonial home);

(e) requiring that some or all of the money payable under the order be paid into court or to another appropriate person or agency for the dependant's benefit;

(f) requiring that support be paid in respect of any period before the date of the order;

(g) requiring payment to an agency referred to in subsection 33(3) of an amount in reimbursement for a benefit or assistance referred to in that subsection, including a benefit or assistance provided before the date of the order;

(h) requiring payment of expenses in respect of a child's prenatal care and birth;

(i) requiring that a spouse who has a policy of life insurance as defined under the *Insurance Act* designate the other spouse or a child as the beneficiary irrevocably;

(j) requiring that a spouse who has an interest in a pension plan or other benefit plan designate the other spouse or a child as beneficiary under the plan and not change that designation; and

(k) requiring the securing of payment under the order, by a charge on property or otherwise.

## Limitation on jurisdiction of Ontario Court of Justice

(2) The Ontario Court of Justice shall not make an order under clause (1)(b), (c), (i), (j) or (k) except for the provision of necessities or to prevent the dependant from becoming or continuing to be a public charge, and shall not make an order under clause (d).

## Assignment of support

(3) An order for support may be assigned to an agency referred to in subsection 33(3).

## Same

(3.1) An agency referred to in subsection 33(3) to whom an order for support is assigned is entitled to the payments due under the order and has the same right to be notified of and to participate in proceedings under this Act to vary, rescind, suspend or enforce the order as the person who would otherwise be entitled to the payments.

## Support order binds estate

(4) An order for support binds the estate of the person having the support obligation unless the order provides otherwise.

## Indexing of support payments

(5) In an order made under clause (1)(a), other than an order for the support of a child, the court may provide that the amount payable shall be increased annually on the order's anniversary date by the indexing factor, as defined in subsection (6), for November of the previous year.

## Definition

(6) The indexing factor for a given month is the percentage change in the Consumer Price Index for Canada for prices of all items since the same month of the previous year, as published by Statistics Canada.

## Domestic contract, etc., may be filed with court

**35.** (1) A person who is a party to a domestic contract may file the contract with the clerk of the Ontario Court of Justice or of the Family Court of the Superior Court of Justice together with the person's affidavit stating that the contract is in effect and has not been set aside or varied by a court or agreement.

## Interpretation

(1.1) For the purposes of subsection (1), a party to a domestic contract includes a party's guardian of property or attorney for property, if the guardian or attorney entered into the domestic contract on behalf of the party under the authority of subsection 55(3).

## Effect of filing

(2) A provision for support or maintenance contained in a contract that is filed in this manner,

(a) may be enforced;

(b) may be varied under section 37;

(c) except in the case of a provision for the support of a child, may be increased under section 38; and

(d) in the case of a provision for the support of a child, may be recalculated under section 39.1,

as if it were an order of the court where it is filed.

## Setting aside available

(3) Subsection 33(4) (setting aside in unconscionable circumstances, etc.) applies to a contract that is filed in this manner.

## Enforcement available despite waiver

(4) Subsection (1) and clause (2)(a) apply despite an agreement to the contrary.

## Existing contracts, etc.

(5) Subsections (1) and (2) also apply to contracts made before the 1st day of March, 1986.

## Existing arrears

(6) Clause (2)(a) also applies to arrears accrued before the 1st day of March, 1986.

## Effect of divorce proceeding

**36.** (1) When a divorce proceeding is commenced under the *Divorce Act* (Canada), an application for support under this Part that has not been adjudicated is stayed, unless the court orders otherwise.

### Arrears may be included in order

(2) The court that deals with a divorce proceeding under the *Divorce Act* (Canada) may determine the amount of arrears owing under an order for support made under this Part and make an order respecting that amount at the same time as it makes an order under the *Divorce Act* (Canada).

### Idem

(3) If a marriage is terminated by divorce or judgment of nullity and the question of support is not adjudicated in the divorce or nullity proceedings, an order for support made under this Part continues in force according to its terms.

### Application for variation

**37.** (1) An application to the court for variation of an order made or confirmed under this Part may be made by,

(a) a dependant or respondent named in the order;

(b) a parent of a dependant referred to in clause (a);

(c) the personal representative of a respondent referred to in clause (a); or

(d) an agency referred to in subsection 33(3).

### Powers of court: spouse and parent support

(2) In the case of an order for support of a spouse or parent, if the court is satisfied that there has been a material change in the dependant's or respondent's circumstances or that evidence not available on the previous hearing has become available, the court may,

(a) discharge, vary or suspend a term of the order, prospectively or retroactively;

(b) relieve the respondent from the payment of part or all of the arrears or any interest due on them; and

(c) make any other order under section 34 that the court considers appropriate in the circumstances referred to in section 33.

### Powers of court: child support

(2.1) In the case of an order for support of a child, if the court is satisfied that there has been a change in circumstances within the meaning of the child support guidelines or that evidence not available on the previous hearing has become available, the court may,

(a) discharge, vary or suspend a term of the order, prospectively or retroactively;

(b) relieve the respondent from the payment of part or all of the arrears or any interest due on them; and

(c) make any other order for the support of a child that the court could make on an application under section 33.

### Application of child support guidelines

(2.2) A court making an order under subsection (2.1) shall do so in accordance with the child support guidelines.

### Exception: special provisions

(2.3) Despite subsection (2.2), a court may award an amount that is different from the amount that would be determined in accordance with the child support guidelines if the court is satisfied,

(a) that special provisions in an order or a written agreement respecting the financial obligations of the parents, or the division or transfer of their property, directly or indirectly benefit a child, or that special provisions have otherwise been made for the benefit of a child; and

(b) that the application of the child support guidelines would result in an amount of child support that is inequitable given those special provisions.

### Reasons

(2.4) Where the court awards, under subsection (2.3), an amount that is different from the amount that would be determined in accordance with the child support guidelines, the court shall record its reasons for doing so.

### Exception: consent orders

(2.5) Despite subsection (2.2), a court may award an amount that is different from the amount that would be determined in accordance with the child support guidelines on the consent of both parents if the court is satisfied that,

(a) reasonable arrangements have been made for the support of the child to whom the order relates; and

(b) where support for the child is payable out of public money, the arrangements do not provide for an amount less than the amount that would be determined in accordance with the child support guidelines.

### Reasonable arrangements

(2.6) For the purposes of clause (2.5)(a), in determining whether reasonable arrangements have been made for the support of a child,

(a) the court shall have regard to the child support guidelines; and

(b) the court shall not consider the arrangements to be unreasonable solely because the amount of support agreed to is not the same as the amount that would otherwise have been determined in accordance with the child support guidelines.

### Limitation on applications for variation

(3) No application for variation shall be made within six months after the making of the order for support or the disposition of another application for variation in respect of the same order, except by leave of the court.

### Indexing existing orders

### Non-application to orders for child support

**38.** (1) This section does not apply to an order for the support of a child.

### Application to have existing order indexed

(2) If an order made or confirmed under this Part is not indexed under subsection 34(5), the dependant, or an agency referred to in subsection 33(3), may apply to the court to have the order indexed in accordance with subsection 34(5).

### Power of court

(3) The court shall, unless the respondent shows that his or her income, assets and means have not increased sufficiently to permit the increase, order that the amount payable be increased by the indexing factor, as defined in subsection 34(6), for November of the year before the year in which the application is made and be increased in the same way annually thereafter on the anniversary date of the order under this section.

### Priority to child support

**38.1** (1) Where a court is considering an application for the support of a child and an application for the support of a spouse, the court shall give priority to the support of the child in determining the applications.

### Reasons

(2) Where as a result of giving priority to the support of a child, the court is unable to make an order for the support of a spouse or the court makes an order for the support of a spouse in an amount less than it otherwise would have, the court shall record its reasons for doing so.

### Consequences of reduction or termination of child support

(3) Where as a result of giving priority to the support of a child, an order for the support of a spouse is not made or the amount of the order for the support of a spouse is less than it otherwise would have been, any material reduction or termination of the support for the child constitutes a material change of circumstances for the purposes of an application for the support of the spouse or for variation of an order for the support of the spouse.

(4) Repealed.

### Administrative calculation of child support

### Definition

**39.** (1) In this section,

"child support calculation service" means the service established by the Government of Ontario for the purposes of this section.

### Application for calculation

(2) Subject to subsection (3), a parent of a child may apply in accordance with the regulations for a calculation by the child support calculation service of an amount to be paid for the support of the child.

### Requirements

(3) Subsection (2) does not apply unless the following requirements are met:

1. The applicant is a parent of the child as set out in section 4 of the *Children's Law Reform Act*, or has custody of the child under an order or domestic contract.
2. If the applicant is a parent of the child as set out in section 4 of the *Children's Law Reform Act*,
   i. the parents of the child live separate and apart, and
   ii. the child lives with one of the parents with the consent, implied consent or acquiescence of the other parent.
3. No order has been made by a court providing for the support of the child, and no domestic contract containing a provision for support of the child has been filed under subsection 35(1).
4. Any other requirement specified by the regulations.

### Information to be provided

(4) The child support calculation service shall not calculate an amount under this section unless each parent of the child has provided the income information and any other information that is required by the regulations, in the manner or form specified by the regulations.

### Application of child support guidelines

(5) Amounts calculated by the child support calculation service shall be determined in accordance with the child support guidelines as if the amounts were being calculated for the purposes of an order under this Part for the support of a child, subject to such modifications in the application of the child support guidelines as the regulations may specify.

### Periodic payments

(6) Amounts calculated under this section are payable on a monthly basis, or on such other periodic basis as may be specified by the regulations.

### Notice

(7) The child support calculation service shall give notice to the parents of a calculation of support payable in respect of a child, showing,

(a) the date on which the calculation was made;

(b) the income information on which the calculation was based;

(c) the amount payable for support and by which parent;

(d) the child's name and birthdate;

(e) the date on which the first payment is due and when subsequent payments become due; and

(f) any other information required by the regulations to be provided in the notice.

## When amount becomes due

(8) The first payment under a notice of calculation is due,

(a) on the 31st day after the day the notice is given, as determined by the regulations; or

(b) on the first instance of a day consented to by the parents in the application for calculation that follows the day described in clause (a).

## Corrections to notice

(9) If the notice of calculation contains an error respecting the amount payable or to whom, any parent affected by the error may, subject to subsection (10), apply in accordance with the regulations to have the error corrected.

## Limitation on corrections

(10) An application for a correction under subsection (9) may be made no later than the time specified by the regulations.

## No error respecting payment

(11) If the correction of the error does not result in a change to the amount to be paid under the notice or to whom, or if there is in fact no error, the child support calculation service shall give notice to that effect to the parents.

## Copies to Director

(12) The child support calculation service shall, on receiving an application under subsection (9) or on giving notice under subsection (11), file a copy of the application or notice with the office of the Director of the Family Responsibility Office.

## Effect of correction

(13) If a notice of calculation is corrected and the correction results in a change to the amount to be paid or to whom,

(a) the child support calculation service shall give a new notice under subsection (7) to the parents;

(b) subsections (8), (9), (10), (11), (12) and this subsection apply with respect to the new notice; and

(c) the original notice of calculation ceases to have effect.

## Effect of notice of calculation

(14) A notice of calculation shall be treated as if it were an order of a court for the purposes of,

(a) enforcement;

(b) subsections 34(3), (3.1) and (4); and

(c) recalculation under section 39.1.

## Enforcement by Director

(15) For the purposes of clause (14)(a), a notice of calculation shall be enforced by the Director of the Family Responsibility Office in accordance with and subject to the *Family Responsibility and Support Arrears Enforcement Act, 1996*.

## Ongoing disclosure of information

(16) Each party to a notice of calculation shall provide information, including income information, to the other party on an ongoing basis, in accordance with the regulations.

## Administrative recalculation of child support

## Definition

**39.1** (1) In this section,

"child support recalculation service" means the service established by the Government of Ontario for the purposes of this section.

## Application for recalculation

(2) If a party to an order for the support of a child believes that the income information on which the order was based has changed, the party may apply in accordance with the regulations for a recalculation by the child support recalculation service of the amount payable under the order.

## Ineligible

(3) Subsection (2) does not apply with respect to any order or child support obligation that is prescribed by the regulations as being ineligible for recalculation under this section.

## Information to be provided

(4) In an application under subsection (2), every party shall provide the income information and any other information that is required by the regulations, in the manner or form and within the timelines specified by the regulations.

## If income information not provided

(5) If a party does not provide income information in accordance with subsection (4), the child support recalculation service shall determine an income amount in accordance with the regulations, and that amount is deemed to be the person's income for the purposes of the recalculation.

## Application of child support guidelines

(6) Amounts calculated by the child support recalculation service shall be determined in accordance with the child support guidelines as if the amounts were being calculated for the purposes of an order for the support of a child, subject to such modifications in the application of the child support guidelines as the regulations may specify.

## Notice

(7) Subject to subsection (8), the child support recalculation service shall give notice of a recalculation to the parties and to any agency to which the order is assigned showing,

(a) the date on which the recalculation was made;

(b) the income information on which the recalculation was based;

(c) the recalculated amount payable for support and by which parent;

(d) the name and birthdate of each child in respect of whom the support is payable;

(e) the date on which the first payment is due and when subsequent payments become due; and

(f) any other information required by the regulations to be provided in the notice.

### No recalculated amount

(8) If the difference between an amount payable for support under the order and the recalculated amount is less than an amount specified by the regulations,

(a) the amount payable for support remains unchanged; and

(b) the child support recalculation service shall give notice to that effect to the parties and to any agency to which the order is assigned, and the notice shall set out how the recalculated amount was determined and any other related information.

### Copy to Director

(9) On giving a notice under subsection (8) in relation to a support order that is being enforced by the Director of the Family Responsibility Office, the child support recalculation service shall file a copy of the notice with the Director's office.

### When recalculated amount becomes due

(10) The first payment of the recalculated amount is due,

(a) on the first instance of the due date specified in the order that follows the 31st day after the day the notice of recalculation is given, as determined by the regulations; or

(b) on the first instance of another day consented to by the parties in the application for recalculation that follows the 31st day after the day the notice of recalculation is given, as determined by the regulations.

### Corrections to notice

(11) If the notice of recalculation or a notice given under subsection (8) contains an error respecting the amount payable or to whom, any party or any agency to which the order is assigned may, subject to subsection (12), apply in accordance with the regulations to have the error corrected.

### Limitation on corrections

(12) An application for a correction under subsection (11) may be made no later than the time specified by the regulations.

### No error respecting payment

(13) If the correction of the error does not result in a change to the amount to be paid in accordance with the notice or to whom, or if there is in fact no error, the child support recalculation service shall give notice to that effect to the parties and to any agency to which the order is assigned.

### Copies to Director

(14) The child support recalculation service shall, on receiving an application under subsection (11) or giving notice under subsection (13) in relation to a support order that is being enforced by the Director of the Family Responsibility Office, file a copy of the application or notice with the Director's office.

### Effect of correction

(15) If a notice of recalculation or a notice given under subsection (8) is corrected and the correction results in a change to the amount to be paid or to whom,

(a) the child support recalculation service shall give a new notice under subsection (7) or (8), as the case may be;

(b) subsections (9), (10), (11), (12), (13), (14) and this subsection apply with respect to the new notice as applicable; and

(c) if the error was in a notice of recalculation, that notice ceases to have effect.

### Recalculation deemed to be part of order

(16) Subject to subsection 25.1(5) of the *Divorce Act* (Canada), on the day that the first payment of the recalculated amount becomes payable in accordance with subsection (10), the recalculated amount is deemed to be the amount payable under the order for the support of the child and, if the due date for payments under the order is changed in accordance with clause (10)(b), the new due date is deemed to be the date on which payments are due under the order.

### Restraining orders

**40.** The court may, on application, make an interim or final order restraining the depletion of a spouse's property that would impair or defeat a claim under this Part.

### Financial statement

**41.** In an application under section 33 or 37, each party shall serve on the other and file with the court a financial statement verified by oath or statutory declaration in the manner and form prescribed by the rules of the court.

### Obtaining information

### Order for return by employer

**42.** (1) In an application under section 33 or 37, the court may order the employer of a party to the application to make a written return to the court showing the party's wages or other remuneration during the preceding twelve months.

### Return as evidence

(2) A return purporting to be signed by the employer may be received in evidence as proof, in the absence of evidence to the contrary, of its contents.

### Order for access to information

(3) The court may, on motion, make an order under subsection (4) if it appears to the court that, in order to make an application under section 33 or 37, the moving party needs to learn or confirm the proposed respondent's whereabouts.

### Idem

(4) The order shall require the person or public body to whom it is directed to provide the court or the moving party with any information that is shown on a record in the person's or public body's possession or control and that indicates the proposed respondent's place of employment, address or location.

### Crown bound

(5) This section binds the Crown in right of Ontario.

### Arrest of absconding debtor

**43.** (1) If an application is made under section 33 or 37 and the court is satisfied that the respondent is about to leave Ontario and that there are reasonable grounds for believing that the respondent intends to evade his or her responsibilities under this Act, the court may issue a warrant for the respondent's arrest for the purpose of bringing him or her before the court.

### Bail

(2) Section 150 (interim release by justice of the peace) of the *Provincial Offences Act* applies with necessary modifications to an arrest under the warrant.

### Provisional orders

**44.** (1) In an application under section 33 or 37 in the Ontario Court (Provincial Division) or the Unified Family Court, the court shall proceed under this section, whether or not the respondent in the application files a financial statement, if,

(a) the respondent fails to appear;

(b) it appears to the court that the respondent resides in a locality in Ontario that is more than 150 kilometres away from the place where the court sits; and

(c) the court is of the opinion, in the circumstances of the case, that the issues can be adequately determined by proceeding under this section.

### Idem

(2) If the court determines that it would be proper to make a final order, were it not for the respondent's failure to appear, the court shall make an order for support that is provisional only and has no effect until it is confirmed by the Ontario Court (Provincial Division) or the Unified Family Court sitting nearest the place where the respondent resides.

### Transmission for hearing

(3) The court that makes a provisional order shall send to the court in the locality in which the respondent resides copies of such documents and records, certified in such manner, as are prescribed by the rules of the court.

### Show cause

(4) The court to which the documents and records are sent shall cause them to be served upon the respondent, together with a notice to file with the court the financial statement required by section 41, and to appear and show cause why the provisional order should not be confirmed.

### Confirmation of order

(5) At the hearing, the respondent may raise any defence that might have been raised in the original proceeding, but if the respondent fails to satisfy the court that the order ought not to be confirmed, the court may confirm the order without variation or with the variation that the court considers proper having regard to all the evidence.

### Adjournment for further evidence

(6) If the respondent appears before the court and satisfies the court that for the purpose of a defence or for the taking of further evidence or otherwise it is necessary to remit the case to the court where the applicant resides, the court may remit the case and adjourn the proceeding for that purpose.

### Where order not confirmed

(7) If the respondent appears before the court and the court, having regard to all the evidence, is of the opinion that the order ought not to be confirmed, the court shall remit the case to the court sitting where the order was made with a statement of the reasons for doing so, and the court sitting where the order was made shall dispose of the application in accordance with the statement.

### Certificates as evidence

(8) A certificate certifying copies of documents or records for the purpose of this section and purporting to be signed by the clerk of the court is, without proof of the clerk's office or signature, admissible in evidence in a court to which it is transmitted under this section as proof, in the absence of evidence to the contrary, of the copy's authenticity.

### Right of appeal

(9) No appeal lies from a provisional order made under this section, but a person bound by an order confirmed under this section has the same right of appeal as he or she would have had if the order had been made under section 34.

## Necessities of life
### Pledging credit of spouse

**45.** (1) During cohabitation, a spouse has authority to render himself or herself and his or her spouse jointly and severally liable to a third party for necessities of life, unless the spouse has notified the third party that he or she has withdrawn the authority.

### Liability for necessities of minor

(2) If a person is entitled to recover against a minor in respect of the provision of necessities for the minor, every parent who has an obligation to support the minor is liable for them jointly and severally with the minor.

### Recovery between persons jointly liable

(3) If persons are jointly and severally liable under this section, their liability to each other shall be determined in accordance with their obligation to provide support.

### Common law supplanted

(4) This section applies in place of the rules of common law by which a wife may pledge her husband's credit.

### Restraining order

**46.** (1) On application, the court may make an interim or final restraining order against a person described in subsection (2) if the applicant has reasonable grounds to fear for his or her own safety or for the safety of any child in his or her lawful custody.

### Same

(2) A restraining order under subsection (1) may be made against,

    (a) a spouse or former spouse of the applicant; or

    (b) a person other than a spouse or former spouse of the applicant, if the person is cohabiting with the applicant or has cohabited with the applicant for any period of time.

### Provisions of order

(3) A restraining order made under subsection (1) shall be in the form prescribed by the rules of court and may contain one or more of the following provisions, as the court considers appropriate:

1. Restraining the respondent, in whole or in part, from directly or indirectly contacting or communicating with the applicant or any child in the applicant's lawful custody.
2. Restraining the respondent from coming within a specified distance of one or more locations.
3. Specifying one or more exceptions to the provisions described in paragraphs 1 and 2.
4. Any other provision that the court considers appropriate.

### Transition

(4) This section, as it read on October 14, 2009, continues to apply to,

    (a) any prosecution or other proceeding begun under this section before October 15, 2009; and

    (b) any order made under this section that was in force on October 14, 2009.

### Application for custody

**47.** The court may direct that an application for support stand over until an application for custody under the *Children's Law Reform Act* has been determined.

### Order regarding conduct

**47.1** In making any order under this Part, other than an order under section 46, the court may also make an interim order prohibiting, in whole or in part, a party from directly or indirectly contacting or communicating with another party, if the court determines that the order is necessary to ensure that an application under this Part is dealt with justly.

### Appeal from Ontario Court of Justice

**48.** An appeal lies from an order of the Ontario Court of Justice under this Part to the Superior Court of Justice.

### Contempt of orders of Ontario Court of Justice

**49.** (1) In addition to its powers in respect of contempt, the Ontario Court of Justice may punish by fine or imprisonment, or by both, any wilful contempt of or resistance to its process, rules or orders under this Act, other than orders under section 46, but the fine shall not exceed $5,000 nor shall the imprisonment exceed ninety days.

### Conditions of imprisonment

(2) An order for imprisonment under subsection (1) may be conditional upon default in the performance of a condition set out in the order and may provide for the imprisonment to be served intermittently.

(3) This section, as it read on October 14, 2009, continues to apply to orders referred to in clause 46(4)(b).

**50.** Repealed.

## PART IV  DOMESTIC CONTRACTS
### Definitions

**51.** In this Part,

"cohabitation agreement" means an agreement entered into under section 53;

"domestic contract" means a marriage contract, separation agreement, cohabitation agreement, paternity agreement or family arbitration agreement;

"family arbitration" means an arbitration that,

(a) deals with matters that could be dealt with in a marriage contract, separation agreement, cohabitation agreement or paternity agreement under this Part, and

(b) is conducted exclusively in accordance with the law of Ontario or of another Canadian jurisdiction;

"family arbitration agreement" and "family arbitration award" have meanings that correspond to the meaning of "family arbitration";

"marriage contract" means an agreement entered into under section 52;

"paternity agreement" means an agreement entered into under section 59;

"separation agreement" means an agreement entered into under section 54.

## Marriage contracts

**52.** (1) Two persons who are married to each other or intend to marry may enter into an agreement in which they agree on their respective rights and obligations under the marriage or on separation, on the annulment or dissolution of the marriage or on death, including,

(a) ownership in or division of property;

(b) support obligations;

(c) the right to direct the education and moral training of their children, but not the right to custody of or access to their children; and

(d) any other matter in the settlement of their affairs.

## Rights re matrimonial home excepted

(2) A provision in a marriage contract purporting to limit a spouse's rights under Part II (Matrimonial Home) is unenforceable.

## Cohabitation agreements

**53.** (1) Two persons who are cohabiting or intend to cohabit and who are not married to each other may enter into an agreement in which they agree on their respective rights and obligations during cohabitation, or on ceasing to cohabit or on death, including,

(a) ownership in or division of property;

(b) support obligations;

(c) the right to direct the education and moral training of their children, but not the right to custody of or access to their children; and

(d) any other matter in the settlement of their affairs.

## Effect of marriage on agreement

(2) If the parties to a cohabitation agreement marry each other, the agreement shall be deemed to be a marriage contract.

## Separation agreements

**54.** Two persons who cohabited and are living separate and apart may enter into an agreement in which they agree on their respective rights and obligations, including,

(a) ownership in or division of property;

(b) support obligations;

(c) the right to direct the education and moral training of their children;

(d) the right to custody of and access to their children; and

(e) any other matter in the settlement of their affairs.

## Form and capacity
### Form of contract

**55.** (1) A domestic contract and an agreement to amend or rescind a domestic contract are unenforceable unless made in writing, signed by the parties and witnessed.

### Capacity of minor

(2) A minor has capacity to enter into a domestic contract, subject to the approval of the court, which may be given before or after the minor enters into the contract.

### Guardian, attorney

(3) If a mentally incapable person has a guardian of property or an attorney under a continuing power of attorney for property, and the guardian or attorney is not his or her spouse, the guardian or attorney may enter into a domestic contract or give any waiver or consent under this Act on the person's behalf, subject to the court's prior approval.

### P.G.T.

(4) In all other cases of mental incapacity, the Public Guardian and Trustee has power to act on the person's behalf in accordance with subsection (3).

## Provisions that may be set aside or disregarded
### Contracts subject to best interests of child

**56.** (1) In the determination of a matter respecting the education, moral training or custody of or access to a child, the court may disregard any provision of a domestic contract pertaining to the matter where, in the opinion of the court, to do so is in the best interests of the child.

### Contracts subject to child support guidelines

(1.1) In the determination of a matter respecting the support of a child, the court may disregard any provision of a domestic contract pertaining to the matter where the provision is unreasonable having regard to the child support guidelines, as well as to any other provision relating to support of the child in the contract.

### Clauses requiring chastity

(2) A provision in a domestic contract to take effect on separation whereby any right of a party is dependent upon remaining chaste is unenforceable, but this subsection shall not be construed to affect a contingency upon marriage or cohabitation with another.

### Idem

(3) A provision in a domestic contract made before the 1st day of March, 1986 whereby any right of a party is dependent upon remaining chaste shall be given effect as a contingency upon marriage or cohabitation with another.

### Setting aside domestic contract

(4) A court may, on application, set aside a domestic contract or a provision in it,

(a) if a party failed to disclose to the other significant assets, or significant debts or other liabilities, existing when the domestic contract was made;

(b) if a party did not understand the nature or consequences of the domestic contract; or

(c) otherwise in accordance with the law of contract.

### Barriers to remarriage

(5) The court may, on application, set aside all or part of a separation agreement or settlement, if the court is satisfied that the removal by one spouse of barriers that would prevent the other spouse's remarriage within that spouse's faith was a consideration in the making of the agreement or settlement.

### Idem

(6) Subsection (5) also applies to consent orders, releases, notices of discontinuance and abandonment and other written or oral arrangements.

### Application of subss. (4, 5, 6)

(7) Subsections (4), (5) and (6) apply despite any agreement to the contrary.

### Provisions re pension plan
### Family law valuation date

**56.1** (1) In this section,

"family law valuation date" means, with respect to the parties to a domestic contract,

(a) the valuation date under Part I (Family Property) that applies in respect of the parties, or

(b) for parties to whom Part I does not apply, the date on which they separate and there is no reasonable prospect that they will resume cohabitation.

### Immediate transfer of lump sum

(2) A domestic contract may provide for the immediate transfer of a lump sum out of a pension plan, but, except as permitted under subsection (3), not for any other division of a party's interest in the plan.

### Division of pension payments

(3) If payment of the first instalment of a party's pension under a pension plan is due on or before the family law valuation date, the domestic contract may provide for the division of pension payments, but not for any other division of the party's interest in the plan.

### Restrictions re certain pension plans

(4) If the *Pension Benefits Act* applies to the pension plan, the restrictions under sections 67.3 and 67.4 of that Act apply with respect to the division of the party's interest in the plan under a family arbitration award.

> **Note: On a day to be named by proclamation of the Lieutenant Governor, subsection 59.4.1(4) of the Act is amended by adding "or under sections 67.8 and 67.9 of that Act in relation to variable benefits" after "of that Act."**
>
> **See: 2017, c. 8, Sched. 27, s. 21 (2).**

### Same

(4.1) If the *Pooled Registered Pension Plans Act, 2015* applies to the pension plan, the restrictions under sections 19 and 20 of that Act apply with respect to the division of the party's interest in the plan under a family arbitration award.

### Valuation

(5) Subsections 10.1(1) and (2) apply, with necessary modifications, with respect to the valuation of a party's interest in a pension plan.

### Same, pooled registered pension plans

(5.1) Subsection 10.1 (1.1) applies, with necessary modifications, with respect to the valuation of a party's interest in a pension plan to which the *Pooled Registered Pension Plans Act, 2015* applies.

### Transition, family law valuation date

(6) This section applies whether the family law valuation date is before, on or after the date on which this section comes into force.

### Transition, previous domestic contracts

(7) This section does not apply to a domestic contract that provided, before the date on which this section comes into force, for the division of a party's interest in a pension plan.

### Rights of donors of gifts

**57.** If a domestic contract provides that specific gifts made to one or both parties may not be disposed of or encumbered without the consent of the donor, the donor shall be deemed to be a party to the contract for the purpose of enforcement or amendment of the provision.

### Contracts made outside Ontario

**58.** The manner and formalities of making a domestic contract and its essential validity and effect are governed by the proper law of the contract, except that,

(a) a contract of which the proper law is that of a jurisdiction other than Ontario is also valid and enforceable in Ontario if entered into in accordance with Ontario's internal law;

(b) subsection 33(4) (setting aside provision for support or waiver) and section 56 apply in Ontario to contracts for which the proper law is that of a jurisdiction other than Ontario; and

(c) a provision in a marriage contract or cohabitation agreement respecting the right to custody of or access to children is not enforceable in Ontario.

## Paternity agreements

**59.** (1) If a man and a woman who are not spouses enter into an agreement for,

(a) the payment of the expenses of a child's prenatal care and birth;

(b) support of a child; or

(c) funeral expenses of the child or mother,

on the application of a party, or a children's aid society, to the Ontario Court of Justice or the Family Court of the Superior Court of Justice, the court may incorporate the agreement in an order, and Part III (Support Obligations) applies to the order in the same manner as if it were an order made under that Part.

## Child support guidelines

(1.1) A court shall not incorporate an agreement for the support of a child in an order under subsection (1) unless the court is satisfied that the agreement is reasonable having regard to the child support guidelines, as well as to any other provision relating to support of the child in the agreement.

## Absconding respondent

(2) If an application is made under subsection (1) and a judge of the court is satisfied that the respondent is about to leave Ontario and that there are reasonable grounds to believe that the respondent intends to evade his or her responsibilities under the agreement, the judge may issue a warrant in the form prescribed by the rules of the court for the respondent's arrest.

## Bail

(3) Section 150 (interim release by justice of the peace) of the *Provincial Offences Act* applies with necessary modifications to an arrest under the warrant.

## Capacity of minor

(4) A minor has capacity to enter into an agreement under subsection (1) that is approved by the court, whether the approval is given before or after the minor enters into the agreement.

## Application to existing agreements

(5) This section applies to paternity agreements that were made before the 1st day of March, 1986.

## Transitional provision

(6) A paternity agreement that is made before the day section 4 of the *Family Statute Law Amendment Act, 2006* comes into force is not invalid for the reason only that it does not comply with subsection 55(1).

## Family arbitrations, agreements and awards

**59.1** (1) Family arbitrations, family arbitration agreements and family arbitration awards are governed by this Act and by the *Arbitration Act, 1991*.

## Conflict

(2) In the event of conflict between this Act and the *Arbitration Act, 1991*, this Act prevails.

## Other third-party decision-making processes in family matters

**59.2** (1) When a decision about a matter described in clause (a) of the definition of "family arbitration" in section 51 is made by a third person in a process that is not conducted exclusively in accordance with the law of Ontario or of another Canadian jurisdiction,

(a) the process is not a family arbitration; and

(b) the decision is not a family arbitration award and has no legal effect.

## Advice

(2) Nothing in this section restricts a person's right to obtain advice from another person.

## Contracting out

**59.3** Any express or implied agreement by the parties to a family arbitration agreement to vary or exclude any of sections 59.1 to 59.7 is without effect.

## No agreement in advance of dispute

**59.4** A family arbitration agreement and an award made under it are unenforceable unless the family arbitration agreement is entered into after the dispute to be arbitrated has arisen.

## Award re pension plan

## Family law valuation date

**59.4.1** (1) In this section,

"family law valuation date" means, with respect to the parties to an arbitration,

(a) the valuation date under Part I (Family Property) that applies in respect of the parties, or

(b) for parties to whom Part I does not apply, the date on which they separate and there is no reasonable prospect that they will resume cohabitation.

## Immediate transfer of lump sum

(2) A family arbitration award may provide for the immediate transfer of a lump sum out of a pension plan, but, except as permitted under subsection (3), not for any other division of a party's interest in the plan.

## Division of pension payments

(3) If payment of the first instalment of a party's pension under a pension plan is due on or before the family law valuation date, the family arbitration award may provide for the division of pension payments, but not for any other division of the party's interest in the plan.

### Restrictions re certain pension plans

(4) If the *Pension Benefits Act* applies to the pension plan, the restrictions under sections 67.3 and 67.4 of that Act apply with respect to the division of the party's interest in the plan under a family arbitration award.

### Valuation

(5) Subsections 10.1(1) and (2) apply, with necessary modifications, with respect to the valuation of a party's interest in a pension plan.

### Transition, family law valuation date

(6) This section applies whether the family law valuation date is before, on or after the date on which this section comes into force.

### Transition, previous family arbitration awards

(7) This section does not apply to a family arbitration award made before the date on which this section comes into force that requires one party to pay to the other party the amount to which that party is entitled under section 5 (equalization of net family properties).

**59.5** Repealed.

### Conditions for enforceability

**59.6** (1) A family arbitration award is enforceable only if,

(a) the family arbitration agreement under which the award is made is made in writing and complies with any regulations made under the *Arbitration Act, 1991*;

(b) each of the parties to the agreement receives independent legal advice before making the agreement;

(c) the requirements of section 38 of the *Arbitration Act, 1991* are met (formal requirements, writing, reasons, delivery to parties); and

(d) the arbitrator complies with any regulations made under the *Arbitration Act, 1991*.

### Certificate of independent legal advice

(2) When a person receives independent legal advice as described in clause (1)(b), the lawyer who provides the advice shall complete a certificate of independent legal advice, which may be in a form approved by the Attorney General.

### Secondary arbitration

**59.7** (1) The following special rules apply to a secondary arbitration and to an award made as the result of a secondary arbitration:

1. Despite section 59.4, the award is not unenforceable for the sole reason that the separation agreement was entered into or the court order or earlier award was made before the dispute to be arbitrated in the secondary arbitration had arisen.

2. Despite clause 59.6(1)(b), it is not necessary for the parties to receive independent legal advice before participating in the secondary arbitration.

3. Despite clause 59.6(1)(c), the requirements of section 38 of the *Arbitration Act, 1991* need not be met.

### Definition

(2) In this section,

"secondary arbitration" means a family arbitration that is conducted in accordance with a separation agreement, a court order or a family arbitration award that provides for the arbitration of possible future disputes relating to the ongoing management or implementation of the agreement, order or award.

### Enforcement

**59.8** (1) A party who is entitled to the enforcement of a family arbitration award may make an application to the Superior Court of Justice or the Family Court to that effect.

### Application or motion

(2) If there is already a proceeding between the parties to the family arbitration agreement, the party entitled to enforcement shall make a motion in that proceeding rather than an application.

### Notice, supporting documents

(3) The application or motion shall be made on notice to the person against whom enforcement is sought and shall be supported by,

(a) the original award or a certified copy;

(b) a copy of the family arbitration agreement; and

(c) copies of the certificates of independent legal advice.

### Order

(4) If the family arbitration award satisfies the conditions set out in subsection 59.6(1), the court shall make an order in the same terms as the award, unless,

(a) the period for commencing an appeal or an application to set the award aside has not yet elapsed;

(b) there is a pending appeal, application to set the award aside or application for a declaration of invalidity; or

(c) the award has been set aside or the arbitration is the subject of a declaration of invalidity.

### Pending proceeding

(5) If clause (4)(a) or (b) applies, the court may,

(a) make an order in the same terms as the award; or

(b) order, on such conditions as are just, that enforcement of the award is stayed until the period has elapsed without an appeal or application being commenced or until the pending proceeding is finally disposed of.

### Unusual remedies

(6) If the family arbitration award gives a remedy that the court does not have jurisdiction to grant or would not grant in a proceeding based on similar circumstances, the court may,

(a) make an order granting a different remedy, if the applicant requests it; or

(b) remit the award to the arbitrator with the court's opinion, in which case the arbitrator may award a different remedy.

## Application of Act to existing contracts

**60.** (1)  A domestic contract validly made before the 1st day of March, 1986 shall be deemed to be a domestic contract for the purposes of this Act.

## Contracts entered into before the 1st day of March, 1986

(2)  If a domestic contract was entered into before the 1st day of March, 1986 and the contract or any part would have been valid if entered into on or after that day, the contract or part is not invalid for the reason only that it was entered into before that day.

## Idem

(3)  If property is transferred, under an agreement or understanding reached before the 31st day of March, 1978, between spouses who are living separate and apart, the transfer is effective as if made under a domestic contract.

## PART V  DEPENDANTS' CLAIM FOR DAMAGES

## Right of dependants to sue in tort

**61.** (1)  If a person is injured or killed by the fault or neglect of another under circumstances where the person is entitled to recover damages, or would have been entitled if not killed, the spouse, as defined in Part III (Support Obligations), children, grandchildren, parents, grandparents, brothers and sisters of the person are entitled to recover their pecuniary loss resulting from the injury or death from the person from whom the person injured or killed is entitled to recover or would have been entitled if not killed, and to maintain an action for the purpose in a court of competent jurisdiction.

## Damages in case of injury

(2)  The damages recoverable in a claim under subsection (1) may include,

  (a)  actual expenses reasonably incurred for the benefit of the person injured or killed;

  (b)  actual funeral expenses reasonably incurred;

  (c)  a reasonable allowance for travel expenses actually incurred in visiting the person during his or her treatment or recovery;

  (d)  where, as a result of the injury, the claimant provides nursing, housekeeping or other services for the person, a reasonable allowance for loss of income or the value of the services; and

  (e)  an amount to compensate for the loss of guidance, care and companionship that the claimant might reasonably have expected to receive from the person if the injury or death had not occurred.

## Contributory negligence

(3)  In an action under subsection (1), the right to damages is subject to any apportionment of damages due to contributory fault or neglect of the person who was injured or killed.

(4)  Repealed.

## Offer to settle for global sum

**62.** (1)  The defendant may make an offer to settle for one sum of money as compensation for his or her fault or neglect to all plaintiffs, without specifying the shares into which it is to be divided.

## Apportionment

(2)  If the offer is accepted and the compensation has not been otherwise apportioned, the court may, on motion, apportion it among the plaintiffs.

## Payment before apportionment

(3)  The court may direct payment from the fund before apportionment.

## Payment may be postponed

(4)  The court may postpone the distribution of money to which minors are entitled.

## Assessment of damages, insurance

**63.**  In assessing damages in an action brought under this Part, the court shall not take into account any sum paid or payable as a result of the death or injury under a contract of insurance.

## PART VI  AMENDMENTS TO THE COMMON LAW

## Unity of legal personality abolished

**64.** (1)  For all purposes of the law of Ontario, a married person has a legal personality that is independent, separate and distinct from that of his or her spouse.

## Capacity of married person

(2)  A married person has and shall be accorded legal capacity for all purposes and in all respects as if he or she were an unmarried person and, in particular, has the same right of action in tort against his or her spouse as if they were not married.

## Purpose of subss. (1, 2)

(3)  The purpose of subsections (1) and (2) is to make the same law apply, and apply equally, to married men and married women and to remove any difference in it resulting from any common law rule or doctrine.

## Actions between parent and child

**65.**  No person is disentitled from bringing an action or other proceeding against another for the reason only that they are parent and child.

## Recovery for prenatal injuries

**66.**  No person is disentitled from recovering damages in respect of injuries for the reason only that the injuries were incurred before his or her birth.

## Domicile of minor

**67.**  The domicile of a person who is a minor is,

  (a)  if the minor habitually resides with both parents and the parents have a common domicile, that domicile;

(b) if the minor habitually resides with one parent only, that parent's domicile;

(c) if the minor resides with another person who has lawful custody of him or her, that person's domicile; or

(d) if the minor's domicile cannot be determined under clause (a), (b) or (c), the jurisdiction with which the minor has the closest connection.

**68.** Repealed.

## General

### Regulations

**69.** (1) The Lieutenant Governor in Council may make regulations respecting any matter referred to as prescribed by the regulations.

### Same

(2) The Lieutenant Governor in Council may make regulations establishing,

(a) guidelines respecting the making of orders for child support under this Act; and

(b) guidelines that may be designated under subsection 2(5) of the *Divorce Act* (Canada).

### Same

(3) Without limiting the generality of subsection (2), guidelines may be established under subsection (2),

(a) respecting the way in which the amount of an order for child support is to be determined;

(b) respecting the circumstances in which discretion may be exercised in the making of an order for child support;

(c) respecting the circumstances that give rise to the making of a variation order in respect of an order for the support of a child;

(d) respecting the determination of income for the purposes of the application of the guidelines;

(e) authorizing a court to impute income for the purposes of the application of the guidelines;

(f) respecting the production of income information and providing for sanctions when that information is not provided.

### Same

(4) The Lieutenant Governor in Council may make regulations respecting the production of information, including income information, relating to child support obligations created by domestic contracts or by written agreements that are not domestic contracts, and providing for enforcement procedures when that information is not provided.

### Same

(5) The Lieutenant Governor in Council may make regulations governing the calculation of amounts payable for the support of a child for the purposes of section 39, including regulations,

(a) governing applications for a calculation;

(b) prescribing additional requirements for the purposes of paragraph 4 of subsection 39(3);

(c) governing the provision of information under subsection 39 (4), including specifying the income information and other information that is required to be provided, providing for the collection of a person's income information from the Canada Revenue Agency on the person's consent, and setting out the manner or form in which information must be provided;

(d) governing the determination of amounts payable for the support of a child in accordance with the child support guidelines by the child support calculation service, including,

(i) providing that any part of the child support guidelines do not apply or apply subject to specified modifications,

(ii) excluding specified special or extraordinary expenses, within the meaning of section 7 of the child support guidelines, from calculation under section 39 of this Act, and providing for methods of calculating special or extraordinary expenses that are not excluded;

(e) specifying periods for the purposes of subsection 39 (6);

(f) respecting additional information to be provided in a notice of calculation for the purposes of clause 39 (7) (f);

(g) governing the determination of the day on which a notice of calculation is given, for the purposes of subsection 39 (8);

(h) governing the making of corrections under subsection 39 (9), including the process for applying for a correction;

(i) specifying times for the purposes of subsection 39 (10);

(j) providing for the correction of errors in notices of calculation other than errors described in subsection 39 (9) and governing the making of such corrections, including,

(i) providing for procedures to correct such errors,

(ii) setting out a time limit on having such errors corrected,

(iii) providing for the issuance of new or corrected notices of calculation, and

(iv) specifying the effect of a correction on a notice of calculation, including providing that the notice of calculation containing the error ceases to have effect;

(k) providing that an obligation to pay child support under a notice of calculation terminates on a specified date or event, and governing the determination of dates and events for the purpose;

(l) governing the payment of fees in relation to calculations under section 39, including prescribing fees and requiring their payment, setting out the time or manner of payment, and providing for exemptions from payment and setting out conditions or circumstances for any exemption;

(m) respecting the production of information, including income information, by parties to a notice of calculation for the purposes of subsection 39 (16), and providing for enforcement procedures when that information is not provided. 2014, c. 7, Sched. 9, s. 10 (1); 2015, c. 27, Sched. 1, s. 2 (2).

**Same**

(6) Regulations made under clause (5) (c) may require a parent of a child to provide personal information, within the meaning of section 38 of the *Freedom of Information and Protection of Privacy Act*, respecting the child, another parent of the child, or any other person whose personal information is relevant to the calculation of child support under section 39 of this Act.

**Same**

(7) The Lieutenant Governor in Council may make regulations governing the recalculation of amounts payable for the support of a child for the purposes of section 39.1, including regulations,

(a) governing applications for a recalculation, including limiting when or how frequently a person can apply for a recalculation;

(b) prescribing orders or child support obligations for the purposes of subsection 39.1(3);

(c) governing the provision of information under subsection 39.1 (4), including specifying the income information and other information that is required to be provided, providing for the collection of a person's income information from the Canada Revenue Agency on the person's consent, setting out the manner or form in which information must be provided, and specifying timelines by which it must be provided;

(d) governing the determination of income amounts for the purposes of subsection 39.1 (5);

(e) governing the determination of amounts payable for the support of a child in accordance with the child support guidelines by the child support recalculation service, including,

(i) providing that any part of the child support guidelines do not apply or apply subject to specified modifications,

(ii) excluding specified special or extraordinary expenses, within the meaning of section 7 of the child support guidelines, from recalculation under section 39.1 of this Act, and providing for methods of recalculating special or extraordinary expenses that are not excluded;

(f) respecting additional information to be provided in a notice of recalculation for the purposes of clause 39.1 (7) (f);

(g) respecting the determination of amounts for the purposes of subsection 39.1 (8);

(h) governing the determination of the day on which a notice of recalculation is given, for the purposes of subsection 39.1 (10);

(i) governing the making of corrections under subsection 39.1 (11), including the process for applying for a correction;

(j) specifying times for the purposes of subsection 39.1 (12);

(k) providing for the correction of errors in notices of recalculation other than errors described in subsection 39.1 (11) and governing the making of such corrections, including,

(i) providing for procedures to correct such errors,

(ii) setting out a time limit on having such errors corrected,

(iii) providing for the issuance of new or corrected notices of recalculation or notices under subsection 39.1 (8), and

(iv) specifying the effect of a correction on a notice of recalculation, including providing that the notice of recalculation containing the error ceases to have effect;

(l) providing that an obligation to pay child support in accordance with a notice of recalculation terminates on a specified date or event, and governing the determination of dates and events for the purpose;

(m) providing that amounts recalculated under section 39.1 are subject to automatic recalculation under that section by or on a specified date or event, governing the determination of dates and events for the purpose, and governing procedures for such a recalculation, including specifying that any part of section 39.1 or the regulations made under this subsection do not apply to such a recalculation or apply subject to specified modifications;

(n) governing the payment of fees in relation to recalculations under section 39.1, including prescribing fees and requiring their payment, setting out the time or manner of payment, and providing for exemptions from payment and setting out conditions or circumstances for any exemption. 2014, c. 7, Sched. 9, s. 10 (2).

**Same**

(8) Regulations made under clause (7)(c) may require a person to provide personal information, within the meaning of section 38 of the *Freedom of Information and Protection of Privacy Act*, respecting the child, a parent of the child, or any other person whose personal information is relevant to the recalculation of child support under section 39.1 of this Act.

## Transition

### Application of ss. 5-8

**70.** (1) Sections 5 to 8 apply unless,

(a) an application under section 4 of the *Family Law Reform Act*, being chapter 152 of the Revised Statutes of Ontario, 1980 was adjudicated or settled before the 4th day of June, 1985; or

(b) the first spouse's death occurred before the 1st day of March, 1986.

### Application of Part II

(2) Part II (Matrimonial Home) applies unless a proceeding under Part III of the *Family Law Reform Act*, being chapter 152 of the Revised Statutes of Ontario, 1980 to determine the rights between spouses in respect of the property concerned was adjudicated or settled before the 4th day of June, 1985.

### Interpretation of existing contracts

(3) A separation agreement or marriage contract that was validly made before the 1st day of March, 1986 and that excludes a spouse's property from the application of sections 4 and 8 of the *Family Law Reform Act*, being chapter 152 of the Revised Statutes of Ontario, 1980,

(a) shall be deemed to exclude that property from the application of section 5 of this Act; and

(b) shall be read with necessary modifications.

# Family Law Rules

O Reg 114/99

| 1. | General | 196 |
|---|---|---|
| 2. | Interpretation | 198 |
| 3. | Time | 200 |
| 4. | Representation | 201 |
| 5. | Where a Case Starts and Is To Be Heard | 202 |
| 6. | Service of documents | 203 |
| 7. | Parties | 206 |
| 8. | Starting a case | 206 |
| 8.1 | Mandatory Information Program | 208 |
| 9. | Continuing Record | 208 |
| 10. | Answering a Case | 210 |
| 11. | Amending an Application, Answer or Reply | 210 |
| 12. | Withdrawing, Combining or Splitting Cases | 211 |
| 13. | Financial Disclosure | 211 |
| 14. | Motions for Temporary Orders | 216 |
| 15. | Motions to Change a Final Order or Agreement | 217 |
| 16. | Summary Judgment | 220 |
| 17. | Conferences | 221 |
| 18. | Offers To Settle | 224 |
| 19. | Document Disclosure | 225 |
| 20. | Questioning a Witness and Disclosure | 226 |
| 20.1 | Experts | 228 |
| 21. | Report of Children's Lawyer | 229 |
| 22. | Admission of Facts | 229 |
| 23. | Evidence and Trial | 229 |
| 24. | Costs | 231 |
| 25. | Orders | 233 |
| 25.1 | Payment Into and Out of Court | 234 |
| 26. | Enforcement of Orders | 235 |
| 27. | Requiring Financial Information | 236 |
| 28. | Seizure and Sale | 238 |
| 29. | Garnishment | 239 |
| 30. | Default Hearing | 242 |
| 31. | Contempt of Court | 242 |
| 32. | Bonds, Recognizances and Warrants | 243 |
| 32.1 | Enforcement of Family Arbitration Awards | 244 |
| 33. | Child Protection | 245 |

| | | |
|---|---|---|
| 34. | Adoption. | 246 |
| 35. | Change of Name | 248 |
| 35.1 | Custody and Access | 248 |
| 36. | Divorce | 249 |
| 37. | Interjurisdictional Support Orders Act, 2002 | 250 |
| 37.1 | Provisional Orders and Confirmation of Provisional Orders—Divorce Act, Family Law Act | 252 |
| 38. | Appeals | 253 |
| 39. | Case Management in Family Court of Superior Court of Justice. | 257 |
| 40. | Case Management in Ontario Court of Justice | 258 |
| 41. | Case Management in the Superior Court of Justice (Other Than the Family Court of the Superior Court of Justice) | 259 |
| 42. | Appointment of Family Case Manager in the Family Court of the Superior Court of Justice in Ottawa | 260 |
| 43. | Table of Forms. | 262 |

## RULE 1: GENERAL

### Citation

**1.** (1) These rules may be cited as the *Family Law Rules*.

### Cases and courts to which rules apply

(2) These rules apply to all family law cases in the Family Court of the Superior Court of Justice, in the Superior Court of Justice and in the Ontario Court of Justice,

(a) under,

(i) the *Change of Name Act*,

(ii) Parts III, VI and VII of the *Child and Family Services Act*,

(iii) the *Children's Law Reform Act*, except sections 59 and 60,

(iii.1) the *Civil Marriage Act* (Canada),

(iv) the *Divorce Act* (Canada),

(iv.1) the *Family Homes on Reserves and Matrimonial Interests or Rights Act* (Canada),

(v) the *Family Law Act*, except Part V,

(vi) the *Family Responsibility and Support Arrears Enforcement Act, 1996*,

(vii) sections 6 of the *Marriage Act*, and

(viii) the *Interjurisdictional Support Orders Act, 2002*;

(b) for the interpretation, enforcement or variation of a marriage contract, cohabitation agreement, separation agreement, paternity agreement, family arbitration agreement or family arbitration award;

(c) for a constructive or resulting trust or a monetary award as compensation for unjust enrichment between persons who have cohabited; and

(d) for annulment of a marriage or a declaration of validity or invalidity of a marriage; and

(e) for appeals of family arbitration awards under the *Arbitration Act, 1991*, and

(f) for proceedings under First Nation laws made under,

(i) the *Family Homes on Reserves and Matrimonial Interests or Rights Act* (Canada), or

(ii) the *First Nations Land Management Act* (Canada), with respect to the effect of relationship breakdown on matrimonial real property.

(2.1) Revoked.

### Case management in Family Court of Superior Court of Justice

(3) Despite subrule (2), rule 39 (case management in the Family Court of the Superior Court of Justice) applies only to cases in the Family Court of the Superior Court of Justice, which has jurisdiction in the following municipalities:

Regional Municipality of Durham
County of Frontenac
County of Haliburton
City of Hamilton
County of Lanark
United Counties of Leeds and Grenville
County of Lennox and Addington
County of Middlesex
Territorial District of Muskoka
The part of The Regional Municipality of Niagara that was the County of Lincoln as it existed on December 31, 1969
County of Northumberland
City of Ottawa

County of Peterborough
United Counties of Prescott and Russell
County of Simcoe
United Counties of Stormont, Dundas and Glengarry
City of Kawartha Lakes
Regional Municipality of York.

### Case management in Ontario Court of Justice

(4) Despite subrule (2), rule 40 (case management in the Ontario Court of Justice) applies only to cases in the Ontario Court of Justice.

### Case management in the Superior Court of Justice

(4.1) Despite subrule (2), rule 41 (case management in the Superior Court of Justice, other than the Family Court of the Superior Court of Justice) applies only to cases in the Superior Court of Justice that are not in the Family Court of the Superior Court of Justice.

### Family law case combined with other matter

(5) If a case in the court combines a family law case to which these rules apply with another matter to which these rules would not otherwise apply, the parties may agree or the court on motion may order that these rules apply to the combined case or part of it.

### Conditions and directions

(6) When making an order, the court may impose conditions and give directions as appropriate.

### Matters not covered in rules

(7) If these rules do not cover a matter adequately, the court may give directions, and the practice shall be decided by analogy to these rules, by reference to the *Courts of Justice Act* and the Act governing the case and, if the court considers it appropriate, by reference to the Rules of Civil Procedure.

### Certain orders that may be made at any time

(7.1) For greater certainty, a court may make an order under subrule (7.2), (8), (8.1) or (8.2) at any time during a case, and the power to make such an order,

(a) is in addition to any other power to make an order that these rules may specify in the circumstances; and

(b) exists unless these rules expressly provide otherwise.

### Procedural orders

(7.2) For the purposes of promoting the primary objective of these rules as required under subrules 2(4) and, particularly, (5), the court may make orders giving such directions or imposing such conditions respecting procedural matters as are just, including an order,

(a) that a party give to another party an affidavit listing documents that are relevant to the issues in a case and that are in the party's control or available to the party on request, or that a party make any other disclosure, within a specified time;

(b) limiting the number of affidavits that a party may file, or limiting the length of affidavits that a party may file (excluding any exhibits);

(c) that any motions be brought within a specified time;

(d) that a statement setting out what material facts are not in dispute be filed within a specified time (in which case the facts are deemed to be established unless a judge orders otherwise);

(e) that questioning be conducted in accordance with a plan established by the court, be subject to a time limit or be limited with respect to scope;

(f) limiting the number of witnesses;

(g) that all or part of an affidavit or any other evidence filed at any stage in a case, and any cross-examinations on it, may be used at a hearing;

(h) that a party serve and file, within a specified time, a written summary of the anticipated evidence of a witness;

(i) that a witness give all or part of his or her evidence by affidavit or another method not requiring the witness to attend in person;

(j) that oral evidence be presented, or that any oral evidence be subject to a time limit;

(k) that any expert witnesses for the parties meet to discuss the issues, and prepare a joint statement setting out the issues on which they agree and the issues that are in dispute;

(l) that a party serve and file a summary of argument;

(m) that a party provide to the court a draft order (Form 25, 25A, 25B, 25C or 25D) setting out the relief that he or she is seeking;

(n) identifying the issues to be decided at a particular hearing;

(o) that the parties appear before the court by a specified date;

(p) that a case be scheduled for trial or that a trial management conference be conducted; and

(q) that a trial be limited to a specified number of days and apportioning those days between the parties.

### Effect of order at trial

(7.3) An order made under clause (7.2)(i) does not apply to the giving of evidence on cross-examination unless the order states so expressly.

(7.4) An order made under subrule (7.2) respecting how a trial is to proceed applies unless the trial judge orders otherwise.

### Failure to obey order

(8) If a person fails to obey an order in a case or a related case, the court may deal with the failure by making any order that it considers necessary for a just determination of the matter, including,

(a) an order for costs;

(b) an order dismissing a claim;

(c) an order striking out any application, answer, notice of motion, motion to change, response to motion to change, financial statement, affidavit, or any other document filed by a party;

(d) an order that all or part of a document that was required to be provided but was not, may not be used in the case;

(e) if the failure to obey was by a party, an order that the party is not entitled to any further order from the court unless the court orders otherwise;

(f) an order postponing the trial or any other step in the case; and

(g) on motion, a contempt order.

### Failure to follow rules

(8.1) If a person fails to follow these rules, the court may deal with the failure by making any order described in subrule (8), other than a contempt order under clause (8)(g).

### Document that may delay or is inflammatory, etc.

(8.2) The court may strike out all or part of any document that may delay or make it difficult to have a fair trial or that is inflammatory, a waste of time, a nuisance or an abuse of the court process.

(8.3) Revoked.

### Consequences of striking out certain documents

(8.4) If an order is made striking out a party's application, answer, motion to change or response to motion to change in a case, the following consequences apply unless a court orders otherwise:

1. The party is not entitled to any further notice of steps in the case, except as provided by subrule 25(13) (service of order).
2. The party is not entitled to participate in the case in any way.
3. The court may deal with the case in the party's absence.
4. A date may be set for an uncontested trial of the case.

### Reference to forms

(9) In these rules, when a form is referred to by number, the reference is to the form with that number that is described in the Table of Forms at the end of these rules and is available on the Internet through www.ontariocourtforms.on.ca.

### Use of forms

(9.1) The forms authorized by these rules and set out in the Table of Forms shall be used where applicable and may be adjusted as needed to fit the situation.

(9.2) A party who is required by these rules to provide a form shall, subject to subrule (9.1),

(a) follow the instructions set out in the form;

(b) fully complete all portions of the form; and

(c) attach to the form any documents that the form requires.

### Format of written documents

(10) Every written document in a case,

(a) shall be legibly typed or printed; and

(b) in the case of a document in paper format,

(i) shall be on white paper, or on white or nearly white paper with recycled paper content, and

(ii) may appear on one or both sides of the page.

(c) Revoked.

### Practice directions

(11) In subrules (12), (12.1) and (12.2),

"practice direction" means a direction, notice, memorandum or guide for the purpose of governing, subject to these rules, the conduct of cases in any area.

### Requirements for practice direction

(12) A practice direction shall be approved in advance by the Chief Justice or Chief Judge of the court, filed with the secretary of the Family Rules Committee and posted on the Ontario Courts website, and notice of the practice direction shall be published in the *Ontario Reports*.

### Effective date of practice direction

(12.1) A practice direction does not come into effect before it is filed and posted and notice of it is published as described in subrule (12).

### Old practice directions

(12.2) Practice directions that were issued before these rules take effect no longer apply.

(13) Revoked.

## RULE 2: INTERPRETATION

### Definitions

**2.** (1) In these rules,

"address" means a person's street or municipal address, mailing address, telephone number, fax number and email address;

"appellant" means a person who starts an appeal;

"applicant" means a person who starts an application;

"application" means, as the context requires, the document that starts a case or the procedure by which new cases are brought to the court for a final order or provisional order;

"arbitration agreement" means an agreement by which two or more persons agree to submit to arbitration a dispute that has arisen or may arise between them;

"bond" includes a recognizance, and expressions that refer to the posting of a bond include the act of entering into a recognizance;

"case" means an application or any other method allowed in law for bringing a matter to the court for a final order or provisional order, and includes all motions, enforcements and appeals;

"change," when used to refer to an order or agreement, means to vary, suspend or discharge, or a variation, suspension or discharge (depending on whether the word is used as a verb or as a noun);

"child" means a child as defined in the Act governing the case or, if not defined in that Act, a person under the age of 18 years, and in a case under the *Divorce Act* (Canada) includes a "child of the marriage" within the meaning of that Act;

"child protection case" means a case under Part III of the *Child and Family Services Act*;

"child support guidelines" means Ontario Regulation 391/97 (Child Support Guidelines) made under the *Family Law Act*, or the Federal Child Support Guidelines, as the case may be;

"clerk" means a person who has the authority of a clerk or a registrar of the court;

"contempt motion" means a motion for a contempt order;

"contempt order" means an order finding a person in contempt of court;

"continuing record" means the record made under Rule 9 containing, in accordance with these rules, written documents in a case that are filed with the court;

"corporation" *French version only.*

"court" means the court in which a case is being heard;

"default hearing" means a hearing under section 41 of the *Family Responsibility and Support Arrears Enforcement Act, 1996* in which a payor is required to come to court to explain why payment has not been made as required by a support order;

"Director of the Family Responsibility Office" means the Director of the Family Responsibility Office under the *Family Responsibility and Support Arrears Enforcement Act, 1996*, and "Director" has the same meaning, unless the context requires otherwise;

"document" means information, sound or images recorded by any method;

"enforcement" means the use of one or more remedies mentioned in rule 26 (enforcement of orders) to enforce an order;

"family arbitration" means an arbitration that,

(a) deals with matters that could be dealt with in a marriage contract, separation agreement, cohabitation agreement or paternity agreement under Part IV of the *Family Law Act*, and

(b) is conducted exclusively in accordance with the law of Ontario or of another Canadian jurisdiction;

"family arbitration agreement" and "family arbitration award" have meanings that correspond to the meaning of "family arbitration";

"file" means to file with proof of service in the court office in the municipality,

(a) where the case or enforcement is started, or

(b) to which the case or enforcement is transferred;

"final order" means an order, other than a temporary order, that decides a claim in an application, including,

(a) an order made on motion that changes a final order,

(b) a judgment, and

(c) an order that decides a party's rights, in an issue between the parties or between a party and a non-party;

"government agency" means the Crown, a Crown agency, a municipal government or agency, a children's aid society or any other public body;

"income source" has the same meaning as in the *Family Responsibility and Support Arrears Enforcement Act, 1996*;

"lawyer" means a person authorized under the *Law Society Act* to practise law in Ontario;

"legal aid rate" means the rate payable by the Ontario Legal Aid Plan on an account submitted by a lawyer for copying in the lawyer's office;

"mail," when used as a noun, means ordinary or regular mail, and when used as a verb means to send by ordinary or regular mail;

"municipality" means a county, district, district municipality, regional municipality, the City of Toronto or a municipal corporation formed from the amalgamation of all the municipalities of a county, district, district municipality or regional municipality, and includes,

(a) an Indian reserve within the territorial area of a municipality, and

(b) the part of The Regional Municipality of Niagara that was the County of Lincoln as it existed on December 31, 1969;

"on motion" means on motion of a party or a person having an interest in the case;

"payment order" means a temporary or final order, but not a provisional order, requiring a person to pay money to another person, including,

(a) an order to pay an amount under Part I or II of the *Family Law Act* or the corresponding provisions of a predecessor Act,

(b) a support order,

(c) a support deduction order,

(d) an order under section 60 or subsection 154(2) of the *Child and Family Services Act*, or under the corresponding provision of a predecessor Act,

(e) a payment order made under rules 26 to 32 (enforcement measures) or under section 41 of the *Family Responsibility and Support Arrears Enforcement Act, 1996*,

(f) a fine for contempt of court,

(g) an order of forfeiture of a bond or recognizance,

(h) an order requiring a party to pay the fees and expenses of,

(i) an assessor, mediator or other expert named by the court, or

(ii)  a person conducting a blood test to help determine a child's parentage, and

(i)  the costs and disbursements in a case;

"payor" means a person required to pay money under an order or agreement, and includes the estate trustee of a payor who died;

"periodic payment" means an amount payable at regular intervals and includes an amount payable in instalments;

"property claim" means a claim,

(a)  under Part I of the *Family Law Act*,

(b)  for a constructive or resulting trust, or

(c)  for a monetary award as compensation for unjust enrichment;

"provisional order" means an order that is not effective until confirmed by a court;

"recipient" means a person entitled to receive money or costs under a payment order or agreement, including,

(a)  a guardian or person with custody of a child who is entitled to money for the child's benefit under an order,

(b)  in the case of a support order made under the *Family Law Act*, an agency referred to in subsection 33(3) of that Act,

(c)  in the case of a support order made under the *Divorce Act* (Canada), an agency referred to in subsection 20.1(1) of that Act,

(d)  a children's aid society entitled to money under an order made under section 60 or subsection 154(2) of the *Child and Family Services Act*, or the corresponding provision in a predecessor Act,

(e)  an assessor, mediator or other expert entitled to fees and expenses from the party named in the order, and

(f)  the estate trustee of a person who was entitled to money under an order at the time of his or her death;

"Registrar General" means the Registrar General under the *Vital Statistics Act*;

"respondent" means a person against whom a claim is made in an application, answer or appeal;

"special party" means a party who is a child or who is or appears to be mentally incapable for the purposes of the *Substitute Decisions Act, 1992* in respect of an issue in the case and who, as a result, requires legal representation, but does not include a child in a custody, access, child protection, adoption or child support case;

"support deduction order" means a support deduction order as defined in section 1 of the *Family Responsibility and Support Arrears Enforcement Act, 1996*;

"support order" means an order described in subsection 34(1) of the *Family Law Act* or a support order as defined in subsection 2(1) of the *Divorce Act* (Canada) or in section 1 of the *Family Responsibility and Support Arrears Enforcement Act, 1996*;

"temporary order" means an order that says it is effective only for a limited time, and includes an interim order;

"trial" includes a hearing;

"uncontested trial" means a trial at which only the party making the claim provides evidence and submissions.

### Primary objective

(2)  The primary objective of these rules is to enable the court to deal with cases justly.

### Dealing with cases justly

(3)  Dealing with a case justly includes,

(a)  ensuring that the procedure is fair to all parties;

(b)  saving expense and time;

(c)  dealing with the case in ways that are appropriate to its importance and complexity; and

(d)  giving appropriate court resources to the case while taking account of the need to give resources to other cases.

### Duty to promote primary objective

(4)  The court is required to apply these rules to promote the primary objective, and parties and their lawyers are required to help the court to promote the primary objective.

### Duty to manage cases

(5)  The court shall promote the primary objective by active management of cases, which includes,

(a)  at an early stage, identifying the issues, and separating and disposing of those that do not need full investigation and trial;

(b)  encouraging and facilitating use of alternatives to the court process;

(c)  helping the parties to settle all or part of the case;

(d)  setting timetables or otherwise controlling the progress of the case;

(e)  considering whether the likely benefits of taking a step justify the cost;

(f)  dealing with as many aspects of the case as possible on the same occasion; and

(g)  if appropriate, dealing with the case without parties and their lawyers needing to come to court, on the basis of written documents or by holding a telephone or video conference.

### RULE 3: TIME

### Counting days

**3.**  (1)  In these rules or an order, the number of days between two events is counted as follows:

1.  The first day is the day after the first event.

2.  The last day is the day of the second event.

## Counting days—Short periods

(2) If a rule or order provides a period of less than seven days for something to be done, Saturdays, Sundays and other days when all court offices are closed do not count as part of the period.

## Day when court offices closed

(3) If the last day of a period of time under these rules or an order falls on a day when court offices are closed, the period ends on the next day they are open.

## Counting days—Examples

(4) The following are examples of how time is counted under these rules:

1. Notice of a motion must be served not later than four days before the motion date (see subrule 14(11)). Saturday and Sunday are not counted, because the notice period is less than seven days (see subrule (2)). Service on the day set out in the left column below is in time for the motion to be heard on the day set out in the right column below.

| Service on | Motion may be heard on the following |
|:---:|:---:|
| Monday | Friday |
| Tuesday | Monday |
| Wednesday | Tuesday |
| Thursday | Wednesday |
| Friday | Thursday |
| Saturday | Friday |
| Sunday | Friday |

2. A respondent who is served with an application in Canada has 30 days to serve an answer (see subrule 10(1)). A respondent who is served with an application on October 1 is in time if the answer is served on or before October 31. A respondent served on November 1 is in time if the answer is served on or before December 1.
3. If the last day for doing something under these rules or an order is New Year's Day, January 1, which is a day when court offices are closed, the time expires on January 2. If January 2 is a Saturday, Sunday or other day when court offices are closed, the time expires on January 3. If January 3 is a day when court offices are closed, the time expires on January 4.

## Order to lengthen or shorten time

(5) The court may make an order to lengthen or shorten any time set out in these rules or an order, except that it may lengthen a time set out in subrule 33(1) (timetable for child protection cases) only if the best interests of the child require it.

## Written consent to change time

(6) The parties may, by consent in writing, change any time set out in these rules, except that they may not change a time set out in,

   (a) clause 14(11)(c) (confirmation of motion);

   (b) subrules 17(14) and (14.1) (confirmation of conference, late briefs);

   (c) subrule 33(1) (timetable for child protection cases);

   (d) rule 39 (case management in Family Court of Superior Court of Justice);

   (e) rule 40 (case management in Ontario Court of Justice); or

   (f) rule 41 (case management in the Superior Court of Justice (other than the Family Court of the Superior Court of Justice)).

## Late documents refused by court office

(7) The staff at a court office shall refuse to accept a document that a person asks to file after,

   (a) the time specified in these rules; or

   (b) the later time specified in a consent under subrule (6), a statute that applies to the case, or a court order.

## RULE 4: REPRESENTATION

### Definition

**4.** (0.1) In this rule,

"limited scope retainer" means the provision of legal services by a lawyer for part, but not all, of a party's case by agreement between the lawyer and the party.

### Representation for a party

(1) A party may,

   (a) act in person;

   (b) be represented by a lawyer; or

   (c) be represented by a person who is not a lawyer, but only if the court gives permission in advance.

### Interpretation, acting in person

(1.1) Where a party acts in person, anything these rules require or permit a lawyer or other representative to do shall be done by the party.

### Limited scope retainer

(1.2) Clause (1)(b) permits a party to be represented by a lawyer acting under a limited scope retainer.

### Interpretation, limited scope retainer

(1.3) A party who is represented by a lawyer acting under a limited scope retainer is considered for the purposes of these rules to be acting in person, unless the lawyer is acting as the party's lawyer of record.

### Private representation of special party

(2) The court may authorize a person to represent a special party if the person is,

   (a) appropriate for the task; and

   (b) willing to act as representative.

**Public law officer to represent special party**

(3) If there is no appropriate person willing to act as a special party's representative, the court may authorize the Children's Lawyer or the Public Guardian and Trustee to act as representative, but only with that official's consent.

**Service of authorization to represent**

(4) An order under subrule (2) or (3) shall be served immediately, by the person who asked for the order or by any other person named by the court,

(a) on the representative; and

(b) on every party in the case.

**Representation of party who dies**

(5) If a party dies after the start of a case, the court may make the estate trustee a party instead, on motion without notice.

**Authorizing representative for party who dies**

(6) If the party has no estate trustee, the court may authorize an appropriate person to act as representative, with that person's consent, given in advance.

**Lawyer for child**

(7) In a case that involves a child who is not a party, the court may authorize a lawyer to represent the child, and then the child has the rights of a party, unless the court orders otherwise.

**Child's rights subject to statute**

(8) Subrule (7) is subject to section 38 (legal representation of child, protection hearing) and subsection 114(6) (legal representation of child, secure treatment hearing) of the *Child and Family Services Act*.

**Choice of lawyer**

(9) A party who is acting in person may choose a lawyer by serving on every other party and filing a notice of change in representation (Form 4) containing the lawyer's consent to act.

**Non-application**

(9.1) Subrule (9) does not apply if the party chooses a lawyer acting under a limited scope retainer and that lawyer is not the lawyer of record for the party.

**Change in representation**

(10) Except as subrule (10.1) provides, a party represented by a lawyer may, by serving on every other party and filing a notice of change in representation (Form 4),

(a) change lawyers; or

(b) act in person.

**Exception, child protection case scheduled for trial**

(10.1) In a child protection case that has been scheduled for trial or placed on a trial list, a party may act under clause (10)(b) only with the court's permission, obtained in advance by motion made with notice.

**Notice of change in representation**

(11) A notice of change in representation shall,

(a) contain the party's address for service, if the party wants to appear without a lawyer; or

(b) show the name and address of the new lawyer, if the party wants to change lawyers.

**Lawyer's removal from the case**

(12) A lawyer may make a motion for an order to be removed from the case, with notice to the client and to,

(a) the Children's Lawyer, if the client is a child;

(b) the Public Guardian and Trustee, if the client is or appears to be mentally incapable in respect of an issue in the case.

**Notice of motion to remove lawyer**

(13) Notice of a motion to remove a lawyer shall also be served on the other parties to the case, but the evidence in support of the motion shall not be served on them, shall not be put into the continuing record and shall not be kept in the court file after the motion is heard.

**Affidavit in support of motion to remove lawyer**

(14) The affidavit in support of the motion shall indicate what stage the case is at, the next event in the case and any scheduled dates.

**Contents and service of order removing lawyer**

(15) The order removing the lawyer from the case shall,

(a) set out the client's last known address for service; and

(b) be served on all other parties, served on the client by mail, fax or email at the client's last known address and filed immediately.

## RULE 5: WHERE A CASE STARTS AND IS TO BE HEARD

**Where case starts**

5. (1) Subject to sections 21.8 and 21.11 of the *Courts of Justice Act* (territorial jurisdiction—Family Court), a case shall be started,

(a) in the municipality where a party resides;

(b) if the case deals with custody of or access to a child, in the municipality where the child ordinarily resides, except for cases described in,

(i) section 22 (jurisdiction of an Ontario court) of the *Children's Law Reform Act*, and

(ii) subsection 48(2) (place for child protection hearing) and subsection 150(1) (place for adoption proceeding) of the *Child and Family Services Act*; or

(c) in a municipality chosen by all parties, but only with the court's permission given in advance in that municipality.

### Starting case—Danger to child or party

(2) Subject to sections 21.8 and 21.11 of the *Courts of Justice Act*, if there is immediate danger that a child may be removed from Ontario or immediate danger to a child's or party's health or safety, a party may start a case in any municipality and a motion may be heard in that municipality, but the case shall be transferred to a municipality referred to in subrule (1) immediately after the motion is heard, unless the court orders otherwise.

### Clerk to refuse documents if case in wrong place

(3) The clerk shall refuse to accept an application for filing unless,

(a) the case is started in the municipality where a party resides;

(b) the case deals with custody of or access to a child and is started in the municipality where the child ordinarily resides;

(c) the case is started in a municipality chosen by all parties and the order permitting the case to be started there is filed with the application; or

(d) the lawyer or party asking to file the application says in writing that the case is one that is permitted by clause (1)(b) or subrule (2) to be started in that municipality.

### Place for steps other than enforcement

(4) All steps in the case, other than enforcement, shall take place in the municipality where the case is started or transferred.

### Place for enforcement—Payment orders

(5) All steps in enforcement of a payment order, including a motion to suspend a support deduction order, shall take place,

(a) in the municipality where the recipient resides;

(b) if the recipient does not reside in Ontario, in the municipality where the order is filed with the court for enforcement;

(c) if the person enforcing the order so chooses, in the municipality where the payor resides; or

(d) in a motion under section 26 (income source dispute) of the *Family Responsibility and Support Arrears Enforcement Act, 1996*, in the municipality where the income source resides.

### Place for enforcement—Other orders

(6) All steps in the enforcement of an order other than a payment order shall take place,

(a) if the order involves custody of or access to a child,

(i) in the municipality where the child ordinarily resides, or

(ii) if the child does not ordinarily reside in Ontario, in the municipality to which the child has the closest connection;

(b) if the order involves property, in the municipality where the person enforcing the order resides or the municipality where the property is located; or

(c) in a municipality chosen by all parties, but only with the court's permission given in advance in that municipality.

### Filing writ with sheriff

(6.1) Despite subrules (5) and (6), a writ of seizure and sale (Form 28) may be filed with a sheriff in a different municipality.

### Alternative place for enforcement—Order enforced by contempt motion

(7) An order, other than a payment order, that is being enforced by a contempt motion may also be enforced in the municipality in which the order was made.

### Place for enforcement—Electronic writ

(7.1) A writ of seizure and sale that is issued electronically under rule 28 (seizure and sale),

(a) shall specify the municipality in which the enforcement is taking place under subrule (5), (6) or (7), as the case may be; and

(b) is deemed to have been issued in that municipality.

### Transfer to another municipality

(8) If it is substantially more convenient to deal with a case or any step in the case in another municipality, the court may, on motion, order that the case or step be transferred there.

### Change of place for child protection case

(9) Notice of a motion under subsection 48(3) of the *Child and Family Services Act* to transfer a case to a place within the jurisdiction of another children's aid society shall be served on the parties and the other children's aid society, with the evidence in support of the motion.

## RULE 6: SERVICE OF DOCUMENTS

### Methods of service

**6.** (1) Service of a document under these rules may be carried out by regular service or by special service in accordance with this rule, unless an Act, rule or order provides otherwise.

### Age restriction

(1.1) No person shall serve a document under these rules unless he or she is at least 18 years of age.

### Regular service

(2) Regular service of a document on a person is carried out by,

(a) mailing a copy to the person's lawyer or, if none, to the person;

(b) sending a copy by same- or next-day courier to the person's lawyer or, if none, to the person;

(c) depositing a copy at a document exchange to which the person's lawyer or, if none, the person belongs;

(c.1) if the person consents or the court orders, using an electronic document exchange;

(d) faxing a copy to the person's lawyer or, if none, to the person; or

(e) if the person consents or the court orders, emailing a copy to the person's lawyer or, if none, to the person.

## Special service

(3) Special service of a document on a person is carried out by,

(a) leaving a copy,

(i) with the person to be served,

(ii) if the person is or appears to be mentally incapable in respect of an issue in the case, with the person and with the guardian of the person's property or, if none, with the Public Guardian and Trustee,

(iii) if the person is a child, with the child and with the child's lawyer, if any,

(iv) if the person is a corporation, with an officer, director or agent of the corporation, or with a person at any place of business of the corporation who appears to be managing the place, or

(v) if the person is a children's aid society, with an officer, director or employee of the society;

(b) leaving a copy with the person's lawyer of record in the case, or with a lawyer who accepts service in writing on a copy of the document;

(c) mailing a copy to the person, together with an acknowledgment of service in the form of a prepaid return postcard (Form 6), all in an envelope that is addressed to the person and has the sender's return address (but service under this clause is not valid unless the return postcard, signed by the person, is filed in the continuing record); or

(d) leaving a copy at the person's place of residence, in an envelope addressed to the person, with anyone who appears to be an adult person resident at the same address and, on the same day or on the next, mailing another copy to the person at that address.

## Special service—Documents that could lead to imprisonment

(4) Special service of the following documents shall be carried out only by a method set out in clause (3)(a), unless the court orders otherwise:

1. A notice of contempt motion.
2. A summons to witness.
3. A notice of motion or notice of default hearing in which the person to be served faces a possibility of imprisonment.

## Special service—Restriction on who may serve

(4.1) Subject to subrule (4.2), special service of the following documents shall be carried out by a person other than the party required to serve the document:

1. An application (Form 8, 8A, 8B, 8B.1, 8B.2, 8C, 8D, 8D.1, 34L or 34N).
2. A motion to change (Form 15) and change information form (Form 15A) or affidavit permitted under subrule 15(22), with required attachments.
3. A document listed in subrule (4).

## Exceptions

(4.2) Subrule (4.1) does not apply if,

(a) the party required to serve the document or the person being served is a person referred to in clause 8(6)(c) (officials, agencies, etc.); or

(b) the court orders otherwise.

## Regular service at address on latest document

(5) Regular service may be carried out at the address for service shown on the latest document filed by the person to be served.

## Notice of address change

(6) A party whose address for service changes shall immediately serve notice of the change on the other parties and file it.

## Service by mail, when effective

(7) Service of a document by mail is effective on the fifth day after it was mailed.

## Service by courier, when effective

(8) Service of a document by courier is effective on

(a) the day after the day the courier picks it up, in the case of same-day courier service; or

(b) two days after the day the courier picks it up, in the case of next-day courier service.

## Service by document exchange, when effective

(9) Service of a document by deposit at a document exchange is effective only if the copy deposited and an additional copy of the document are date-stamped by the document exchange in the presence of the person depositing the copy, and then service is effective on the day after the date on the stamp.

## Service by electronic document exchange, when effective

(10) Service of a document through an electronic document exchange is effective only if the electronic document exchange provides a record of service showing the date and time of service, as well as the information listed in subrule (11.4), and then service is effective on,

(a) the date shown on the record of service; or

(b) if the record of service shows that the document was served after 4 p.m., the following day.

## Service by fax or email, when effective

(11) Service of a document by fax or email is effective on,

(a) the date shown on the first page of the fax or in the email message, as the case may be; or

(b) if the first page of the fax or the email message shows that the document was served after 4 p.m., the following day.

## Special service by leaving copy, when effective

(11.1) Special service of a document under clause (3) (a) or (b) is effective on the day the copy of the document was left in accordance with those clauses or, if the document was left after 4 p.m., the following day.

## Special service by leaving copy and mailing, when effective

(11.2) Special service of a document under clause (3) (d) is effective on the fifth day after it was mailed.

## Exception, if effective date is a holiday

(11.3) Despite subrules (7) to (11.2), if the effective date of service under one of those subrules would be a day on which court offices are closed, service is instead effective on the next day on which they are open.

## Information to be included in record of service

(11.4) A record of service for service of a document through an electronic document exchange shall, in addition to the date and time of service, include,

(a) the total number of pages served;

(b) the name and email address of the person who served the document;

(c) the name of the person or lawyer who was served; and

(d) the title or a description of the nature of the document.

## Information to be included with document served by fax

(12) A document that is served by fax shall show, on its first page,

(a) the sender's name, telephone number and fax number;

(b) the name of the person or lawyer to be served;

(c) the date and time of the fax;

(d) the total number of pages faxed; and

(e) the name and telephone number of a person to contact in case of transmission difficulties.

## Maximum length of document that may be faxed

(13) Service of a document or documents relating to a single step in a case may be carried out by fax only if the total number of pages (including any cover page or back sheet) is not more than 20, unless the parties consent in advance or the court orders otherwise.

## Documents that may not be faxed

(14) A trial record, appeal record, factum or book of authorities may not be served by fax at any time unless the person to be served consents in advance.

## Information to be included with document served by email

(14.1) Unless the court orders otherwise, the email message to which a document served by email is attached shall include,

(a) the name of the person or lawyer to be served;

(b) the title or a description of the nature of the document;

(c) the date and time of the email; and

(d) the name and telephone number of a person to contact in case of transmission difficulties.

## Substituted service

(15) The court may order that a document be served by substituted service, using a method chosen by the court, if the party making the motion,

(a) provides detailed evidence showing,

(i) what steps have been taken to locate the person to be served, and

(ii) if the person has been located, what steps have been taken to serve the document on that person; and

(b) shows that the method of service could reasonably be expected to bring the document to the person's attention.

## Same, notice

(15.1) An order under subrule (15) may be obtained on motion without notice, except where the person to be served is a government agency.

## Service not required

(16) The court may, on motion without notice, order that service is not required if,

(a) reasonable efforts to locate the person to be served have not been or would not be successful; and

(b) there is no method of substituted service that could reasonably be expected to bring the document to the person's attention.

## Service by advertisement

(17) If the court orders service by advertisement, Form 6A shall be used.

## Approving irregular service

(18) When a document has been served by a method not allowed by these rules or by an order, the court may make an order approving the service if the document,

(a) came to the attention of the person to be served; or

(b) would have come to the person's attention if the person had not been evading service.

### Proof of service

(19) Service of a document may be proved by,

(a) an acceptance or admission of service, written by the person to be served or the person's lawyer;

(b) an affidavit of service (Form 6B);

(c) the return postcard mentioned in clause (3)(c);

(d) the date stamp on a copy of the document served by deposit at a document exchange; or

(e) a record of service provided by an electronic document exchange that meets the requirements of this rule.

### Document that was not seen on effective date

(20) The court may, on motion, lengthen a time, set aside the consequences of failing to take a step by a specified time, order an adjournment, or make any other order that is just, if, despite service of a document having been effected on a person in accordance with this rule, the person shows that the document,

(a) did not come to his or her notice; or

(b) came to his or her notice only after the effective date of service.

## RULE 7: PARTIES

### Who are parties—Case

**7.** (1) A person who makes a claim in a case or against whom a claim is made in a case is a party to the case.

### Who are parties—Motion

(2) For purposes of a motion only, a person who is affected by a motion is also a party, but this does not apply to a child affected by a motion relating to custody, access, child protection, adoption or child support.

### Persons who must be named as parties

(3) A person starting a case shall name,

(a) as an applicant, every person who makes a claim;

(b) as a respondent,

(i) every person against whom a claim is made, and

(ii) every other person who should be a party to enable the court to decide all the issues in the case.

### Parties in cases involving children

(4) In any of the following cases, every parent or other person who has care and control of the child involved, except a foster parent under the *Child and Family Services Act*, shall be named as a party, unless the court orders otherwise:

1. A case about custody of or access to a child.
2. A child protection case.
3. A secure treatment case (Part VI of the *Child and Family Services Act*).

### Motion to change order under s. 57.1 of the *Child and Family Services Act*

(4.1) In a motion to change an order made under section 57.1 of the *Child and Family Services Act*, the children's aid society that was a party to the case in which the order was made is not a party to the motion to change the order, unless the court orders otherwise.

### Party added by court order

(5) The court may order that any person who should be a party shall be added as a party, and may give directions for service on that person.

### Permanent case name and court file number

(6) The court file number given to a case and the description of the parties as applicants and respondents in the case shall remain the same on a motion to change an order, a status review application, an application (general) for *Child and Family Services Act* cases other than child protection and status review, an application for an openness order, an enforcement or an appeal, no matter who starts it, with the following exceptions:

1. In an enforcement of a payment order, the parties may be described instead as payors, recipients and garnishees.
2. In an appeal, the parties shall also be described as appellants and respondents.
3. When a case is transferred to another municipality, it may be given a new court file number.
4. An application under section 153.1 of the *Child and Family Services Act* to change or terminate an openness order shall be given a new court file number.
5. In a motion to change an order made under section 57.1 of the *Child and Family Services Act*,
    i. the person making the motion shall be named as the applicant and every other party to the motion shall be named as the respondents, and
    ii. the motion shall be given a new court file number.
6. In an application brought under section 145.1.2 of the Child and Family Services Act, the person bringing the application shall be named as the applicant and the children's aid society and any other party entitled to notice shall be named as the respondents.

## RULE 8: STARTING A CASE

### Filing an application

**8.** (1) To start a case, a person shall file an application (Form 8, 8A, 8B, 8B.1, 8B.2, 8C, 8D, 8D.1, 34L or 34N).

### Enforcement of family arbitration award

(1.1) Despite subrule (1), a person who is entitled to the enforcement of a family arbitration award and who wants to ask the court to enforce the award under section 59.8 of the *Family Law Act* may do so by filing a request to enforce a family arbitration award (Form 32.1) under rule 32.1.

### When required to proceed by motion

(1.2) Despite subrules (1) and (1.1), if there is already a family law case to which these rules apply between the parties to the family arbitration agreement in the Superior Court of Justice or the Family Court of the Superior Court of Justice, the party entitled to enforcement shall make a motion in that case rather than an application under this rule or a request under rule 32.1, and subrule 14(24) applies in respect of the motion.

### Change to final order or agreement

(2) Subject to subrule 25(19) (changing order—fraud, mistake, lack of notice), a party who wants to ask the court to change a final order or an agreement for support filed under section 35 of the *Family Law Act* may do so only by a motion under rule 15 (if permitted to do so by that rule).

### Exception

(2.1) Despite subrule (2), if a party who wants to ask the court to change a final order or agreement to which rule 15 applies also wants to make one or more related claims to which rule 15 does not apply, the party may file an application under subrule (1) to deal with the request for a change together with the related claim or claims and, in that case, subrules 15(11) to (13) apply with necessary changes to the request.

### Claims in application

(3) An application may contain,

(a) a claim against more than one person; and

(b) more than one claim against the same person.

### Claim for custody or access

(3.1) An application containing a claim for custody of or access to a child shall be accompanied by the applicable documents referred to in rule 35.1.

### Claim relating to family arbitration

(3.2) An application containing a claim under the *Arbitration Act, 1991* or the *Family Law Act* relating to a family arbitration, family arbitration agreement or family arbitration award shall be accompanied by,

(a) copies of the certificates of independent legal advice required by the *Family Law Act* for the parties;

(b) a copy of the family arbitration agreement; and

(c) if an award has been made, the original award or a certified copy.

### Court date set when application filed

(4) When an application is filed, the clerk shall,

(a) set a court date, except as provided by subrule 39(7) (case management, standard track) and subrule 41(4) (case management, clerk's role); and

(b) seal the application with the court seal.

### Service of application

(5) The application shall be served immediately on every other party, and special service shall be used unless the party is listed in subrule (6).

### Service on officials, agencies, etc.

(6) The application may be served,

(a) on a foster parent, at the foster parent's residence;

(b) on a representative of a band or native community, by serving the chief or other person who appears to be in charge of its management;

(c) on any of the following persons, at their place of business:

1. A Director appointed under section 5 of the *Child and Family Services Act*.

2. A local director appointed under section 16 of the *Child and Family Services Act*.

3. An administrator in charge of a secure treatment program under Part VI of the *Child and Family Services Act*.

4. A children's aid society.

5. The Minister of Community and Social Services.

6. An agency referred to in subsection 33(3) of the *Family Law Act* or subsection 20.1(1) of the *Divorce Act* (Canada).

7. The Director of the Family Responsibility Office.

8. The Children's Lawyer.

9. The Public Guardian and Trustee.

10. The Registrar General.

### Serving protection application on child

(7) In a child protection case in which the child is entitled to notice, the application shall be served on the child by special service.

### Serving secure treatment application on child

(8) An application for secure treatment (Part VI of the *Child and Family Services Act*) shall be served on the child by special service.

### Serving application on child's lawyer

(9) If an order has been made for legal representation of a child under section 38 or subsection 114(6) of the *Child and Family Services Act* or under subrule 4(7), the applicant, or another party directed by the court, shall serve all documents in the continuing record and any status review application on the child's lawyer.

### Serving protection application before start of case

(10) If a child is brought to a place of safety (section 40, 42 or 43 of the *Child and Family Services Act*) or a homemaker remains or is placed on premises (subsection 78(2) of that Act), an application may be served without being sealed by the clerk, if it is filed on or before the court date.

### Application not served on or before court date

(11) If an application is not served on a respondent on or before the court date, at the applicant's request the clerk shall set a new court date for that respondent and the applicant shall make the necessary change to the application and serve it immediately on that respondent.

## RULE 8.1: MANDATORY INFORMATION PROGRAM
### Application of rule

**8.1** (1) This rule applies to cases started after August 31, 2011 that deal with any of the following:

1. A claim for custody of or access to a child under the *Divorce Act* (Canada) or Part III of the *Children's Law Reform Act*.
2. A claim respecting net family property under Part I of the *Family Law Act*.
3. A claim respecting a matrimonial home under Part II of the *Family Law Act*.
4. A claim for support under the *Divorce Act* (Canada) or Part III of the *Family Law Act*.
5. A restraining order under the *Family Law Act* or the *Children's Law Reform Act*.
6. A motion to change a final order or agreement under rule 15, except motions that deal only with changing child or spousal support.

### Exception

(2) Subrules (4) to (7) do not apply to,

(a) a person or agency referred to in subsection 33(3) of the *Family Law Act*;

(b) the Director of the Family Responsibility Office;

(c) parties in cases that are proceeding on consent;

(d) parties in cases in which the only claims made are for a divorce, costs or the incorporation of the terms of an agreement or prior court order;

(d.1) parties to an application in which the only claims made in the application and any answer relate to a family arbitration, family arbitration agreement or family arbitration award, unless the court orders otherwise; or

(e) parties who have already attended a mandatory information program.

### Content of program

(3) The program referred to in this rule shall provide parties to cases referred to in subrule (1) with information about separation and the legal process, and may include information on topics such as,

(a) the options available for resolving differences, including alternatives to going to court;

(b) the impact the separation of parents has on children; and

(c) resources available to deal with problems arising from separation.

### Attendance compulsory

(4) Each party to a case shall attend the program no later than 45 days after the case is started.

### Appointments to attend

(5) The applicant shall arrange his or her own appointment to attend the program, obtain an appointment for the respondent from the person who conducts the program, and serve notice of the respondent's appointment with the application.

### Certificate

(6) The person who conducts the program shall provide for each party who attends a certificate of attendance, which shall be filed as soon as possible, and in any event not later than 2 p.m. on the second day before the day of the case conference, if one is scheduled.

### No other steps

(7) A party shall not take any step in the case before his or her certificate of attendance is filed, except that a respondent may serve and file an answer and a party may make an appointment for a case conference.

### Exception

(8) The court may, on motion, order that any or all of subrules (4) to (7) do not apply to the party because of urgency or hardship or for some other reason in the interest of justice.

(9) Revoked.

## RULE 9: CONTINUING RECORD
### Continuing record created

**9.** (1) A person starting a case shall,

(a) prepare a single continuing record of the case, to be the court's permanent record of the case; and

(b) serve it on all other parties and file it, along with the affidavits of service or other documents proving that the continuing record was served.

(2) Revoked.

### Support enforcement continuing record

(3) If a support order is filed with the Director of the Family Responsibility Office, the person bringing the case before the court shall prepare the continuing record, and the continuing record shall be called the support enforcement continuing record.

### Child protection continuing record

(4) In an application for a child protection order or an application for a status review of a child protection order, the continuing record shall be called the child protection continuing record.

(5) Revoked.

### Formal requirements of continuing record

(6) In preparing and maintaining a continuing record and support enforcement continuing record under this rule, the parties shall meet the requirements set out in the document entitled "Formal Requirements of the Continuing Record under the *Family Law Rules*," dated October 21, 2013, published by the Family Rules Committee and available on the Internet through www.ontariocourtforms.on.ca.

### Formal requirements of child protection continuing record

(6.1) In preparing and maintaining a child protection continuing record under this rule, the parties shall meet the requirements set out in the document entitled "Formal Requirements of the Child Protection Continuing Record under the *Family Law Rules*," dated November 1, 2005, published by the Family Rules Committee and available on the Internet through www.ontariocourtforms.on.ca.

### Separation of single record

(7) Instead of the single continuing record mentioned in subrule (1), the continuing record may be separated into separate records for the applicant and the respondent, in accordance with the following:

1. In a case other than a child protection case, the court may order separate records on its own initiative or at the request of either party on motion or at a case conference, settlement conference or trial management conference.
2. Revoked.
3. If the court orders separate records and there is more than one applicant and respondent, the court may order separate records for each applicant and respondent.
4. If the record consists of separate records, the separate records are called the applicant's record and the respondent's record.

### Combining separated records

(8) If the continuing record has been separated, the court may order the records to be combined into a single record on its own initiative or at the request of either party at a case conference, settlement conference or trial management conference.

### Combining separated records on consent

(9) If the continuing record has been separated, the parties may, if they agree, combine the separate records into a single continuing record, in which case the parties shall arrange together for the combining of the records.

### By whom record is separated or combined

(10) If the court orders that the continuing record,

(a) be separated or combined on its own initiative, the court shall give directions as to which party shall separate or combine the record, as the case requires;

(b) be separated or combined at the request of a party at a case conference, settlement conference or trial management conference, the party that makes the request shall separate or combine the record, as the case requires, unless the court orders otherwise.

### Maintaining continuing record

(11) The parties are responsible, under the clerk's supervision, for adding to a continuing record that has not been separated all documents filed in the case and, in the case of separated records, each party is responsible, under the clerk's supervision, for adding the documents the party files to the party's own record.

### Duties of party serving documents

(12) A party serving documents shall,

(a) if the continuing record has not been separated,

(i) serve and file any documents that are not already in the continuing record, and

(ii) serve with the documents an updated cumulative table of contents listing the documents being filed; and

(b) if the continuing record has been separated,

(i) serve and file any documents that are not already in the party's separate record, and

(ii) serve with the documents an updated cumulative table of contents listing the documents being filed in the party's separate record.

### No service or filing of documents already in record

(13) A party shall not serve or file any document that is already in the record, despite any requirement in these rules that the document be served and filed.

(14) Revoked.

### Documents referred to by tab in record

(15) A party who is relying on a document in the record shall refer to it by its tab in the record, except in a support enforcement continuing record.

### Documents not to be removed from record

(16) No document shall be removed from the continuing record except by order.

### Written reasons for order

(17) If the court gives written reasons for making an order,

(a) they may be endorsed by hand on an endorsement sheet, or the endorsement may be a short note on the endorsement sheet saying that written reasons are being given separately;

(b) the clerk shall add a copy of the reasons to the endorsements section of the record; and

(c) the clerk shall send a copy to the parties by mail, fax or email.

(18) Revoked.

### Appeal

(19) If a final order is appealed, only the notice of appeal and any order of the appeal court (and no other appeal document) shall be added to the record.

### Transfer of record if case transferred

(20) If the court transfers a case to another municipality the clerk shall, on request, transfer the record to the clerk at the court office in the other municipality, and the record shall be used there as if the case had started in the other municipality.

## Confirmation of support order

(21) When a provisional support order or a provisional change to a support order is sent to a court in Ontario for confirmation,

(a) if the provisional order or change was made in Ontario, the clerk shall send the continuing record to the court office where the confirmation is to take place and the respondent shall update it as this rule requires; and

(b) if the provisional order or change was not made in Ontario, the clerk shall prepare the continuing record and the respondent shall update it as this rule requires.

## Cases started before January 1, 2007

(22) Despite this rule, if a case was started before January 1, 2007, the version of this rule that applied to the case on December 31, 2006 as its application may have been modified by the court continues, subject to subrule (23), to apply to the case unless the court orders otherwise.

## Exception, cases started before January 1, 2007

(23) If a motion to change a final order is made on or after January 1, 2007 in respect of a case started before that date, this rule shall apply to the motion and to all documents filed afterwards.

(24) Revoked.

## RULE 10: ANSWERING A CASE

### Serving and filing answer

10. (1) A person against whom an application is made shall serve an answer (Form 10, 33B, 33B.1 or 33B.2) on every other party and file it within 30 days after being served with the application.

### Time for answer—Application served outside Canada or U.S.A.

(2) If an application is served outside Canada or the United States of America, the time for serving and filing an answer is 60 days.

### Exception—Placement for adoption

(2.1) In an application to dispense with a parent's consent before adoption placement, (Form 8D.1), the time for serving the answer is,

(a) 20 days, if the application is served in Canada or the United States of America;

(b) 40 days, if the application is served outside Canada or the United States of America.

### Answer may include claim

(3) A respondent may include in the answer,

(a) a claim against the applicant;

(b) a claim against any other person, who then also becomes a respondent in the case.

### Answer by added respondent

(4) Subrules (1) to (3) apply to a respondent added under subrule (3), except that the time for serving and filing an answer is 14 days after service on the added respondent, or 30 days if the added respondent is served outside Canada or the United States of America.

### Claim for custody or access

(4.1) An answer that includes a claim for custody of or access to a child shall be accompanied by the applicable documents referred to in rule 35.1.

### No answer

(5) The consequences set out in paragraphs 1 to 4 of subrule 1(8.4) apply, with necessary changes, if a respondent does not serve and file an answer.

### Reply

(6) A party may, within 10 days after being served with an answer, serve and file a reply (Form 10A) in response to a claim made in the answer.

## RULE 11: AMENDING AN APPLICATION, ANSWER OR REPLY

### Amending application without court's permission

11. (1) An applicant may amend the application without the court's permission as follows:

1. If no answer has been filed, by serving and filing an amended application in the manner set out in rule 8 (starting a case).
2. If an answer has been filed, by serving and filing an amended application in the manner set out in rule 8 and also filing the consent of all parties to the amendment.

### Amending answer without court's permission

(2) A respondent may amend the answer without the court's permission as follows:

1. If the application has been amended, by serving and filing an amended answer within 14 days after being served with the amended application.
2. If the application has not been amended, by serving and filing an amended answer and also filing the consent of all parties to the amendment.

### Child protection, amendments without court's permission

(2.1) In a child protection case, if a significant change relating to the child happens after the original document is filed,

(a) the applicant may serve and file an amended application, an amended plan of care or both; and

(b) the respondent may serve and file an amended answer and plan of care.

### Amending application or answer with court's permission

(3) On motion, the court shall give permission to a party to amend an application, answer or reply, unless the amendment would disadvantage another party in a way for which costs or an adjournment could not compensate.

### Claim for custody or access

(3.1) If an application or answer is amended to include a claim for custody of or access to a child that was not in the original application or answer, the amended application or amended answer shall be accompanied by the applicable documents referred to in rule 35.1.

### How amendment is shown

(4) An amendment shall be clearly shown by underlining all changes, and the rule or order permitting the amendment and the date of the amendment shall be noted in the margin of each amended page.

## RULE 12: WITHDRAWING, COMBINING OR SPLITTING CASES

### Withdrawing application, answer or reply

**12.** (1) A party who does not want to continue with all or part of a case may withdraw all or part of the application, answer or reply by serving a notice of withdrawal (Form 12) on every other party and filing it.

### Withdrawal—Special party's application, answer or reply

(2) A special party's application, answer or reply may be withdrawn (whether in whole or in part) only with the court's permission, and the notice of motion for permission shall be served on every other party and on,

(a) the Children's Lawyer, if the special party is a child;

(b) the Public Guardian and Trustee, if the special party is not a child.

### Costs payable on withdrawal

(3) A party who withdraws all or part of an application, answer or reply shall pay the costs of every other party in relation to the withdrawn application, answer, reply or part, up to the date of the withdrawal, unless the court orders or the parties agree otherwise.

### Costs on withdrawal by government agency

(4) Despite subrule (3), if the party is a government agency, costs are in the court's discretion.

### Combining and splitting cases

(5) If it would be more convenient to hear two or more cases, claims or issues together or to split a case into two or more separate cases, claims or issues, the court may, on motion, order accordingly.

### Splitting divorce from other issues

(6) The court may, on motion, make an order splitting a divorce from the other issues in a case if,

(a) neither spouse will be disadvantaged by the order; and

(b) reasonable arrangements have been made for the support of any children of the marriage.

## RULE 13: FINANCIAL DISCLOSURE

### Financial statement with application, answer or motion

**13.** (1) If an application, answer or motion contains a claim for support, a property claim, or a claim for exclusive possession of the matrimonial home and its contents,

(a) the party making the claim shall serve and file a financial statement (Form 13 or 13.1) with the document that contains the claim; and

(b) the party against whom the claim is made shall serve and file a financial statement within the time for serving and filing an answer, reply or affidavit or other document responding to the motion, whether the party is serving an answer, reply or affidavit or other document responding to the motion or not.

### Form 13 for support claim without property claim

(1.1) If the application, answer or motion contains a claim for support but does not contain a property claim or a claim for exclusive possession of the matrimonial home and its contents, the financial statement used by the parties under these rules shall be in Form 13.

### Form 13.1 for property claim with or without support claim

(1.2) If the application, answer or motion contains a property claim or a claim for exclusive possession of the matrimonial home and its contents, the financial statement used by the parties under these rules shall be in Form 13.1, whether a claim for support is also included or not.

### Exception, certain support claims

(1.3) If the only claim for support contained in the application, answer or motion is a claim for child support in the amount specified in the table of the applicable child support guidelines, the party making the claim is not required to file a financial statement, unless the application, answer or motion also contains a property claim or a claim for exclusive possession of the matrimonial home and its contents.

### Exception, family arbitration claim

(1.4) If the only claim contained in the application, answer or motion is a claim under the *Arbitration Act, 1991* or the *Family Law Act* relating to a family arbitration, family arbitration agreement or family arbitration award, the party making the claim is not required to file a financial statement, unless the court orders otherwise.

### Claim for payment order under CFSA

(2) If an application, answer or notice of motion contains a claim for a payment order under section 60 of the *Child and Family Services Act*, clause (1)(a) does not apply to the children's aid society but clause (1)(b) applies to the party against whom the claim is made.

### Financial statements in custody and access cases

(3) If an application, answer or motion contains a claim for custody of or access to a child and this rule does not otherwise require the parties to serve and file financial statements, the court may order each party to serve and file a financial statement in Form 13 within the time decided by the court.

### Additional required financial disclosure, support claim

(3.1) A party who is required under subrules (1) to (3) to serve and file a financial statement in relation to a claim for support shall, before the deadline set out in subrule (3.2), serve with the financial statement the following information, unless the court orders otherwise:

1. The income and financial information referred to in subsection 21(1) of the child support guidelines.
2. If the party became unemployed within the last three years,
   i. a complete copy of the party's Record of Employment, or other evidence of termination, and
   ii. a statement of any benefits or income that the party is still entitled to receive from his or her former employer despite or as a result of the termination.
3. In the case of a claim for the support of a child, proof of the amount of any special or extraordinary expenses, within the meaning of section 7 of the child support guidelines.

### Timing of requirement

(3.2) The party shall serve the information referred to in subrule (3.1),

(a) with the financial statement, if the application, answer or motion contains a claim for support but does not contain a property claim; or

(b) with the documents required to be served under subrule (3.3) or (3.4), as the case may be, if the application, answer or motion contains a property claim.

### Additional required financial disclosure, claim under Part I of the Family Law Act

(3.3) A party who is required under subrules (1) to (3) to serve and file a financial statement in relation to a claim under Part I of the *Family Law Act* shall, no later than 30 days after the day by which the financial statement is required to be served, serve on the other party the following information, unless the court orders otherwise:

1. The statement issued closest to the valuation date for each bank account or other account in a financial institution, pension, registered retirement or other savings plan, and any other savings or investments in which the party had an interest on that date.
2. A copy of an application or request made by the party to obtain a valuation of his or her own pension benefits, deferred pension or pension, as the case may be, if any, as of the valuation date.
3. A copy of the Municipal Property Assessment Corporation's assessment of any real property in Ontario in which the party had a right or interest on the valuation date, for the year in which that date occurred.
4. If the party owned a life insurance policy on the valuation date, the statement issued closest to that date showing the face amount and cash surrender value, if any, of the policy, and the named beneficiary.
5. If the party had an interest in a sole proprietorship or was self-employed on the valuation date, for each of the three years preceding that date,
   i. the financial statements of the party's business or professional practice, other than a partnership, and
   ii. a copy of every personal income tax return filed by the party, including any materials that were filed with the return.
6. If the party was a partner in a partnership on the valuation date, a copy of the partnership agreement and, for each of the three years preceding the valuation date,
   i. a copy of every personal income tax return filed by the party, including any materials that were filed with the return, and
   ii. the financial statements of the partnership.
7. If the party had an interest in a corporation on the valuation date, documentation showing the number and types of shares of the corporation and any other interests in the corporation that were owned by the party on that date.
8. If the corporation in which a party had an interest was privately held, for each of the three years preceding the valuation date,
   i. the financial statements for the corporation and its subsidiaries, and
   ii. if the interest was a majority interest, a copy of every income tax return filed by the corporation.
9. If the party was a beneficiary under a trust on the valuation date, a copy of the trust settlement agreement and the trust's financial statements for each of the three years preceding that date.

10. Documentation showing the value, on the valuation date, of any property not referred to in paragraphs 1 to 9 in which the party had an interest on that date.
11. Documentation that supports a claim, if any, for an exclusion under subsection 4 (2) of the *Family Law Act*.
12. The statements or invoices issued closest to the valuation date in relation to any mortgage, line of credit, credit card balance or other debt owed by the party on that date.
13. Any available documentation showing the value, on the date of marriage, of property that the party owned or in which he or she had an interest on that date, and the amount of any debts owed by the party on that date.

### Additional required financial disclosure, other property claims

(3.4) A party who is required under subrules (1) to (3) to serve and file a financial statement in relation to a property claim other than a claim under Part I of the *Family Law Act* shall, no later than 30 days after the day by which the financial statement is required to be served, serve on the other party any information necessary to support the claim, unless the court orders otherwise.

### Financial statement with motion to change temporary support order

(4) Subject to subrule (1.3), the following rules respecting financial statements apply if a motion contains a request for a change in a temporary support order:

1. The party making the motion shall serve and file a financial statement (Form 13 or 13.1) with the notice of motion.
2. The party responding to the motion shall serve and file a financial statement as soon as possible after being served with the notice of motion, but in any event no later than two days before the motion date. Any affidavit in response to the motion shall be served and filed at the same time as the financial statement.

### Exception—by consent

(4.1) Parties to a consent motion to change a temporary support order do not need to serve and file financial statements if they file a consent agreeing not to serve and file them.

### Financial statement with motion to change final support order or support agreement

(4.2) Subject to subrule (1.3), the following rules respecting financial statements apply if a motion is made under rule 15 requesting a change to a final support order or a support agreement:

1. The party making the motion shall serve and file a financial statement (Form 13 or 13.1) with the motion to change (Form 15).

2. The party responding to the motion shall serve and file a financial statement within the time for serving and filing the response to motion to change (Form 15B) or returning the consent motion to change (Form 15C) to the party making the motion, as set out in subrule 15(10). Any response to motion to change (Form 15B) shall be served and filed at the same time as the financial statement.
3. Parties who bring the motion by filing a consent motion to change (Form 15C) shall each file a financial statement with the form, unless they indicate in the form that they agree not to do so.
4. Parties who bring the motion by filing a consent motion to change child support (Form 15D) do not need to serve or file financial statements.

### Financial statement required by response

(4.3) Subrules (4) or (4.2), as the case may be, apply with necessary changes if a party makes a motion to change an order or agreement for which the party is not required by this rule to file a financial statement, and the party responding to the motion requests a change to a support order or support agreement.

### No financial statement from assignee

(5) The assignee of a support order is not required to serve and file a financial statement under subrule (4) or (4.2).

### Additional required financial disclosure, motion to change support

(5.0.1) A party who is required under subrules (4) to (4.3) to serve and file a financial statement shall serve with the financial statement the following information, unless the court orders otherwise:

1. The documents referred to in subrule (3.1).
2. A current statement of arrears from the Family Responsibility Office.
3. One of the following for each year for which the party is seeking to change or cancel arrears, as proof of the party's income:
    i. The party's income tax return and,
        A. the party's notice of assessment and, if any, notice of reassessment, or
        B. if a notice of assessment and a notice of reassessment are unavailable for the year, a copy of the Income and Deductions printout provided by the Canada Revenue Agency for the party.
    ii. If the party is not required to and has chosen not to file an income tax return because of the Indian Act (Canada), some other proof of income.

### Requirement to certify financial disclosure

(5.0.2) A party who is required to serve documents under subrule (3.1), (3.3), (3.4) or (5.0.1) shall confirm service by,

(a) serving a certificate of financial disclosure (Form 13A) together with the documents; and

(b) filing the certificate no later than,

(i) seven days before a case conference, in the case of the applicant or the party making the motion, as the case may be, and

(ii) four days before the case conference, in the case of the other party.

### Financial statement with motion to refrain

(5.1) A payor who makes a motion to require the Director of the Family Responsibility Office to refrain from suspending the payor's driver's licence shall, in accordance with subsection 35(7) of the *Family Responsibility and Support Arrears Enforcement Act, 1996*, serve and file with the notice of motion,

(a) a financial statement (Form 13 or 13.1) or a financial statement incorporated as Form 4 in Ontario Regulation 167/97 (General) made under that Act; and

(b) the proof of income specified in section 15 of the regulation referred to in clause (a).

(6) Revoked.

### Requirements for filing

(7) The clerk shall not accept the financial statement of a party making or responding to a claim for support unless the following are attached to the form:

1. Proof of the party's current income.
2. One of the following, as proof of the party's income for the three previous years:

i. For each of the three previous taxation years,

A. the party's notice of assessment and, if any, notice of reassessment, or

B. if a notice of assessment and a notice of reassessment are unavailable for a taxation year, a copy of the Income and Deductions printout provided by the Canada Revenue Agency for the party for the taxation year.

ii. If the party swears or affirms a statement in the form that he or she is not required to and has chosen not to file an income tax return because of the *Indian Act* (Canada), some other proof of income for the three previous years.

### Exception

(7.0.1) Subrule (7) does not apply to a financial statement filed under subrule (5.1).

### Documents that are not required to be filed

(7.1) The following documents are not required to be filed in the continuing record unless the court orders otherwise:

1. Income tax returns, except in the case of a filing under subrule (5.1).
2. Any other document referred to in subrule (3.1), (3.3), (3.4) or (5.0.1), unless these rules provide otherwise

### No financial disclosure by consent—Spousal support in divorce

(8) Parties to a claim for spousal support under the *Divorce Act* (Canada) do not need to serve and file financial statements or provide additional financial disclosure under this rule if they file a consent,

(a) agreeing to not serve and file financial statements or provide additional financial disclosure under this rule; or

(b) agreeing to a specified amount of support, or to no support.

(9) Revoked.

### Documents not to be filed without financial statement

(10) The clerk shall not accept a document for filing without a financial statement if these rules require the document to be filed with a financial statement.

### Insufficient financial information

(11) If a party believes that the financial disclosure provided by another party under this rule, whether in a financial statement or otherwise, does not provide enough information for a full understanding of the other party's financial circumstances,

(a) the party shall ask the other party to give the necessary additional information; and

(b) if the other party does not give it within seven days, the court may, on motion, order the other party to give the information or to serve and file a new financial statement.

### Same

(11.1) For greater certainty, a motion form (Form 14B) may be used if making a motion for an order under subrule (3.1), (3.3), (3.4) or (5.0.1) or an order under clause (11)(b).

### Updating financial statement

(12) Before any case conference, motion, settlement conference or trial, each party shall update the information in any financial statement that is more than 30 days old by serving and filing,

(a) a new financial statement; or

(b) an affidavit saying that the information in the last statement has not changed and is still true.

## Minor changes

(12.1)  If there have been minor changes but no major changes to the information in a party's past statement, the party may serve and file, instead of a new financial statement, an affidavit with details of the changes.

## Time for updating

(12.2)  The material described in subrules (12) and (12.1) shall be served and filed as follows:

1. For a case conference or settlement conference requested by a party, the requesting party shall serve and file at least seven days before the conference date and the other party shall serve and file at least four days before that date.

2. For a case conference or settlement conference that is not requested by a party, the applicant shall serve and file at least seven days before the conference date and the respondent shall serve and file at least four days before that date.

3. For a motion, the party making the motion shall serve and file at least seven days before the motion date and the other party shall serve and file at least four days before that date.

4. For a trial, the applicant shall serve and file at least seven days before the trial date and the respondent shall serve and file at least four days before that date.

## Questioning on financial statement

(13)  A party may be questioned under rule 20 on a financial statement provided under this rule, but only after a request for information has been made under clause (11)(a).

## Updating certificate of financial disclosure

(13.1)  Before any settlement conference or trial management conference, a party who has served a corrected, updated or new version of a document referred to in subrule (3.1), (3.3), (3.4) or (5.0.1) in accordance with subrule (15), or additional documents in accordance with subrule (16), shall serve and file an updated certificate of financial disclosure (Form 13A), no later than,

(a)  seven days before the conference, in the case of the party requesting the conference or, if the conference is not requested by a party, the applicant or the party making the motion, as the case may be; and

(b)  four days before the conference, in the case of the other party.

## Net family property statement

(14)  Each party to a property claim under Part I of the *Family Law Act* shall serve and file a net family property statement (Form 13B) or, if the party has already served a net family property statement, an affidavit saying that the information in that statement has not changed and is still true,

(a)  not less than 30 days before a settlement conference; and

(b)  not more than 30 days and not less than seven days before a trial.

## Exception, family arbitration claim

(14.1)  Subrule (14) does not apply if the property claim arises within a claim under the *Arbitration Act, 1991* or the *Family Law Act* relating to a family arbitration, family arbitration agreement or family arbitration award.

## Comparison of net family properties, joint

(14.2)  Parties who have served and filed net family property statements in accordance with subrule (14) shall file a joint comparison of net family property statements (Form 13C) no later than seven days before a settlement conference, subject to subrule (14.3).

## Comparison of net family properties, separate

(14.3)  If the parties fail to agree on a joint comparison of net family properties, each party shall serve and file his or her own comparison of net family property statements (Form 13C) no later than,

(a)  seven days before a settlement conference, in the case of the party requesting the conference or, if the settlement conference is not requested by a party, the applicant or the party making the motion, as the case may be; and

(b)  four days before the settlement conference, in the case of the other party.

## Duty to correct, update documents

(15)  As soon as a party discovers that a document that he or she has served under this rule is incorrect, incomplete or out of date, the party shall serve on the other party and, if applicable, file, a corrected, updated or new document, as the circumstances require].

## Duty to address omissions in financial disclosure

(16)  As soon as a party discovers that he or she failed to serve a document required to be served under subrule (3.1), (3.3), (3.4) or (5.0.1), the party shall serve the document on the other party.

## Order, if document not provided

(17)  If a party has not served or filed a document in accordance with the requirements of this rule or an Act or regulation, the court may on motion order the party to serve or file the document and, if the court makes that order, it shall also order the party to pay costs.

## Other obligations continue to apply

(18)  The duty to provide information under this rule does not affect any other duty set out in any other Act or regulation for the party to provide information to the other party in relation to a claim to which this rule applies.

## RULE 14: MOTIONS FOR TEMPORARY ORDERS

### When to make motion

**14.** (1) A person who wants any of the following may make a motion:

1. A temporary order for a claim made in an application.
2. Directions on how to carry on the case.
3. A change in a temporary order.

### Who may make motion

(2) A motion may be made by a party to the case or by a person with an interest in the case.

### Parties to motion

(3) A person who is affected by a motion is also a party, for purposes of the motion only, but this does not apply to a child affected by a motion relating to custody, access, child protection, adoption or child support.

### No motion before case conference on substantive issues completed

(4) No notice of motion or supporting evidence may be served and no motion may be heard before a conference dealing with the substantive issues in the case has been completed.

(4.1) Revoked.

### Urgency, hardship etc.

(4.2) Subrule (4) does not apply if the court is of the opinion that there is a situation of urgency or hardship or that a case conference is not required for some other reason in the interest of justice.

(5) Revoked.

### Other motions

(6) Subrule (4) does not apply to a motion,

(a) to change a temporary order under subrule 25(19) (fraud, mistake, lack of notice);

(b) for a contempt order under rule 31 or an order striking out a document under subrule (22);

(c) for summary judgment under rule 16;

(d) to require the Director of the Family Responsibility Office to refrain from suspending a licence;

(e) to limit or stay a support order, the enforcement of arrears under a support order, or an alternative payment order under the *Family Responsibility and Support Arrears Enforcement Act, 1996*;

(e.1) in a child protection case;

(e.2) made without notice, made on consent, that is unopposed or that is limited to procedural, uncomplicated or unopposed matters (Form 14B);

(e.3) made in an appeal;

(f) for an oral hearing under subrule 32.1(10), 37(8) or 37.1(8); or

(g) to set aside the registration of an interjurisdictional support order made outside Canada.

### Motion involving complicated matters

(7) The judge who hears a motion involving complicated matters may,

(a) order that the motion or any part of it be heard as a trial; and

(b) give any directions that are necessary.

### Motion by telephone or video conference

(8) A party who wants a motion to be heard by telephone or video conference shall,

(a) obtain an appointment from the clerk for the hearing of the motion;

(b) make the necessary arrangements;

(c) serve a notice of the appointment and arrangements on all other parties, and file it; and

(d) participate in the motion as the notice specifies.

### Documents for a motion

(9) A motion, whether made with or without notice,

(a) requires a notice of motion (Form 14) and an affidavit (Form 14A); and

(b) may be supported by additional evidence.

### Procedural, uncomplicated or unopposed matters—Motion form

(10) If a motion is limited to procedural, uncomplicated or unopposed matters, the party making the motion may use a motion form (Form 14B) instead of a notice of motion and affidavit.

### Response to motion form

(10.1) If a party uses a motion form (Form 14B) and no person served with the motion form serves and files a response within four days after being served, the motion shall be dealt with by the court as an unopposed motion.

### Where no reply permitted

(10.2) A party who uses a motion form (Form 14B) and who is served with a response to it may not serve or file a reply.

### Motion with notice

(11) A party making a motion with notice shall,

(a) serve the documents mentioned in subrule (9) or (10) on all other parties, not later than four days before the motion date;

(b) file the documents as soon as possible after service, but not later than two days before the motion date; and

(c) file a confirmation (Form 14C) not later than 2 p.m. two days before the motion date.

### No late documents

(11.1) No documents for use on the motion may be served or filed after 2 p.m. two days before the motion date.

### Motion without notice

(12) A motion may be made without notice if,

(a) the nature or circumstances of the motion make notice unnecessary or not reasonably possible;

(b) there is an immediate danger of a child's removal from Ontario, and the delay involved in serving a notice of motion would probably have serious consequences;

(c) there is an immediate danger to the health or safety of a child or of the party making the motion, and the delay involved in serving a notice of motion would probably have serious consequences; or

(d) service of a notice of motion would probably have serious consequences.

### Filing for motion without notice

(13) The documents for use on a motion without notice shall be filed on or before the motion date, unless the court orders otherwise.

### Order made on motion without notice

(14) An order made on motion without notice (Form 14D) shall require the matter to come back to the court and, if possible, to the same judge, within 14 days or on a date chosen by the court.

### Service of order made without notice

(15) An order made on motion without notice shall be served immediately on all parties affected, together with all documents used on the motion, unless the court orders otherwise.

### Withdrawing a motion

(16) A party making a motion may withdraw it in the same way as an application or answer is withdrawn under rule 12.

### Evidence on a motion

(17) Evidence on a motion may be given by any one or more of the following methods:

1. An affidavit or other admissible evidence in writing.
2. A transcript of the questions and answers on a questioning under rule 20.
3. With the court's permission, oral evidence.

### Affidavit based on personal knowledge

(18) An affidavit for use on a motion shall, as much as possible, contain only information within the personal knowledge of the person signing the affidavit.

### Affidavit based on other information

(19) The affidavit may also contain information that the person learned from someone else, but only if,

(a) the source of the information is identified by name and the affidavit states that the person signing it believes the information is true; and

(b) in addition, if the motion is a contempt motion under rule 31, the information is not likely to be disputed.

### Restrictions on evidence

(20) The following restrictions apply to evidence for use on a motion, unless the court orders otherwise:

1. The party making the motion shall serve all the evidence in support of the motion with the notice of motion.
2. The party responding to the motion shall then serve all the evidence in response.
3. The party making the motion may then serve evidence replying to any new matters raised by the evidence served by the party responding to the motion.
4. No other evidence may be used.

### No motions without court's permission

(21) If a party tries to delay the case or add to its costs or in any other way to abuse the court's process by making numerous motions without merit, the court may order the party not to make any other motions in the case without the court's permission.

(22), (23) Revoked.

### Motion relating to family arbitration

(24) A party who wishes to make a claim under the *Arbitration Act, 1991* or the *Family Law Act* relating to a family arbitration, family arbitration agreement or family arbitration award that must or may be commenced by way of a motion may do so under this rule, even if the order being sought is a final order and, for the purpose, this rule applies with the following and any other necessary changes:

1. In addition to the documents referred to in subrule (9) or (10), the motion also requires,

    i. copies of the certificates of independent legal advice required by the *Family Law Act* for the parties,

    ii. a copy of the family arbitration agreement, and

    iii. if an award has been made, the original award or a certified copy.

2. The documents referred to in subparagraphs 1 i, ii and iii shall be served and filed in accordance with subrule (11).

3. In the case of a motion to enforce a family arbitration award under section 59.8 of the *Family Law Act*, subrules (12) to (15) do not apply.

## RULE 15: MOTIONS TO CHANGE A FINAL ORDER OR AGREEMENT

### Definition

**15.** (1) In this rule,

"assignee" means an agency or person to whom a support order or agreement that is the subject of a motion under this rule is assigned under the *Family Law Act* or the *Divorce Act* (Canada).

### Application

(2) Subject to subrule (3), this rule only applies to a motion to change,

(a) a final order; or

(b) an agreement for support filed under section 35 of the *Family Law Act*.

### Same, notice of recalculation

(2.1) Subrule (2) applies regardless of whether a child support obligation set out in the order or agreement has been recalculated under section 39.1 of the Family Law Act.

### Exception

(3) This rule does not apply to a motion or application to change an order made under the *Child and Family Services Act*, other than a final order made under section 57.1 of that Act.

### Place of motion

(4) Rule 5 (where a case starts) applies to a motion to change a final order or agreement as if the motion were a new case.

### Motion to change

(5) Subject to subrules (17) and (18), a party who wants to ask the court to change a final order or agreement shall serve and file,

(a) a motion to change (Form 15); and

(b) a change information form (Form 15A), with all required attachments.

### Claim for custody or access

(5.1) If the motion includes a claim for custody of or access to a child, the documents referred to in subrule (5) shall be accompanied by the applicable documents referred to in rule 35.1.

### Service to include blank forms

(6) The party making the motion shall serve on the other party a blank response to motion to change (Form 15B) and a blank consent motion to change (Form 15C) together with the documents referred to in subrule (5).

### Special service

(7) The documents referred to in subrules (5), (5.1) and (6) shall be served by special service (subrule 6(3)), and not by regular service.

### Exception

(8) Despite subrule (7), service on the persons mentioned in subrule 8(6) (officials, agencies, etc.) may be made by regular service.

### Service on family responsibility office required

(8.1) The documents referred to in subrule (5) shall be served on the Director of the Family Responsibility Office if the motion to change includes a request to change a child support obligation that,

(a) is set out in an order made under the *Divorce Act* (Canada); and

(b) was recalculated under section 39.1 of the *Family Law Act* within the 35-day period before the motion is filed.

### Response or consent to motion

(9) The following rules apply to a party who is served with a motion to change a final order or agreement:

1. If the party does not agree to the change or if the party wants to ask the court to make an additional or a different change to the final order or agreement, the party shall serve and file a response to motion to change (Form 15B), with all required attachments, within the time set out in clause (10)(a) or (b), as the case may be.

2. If the party agrees to the change or if the parties agree to a different change, the party shall complete the applicable portions of the consent motion to change (Form 15C) and shall, within the time set out in clause (10)(a) or (b), as the case may be,

   i. return a signed copy of the consent motion to change to the party making the motion, and

   ii. provide a copy of the signed consent motion to change to the assignee, if any.

### Same

(10) The documents referred to in paragraphs 1 and 2 of subrule (9) shall be served and filed or returned and provided,

(a) no later than 30 days after the party responding to the motion receives the motion to change and the supporting documents, if that party resides in Canada or the United States of America; or

(b) no later than 60 days after the party responding to the motion receives the motion to change and the supporting documents, in any other case.

### Service on assignee required

(11) In a motion to change a final order or agreement that has been assigned to an assignee, a party shall, in serving documents under subrule (5) or paragraph 1 of subrule (9), serve the documents on the assignee as if the assignee were also a party.

### Assignee may become party

(12) On serving and filing a notice claiming a financial interest in the motion, an assignee becomes a respondent to the extent of the financial interest.

### Sanctions if assignee not served

(13) If an assignee is not served as required by subrule (11), the following rules apply:

1. The court may at any time, on motion by the assignee with notice to the other parties, set aside the changed order to the extent that it affects the assignee's financial interest.

2. The party who asked for the change has the burden of proving that the changed order should not be set aside.

3. If the changed order is set aside, the assignee is entitled to full recovery of its costs of the motion to set aside, unless the court orders otherwise.

## No response or consent

(14) The consequences set out in paragraphs 1 to 4 of subrule 1(8.4) apply, with necessary changes, if a party does not serve and file a response to motion to change (Form 15B) or return a consent motion to change (Form 15C) to the party making the motion as required under subrule (9).

## Request for order

(15) If a party does not serve and file a response to motion to change (Form 15B) or return a consent motion to change (Form 15C) to the party making the motion as required under subrule (9), or if the party's response is struck out by an order, the party making the motion to change may file a motion form (Form 14B) asking that the court make the order requested in the materials filed by the party, unless an assignee has filed a notice of financial interest in the motion and opposes the change.

## Consent to motion

(16) If a party returns to the party making the motion a consent motion to change (Form 15C) in accordance with subparagraph 2 i of subrule (9), the party making the motion shall complete and file the consent motion to change and, unless any assignee refuses to consent to the change being requested, the party making the motion shall file with the consent motion to change,

(a) a motion form (Form 14B) asking that the court make the order described in the consent motion to change;

(b) five copies of a draft order;

(c) a stamped envelope addressed to each party and to the assignee, if any; and

(d) if the order that is agreed on relates in whole or in part to a support obligation,

(i) a support deduction order information form prescribed under the *Family Responsibility and Support Arrears Enforcement Act, 1996*, and

(ii) a draft support deduction order.

## Motion to change on consent

(17) Subject to subrule (18), if the parties to a final order or agreement want to ask the court to change the final order or agreement and the parties and any assignee agree to the change, the parties shall file,

(a) a change information form (Form 15A), with all required attachments;

(b) a consent motion to change (Form 15C);

(c) a motion form (Form 14B) asking that the court make the order described in the consent motion to change;

(d) five copies of a draft order;

(e) a stamped envelope addressed to each party and to the assignee, if any; and

(f) if the order that is agreed on relates in whole or in part to a support obligation,

(i) a support deduction order information form prescribed under the *Family Responsibility and Support Arrears Enforcement Act, 1996*, and

(ii) a draft support deduction order.

## Motion to change on consent—Child support only

(18) If the parties to a final order or agreement want to ask the court to change the final order or agreement in relation only to a child support obligation, and the parties and any assignee agree to the change, the parties shall file,

(a) a consent motion to change child support (Form 15D), with all required attachments;

(b) five copies of a draft order;

(c) a stamped envelope addressed to each party and to the assignee, if any;

(d) a support deduction order information form prescribed under the *Family Responsibility and Support Arrears Enforcement Act, 1996*; and

(e) a draft support deduction order.

## Consent after response filed

(19) If, at any time after a party has served and filed a response under paragraph 1 of subrule (9) and before the motion to change is heard, the parties and any assignee agree to an order that changes the final order or agreement that is the subject of the motion, the parties may proceed on consent by filing,

(a) a consent motion to change (Form 15C);

(b) a motion form (Form 14B) asking that the court make the order described in the consent motion to change;

(c) five copies of a draft order;

(d) a stamped envelope addressed to each party and to the assignee, if any; and

(e) if the order that is agreed on relates in whole or in part to a support obligation,

(i) a support deduction order information form prescribed under the *Family Responsibility and Support Arrears Enforcement Act, 1996*, and

(ii) a draft support deduction order.

## Order, agreement to be attached

(20) A copy of any existing order or agreement that deals with custody, access or support shall be attached to every change information form (Form 15A) or consent motion to change child support (Form 15D).

## Change not in accordance with child support guidelines

(21) Unless a motion to change a child support order or agreement is proceeding on the consent of the parties and any assignee, if a party asks that an order be made under this rule that is not in accordance with the tables in the applicable child support guidelines, the support recipient and the support payor shall each serve and file the evidence required by the

following sections of the applicable child support guidelines, or the evidence that is otherwise necessary to satisfy the court that it should make the order asked for:

1. Section 4 (income over $150,000).
2. Section 5 (step-parent).
3. Section 7 (special expenses).
4. Section 8 (split custody).
5. Section 9 (shared custody).
6. Section 10 (undue hardship).
7. Section 21 (income and financial information), subject to subrule (21.1).

### Financial disclosure

(21.1) Subrule (21) does not require that any documents already served on the other party under subrule 13 (5.0.1) be served again, but any such documents are required to be filed.

### Affidavit may be filed

(22) A party or parties who want to ask the court to change a final order or agreement may, instead of using a change information form (Form 15A), use an affidavit containing evidence necessary to satisfy the court that it should make the order asked for and, in that case, these rules apply to the affidavit as if it were a change information form.

### Same

(23) A party who responds to a motion to change a final order or agreement by serving and filing a response to motion to change (Form 15B) may use an affidavit to provide evidence supporting his or her position instead of relying on the relevant portions of the form to provide the evidence or in addition to those portions of the form and, in that case, the affidavit is deemed to be part of the form.

### Requirements for affidavit

(24) Subrules 14(18) and (19) apply with necessary changes to an affidavit provided in accordance with subrule (22) or (23).

### Powers of court—Motion on consent or unopposed

(25) If a motion to change a final order or agreement proceeds on the consent of the parties and any assignee or is unopposed, the clerk shall present the filed materials to a judge and the judge may,

(a) make the order asked for;

(b) require one or both parties to file further material; or

(c) require one or both parties to come to court.

### Powers of court—Directions

(26) If the court is of the opinion that a motion, whether proceeding on consent or not, cannot be properly dealt with because of the material filed, because of the matters in dispute or for any other reason, the court may give directions, including directions for a trial.

### Application of subrule 14(21)

(27) Subrule 14(21) applies with necessary changes to a motion to change a final order or agreement.

### Motion under rule 14

(28) A motion under rule 14 may be made on a motion to change a final order or agreement.

### Access to listed documents

(29) Subrule 19(2) (access to listed documents) applies with necessary changes to a document mentioned in a form or affidavit used under this rule.

## RULE 16: SUMMARY JUDGMENT

### When available

16. (1) After the respondent has served an answer or after the time for serving an answer has expired, a party may make a motion for summary judgment for a final order without a trial on all or part of any claim made or any defence presented in the case.

### Available in any case except divorce

(2) A motion for summary judgment under subrule (1) may be made in any case (including a child protection case) that does not include a divorce claim.

### Divorce claim

(3) In a case that includes a divorce claim, the procedure provided in rule 36 (divorce) for an uncontested divorce may be used, or the divorce claim may be split from the rest of the case under subrule 12(6).

### Evidence required

(4) The party making the motion shall serve an affidavit or other evidence that sets out specific facts showing that there is no genuine issue requiring a trial.

### Evidence of responding party

(4.1) In response to the affidavit or other evidence served by the party making the motion, the party responding to the motion may not rest on mere allegations or denials but shall set out, in an affidavit or other evidence, specific facts showing that there is a genuine issue for trial.

### Evidence not from personal knowledge

(5) If a party's evidence is not from a person who has personal knowledge of the facts in dispute, the court may draw conclusions unfavourable to the party.

### No genuine issue for trial

(6) If there is no genuine issue requiring a trial of a claim or defence, the court shall make a final order accordingly.

### Powers

(6.1) In determining whether there is a genuine issue requiring a trial, the court shall consider the evidence submitted by the parties, and the court may exercise any of the following powers for the purpose, unless it is in the interest of justice for such powers to be exercised only at a trial:

1. Weighing the evidence.
2. Evaluating the credibility of a deponent.
3. Drawing any reasonable inference from the evidence. O. Reg. 69/15, s. 5 (1).

### Oral evidence (mini-trial)

(6.2) The court may, for the purposes of exercising any of the powers set out in subrule (6.1), order that oral evidence be presented by one or more parties, with or without time limits on its presentation.

### Only issue amount of entitlement

(7) If the only genuine issue is the amount to which a party is entitled, the court shall order a trial to decide the amount.

### Only issue question of law

(8) If the only genuine issue is a question of law, the court shall decide the issue and make a final order accordingly.

### Order giving directions

(9) If the court does not make a final order, or makes an order for a trial of an issue, the court may, in addition to exercising a power listed in subrule 1(7.2),

(a) specify what facts are not in dispute, state the issues and give directions about how and when the case will go to trial (in which case the order governs how the trial proceeds, unless the trial judge orders otherwise to prevent injustice);

(b) give directions; and

(c) impose conditions (for example, require a party to pay money into court as security, or limit a party's pretrial disclosure).

(10), (11) Revoked.

### Motion for summary decision on legal issue

(12) The court may, on motion,

(a) decide a question of law before trial, if the decision may dispose of all or part of the case, substantially shorten the trial or save substantial costs;

(b) strike out an application, answer or reply because it sets out no reasonable claim or defence in law; or

(c) dismiss or suspend a case because,

(i) the court has no jurisdiction over it,

(ii) a party has no legal capacity to carry on the case,

(iii) there is another case going on between the same parties about the same matter, or

(iv) the case is a waste of time, a nuisance or an abuse of the court process.

### Evidence on motion for summary decision of legal issue

(13) On a motion under subrule (12), evidence is admissible only if the parties consent or the court gives permission.

## RULE 17: CONFERENCES

### Conferences in defended cases

**17.** (1) Subject to subrule (1.1), in each case in which an answer is filed, a judge shall conduct at least one conference.

### Exception, case conference optional in child protection case

(1.1) In a child protection case, a case conference may be conducted if,

(a) a party requests it; or

(b) the court considers it appropriate.

### Undefended cases

(2) If no answer is filed,

(a) the clerk shall, on request, schedule a case conference or set a date for an uncontested trial or, in an uncontested divorce case, prepare the documents for a judge; and

(b) a settlement conference or trial management conference shall be conducted only if the court orders it.

### Motions to change final order or agreement

(3) Subrule (1) applies, with necessary changes, to a motion to change a final order or agreement under rule 15, unless the motion is proceeding on the consent of the parties and any assignee or is unopposed.

### Purposes of case conference

(4) The purposes of a case conference include,

(a) exploring the chances of settling the case;

(b) identifying the issues that are in dispute and those that are not in dispute;

(c) exploring ways to resolve the issues that are in dispute;

(d) ensuring disclosure of the relevant evidence;

(d.1) identifying any issues relating to any expert evidence or reports on which the parties intend to rely at trial;

(e) noting admissions that may simplify the case;

(f) setting the date for the next step in the case;

(g) setting a specific timetable for the steps to be taken in the case before it comes to trial;

(h) organizing a settlement conference, or holding one if appropriate; and

(i) giving directions with respect to any intended motion, including the preparation of a specific timetable for the exchange of material for the motion and ordering the filing of summaries of argument, if appropriate.

### Case conference notice

(4.1) A party who asks for a case conference shall serve and file a case conference notice (Form 17).

### Purposes of settlement conference

(5) The purposes of a settlement conference include,

(a) exploring the chances of settling the case;

(b) settling or narrowing the issues in dispute;

(c) ensuring disclosure of the relevant evidence;

(c.1) settling or narrowing any issues relating to any expert evidence or reports on which the parties intend to rely at trial;

(d) noting admissions that may simplify the case;

(e) if possible, obtaining a view of how the court might decide the case;

(f) considering any other matter that may help in a quick and just conclusion of the case;

(g) if the case is not settled, identifying the witnesses and other evidence to be presented at trial, estimating the time needed for trial and scheduling the case for trial; and

(h) organizing a trial management conference, or holding one if appropriate.

### Purposes of trial management conference

(6) The purposes of a trial management conference include,

(a) exploring the chances of settling the case;

(b) arranging to receive evidence by a written report, an agreed statement of facts, an affidavit or another method, if appropriate;

(c) deciding how the trial will proceed;

(c.1) exploring the use of expert evidence or reports at trial, including the timing requirements for service and filing of experts' reports;

(d) ensuring that the parties know what witnesses will testify and what other evidence will be presented at trial;

(e) estimating the time needed for trial; and

(f) setting the trial date, if this has not already been done.

### Combined conference

(7) At any time on the direction of a judge, part or all of a case conference, settlement conference and trial management conference may be combined.

### Orders at conference

(8) At a case conference, settlement conference or trial management conference the judge may, if it is appropriate to do so,

(a) make an order for document disclosure (rule 19), questioning (rule 20) or filing of summaries of argument on a motion, set the times for events in the case or give directions for the next step or steps in the case;

(a.0.1) make an order respecting the use of expert witness evidence at trial or the service and filing of experts' reports;

(a.1) make an order requiring the parties to file a trial management endorsement or trial scheduling endorsement in a form determined by the court;

(b) make an order requiring one or more parties to attend,

(i) a mandatory information program,

(ii) a case conference or settlement conference conducted by a person named under subrule (9),

(iii) an intake meeting with a court-affiliated mediation service, or

(iv) a program offered through any other available community service or resource;

(b.1) if notice has been served, make a final order or any temporary order, including any of the following temporary orders to facilitate the preservation of the rights of the parties until a further agreement or order is made:

(i) an order relating to the designation of beneficiaries under a policy of life insurance, registered retirement savings plan, trust, pension, annuity or a similar financial instrument,

(ii) an order preserving assets generally or particularly,

(iii) an order prohibiting the concealment or destruction of documents or property,

(iv) an order requiring an accounting of funds under the control of one of the parties,

(v) an order preserving the health and medical insurance coverage for one of the parties and the children of the relationship, and

(vi) an order continuing the payment of periodic amounts required to preserve an asset or a benefit to one of the parties and the children;

(c) make an unopposed order or an order on consent; and

(d) on consent, refer any issue for alternative dispute resolution.

### Conferences with a non-judge

(9) A case conference or settlement conference may be conducted by a person referred to in subrule (9.1) who has been named by the appropriate regional senior judge, unless a party requests a conference with a judge.

### Same

(9.1) For the purposes of subrule (9), the following persons may conduct a conference:

1. A person who is licensed under the *Law Society Act* to practice law in Ontario as a barrister and solicitor and whose licence is not suspended, if he or she has at least 10 years experience in the practice of family law.

2. A person who was licensed under the *Law Society Act* to practice law in Ontario as a barrister and solicitor but who has since retired, if, at the time of retirement,

   i. his or her license was not suspended, and
   ii. he or she had at least 10 years experience in the practice of family law.

3. A master or retired master of the Superior Court of Justice.

4. A retired judge of the Superior Court of Justice.

### Settlement conference with judge before case set for trial

(10) A case shall not be scheduled for trial unless,

(a) a judge has conducted a settlement conference; or

(b) a judge has ordered that the case be scheduled for trial.

(11) Revoked.

### When conferences optional

(12) A case conference, settlement conference or trial management conference is not required, but may be held at a party's request or on a judge's direction in the following circumstances:

1. In an enforcement.
2. In a request to enforce a family arbitration award under rule 32.1.

### Parties to serve briefs

(13) For each conference, each party shall serve and file a case conference brief (Form 17A or Form 17B), settlement conference brief (Form 17C or Form 17D) or trial management conference brief (Form 17E), as appropriate.

### Case conference brief in child protection case

(13.0.1) In a child protection case, a case conference brief shall be served and filed only if a case conference is being held under subrule (1.1).

### Time for service of briefs

(13.1) The party requesting the conference (or, if the conference is not requested by a party, the applicant or party making the motion) shall serve and file a brief not later than seven days before the date scheduled for the conference and the other party shall do so not later than four days before that date.

### Parties to confirm attendance

(14) Not later than 2 p.m. two days before the date scheduled for the conference, each party shall file a confirmation (Form 14C).

### No late briefs

(14.1) No brief or other document for use at the conference that is required to be served or filed may be served or filed after 2 p.m. two days before the date scheduled for the conference.

### Requirement to bring documents to settlement conference

(14.2) The following documents shall be brought to a settlement conference:

1. Any document that supports a party's position in respect of a dispute regarding the value of property or regarding the amount of a debt, in the case of a property claim under Part I of the *Family Law Act*.

2. Any document required to be served under rule 13 (financial disclosure), if there is a dispute as to whether it was served.

### Parties and lawyers to come to conference

(15) The following shall come to each conference:

1. The parties, unless the court orders otherwise.
2. For each represented party, the lawyer with full knowledge of and authority in the case.

### Participation by telephone or video conference

(16) With permission obtained in advance from the judge who is to conduct a conference, a party or lawyer may participate in the conference by telephone or video conference.

### Setting up telephone or video conference

(17) A party or lawyer who has permission to participate by telephone or video conference shall,

(a) make the necessary arrangements;

(b) serve a notice of the arrangements on all other parties and file it; and

(c) participate in the conference as the notice specifies.

### Costs of adjourned conference

(18) If a conference is adjourned because a party is not prepared, has not served the required brief, has not made the required disclosure has otherwise contributed to the conference being unproductive or has otherwise not followed these rules, the judge shall,

(a) order the party to pay the costs of the conference immediately;

(b) decide the amount of the costs; and

(c) give any directions that are needed.

### Conference agreement

(19) No agreement reached at a conference is effective until it is signed by the parties, witnessed and, in a case involving a special party, approved by the court.

### Agreement filed in continuing record

(20) The agreement shall be filed as part of the continuing record, unless the court orders otherwise.

### Continuing record, trial management conference briefs

(21) Trial management conference briefs form part of the continuing record.

### Continuing record, case conference briefs

(22) Case conference briefs do not form part of the continuing record unless the court orders otherwise and shall be returned at the end of the conference to the parties who filed them or be destroyed by court staff immediately after the conference.

### Deletions from case conference brief included in record

(22.1)  If the court orders that a case conference brief form part of the continuing record, that portion of the brief that deals with settlement of the case shall be deleted.

### Continuing record, settlement conference briefs

(22.2)  Settlement conference briefs do not form part of the continuing record and shall be returned at the end of the conference to the parties who filed them or be destroyed by the court staff immediately after the conference.

### Confidentiality of settlement conference

(23)  No brief or evidence prepared for a settlement conference and no statement made at a settlement conference shall be disclosed to any other judge, except in,

(a)  an agreement reached at a settlement conference; or

(b)  an order.

### Settlement conference judge cannot hear issue

(24)  A judge who conducts a settlement conference about an issue shall not hear the issue, except as subrule (25) provides.

### Exception, child protection case

(25)  In a child protection case, if a finding that the child is in need of protection is made without a trial and a trial is needed to determine which order should be made under section 57 of the *Child and Family Services Act*, any judge who has not conducted a settlement conference on that issue may conduct the trial.

## RULE 18: OFFERS TO SETTLE

### Definition

**18.** (1)  In this rule,

"offer" means an offer to settle one or more claims in a case, motion, appeal or enforcement, and includes a counter-offer.

### Application

(2)  This rule applies to an offer made at any time, even before the case is started.

### Making an offer

(3)  A party may serve an offer on any other party.

### Offer to be signed by party and lawyer

(4)  An offer shall be signed personally by the party making it and also by the party's lawyer, if any.

### Withdrawing an offer

(5)  A party who made an offer may withdraw it by serving a notice of withdrawal, at any time before the offer is accepted.

### Time-limited offer

(6)  An offer that is not accepted within the time set out in the offer is considered to have been withdrawn.

### Offer expires when court begins to give decision

(7)  An offer may not be accepted after the court begins to give a decision that disposes of a claim dealt with in the offer.

### Confidentiality of offer

(8)  The terms of an offer,

(a)  shall not be mentioned in any document filed in the continuing record; and

(b)  shall not be mentioned to the judge hearing the claim dealt with in the offer, until the judge has dealt with all the issues in dispute except costs.

### Accepting an offer

(9)  The only valid way of accepting an offer is by serving an acceptance on the party who made the offer, at any time before,

(a)  the offer is withdrawn; or

(b)  the court begins to give a decision that disposes of a claim dealt with in the offer.

### Offer remains open despite rejection or counter-offer

(10)  A party may accept an offer in accordance with sub-rule (9) even if the party has previously rejected the offer or made a counter-offer.

### Costs not dealt with in offer

(11)  If an accepted offer does not deal with costs, either party is entitled to ask the court for costs.

### Court approval, offer involving special party

(12)  A special party may make, withdraw and accept an offer, but another party's acceptance of a special party's offer and a special party's acceptance of another party's offer are not binding on the special party until the court approves.

### Failure to carry out terms of accepted offer

(13)  If a party to an accepted offer does not carry out the terms of the offer, the other party may,

(a)  make a motion to turn the parts of the offer within the court's jurisdiction into an order; or

(b)  continue the case as if the offer had never been accepted.

### Costs consequences of failure to accept offer

(14)  A party who makes an offer is, unless the court orders otherwise, entitled to costs to the date the offer was served and full recovery of costs from that date, if the following conditions are met:

1.  If the offer relates to a motion, it is made at least one day before the motion date.
2.  If the offer relates to a trial or the hearing of a step other than a motion, it is made at least seven days before the trial or hearing date.
3.  The offer does not expire and is not withdrawn before the hearing starts.

4. The offer is not accepted.

5. The party who made the offer obtains an order that is as favourable as or more favourable than the offer.

## Costs consequences—Burden of proof

(15) The burden of proving that the order is as favourable as or more favourable than the offer to settle is on the party who claims the benefit of subrule (14).

## Costs—Discretion of court

(16) When the court exercises its discretion over costs, it may take into account any written offer to settle, the date it was made and its terms, even if subrule (14) does not apply.

## RULE 19: DOCUMENT DISCLOSURE

### Affidavit listing documents

**19.** (1) Subject to subrule (1.1), every party shall, within 10 days after another party's request, give the other party an affidavit listing every document that is,

(a) relevant to any issue in the case; and

(b) in the party's control, or available to the party on request.

### Exceptions

(1.1) Subrule (1) does not apply,

(a) to the Office of the Children's Lawyer or to children's aid societies; and

(b) in respect of documents required to be served under rule 13 (financial disclosure).

### Access to listed documents

(2) The other party is entitled, on request,

(a) to examine any document listed in the affidavit, unless it is protected by a legal privilege; and

(b) to receive, at the party's own expense at the legal aid rate, a copy of any document that the party is entitled to examine under clause (a).

### Access to documents mentioned in court papers

(3) Subrule (2) also applies, with necessary changes, to a document mentioned in a party's application, answer, reply, notice of motion or affidavit.

### Documents protected by legal privilege

(4) If a party claims that a document is protected by a legal privilege, the court may, on motion, examine it and decide the issue.

### Use of privileged documents

(5) A party who claims that a document is protected by a legal privilege may use it at trial only,

(a) if the other party has been allowed to examine the document and been supplied with a copy, free of charge, at least 30 days before the settlement conference; or

(b) on the conditions the trial judge considers appropriate, including an adjournment if necessary.

### Documents of subsidiary or affiliated corporation

(6) The court may, on motion, despite clause 1(7.2)(a), order a party to give another party an affidavit listing the documents that are,

(a) relevant to any issue in the case; and

(b) in the control of, or available on request to a corporation that is controlled, directly or indirectly, by the party or by another corporation that the party controls directly or indirectly.

### Documents of Office of the Children's Lawyer or children's aid society

(6.1) The court may, on motion, despite clause 1(7.2)(a), order the Office of the Children's Lawyer or a children's aid society to give another party an affidavit listing the documents that are,

(a) relevant to any issue in the case; and

(b) in the control of, or available on request to, the Office of the Children's Lawyer or the children's aid society.

### Access to listed documents

(7) Subrule (2) also applies, with necessary changes, to any document listed in an affidavit ordered under subrule (6) or (6.1).

### Documents omitted from affidavit or found later

(8) A party who, after serving an affidavit required under subrule (1), (6) or (6.1), finds a document that should have been listed in it, or finds that the list is not correct or not complete, shall immediately serve on the other party a new affidavit listing the correct information.

### Access to additional documents

(9) The other party is entitled, on request,

(a) to examine any document listed in an affidavit served under subrule (8), unless it is protected by a legal privilege; and

(b) to receive, free of charge, a copy of any document that the party is entitled to examine under clause (a).

### Failure to follow rule 19 or obey order

(10) If a party does not follow this rule or obey an order made under this rule, the court may, in addition to any power to make an order under subrule 1(8) or (8.1),

(a) order the party to give another party an affidavit, let the other party examine a document or supply the other party with a copy free of charge;

(b) order that a document favourable to the party's case may not be used except with the court's permission; or

(c) order that the party is not entitled to obtain disclosure under these rules until the party follows the rule or obeys the order.

### Document in non-party's control

(11) If a document is in a non-party's control, or is available only to the non-party, and is not protected by a legal

privilege, and it would be unfair to a party to go on with the case without the document, the court may, on motion with notice served on every party and served on the non-party by special service,

(a) order the non-party to let the party examine the document and to supply the party with a copy at the legal aid rate; and

(b) order that a copy be prepared and used for all purposes of the case instead of the original.

## RULE 20: QUESTIONING A WITNESS AND DISCLOSURE

### Questioning—Procedure

**20.** (1) Questioning under this rule shall take place orally under oath or affirmation.

### Cross-examination

(2) The right to question a person includes the right to cross-examine.

### Child protection case—Available as of right

(3) In a child protection case, a party is entitled to obtain information from another party about any issue in the case,

(a) by questioning the other party, in which case the party shall serve the other party with a summons to witness (Form 23) by special service in accordance with subrule 6(4); or

(b) by affidavit or by another method, in which case the party shall serve the other party with a request for information (Form 20).

### Other cases—Consent or order

(4) In a case other than a child protection case, a party is entitled to obtain information from another party about any issue in the case,

(a) with the other party's consent; or

(b) by an order under subrule (5).

### Order for questioning or disclosure

(5) The court may, on motion, order that a person (whether a party or not) be questioned by a party or disclose information by affidavit or by another method about any issue in the case, if the following conditions are met:

1. It would be unfair to the party who wants the questioning or disclosure to carry on with the case without it.
2. The information is not easily available by any other method.
3. The questioning or disclosure will not cause unacceptable delay or undue expense.

### Questioning special party

(6) If a person to be questioned is a special party, the court may, on motion, order that someone else be questioned in addition to or in place of the person.

### Questioning about affidavit or net family property statement

(7) The court may make an order under subrule (5) that a person be questioned or disclose details about information in an affidavit or net family property statement.

### Questioning or disclosure—Preconditions

(8) A party who wants to question a person or obtain information by affidavit or by another method may do so only if the party,

(a) has served and filed any answer, financial statement or net family property statement that these rules require; and

(b) promises in writing not to serve or file any further material for the next step in the case, except in reply to the answers or information obtained.

### Notice and summons to non-party

(9) The court may make an order under this rule affecting a non-party only if the non-party has been served with the notice of motion, a summons to witness (Form 23) and the witness fee required by subrule 23(4), all by special service (subrules 6(3) and (4)).

### Penalty for failure to obey summons

(10) Subrule 23(7) (failure to obey summons to witness) applies, with necessary changes, if a person summoned under subrule (9) fails to obey the summons.

### Place of questioning

(11) The questioning shall take place in the municipality in which the person to be questioned lives, unless that person and the party who wants to do the questioning agree to hold it in another municipality.

### Other arrangements for questioning

(12) If the person to be questioned and the party who wants to do the questioning do not agree on one or more of the following matters, the court shall, on motion, make an order to decide the matter:

1. The date and time for the questioning.
2. The person responsible for recording the questioning.
3. The method for recording the questioning.
4. Payment of the expenses of the person to be questioned, if a non-party.

### Notice to parties

(13) The parties shall, not later than three days before the questioning, be served with notice of the name of the person to be questioned and the address, date and time of the questioning.

### Questioning person outside Ontario

(14) If a person to be questioned lives outside Ontario and will not come to Ontario for questioning, the court may decide,

(a) the date, time and place for the questioning;

(b) how much notice the person should be given;

(c) the person before whom the questioning will be held;

(d) the amount of the witness fee to be paid to the person to be questioned;

(e) the method for recording the questioning;

(f) where necessary, that the clerk shall issue,

(i) an authorization to a commissioner (Form 20A) who is to supervise the questioning outside Ontario, and

(ii) a letter of request (Form 20B) to the appropriate court or authorities outside Ontario, asking for their assistance in getting the person to be questioned to come before the commissioner; and

(g) any other related matter.

### Commissioner's duties

(15) A commissioner authorized under subrule (14) shall,

(a) supervise the questioning according to the terms of the court's authorization, these rules and Ontario's law of evidence, unless the law of the place where the questioning is to be held requires some other manner of questioning;

(b) make and keep a copy of the record of the questioning and, if possible, of the exhibits, if any;

(c) deliver the original record, any exhibits and the authorization to the clerk who issued it; and

(d) notify the party who asked for the questioning that the record has been delivered to the clerk.

### Order to bring documents or things

(16) An order for questioning and a summons to witness may also require the person to bring any document or thing that is,

(a) relevant to any issue in the case; and

(b) in the person's control or available to the person on request.

### Other rules apply

(17) Subrules 19(2), (4) and (5) (right to examine document and obtain copy, documents protected by legal privilege, use of privileged documents) apply, with necessary changes, to the documents mentioned in the order.

### Scope of questions

(18) Unless the court orders otherwise, a person to be questioned may be asked about,

(a) the names of persons who might reasonably be expected to know about the claims in the case and, with the court's permission, their addresses;

(b) the names of the witnesses whom a party intends to call at trial and, with the court's permission, their addresses;

(c) the names, addresses, findings, conclusions and opinions of expert witnesses whom a party intends to call or on whose reports the party intends to rely at trial;

(d) if it is relevant to the case, the existence and details of any insurance policy under which the insurance company may be required to pay all or part of an order for the payment of money in the case or to pay back to a party money that the party has paid under an order; and

(e) any other matter in dispute in the case.

### Refusal to answer question

(19) If a person being questioned refuses to answer a question,

(a) the court may, on motion,

(i) decide whether the question is proper,

(ii) give directions for the person's return to the questioning, and

(iii) make a contempt order against the person; and

(b) if the person is a party or is questioned on behalf or in place of a party, the party shall not use the information that was refused as evidence in the case, unless the court gives permission under subrule (20).

### Court's permission

(20) The court shall give permission unless the use of the information would cause harm to another party or an unacceptable delay in the trial, and may impose any appropriate conditions on the permission, including an adjournment if necessary.

### Duty to correct or update answers

(21) A person who has been questioned or who has provided information in writing by affidavit or by another method and who finds that an answer or information given was incorrect or incomplete, or is no longer correct or complete, shall immediately provide the correct and complete information in writing to all parties.

### Lawyer answering

(22) If there is no objection, questions may be answered by the lawyer for a person being questioned, and the answer shall be taken as the person's own answer unless the person corrects or changes it before the questioning ends.

### Method for recording questioning

(23) All the questions and answers at a questioning shall be recorded electronically or manually.

### Obligation to keep information confidential

(24) When a party obtains evidence under this rule, rule 13 (financial disclosure) or rule 19 (document disclosure), the party and the party's lawyer may use the evidence and any information obtained from it only for the purposes of the case in which the evidence was obtained, subject to the exceptions in subrule (25).

### Use of information permitted

(25) Evidence and any information obtained from it may be used for other purposes,

    (a) if the person who gave the evidence consents;

    (b) if the evidence is filed with the court, given at a hearing or referred to at a hearing;

    (c) to impeach the testimony of a witness in another case; or

    (d) in a later case between the same parties or their successors, if the case in which the evidence was obtained was withdrawn or dismissed.

### Court may lift obligation of confidentiality

(26) The court may, on motion, give a party permission to disclose evidence or information obtained from it if the interests of justice outweigh any harm that would result to the party who provided the evidence.

## RULE 20.1: EXPERTS

### Duty of expert

**20.1** (1) It is the duty of every expert who provides evidence in relation to a case under these rules,

    (a) to provide opinion evidence that is fair, objective and non-partisan;

    (b) to provide opinion evidence that is related only to matters that are within the expert's area of expertise; and

    (c) to provide such additional assistance as the court may reasonably require to determine a matter in issue.

### Duty prevails

(2) In the case of an expert engaged by or on behalf of a party, the duty in subrule (1) prevails over any obligation owed by the expert to that party.

### Court appointed experts

(3) The court may, on motion or on its own initiative, appoint one or more independent experts to inquire into and report on any question of fact or opinion relevant to an issue in a case.

### Expert to be named

(4) An order under subrule (3) appointing an expert shall name the expert and, where possible, the expert shall be a person agreed on by the parties.

### Instructions

(5) An order under subrule (3) appointing an expert shall contain the instructions to be given to the expert, and the court may make any further orders that it considers necessary to enable the expert to carry out the instructions.

### Fees and expenses

(6) The court shall require the parties to pay the fees and expenses of an expert appointed under subrule (3), and shall specify the proportions or amounts of the fees and expenses that each party is required to pay.

### Security

(7) If a motion by a party for the appointment of an expert under subrule (3) is opposed, the court may, as a condition of making the appointment, require the party seeking the appointment to give such security for the expert's fees and expenses as is just.

### Serious financial hardship

(8) The court may relieve a party from responsibility for payment of any of the expert's fees and expenses, if the court is satisfied that payment would cause serious financial hardship to the party.

### Report

(9) The expert shall prepare a report of the results of his or her inquiry, and shall,

    (a) file the report with the clerk of the court; and

    (b) provide a copy of the report to each of the parties.

### Content of report

(10) A report provided by an expert shall contain the following information:

1. The expert's name, address and area of expertise.
2. The expert's qualifications, including his or her employment and educational experiences in his or her area of expertise.
3. The instructions provided to the expert in relation to the proceeding.
4. The nature of the opinion being sought and each issue in the proceeding to which the opinion relates.
5. The expert's opinion respecting each issue and, where there is a range of opinions given, a summary of the range and the reasons for the expert's own opinion within that range.
6. The expert's reasons for his or her opinion, including,

    i. a description of the factual assumptions on which the opinion is based,

    ii. a description of any research conducted by the expert that led him or her to form the opinion, and

    iii. a list of every document relied on by the expert in forming the opinion.

7. An acknowledgement of expert's duty (Form 20.1) signed by the expert.

### Admissibility

(11) The expert's report is admissible in evidence in the case.

### Cross-examination

(12) Any party may cross-examine the expert at the trial.

**Non-application**

(13) For greater certainty, subrules (3) to (12) do not apply in respect of,

(a) appointments of persons by the court under subsection 54(1.2) of the *Child and Family Services Act* or subsection 30(1) of the *Children's Law Reform Act*; or

(b) requests by the court that the Children's Lawyer act under subsection 112(1) of the *Courts of Justice Act*.

## RULE 21: REPORT OF CHILDREN'S LAWYER

**Report of Children's Lawyer**

**21.** When the Children's Lawyer investigates and reports on custody of or access to a child under section 112 of the *Courts of Justice Act*,

(a) the Children's Lawyer shall first serve notice on the parties and file it;

(b) the parties shall, from the time they are served with the notice, serve the Children's Lawyer with every document in the case that involves the child's custody, access, support, health or education, as if the Children's Lawyer were a party in the case;

(c) the Children's Lawyer has the same rights as a party to document disclosure (rule 19) and questioning witnesses (rule 20) about any matter involving the child's custody, access, support, health or education;

(d) within 90 days after serving the notice under clause (a), the Children's Lawyer shall serve a report on the parties and file it;

(e) within 30 days after being served with the report, a party may serve and file a statement disputing anything in it; and

(f) the trial shall not be held and the court shall not make a final order in the case until the 30 days referred to in clause (e) expire or the parties file a statement giving up their right to that time.

## RULE 22: ADMISSION OF FACTS

**Meaning of admission that document genuine**

**22.** (1) An admission that a document is genuine is an admission,

(a) if the document is said to be an original, that it was written, signed or sealed as it appears to have been;

(b) if it is said to be a copy, that it is a complete and accurate copy; and

(c) if it is said to be a copy of a document that is ordinarily sent from one person to another (for example, a letter, fax or electronic message), that it was sent as it appears to have been sent and was received by the person to whom it is addressed.

**Request to admit**

(2) At any time, by serving a request to admit (Form 22) on another party, a party may ask the other party to admit, for purposes of the case only, that a fact is true or that a document is genuine.

**Copy of document to be attached**

(3) A copy of any document mentioned in the request to admit shall be attached to it, unless the other party already has a copy or it is impractical to attach a copy.

**Response required within 20 days**

(4) The party on whom the request to admit is served is considered to have admitted, for purposes of the case only, that the fact is true or that the document is genuine, unless the party serves a response (Form 22A) within 20 days,

(a) denying that a particular fact mentioned in the request is true or that a particular document mentioned in the request is genuine; or

(b) refusing to admit that a particular fact mentioned in the request is true or that a particular document mentioned in the request is genuine, and giving the reasons for each refusal.

**Withdrawing admission**

(5) An admission that a fact is true or that a document is genuine (whether contained in a document served in the case or resulting from subrule (4)), may be withdrawn only with the other party's consent or with the court's permission.

## RULE 23: EVIDENCE AND TRIAL

**Trial record**

**23.** (1) At least 30 days before the start of the trial, the applicant shall serve and file a trial record containing a table of contents and the following documents:

1. The application, answer and reply, if any.
2. Any agreed statement of facts.
3. If relevant to an issue at trial, financial statements and net family property statements by all parties, completed not more than 30 days before the record is served.
3.1 If the trial involves a claim for custody of or access to a child, the applicable documents referred to in rule 35.1.
4. Any assessment report ordered by the court or obtained by consent of the parties.
5. Any temporary order relating to a matter still in dispute.
6. Any order relating to the trial.
7. The relevant parts of any transcript on which the party intends to rely at trial.
8. Any evidence that is the subject of an order made under clause 1(7.2)(g).

**Respondent may add to trial record**

(2) Not later than seven days before the start of the trial, a respondent may serve, file and add to the trial record any document referred to in subrule (1) that is not already in the trial record.

## Summons to witness

(3) A party who wants a witness to give evidence in court or to be questioned and to bring documents or other things shall serve on the witness a summons to witness (Form 23) by special service in accordance with subrule 6(4), together with the witness fee set out in subrule (4).

## Witness fee

(4) A person summoned as a witness shall be paid, for each day that the person is needed in court or to be questioned,

(a) $50 for coming to court or to be questioned;

(b) travel money in the amount of,

(i) $5, if the person lives in the city or town where the person gives evidence,

(ii) 30 cents per kilometre each way, if the person lives elsewhere but within 300 kilometres of the court or place of questioning,

(iii) the cheapest available air fare plus $10 a day for airport parking and 30 cents per kilometre each way from the person's home to the airport and from the airport to the court or place of questioning, if the person lives 300 or more kilometres from the court or place of questioning; and

(c) $100 per night for meals and overnight stay, if the person does not live in the city or town where the trial is held and needs to stay overnight.

## Meaning of "city or town"

(4.1) For the purposes of subrule (4), a municipality shall be considered a city or town if it was a city or town on December 31, 2002.

## Continuing effect of summons

(5) A summons to witness remains in effect until it is no longer necessary to have the witness present.

## Summons for original document

(6) If a document can be proved by a certified copy, a party who wants a witness to bring the original shall not serve a summons on the witness for that purpose without the court's permission.

## Failure to obey summons

(7) The court may issue a warrant for arrest (Form 32B) to bring a witness before the court if,

(a) the witness has been served as subrule (3) requires, but has not obeyed the summons; and

(b) it is necessary to have the witness present in court or at a questioning.

## Interprovincial summons to witness

(8) A summons to a witness outside Ontario under the *Interprovincial Summonses Act* shall be in Form 23A.

## Setting aside summons to witness

(9) The court may, on motion, order that a summons to witness be set aside.

## Attendance of a prisoner

(10) If it is necessary to have a prisoner come to court or to be questioned, the court may order (Form 23B) the prisoner's custodian to deliver the prisoner on payment of the fee set out in the regulations under the *Administration of Justice Act*.

## Calling opposing party as witness

(11) A party may call the opposing party as a witness and may cross-examine the opposing party.

## Attendance of opposing party

(11.1) A party who wishes to call an opposing party as a witness may have the opposing party attend,

(a) by serving a summons under subrule (3) on the opposing party; or

(b) by serving on the opposing party's lawyer, at least 10 days before the start of the trial, a notice of intention to call the opposing party as a witness.

## Opposing party disobeying summons

(12) When an opposing party has been served with a summons under subrule (3), the court may make a final order in favour of the party calling the witness, adjourn the case or make any other appropriate order, including a contempt order, if the opposing party,

(a) does not come to or remain in court as required by the summons; or

(b) refuses to be sworn or to affirm, to answer any proper question or to bring any document or thing named in the summons.

## Reading opposing party's answers into evidence

(13) An answer or information given under rule 20 (questioning) by an opposing party may be read into evidence at trial if it is otherwise proper evidence, even if the opposing party has already testified at trial.

## Reading other person's answers into evidence

(14) Subrule (13) also applies, with necessary changes, to an answer or information given by a person questioned on behalf of or in place of an opposing party, unless the trial judge orders otherwise.

## Using answers—Special circumstances

(15) Subrule (13) is subject to the following:

1. If the answer or information is being read into evidence to show that a witness's testimony at trial is not to be believed, answers or information given by the witness earlier must be put to the witness as sections 20 and 21 of the *Evidence Act* require.

2. At the request of an opposing party, the trial judge may direct the party reading the answer or information into evidence to read in, as well, any other answer or information that qualifies or explains what the party has read into evidence.

3. A special party's answer or information may be read into evidence only with the trial judge's permission.

### Rebutting answers

(16) A party who has read answers or information into evidence at trial may introduce other evidence to rebut the answers or information.

### Using answers of witness not available for trial

(17) The trial judge may give a party permission to read into evidence all or part of the answers or information given under rule 20 (questioning) by a person who is unable or unwilling to testify at the trial, but before doing so the judge shall consider,

> (a) the importance of the evidence;
> (b) the general principle that trial evidence should be given orally in court;
> (c) the extent to which the person was cross-examined; and
> (d) any other relevant factor.

### Taking evidence before trial

(18) The court may order that a witness whose evidence is necessary at trial may give evidence before trial at a place and before a person named in the order, and then may accept the transcript as evidence.

### Taking evidence before trial outside Ontario

(19) If a witness whose evidence is necessary at trial lives outside Ontario, subrules 20(14) and (15) (questioning person outside Ontario, commissioner's duties) apply, with necessary changes.

### Evidence by affidavit, other method

(20) A party may request that the court make an order under clause 1 (7.2) (i) permitting the evidence of a witness to be heard by affidavit or another method not requiring the witness to attend in person.

(20.1) Revoked.

### Conditions for use of affidavit or other method

(21) Evidence at trial by affidavit or another method not requiring a witness to attend in person may be used only if,

> (a) the use is in accordance with an order under clause 1(7.2)(i);
> (b) the evidence is served at least 30 days before the start of the trial; and
> (c) the evidence would have been admissible if given by the witness in court.

### Affidavit evidence at uncontested trial

(22) At an uncontested trial, evidence by affidavit in Form 14A or Form 23C and, if applicable, Form 35.1 may be used without an order under clause 1(7.2)(i), unless the court directs that oral evidence must be given.

### Expert witness reports

(23) A party who wants to call an expert witness at trial shall serve on all other parties a report signed by the expert and containing the information listed in subrule (25),

> (a) at least 90 days before the start of the trial; or
> (b) in the case of a child protection case, at least 30 days before the start of the trial.

### Same, response

(24) A party who wants to call an expert witness at trial to respond to the expert witness of another party shall serve on all other parties a report signed by the expert and containing the information listed in subrule (25),

> (a) at least 60 days before the start of the trial; or
> (b) in the case of a child protection case, at least 14 days before the start of the trial.

### Same, contents

(25) A report provided for the purposes of subrule (1) or (2) shall contain the following information:

1. The expert's name, address and area of expertise.
2. The expert's qualifications and employment and educational experiences in his or her area of expertise.
3. The substance of the expert's proposed evidence.

### Supplementary report

(26) Any supplementary expert witness report shall be signed by the expert and served on all other parties,

> (a) at least 30 days before the start of the trial; or
> (b) in the case of a child protection case, at least 14 days before the start of the trial.

### Failure to serve expert witness report

(27) A party who has not followed a requirement under subrule (23), (24), or (26) to serve and file an expert witness report, may not call the expert witness unless the trial judge allows otherwise.

## RULE 24: COSTS

### Successful party presumed entitled to costs

**24.** (1) There is a presumption that a successful party is entitled to the costs of a motion, enforcement, case or appeal.

### No presumption in child protection case or if party is government agency

(2) The presumption does not apply in a child protection case or to a party that is a government agency.

### Court's discretion—Costs for or against government agency

(3) The court has discretion to award costs to or against a party that is a government agency, whether it is successful or unsuccessful.

### Successful party who has behaved unreasonably

(4) Despite subrule (1), a successful party who has behaved unreasonably during a case may be deprived of all or part of the party's own costs or ordered to pay all or part of the unsuccessful party's costs.

### Decision on reasonableness

(5) In deciding whether a party has behaved reasonably or unreasonably, the court shall examine,

(a) the party's behaviour in relation to the issues from the time they arose, including whether the party made an offer to settle;

(b) the reasonableness of any offer the party made; and

(c) any offer the party withdrew or failed to accept.

### Divided success

(6) If success in a step in a case is divided, the court may apportion costs as appropriate.

### Absent or unprepared party

(7) If a party does not appear at a step in the case, or appears but is not properly prepared to deal with the issues at that step or otherwise contributes to that step being unproductive, the court shall award costs against the party unless the court orders otherwise in the interests of justice.

### Bad faith

(8) If a party has acted in bad faith, the court shall decide costs on a full recovery basis and shall order the party to pay them immediately.

### Costs caused by fault of lawyer or agent

(9) If a party's lawyer or agent has run up costs without reasonable cause or has wasted costs, the court may, on motion or on its own initiative, after giving the lawyer or agent an opportunity to be heard,

(a) order that the lawyer or agent shall not charge the client fees or disbursements for work specified in the order, and order the lawyer or agent to repay money that the client has already paid toward costs;

(b) order the lawyer or agent to repay the client any costs that the client has been ordered to pay another party;

(c) order the lawyer or agent personally to pay the costs of any party; and

(d) order that a copy of an order under this subrule be given to the client.

### Deciding costs

(10) Promptly after Promptly after dealing with a step in the case, the court shall,

(a) make a decision on costs in relation to that step; or

(b) reserve the decision on costs for determination at a later stage in the case.

### Same

(10.1) In making a decision on costs in relation to a step in a case, the court shall decide in a summary manner whether anyone is entitled to costs and, if so, determine who is entitled and set the amount of the costs.

### Factors in costs

(11) In setting the amount of costs, the court shall consider,

(a) the importance, complexity or difficulty of the issues;

(b) the reasonableness or unreasonableness of each party's behaviour in the case;

(c) the lawyer's rates;

(d) the time properly spent on the case, including conversations between the lawyer and the party or witnesses, drafting documents and correspondence, attempts to settle, preparation, hearing, argument, and preparation and signature of the order;

(e) expenses properly paid or payable; and

(f) any other relevant matter.

### Payment of expenses

(12) The court may make an order that a party pay an amount of money to another party to cover part or all of the expenses of carrying on the case, including a lawyer's fees.

### Order for security for costs

(13) A judge may, on motion, make an order for security for costs that is just, based on one or more of the following factors:

1. A party ordinarily resides outside Ontario.
2. A party has an order against the other party for costs that remains unpaid, in the same case or another case.
3. A party is a corporation and there is good reason to believe it does not have enough assets in Ontario to pay costs.
4. There is good reason to believe that the case is a waste of time or a nuisance and that the party does not have enough assets in Ontario to pay costs.
5. A statute entitles the party to security for costs.

### Amount and form of security

(14) The judge shall determine the amount of the security, its form and the method of giving it.

### Effect of order for security

(15) Until the security has been given, a party against whom there is an order for security for costs may not take any step in the case, except to appeal from the order, unless a judge orders otherwise.

### Failure to give security

(16) If the party does not give the security as ordered and, as a result, a judge makes an order dismissing the party's case or striking out the party's answer or any other document filed by the party, then subrule (15) no longer applies.

### Security may be changed

(17) The amount of the security, its form and the method of giving it may be changed by order at any time.

## RULE 25: ORDERS

### Consent order

**25.** (1) If the parties agree, the court may make an order under these rules or an Act without having the parties or their lawyers come to court.

### Successful party prepares draft order

(2) The party in whose favour an order is made shall prepare a draft of the order (Form 25, 25A, 25B, 25C or 25D), unless the court orders otherwise.

### Other party may prepare draft order

(3) If the party in whose favour an order is made does not have a lawyer or does not prepare a draft order within 10 days after the order is made, any other party may prepare the draft order, unless the court orders otherwise.

### Approval of draft order

(4) A party who prepares an order shall serve a draft, for approval of its form and content, on every other party who was in court or was represented when the order was made (including a child who has a lawyer).

### Settling contents of disputed order

(5) Unless the court orders otherwise, a party who disagrees with the form or content of a draft order shall serve, on every party who was served under subrule (4) and on the party who served the draft order,

(a) a notice disputing approval (Form 25E);

(b) a copy of the order, redrafted as proposed; and

(c) notice of a time and date at which the clerk will settle the order by telephone conference.

### Time and date

(6) The time and date shall be set by the clerk and shall be within five days after service of the notice disputing approval.

### Disputed order—Settlement by judge

(7) If unable to settle the order at the telephone conference, the clerk shall, as soon as possible, refer the order to the judge who made it, to be settled at a further telephone conference, unless the judge orders the parties to come to court for settlement of the order.

### No approval required if no response from other party

(8) If no approval or notice disputing approval (Form 25E) is served within 10 days after the draft order is served for approval, it may be signed without approval.

### No approval required for certain orders

(9) If an order dismisses a motion, case or appeal, without costs, or is prepared by the clerk under subrule (11), it may be signed without approval.

### No approval required in emergencies

(10) If the delay involved in getting an order approved would have serious consequences, the judge who made it may sign it without approval.

### When clerk prepares order

(11) The clerk shall prepare the order for signature,

(a) within 10 days after it is made, if no party has a lawyer;

(b) as soon as it is made,

(i) if it is a support deduction order or alternative payment order under the *Family Responsibility and Support Arrears Enforcement Act, 1996* or an order under the *Interjurisdictional Support Orders Act, 2002,*

(i.1) if it is a restraining order under section 35 of the *Children's Law Reform Act* or section 46 of the *Family Law Act,*

(i.2) if it is an order terminating a restraining order referred to in subclause (i.1), or

(ii) if the judge directs the clerk to do so.

### Restraining orders

(11.1) A restraining order referred to in subclause 11(b)(i.1) shall be in Form 25F or 25G.

(11.2) An order terminating a restraining order referred to in subclause 11(b)(i.1) shall be in Form 25H.

### Who signs order

(12) An order may be signed by the judge who made it or by the clerk.

### Service of order

(13) Unless the court orders otherwise, the person who prepared an order shall serve it,

(a) on every other party, including a party to whom paragraph 1 of subrule 1(8.4) (no notice to party) applies;

(b) if a child involved in the case has a lawyer, on the lawyer; and

(c) on any other person named by the court.

### Support deduction order not served

(14) A support deduction order under the *Family Responsibility and Support Arrears Enforcement Act, 1996* does not have to be served.

### Service of Crown wardship order

(15) An order for Crown wardship under Part III of the *Child and Family Services Act* shall be served on the following persons, in addition to the ones mentioned in subrule (13):

1. The child, if that Act requires notice to the child.

2. Any foster parent or other person who is entitled to notice under subsection 39(3) of that Act.

3. A Director appointed under that Act.

### Service of secure treatment order

(16) An order for secure treatment under Part VI of the *Child and Family Services Act* shall be served on the administrator of the secure treatment program, in addition to the persons mentioned in subrule (13).

### Service of adoption order

(17) An adoption order shall be served on the following persons, in addition to the ones mentioned in subrule (13):

1. The adopted child, if the child gave consent under subsection 137(6) of the *Child and Family Services Act.*
2. The persons mentioned in subsection 162(3) of that Act.

### Effective date

(18) An order is effective from the date on which it is made, unless it states otherwise.

### Changing order—Fraud, mistake, lack of notice

(19) The court may, on motion, change an order that,

(a) was obtained by fraud;

(b) contains a mistake;

(c) needs to be changed to deal with a matter that was before the court but that it did not decide;

(d) was made without notice; or

(e) was made with notice, if an affected party was not present when the order was made because the notice was inadequate or the party was unable, for a reason satisfactory to the court, to be present.

### Same

(20) Rule 14 applies with necessary changes to a motion to change a final order under subrule (19) and, for the purpose, clause 14(6)(a) shall be read as if the reference to a temporary order were a reference to a final order.

## RULE 25.1: PAYMENT INTO AND OUT OF COURT

### Definition

**25.1** (1) In this rule,

"Accountant" means the Accountant of the Superior Court of Justice.

### Non-application of rule

(2) This rule does not apply to,

(a) money paid or to be paid into court for the enforcement of an order for the payment or recovery of money, including enforcement by garnishment; or

(b) money for the support of a child or spouse that is paid or to be paid into court by the payor on behalf of a recipient.

### Payment into court, filing in person with clerk or accountant

(3) Subject to subrule (9), a party who is required to pay money into court shall do so in accordance with subrules (4) to (8).

### Documents to be filed

(4) The party shall file with the clerk or Accountant a written request for payment into court and a copy of the order under which the money is payable.

### Direction

(5) On receiving the documents filed under subrule (4), the clerk or Accountant shall give the party a direction to receive the money, addressed to a bank listed in Schedule I or II to the *Bank Act* (Canada) and specifying the account in the Accountant's name into which the money is to be paid.

### Clerk to forward documents

(6) If the documents are filed with the clerk, the clerk shall forward the documents to the Accountant.

### Payment

(7) On receiving from the clerk or Accountant the direction referred to in subrule (5), the party shall pay the money into the specified bank account in accordance with the direction.

### Bank's duties

(8) On receiving the money, the bank shall give a receipt to the party paying the money and immediately send a copy of the receipt to the Accountant.

### Payment into court, payment by mail to accountant

(9) A party may pay money into court by mailing to the Accountant the documents referred to in subrule (4), together with the money that is payable.

### Accountant to provide receipt

(10) On receiving money under subrule (9), the Accountant shall give a receipt to the party paying the money.

### Payment out of court, authority

(11) Money may only be paid out of court under an order or on consent of all parties.

### Payment out under an order

(12) A person who seeks payment of money out of court under an order shall file with the Accountant,

(a) a written request for payment out naming the person to whom the money is to be paid under the order;

(b) the original order for payment out or a copy certified by an official of the court, unless one or the other has already been filed with the Accountant; and

(c) an affidavit stating that the order for payment out is not under appeal and that the time for appealing the order has expired, or that any appeal of the order has been disposed of.

### Children's Lawyer, Public Guardian and Trustee

(13) If the person seeking payment out under an order is the Children's Lawyer or the Public Guardian and Trustee, the documents referred to in clauses (12)(a) and (c) are not required to be filed.

### Payment out on consent

(14)  A person who seeks payment of money out of court on consent shall file with the Accountant,

(a)  a written request for payment out naming the person to whom the money is to be paid, and an affidavit stating that neither the person making the request nor the person to whom the money is to be paid is a special party or a child under the age of 18 years who is not a party, with copies of the following attached as exhibits:

(i)  photo identification of the requesting person,

(ii)  proof of that person's date of birth,

(iii)  proof of that person's current address; and

(b)  the affidavit of each party or each of the other parties, as the case may be, stating that the party consents to the payment out as set out in the request and that neither the party nor the person to whom the money is to be paid is a special party or a child under the age of 18 years who is not a party, with copies of the documents referred to in subclauses (a) (i), (ii) and (iii), as they relate to the party providing the affidavit, attached as exhibits.

### Accountant's duties

(15)  If the requirements of subrule (12) or (14), as the case may be, are met, the Accountant shall pay the money to the person named in the order or request for payment out, and the payment shall include any accrued interest, unless a court orders otherwise.

### Order for payment out, special party or non-party child

(16)  The court may, on motion, order payment out of court of money for or on behalf of a special party or a child who is not a party.

### Where notice is not required

(17)  A motion under subrule (16) by the Children's Lawyer or the Public Guardian and Trustee may be made without notice, unless the court orders otherwise.

### Costs

(18)  In making an order under subrule (16), the court may order that costs payable to the person who made the motion be paid directly to that person's representative out of the money in court.

### Application

(19)  This rule applies to the payment into and out of court of money paid into court on and after the day on which Ontario Regulation 389/12 comes into force.

### RULE 26: ENFORCEMENT OF ORDERS

### Where to enforce an order

**26.**  (1)  The place for enforcement of an order is governed by subrules 5(5), (6), (7), and (7.1) (place for starting enforcement).

### How to enforce an order

(2)  An order that has not been obeyed may, in addition to any other method of enforcement provided by law, be enforced as provided by subrules (3) and (4).

### Payment orders

(3)  A payment order may be enforced by,

(a)  a request for a financial statement (subrule 27(1));

(b)  a request for disclosure from an income source (subrule 27(7));

(c)  a financial examination (subrule 27(11));

(d)  seizure and sale (rule 28);

(e)  garnishment (rule 29);

(f)  a default hearing (rule 30), if the order is a support order;

(g)  the appointment of a receiver under section 101 of the *Courts of Justice Act*; and

(h)  registration under section 42 of the *Family Responsibility and Support Arrears Enforcement Act, 1996*.

### Other orders

(4)  An order other than a payment order may be enforced by,

(a)  a writ of temporary seizure of property (subrule 28(10));

(b)  a contempt order (rule 31); and

(c)  the appointment of a receiver under section 101 of the *Courts of Justice Act*.

### Statement of money owed

(5)  A statement of money owed shall be in Form 26, with a copy of the order that is in default attached.

### Special forms for statement of money owed

(6)  Despite subrule (5),

(a)  if the *Family Responsibility and Support Arrears Enforcement Act, 1996* applies, a statement of arrears in the form used by the Director may be used instead of Form 26;

(b)  if the *Interjurisdictional Support Orders Act, 2002* applies, a document receivable under section 49 of that Act may be used instead of Form 26.

### Recipient's or Director's entitlement to costs

(7)  Unless the court orders otherwise, the recipient or the Director is entitled to the costs,

(a)  of carrying out a financial examination; and

(b)  of issuing, serving, filing and enforcing a writ of seizure and sale, a writ of temporary seizure and a notice of garnishment and of changing them by statutory declaration.

### Enforcement of administrative costs

(8)  For the purpose of subrule (7), the recipient or the Director may collect under a writ of seizure and sale, a notice of garnishment or a statutory declaration changing either of them,

(a) the amounts set out in the regulations under the *Administration of Justice Act* and awarded under rule 24 (costs) for filing and renewing with the sheriff a writ of seizure and sale or a writ of temporary seizure;

(b) payments made to a sheriff, clerk, official examiner, authorized court transcriptionist or other public officer in accordance with the regulations under the *Administration of Justice Act* and awarded under rule 24 (costs), on filing with the sheriff or clerk a copy of a receipt for each payment or an affidavit setting out the payments made; and

(c) the actual expense for carrying out a financial examination, or any other costs to which the recipient or the Director is entitled under subrule (7), on filing with the sheriff or clerk an affidavit (Form 26A) setting out the items of expense in detail.

### Affidavit for filing domestic contract

(9) An affidavit for filing a domestic contract or paternity agreement under subsection 35(1) of the *Family Law Act* shall be in Form 26B.

### Director's status

(10) If the Director enforces an order under the *Family Responsibility and Support Arrears Enforcement Act, 1996*, anything in these rules relating to enforcement by the person in whose favour the order was made applies to the Director.

### Filing and refiling with the Director

(11) A person who files or refiles a support order in the Director's office shall immediately send notice of the filing, by mail, fax or email, to the clerk at any court office where the recipient is enforcing the order.

### Transferring enforcement from recipient to Director

(12) A recipient who files a support order in the Director's office shall, on the Director's request, assign to the Director any enforcement that the recipient has started, and then the Director may continue with the enforcement as if the Director had started it.

### Transferring enforcement from Director to recipient

(13) If the parties withdraw a support order from the Director's office, the Director shall, on the recipient's request, given to the Director at the same time as the notice of withdrawal, assign to the recipient any enforcement that the Director has started, and then the recipient may continue with the enforcement as if the recipient had started it.

### Notice of transfer of enforcement

(14) A person who continues an enforcement under subrule (12) or (13) shall immediately send a notice of transfer of enforcement (Form 26C), by mail, fax or email to,

(a) all parties to the enforcement;

(b) the clerk at every court office where the enforcement is being carried on; and

(c) every sheriff who is involved with the enforcement at the time of transfer.

### Place of registration of support order under the Divorce Act (Canada)

(15) If a person wants to enforce an order for support made outside Ontario under the *Divorce Act* (Canada), the order shall be registered in a court, as defined in subsection 20(1) of that Act, as follows:

1. If the recipient resides in Ontario, in the municipality where the recipient resides.
2. If the recipient does not reside in Ontario, in the municipality where the payor resides.
3. If neither the recipient nor the payor resides in Ontario, in the municipality where any property owned by the payor is located or, if the payor doesn't have any property, in any municipality.

### Place of registration of custody or access order under the Divorce Act (Canada)

(16) If a person wants to enforce an order involving custody of or access to a child that is made outside Ontario under the *Divorce Act* (Canada), the order shall be registered in a court, as defined in subsection 20(1) of that Act, in accordance with clause 5(6)(a) of these rules.

### Registration requirements

(17) The person requesting the registration shall send to the court a certified copy of the order and a written request that the order be registered under paragraph 20(3)(a) of the *Divorce Act* (Canada).

### RULE 27: REQUIRING FINANCIAL INFORMATION
### Request for financial statement

27. (1) If a payment order is in default, a recipient may serve a request for a financial statement (Form 27) on the payor.

### Effect of request for financial statement

(2) Within 15 days after being served with the request, the payor shall send a completed financial statement (Form 13) to the recipient by mail, fax or email.

### Frequency of requests for financial statements

(3) A recipient may request a financial statement only once in a six-month period, unless the court gives the recipient permission to do so more often.

### Application of rule 13

(4) If a party is required under this rule to give a financial statement, the following subrules apply with necessary changes:

13(6) (full disclosure)
13(7) or (7.1) (income tax documents)
13(11) (insufficient financial information)
13(12) (updating financial statement)
13(15) (correcting and updating)
13(16) (order to file statement).

### Order for financial statement

(5) The court may, on motion, order a payor to serve and file a financial statement.

## Failure to obey order

(6) If the payor does not serve and file a financial statement within 10 days after being served with the order, the court may, on motion with special service (subrule 6(3)), order that the payor be imprisoned continuously or intermittently for not more than 40 days.

## Request for statement of income from income source

(7) If a payment order is in default, the recipient may serve a request for a statement of income (Form 27A) on an income source of the payor, requiring the income source to prepare and send to the recipient, by mail, fax or email, a statement of income (Form 27B).

## Frequency of requests for statement of income

(8) A recipient may request a statement of income from an income source only once in a six-month period, unless the court gives the recipient permission to do so more often.

## Order for statement of income

(9) The court may, on the recipient's motion, order an income source to serve and file a statement of income.

## Income source's failure to obey order

(10) If the income source does not serve and file a statement of income within 10 days after being served with the order, the court may, on the recipient's motion, order the income source to post a bond (Form 32).

## Appointment for financial examination

(11) If a payment order is in default, the recipient may serve on the payor, by special service (subrule 6(3)), an appointment for a financial examination (Form 27C), requiring the payor to,

(a) come to a financial examination;

(b) bring to the examination any document or thing named in the appointment that is in the payor's control or available to the payor on request, relevant to the enforcement of the order, and not protected by a legal privilege; and

(c) serve a financial statement (Form 13) on the recipient, not later than seven days before the date of the examination.

## Financial examination of person other than payor

(12) If a payment order is in default and a person other than the payor may know about the matters listed in subrule (17), the recipient may require that person to come to a financial examination by serving a summons to witness (Form 23) and the witness fee (subrule 23(4)) on the person by special service (subrules 6(3) and (4)).

## Place where financial examination held

(13) A financial examination shall be held,

(a) in a place where the parties and the person to be examined agree;

(b) where the person to be examined lives in Ontario, in the municipality where the person lives; or

(c) in a place chosen by the court.

## Other rules apply

(14) Subrules 19(4), (5) and (8) (documents protected by legal privilege, use of privileged documents, documents omitted from affidavit) and 23(7) (failure to obey summons) apply to a financial examination, with necessary changes.

## Notice of time and place of examination

(15) A payor who is served with an appointment or a person who is served with a summons for a financial examination shall have at least 10 days' notice of the time and place of the examination.

## Before whom examination is held, method of recording

(16) A financial examination shall be held under oath or affirmation, before a person chosen by agreement of the payor and recipient or in accordance with subrule 20(12) (other arrangements for questioning), and shall be recorded by a method chosen in the same way.

## Scope of examination

(17) On a financial examination, the payor or other person may be questioned about,

(a) the reason for the payor's default;

(b) the payor's income and property;

(c) the debts owed to and by the payor;

(d) the disposal of any property by the payor either before or after the making of the order that is in default;

(e) the payor's past, present and future ability to pay under the order;

(f) whether the payor intends to obey the order, and any reason for not doing so; and

(g) any other matter relevant to the enforcement of the order.

## Resistance to examination

(18) Subrule (19) applies if a payor who is served with an appointment or a person who is served with a summons for a financial examination,

(a) does not come to the examination as required by the appointment or summons;

(b) does not serve on the recipient a financial statement as required by the appointment;

(c) comes to the examination, but does not bring a document or thing named in the appointment or summons; or

(d) comes to the examination, but refuses to take an oath or affirm or to answer a question.

## Order for another examination

(19) The court may, on motion, make an order and give directions for another financial examination of the payor or other person and may in addition require the payor or person to post a bond (Form 32).

## Imprisonment

(20) If a payor or other person, without sufficient excuse, fails to obey an order or direction made under subrule (19),

the court may, on motion with special service (subrule 6(3)), order that the payor or person be imprisoned continuously or intermittently for not more than 40 days.

### Imprisonment power is additional

(21) The court may exercise its power under subrule (20) in addition to or instead of its power of forfeiture under rule 32 (bonds, recognizances and warrants).

### Frequency of examinations

(22) A recipient may conduct only one financial examination of a payor and one financial examination of any other person in a six-month period, or more often with the court's permission.

## RULE 28: SEIZURE AND SALE

### Issue of writ of seizure and sale

**28.** (1) The clerk shall issue a writ of seizure and sale (Form 28) if a recipient files,

(a) a request for a writ of seizure and sale (Form 28A); and

(b) a statement of money owed (subrules 26(5) and (6)).

### Electronic filing of writ

(1.1) Subject to subrule (11), a writ of seizure and sale issued under subrule (1) may be filed with a sheriff electronically.

### Electronic filing of request, issuance of writ

(1.2) Subject to subrule (11), a recipient may file a request for a writ of seizure and sale electronically, in which case,

(a) clause (1)(b) does not apply to the request;

(b) the writ shall be issued electronically; and

(c) the issued writ shall automatically be filed electronically with the sheriff specified in the writ.

### Deemed issuance by court

(1.3) A writ issued electronically is deemed to have been issued by the court.

### Error in writ issued electronically

(1.4) If a person who obtained an electronically issued writ of seizure and sale discovers that the writ contains an error, the person may, no later than 5 p.m. eastern standard or daylight saving time, as the case may be, on the second day after the day on which the writ is considered under subrule (13) to have been filed with a sheriff, correct the error by using the software that was used for the issuance of the writ.

### Statutory declaration under the Family Responsibility and Support Arrears Enforcement Act, 1996

(2) The statutory declaration to sheriff mentioned in section 44 of the *Family Responsibility and Support Arrears Enforcement Act, 1996* shall be in Form 28B.

### Statutory declaration if order changed

(3) If a court changes a payment order that is being enforced by a writ of seizure and sale, a statutory declaration to sheriff (Form 28B) may be filed with the sheriff and once

filed, it has the same effect as a declaration mentioned in subrule (2).

### Electronic filing

(3.1) A statutory declaration referred to in subrule (2) or (3) may be filed electronically.

### Duration of writ

(4) A writ of seizure and sale continues in effect until,

(a) the writ is withdrawn under subrule (7); or

(b) the court orders otherwise under subrule (8).

### Writ issued under former rules

(5) A writ directing the sheriff to seize and sell a payor's property that was issued by the court under the rules that applied before these rules take effect has the same legal effect as a writ of seizure and sale issued under these rules, and does not expire except as subrule (4) provides.

### Notifying sheriff of payment received

(6) If a writ of seizure and sale has been filed with a sheriff,

(a) the recipient shall, on the sheriff's request, provide a statutory declaration setting out details of all payments received by or on behalf of the recipient; and

(b) the sheriff shall update the writ accordingly.

### May be filed electronically

(6.1) Subject to subrule (11), the statutory declaration referred to in clause (6)(a) may be filed with the sheriff electronically.

### Change of address

(6.2) If the address of the recipient or his or her lawyer changes after a writ has been filed with a sheriff, the recipient shall give written notice of the new address to the sheriff, and the sheriff shall update the writ accordingly.

### May be filed electronically

(6.3) Subject to subrule (11), notice of the new address may be filed with the sheriff electronically.

### Confirmation of electronically filed writ

(6.4) In order to confirm whether a writ of seizure and sale filed with a sheriff electronically has been properly issued and filed, the sheriff may require the recipient to provide to the sheriff, in the manner and within the time the sheriff specifies, a statement of money owed (subrule 26(5) or (6)).

### Withdrawal by sheriff

(6.5) The sheriff may withdraw an electronically filed writ of seizure and sale if,

(a) the sheriff determines that the writ was improperly issued or filed; or

(b) the recipient fails to comply with subrule (6.4).

### Same

(6.6) A writ may be withdrawn under subrule (6.5) at any time during its enforcement.

## Corrections by sheriff

(6.7) If the sheriff makes a determination that a writ of seizure and sale filed with the sheriff electronically was properly issued or filed but contains an error or otherwise differs from the order to which the writ relates, the sheriff may correct the writ to make it consistent with the order.

## Notice

(6.8) The sheriff shall give notice of a withdrawal under subrule (6.5) or a correction under subrule (6.7) to the recipient.

## Withdrawing writ

(7) The person who obtained a writ to enforce an order shall immediately withdraw it from every sheriff's office where it has been filed if,

(a) the person no longer wants to enforce the order by a writ;

(b) in the case of a payment order, the payor's obligation to make periodic payments under the order has ended and all other amounts owing under it have been paid; or

(c) in the case of any other order, the person against whom the writ was issued has obeyed the order.

## Same

(7.1) A writ may be withdrawn under subrule (7) by,

(a) giving written notice to the sheriff that the writ should be withdrawn; or

(b) subject to subrule (11), filing notice of a withdrawal of writ electronically.

## Order changing, withdrawing or suspending writ

(8) The court may, on motion, make an order changing the terms of a writ, withdrawing it or temporarily suspending it, even if the writ was issued by another court in Ontario.

## Service of order

(9) The person making the motion, or another person named by the court, shall serve a copy of the order on,

(a) every sheriff in whose office the writ has been filed; and

(b) if the writ was issued by the court in another place, or by another court, on the clerk of the court in the other place or the clerk of the other court.

## Electronic filing of changes

(9.1) If the court makes an order under subrule (8) making any of the following changes to a writ that has been filed with a sheriff, the person required to serve a copy of the order under subrule (9) may, subject to subrule (11), file the changes to the writ with the sheriff electronically instead of serving a copy of the order on the sheriff under clause (9)(a):

1. The name of a party.
2. The recipient's lawyer or other representative.
3. The amount owing under the writ.

## Writ of temporary seizure of property

(10) The court may, on motion with special service (subrule 6(3)), give permission to issue a writ of temporary

seizure (Form 28C) directing the sheriff to take possession of and hold all or part of the land and other property of a person against whom an order has been made and to hold any income from the property until the writ is withdrawn or the court orders otherwise.

## Limit on who may file electronically

(11) The electronic filing and issuance of documents under this rule is only available for,

(a) lawyers;

(b) the Director of the Family Responsibility Office; and

(c) Ministers or bodies acting under the authority of an Act of Canada or Ontario.

## Electronic filing, issuance—Authorized software

(12) If this rule permits or requires a document to be filed or issued electronically, the software authorized by the Ministry of the Attorney General for the purpose shall be used for the filing or issuance.

## Date of electronic filing, issuance

(13) The date on which a document that is filed or issued electronically under this rule is considered to have been filed or issued, as the case may be, is the date indicated for the document by the authorized software.

## Electronic filing and signatures, swearing

(14) The following requirements are deemed to have been met if a document is filed or issued under this rule electronically using the authorized software:

1. A requirement that the document be signed.
2. A requirement that the document be sworn or affirmed.

## RULE 29: GARNISHMENT

### Issue of notice or notices of garnishment

**29.** (1) The clerk shall issue as many notices of garnishment (Form 29A or 29B) as a recipient requests if the recipient files,

(a) a request for garnishment (Form 29) or an extra-provincial garnishment process referred to in section 50 of the *Family Responsibility and Support Arrears Enforcement Act, 1996*; and

(b) a statement of money owed (subrules 26(5) and (6)).

### One recipient and one garnishee per notice

(2) Each notice of garnishment shall name only one recipient and one garnishee.

### Service on payor and garnishee

(3) The notice of garnishment shall be served on the payor and on the garnishee but the payor shall, in addition, be served with the documents filed under subrule (1).

### Effect of notice of garnishment

(4) A notice of garnishment attaches,

(a) every debt that is payable by the garnishee to the payor at the time the notice is served; and

(b) every debt that is payable by the garnishee to the payor,

    (i) after the notice is served, or

    (ii) on the fulfilment of a condition after the notice is served.

### Duration

(5) The notice of garnishment continues in effect from the time of service on the garnishee until it is withdrawn or stopped under this rule or until the court orders otherwise under this rule.

### Financial institution

(6) If the garnishee is a financial institution, the notice of garnishment and all further notices required to be served under this rule shall be served at the branch of the institution where the debt to the payor is payable, unless subrule (6.1) applies.

### Federally regulated financial institution— Garnishment re support

(6.1) If the garnishee is a financial institution to which the *Bank Act* (Canada), the *Cooperative Credit Associations Act* (Canada) or the *Trust and Loan Companies Act* (Canada) applies and the garnishment enforces a support order, the notice of garnishment and all further notices required to be served under this rule,

    (a) shall be served at the designated office of the institution established for this purpose; and

    (b) shall be accompanied by a statement to garnishee financial institution re support (Form 29J).

### New accounts

(6.2) Subrules (4) and (5) do not apply to money in an account opened after a notice of garnishment is served as described in subrule (6) or (6.1).

### Joint debts garnishable

(7) Subrules (4) and (5) also apply to debts owed to the payor and another person jointly.

### Procedure when joint debt garnished

(8) If a garnishee has been served with a notice of garnishment and the garnishee owes a debt to which subrules (4) and (5) apply to the payor and another person jointly,

    (a) the garnishee shall pay, in accordance with subrule (11), half of the debt, or the larger or smaller amount that the court orders;

    (b) the garnishee shall immediately send the other person a notice to co-owner of debt (Form 29C) by mail, fax or email, to the person's address in the garnishee's records; and

    (c) the garnishee shall immediately serve the notice to co-owner of debt on the recipient or the Director, depending on who is enforcing the order, and on the sheriff or clerk if the sheriff or clerk is to receive the money under subrule (11) or (12).

### Joint debt—Money to be held

(9) Despite subrule (12), if served with notice under clause (8)(c), the sheriff, clerk or Director shall hold the money received for 30 days, and may pay it out when the 30 days expire, unless the other person serves and files a dispute within the 30 days.

### Payment of arrears does not end garnishment

(10) A notice of garnishment continues to attach future periodic payments even though the total amount owed when it was served is fully paid up.

### Persons to whom garnishee makes payments

(11) A garnishee who has been served with a notice of garnishment shall make the required payments to,

    (a) the Director, if the notice of garnishment relates to an order being enforced by the Director;

    (b) the clerk, if the notice of garnishment does not relate to an order being enforced by the Director.

### Clerk or Director to pay out money

(12) On receiving money under a notice of garnishment, the Director or clerk shall, even if a dispute has been filed, but subject to subrules (9) and (13), immediately pay,

    (a) to the recipient, any part of the money that comes within the priority created by subsection 2(3) of the *Creditors' Relief Act, 2010*; and

    (b) to the sheriff, any part of the money that exceeds that priority.

### Order that subrule (12) does not apply

(13) The court may, at a garnishment hearing or on a motion to change the garnishment under this rule, order that subrule (12) does not apply.

### Change in garnishment, indexed support

(14) If a notice of garnishment enforces a support order that indexes periodic payments for inflation, the recipient may serve on the garnishee and on the payor a statutory declaration of indexed support (Form 29D) setting out the new amount to be paid under the order, and file the declaration with the court.

### Effect of statutory declaration of indexed support

(15) A statutory declaration of indexed support requires the garnishee to pay the new amount set out in the declaration from the time it is served on the garnishee.

### Garnishment dispute

(16) Within 10 days after being served with a notice of garnishment or a statutory declaration of indexed support, a payor, garnishee or co-owner of a debt may serve on the other parties and file a dispute (Form 29E, 29F or 29G).

### Notice of garnishment hearing

(17) The clerk shall, on request, issue a notice of garnishment hearing (Form 29H),

(a) within 10 days after a dispute is served and filed; or

(b) if the recipient says that the garnishee has not paid any money or has not paid enough money.

## Service of notice

(18) The clerk shall serve and file the notice not later than 10 days before the hearing.

## Garnishment hearing

(19) At a garnishment hearing, the court may make one or more of the following temporary or final orders:

1. An order dismissing the dispute.
2. An order that changes how much is being garnished on account of a periodic payment order. The court may make an order under this paragraph even if it does not have the authority to change the payment order itself.
2.1 An order that changes how much is being garnished on account of a periodic payment order and that, at the same time, changes the payment order itself. The court may make an order under this paragraph only if,
   i. the payment order is one that the court has the authority to change, and
   ii. the parties to the payment order agree to the change, or one of those parties has served and filed notice of a motion to have the change made.
3. An order changing how much is being garnished on account of a non-periodic payment order.
4. An order suspending the garnishment or any term of it, while the hearing is adjourned or until the court orders otherwise.
5. An order setting aside the notice of garnishment or any statutory declaration of indexed support.
6. An order that garnished money held or received by the clerk, Director or sheriff be held in court.
7. An order that garnished money that has been paid out in error to the recipient be paid into and held in court, returned to the garnishee or sent to the payor or to the co-owner of the debt.
8. An order that garnished money held in court be returned to the garnishee or be sent to the payor, the co-owner of the debt, the sheriff, the clerk or the Director.
9. An order deciding how much remains owing under a payment order that is being enforced by garnishment against the payor or garnishee.
10. If the garnishee has not paid what was required by the notice of garnishment or statutory declaration of indexed support, an order that the garnishee pay all or part of what was required.
11. An order deciding who is entitled to the costs of the garnishment hearing and setting the amount of the costs.

## Changing garnishment at other times

(20) The court may also use the powers listed in subrule (19), on motion or on its own initiative, even if the notice of garnishment was issued by another court,

(a) on a motion under section 7 of the *Wages Act;*

(b) if the court replaces a temporary payment order with a final payment order;

(c) if the court indexes or changes a payment order; or

(d) if the court allows an appeal.

## Changing garnishment when ability to pay changes

(21) If there has been a material change in the payor's circumstances affecting the payor's ability to pay, the court may, on motion, use the powers listed in subrule (19).

## Garnishee's payment pays debt

(22) Payment of a debt by a garnishee under a notice of garnishment or statutory declaration of indexed support pays off the debt between the garnishee and the payor to the extent of the payment.

## Notice by garnishee—Payor not working or receiving money

(23) Within 10 days after a payor stops working for or is no longer receiving any money from a garnishee, the garnishee shall send a notice as subrule (27) requires,

(a) saying that the payor is no longer working for or is no longer receiving any money from the garnishee;

(b) giving the date on which the payor stopped working for or receiving money from the garnishee and the date of the last payment to the payor from the garnishee; and

(c) giving the name and address of any other income source of the payor, if known.

## Notice by garnishee—Payor working or receiving money again

(24) Within 10 days after the payor returns to work for or starts to receive money again from the garnishee, the garnishee shall send another notice as subrule (27) requires, saying that the payor has returned to work for or started to receive money again from the garnishee.

## Notice by payor—Working or receiving money again

(25) Within 10 days after returning to work for or starting to receive money again from the garnishee, the payor shall send a notice as subrule (27) requires, saying that the payor has returned to work for or started to receive money again from the garnishee.

## Notice by payor—New income source

(26) Within 10 days after starting to work for or receive money from a new income source, the payor shall send a notice as subrule (27) requires, saying that the payor has started to work for or to receive money from the new income source.

## Notice sent to clerk and recipient or Director

(27) A notice referred to in subrule (23), (24), (25) or (26) shall be sent to the clerk, and to the recipient or the Director (depending on who is enforcing the order), by mail, fax or email.

## Notice by clerk

(28) When the clerk receives a notice under subrule (26), the clerk shall immediately notify the recipient or the

Director (depending on who is enforcing the order) by mail, fax or electronic mail.

### New notice of garnishment

(29)  If no written objection is received within 10 days of the clerk notifying the recipient or the Director that a notice under subrule (26) was received, the clerk shall,

  (a)  issue a new notice of garnishment directed to the new garnishee, requiring the same deductions as were required to be made, under the previous notice of garnishment or statutory declaration of indexed support, on the day that the notice under subrule (26) was received; and

  (b)  send a copy of the new notice of garnishment to the payor and the new garnishee, by mail, fax or email.

### Effect of new notice of garnishment

(30)  Issuing a new notice of garnishment under clause (29)(a) does not cancel any previous notice of garnishment or statutory declaration of indexed support.

### Notice to stop garnishment

(31)  The recipient shall immediately send a notice to stop garnishment (Form 29I), by mail, fax or email, to the garnishee and payor and file it with the clerk if,

  (a)  the recipient no longer wants to enforce the order by garnishment; or

  (b)  the requirement to make periodic payments under the order has ended and all other amounts owing under the order have been paid.

### Old orders

(32)  This rule applies, with necessary changes, to,

  (a)  an attachment order made under section 30 of the *Family Law Reform Act* (chapter 152 of the Revised Statutes of Ontario, 1980); and

  (b)  a garnishment order issued by the court under the rules that were in effect before January 1, 1985.

### RULE 30: DEFAULT HEARING

#### Issuing notice of default hearing

**30.** (1)  The clerk shall issue a notice of default hearing (Form 30),

  (a)  if the support order is being enforced by the recipient, when the recipient files a request for a default hearing (Form 30A) and a statement of money owed (subrule 26(5));

  (b)  if it is being enforced by the Director, when the Director files a statement of money owed.

#### Serving notice of default hearing

(2)  The notice of default hearing shall be served on the payor by special service in accordance with subrule 6(4) and filed.

#### Payor's dispute

(3)  Within 10 days after being served with the notice, the payor shall serve on the recipient and file,

  (a)  a financial statement (Form 13); and

  (b)  a default dispute (Form 30B).

### Updating statement of money owed

(4)  The recipient shall serve and file a new statement of money owed (subrule 26(5)) not more than seven days before the default hearing.

### When Director to update statement

(5)  Despite subrule 26(10), subrule (4) applies to the Director only if,

  (a)  the amount the Director is asking the court to enforce is greater than the amount shown in the notice of default hearing; or

  (b)  the court directs it.

### Statement of money owed presumed correct

(6)  The payor is presumed to admit that the recipient's statement of money owed is correct, unless the payor has filed a default dispute stating that the statement of money owed is not correct and giving detailed reasons.

### Arrears enforceable to date of hearing

(7)  At the default hearing, the court may decide and enforce the amount owing as of the date of the hearing.

### Conditional imprisonment

(8)  The court may make an order under clause 41(10)(h) or (i) of the *Family Responsibility and Support Arrears Enforcement Act, 1996*, suspending the payor's imprisonment on appropriate conditions.

### Issuing warrant of committal

(9)  If the recipient, on a motion with special service in accordance with subrule 6(4) on the payor, states by affidavit (or by oral evidence, with the court's permission) that the payor has not obeyed a condition that was imposed under subrule (8), the court may issue a warrant of committal against the payor, subject to subsection 41(15) (power to change order) of the *Family Responsibility and Support Arrears Enforcement Act, 1996*.

### RULE 31: CONTEMPT OF COURT

#### When contempt motion available

**31.** (1)  An order, other than a payment order, may be enforced by a contempt motion made in the case in which the order was made, even if another penalty is available.

#### Notice of contempt motion

(2)  The notice of contempt motion (Form 31) shall be served together with a supporting affidavit, by special service in accordance with subrule 6(4), unless the court orders otherwise.

#### Affidavit for contempt motion

(3)  The supporting affidavit may contain statements of information that the person signing the affidavit learned from someone else, but only if the requirements of subrule 14(19) are satisfied.

### Warrant to bring to court

(4) To bring before the court a person against whom a contempt motion is made, the court may issue a warrant for the person's arrest if,

(a) the person's attendance is necessary in the interest of justice; and

(b) the person is not likely to attend voluntarily.

### Contempt orders

(5) If the court finds a person in contempt of the court, it may order that the person,

(a) be imprisoned for any period and on any conditions that are just;

(b) pay a fine in any amount that is appropriate;

(c) pay an amount to a party as a penalty;

(d) do anything else that the court decides is appropriate;

(e) not do what the court forbids;

(f) pay costs in an amount decided by the court; and

(g) obey any other order.

### Writ of temporary seizure

(6) The court may also give permission to issue a writ of temporary seizure (Form 28C) against the person's property.

### Limited imprisonment or fine

(7) In a contempt order under one of the following provisions, the period of imprisonment and the amount of a fine may not be greater than the relevant Act allows:

1. Section 38 of the *Children's Law Reform Act*.
2. Section 49 of the *Family Law Act*.
3. Section 53 of the *Family Responsibility and Support Arrears Enforcement Act, 1996*.

### Conditional imprisonment or fine

(8) A contempt order for imprisonment or for the payment of a fine may be suspended on appropriate conditions.

### Issuing warrant of committal

(9) If a party, on a motion with special service (subrule 6(3)) on the person in contempt, states by an affidavit in Form 32C (or by oral evidence, with the court's permission) that the person has not obeyed a condition imposed under subrule (8), the court may issue a warrant of committal against the person.

### Payment of fine

(10) A contempt order for the payment of a fine shall require the person in contempt to pay the fine,

(a) in a single payment, immediately or before a date that the court chooses; or

(b) in instalments, over a period of time that the court considers appropriate.

### Corporation in contempt

(11) If a corporation is found in contempt, the court may also make an order under subrule (5), (6) or (7) against any officer or director of the corporation.

### Change in contempt order

(12) The court may, on motion, change an order under this rule, give directions and make any other order that is just.

## RULE 32: BONDS, RECOGNIZANCES AND WARRANTS

### Warrant to bring a person to court

**32.** (1) If a person does not come to court after being served with notice of a case, enforcement or motion that may result in an order requiring the person to post a bond,

(a) the court may issue a warrant for the person's arrest, to bring the person before the court, and adjourn the case to await the person's arrival; or

(b) the court may,

(i) hear and decide the case in the person's absence and, if appropriate, make an order requiring the person to post a bond, and

(ii) if the person has been served with the order and does not post the bond by the date set out in the order, issue a warrant for the person's arrest, on motion without notice, to bring the person before the court.

### Form of bond and other requirements

(2) A bond shall be in Form 32, does not need a seal, and shall,

(a) have at least one surety, unless the court orders otherwise;

(b) list the conditions that the court considers appropriate;

(c) set out an amount of money to be forfeited if the conditions are not obeyed;

(d) shall require the person posting the bond to deposit the money with the clerk immediately, unless the court orders otherwise; and

(e) name the person to whom any forfeited money is to be paid out.

### Person before whom recognizance to be entered into

(3) A recognizance shall be entered into before a judge, a justice of the peace or the clerk.

### Change of conditions in a bond

(4) The court may, on motion, change any condition in a bond if there has been a material change in a party's circumstances since the date of the order for posting the bond or the date of an order under this subrule, whichever is more recent.

### Change in bond under Children's Law Reform Act

(5) In the case of a bond under the *Children's Law Reform Act*, subrule (4) also applies to a material change in circumstances that affects or is likely to affect the best interests of the child.

### Removal or replacement of surety

(6) The court may, on motion, order that a surety be removed or be replaced by another person as surety, in which

case as soon as the order is made, the surety who is removed or replaced is free from any obligation under the bond.

### Motion to enforce bond

(7) A person requesting the court's permission to enforce a bond under subsection 143(1) (enforcement of recognizance or bond) of the *Courts of Justice Act* shall serve a notice of forfeiture motion (Form 32A), with a copy of the bond attached, on the person said to have broken the bond and on each surety.

### Forfeiture if no deposit made

(8) If an order of forfeiture of a bond is made and no deposit was required, or a deposit was required but was not made, the order shall require the payor or surety to pay the required amount to the person to whom the bond is payable,

(a) in a single payment, immediately or before a date that the court chooses; or

(b) in instalments, over a period of time that the court considers appropriate.

### Change in payment schedule

(9) If time is allowed for payment under subrule (8), the court may, on a later motion by the payor or a surety, allow further time for payment.

### Order for forfeiture of deposit

(10) If an order of forfeiture of a bond is made and a deposit was required and was made, the order shall direct the clerk to pay the required amount immediately to the person to whom the bond is made payable.

### Cancelling bond

(11) The court may, on motion, make an order under subrule (4), or an order cancelling the bond and directing a refund of all or part of the deposit, if,

(a) a payor or surety made a deposit under the bond;

(b) the conditions of the bond have not been broken; and

(c) the conditions have expired or, although they have not expired or do not have an expiry date, the payor or surety has good reasons for getting the conditions of the bond changed.

### Form of warrant for arrest

(12) A warrant for arrest issued against any of the following shall be in Form 32B:

1. A payor who does not file a financial statement ordered under subsection 40(4) of the *Family Responsibility and Support Arrears Enforcement Act, 1996* or under these rules.

2. A payor who does not come to a default hearing under section 41 of the *Family Responsibility and Support Arrears Enforcement Act, 1996.*

3. An absconding respondent under subsection 43(1) or 59(2) of the *Family Law Act.*

4. An absconding payor under subsection 49(1) of the *Family Responsibility and Support Arrears Enforcement Act, 1996.*

5. A witness who does not come to court or remain in attendance as required by a summons to witness.

6. A person who does not come to court in a case that may result in an order requiring the person to post a bond under these rules.

7. A person who does not obey an order requiring the person to post a bond under these rules.

8. A person against whom a contempt motion is made.

9. Any other person liable to arrest under an order.

10. Any other person liable to arrest for committing an offence.

### Bail on arrest

(13) Section 150 (interim release by justice of the peace) of the *Provincial Offences Act* applies, with necessary changes, to an arrest made under a warrant mentioned in paragraph 1, 2, 3 or 4 of subrule (12).

### Affidavit for warrant of committal

(14) An affidavit in support of a motion for a warrant of committal shall be in Form 32C.

### Form of warrant of committal

(15) A warrant of committal issued to enforce an order of imprisonment shall be in Form 32D.

## RULE 32.1: ENFORCEMENT OF FAMILY ARBITRATION AWARDS

### Requesting enforcement

**32.1** (1) A party who is entitled to the enforcement of a family arbitration award and who wants to ask the court to enforce the award under section 59.8 of the *Family Law Act* may file a request to enforce a family arbitration award (Form 32.1), together with,

(a) copies of the certificates of independent legal advice required by the *Family Law Act* for the parties to the family arbitration agreement;

(b) a copy of the family arbitration agreement; and

(c) the original award or a certified copy.

### When required to proceed by motion

(2) Despite subrule (1), if there is already a family law case to which these rules apply between the parties to the family arbitration agreement in the Superior Court of Justice or the Family Court of the Superior Court of Justice, the party entitled to enforcement shall make a motion in that case rather than a request under this rule, and subrule 14(24) applies in respect of the motion.

### Application of other rules

(3) The rules that apply to an application apply to a request to enforce a family arbitration award that is proceeding under this rule, unless these rules provide otherwise.

### Hearing date

(4) When a request to enforce a family arbitration award is filed, the clerk shall set a hearing date.

**Service**

(5) The request shall be served immediately on every other party.

**Request not served on or before hearing date**

(6) If a request to enforce a family arbitration award is not served on a respondent on or before the hearing date, the clerk shall, at the applicant's request, set a new hearing date for that respondent, and the applicant shall make the necessary change to the request and serve it immediately on that respondent.

**Opposing a request**

(7) Despite subrule 10(1) (serving and filing answer), a respondent who wants to oppose a request to enforce a family arbitration award shall serve a dispute of request for enforcement (Form 32.1A) on every other party and file it,

(a) no later than 30 days after being served with the request; or

(b) if the request is served outside Canada or the United States of America, no later than 60 days after being served with the request.

**Written hearing**

(8) Unless the court orders otherwise under subrule (10), the request shall be dealt with on the basis of written documents without the parties or their lawyers needing to come to court.

**Request for oral hearing**

(9) A respondent may request an oral hearing by filing a motion (Form 14B) within seven days after being served with the request to enforce a family arbitration award.

**Order for oral hearing**

(10) The court may order an oral hearing, on motion or on its own initiative, if it is satisfied that an oral hearing is necessary to deal with the case justly.

### RULE 33: CHILD PROTECTION

**Timetable**

**33.** (1) Every child protection case, including a status review application, is governed by the following timetable:

| Step in the case | Maximum time for completion, from start of case |
|---|---|
| First hearing, if child has been apprehended | 5 days |
| Service and filing of answers and plans of care | 30 days |
| Temporary care and custody hearing | 35 days |
| Settlement conference | 80 days |
| Hearing | 120 days |

**Case management judge**

(2) Wherever possible, at the start of the case a judge shall be assigned to manage it and monitor its progress.

**Court may lengthen times only in best interests of child**

(3) The court may lengthen a time shown in the timetable only if the best interests of the child require it.

**Parties may not lengthen times**

(4) The parties may not lengthen a time shown in the timetable by consent under subrule 3(6).

**Plan of care or supervision to be served**

(5) A party who wants the court to consider a plan of care or supervision shall serve it on the other parties and file it not later than seven days before a conference, even if that is sooner than the timetable would require.

**Temporary care and custody hearing— Affidavit evidence**

(6) The evidence at a temporary care and custody hearing shall be given by affidavit, unless the court orders otherwise.

**Status review**

(6.1) A status review application under clause 64(2)(a) or (b) of the *Child and Family Services Act* shall be served at least 30 days before the date the order for society supervision or society wardship expires.

**Forms for child protection cases**

(7) In a child protection case,

(a) an information for a warrant to apprehend a child shall be in Form 33;

(b) a warrant to apprehend a child shall be in Form 33A;

(c) an applicant's plan of care for a child shall be,

(i) if the applicant is a children's aid society, in Form 33B, and

(ii) if the applicant is not a children's aid society, in Form 33B.1;

(c.1) a respondent's answer and plan of care for a child shall be,

(i) if the respondent is not a children's aid society, in Form 33B.1,

(ii) if the respondent is a children's aid society, in Form 10 and Form 33B;

(d) an agreed statement of facts in a child protection case shall be in Form 33C; and

(e) an agreed statement of facts in a status review application shall be in Form 33D.

**Forms for secure treatment cases**

(8) In an application under Part VI (secure treatment) of the *Child and Family Services Act*, a consent signed by the child shall be in Form 33E and a consent signed by any other person shall be in Form 33F.

## RULE 34: ADOPTION

### CFSA definitions apply

**34.** (1) The definitions in the *Child and Family Services Act* apply to this rule and, in particular,

"Director" means a Director within the meaning of the Act.

### Meaning of "act"

(2) In this rule,

"Act" means the *Child and Family Services Act*.

### Use of initials in documents

(2.1) An applicant or respondent may be referred to by only the first letter of his or her surname in any document in the case, except that,

    (a) the applicant's full names shall appear in the adoption order; and

    (b) the child's full names shall appear in the adoption order, unless the court orders that the child's first name and the first letter of his or her surname be used.

### Certified copy of order from outside Ontario

(3) When this rule requires a copy of an order to be filed and the order in question was made outside Ontario, it shall be a copy that is certified by an official of the court or other authority that made it.

### Material to be filed with adoption applications

(4) The following shall be filed with every application for an adoption:

1. A certified copy of the statement of live birth of the child, or an equivalent that satisfies the court.
2. If required, the child's consent to adoption (Form 34) or a notice of motion and supporting affidavit for an order under subsection 137(9) of the Act dispensing with the child's consent.
3. If the child is not a Crown ward, an affidavit of parentage (Form 34A) or any other evidence about parentage that the court requires from the child's parent or a person named by the court.
4. If the applicant has a spouse who has not joined in the application, a consent to the child's adoption by the spouse (Form 34B).
5. If required by the Act or by an order, a Director's or local director's statement on adoption (Form 34C) under subsection 149(1) or (6) of the Act.
6. An affidavit signed by the applicant (Form 34D) that includes details about the applicant's education, employment, health, background and ability to support and care for the child, a history of the relationship between the parent and the child and any other evidence relating to the best interests of the child, and states whether the child is an Indian or a native person.

### Report of child's adjustment

(5) A report under subsection 149(5) or (6) of the Act of the child's adjustment in the applicant's home shall also be filed with the application if the child is under 16 years of age, or is 16 years of age or older but has not withdrawn from parental control and has not married.

### Additional material—Crown ward

(6) If the child is a Crown ward, the following shall also be filed with the application:

1. A Director's consent to adoption (Form 34E).
1.1 If an access order was made under subsection 58(1) of the Act,

    i. copies of each notice of intention to place a child for adoption (Form 8D.2) or of the notice to child of intention to place for adoption (Form 8D.3) that was sent to a person who was granted an access order,

    ii. copies of each notice of termination of access (Form 8D.4) that was sent to a person who was the subject of an access order but was not entitled to bring an application for an openness order,

    iii. for each notice,

        A. proof of service of the notice in accordance with subsection 145.1.1(4) of the Act,

        B. a copy of an order permitting another method of service under subsection 145.1.1(5) of the Act and proof of such service, or

        C. a copy of an order under subsection 145.1.1(6) of the Act that notice is not required, and

    iv. an affidavit (Form 34G.1) signed by an employee of a children's aid society stating that,

        A. no application for an openness order has been filed, or

        B. if any applications for openness orders have been filed, the status of those applications, including details of any openness orders that have been made.

2. A copy of any order under subsection 58(1) of the Act ending access to the child.
3. A copy of the order of Crown wardship.
4. Proof of service of the orders referred to in paragraphs 2 and 3, or a copy of any order dispensing with service.
5. An affidavit (Form 34G.1), signed by a person delegated by the local director of the children's aid society that has placed the child for adoption, stating that there is no appeal in progress from an order referred to in paragraph 2 or 3, or that the appeal period has expired without an appeal being filed, or that an appeal was filed but has been withdrawn or finally dismissed.
6. If the child is an Indian or native person, proof of 30 days written notice to the child's band or native community of the intention to place the child for adoption.

### Additional material—Child not Crown ward

(7) If the child is not a Crown ward and is placed for adoption by a licensee or children's aid society, the following shall also be filed with the application:

1. A copy of any custody or access order that is in force and is known to the person placing the child, or to an applicant.
2. Revoked.
3. A consent to adoption (Form 34F) under section 137 of the Act from every parent, other than the applicant, of whom the person placing the child or an applicant is aware. An order under section 138 of the Act dispensing with a parent's consent may be filed instead of the consent.
4. An affidavit (Form 34G) signed by the licensee or by an authorized employee of the children's aid society (depending on who is placing the child).
5. If the child is placed by a licensee, a copy of the licensee's licence to make the placement at the time of placing the child for adoption.
6. If the child is an Indian or native person, proof of 30 days written notice to the child's band or native community of the intention to place the child for adoption.

### Additional material—Relative or step-parent

(8) If the applicant is the child's relative or the spouse of the child's parent, an affidavit from each applicant (Form 34H) shall also be filed with the application.

### Application by step-parent or relative

(9) An application by a relative of the child or the spouse of the child's parent,

(a) shall not be commenced until the 21-day period referred to in subsection 137(8) of the Act has expired; and

(b) shall be accompanied by the applicant's affidavit confirming that he or she did not receive a withdrawal of consent during the 21-day period.

### Step-parent adoption, parent's consent

(10) An application by the spouse of the child's parent shall be accompanied by the parent's consent (Form 34I).

### Independent legal advice, child's consent

(11) The consent of a child to be adopted (Form 34) shall be witnessed by a representative of the Children's Lawyer, who shall complete the affidavit of execution and independent legal advice contained in the form.

### Independent legal advice, consent of parent under 18

(11.1) The consent of a person under the age of 18 years who is a parent of the child to be adopted (Form 34F) shall be witnessed by a representative of the Children's Lawyer, who shall complete an affidavit of execution and independent legal advice (Form 34J).

### Independent legal advice, adult parent's consent

(12) The consent of an adult parent of the child to be adopted shall be witnessed by an independent lawyer, who shall complete the affidavit of execution and independent legal advice.

### Copy of consent for person signing

(13) A person who signs a consent to an adoption shall be given a copy of the consent and of the affidavit of execution and independent legal advice.

### Withdrawal of consent by parent

(13.1) A parent who has given consent to an adoption under subsection 137(2) of the Act may withdraw the consent under subsection 137(8) of the Act in accordance with the following:

1. If the child is placed for adoption by a children's aid society, the parent who wishes to withdraw the consent shall ensure that the children's aid society receives the written withdrawal within 21 days after the consent was given.
2. If the child is placed for adoption by a licensee, the parent who wishes to withdraw the consent shall ensure that the licensee receives the written withdrawal within 21 days after the consent was given.
3. If a relative of the child or a spouse of a parent proposes to apply to adopt the child, the parent who wishes to withdraw the consent shall ensure that the relative or spouse receives the written withdrawal within 21 days after the consent was given.

### Withdrawal of consent by child aged seven or older

(13.2) A child who has given consent to an adoption under subsection 137(6) of the Act may withdraw the consent under subsection 137(8) of the Act in accordance with the following:

1. The withdrawal shall be signed within 21 days after the consent was given, and witnessed by the person who witnessed the consent under subrule (11) or by another representative of the Children's Lawyer.
2. The person who witnesses the withdrawal shall give the original withdrawal document to the child and promptly serve a copy on the children's aid society, licensee, relative or spouse, as the case may be.

### Motion to withdraw consent

(14) Despite subrule 5(4) (place for steps other than enforcement), a motion to withdraw a consent to an adoption under subsection 139(1) of the Act shall be made in,

(a) the municipality where the person who gave the consent lives; or

(b) in any other place that the court decides.

### Clerk to check adoption application

(15)  Before the application is presented to a judge, the clerk shall,

(a)  review the application and other documents filed to see whether they are in order; and

(b)  prepare a certificate (Form 34K).

### Dispensing with consent before placement

(16)  In an application to dispense with a parent's consent before placement for adoption,

(a)  the applicant may be the licensee, a parent, the children's aid society or the person who wants to adopt;

(b)  the respondent is the person who has not given consent;

(c)  if an order that service is not required is sought, the request shall be made in the application and not by motion;

(d)  if the application is being served, the applicant shall serve and file with it an affidavit (Form 14A) setting out the facts of the case;

(e)  if the application is not being served, the applicant shall file with it an affidavit (Form 14A) setting out the facts of the case, and the clerk shall send the case to a judge for a decision on the basis of affidavit evidence.

### Forms for openness applications

(17)  In a case about an openness order under Part VII of the Act,

(a)  an application for an openness order shall be in Form 34L;

(b)  a consent to an openness order under section 145.1 of the Act shall be in Form 34M;

(b.1)  a consent to an openness order under section 145.1.2 of the Act shall be in Form 34M.1;

(c)  an application to change or terminate an openness order shall be in Form 34N; and

(d)  an answer to an application for an openness order or an answer to an application to change or terminate an openness order shall be in Form 33B.2.

(e)  the notice of intention to place a child for adoption to be served on persons entitled to access, other than the child, shall be in Form 8D.2;

(f)  the notice to a child who is entitled to access that he or she will be placed for adoption shall be in Form 8D.3; and

(g)  the notice of termination of access to be served on a person who is the subject of an access order and not entitled to bring an application for an openness order shall be in Form 8D.4.

### Service of notice of intention to place a child for adoption

(18)  In an application for an order under subsection 145.1.1(5) of the Act to allow another method of service of the notice of intention to place a child for adoption or of the notice

of termination of access (Form 8D.4), or for an order under subsection 145.1.1 (6) of the Act that notice is not required,

(a)  the applicant is the children's aid society;

(b)  the respondent is the person who is entitled to have access to, or contact with, the child;

(c)  the application shall be made using Form 8B.2—Application (general) (*Child and Family Services Act* cases other than child protection and status review);

(d)  the application shall be filed in the same court file as the child protection case in which the child was made a Crown ward;

(e)  the applicant shall file an affidavit (Form 14A) setting out the facts in support of the order being requested and the clerk shall send the case to a judge for a decision on the basis of the affidavit evidence.

### Timelines for openness applications

(19)  Every application for an openness order is governed by the following timetable:

| Step in the case | Maximum time for completion, from the date the application is filed |
|---|---|
| Service and filing of answers | 30 days |
| First hearing or settlement conference | 50 days |
| Hearing | 90 days |

## RULE 35: CHANGE OF NAME

### Time for application

**35.**  (1)  An application under subsection 7(3) (application to court for change of name) of the *Change of Name Act* shall be made within 30 days after the applicant is notified that the Registrar General has refused to make the requested change of name.

### Service on the registrar general

(2)  The applicant shall serve the application and any supporting material on the Registrar General by delivering or mailing a copy of the documents to the Deputy Registrar General.

### Registrar general's reasons for refusal

(3)  Within 15 days after being served under subrule (2), the Registrar General may file reasons for refusing to make the requested change of name.

## RULE 35.1: CUSTODY AND ACCESS

### Definition

**35.1**  (1)  In this rule,

"parent" means,

(a) a biological parent of a child,

(b) an adoptive parent of a child,

(c) an individual declared under Part II of the *Children's Law Reform Act* to be a parent of a child, and

(d) an individual presumed under section 8 of the *Children's Law Reform Act* to be the father of a child.

### Affidavit in support of custody or access claim

(2) If an application, answer or motion to change a final order contains a claim for custody of or access to a child, the party making the claim shall serve and file an affidavit in support of claim for custody or access (Form 35.1), together with any other documents required by this rule, with the document that contains the claim.

### Police records check

(3) Every person who makes a claim for custody of a child and who is not a parent of the child shall attach to the affidavit in support of claim for custody or access,

(a) a police records check obtained not more than 60 days before the person starts the claim; or

(b) if the person requested the police records check for the purposes of the claim but has not received it by the time he or she starts the claim, proof of the request.

### Same

(4) If clause (3)(b) applies, the person shall serve and file the police records check no later than 10 days after receiving it.

### Request for report from children's aid society

(5) Every person required to submit a request under subsection 21.2(2) of the *Children's Law Reform Act* for a report from a children's aid society shall provide to the court a copy of the request together with the affidavit in support of claim for custody or access.

### Documents shall be refused

(6) If these rules require a document to be accompanied by the applicable documents referred to in this rule, the clerk shall not accept the document for filing without,

(a) an affidavit in support of claim for custody or access; and

(b) the documents referred to in subrules (3) and (5), if applicable.

### Corrections and updates

(7) As soon as a person discovers that information in his or her affidavit in support of claim for custody or access is incorrect or incomplete, or that there has been a change in the information provided in the affidavit, he or she shall immediately serve and file,

(a) a new affidavit in support of claim for custody or access (Form 35.1) containing the correct or updated information; or

(b) if the correction or change is minor, an affidavit in Form 14A describing the correction or change and indicating any effect it has on the person's plan for the care and upbringing of the child.

### Associated cases

(8) If the clerk provides to a person making a claim for custody of a child information in writing under subsection 21.3(1) of the *Children's Law Reform Act* respecting any current or previous family proceedings involving the child or any person who is a party to the claim and who is not a parent of the child, the person shall serve a copy of the written information on every other party.

### Same

(9) If the written information provided by the clerk contains information indicating that the person making the claim was or is involved in family proceedings in which he or she was or is not involved, the person making the claim may serve with the copy of the written information an affidavit identifying those proceedings.

## RULE 36: DIVORCE

### Application for divorce

**36.** (1) Either spouse may start a divorce case by,

(a) filing an application naming the other spouse as a respondent; or

(b) filing a joint application with no respondent.

### Joint application

(2) In a joint application, the divorce and any other order sought shall be made only with the consent of both spouses.

### Allegation of adultery

(3) In an application for divorce claiming that the other spouse committed adultery with another person, that person does not need to be named, but if named, shall be served with the application and has all the rights of a respondent in the case.

### Marriage certificate and central divorce registry certificate

(4) The court shall not grant a divorce until the following have been filed:

1. A marriage certificate or marriage registration certificate, unless the application states that it is impractical to obtain a certificate and explains why.

2. A report on earlier divorce cases started by either spouse, issued under the *Central Registry of Divorce Proceedings Regulations* (Canada).

### Divorce based on affidavit evidence

(5) If the respondent files no answer, or files one and later withdraws it, the applicant shall file an affidavit (Form 36) that,

(a) confirms that all the information in the application is correct, except as stated in the affidavit;

(b) if no marriage certificate or marriage registration certificate has been filed, provides sufficient information to prove the marriage;

(c) contains proof of any previous divorce or the death of a party's previous spouse, unless the marriage took place in Canada;

(d) contains the information about arrangements for support of any children of the marriage required by paragraph 11(1)(b) of the *Divorce Act* (Canada), and attaches as exhibits the income and financial information required by section 21 of the child support guidelines; and

(e) contains any other information necessary for the court to grant the divorce.

### Draft divorce order

(6) The applicant shall file with the affidavit,

(a) three copies of a draft divorce order (Form 25A);

(b) a stamped envelope addressed to each party; and

(c) if the divorce order is to contain a support order,

(i) an extra copy of the draft divorce order for the clerk to file with the Director of the Family Responsibility Office, and

(ii) two copies of a draft support deduction order.

### Clerk to present papers to judge

(7) When the documents mentioned in subrules (4) to (6) have been filed, the clerk shall prepare a certificate (Form 36A) and present the documents to a judge, who may,

(a) grant the divorce as set out in the draft order;

(b) have the clerk return the documents to the applicant to make any needed corrections; or

(c) grant the divorce but make changes to the draft order, or refuse to grant the divorce, after giving the applicant a chance to file an additional affidavit or come to court to explain why the order should be made without change.

### Divorce certificate

(8) When a divorce takes effect, the clerk shall, on either party's request,

(a) check the continuing record to verify that,

(i) no appeal has been taken from the divorce order, or any appeal from it has been disposed of, and

(ii) no order has been made extending the time for an appeal, or any extended time has expired without an appeal; and

(b) if satisfied of those matters, issue a divorce certificate (Form 36B) and mail it to the parties, unless the court orders otherwise.

(9) Revoked.

## RULE 37: INTERJURISDICTIONAL SUPPORT ORDERS ACT, 2002

### Application

**37.** (1) This rule applies to cases under the Act.

### Definitions

(2) In this rule,

"Act" means the *Interjurisdictional Support Orders Act, 2002*;

"appropriate authority" has the same meaning as in the Act;

"designated authority" has the same meaning as in the Act;

"general regulation" means Ontario Regulation 55/03;

"send," when used in reference to a person, means to,

(a) mail to the person's lawyer or, if none, to the person,

(b) send by courier to the person's lawyer or, if none, to the person,

(c) deposit at a document exchange to which the person's lawyer belongs, or

(d) fax to the person's lawyer or, if none, to the person.

### Notice of hearing

(3) When the court receives a support application or a support variation application the clerk shall, under section 10 or 33 of the Act,

(a) serve on the respondent, by special service,

(i) the notice of hearing mentioned in clause 10(b) or 33(b) of the Act (Form 37),

(ii) a copy of the documents sent by the designated authority, and

(iii) blank response forms; and

(b) send to the designated authority a copy of the notice of hearing and an information sheet (Form 37A).

### Information and documents to be provided by respondent

(4) The respondent shall file, within 30 days after service of the notice of hearing,

(a) an answer in Form N under the general regulation,

(i) identifying any issues the respondent intends to raise with respect to the support application, and

(ii) containing the financial information referred to in subsection 21(1) of Ontario Regulation 391/97 (Child Support Guidelines), if the support application includes a claim for child support;

(b) an affidavit (Form 14A) setting out the evidence on which the respondent relies; and

(c) a financial statement in Form K under the general regulation.

### Respondent's financial statement

(5) The respondent is required to file a financial statement whether he or she intends to dispute the claim or not.

### Applicant's financial statement

(6) The fact that the applicant has provided financial information in a form different than that required by these rules does not affect the case.

### Written hearing

(7) Unless the court orders otherwise under subrule (9), the application shall be dealt with on the basis of written documents without the parties or their lawyers needing to come to court.

### Request for oral hearing

(8) The respondent may request an oral hearing by filing a motion (Form 14B) within 30 days after being served with the notice of hearing.

### Order for oral hearing

(9) The court may order an oral hearing, on the respondent's motion or on its own initiative, if it is satisfied that an oral hearing is necessary to deal with the case justly.

### Direction to request further information or documents

(10) A direction to request further information or documents under clause 11(2)(a) or 34(2)(a) of the Act shall be in Form 37B, and a statement of the court's reasons for requesting further evidence shall be attached to the direction.

### Direction to be sent to respondent

(11) When a direction is sent to the designated authority under clause 11(2)(a) of the Act, the clerk shall also send a copy to the respondent.

### Adjournment

(12) When the court adjourns the hearing under clause 11(2)(b) or 34(2)(b) of the Act, it shall specify the date on which the hearing is to continue.

### Copies of further information or documents

(13) When the court receives the further information or documents, the clerk shall promptly prepare a notice of continuation of hearing (Form 37C) and send it, with copies of the information or documents, to the respondent and to the designated authority.

### Respondent's affidavit

(14) If the respondent wishes to respond to the further information or documents, he or she shall file an affidavit (Form 14A) containing the response with the court, within 30 days after receiving the notice of continuation of hearing.

### Preparation of order

(15) The clerk shall prepare the order for signature as soon as it is made, in accordance with subrule 25(11).

### Sending copies of order to respondent and designated authority

(16) The court shall send,

(a) a copy of the order to the respondent, addressed to the respondent's last known address if sent by mail; and

(b) a certified copy of the order to the designated authority.

### Sending copy of order to appropriate authority

(17) The designated authority shall send the certified copy of the order to the appropriate authority.

### Notice of registration, order made outside Canada

(18) For the purpose of subsection 20(1) of the Act, the clerk of the Ontario court shall give notice of the registration of an order made outside Canada by providing a notice in Form 37D, as described in subrule (19), to any party to the order who is believed to ordinarily reside in Ontario.

### Sending or special service

(19) If the party to whom notice is to be provided applied for the order in Ontario, the clerk shall send the notice to the party, but in any other case, the clerk shall serve the notice on the party by special service.

### Motion to set aside registration

(20) For the purpose of subsection 20(3) of the Act, a party shall give notice of a motion to set aside the registration of an order made outside Canada by,

(a) filing in the Ontario court a notice of motion (Form 14) setting out the grounds for the motion;

(b) sending the notice of motion and supporting documents to the claimant at the address shown in the order; and

(c) serving the notice of motion and supporting documents on the designated authority at least 10 days before the motion hearing date.

### Designated authority need not appear on motion

(21) The designated authority is not required to appear on the motion to set aside registration.

### Notice of decision or order

(22) When the court makes a decision or order under section 20 of the Act, the clerk shall send copies of the order, with the court's reasons, if any,

(a) to each party, addressed to the party's last known address if sent by mail; and

(b) to the designated authority.

### Party in reciprocating jurisdiction

(23) If a party ordinarily resides in a reciprocating jurisdiction and the order was originally sent to Ontario for registration by the appropriate authority there, the clerk may send it to that appropriate authority rather than sending it to the party as set out in clause (22)(a).

### Provisional orders

(24) When the court makes a provisional order under section 7 or 30 of the Act, the clerk shall send the following to the designated authority, to be sent to the reciprocating jurisdiction:

1. One copy of,

   i. the application (Form A under the general regulation),

ii.   the applicant's financial statement (Form K under the general regulation), and

iii.   a statement giving any information about the respondent's identification, whereabouts, income, assets and liabilities.

2.   Three certified copies of,

i.   the applicant's evidence and, if reasonably possible, the exhibits, and

ii.   the provisional order.

### Further evidence

(25)   When the court that made a provisional order receives a request for further evidence from the confirming court under subsection 7(4) or 30(4) of the Act, the clerk shall send to the applicant a notice for taking further evidence (Form 37E) and a copy of the documents sent by the confirming court.

## RULE 37.1: PROVISIONAL ORDERS AND CONFIRMATION OF PROVISIONAL ORDERS— DIVORCE ACT, FAMILY LAW ACT

### Application

**37.1** (1)   This rule applies to orders made under sections 18 and 19 of the *Divorce Act* (Canada) and under section 44 of the *Family Law Act*.

### Definitions

(2)   In this rule,

"confirming court" means,

(a)   in the case of an order under section 19 of the *Divorce Act* (Canada), the court in Ontario or another province or territory of Canada that has jurisdiction to confirm a provisional variation of the order, or

(b)   for the purpose of section 44 of the *Family Law Act*,

(i)   the Ontario Court of Justice sitting in the municipality where the respondent resides, or

(ii)   the Family Court of the Superior Court of Justice, if the respondent resides in an area where that court has jurisdiction;

"originating court" means,

(a)   in the case of an order under section 18 of the *Divorce Act* (Canada), the court in Ontario or another province or territory of Canada that has jurisdiction under section 5 of that Act to deal with an application for a provisional variation of the order, or

(b)   for the purpose of section 44 of the *Family Law Act*,

(i)   the Ontario Court of Justice sitting in the municipality where the provisional order is made, or

(ii)   the Family Court of the Superior Court of Justice when it makes the provisional order;

"send," when used in reference to a person, means to,

(a)   mail to the person's lawyer or, if none, to the person,

(b)   send by courier to the person's lawyer or, if none, to the person,

(c)   deposit at a document exchange to which the person's lawyer belongs, or

(d)   fax to the person's lawyer or, if none, to the person.

### Documents to be sent to confirming court

(3)   When the court makes a provisional order under section 18 of the *Divorce Act* (Canada) or section 44 of the *Family Law Act*, the clerk shall send the following to the confirming court (if it is in Ontario) or to the Attorney General to be sent to the confirming court (if it is outside Ontario):

1.   One copy of,

i.   the application (Form 8),

ii.   the applicant's financial statement (Form 13),

iii.   a statement giving any information about the respondent's identification, whereabouts, income, assets and liabilities, and

iv.   if the confirming court is in another municipality in Ontario, proof that the application was served on the respondent.

2.   Three certified copies of,

i.   the applicant's evidence and, if reasonably possible, the exhibits, and

ii.   the provisional order.

### No financial statement from foreign applicant

(4)   When a confirming court in Ontario receives a provisional order made outside Ontario, the applicant does not have to file a financial statement.

### Notice of confirmation hearing

(5)   A clerk of a confirming court in Ontario who receives a provisional order shall,

(a)   serve on the respondent, by special service (subrule 6(3)),

(i)   a notice of hearing (Form 37),

(ii)   a copy of the documents sent by the originating court, and

(iii)   blank response forms; and

(b)   send a notice of hearing and an information sheet (Form 37A) to,

(i)   the applicant,

(ii)   the clerk of the originating court, and

(iii)   the Attorney General, if the provisional order was made outside Ontario.

### Respondent's financial statement

(6)   A respondent at a confirmation hearing under section 19 of the *Divorce Act* (Canada) shall serve and file a financial statement (Form 13) within 30 days after service of the notice of confirmation hearing.

### Written hearing

(7) Unless the court orders otherwise under subrule (9), the application shall be dealt with on the basis of written documents without the parties or their lawyers needing to come to court.

### Request for oral hearing

(8) The respondent may request an oral hearing by filing a motion (Form 14B) within 30 days after being served with the notice of hearing.

### Order for oral hearing

(9) The court may order an oral hearing, on the applicant's motion or on its own initiative, if it is satisfied that an oral hearing is necessary to deal with the case justly.

### Court receives request for further evidence

(10) When an originating court in Ontario receives a request for further evidence from the confirming court, the clerk shall send to the applicant a notice for taking further evidence (Form 37E) and a copy of the documents sent by the confirming court.

### Court sends request for further evidence

(11) When a confirming court in Ontario requests further evidence from the originating court,

    (a) the confirming court shall adjourn the confirmation hearing to a new date; and

    (b) the clerk shall send to the originating court two certified copies of the evidence taken in the confirming court.

### Continuing the Confirmation Hearing

(12) When a confirming court in Ontario receives further evidence from the originating court, the clerk shall promptly prepare a notice of continuation of hearing (Form 37C) and send it, with copies of the evidence, to the respondent and, if the provisional order was made outside Ontario, to the Attorney General.

### Respondent's affidavit

(13) If the respondent wishes to respond to the further evidence, he or she shall file an affidavit containing the response with the court, within 30 days after receiving the notice of continuation of hearing.

## RULE 38: APPEALS

### Rules that apply in appeals to Divisional Court and Court of Appeal

**38.** (1) Rules 61, 62 and 63 of the Rules of Civil Procedure apply with necessary changes, including those modifications set out in subrules (2) and (3),

    (a) if an appeal lies to the Divisional Court or the Court of Appeal;

    (b) if leave to appeal to the Divisional Court or the Court of Appeal is required,

in a family law case as described in subrule 1(2).

### Modifications in child protection appeals

(2) If the appeal is brought in a case under the *Child and Family Services Act*, the following time periods apply instead of the time periods mentioned in the referenced provisions of the Rules of Civil Procedure:

1. The time period referred to in clause 61.09(1)(a) shall be 14 days after filing the notice of appeal if there is no transcript.
2. The time period referred to in clause 61.09(1)(b) shall be 30 days after receiving notice that the evidence has been transcribed.
3. The time period referred to in clause 61.12(2) shall be 30 days after service of the appeal book and compendium, exhibit book, transcript of evidence, if any, and appellant's factum.
4. The time period referred to in clause 61.13(2)(a) shall be 30 days after the registrar receives notice that the evidence has been transcribed.
5. The time period referred to in clause 61.13(2)(b) shall be six months after filing the notice of appeal.
6. The time period referred to in subrule 62.02(2) for serving the notice of motion for leave to appeal shall be 30 days.

### Appeal of temporary order in *Child and Family Services Act* case

(3) In an appeal of a temporary order made in a case under the *Child and Family Services Act* and brought to the Divisional Court under clause 19(1)(b) of the *Courts of Justice Act*, the motion for leave to appeal shall be combined with the notice of appeal and heard together with the appeal.

### Appeals to the superior court of justice

(4) Subrules (5) to (45) apply to an appeal from an order of the Ontario Court of Justice to the Superior Court of Justice under,

    (a) section 48 of the *Family Law Act*;

    (b) section 73 of the *Children's Law Reform Act*;

    (c) sections 69 and 156 of the *Child and Family Services Act*;

    (d) section 40 of the *Interjurisdictional Support Orders Act, 2002*;

    (e) section 40 of the *Courts of Justice Act*; and

    (f) any other statute to which these rules apply, unless the statute provides for another procedure.

### How to start appeal

(5) To start an appeal from a final order of the Ontario Court of Justice to the Superior Court of Justice under any of the provisions listed in subrule (4), a party shall,

    (a) within 30 days after the date of the order or decision being appealed from, serve a notice of appeal (Form 38) on,

        (i) every other party affected by the appeal or entitled to appeal,

(ii) the clerk of the court in the place where the order was made, and

(iii) if the appeal is under section 69 of the *Child and Family Services Act*, every other person entitled to notice under subsection 39(3) of that Act who appeared at the hearing; and

(b) within 10 days after serving the notice of appeal, file it.

### Starting appeal of temporary order

(6) Subrule (5) applies to the starting of an appeal from a temporary order of the Ontario Court of Justice to the Superior Court of Justice except that the notice of appeal shall be served within seven days after the date of the temporary order.

### Same, *Child and Family Services Act* case

(7) To start an appeal from a temporary order of the Ontario Court of Justice to the Superior Court of Justice in a case under the *Child and Family Services Act*, subrule (5) applies and the notice of appeal shall be served within 30 days after the date of the temporary order.

### Name of case unchanged

(8) The name of a case in an appeal shall be the same as the name of the case in the order appealed from and shall identify the parties as appellant and respondent.

### Appeal by respondent

(9) If the respondent in an appeal also wants to appeal the same order, this rule applies, with necessary changes, to the respondent's appeal, and the two appeals shall be heard together.

### Grounds stated in notice of appeal

(10) The notice of appeal shall state the order that the appellant wants the appeal court to make and the legal grounds for the appeal.

### Other grounds

(11) At the hearing of the appeal, no grounds other than the ones stated in the notice of appeal may be argued unless the court gives permission.

### Transcript of evidence

(12) If the appeal requires a transcript of evidence, the appellant shall, within 30 days after filing the notice of appeal, file proof that the transcript has been ordered.

### Consultation with respondent

(13) The appellant shall determine if the appeal requires a transcript of evidence in consultation with the respondent.

### Agreement on evidence to be transcribed

(14) If the appellant and respondent agree about what evidence needs to be transcribed, the appellant shall order the agreed evidence transcribed.

### No agreement

(15) If the appellant and respondent cannot agree, the appellant shall order a transcript of all of the oral evidence from the hearing of the decision under appeal unless the court orders otherwise.

### Once transcript completed

(16) When the authorized court transcriptionist has completed the transcript, he or she shall promptly notify the appellant, the respondent and the court office in the court where the appeal will be heard.

### Contents of appellant's appeal record

(17) The appellant's appeal record shall contain a copy of the following documents, in the following order:

1. A table of contents describing each document, including each exhibit, by its nature and date and, for an exhibit, by exhibit number or letter.
2. The notice of appeal.
3. The order being appealed, as signed, and any reasons given by the court appealed from, as well as a further printed copy of the reasons if they are handwritten.
4. A transcript of the oral evidence.
5. Any other material that was before the court appealed from and that is necessary for the appeal.

### Contents of appellant's factum

(18) The appellant's factum shall be not more than 30 pages long, shall be signed by the appellant's lawyer or, if none, by the appellant and shall consist of the following parts, containing paragraphs numbered consecutively from the beginning to the end of the factum:

1. Part 1: Identification. A statement identifying the appellant and respondent and the court appealed from, and stating the result in that court.
2. Part 2: Overview. A brief overview of the case and the issues on the appeal.
3. Part 3: Facts. A brief summary of the facts relevant to the appeal, with reference to the evidence by page and line as necessary.
4. Part 4: Issues. A brief statement of each issue, followed by a brief argument referring to the law relating to that issue.
5. Part 5: Order. A precise statement of the order the appeal court is asked to make, including any order for costs.
6. Part 6: Time estimate. An estimate of how much time will be needed for the appellant's oral argument, not including reply to the respondent's argument.
7. Part 7: List of authorities. A list of all statutes, regulations, rules, cases and other authorities referred to in the factum.
8. Part 8: Legislation. A copy of all relevant provisions of statutes, regulations and rules.

## Respondent's factum and appeal record

(19) The respondent shall, within the timeline set out in subrule (21) or (22), serve on every other party to the appeal and file,

(a) a respondent's factum (subrule (20)); and

(b) if applicable, a respondent's appeal record containing a copy of any material that was before the court appealed from which are necessary for the appeal but are not included in the appellant's appeal record.

## Contents of respondent's factum

(20) The respondent's factum shall be not more than 30 pages long, shall be signed by the respondent's lawyer or, if none, by the respondent and shall consist of the following parts, containing paragraphs numbered consecutively from the beginning to the end of the factum:

1. Part 1: Overview. A brief overview of the case and the issues on the appeal.
2. Part 2: Facts. A brief statement of the facts in the appellant's factum that the respondent accepts as correct and the facts that the respondent says are incorrect, and a brief summary of any additional facts relied on by the respondent, with reference to the evidence by page and line as necessary.
3. Part 3: Issues. A statement of the respondent's position on each issue raised by the appellant, followed by a brief argument referring to the law relating to that issue.
4. Part 4: Additional issues. A brief statement of each additional issue raised by the respondent, followed by a brief argument referring to the law relating to that issue.
5. Part 5: Order. A precise statement of the order the appeal court is asked to make, including any order for costs.
6. Part 6: Time estimate. An estimate of how much time will be needed for the respondent's oral argument.
7. Part 7: List of authorities. A list of all statutes, regulations, rules, cases and other authorities referred to in the factum.
8. Part 8: Legislation. A copy of all relevant provisions of statutes, regulations and rules not included in the appellant's factum.

## Timelines for serving and filing of records and factums other than in *Child and Family Services Act* cases

(21) Except for appeals in cases under the *Child and Family Services Act*, the following timelines for serving appeal records and factums apply:

1. If a transcript is required, the appellant's appeal record and factum shall be served on the respondent and any other person entitled to be heard in the appeal and filed within 60 days from the date of receiving notice that evidence has been transcribed.
2. If no transcript is required, the appellant's appeal record and factum shall be served on the respondent and any other person entitled to be heard in the appeal and filed within 30 days of filing of the notice of appeal.
3. The respondent's appeal record and factum shall be served on the appellant and any other person entitled to be heard on the appeal and filed within 60 days from the serving of the appellant's appeal record and factum.

## Timelines for serving and filing of records and factums in *Child and Family Services Act* cases

(22) For appeals of cases under the *Child and Family Services Act*, the following timelines for serving appeal records and factums apply:

1. If a transcript is required, the appellant's appeal record and factum shall be served on the respondent and any other person entitled to be heard in the appeal and filed within 30 days from the date of receiving notice that evidence has been transcribed.
2. If no transcript is required, the appellant's appeal record and factum shall be served on the respondent and any other person entitled to be heard in the appeal and filed within 14 days of filing of the notice of appeal.
3. The respondent's appeal record and factum shall be served on the appellant and any other person entitled to be heard on the appeal and filed within 30 days from the serving of the appellant's appeal record and factum.

## Scheduling of hearing

(23) When the appellant's appeal record and factum have been filed and the respondent's factum and appeal record, if any, have been filed, or the time for their filing has expired, the clerk shall schedule the appeal for hearing.

## Prompt hearing of CFSA appeals

(24) An appeal under the *Child and Family Services Act* shall be heard within 60 days after the appellant's factum and appeal record are filed.

## Motions in appeals

(25) If a person needs to bring a motion in an appeal, rule 14 applies with necessary changes to the motion.

## Security for costs of appeal

(26) On a motion by the respondent for security for costs, the court may make an order for security for costs that is just, if it is satisfied that,

(a) there is good reason to believe that the appeal is a waste of time, a nuisance, or an abuse of the court process and that the appellant has insufficient assets in Ontario to pay the costs of the appeal;

(b) an order for security for costs could be made against the appellant under subrule 24(13); or

(c) for other good reason, security for costs should be ordered.

## Dismissal for failure to obey order

(27) If an appellant does not obey an order under subrule (26), the court may on motion dismiss the appeal.

## Motion for summary judgment in appeal

(28) After the notice of appeal is filed, the respondent or any other person who is entitled to be heard on the appeal may make a motion for summary judgment or for summary decision on a legal issue without a hearing of the appeal, and rule 16 applies to the motion with necessary changes.

## Motion to receive further evidence

(29) Any person entitled to be heard in the appeal may bring a motion to admit further evidence under clause 134(4)(b) of the *Courts of Justice Act*.

## Motion for dismissal for delay

(30) If the appellant has not,

(a) filed proof that a transcript of evidence was ordered under subrule (12);

(b) served and filed the appeal record and factum within the timelines set out in subrule (21) or (22) or such longer time as may have been ordered by the court,

the respondent may file a motion form (Form 14B) to have the appeal dismissed for delay.

## Withdrawal of appeal

(31) The appellant may withdraw an appeal by serving a notice of withdrawal (Form 12) on every other party and filing it.

## Deemed withdrawal

(32) If a person serves a notice of appeal and does not file it within 10 days as required by clause (5)(b), the appeal shall be deemed to be withdrawn unless the court orders otherwise.

## Automatic stays pending appeal, support orders

(33) The service of a notice of appeal from a temporary or final order does not stay a support order or an order that enforces a support order.

## Other payment orders

(34) The service of a notice of appeal from a temporary or final order stays, until the disposition of the appeal, any other payment order made under the temporary or final order.

## Stay by order of court

(35) A temporary or final order may be stayed on any conditions that the court considers appropriate,

(a) by an order of the court that made the order; or

(b) by an order of the Superior Court of Justice.

## Expiry of stay granted by court that made order

(36) A stay granted under clause (35)(a) expires if no notice of appeal is served and the time for service has expired.

## Powers of superior court of justice

(37) A stay granted under subrule (35) may be set aside or changed by the Superior Court of Justice.

## Effect of stay generally

(38) If an order is stayed, no steps may be taken under the order or for its enforcement, except,

(a) by order of the Superior Court of Justice; or

(b) as provided in subrules (39) and (40).

## Settling of order

(39) A stay does not prevent the settling or signing of the order.

## Writ of execution

(40) A stay does not prevent the issue of a writ of seizure and sale or the filing of the writ in a sheriff's office or land registry office, but no instruction or direction to enforce the writ shall be given to a sheriff while the stay remains in effect.

## Certificate of stay

(41) If an order is stayed, the clerk of the court that granted the stay shall, if requested by a party to the appeal, issue a certificate of stay in Form 63A under the Rules of Civil Procedure with necessary changes.

## Stay of support order

(42) A party who obtains a stay of a support order shall obtain a certificate of stay under subrule (41) and file it immediately in the office of the Director of the Family Responsibility Office if the stay relates to a support order being enforced by the Director.

## Certificate filed with sheriff's office

(43) If a certificate of stay is filed with the sheriff's office, the sheriff shall not begin or continue enforcement of the order until satisfied that the stay is no longer in effect.

## Request for certificate

(44) A request for a certificate of stay under subrule (41) shall state whether the stay is under subrule (34) or by order under subrule (35) and, if under subrule (35), shall set out the particulars of the order.

## Setting aside writ of execution

(45) The court may set aside the issue or filing of a writ of seizure and sale if the party making the motion or the appellant gives security satisfactory to the court.

## Appeals, family arbitration awards

(46) Subrules (5), (8) to (21), (23) and (25) to (32) apply, with necessary changes, including the modifications set out in subrules (47) to (55), to the appeal of a family arbitration award under section 45 of the *Arbitration Act, 1991* and, for the purpose,

(a) a reference to the Ontario Court of Justice or to the court being appealed from shall be read as a reference to the arbitrator who made the family arbitration award; and

(b) a reference to the order or decision being appealed from shall be read as a reference to the family arbitration award.

### Same, service

(47) In addition to the persons listed under clause (5)(a), the appellant shall serve the notice of appeal on the arbitrator.

### Same, contents of appellant's appeal record

(48) The material referred to in paragraph 5 of subrule (17) shall include,

(a) copies of the certificates of independent legal advice required by the *Family Law Act* for the parties;

(b) a copy of the family arbitration agreement; and

(c) the original family arbitration award or a certified copy.

### Same, if leave required

(49) If the appeal of a family arbitration award requires the leave of the court, rule 14 applies, with necessary changes, including the modifications set out in subrules (50) to (55), to the motion for leave to appeal, other than subrules 14(4), (4.2), (6), (7), (10) to (15) and (17).

### Same

(50) The notice of motion (Form 14) shall,

(a) be served on every other party affected by the appeal or entitled to appeal and on the arbitrator no later than 15 days after the making of the family arbitration award; and

(b) be filed no later than five days after service.

### Same

(51) The affidavit (Form 14A) and any additional evidence mentioned in clause 14(9)(b) shall be served and filed no later than 30 days after the filing of the notice of motion for leave to appeal, together with,

(a) a copy of the notice of motion;

(b) the documents listed in subrule (48); and

(c) a factum consisting of a concise argument stating the facts and law relied on by the party making the motion.

### Same

(52) The notice of motion and factum shall set out the specific questions that it is proposed the court should answer on appeal if leave to appeal is granted.

### Same

(53) Any response to the motion for leave to appeal by a party shall be served and filed no later than 15 days after the materials referred to in subrule (51) were served on the party.

### Same

(54) The clerk shall fix a date for the hearing of the motion, which shall not, except with the consent of the party responding to the motion, be earlier than 15 days after the filing of the materials referred to in subrule (51).

### Same

(55) If leave to appeal is granted,

(a) the notice of appeal shall be served no later than seven days after the granting of leave; and

(b) the 30-day deadline set out in clause (5)(a) does not apply, but the filing deadline set out in clause (5)(b) continues to apply.

## RULE 39: CASE MANAGEMENT IN FAMILY COURT OF SUPERIOR COURT OF JUSTICE

### Case management in certain areas only

**39.** (1) This rule applies only to cases in the Family Court of the Superior Court of Justice, which has jurisdiction in the municipalities listed in subrule 1(3).

### Excluded cases

(2) This rule does not apply to,

(a) enforcements;

(b) cases under rule 32.1, 37 or 37.1; or

(c) cases under the *Child and Family Services Act*.

### Parties may not lengthen times

(3) A time set out in this rule may be lengthened only by order of the case management judge and not by the parties' consent under subrule 3(6).

### Fast track

(4) Applications to which this rule applies, except the ones mentioned in subrule (7), and motions to change a final order or agreement are fast track cases (subrules (5) and (6)).

### Fast track—First court date

(5) In a fast track case the clerk shall, on or before the first court date,

(a) confirm that all necessary documents have been served and filed;

(b) refer the parties to sources of information about the court process, alternatives to court (including mediation), the effects of separation and divorce on children and community resources that may help the parties and their children;

(c) if an answer has been filed in response to an application, or if a response to motion to change (Form 15B) or a notice of financial interest has been filed in a motion to change a final order or agreement under rule 15, confirm that the case is ready for a hearing, case conference or settlement conference and schedule it accordingly;

(d) if no answer has been filed in response to an application, send the case to a judge for a decision on the basis of affidavit evidence or, on request of the applicant, schedule a case conference; and

(e) if no response to motion to change (Form 15B), consent motion to change (Form 15C) or notice of financial interest is filed in response to a motion to change a final order or agreement under rule 15, send the case to a judge for a decision on the basis of the evidence filed in the motion.

### Fast track—Case management judge assigned at start

(6) In a fast track case, a case management judge shall be assigned by the first time the case comes before a judge.

### Standard track

(7) Applications in which the applicant makes any of the following claims are standard track cases (subrule (8)).

1. A claim for divorce.
2. A property claim.
3. A claim under the *Arbitration Act, 1991* or the *Family Law Act* relating to a family arbitration, family arbitration agreement or family arbitration award.

### Features of standard track

(8) In a standard track case,

(a) the clerk shall not set a court date when the application is filed;

(b) a case management judge shall be assigned when a case conference or a motion is scheduled, whichever comes first; and

(c) the clerk shall schedule a case conference on any party's request.

### Functions of case management judge

(9) The case management judge assigned to a case,

(a) shall generally supervise its progress;

(b) shall conduct the case conference and the settlement conference;

(c) may schedule a case conference or settlement conference at any time, on the judge's own initiative; and

(d) shall hear motions in the case, when available to hear motions.

(e) Revoked.

### Substitute case management judge

(10) If the case management judge is, for any reason, unavailable to continue as the case management judge, another case management judge may be assigned for part or all of the case.

### Notice of approaching dismissal after 365 days

(11) The clerk shall serve a notice of approaching dismissal (Form 39) for a case on the parties by mail, fax or email if the case has not been settled, withdrawn or scheduled or adjourned for trial before the 365th day after the date the case was started, and that time has not been lengthened by an order under subrule (3).

### Exception

(11.1) Despite subrule (11), if a case conference or settlement conference is arranged before the 365th day after the date the case was started for a date on or later than the 365th

day, the clerk shall not serve a notice of approaching dismissal except as set out in subrule (11.2).

### Notice sent if conference does not take place

(11.2) If a case conference or settlement conference is arranged for a date on or later than the 365th day after the date the case was started, but the hearing does not take place on that date and is not adjourned by a judge, the clerk shall serve the notice of approaching dismissal on the parties by mail, fax or email.

### Dismissal of case

(12) A case for which a notice of approaching dismissal has been served shall be dismissed without further notice, unless one of the parties, within 60 days after the notice is served,

(a) obtains an order under subrule (3) to lengthen that time;

(b) files an agreement signed by all parties and their lawyers, if any, for a final order disposing of all issues in the case, and a notice of motion for an order carrying out the agreement;

(c) serves on all parties and files a notice of withdrawal (Form 12) that discontinues all outstanding claims in the case;

(d) schedules or adjourns the case for trial; or

(e) arranges a case conference or settlement conference for the first available date.

### Same

(12.1) If a case conference or settlement conference is arranged for a date as described in clause (12)(e), but the hearing does not take place on that date and is not adjourned by a judge, the case shall be dismissed without further notice.

### Dismissal after notice

(12.2) The clerk shall dismiss a case under subrule (12) or (12.1) by preparing and signing an order dismissing the case, with no costs payable by any party.

### Service of dismissal order by clerk

(13) The clerk shall serve the order on each party by mail, fax or email.

### Service of dismissal order by lawyer on client

(14) A lawyer who is served with a dismissal order on behalf of a client shall serve it on the client by mail, fax or email and file proof of service of the order.

### Judge may set clerk's order aside

(14.1) The case management judge or another judge may, on motion, set aside an order of the clerk under subrule (12).

(15) Revoked.

### RULE 40: CASE MANAGEMENT IN ONTARIO COURT OF JUSTICE

### Case management in certain areas only

**40.** (1) This rule applies only to cases in the Ontario Court of Justice.

**Excluded cases**

(2)  This rule does not apply to,

(a)  enforcements;

(b)  cases under rule 37 or 37.1; or

(c)  cases under the *Child and Family Services Act.*

**Parties may not lengthen times**

(3)  A time set out in this rule may be lengthened only by order and not by the parties' consent under subrule 3(6).

**First court date**

(4)  The clerk shall, on or before the first court date,

(a)  confirm that all necessary documents have been served and filed;

(b)  refer the parties to sources of information about the court process, alternatives to court (including mediation), the effects of separation and divorce on children and community resources that may help the parties and their children;

(c)  if an answer has been filed in response to an application, or if a response to motion to change (Form 15B) or a notice of financial interest has been filed in a motion to change a final order or agreement under rule 15, confirm that the case is ready for a hearing, case conference or settlement conference and schedule it accordingly;

(d)  if no answer has been filed in response to an application, send the case to a judge for a decision on the basis of affidavit evidence or, on request of the applicant, schedule a case conference; and

(e)  if no response to motion to change (Form 15B), consent motion to change (Form 15C) or notice of financial interest is filed in response to a motion to change a final order or agreement under rule 15, send the case to a judge for a decision on the basis of the evidence filed in the motion.

**Notice of approaching dismissal after 365 days**

(5)  The clerk shall serve a notice of approaching dismissal (Form 39) for a case on the parties by mail, fax or email if the case has not been settled, withdrawn or scheduled or adjourned for trial before the 365th day after the date the case was started, and that time has not been lengthened by an order under subrule (3).

**Exception**

(5.1)  Despite subrule (5), if a case conference or settlement conference is arranged before the 365th day after the date the case was started for a date on or later than the 365th day, the clerk shall not serve a notice of approaching dismissal except as set out in subrule (5.2).

**Notice sent if conference does not take place**

(5.2)  If a case conference or settlement conference is arranged for a date on or later than the 365th day after the date the case was started, but the hearing does not take place on that date and is not adjourned by a judge, the clerk shall serve the notice of approaching dismissal on the parties by mail, fax or email.

**Dismissal of case**

(6)  A case for which a notice of approaching dismissal has been served shall be dismissed without further notice, unless one of the parties, within 60 days after the notice is served,

(a)  obtains an order under subrule (3) to lengthen that time;

(b)  files an agreement signed by all parties and their lawyers, if any, for a final order disposing of all issues in the case, and a notice of motion for an order carrying out the agreement;

(c)  serves on all parties and files a notice of withdrawal (Form 12) that discontinues all outstanding claims in the case;

(d)  schedules or adjourns the case for trial; or

(e)  arranges a case conference or settlement conference for the first available date.

**Same**

(6.1)  If a case conference or settlement conference is arranged for a date as described in clause (6)(e), but the hearing does not take place on that date and is not adjourned by a judge, the case shall be dismissed without further notice.

**Dismissal after notice**

(6.2)  The clerk shall dismiss a case under subrule (6) or (6.1) by preparing and signing an order dismissing the case, with no costs payable by any party.

**Service of dismissal order by clerk**

(7)  The clerk shall serve the order on each party by mail, fax or email.

**Service of dismissal order by lawyer on client**

(8)  A lawyer who is served with a dismissal order on behalf of a client shall serve it on the client by mail, fax or email and file proof of service of the order.

**Judge may set clerk's order aside**

(9)  A judge may, on motion, set aside an order of the clerk under subrule (6).

(10)  Revoked.

### RULE 41: CASE MANAGEMENT IN THE SUPERIOR COURT OF JUSTICE (OTHER THAN THE FAMILY COURT OF THE SUPERIOR COURT OF JUSTICE)

**Case management**

**41.** (1)  This rule applies only to cases in the Superior Court of Justice, other than cases in the Family Court of the Superior Court of Justice, started on or after July 1, 2004.

**Excluded cases**

(2)  This rule does not apply to,

(a)  enforcements; or

(b)  cases under rule 32.1, 37 or 37.1.

### Parties may not lengthen times

(3) A time set out in this rule may be lengthened only by order of the court and not by the parties' consent under subrule 3(6).

### Clerk's role

(4) The clerk shall not set a court date when the application is filed, and the case shall come before the court when a case conference or a motion is scheduled, whichever comes first, and the clerk shall schedule a case conference on any party's request.

### Notice of approaching dismissal after 365 days

(5) The clerk shall serve a notice of approaching dismissal (Form 39) for a case on the parties by mail, fax or email if the case has not been settled, withdrawn or scheduled or adjourned for trial before the 365th day after the date the case was started, and that time has not been lengthened by an order under subrule (3).

### Exception

(5.1) Despite subrule (5), if a case conference or settlement conference is arranged before the 365th day after the date the case was started for a date on or later than the 365th day, the clerk shall not serve a notice of approaching dismissal except as set out in subrule (5.2).

### Notice sent if conference does not take place

(5.2) If a case conference or settlement conference is arranged for a date on or later than the 365th day after the date the case was started, but the hearing does not take place on that date and is not adjourned by a judge, the clerk shall serve the notice of approaching dismissal on the parties by mail, fax or email.

### Dismissal of case

(6) A case for which a notice of approaching dismissal has been served shall be dismissed without further notice, unless one of the parties, within 60 days after the notice is served,

(a) obtains an order under subrule (3) to lengthen that time;

(b) files an agreement signed by all parties and their lawyers, if any, for a final order disposing of all issues in the case, and a notice of motion for an order carrying out the agreement;

(c) serves on all parties and files a notice of withdrawal (Form 12) that discontinues all outstanding claims in the case;

(d) schedules or adjourns the case for trial; or

(e) arranges a case conference or settlement conference for the first available date.

### Same

(6.1) If a case conference or settlement conference is arranged for a date as described in clause (6)(e), but the hearing does not take place on that date and is not adjourned by a judge, the case shall be dismissed without further notice.

### Dismissal after notice

(6.2) The clerk shall dismiss a case under subrule (6) or (6.1) by preparing and signing an order dismissing the case, with no costs payable by any party.

### Service of dismissal order

(7) The clerk shall serve the order on each party by mail, fax or email.

### Service of dismissal order by lawyer on client

(8) A lawyer who is served with a dismissal order on behalf of a client shall serve it on the client by mail, fax or email and file proof of service of the order.

### Judge may set clerk's order aside

(9) A judge may, on motion, set aside an order of the clerk under subrule (6).

(10) Revoked.

## RULE 42: APPOINTMENT OF FAMILY CASE MANAGER IN THE FAMILY COURT OF THE SUPERIOR COURT OF JUSTICE IN OTTAWA

### Scope

42. (1) This rule applies to cases in the Family Court of the Superior Court of Justice in the City of Ottawa if the cases relate to matters under the following Acts:

1. Revoked.
2. The *Children's Law Reform Act*.
3. The *Divorce Act* (Canada).
4. The *Family Law Act*.
5. The *Family Responsibility and Support Arrears Enforcement Act, 1996*.

### Same

(1.1) This rule applies in respect of a case regardless of whether it is a fast track case (rule 39) or a standard track case.

### Purpose

(2) The purpose of this rule is to promote the active management, in accordance with subrule 2(5), of cases to which this rule applies by conferring specified family law jurisdiction on a Family Case Manager.

### Definition

(3) In this rule,

"Family Case Manager" means a person appointed under section 86.1 of the *Courts of Justice Act* by the Lieutenant Governor in Council as a case management master who is assigned to manage cases for the purposes of this rule.

### Family case manager, powers and duties

(4) In a case to which this rule applies,

(a) the Family Case Manager may only exercise the powers and carry out the duties and functions that are specified in this rule; and

(b) the exercise of those powers and the performance of those duties and functions are subject to the restrictions specified in subrule (5).

### No jurisdiction

(5) The Family Case Manager has no jurisdiction in respect of,

(a) a power, duty or function that is conferred exclusively on a judge of a superior court by law or expressly on a judge by an Act;

(b) a case involving a special party;

(c) the determination of a right or interest of a party in real property; or

(d) the making of an order or hearing of a motion for an order,

(i) to change, set aside, stay or confirm an order of a judge,

(ii) to find a person in contempt of court,

(iii) to restrain the liberty of a person, including an order for imprisonment, a warrant for arrest or a warrant of committal,

(iv) to dismiss all or part of a party's case for a failure by the party to follow these rules or obey an order in the case or a related case, if the *Family Responsibility and Support Arrears Enforcement Act, 1996* applies to the party's case,

(v) to split a divorce from other issues in a case under subrule 12(6), or

(vi) Revoked

(vii) to grant summary judgment.

(6) Revoked.

### Motions under rule 14

(7) The Family Case Manager may hear motions under rule 14 relating to matters over which he or she has jurisdiction and, for the purpose, may exercise any power under that rule, other than a power under subrule 14(21).

### Orders on motion under rule 14

(8) If a motion under rule 14 is made in a case under an Act to which this rule applies, the Family Case Manager may make only the following orders:

0.1 Subject to subclause (5)(d)(iv), an order under subrule 1(8), other than a contempt order under clause 1(8)(g), and an order under subrule 1(8.1).

0.2 An order under subrule 1(8.2).

0.3 An order under subrule 1(8.4), if the Family Case Manager made the order striking out the document.

1. An order under rules 3, 4, 5, 6, 7, 9, 10, 11, 12, 13, 18, 19 and 20.

2. An order for costs under rule 24 relating to a step in the case that the Family Case Manager dealt with.

3. An order under rule 25 relating to an order made by the Family Case Manager.

3.1 An order under subrule 39(3) or (14.1).

4. An order to change a temporary order made by the Family Case Manager.

5. An order under section 17.2 (Blood tests and DNA tests) of the *Children's Law Reform Act*.

6. A temporary order for or relating to custody of or access to a child under section 21, 23, 25, 28, 29, 30, 32, 34, 39 or 40 of the *Children's Law Reform Act*.

7. A temporary order for custody of or access to a child under section 16 of the *Divorce Act* (Canada).

8. An order appointing a mediator under section 31 of the *Children's Law Reform Act* or section 3 (Mediation) of the *Family Law Act*.

9. A temporary order for or relating to support under section 33, clause 34(1)(a), (e), (f), (g) or (h), subsection 34(5) or section 37, 42 or 47 of the *Family Law Act*.

10. A temporary order for support under section 15.1 (Child support order) or 15.2 (Spousal support order) of the *Divorce Act* (Canada).

11. A temporary order under section 40 of the *Family Law Act*.

12. A temporary order dealing with property other than real property.

13. A support deduction order under section 10 (Support deduction orders to be made) of the *Family Responsibility and Support Arrears Enforcement Act, 1996*.

14. An order limiting or suspending a support deduction order.

15. An order under section 8 (Director to cease enforcement, termination of support obligation) of the *Family Responsibility and Support Arrears Enforcement Act, 1996* that terminates a support obligation or orders repayment from a person who received support.

15.1 An order under subsection 89(3.1) or 112(2) of the *Courts of Justice Act* requesting the Children's Lawyer to act.

16. An order that is necessary and incidental to the power to make a temporary order that is within the jurisdiction of the Family Case Manager.

(9), (10) Revoked.

(11) Revoked.

### Conferences

(12) The Family Case Manager may conduct a case conference, settlement conference or trial management conference instead of a judge under rule 17.

(13) Revoked.

### Application of Rule 17

(14) At a case conference, settlement conference or trial management conference conducted by the Family Case Manager, rule 17 applies subject to the following changes:

1. In a case to which this rule applies, the Family Case Manager may make any order described in rule 17 and,

with respect to the temporary and final orders referred to in clause 17(8)(b),

    i. the only temporary or final orders that the Family Case Manager may make are those described in subrule (8) of this rule, and

    ii. the Family Case Manager shall not make a final order unless the parties consent to the order.

2. Revoked.

3. A party to the conference may not request that the conference be conducted by a judge under subrule 17(9).

4. Despite clause 17(10)(a), a case may be scheduled for trial if the Family Case Manager conducted a settlement conference.

### Enforcement powers

(15) The Family Case Manager may exercise,

    (a) any power that a court may exercise under rule 27 (requiring financial information) other than a power to order a person imprisoned under subrule 27(6), (20) or (21); and

    (b) the powers relating to garnishment orders set out in subrules 29(5) and (19).

### Sending case to judge

(16) Despite anything to the contrary in this rule, the Family Case Manager may at any time order that a matter assigned to him or her be adjourned and sent to a judge.

### Appeal from temporary order

(17) Subrules 38(5) to (45) apply with necessary changes to an appeal from a temporary order of the Family Case Manager.

### Appeal from final order

(18) Subrules 38(1), (2) and (3) apply with necessary changes to an appeal from a final order of the Family Case Manager.

### Revocation

(19) This rule is revoked on July 1, 2021.

**43.** Omitted (provides for coming into force of provisions of this Regulation).

### TABLE OF FORMS

| Form Number | Form Title | Date of Form |
| --- | --- | --- |
| 4 | Notice of change in representation | October 21, 2013 |
| 6 | Acknowledgment of service | September 1, 2005 |
| 6A | Advertisement | March 19, 2015 |
| 6B | Affidavit of service | April 12, 2016 |
| 8 | Application (general) | April 12, 2016 |
| 8A | Application (divorce) | April 12, 2016 |
| 8B | Application (child protection and status review) | April 15, 2017 |
| 8B.1 | Application (status review for Crown ward and former Crown ward) | April 15, 2017 |
| 8B.2 | Application (general) (*Child and Family Services Act* cases other than child protection and status review) | April 15, 2017 |
| 8C | Application (secure treatment) | November 15, 2009 |
| 8D | Application (adoption) | April 23, 2012 |
| 8D.1 | Application (dispense with parent's consent to adoption before placement) | September 1, 2005 |
| 8D.2 | Notice of intention to place a child for adoption | August 2, 2011 |
| 8D.3 | Notice to child of intention to place for adoption | August 2, 2011 |
| 8D.4 | Notice of termination of access | August 2, 2011 |
| 8E | Revoked. | |
| 10 | Answer | October 1, 2012 |
| 10A | Reply | September 1, 2005 |
| 12 | Notice of withdrawal | September 1, 2005 |
| 13 | Financial statement (support claims) | January 6, 2015 |
| 13.1 | Financial statement (property and support claims) | January 6, 2015 |

| Form Number | Form Title | Date of Form |
|---|---|---|
| 13A | Certificate of financial disclosure | January 6, 2015 |
| 13B | Net family property statement | May 15, 2009 |
| 13C | Comparison of net family property statements | January 6, 2015 |
| 14 | Notice of motion | June 15, 2007 |
| 14A | Affidavit (general) | September 1, 2005 |
| 14B | Motion form | September 1, 2005 |
| 14C | Confirmation | September 1, 2005 |
| 14D | Order on motion without notice | September 1, 2005 |
| 15 | Motion to change | April 12, 2016 |
| 15A | Change information form | April 12, 2016 |
| 15B | Response to motion to change | April 12, 2016 |
| 15C | Consent motion to change | April 12, 2016 |
| 15D | Consent motion to change child support | April 12, 2016 |
| 17 | Conference notice | September 1, 2005 |
| 17A | Case conference brief—General | November 15, 2009 |
| 17B | Case conference brief for protection application or status review | November 15, 2009 |
| 17C | Settlement conference brief—General | November 15, 2009 |
| 17D | Settlement conference brief for protection application or status review | November 15, 2009 |
| 17E | Trial management conference brief | November 15, 2009 |
| 20 | Request for information | September 1, 2005 |
| 20.1 | Acknowledgement of expert's duty | August 2, 2011 |
| 20A | Authorization to commissioner | September 1, 2005 |
| 20B | Letter of request | September 1, 2005 |
| 22 | Request to admit | September 1, 2005 |
| 22A | Response to request to admit | September 1, 2005 |
| 23 | Summons to witness | September 1, 2005 |
| 23A | Summons to witness outside Ontario | September 1, 2005 |
| 23B | Order for prisoner's attendance | September 1, 2005 |
| 23C | Affidavit for uncontested trial | September 1, 2009 |
| 25 | Order (general) | September 1, 2005 |
| 25A | Divorce order | September 1, 2005 |
| 25B | Secure treatment order | September 1, 2005 |
| 25C | Adoption order | April 23, 2012 |
| 25D | Order (uncontested trial) | September 1, 2005 |
| 25E | Notice disputing approval of order | September 1, 2005 |
| 25F | Restraining order | September 1, 2009 |
| 25G | Restraining order on motion without notice | September 1, 2009 |
| 25H | Order terminating restraining order | September 1, 2009 |

| Form Number | Form Title | Date of Form |
| --- | --- | --- |
| 26 | Statement of money owed | April 12, 2016 |
| 26A | Affidavit of enforcement expenses | April 12, 2016 |
| 26B | Affidavit for filing domestic contract with court | April 12, 2016 |
| 26C | Notice of transfer of enforcement | April 12, 2016 |
| 27 | Request for financial statement | April 12, 2016 |
| 27A | Request for statement of income | April 12, 2016 |
| 27B | Statement of income from income source | September 1, 2005 |
| 27C | Appointment for financial examination | April 12, 2016 |
| 28 | Writ of seizure and sale | April 12, 2016 |
| 28A | Request for writ of seizure and sale | September 1, 2005 |
| 28B | Statutory declaration to sheriff | June 15, 2007 |
| 28C | Writ of temporary seizure | September 1, 2005 |
| 29 | Request for garnishment | April 12, 2016 |
| 29A | Notice of garnishment (lump-sum debt) | April 12, 2016 |
| 29B | Notice of garnishment (periodic debt) | April 12, 2016 |
| 29C | Notice to co-owner of debt | September 1, 2005 |
| 29D | Statutory declaration of indexed support | April 12, 2016 |
| 29E | Dispute (payor) | September 1, 2005 |
| 29F | Dispute (garnishee) | September 1, 2005 |
| 29G | Dispute (co-owner of debt) | September 1, 2005 |
| 29H | Notice of garnishment hearing | September 1, 2005 |
| 29I | Notice to stop garnishment | September 1, 2005 |
| 29J | Statement to garnishee financial institution re support | April 12, 2016 |
| 30 | Notice of default hearing | April 12, 2016 |
| 30A | Request for default hearing | September 1, 2005 |
| 30B | Default dispute | September 1, 2005 |
| 31 | Notice of contempt motion | September 1, 2005 |
| 32 | Bond (recognizance) | September 1, 2005 |
| 32A | Notice of forfeiture motion | September 1, 2005 |
| 32B | Warrant for arrest | April 12, 2016 |
| 32C | Affidavit for warrant of committal | September 1, 2005 |
| 32D | Warrant of committal | April 12, 2016 |
| 32.1 | Request to enforce a family arbitration award | October 1, 2012 |
| 32.1A | Dispute of request for enforcement | October 1, 2012 |
| 33 | Information for warrant to apprehend child | September 1, 2005 |
| 33A | Warrant to apprehend child | September 1, 2005 |
| 33B | Plan of care for child(ren) (Children's Aid Society) | October 1, 2006 |
| 33B.1 | Answer and plan of care (parties other than Children's Aid Society) | April 15, 2017 |

| Form Number | Form Title | Date of Form |
|---|---|---|
| 33B.2 | Answer (*Child and Family Services Act* cases other than child protection and status review) | April 15, 2017 |
| 33C | Statement of agreed facts (child protection) | April 15, 2017 |
| 33D | Statement of agreed facts (status review) | April 15, 2017 |
| 33E | Child's consent to secure treatment | September 1, 2005 |
| 33F | Consent to secure treatment (person other than child) | September 1, 2005 |
| 34 | Child's consent to adoption | April 1, 2009 |
| 34A | Affidavit of parentage | April 15, 2017 |
| 34B | Non-parent's consent to adoption by spouse | June 15, 2007 |
| 34C | Director's or local director's statement on adoption | September 1, 2005 |
| 34D | Affidavit of adoption applicant(s), sworn/affirmed | April 1, 2009 |
| 34E | Director's consent to adoption | August 2, 2011 |
| 34F | Parent's or custodian's consent to adoption | April 15, 2017 |
| 34G | Affidavit of adoption licensee or society employee | September 1, 2005 |
| 34G.1 | Affidavit of society employee for adoption of a Crown ward | August 2, 2011 |
| 34H | Affidavit of adopting relative or stepparent | April 1, 2009 |
| 34I | Parent's consent to adoption by spouse | April 15, 2017 |
| 34J | Affidavit of execution and independent legal advice (Children's Lawyer) | April 1, 2009 |
| 34K | Certificate of clerk (adoption) | August 2, 2011 |
| 34L | Application for openness order | August 2, 2011 |
| 34M | Consent to openness order under s. 145.1 of the *Child and Family Services Act* | August 2, 2011 |
| 34M.1 | Consent to openness order under s. 145.1.2 of the *Child and Family Services Act* | August 2, 2011 |
| 34N | Application to change or terminate openness order | October 1, 2006 |
| 35.1 | Affidavit in support of claim for custody or access | April 15, 2017 |
| 36 | Affidavit for divorce | September 1, 2005 |
| 36A | Certificate of clerk (divorce) | September 1, 2005 |
| 36B | Certificate of divorce | September 1, 2005 |
| 37 | Notice of hearing | September 1, 2005 |
| 37A | Information sheet | September 1, 2005 |
| 37B | Direction to request further information | September 1, 2005 |
| 37C | Notice of continuation of hearing | September 1, 2005 |
| 37D | Notice of registration of order | September 1, 2005 |
| 37E | Notice for taking further evidence | September 1, 2005 |
| 38 | Notice of appeal | September 1, 2005 |
| 39 | Notice of approaching dismissal | June 15, 2007 |

FORMS 4-39 Revoked.

# Family Responsibility and Support Arrears Enforcement Act, 1996

SO 1996, c 31

## PART I INTERPRETATION

### Definitions

**1.** (1) In this Act,

"Director" means the Director of the Family Responsibility Office;

"income source" means an individual, corporation or other entity that owes or makes any payment, whether periodically or in a lump sum, to or on behalf of a payor of,

    (a) wages, wage supplements or salary, or draws or advances on them,

    (b) a commission, bonus, piece-work allowance or similar payment,

    (c) a payment made under a contract for service,

    (d) a benefit under an accident, disability or sickness plan,

    (e) a disability, retirement or other pension,

    (f) an annuity,

    (g) vacation pay, termination pay and severance pay,

    (h) an employee loan,

    (i) a shareholder loan or dividends on shares, if the corporation that issued the shares is effectively controlled by the payor or the payor and the payor's parent, spouse, child or other relative or a body corporate which the payor and his or her parent, spouse, child or other relative effectively control, directly or indirectly,

    (j) refunds under the *Income Tax Act* (Canada),

    (k) lump sum payments under the *Family Orders and Agreements Enforcement Assistance Act* (Canada),

    (l) income of a type described in the regulations;

"payor" means a person who is required to pay support under a support order;

"provisional order" means an order that has no effect until it is confirmed by another court and includes orders made under subsection 18(2) of the *Divorce Act* (Canada), sections 7 and 30 of the *Interjurisdictional Support Orders Act, 2002* and section 44 of the *Family Law Act*;

"recipient" means a person entitled to support under a support order or the parent, other than the payor, of a child entitled to support under a support order;

"reciprocating jurisdiction" has the same meaning as in the *Interjurisdictional Support Orders Act, 2002*;

"regulations" means the regulations made under this Act;

"spouse" means,

    (a) a spouse as defined in section 1 of the *Family Law Act*, or

    (b) either of two persons who live together in a conjugal relationship outside marriage;

"support deduction order" means a support deduction order made or deemed to have been made under this Act or its predecessor;

"support order" means a provision in an order made in or outside Ontario and enforceable in Ontario for the payment of money as support or maintenance, and includes a provision for,

    (a) the payment of an amount periodically, whether annually or otherwise and whether for an indefinite or limited period, or until the happening of a specified event,

    (b) a lump sum to be paid or held in trust,

    (c) payment of support or maintenance in respect of a period before the date of the order,

(d) payment to an agency of an amount in reimbursement for a benefit or assistance provided to a party under a statute, including a benefit or assistance provided before the date of the order,

(e) payment of expenses in respect of a child's prenatal care and birth,

(e.1) payment of expenses in respect of DNA testing to establish parentage,

(f) the irrevocable designation, by a spouse who has a policy of life insurance or an interest in a benefit plan, of the other spouse or a child as the beneficiary, or

(g) interest or the payment of legal fees or other expenses arising in relation to support or maintenance, and includes such a provision in,

(h) a domestic contract that is enforceable under section 35 of the *Family Law Act*, or

(i) a notice of calculation that is enforceable under section 39 of the *Family Law Act*.

### Interpretation—income source

(2) An individual, corporation or other entity continues to be an income source despite temporary interruptions in the payments owed to a payor.

### Same—related orders

(3) A support deduction order is related to the support order on which it is based and a support order is related to the support deduction order that is based on it.

(4) A reference in this Act to a support order that is changed includes reference to a support order that is subject to a recalculation under section 39.1 of the Family Law Act.

### PART II  DIRECTOR OF THE FAMILY RESPONSIBILITY OFFICE

### Director of Family Responsibility Office

**2.** There shall be a Director of the Family Responsibility Office who shall be appointed by the Lieutenant Governor in Council.

### Delegation

**3.** (1) The Director may, in writing, authorize a person or class of persons employed in the Director's office to exercise any of the powers or perform any of the duties of the Director.

### Decisions

(2) A decision made by a person exercising the Director's powers or performing the Director's duties under subsection (1) shall be deemed to be a decision of the Director.

### Assignment of Director's powers, etc.

**4.** (1) The Minister responsible for the administration of this Act may, subject to the approval of the Lieutenant Governor in Council, assign to any person, agency or body, or class thereof, any of the powers, duties or functions of the Director under this Act, subject to the limitations, conditions and requirements set out in the assignment.

### Same

(2) An assignment may include powers, duties or functions that are not purely administrative in nature, including statutory powers of decision and discretionary powers given to the Director under this Act, and may provide that an assignee may be a party in any action or proceeding instead of the Director.

### Fees, etc.

(3) An assignment may, subject to any regulation made under clause 63(1), set out the fees, costs, disbursements, surcharges and other charges that the assignee may charge to the payor, or a method for determining them, how and when they may be collected, and may exempt the assignee from clause 22(a) of the *Collection and Debt Settlement Services Act*.

### Same

(4) An assignee may charge fees, costs, disbursements, surcharges and other charges as set out in the assignment and such fees, costs, disbursements, surcharges and other charges may,

(a) be in respect of services for which the Director may not charge anything;

(b) be higher than a fee, cost, disbursement, surcharge or other charge that the Director is permitted to charge for the same service; and

(c) be applied in a manner other than that provided in section 57.

### Same

(5) Any fees, costs, disbursements, surcharges or other charges charged by an assignee must be charged to the payor and may be added to the amount of arrears owing by the payor and may be collected in like manner as arrears.

### Interest

(6) For the purposes of subsections (3), (4) and (5),

"other charges" includes interest at a rate prescribed by regulation.

### Use of information restricted

(7) An assignee shall not use or disclose the information it has collected in carrying out any power, duty or function assigned to the assignee under subsection (1) except for the purposes of this Act.

### Duty of Director

**5.** (1) It is the duty of the Director to enforce support orders where the support order and the related support deduction order, if any, are filed in the Director's office and to pay the amounts collected to the person to whom they are owed.

### Transition

(2) Subject to subsection (4), a support order or support deduction order that is filed in the office of the Director of the Family Support Plan immediately before the day this section

comes into force shall be deemed to be filed in the Director's office on the day this section comes into force.

#### Same

(3) If a support deduction order is filed in the office of the Director of the Family Support Plan immediately before the day this section comes into force and the related support order was never filed in his or her office before that day, it is the duty of the Director to enforce the support deduction order so long as it is filed in the Director's office.

#### Same

(4) If a support deduction order is filed in the office of the Director of the Family Support Plan immediately before the day this section comes into force and the related support order was withdrawn from his or her office before that day, either when the support order was made or later, the support deduction order shall be deemed to be withdrawn from the Director's office on the day this section comes into force.

#### Powers

**6.** (1) The Director shall carry out his or her duties in the manner, if any, that appears practical to the Director and, for the purpose, may commence and conduct a proceeding and take any steps in the Director's name for the benefit of recipients, including,

(a) enforcing support deduction orders that are filed in the Director's office, as provided by this Act;

(b) employing any other enforcement mechanisms expressly provided for in this Act;

(c) employing any other enforcement mechanisms not expressly provided for in this Act.

#### Policies and procedures

(1.1) The Director may establish policies and procedures respecting subsection (1) and the policies and procedures shall be considered in the exercise of the Director's powers and the performance of the Director's duties under that subsection.

#### Transition

(2) The Director may enforce the payment of arrears of support under a support order although they were incurred before the order was filed in the Director's office or before July 2, 1987.

#### Same

(3) The Director may enforce the payment of the arrears of support owed on the day this section comes into force under an order that,

(a) is not a support order as defined in subsection 1(1) but was a support order within the meaning of the *Family Support Plan Act*, as it read immediately before its repeal by this Act; and

(b) is filed in the office of the Director of the Family Support Plan immediately before such repeal.

#### Same

(4) For the purpose of subsection (3), an order described in that subsection shall be deemed to be a support order as defined in subsection 1(1).

(5) Repealed. See: Table of Public Statute Provisions Repealed Under Section 10.1 of the *Legislation Act, 2006*—December 31, 2011.

#### Enforcement alternatives

(6) Enforcement of a support order or support deduction order by one means does not prevent enforcement by other means at the same time or different times.

#### Enforcement by Director exclusive

(7) Subject to section 4, no person other than the Director shall enforce a support order that is filed in the Director's office.

#### Same

(8) Subject to section 4, no person other than the Director shall enforce a support deduction order, whether the order is filed in the Director's office or not.

#### Director may refuse to enforce

**7.** (1) Despite section 5, the Director may at any time refuse to enforce a support order or support deduction order that is filed in the Director's office if, in his or her opinion,

(a) the amount of the support is nominal;

(b) the amount of the support cannot be determined from the face of the order because it is expressed as a percentage of the payor's income or it is dependent on another variable that does not appear on the order;

(c) the meaning of the order is unclear or ambiguous;

(d) the recipient has not complied with reasonable requests to provide the Director with accurate or sufficient information as may be needed in order to enforce the order or respecting the amount of arrears owed under the order;

(e) the whereabouts of the recipient cannot be determined after reasonable efforts have been made;

(f) the payor is in prison serving a sentence of five years or longer and has no assets or income available to satisfy the support order and any arrears under the order;

(g) the payor is receiving benefits under the *Family Benefits Act*, assistance under the *General Welfare Assistance Act* or the *Ontario Works Act, 1997* or income support under the *Ontario Disability Support Program Act, 1997* and has no assets or income available to satisfy the support order and any arrears under the order;

(h) the recipient repeatedly accepts payment of support directly from the payor;

(i) the recipient consents to a limitation of enforcement of the support order by the Director;

(j) enforcement of the support order has been stayed by a court; or

(k) enforcement of the order is otherwise unreasonable or impractical.

## Policies and procedures

(2) The Director may establish policies and procedures respecting subsection (1) and the policies and procedures shall be considered in the exercise of the Director's discretion under that subsection.

## Order deemed withdrawn

(3) If the Director refuses to enforce an order under subsection (1), the Director shall notify the payor and the recipient and the support order and the related support deduction order, if any, shall be deemed to be withdrawn from the Director's office on the date set out in the notice.

## Cost of living clauses

(4) The Director shall not enforce a cost of living clause in a support order or support deduction order made in Ontario unless it is calculated in accordance with subsection 34(5) of the *Family Law Act* or in a manner prescribed by regulation.

## Same

(5) The Director shall not enforce a cost of living clause in a support order or a support deduction order if the support order was made outside Ontario unless it is calculated in a manner that the Director considers similar to that provided in subsection 34(5) of the *Family Law Act* or in a manner prescribed by regulation.

## Same

(6) Where the cost of living clause in an order is not calculated in accordance with subsection 34(5) of the *Family Law Act* or in a manner prescribed by regulation or, if the order was made outside Ontario, in a manner that the Director considers similar, the Director shall, subject to subsection (1), enforce the order as if it contained no cost of living clause.

## Transition

(7) Despite subsections (5) and (6), if an order contains a cost of living clause that is not calculated in accordance with subsection 34(5) of the *Family Law Act* or in a manner prescribed by regulation or, if the order was made outside Ontario, in a manner that the Director considers similar, which became effective before this section came into force,

(a) the Director shall continue to enforce the order and the cost of living clause at the same amount at which the Director of the Family Support Plan was enforcing them immediately before this section came into force; and

(b) the Director shall not make any further adjustments under the cost of living clause after this section comes into force.

## Same

(8) This section applies even if the order was filed in the Director's office before this section comes into force.

## Director to cease enforcement
## Termination of support obligation

**8.** (1) Subject to section 8.3, the Director shall cease enforcement of a support obligation provided for in a support order or support deduction order filed in the Director's office if the support obligation has terminated.

## How termination is determined

(2) For the purpose of subsection (1), a support obligation is terminated if,

(a) the parties to the support order or support deduction order agree, in the manner prescribed by the regulations, that the support obligation has terminated;

(b) the support order or support deduction order states that the support obligation terminates on a set calendar date, and that date arrives; or

(c) a court orders that the obligation has terminated; or

(d) in the case of an obligation for the support of a child, the Director receives notice, in accordance with the regulations, of the child's death.

## Payor's death

(3) The Director shall not enforce a support order or support deduction order against the estate of a payor after he or she is notified, in accordance with the regulations, of the payor's death.

## Notice to Director

(4) For the purposes of clause (2)(a), if a support order or related support deduction order is filed in the Director's office, each party to the support order shall give the Director notice of a termination of a support obligation under the order, in the manner and at the time prescribed by the regulations.

## Director's discretion

**8.1** (1) Despite section 5 and subject to section 8.3, the Director has discretion to discontinue enforcement of a support order or support deduction order that is filed in the Director's office if,

(a) the payor notifies the Director in accordance with subsection 8(4) that the support obligation has terminated;

(b) the Director serves on the recipient a request to confirm or deny that the support obligation has terminated; and

(c) the recipient does not respond within 20 days after being served.

## Written response

(1.1) For the purposes of clause (1)(c), the response must be in writing.

## Reinstatement

(2) If, after enforcement has been discontinued in accordance with subsection (1), the Director receives a written

notice from the recipient denying that the support obligation has terminated, the Director may resume enforcement.

## Discretion to enforce for lesser amount if child's entitlement ceases

**8.2** (1) Subject to section 8.3, if the conditions set out in subsection (2) are satisfied with respect to a support order or support deduction order, the Director may exercise discretion to enforce a lesser amount of support in accordance with the table set out in the applicable child support guidelines.

## Conditions

(2) The conditions referred to in subsection (1) are:

1. The order was made in accordance with the table set out in the applicable child support guidelines.
2. One of the following applies:
    i. It has been agreed under clause 8(2)(a) that the support obligation under the order has terminated with respect to a child.
    ii. The payor notifies the Director in accordance with subsection 8(4) that the support obligation has terminated, the Director serves on the recipient a request to confirm or deny that the support obligation has terminated, and the recipient does not respond within 20 days after being served.
3. The support obligation under the order still continues with respect to another child.
4. The order states,
    i. the number of children, and
    ii. the total amount of support determined in accordance with the table.

## Written response

(3) For the purposes of subparagraph 2 ii of subsection (2), the response must be in writing.

## Reinstatement

(4) If, after the Director exercises the discretion to enforce a lesser amount in reliance on subparagraph 2 ii of subsection (2), the Director receives a written notice from the recipient denying that the support obligation has terminated, the Director may reinstate the amount enforced before the reduction.

## Agency's consent required

**8.3** If a support order has been assigned to an agency described in subsection 33(3) of the *Family Law Act*, the Director shall not cease, discontinue or reduce enforcement of the support order without the agency's consent.

## Disputes

**8.4** (1) If the parties to a support order do not agree that a support obligation has terminated or if the agency referred to in section 8.3 does not provide its consent under that section, the court that made the support order shall, on the motion of a party to the support order or of the agency,

(a) decide whether the support obligation has terminated; and

(b) make an order to that effect.

## Same

(2) If the support order was not made by a court, the order described in subsection (1) shall be made by the Ontario Court of Justice or the Family Court.

## Same

(3) If an issue as to whether the support obligation has terminated arises within an application between the parties, it is not necessary to make a separate motion under subsection (1).

## Order to repay

(4) A court that finds that a support obligation has terminated may order repayment in whole or in part from a person who received support after the obligation was terminated if the court is of the opinion that the person ought to have notified the Director that the support obligation had terminated.

## Same

(5) In determining whether to make an order under subsection (4), the court shall consider the circumstances of each of the parties to the support order.

## Role of Director

(6) An order under subsection (4) is not a support order and shall not be enforced by the Director.

## Continued enforcement

(7) The Director shall continue to enforce the support obligation until he or she receives a copy of the court's order terminating the support obligation.

## Same

(8) Despite the termination of a support obligation, the Director shall continue to enforce the support obligation in respect of any arrears that have accrued.

## Director not a party

(9) The Director is not a party to,

(a) a proceeding to determine a person's entitlement to support under a support order; or

(b) a motion to decide whether a support obligation has terminated.

## PART III  SUPPORT ORDERS AND SUPPORT DEDUCTION ORDERS—MAKING AND FILING

## Contents of support order

**9.** (1) Every support order made by an Ontario court, other than a provisional order, shall state in its operative part that unless the order is withdrawn from the Director's office, it shall be enforced by the Director and that amounts owing under the order shall be paid to the Director, who shall pay them to the person to whom they are owed.

### Court may require that order may not be withdrawn

(2) If the court considers it appropriate to do so, it may state in the operative part of the order, instead of the wording prescribed by subsection (1), that the order and the related support deduction order shall be enforced by the Director and that they cannot be withdrawn from the Director's office.

### Application to notices of calculation

(2.1) The wording required by subsection (1) to be included in every support order made by an Ontario court shall be included in every support order that is a notice of calculation.

### Director retains discretion to not enforce orders

(3) Section 7 applies to every support order worded as provided in subsection (1), (2), or (2.1), whether the order was made before or after this section comes into force and despite the wording of an order made under subsection (2).

### Support deduction orders to be made

**10.** (1) An Ontario court that makes a support order, as defined in subsection 1(1), shall also make a support deduction order.

### New orders to be made

(2) When a support order is changed and the changed order is a support order as defined in subsection 1(1), the court shall also make a support deduction order to reflect the change.

### Transition

(3) When a support order, within the meaning of the *Family Support Plan Act* as it read immediately before its repeal by this Act, is changed and the changed order is a support order as defined in subsection 1(1), the court shall also make a support deduction order to reflect the change.

### Order mandatory

(4) A support deduction order shall be made even though the court cannot identify an income source in respect of the payor at the time the support order is made.

### Exception

(5) A support deduction order shall not be made in respect of a provisional order.

### Same

(6) A notice of recalculation under section 39.1 of the *Family Law Act* does not require a support deduction order reflecting the recalculation.

### Form of support deduction order

**11.** (1) A support deduction order shall be in the form prescribed by the regulations.

### Information re payor, income source

(2) Before making a support deduction order, the court shall make such inquiries of the parties as it considers necessary to determine the names and addresses of each income source of the payor and the amounts paid to the payor by each income source and shall make such other inquiries to obtain information as may be prescribed by the regulations.

### Same

(3) If the support order is sought on consent or by way of motion for judgment or if the making of the support order is uncontested, the parties shall give the court the particulars described in subsection (2) and such other information as may be prescribed by the regulations.

### Completion of form, etc.

(4) The support deduction order shall be completed and signed by the court, or by the clerk or registrar of the court, at the time the support order is made and shall be entered in the court records promptly after it is signed, even if the support order may not have been settled or signed at that time.

### Precedence of orders

**11.1** In the event of a conflict between a support order and the support deduction order made in relation to the support order, the support order prevails.

### Court to file orders

### Support orders

**12.** (1) The clerk or registrar of the court that makes a support order shall file it with the Director's office promptly after it is signed.

### Support deduction orders

(2) The clerk or registrar of the court that makes a support deduction order shall file it with the Director's office promptly after it is signed, even if the related support order may not have been settled or signed at the time.

### Filing notices of calculation

**12.1** On giving notice of a calculation under section 39 of the *Family Law Act*, the child support calculation service, as defined in that section, shall file a copy of the notice with the Director's office.

### Filing notices of recalculation

**12.2** On giving notice of a recalculation under section 39.1 of the *Family Law Act* that relates to a support order that is being enforced by the Director, the child support recalculation service, as defined in that section, shall file a copy of the notice with the Director's office.

### Orders of other jurisdictions

**13.** (1) When a support order made by a court outside Ontario is registered under subsection 19(1) of the *Interjurisdictional Support Orders Act, 2002*, the clerk who registers the order shall promptly file it with the Director's office, unless the order is accompanied by a notice signed by the person seeking enforcement stating that he or she does not want the order enforced by the Director.

### Same — *Divorce Act* (Canada) orders

(2) A support order made by a court outside Ontario under the *Divorce Act* (Canada) may be filed in the Director's office by the recipient under the order and, for the purpose of subsection 20(3) of the *Divorce Act* (Canada), the order becomes enforceable by the Director upon its filing in the Director's office without it having been registered in a court in Ontario.

### Orders filed by Minister, etc.

**14.** (1) If a recipient has applied and is eligible for, or has received, a benefit under the *Family Benefits Act* or assistance under the *General Welfare Assistance Act* or the *Ontario Works Act, 1997* or income support under the *Ontario Disability Support Program Act, 1997*, a support order may be filed in the Director's office, whether or not the payor and recipient have given a notice to withdraw under subsection 16(1.1), by the following:

1. The Ministry of Community and Social Services in the name of the Minister.
2. A municipality, excluding a lower-tier municipality in a regional municipality.
3. A district social services administration board under the *District Social Services Administration Boards Act*.
4. A band approved under section 15 of the *General Welfare Assistance Act*.
5. A delivery agent under the *Ontario Works Act, 1997*.

### Same, reciprocating jurisdiction

(1.1) If a recipient has applied and is eligible for, or has received, social assistance benefits in a reciprocating jurisdiction, or if a support order has been assigned to a social assistance provider in a reciprocating jurisdiction, the support order may be filed in the Director's office by the social assistance provider in the reciprocating jurisdiction, whether or not the payor and recipient have given a notice to withdraw under subsection 16(1.1).

### Same

(2) If a support order is filed under subsection (1) or (1.1), the related support deduction order, if any, shall be deemed to be filed in the Director's office at the same time.

### Payors, recipients may file support orders

**15.** Subject to sections 12, 12.1, 12.2, 13 and 14, a support order may be filed in the Director's office only by the payor or recipient under the order.

### Withdrawal of orders

**16.** (1) A support order or support deduction order filed in the office of the Director may be withdrawn at any time, as described in subsection (1.1), unless the support order states that it and the related support deduction order cannot be withdrawn from the Director's office.

### Method

(1.1) Withdrawal is effected by a written notice signed by,

(a) the recipient and the payor, if the payor is in compliance as defined in the regulations; or

(b) the recipient, if the payor is not in compliance as defined in the regulations.

### Consent of agency filing order

(2) A support order and related support deduction order, if any, that have been assigned to an agency referred to in subsection 14(1) may not be withdrawn under subsection (1) except by the agency or with the consent of the agency so long as the orders are under assignment.

### Effect of withdrawal

(3) The Director shall cease enforcement of an order upon its withdrawal from the Director's office.

### Same

(4) If there are arrears owing to an agency referred to in subsection 14(1) from a past assignment, the Director may continue to enforce the support order and related support deduction order, if any, to collect the arrears owed to the agency, even if the payor and recipient have withdrawn the orders under this section.

### Support and support deduction order must be withdrawn together

(5) A support order cannot be withdrawn under subsection (1) unless the related support deduction order, if any, is also withdrawn and a support deduction order cannot be withdrawn under subsection (1) unless the related support order, if any, is also withdrawn.

### Filing after withdrawal

(6) A support order or support deduction order that has been withdrawn under subsection (1) or that has been deemed to have been withdrawn under subsection 7(3) may be filed in the office of the Director at any time by a written notice signed by either the payor or the recipient.

### Effect

(7) Filing under subsection (6) has the same effect for all purposes, including the purposes of subsection 6(2), as filing under sections 12 to 15.

### Application

(7.1) Subsection (7) applies whether the order was filed under subsection (6) before or after the day the *Government Efficiency Act, 2001* receives Royal Assent.

### Support and support deduction orders, filing together after withdrawal

(7.2) A support order cannot be filed under subsection (6) unless the related support deduction order, if any, is also filed and a support deduction order cannot be filed under subsection (6) unless the related support order is also filed.

### Notice of recalculation

(7.3)  In the case of a support order that was subject to a recalculation under section 39.1 of the *Family Law Act* after the support order or support deduction order was withdrawn, the notice of recalculation shall also be filed.

### Transition

(8)  Despite subsection 6(4), subsection (7) does not apply to an order that is not a support order as defined in subsection 1(1), but was a support order within the meaning of the *Family Support Plan Act*, as it read immediately before its repeal by this Act, and was filed in the office of the Director of the Family Support Plan immediately before this section came into force.

### Notice of filings and withdrawals

**17.**  The Director shall give notice of the filing or withdrawal of a support order or support deduction order to all the parties to the order, and at the request of any agency referred to in subsection 14(1), to the agency.

### Duty to advise re unfiled support orders

**18.**  Where a support deduction order that was made before this section came into force is filed in the Director's office but the related support order was never filed in the Director's office, the recipient shall inform the Director in writing of,

    (a)  the amount of money received on account of the support order other than by means of the support deduction order; and

    (b)  any changes in the amount to be paid under the support order.

### Updating contact information

**19.**  A payor or recipient under a support order or support deduction order that is filed in the Director's office shall advise the Director of any changes to the following, within 10 days after the change:

1. Any name or alias used by the payor or recipient, including any spelling variation of any name or alias.
2. The payor's or recipient's home address, and the mailing address if different from the home address.
3. Any telephone number of the payor or recipient.
4. Other contact information, such as the payor's or recipient's work address, fax number or e-mail address, if the payor or recipient has previously provided that contact information to the Director.

### PART IV  SUPPORT DEDUCTION ORDERS—ENFORCEMENT

### Director to enforce support deduction orders

**20.**  (1)  The Director shall enforce a support deduction order that is filed in the Director's office, subject to section 7, to any change made to the support deduction order and to any alternative payment order made under section 28, until the related support order is terminated and there are no arrears owing or until the support order and support deduction order are withdrawn.

### Notice of support deduction order to income sources

(2)  The Director may serve a notice of a support deduction order to each income source from whom the Director is seeking payment, and may serve new notices when the amount to be paid under a support order changes or arrears are owing.

### Contents of notice

(3)  The notice shall set out the amount of support owed by the payor under the support order and may also set out any amount in arrears under the support order and the amount required to be paid by the income source to the Director.

### Notice to payor

(4)  The Director shall send to the payor a copy of every notice sent under subsection (2).

### Notice deemed garnishment for *Family Orders and Agreements Enforcement Assistance Act* (Canada)

(5)  A notice of a support deduction order shall be deemed to be a notice of garnishment made under provincial garnishment law for the purposes of the *Family Orders and Agreements Enforcement Assistance Act* (Canada).

### Support deduction order not affected by stay of enforcement of support order

(6)  The operation or enforcement of a support deduction order is not affected by an order staying the enforcement of the related support order unless the support order is also stayed.

### Support deduction order deemed to be made

**21.**  (1)  A support deduction order shall be deemed to have been made in respect of a support order described in subsection (8) if,

    (a)  the payor or the recipient requests that the Director enforce the support order under this Part and the Director considers it practical to do so; or

    (b)  the Director considers it advisable to enforce the support order under this Part.

### Notice to other party

(2)  The Director shall give notice to the other party of the Director's intention to enforce the support order under this Part.

### Exception

(2.1)  Subsection (2) does not apply in the case of a support order that is a notice of calculation.

### When and by what court deemed order is made

(3)  The support deduction order shall, 30 days after the notice is served, be deemed to have been made by the court that made the support order or,

(a) if the support order was made under the *Divorce Act* (Canada) by a court outside Ontario, by the Superior Court of Justice or, where applicable, the Family Court;

(b) if the support order (other than an order under the *Divorce Act* (Canada)) was made by a court outside Ontario, by a court in Ontario that is the same level as the court that has the jurisdiction to make the order enforceable in Ontario;

(c) if the support order is a domestic contract, by the Ontario Court of Justice or the Family Court.

### Same, notice of calculation

(3.1) If the support order is a notice of calculation, the support deduction order shall be deemed to have been made by the Ontario Court of Justice or the Family Court.

### Alternative payment order

(4) The payor may make a motion for an alternative payment order under section 28, in the court that is deemed to have made the support deduction order.

### Delay of effective date

(5) If a motion is made under subsection (4), a deemed support deduction order does not come into force until the motion is determined.

### Withdrawal of support deduction order

(6) Section 16 applies to a deemed support deduction order.

### No form required

(7) Subsection 11(1) does not apply to a deemed support deduction order.

### Application of this section

(8) This section applies only to support orders filed in the Director's office that are,

(a) support orders made by an Ontario court before March 1, 1992;

(b) domestic contracts that are enforceable under section 35 of the *Family Law Act*;

(b.1) notices of calculation that are enforceable under section 39 of the *Family Law Act*;

(c) support orders made by a court outside Ontario that are enforceable in Ontario.

### Duty of income source

**22.** (1) An income source that receives notice of a support deduction order, whether or not the income source is named in the order, shall, subject to section 23, deduct from the money the income source owes to the payor the amount of the support owed by the payor, or such other amount that is set out in the notice, and shall pay that amount to the Director.

### First payment

(2) The income source shall begin making payments to the Director not later than the day the first payment is to be paid to the payor that falls at least 14 days after the day on which the income source is served with the notice.

### Electronic payment

(2.1) The income source may make the payments by a prescribed method of electronic transmission.

### Payor's duty to pay

(3) Until an income source begins deducting support payments in respect of a support deduction order or if payments by an income source are interrupted or terminated, the payor shall pay the amounts owing under the support order to the Director, if the support order is filed in the Director's office, or to the recipient, if the support order is not filed in the Director's office.

### Maximum deduction by income source

**23.** (1) The total amount deducted by an income source and paid to the Director under a support deduction order shall not exceed 50 per cent of the net amount owed by the income source to the payor.

(2) Repealed. See: Table of Public Statute Provisions Repealed Under Section 10.1 of the *Legislation Act, 2006*—December 31, 2011.

### Exception for certain federal payments

(3) Despite subsection (1), up to 100 per cent of a payor's income tax refund or other lump sum payment that is attachable under the *Family Orders and Agreements Enforcement Assistance Act* (Canada) may be deducted and paid to the Director under a support deduction order.

(4) Repealed. See: Table of Public Statute Provisions Repealed Under Section 10.1 of the *Legislation Act, 2006*—December 31, 2011.

### Interpretation—net amount

(5) For the purposes of this section,

"net amount" means the total amount owed by the income source to the payor at the time payment is to be made to the Director, less the total of the following deductions:

1. Income Tax.
2. Canada Pension Plan.
3. Employment Insurance.
4. Union dues.
5. Such other deductions as may be prescribed by the regulations.

### Same

(6) Despite any other provision of this Act, no deduction shall be made under a support deduction order in respect of amounts owing to a payor as reimbursement for expenses covered by a medical, health, dental or hospital insurance contract or plan.

## Crown bound by support deduction order

**24.** (1) A support deduction order is effective against the Crown only in respect of amounts payable on behalf of the administrative unit served with notice of the support deduction order to the payor named in the notice.

## Social assistance benefits

(2) Despite subsection (1), no amounts shall be deducted from any amount payable to a payor as a benefit under the *Family Benefits Act* or as assistance under the *General Welfare Assistance Act* or the *Ontario Works Act, 1997* or as income support under the *Ontario Disability Support Program Act, 1997,* in order to comply with a support deduction order unless authorized under the *Ontario Works Act, 1997* or the *Ontario Disability Support Program Act, 1997.*

## Definition

(3) In subsection (1),

"administrative unit" means a ministry of the Government of Ontario, a Crown agency within the meaning of the *Crown Agency Act* or the Office of the Assembly.

## Duty to inform re payment interruption

**25.** (1) Within 10 days after the termination or beginning of an interruption of payments by an income source to a payor, both the income source and the payor shall give written notice of the termination or interruption to the Director, together with such other information as may be required by the regulations.

## Same

(2) If notice has been or should have been given under subsection (1),

(a) the payor and the income source, within 10 days after the resumption of payments that have been interrupted, shall give written notice to the Director of the resumption;

(b) the payor, within 10 days of beginning employment with another income source or of becoming entitled to payments from another income source, shall give written notice to the Director of the new employment or entitlement and of the name and address of the income source.

## Disputes re income source

**26.** (1) If an individual, corporation or other entity served with notice of a support deduction order is not an income source of the payor named in the notice, the individual, corporation or other entity shall give written notice in the prescribed form of that fact to the Director within 10 days after the service of the notice.

## Same

(2) The Director or an individual, corporation or other entity who has notified the Director under subsection (1) may, on notice to each other, make a motion to the court that made or is deemed to have made the support deduction order to determine whether the individual, corporation or other entity is an income source.

## Same

(3) The Director or an income source may, on notice to each other, make a motion to the court that made or is deemed to have made the support deduction order to determine,

(a) whether the income source has failed to comply with the order; or

(b) whether the amount the income source is deducting and paying to the Director under the order is correct.

## Determination by court

(4) In a motion under subsection (2) or (3), the court shall determine the issue in a summary manner and make such order as it considers appropriate in the circumstances.

## Limitation

(5) A motion shall not be made under subsection (2) by an individual (other than the Director), corporation or other entity until at least 14 days after the individual, corporation or other entity gave written notice to the Director as required by subsection (1).

## Same

(6) A motion shall not be made by an income source under subsection (3) unless the income source has given written particulars of the proposed motion to the Director at least 14 days before serving the Director with notice of the motion.

## Liability

(7) An income source is liable to pay to the Director any amount that it failed without proper reason to deduct and pay to the Director after receiving notice of a support deduction order and, in a motion under subsection (3), the court may order the income source to pay the amount that it ought to have deducted and paid to the Director.

## Other enforcement

(8) In addition to any other method available to enforce an order in a civil proceeding, any order made under subsection (4) or (7) may be enforced under this Act in the same manner and with the same remedies as a support order.

## Disputes, etc., by payor

**27.** (1) A payor, on motion in the court that made or is deemed to have made the support deduction order,

(a) may dispute the amount being deducted by an income source under a support deduction order if he or she is of the opinion that because of a mistake of fact more is being deducted than is required under this Act;

(b) may dispute whether he or she has defaulted in paying support after an alternative payment order has been made under section 28;

(c) may seek relief regarding the amount that is being deducted by an income source under a support deduction order for arrears under a support order.

### Motion to increase deductions for arrears

(2) If an order has been made on a motion under clause (1)(c), the Director may, on motion in the court that made the order, request that the amount to be deducted by an income source be increased if there has been an improvement in the payor's financial circumstances.

### Dispute over entitlement

(3) On a motion under subsection (1) or (2), the payor shall not dispute the entitlement of a person to support under a support order.

### Necessary party

(4) The Director is a necessary party to a motion under subsection (1) and the payor is a necessary party to a motion under subsection (2).

### Determination by court

(5) The court shall determine the issue in a motion under subsection (1) or (2) in a summary manner and make such order as it considers appropriate in the circumstances.

### Same

(6) On a motion under clause (1)(c), the payor shall be presumed to have the ability to pay the amount being deducted for arrears and the court may change the amount being deducted only if it is satisfied that the payor is unable for valid reasons to pay that amount, but this does not affect the accruing of arrears.

### Variation of support deduction order

(7) A court shall not change the amount to be paid under a support deduction order except under subsection (5) or 23(4) or if the related support order is changed.

### Alternative payment order

**28.** (1) A court that makes a support deduction order may make an order requiring the payor to make payments directly to the Director, at the same time as it makes the support deduction order, or subsequently on motion.

### Same

(2) A court that is deemed to have made a support deduction order may, on a motion made under subsection 21(4), make an order requiring the payor to make payments directly to the Director.

### Effect on support order and support deduction order

(3) An alternative payment order made under subsection (1) or (2) suspends the support deduction order, but it does not affect the payor's obligations under the support order nor does it affect any other means of enforcing the support order.

### Criteria

(4) The court may make an alternative payment order under subsection (1) or (2) only if,

(a) it finds that it would be unconscionable, having regard to all of the circumstances, to require the payor to make support payments by means of a support deduction order; or

(b) the parties to the support order agree that they do not want support payments collected by means of a support deduction order and the court requires the payor to post such security as it considers adequate and in accordance with the regulations.

### Agency's consent required

(5) If the support order has been assigned to an agency described in subsection 33(3) of the *Family Law Act* or if there are arrears owing to the agency from a past assignment, the court shall not make an alternative payment order in the circumstances described in clause (4)(b) without the agency's consent.

### Unconscionable, determination

(6) The following shall not be considered by a court in determining whether it would be unconscionable to require a payor to make support payments by means of a support deduction order:

1. The fact that the payor has demonstrated a good payment history in respect of his or her debts, including support obligations.
2. The fact that the payor has had no opportunity to demonstrate voluntary compliance in respect of support obligations.
3. The fact that the parties have agreed to the making of an alternative payment order.
4. The fact that there are grounds upon which a court might find that the amount payable under the support order should be changed.

### Security

(7) For the purposes of clause (4)(b), security shall be in a minimum amount equal to the support payable for four months and the security shall be in money or in such other form as may be prescribed in the regulations.

### When Director is a party

(8) The Director is not a party to a motion made to obtain an alternative payment order, but if the motion relates to a support deduction order deemed to have been made under section 21, the Director,

(a) shall also be served with notice of the motion; and

(b) may be added as a party.

### When agency is a party

(9) If the support order was filed in the Director's office by an agency under subsection 14(1), or has been assigned to an agency referred to in that subsection, the agency,

(a) shall also be served with notice of the motion; and

(b) may be added as a party.

### Completion of form, etc.

(10) An alternative payment order shall be completed and signed by the court or by the clerk or registrar of the court at the time it is made and shall be entered in the court records promptly after it is signed.

### Prompt filing

(11) The clerk or registrar of the court that makes an alternative payment order shall file it in the Director's office promptly after it is made.

### Form and effective date

(12) An alternative payment order shall be in the form prescribed by the regulations and takes effect only when it is filed in the Director's office and every income source affected by the alternative payment order has received notice of it and of its effect on the support deduction order.

### Termination of alternative payment order

(13) An alternative payment order is automatically terminated if the payor fails to post security of the type or within the time period set out in the alternative payment order or if the payor fails to comply with the support order.

### Effect of termination

(14) When an alternative payment order is terminated under subsection (13), the support deduction order is reinstated and the Director may immediately realize on any security that was posted.

### Effect of withdrawing support order and support deduction order

(15) If the support order and the related support deduction order are withdrawn from the Director's office while an alternative payment order is in effect, the alternative payment order is terminated and the Director shall repay to the payor any security that was posted.

### Effect of changing support order or support deduction order

(16) If the support order or the related support deduction order is changed while an alternative payment order is in effect, the alternative payment order is terminated and the Director shall repay to the payor any security that was posted.

### Transition

(17) A suspension order made under this section as it read on the day before section 15 of the *Family Responsibility and Support Arrears Enforcement Amendment Act, 2005* came into force has the same effect as an alternative payment order, and

this Act applies to the suspension order as if it were an alternative payment order.

### Income source to keep information confidential

29. Information about a payor obtained as a result of the application of this Part by an income source or an individual, corporation or other entity believed to be an income source shall not be disclosed by the income source or the individual, corporation or other entity, as the case may be, or any director, officer, employee or agent thereof, except for the purposes of complying with a support deduction order or this Act.

### Priority of support deduction orders

30. (1) Despite any other Act, a support deduction order has the same priority over other judgment debts as a support order has under the *Creditors' Relief Act, 2010* and all support orders and support deduction orders rank equally with each other.

### Same

(2) If an income source is required to make payments to the Director under a support deduction order and the income source receives a garnishment notice related to the same support obligation, the income source shall make full payment under the support deduction order and the garnishment shall be of no effect until the income source has received notice from the Director that an alternative payment order has been made or that the support deduction order is terminated or withdrawn from the Director's office.

### Anti-avoidance

31. An agreement by the parties to a support order to change enforcement of a support deduction order that is filed in the Director's office and any agreement or arrangement to avoid or prevent enforcement of a support deduction order that is filed in the Director's office are of no effect.

### Conflict with other Acts

32. A support deduction order may be enforced despite any provision in any other Act protecting any payment owed by an income source to a payor from attachment or other process for the enforcement of a judgment debt.

## PART V  SUSPENSION OF DRIVERS' LICENCES

### Definition, Part V

33. In this Part,

"driver's licence" has the same meaning as in subsection 1(1) of the *Highway Traffic Act*.

### First notice

34. When a support order that is filed in the Director's office is in default, the Director may serve a first notice on the payor, informing the payor that his or her driver's licence may be suspended unless, within 30 days after the day the first notice is served,

(a) the payor makes an arrangement satisfactory to the Director for complying with the support order and for paying the arrears owing under the support order;

(b) the payor obtains an order to refrain under subsection 35(1) and files the order in the Director's office; or

(c) the payor pays all arrears owing under the support order.

### Order to refrain

**35.** (1) If a payor is served with a first notice under section 34 and makes a motion to change the support order, the payor may also, on notice to the Director, make a motion for an order that the Director refrain from directing the suspension of the payor's driver's licence under subsection 37(1), on the terms that the court considers just, which may include payment terms.

### Interjurisdictional Support Orders Act, 2002

(2) For the purposes of this section, submitting a support variation application to the designated authority in Ontario under the *Interjurisdictional Support Orders Act, 2002* has the same effect as making a motion to change a support order.

### Effect on arrears

(3) Payment terms that are included in an order to refrain do not affect the accruing of arrears, nor do they affect any other means of enforcing the support order.

### Exceptions

(4) Despite subsection (1), a motion for an order to refrain may be made,

(a) before making a motion to change the support order, on the undertaking of the payor or the payor's lawyer to obtain, within 20 days after the date of the order to refrain, a court date for the motion to change the support order; or

(b) without making a motion to change the support order, if the payor has started an appeal of the support order and the appeal has not been determined.

### Court with jurisdiction to change support order

(5) A motion for an order to refrain shall be made in the court that has jurisdiction to change the support order.

### Same

(6) The court that has jurisdiction to change a support order is,

(a) in the case of a support order that was made in Ontario,

(i) the court that made the support order, unless subclause (ii) applies,

(ii) if the support order is a provision in a domestic contract or paternity agreement, the Ontario Court of Justice or the Family Court; and

(b) in the case of a support order that was made outside Ontario,

(i) if the support order was made under the *Divorce Act* (Canada), the Superior Court of Justice or the Family Court,

(ii) if the support order is registered under the *Interjurisdictional Support Orders Act, 2002*, the court in Ontario that has jurisdiction under that Act to vary the support order.

### Financial statement and proof of income

(7) A payor who makes a motion for an order to refrain shall serve and file together with the notice of motion,

(a) a financial statement, in the form prescribed by the regulations or in the form prescribed by the rules of court; and

(b) such proof of income as may be prescribed by the regulations.

### Exception, undertaking

(8) Despite clause (7)(b), if the payor is unable to serve and file the proof of income before the motion is heard, the court may make the order to refrain subject to the undertaking of the payor or the payor's lawyer to serve and file proof of income within 20 days.

### Court may change or terminate order to refrain

(9) When an undertaking is made under subsection (8), the court may change or terminate the order to refrain, without proof of a material change in circumstances, on motion by the Director, if,

(a) the 20-day period has expired and the proof of income has not been served and filed; or

(b) the proof of income has been served and filed and the court is satisfied that a different order would have been made if the proof of income had been available when the motion for the order to refrain was heard.

### Time limits and changing order to refrain

(10) A court shall not make an order to refrain after the 30-day period referred to in the first notice, but an order to refrain may be changed, on motion by the payor or the Director, at any time before the motion to change support is determined if there is a material change in the payor's circumstances.

### Same

(11) A court may make an order to refrain only within the 30-day period referred to in the first notice and may make only one order to refrain in respect of any first notice.

### Same

(12) For greater certainty, the 30-day period referred to in the first notice can not be extended for the purposes of subsections (10) and (11).

**Same**

(13) For greater certainty, if the 30-day period referred to in the first notice expires on a day when court offices are closed, the last day for making an order to refrain is the last day on which court offices are open before the 30-day period expires.

**Order re arrears**

(14) When a court that has determined a motion for an order to refrain also determines the related motion to change support, the court,

(a) shall state the amount of the arrears owing, after any change to the support order; and

(b) may make an order respecting payment of the arrears.

**Same**

(15) For the purpose of clause (14)(b), the court may make any order that may be made under clause 41(10)(a), (b), (c), (e), (h) or (i) or subsection 41(19) and, in the case of an order provided by clause 41(10)(h) or (i), imprisonment does not discharge arrears under the support order.

**When Director is a party**

(16) The Director is not a party to a motion to change a support order referred to in subsection (1), but the Director and the payor are the only parties to a motion under subsection (1) for an order to refrain.

**Filing with Director's office**

(17) The court shall file a copy of the order in the Director's office promptly after the order is signed.

**Form and effective date**

(18) An order to refrain shall be in the form prescribed by the regulations and takes effect only when it is filed in the Director's office.

**Duration of order**

(19) An order to refrain terminates on the earliest of,

(a) the day the order to refrain is terminated under subsection (9);

(b) the day the motion to change or the appeal is determined;

(c) the day the support order is withdrawn from the Director's office; and

(d) the day that is six months after the order to refrain is made.

**Exception**

(20) Despite subsection (19), an order to refrain made before the making of a motion to change the support order is automatically terminated if the payor does not, within 20 days after the date of the order to refrain, obtain a court date for the motion to change the support order.

**Extension of order**

(21) The court that made an order to refrain may, on a motion made by the payor with notice to the Director, extend the order for one further period of,

(a) three months, unless clause (b) applies; or

(b) six months, if the motion to change is being dealt with under section 44 of the *Family Law Act*, sections 18 and 19 of the *Divorce Act* (Canada) or the *Interjurisdictional Support Orders Act, 2002.*

**Time for extending order**

(22) An extending order under subsection (21) shall not be made after the order to refrain has terminated.

**Same**

(23) For greater certainty, if the order to refrain terminates on a day when court offices are closed, the last day for making an extending order is the last day on which court offices are open before the order terminates.

**Application of order**

(24) An order to refrain is applicable only to the notice in respect of which the motion for an order to refrain was made under subsection (1).

**Final notice**

**36.** (1) The Director may serve a final notice on the payor if, at any time in the 24 months after the payor made an arrangement under clause 34(a) or obtained an order under subsection 35(1) or clause 35(14)(b), the payor fails to comply with,

(a) the terms of the arrangement made with the Director in response to the first notice;

(b) the terms of an order to refrain under subsection 35(1); or

(c) the terms of the changed support order and an order respecting payment of arrears under clause 35(14)(b).

**Contents**

(2) The final notice shall inform the payor that his or her driver's licence may be suspended,

(a) unless, within 15 days after the day the final notice is served,

(i) the payor complies with clause (1)(a), (b) or (c), or

(ii) the payor pays all arrears owing under the support order; or

(b) if, within 24 months after the payor makes an arrangement under clause (1)(a) or obtains an order under subsection 35(1) or clause 35(14)(b), the payor fails to comply with the arrangement or order.

**Interpretation: arrangement in response to notice**

(3) For the purposes of this section, an arrangement is made in response to a first notice if it is made within the time referred to in the first notice.

**Same**

(4) An arrangement that is made in response to a first notice and is then amended by agreement in writing remains an arrangement made in response to the first notice.

## Direction to suspend
### After first notice

**37.** (1) The Director may direct the Registrar of Motor Vehicles to suspend a payor's driver's licence if, within the 30-day period referred to in the first notice, the payor does not,

(a) make an arrangement satisfactory to the Director for complying with the support order;

(b) obtain an order to refrain under subsection 35(1) and file the order in the Director's office; or

(c) pay all arrears owing under the support order.

### After final notice

(2) The Director may direct the Registrar of Motor Vehicles to suspend a payor's driver's licence if, within the 15-day period referred to in the final notice or at any time in the 24-month period referred to in the final notice, the payor does not,

(a) comply with clause 36(1)(a), (b) or (c); or

(b) pay all arrears owing under the support order.

### Form of direction

(3) A direction under this section shall be in a form approved by the Director and the Registrar of Motor Vehicles.

### Direction to reinstate

**38.** (1) The Director shall direct the Registrar of Motor Vehicles to reinstate a driver's licence suspended as a result of a direction under section 37 if,

(a) the payor pays all the arrears owing under the support order;

(b) the payor is complying with the terms of the arrangement made with the Director in response to the first notice;

(c) the payor is complying with the terms of an order to refrain that has not expired;

(d) the support order has been changed and the payor is complying with the terms of the changed support order, including the terms of any order under clause 35(14)(b) that relates to the support order;

(d.1) the payor makes an arrangement satisfactory to the Director for complying with the support order and for paying the arrears owing under the support order; or

(e) the support order is withdrawn under section 16.

### Notice revived if payor breaches arrangement or order

(2) If the Director directs the Registrar of Motor Vehicles to reinstate a driver's licence under clause (1)(b), (c) or (d) and the payor subsequently defaults within 24 months from the date of reinstatement or if the payor subsequently defaults within 24 months after the payor entered into an arrangement under clause 34(a) or obtained an order under clause 35(14)(b), the Director may proceed to act in accordance with the most recent notice that was served on the payor under this Part.

### More than one order in default

(3) If the payor is in default on one or more other support orders, the Director shall not direct the Registrar of Motor Vehicles to reinstate the driver's licence unless,

(a) all arrears under all the support orders are paid;

(b) an arrangement or arrangements have been made, on terms satisfactory to the Director, to pay all arrears under all the support orders, and the payor is in compliance with the arrangement or arrangements; or

(c) all arrears under all the support orders are the subject of a court order or orders for payment and the payor is in compliance with the court order or orders.

### Discretion to reinstate

(4) The Director may direct the Registrar of Motor Vehicles to reinstate a driver's licence suspended as a result of a direction under section 37 if, in the opinion of the Director, it would be unconscionable not to do so.

### Form of direction

(5) A direction under this section shall be in a form approved by the Director and the Registrar of Motor Vehicles.

### Anti-avoidance

**39.** An agreement by the parties to a support order to avoid or prevent its enforcement under this Part is of no effect.

## PART VI  OTHER ENFORCEMENT MECHANISMS
### Financial statements

**40.** (1) The Director may request that a payor who is in default under a support order, where the support order or related support deduction order is filed in the Director's office, complete and deliver to the Director a financial statement in the form prescribed by the regulations together with such proof of income as may be required by the regulations.

### Same

(2) The payor shall deliver the completed financial statement to the Director within 15 days after he or she was served with the request to complete the form.

### Changes in information

(3) If a payor discovers that any information was incomplete or wrong at the time he or she completed the financial statement, he or she shall, within 10 days of the discovery, deliver the corrected information to the Director.

### Failure to comply

(4) The Ontario Court of Justice or the Family Court, on the motion of the Director, may order a payor to comply with a request under subsection (1) and subsections 41(6) and (7) apply with necessary modifications.

### Limitation

(5) The Director may request a financial statement under this section once in any six-month period but this does not restrict the Director's right to obtain a financial statement under section 41.

### Default hearing

**41.** (1) When a support order that is filed in the Director's office is in default, the Director may prepare a statement of the arrears and, by notice served on the payor together with the statement of arrears, may require the payor to deliver to the Director a financial statement and such proof of income as may be required by the regulations and to appear before the court to explain the default.

### Same

(2) When a support order that is not filed in the Director's office is in default, the recipient may file a request with the court, together with a statement of arrears, and, on such filing, the clerk of the court shall, by notice served on the payor together with the statement of arrears, require the payor to file a financial statement and appear before the court to explain the default.

### Persons financially connected to payor

(3) The Director or the recipient may, at any time during a default hearing under subsection (1) or (2), request that the court make an order under subsection (4) or (5) or both.

### Financial statement

(4) The court may, by order, require a person to file a financial statement and any other relevant documents with the court if the court is satisfied that the person is financially connected to the payor.

### Adding party

(5) The court may, by order, add a person as a party to the hearing if the court,

(a) has made or could make an order under subsection (4); and

(b) is satisfied on considering all the circumstances, including the purpose and effect of the dealings between the person and the payor and their benefit or expected benefit to the payor, that there is some evidence that the person has sheltered assets or income of the payor such that enforcement of the support order against the payor may be frustrated.

### Form of statements

(6) A financial statement and statement of arrears required by subsection (2) shall be in the form prescribed by the rules of the court and a financial statement required by subsection (1) or (4) shall be in the form prescribed by the regulations.

### Arrest of payor

(7) If the payor fails to file the financial statement or to appear as the notice under subsection (1) or (2) requires, the court may issue a warrant for the payor's arrest for the purpose of bringing him or her before the court.

### Bail

(8) Section 150 (interim release by justice of the peace) of the *Provincial Offences Act* applies with necessary modifications to an arrest under the warrant.

### Presumptions at hearing

(9) At the default hearing, unless the contrary is shown, the payor shall be presumed to have the ability to pay the arrears and to make subsequent payments under the order, and the statement of arrears prepared and served by the Director shall be presumed to be correct as to arrears accruing while the order is filed in the Director's office.

### Powers of court

(10) The court may, unless it is satisfied that the payor is unable for valid reasons to pay the arrears or to make subsequent payments under the order, order that the payor,

(a) pay all or part of the arrears by such periodic lump sum payments as the court considers just, but an order for partial payment does not rescind any unpaid arrears;

(b) discharge the arrears in full by a specified date;

(c) comply with the order to the extent of the payor's ability to pay;

(d) make a motion to change the support order;

(e) provide security in such form as the court directs for the arrears and subsequent payment;

(f) report periodically to the court, the Director or a person specified in the order;

(g) provide to the court, the Director or a person specified in the order particulars of any future change of address or employment as soon as they occur;

(h) be imprisoned continuously or intermittently until the period specified in the order, which shall not be more than 180 days, has expired, or until the arrears are paid, whichever is sooner; and

(i) on default in any payment ordered under this subsection, be imprisoned continuously or intermittently until the period specified in the order, which shall not be more than 180 days, has expired, or until the payment is made, whichever is sooner.

### No effect on accruing of arrears or other means of enforcement

(11) An order under subsection (10) does not affect the accruing of arrears, nor does it limit or otherwise affect any other means of enforcing the support order.

## Order against person financially connected to payor

(12) If the court is satisfied that a person who was made a party to the hearing under subsection (5) sheltered assets or income of the payor such that enforcement of the support order against the payor has been frustrated, the court may, having regard to all the circumstances, including the purpose and effect of the dealings and the benefit or expected benefit therefrom to the payor, make any order against the person that it may make against the payor under clauses (10)(a), (b), (c), (e), (f) and (g) and subsection (19), to the extent of the value of the sheltered assets or income and, for the purpose, in clause (10) (c), "payor's" shall be read as "person's."

## Same

(13) Subsections (7) and (8) apply with necessary modifications to a person with respect to whom an order is made under subsection (4) or (5).

## Temporary orders

(14) The court may make a temporary order against the payor, or a person who was made a party to the hearing under subsection (5), that includes any order that may be made under subsection (10) or (12), as the case may be.

## Power to change order

(15) The court that made an order under subsection (10) or (12) may change the order on motion if there is a material change in the payor's or other person's circumstances, as the case may be.

## Enforcement of order

(16) The Director may enforce an order against a person made under subsection (12), (14) or (15) in the same manner as he or she may enforce an order against the payor.

## Imprisonment does not discharge arrears

(17) Imprisonment of a payor under clause (10)(h) or (i) does not discharge arrears under an order.

## No early release

(18) Section 28 of the *Ministry of Correctional Services Act* does not apply to the imprisonment of a payor under clause (10)(h) or (i).

## Realizing on security

(19) An order for security under clause (10)(e) or a subsequent order of the court may provide for the realization of the security by seizure, sale or other means, as the court directs.

## Proof of service not necessary

(20) Proof of service of a support order or a changed support order is not necessary for the purpose of a default hearing.

## Joinder of default and change hearings

(21) A default hearing under this section and a hearing on a motion to change the support order may be held together or separately.

## Effect of change on default hearing

(22) If an order changing a support order is made while a default hearing under this section in relation to the support order is under way,

(a) the default hearing continues;

(b) it is not necessary to serve fresh documents under subsection (1) or (2); and

(c) the payment terms of the changed support order shall be incorporated into any subsequent order made under subsection (10).

## Spouses compellable witnesses

(23) Spouses are competent and compellable witnesses against each other on a default hearing.

## Records sealed

(24) A financial statement or other document filed under subsection (4) shall be sealed in the court file and shall not be disclosed except as permitted by the order or a subsequent order or as necessary to enforce an order made under subsection (12) or (14) against a person other than the payor.

## Definition

(25) In this section,

"court" means the Ontario Court of Justice or the Family Court.

## Registration against land

**42.** (1) A support order may be registered in the proper land registry office against the payor's land and on registration the obligation under the order becomes a charge on the property.

## Sale of property

(2) A charge created by subsection (1) may be enforced by sale of the property against which it is registered in the same manner as a sale to realize on a mortgage.

## Discharge or postponement of charge

(3) A court may order the discharge, in whole or in part, or the postponement, of a charge created by subsection (1), on such terms as to security or other matters as the court considers just.

## Notice

(4) An order under subsection (3) may be made only after notice to the Director, if the support order or a related support deduction order is filed with the Director's office for enforcement.

## Registration under the *Personal Property Security Act*

**43.** (1) Arrears owing from time to time under a support order are, upon registration by the Director or the recipient with the registrar under the *Personal Property Security Act* of a notice claiming a lien and charge under this section, a lien and charge on any interest in all the personal property in

Ontario owned or held at the time of registration or acquired afterwards by the payor.

### Amounts included and priority

(2) The lien and charge is in respect of the arrears owed by the payor under a support order at the time of registration of the notice and the arrears owed by the payor under the support order which accrue afterwards while the notice remains registered and, upon registration of a notice of lien and charge, the lien and charge has priority over,

(a) any perfected security interest registered after the notice is registered;

(b) any security interest perfected by possession after the notice is registered; and

(c) any encumbrance or other claim that is registered against or that otherwise arises and affects the payor's property after the notice is registered.

### Exception

(3) For the purpose of subsection (2), the notice of lien and charge does not have priority over a perfected purchase money security interest in collateral or its proceeds and shall be deemed to be a security interest perfected by registration for the purpose of the priority rules under section 28 of the *Personal Property Security Act*.

### Effective period

(4) The notice of lien and charge is effective from the time assigned to its registration by the registrar or branch registrar until its discharge or expiry.

### Secured party

(5) In addition to any other rights and remedies, if any arrears under a support order remain unpaid, the Director or recipient, as the case may be, has, in respect of the lien and charge,

(a) all the rights, remedies and duties of a secured party under sections 17, 59, 61, 62, 63 and 64, subsections 65(4), (5), (6) and (7) and section 66 of the *Personal Property Security Act*;

(b) a security interest in the collateral for the purpose of clause 63(4)(c) of that Act; and

(c) a security interest in the personal property for the purposes of sections 15 and 16 of the *Repair and Storage Liens Act*, if it is an article as defined in that Act.

### Registration of documents

(6) The notice of lien and charge shall be in the form of a financing statement as prescribed by regulation under the *Personal Property Security Act* and may be tendered for registration at a branch office as provided in Part IV of that Act.

### Errors in documents

(7) The notice of lien and charge is not invalidated nor its effect impaired by reason only of an error or omission in the notice or in its execution or registration, unless a reasonable person is likely to be materially misled by the error or omission.

### *Bankruptcy and Insolvency Act* (Canada) unaffected

(8) Subject to Crown rights provided under section 87 of the *Bankruptcy and Insolvency Act* (Canada), nothing in this section affects or purports to affect the rights and obligations of any person under that Act.

### Writs of seizure and sale

**44.** (1) If a writ of seizure and sale is filed with a sheriff in respect of a support order, the person who filed the writ may at any time file with the sheriff a statutory declaration specifying,

(a) the amount currently owing under the order; or

(b) any name, alias or spelling variation of any name or alias used by the payor.

### Same

(2) When a statutory declaration is filed under clause (1)(a), the writ of seizure and sale shall be deemed to be amended to specify the amount owing in accordance with the statutory declaration.

### Same

(2.1) When a statutory declaration is filed under clause (1)(b), the writ of seizure and sale shall be deemed to be amended to include the names specified on the statutory declaration.

### Notice from sheriff of opportunity to amend writ

(3) A sheriff who comes into possession of money to be paid out under a writ of seizure and sale in respect of a support order shall, not later than seven days after making the entry required by subsection 4(1) of the *Creditors' Relief Act, 2010*, give notice to the person who filed the writ of the opportunity to file a statutory declaration under clause (1)(a).

### Same

(4) A sheriff who receives a request for information about the amount owing under a writ of seizure and sale in respect of a support order from a person seeking to have the writ removed from the sheriff's file shall promptly give notice to the person who filed the writ of the opportunity to file a statutory declaration under clause (1)(a).

### Removal of writ from sheriff's file

(5) A sheriff shall not remove a writ of seizure and sale in respect of a support order from his or her file unless,

(a) the writ has expired and has not been renewed;

(b) the sheriff receives written notice from the person who filed the writ to the effect that the writ should be withdrawn;

(c) notice is given under subsection (3) or (4), a statutory declaration is subsequently filed under clause (1)(a) and the writ, as deemed to be amended under subsection (2), has been fully satisfied; or

(d) notice is given under subsection (3) or (4), 10 days have elapsed since the notice was given, no statutory declaration has been filed under clause (1)(a) since the giving of the notice and the writ has been fully satisfied.

### Delivery of statutory declaration to land registrar

(6) If a copy of a writ of seizure and sale has been delivered by the sheriff to a land registrar under section 136 of the *Land Titles Act* and a statutory declaration is filed under subsection (1) in respect of the writ, the sheriff shall promptly deliver a copy of the statutory declaration to the land registrar and the amendment deemed to be made to the writ under subsection (2) or (2.1) does not bind land registered under the *Land Titles Act* until a copy of the statutory declaration has been received and recorded by the land registrar.

### Garnishment of joint accounts

**45.** (1) Upon being served on a financial institution, a notice of garnishment issued by the Director to enforce a support order against a payor attaches 50 per cent of the money credited to a deposit account held in the financial institution in the name of the payor together with one or more other persons as joint or joint and several deposit account holders, and the financial institution shall pay up to 50 per cent of the money credited to the deposit account to the Director in accordance with the notice of garnishment.

### Duties of financial institution

(2) The financial institution shall, within 10 days of being served with the notice of garnishment,

(a) pay the money to the Director and, at the same time, notify the Director if the account is held jointly or jointly and severally in the name of two or more persons; and

(b) notify the co-holders of the account who are not named in the notice of garnishment of the garnishment.

### Dispute by co-holder

(3) Within 30 days after the financial institution notified the Director under clause (2)(a), a co-holder of the deposit account may file a dispute to the garnishment in the Ontario Court of Justice or the Family Court claiming ownership of all or part of the money that the financial institution paid to the Director.

### Director to hold money for 30 days

(4) If the financial institution notifies the Director under clause (2)(a), the Director shall not release the money received under subsection (1) until 30 days after the financial institution so notified the Director, and the Director may release the money after the 30 days unless a co-holder of the deposit account first serves on the Director a copy of the dispute to the garnishment that the co-holder filed under subsection (3).

### Determination by court

(5) In a hearing to determine the dispute to the garnishment, the money paid to the Director shall be presumed to be owned by the payor and the court shall order,

(a) that the garnishment be limited to the payor's interest in the money that was paid to the Director; and

(b) that all or part of the money that was paid to the Director be returned to the co-holder only if it is satisfied that the co-holder owns that money.

### Payment by Director

(6) Upon receipt of a copy of the court's order, the Director shall return to the co-holder any money determined by the court to belong to the co-holder and may release any remaining money, if any, to the recipient.

### Action by joint account co-holder against payor

(7) A co-holder may bring an action against the payor in a court of competent jurisdiction,

(a) to recover any money owned by the co-holder that was paid to the Director under subsection (1);

(b) to recover any interest that the co-holder would have earned on the money owned by the co-holder that was paid to the Director under subsection (1).

### Director and recipient are not parties

(8) The Director and the recipient are not parties to an action under subsection (7).

### Definition

(9) In this section,

"deposit account" includes a deposit as defined in the *Deposits Regulation Act* and a demand account, time account, savings account, passbook account, checking account, current account and other similar accounts in,

(a) a bank listed in Schedule I or II to the *Bank Act* (Canada),

(b) a loan corporation or trust corporation as defined in the *Loan and Trust Corporations Act*,

(c) a credit union as defined in the *Credit Unions and Caisses Populaires Act, 1994*, or

(d) a similar institution.

(e) Repealed.

### Garnishment of lottery prizes

**46.** (1) In this section,

"Corporation" means the Ontario Lottery and Gaming Corporation;

"lottery" means a lottery scheme, as defined in section 1 of the *Ontario Lottery* and Gaming *Corporation Act, 1999*, that is conducted by the Corporation in Ontario and involves the issuance and sale of tickets;

"prize" means a prize in a lottery.

### Deduction of arrears from prize

(2) If a payor who owes arrears under a support order that is filed in the Director's office is entitled to a single monetary prize of $1,000 or more from the Corporation, the Corporation shall,

(a) deduct from the prize the amount of the arrears or the amount of the prize, whichever is less;

(b) pay the amount deducted to the Director; and

(c) pay any balance to the payor.

### Non-monetary prize

(3) If a payor who owes arrears under a support order that is filed in the Director's office is entitled to a non-monetary prize from the Corporation that the Corporation values at $1,000 or more, the Corporation shall promptly disclose to the Director,

(a) any identifying information about the payor from the Corporation's records, including his or her name and address; and

(b) a complete description of the prize.

### Exchange of information

(4) For the purposes of subsections (2) and (3),

(a) the Director shall disclose to the Corporation any identifying information about payors from the Director's records, including their names and addresses and the status and particulars of their support obligations; and

(b) the Corporation shall disclose to the Director any identifying information about prize winners from its records, including their names and addresses.

### Reporting default to consumer reporting agency

**47.** The Director may disclose the information set out in section 47.2 to a consumer reporting agency registered under the *Consumer Reporting Act.*

### Reporting default to prescribed entity

**47.1** (1) The Director may disclose the information set out in section 47.2 to a prescribed entity that is,

(a) a professional or occupational organization;

(b) the governing body of a self-governing or regulated profession; or

(c) an entity that is responsible for licensing or registering individuals for occupational purposes.

### Presumption

(2) In the absence of evidence to the contrary, it shall be presumed that the amount disclosed with respect to arrears as described in clause 47.2(d) is correct.

### Information that may be disclosed

**47.2** The information that may be disclosed under section 47 or 47.1 is,

(a) the name of a payor who is in default on a support order filed in the Director's office;

(b) the date of the support order;

(c) the amount and frequency of the payor's support obligation under the support order;

(d) the amount of the arrears owing under the support order at the time of the disclosure; and

(e) such other information as may be prescribed.

### Restraining order

**48.** A court, including the Ontario Court of Justice, may make an order restraining the disposition or wasting of assets that may hinder or defeat the enforcement of a support order or support deduction order.

### Arrest of absconding payor

**49.** (1) The Ontario Court of Justice or the Family Court may issue a warrant for a payor's arrest for the purpose of bringing him or her before the court if the court is satisfied that the payor is about to leave Ontario and that there are reasonable grounds for believing that the payor intends to evade his or her obligations under the support order.

### Bail

(2) Section 150 (interim release by justice of the peace) of the *Provincial Offences Act* applies with necessary modifications to an arrest under the warrant.

### Powers of court

(3) When the payor is brought before the court, it may make any order provided for in subsection 41(10).

### Recognition of extra-provincial garnishments

**50.** (1) On the filing of a garnishment process that,

(a) is issued outside Ontario and is directed to a garnishee in Ontario;

(b) states that it is issued in respect of support or maintenance; and

(c) is written in or accompanied by a sworn or certified translation into English or French,

the clerk of the Ontario Court of Justice or Family Court shall issue a notice of garnishment to enforce the support or maintenance obligation.

### Foreign currencies

(2) If the garnishment process refers to an obligation in a foreign currency, section 44 of the *Interjurisdictional Support Orders Act, 2002* applies with necessary modifications.

## PART VII OFFENCES AND PENALTIES

### Offences—payors, income sources, etc.

### Payors

**51.** (1) A payor who knowingly contravenes or knowingly fails to comply with section 19 or subsection 25(1) or (2) or 40(2) or (3) is guilty of an offence and on conviction is liable to a fine of not more than $10,000.

### Income sources

(2) An income source who knowingly contravenes or knowingly fails to comply with subsection 22(2) or 25(1)

or (2) or section 29 is guilty of an offence and on conviction is liable to a fine of not more than $10,000.

### Individuals, etc., believed to be an income source

(3) An individual, corporation or other entity that knowingly contravenes or knowingly fails to comply with subsection 26(1) or section 29 is guilty of an offence and on conviction is liable to a fine of not more than $10,000.

### Offences—assignees

**52.** (1) An assignee under section 4 who knowingly contravenes or knowingly fails to comply with this Act or its regulations or the limitations, conditions or requirements set out in the assignment is guilty of an offence and on conviction is liable to a fine of not more than $10,000.

### Same—directors, officers, employees, agents

(2) A director, officer, employee or agent of an assignee who commits an offence described in subsection (1) on conviction is liable to a fine of not more than $10,000.

### Same—directors, officers

(3) A director or officer of an assignee is guilty of an offence if he or she,

(a) knowingly causes, authorizes, permits or participates in the commission of an offence described in subsection (1); or

(b) fails to take reasonable care to prevent the commission of an offence described in subsection (1).

### Penalty

(4) A person who is convicted of an offence under subsection (3) is liable to a fine of not more than $10,000.

### Contempt

**53.** (1) In addition to its powers in respect of contempt, a court, including the Ontario Court of Justice, may punish by fine or imprisonment, or by both, any wilful contempt of, or resistance to, its process, rules or orders under this Act, but the fine shall not exceed $10,000 nor shall the imprisonment exceed 90 days.

### Conditions of imprisonment

(2) An order for imprisonment under subsection (1) may be conditional upon default in the performance of a condition set out in the order and may provide for the imprisonment to be served intermittently.

## PART VIII MISCELLANEOUS
### Director's access to information
### Definitions

**54.** (1) In this section,

"enforcement-related information" means information that indicates any of the following about a payor:

0.1 name, alias or spelling variation of any name or alias,

1. employer or place of employment,

2. wages, salary or other income,

2.1 indexing factors applied to the payor's wages, salary, pension or other income,

3. assets or liabilities,

4. home, work or mailing address, or location,

5. telephone number, fax number or e-mail address;

"recipient information" means information that indicates any of the following about a recipient:

0.1 name, alias or spelling variation of any name or alias,

1. home, work or mailing address, or location,

2. telephone number, fax number or e-mail address.

### Power of Director

(2) The Director may, for the purpose of enforcing a support order or support deduction order filed in the Director's office or for the purpose of assisting an office or person in another jurisdiction performing similar functions to those performed by the Director,

(a) demand enforcement-related information or recipient information from any person, public body or other entity from a record in the possession or control of the person, public body or other entity;

(b) subject to subsections (4) and (5), have access to all records that may contain enforcement-related information or recipient information and that are in the possession or control of any ministry, agency, board or commission of the Government of Ontario in order to search for and obtain the information from the records;

(c) subject to subsections (4) and (5), enter into an agreement with any person, public body or other entity, including the Government of Canada, a Crown corporation, the government of another province or territory or any agency, board or commission of such government, to permit the Director to have access to records in the possession or control of the person, public body or other entity that may contain enforcement-related information or recipient information, in order to search for and obtain the information from the records; and

(d) disclose information obtained under clause (a), (b) or (c) to a person performing similar functions to those of the Director in another jurisdiction.

### 10-day period for response

(3) When the Director demands information under clause (2)(a), the person, public body or other entity shall provide the information within 10 days after being served with the demand.

### Access to part of record

(4) Where the record referred to in clause (2)(b) or (c) is part of a larger record, the Director,

(a) may have access to the part of the record that may

contain enforcement-related information or recipient information; and

(b) may have incidental access to any other information contained in that part of the record, but may not use or disclose that other information.

### Restriction on access to health information

(5) Despite subsection (4), if a record described in clause (2)(b) or (c) contains health information, as defined in the regulations, the Director shall not have access to the health information but shall have access only to the part of the record that may contain enforcement-related information or recipient information.

### Information confidential

(6) Information obtained under subsection (2) shall not be disclosed except,

(a) to the extent necessary for the enforcement of the support order or support deduction order;

(b) as provided in clause (2)(d); or

(c) to a police officer who needs the information for a criminal investigation that is likely to assist the enforcement of the support order or support deduction order.

### Court order for access to information

(7) A court may, on motion, make an order requiring any person, public body or other entity to provide the court or the person whom the court names with any enforcement-related information or recipient information that is shown on a record in the possession or control of the person, public body or other entity if it appears that,

(a) the Director has been refused information after making a demand under clause (2)(a);

(b) the Director has been refused access to a record under clause (2)(b); or

(c) a person needs an order under this subsection for the enforcement of a support order that is not filed in the Director's office.

### Court order re agreement

(8) A court may, on motion, make an order requiring any person, public body or other entity to enter into an agreement described in clause (2)(c) with the Director if it appears that the person, public body or other entity has unreasonably refused to enter into such an agreement.

### Costs

(9) If the Director obtains an order under clause (7)(a) or (b) or under subsection (8), the court shall award the costs of the motion to the Director.

### Information confidential

(10) Information obtained under an order under clause (7)(c) shall be sealed in the court file and shall not be disclosed except,

(a) as permitted by the order or a subsequent order;

(b) to the extent necessary for the enforcement of the support order or support deduction order;

(c) as provided in clause (2)(d); or

(d) to a police officer who needs the information for a criminal investigation that is likely to assist the enforcement of the support order or support deduction order.

### Section governs

(11) This section applies despite any other Act or regulation and despite any common law rule of confidentiality.

### Federal-provincial agreement

**55.** (1) The Minister responsible for the administration of this Act may, on behalf of the Government of Ontario, enter into an agreement with the Government of Canada concerning the searching for and the release of information under Part I of the *Family Orders and Agreements Enforcement Assistance Act* (Canada).

### Information obtained from federal government

(2) The Director shall not disclose information obtained under the *Family Orders and Agreements Enforcement Assistance Act* (Canada) for the enforcement of a support order, except,

(a) to the extent necessary for the enforcement of the order; or

(b) as permitted by the *Freedom of Information and Protection of Privacy Act*.

### Payments pending court decisions

**56.** (1) The Director shall pay any money he or she receives in respect of a support order or a support deduction order to the recipient despite the commencement of any court proceeding in respect of the support obligation or its enforcement, in the absence of a court order to the contrary.

### Exception

(2) If a court orders the Director to hold any of the money received in respect of a support order or a support deduction order pending the disposition of the proceeding, the Director shall, upon receipt of a copy of the order, hold any money he or she receives to the extent required by the court.

### Application of payments

**57.** (1) Money paid to the Director on account of a support order or support deduction order shall be credited as prescribed by the regulations.

### Same

(2) Despite anything in this Act, the payor shall not be credited with making a payment until the money for that payment is received by the Director and if a payment is made but not honoured, the amount of the payment shall be added to the support arrears owed by the payor.

### Fees

**58.** (1) The Director shall not charge any fee to any person for his or her services except as provided by regulation.

## Enforcement of orders to collect fees, etc.

(2) The Director may continue to enforce a support order or support deduction order to collect an amount described in subsection (3), even if,

(a) the support order or support deduction order to which the amount relates has been withdrawn from the Director's office;

(b) there is no current support obligation, and there are no arrears, or any arrears are rescinded by a changed support order; or

(c) the support obligation has terminated and there are no arrears, or any arrears are rescinded by a changed support order.

## Same

(3) Subsection (2) applies with respect to,

(a) fees;

(b) costs awarded to the Director by a court;

(c) any amount owed to the Director as reimbursement for money paid to a recipient; and

(d) any amount similar to the ones described in clauses (a), (b) and (c) that is owed to a support enforcement program in a reciprocating jurisdiction, if the support order to which the amount relates is registered in Ontario under the *Interjurisdictional Support Orders Act, 2002*.

## Protection from personal liability

**59.** (1) No action or other proceeding for damages shall be instituted against the Director or any employee of the Director's office for any act done in good faith in the execution or intended execution of any duty or authority under this Act or for any alleged neglect or default in the execution in good faith of any duty or authority under this Act.

## Crown not relieved of liability

(2) Despite subsections 5(2) and (4) of the *Proceedings Against the Crown Act*, subsection (1) does not relieve the Crown of liability in respect of a tort committed by a person mentioned in subsection (1) to which it would otherwise be subject.

## Acting by lawyer

**60.** Anything that this Act requires to be signed or done by a person, or that is referred to in this Act as signed or done by a person, may be signed or done by a lawyer acting on the person's behalf.

## Disclosure of personal information

**61.** (1) The Director shall collect, disclose and use personal information about an identifiable individual for the purpose of enforcing a support order or a support deduction order under this Act.

## Same

(2) Any person, public body or other entity that is referred to in clause 54(2)(a) shall disclose personal information about an identifiable individual to the Director for the purpose of section 54, within 10 days after being served with the Director's demand.

## Notice to individual not required

(3) Subsection 39(2) of the *Freedom of Information and Protection of Privacy Act* does not apply to the collection of personal information about an identifiable individual under this Act.

## Act prevails over confidentiality provisions

(4) This Act prevails over a confidentiality provision in another Act that would, if not for this Act, prohibit the disclosure of information to the Director.

## Law enforcement

(5) The Director shall be deemed to be engaged in law enforcement for the purposes of section 14 of the *Freedom of Information and Protection of Privacy Act* when collecting information, under section 54 or otherwise, for the purpose of enforcing a support order or support deduction order under this Act.

## Obtaining information about payor by means of Internet posting
### Director's discretion

**61.1** (1) The Director may post a payor's name and other prescribed information relating to the payor on a website on the Internet if,

(a) the payor is in default under a support order;

(b) the support order or a related support deduction order is filed in the Director's office;

(c) the Director has been unsuccessful in locating the payor; and

(d) the prescribed conditions are satisfied.

## Purpose of posting

(2) The sole purpose of posting information under subsection (1) is to assist the Director in locating the payor.

## Confidentiality of information obtained as a result of posting

(3) Subsection 54(6) applies, with necessary modifications, to any information obtained by the Director as a result of the posting.

## Act binds Crown

**62.** This Act binds the Crown.

## Regulations

**63.** (1) The Lieutenant Governor in Council may make regulations,

(a) prescribing forms and providing for their use;

(b) prescribing types of income for the purposes of clause (l) of the definition of "income source" in subsection 1(1);

(c) prescribing the manner of calculating a cost of living clause for the purposes of subsections 7(4), (5), (6) and (7);

(d) prescribing classes of persons and information to be supplied to the court and the manner in which information is to be supplied for the purposes of subsections 11(2) and (3);

(e) prescribing practices and procedures related to the filing and withdrawal of support orders and support deduction orders and to the enforcement, suspension and termination of such orders filed in the Director's office;

(e.1) defining "in compliance" for the purposes of subsection 16(1.1);

(e.2) prescribing methods of electronic transmission for the purpose of subsection 22(2.1);

(f) prescribing deductions for the purposes of subsection 23(5);

(g) prescribing information that shall be supplied under subsection 25(1);

(g.1) prescribing practices and procedures relating to the filing and withdrawal of alternative payment orders under section 28;

(h) governing the form and posting of security by a payor under section 28 and the realization thereon;

(i) respecting proof of income for the purposes of sections 35, 40 and 41;

(j) prescribing, for the purposes of clause 47.2(e), other information that may be disclosed under section 47 or 47.1;

(k) prescribing,

(i) fees to be charged by the Director for administrative services, including preparing and photocopying documents on request, and

(ii) fees for any steps taken by the Director to enforce a support order in response to the persistent or wilful default by a payor;

(k.1) prescribing fees for the repeated filing of a support order or support deduction order, and specifying what constitutes repeated filing;

(l) prescribing the maximum fees, costs, disbursements, surcharges and other charges, or a method for determining the maximum fees, costs, disbursements, surcharges and other charges, that an assignee under section 4 may charge a payor, including fees, costs, disbursements, surcharges and other charges for services for which the Director is not permitted to charge and including fees, costs, disbursements, surcharges or other charges that are higher than the fees, costs, disbursements, surcharges and other charges that the Director may charge for the same

service, prescribing how and when such fees, costs, disbursements, surcharges and other charges may be collected, prescribing the manner in which they may be applied and prescribing the rate of interest to be charged on any of them;

(m) prescribing methods of and rules respecting service, filing and notice for the purposes of this Act, including different methods and rules for different provisions and different methods and rules for service on or notice to the Crown;

(n) providing that a support deduction order is not effective against the Crown unless a statement of particulars in the prescribed form is served with the notice of the order;

(o) defining "health information" for the purposes of subsection 54(5);

(p) prescribing the manner in which payments received by the Director are to be credited;

(p.1) governing the delivery of payments to recipients, including requiring recipients to provide the Director with the information and authorization required to enable the Director to make direct deposits into the recipients' accounts with financial institutions;

(p.2) setting out recommended standard terms for support orders;

(q) prescribing anything that is required or authorized by this Act to be prescribed.

### Repeated filing

(2) A fee prescribed under clause (1)(k.1) may be charged against both the payor and the recipient, regardless of which one of them files the order.

**64.** Repealed. See: Table of Public Statute Provisions Repealed Under Section 10.1 of the *Legislation Act, 2006—*December 31, 2011.

**65.–70.** Omitted (amends or repeals other Acts).

**71.** Repealed. See: Table of Public Statute Provisions Repealed Under Section 10.1 of the *Legislation Act, 2006—*December 31, 2011.

**72., 73.** Omitted (amends or repeals other Acts).

**74.** Omitted (provides for coming into force of provisions of this Act).

**75.** Omitted (enacts short title of this Act).

# Child Support Guidelines

O Reg 391/97

**Objectives**

**1.** The objectives of this Regulation are,

(a) to establish a fair standard of support for children that ensures that they benefit from the financial means of their parents and, in the case of divorce, from the financial means of both spouses after separation;

(b) to reduce conflict and tension between parents or spouses by making the calculation of child support more objective;

(c) to improve the efficiency of the legal process by giving courts, and parents and spouses, guidance in setting the levels of child support and encouraging settlement; and

(d) to ensure consistent treatment of parents or spouses and their children who are in similar circumstances.

## INTERPRETATION

**Definitions**

**2.** (1) In this Regulation,

"child" means, other than in Schedule II to this Regulation,

(a) a child who is a dependant under the Act, or

(b) in cases where the *Divorce Act* (Canada) applies, a child of the marriage under that Act;

"income" means the annual income determined under sections 15 to 20;

"order assignee" means,

(a) an agency to whom an order is assigned under subsection 34(3) of the Act, or

(b) a minister, member or agency referred to in subsection 20.1(1) of the *Divorce Act* (Canada) to whom an order for the support of a child is assigned in accordance with that subsection;

"parent," in a case to which the Act applies, means a parent to whom section 31 of the Act applies;

"spouse," in a case to which the *Divorce Act* (Canada) applies, has the meaning assigned by subsection 2(1) of that Act, and includes a former spouse;

"table" means,

(a) if the parent or spouse against whom an order is sought ordinarily resides in Ontario at the time of the application, the Child Support Table for Ontario set out in Schedule I to this Regulation,

(b) if the parent or spouse against whom an order is sought ordinarily resides elsewhere in Canada, the table set out in the Federal Child Support Guidelines for the province or territory in which the parent or spouse ordinarily resides at the time of the application,

(c) if the court is satisfied that the province or territory in which the parent or spouse against whom an order is sought ordinarily resides has changed since the time of the application, the table set out in the Federal Child Support Guidelines for the province or territory in which the parent or spouse ordinarily resides at the time the amount of support is determined,

(d) if the court is satisfied that the parent or spouse against whom an order is sought will, in the near future after the amount of support is determined, ordinarily reside in another province or territory than the one in which he or she ordinarily resides at the time the amount of support is determined, the table set out in the Federal Child Support Guidelines for that other province or territory,

(e) if the parent or spouse against whom an order is sought ordinarily resides outside of Canada or if the ordinary residence of the parent or spouse is unknown,

(i) the Child Support Table for Ontario set out in Schedule I to this Regulation if the other parent or spouse applying for the order resides in Ontario, or

(ii) the table set out in the Federal Child Support Guidelines for the province or territory in which the parent or spouse applying for the order ordinarily resides.

"universal child care benefit" means a benefit provided under section 4 of the *Universal Child Care Benefit Act* (Canada).

### *Income Tax Act* (Canada)

(2) Words and expressions that are used in sections 15 to 21 and that are not defined in this section have the meanings assigned to them under the *Income Tax Act* (Canada).

### Most current information

(3) Where, for the purposes of the child support guidelines, any amount is determined on the basis of specified information, the most current information must be used.

### Application of guidelines

(4) In addition to their application to orders for support of a child, the child support guidelines apply, with such modifications as the circumstances require, to,

(a) interim orders under subsection 34(1) of the Act or subsections 15.1(2) and 19(9) of the *Divorce Act* (Canada);

(b) orders varying a child support order; and

(c) orders referred to in subsection 19(7) of the *Divorce Act* (Canada).

### AMOUNT OF CHILD SUPPORT

### Presumptive rule

3. (1) Unless otherwise provided under these guidelines, the amount of an order for the support of a child for children under the age of majority is,

(a) the amount set out in the applicable table, according to the number of children under the age of majority to whom the order relates and the income of the parent or spouse against whom the order is sought; and

(b) the amount, if any, determined under section 7.

### Child the age of majority or over

(2) Unless otherwise provided under these guidelines, where a child to whom an order for the support of a child relates is the age of majority or over, the amount of an order for the support of a child is,

(a) the amount determined by applying these guidelines as if the child were under the age of majority; or

(b) if the court considers that approach to be inappropriate, the amount that it considers appropriate, having regard to the condition, means, needs and other circumstances of the child and the financial ability of each parent or spouse to contribute to the support of the child.

### Incomes over $150,000

4. Where the income of the parent or spouse against whom an order for the support of a child is sought is over $150,000, the amount of an order for the support of a child is,

(a) the amount determined under section 3; or

(b) if the court considers that amount to be inappropriate,

(i) in respect of the first $150,000 of the parent's or spouse's income, the amount set out in the table for the number of children under the age of majority to whom the order relates,

(ii) in respect of the balance of the parent's or spouse's income, the amount that the court considers appropriate, having regard to the condition, means, needs and other circumstances of the children who are entitled to support and the financial ability of each parent or spouse to contribute to the support of the children, and

(iii) the amount, if any, determined under section 7.

### Spouse in place of a parent

5. Where the spouse against whom an order for the support of a child is sought stands in the place of a parent for a child or the parent is not a parent of the child as set out in section 4 of the *Children's Law Reform Act*, the amount of the order is, in respect of that parent or spouse, such amount as the court considers appropriate, having regard to these guidelines and any other parent's legal duty to support the child.

### Medical and dental insurance

6. In making an order for the support of a child, where medical or dental insurance coverage for the child is available to either parent or spouse through his or her employer or otherwise at a reasonable rate, the court may order that coverage be acquired or continued.

### Special or extraordinary expenses

7. (1) In an order for the support of a child, the court may, on the request of either parent or spouse or of an applicant under section 33 of the Act, provide for an amount to cover all or any portion of the following expenses, which expenses may be estimated, taking into account the necessity of the expense in relation to the child's best interests and the reasonableness of the expense in relation to the means of the parents or spouses and those of the child and to the spending pattern of the parents or spouses in respect of the child during cohabitation:

(a) child care expenses incurred as a result of the custodial parent's employment, illness, disability or education or training for employment;

(b) that portion of the medical and dental insurance premiums attributable to the child;

(c) health-related expenses that exceed insurance reimbursement by at least $100 annually, including orthodontic treatment, professional counselling provided by a psychologist, social worker, psychiatrist or any other person, physiotherapy, occupational therapy, speech therapy, prescription drugs, hearing aids, glasses and contact lenses;

(d) extraordinary expenses for primary or secondary school education or for any other educational programs that meet the child's particular needs;

(e) expenses for post-secondary education; and

(f) extraordinary expenses for extracurricular activities.

## Definition, "extraordinary expenses"

(1.1) For the purposes of clauses (1)(d) and (f), "extraordinary expenses" means

(a) expenses that exceed those that the parent or spouse requesting an amount for the extraordinary expenses can reasonably cover, taking into account that parent's or spouse's income and the amount that the parent or spouse would receive under the applicable table or, where the court has determined that the table amount is inappropriate, the amount that the court has otherwise determined is appropriate, or

(b) where clause (a) is not applicable, expenses that the court considers are extraordinary taking into account,

(i) the amount of the expense in relation to the income of the parent or spouse requesting the amount, including the amount that the parent or spouse would receive under the applicable table or, where the court has determined that the table amount is inappropriate, the amount that the court has otherwise determined is appropriate,

(ii) the nature and number of the educational programs and extracurricular activities,

(iii) any special needs and talents of the child,

(iv) the overall cost of the programs and activities, and

(v) any other similar factors that the court considers relevant.

## Sharing of expense

(2) The guiding principle in determining the amount of an expense referred to in subsection (1) is that the expense is shared by the parents or spouses in proportion to their respective incomes after deducting from the expense, the contribution, if any, from the child.

## Subsidies, tax deductions, etc.

(3) Subject to subsection (4), in determining the amount of an expense referred to in subsection (1), the court must take into account any subsidies, benefits or income tax deductions or credits relating to the expense, and any eligibility to claim a subsidy, benefit or income tax deduction or credit relating to the expense.

## Universal child care benefit

(4) In determining the amount of an expense referred to in subsection (1), the court shall not take into account any universal child care benefit or any eligibility to claim that benefit.

## Split custody

8. Where each parent or spouse has custody of one or more children, the amount of an order for the support of a child is the difference between the amount that each parent or spouse would otherwise pay if such an order were sought against each of the parents or spouses.

## Shared custody

9. Where a parent or spouse exercises a right of access to, or has physical custody of, a child for not less than 40 per cent of the time over the course of a year, the amount of the order for the support of a child must be determined by taking into account,

(a) the amounts set out in the applicable tables for each of the parents or spouses;

(b) the increased costs of shared custody arrangements; and

(c) the condition, means, needs and other circumstances of each parent or spouse and of any child for whom support is sought.

## Undue hardship

10. (1) On the application of either spouse or an applicant under section 33 of the Act, a court may award an amount of child support that is different from the amount determined under any of sections 3 to 5, 8 or 9 if the court finds that the parent or spouse making the request, or a child in respect of whom the request is made, would otherwise suffer undue hardship.

## Circumstances that may cause undue hardship

(2) Circumstances that may cause a parent, spouse or child to suffer undue hardship include,

(a) the parent or spouse has responsibility for an unusually high level of debts reasonably incurred to support the parents or spouses and their children during cohabitation or to earn a living;

(b) the parent or spouse has unusually high expenses in relation to exercising access to a child;

(c) the parent or spouse has a legal duty under a judgment, order or written separation agreement to support any person;

(d) the spouse has a legal duty to support a child, other than a child of the marriage, who is,

(i) under the age of majority, or

(ii) the age of majority or over but is unable, by reason of illness, disability or other cause, to obtain the necessaries of life;

(e) the parent has a legal duty to support a child, other than the child who is the subject of this application, who is under the age of majority or who is enrolled in a full time course of education;

(f) the parent or spouse has a legal duty to support any person who is unable to obtain the necessaries of life due to an illness or disability.

### Standards of living must be considered

(3) Despite a determination of undue hardship under subsection (1), an application under that subsection must be denied by the court if it is of the opinion that the household of the parent or spouse who claims undue hardship would, after determining the amount of child support under any of sections 3 to 5, 8 or 9, have a higher standard of living than the household of the other parent or spouse.

### Standards of living test

(4) In comparing standards of living for the purpose of subsection (3), the court may use the comparison of household standards of living test set out in Schedule II.

### Reasonable time

(5) Where the court awards a different amount of child support under subsection (1), it may specify, in the order for child support, a reasonable time for the satisfaction of any obligation arising from circumstances that cause undue hardship and the amount payable at the end of that time.

### Reasons

(6) Where the court makes an order for the support of a child in a different amount under this section, it must record its reasons for doing so.

## ELEMENTS OF AN ORDER FOR THE SUPPORT OF A CHILD

### Form of payments

**11.** Where the child support guidelines apply to orders made under the *Divorce Act* (Canada), section 34 of the Act applies.

### Security

**12.** The court may require in the order for the support of a child that the amount payable under the order be paid or secured, or paid and secured, in the manner specified in the order.

### Information to be specified in order

**13.** An order for the support of a child must include,

(a) the name and birth date of each child to whom the order relates;

(b) the income of any parent or spouse whose income is used to determine the amount of the order;

(c) the amount determined under clause 3(1)(a) for the number of children to whom the order relates;

(d) the amount determined under clause 3(2)(b) for a child the age of majority or over;

(e) the particulars of any expense described in subsection 7(1), the child to whom the expense relates and the amount of the expense or, where that amount cannot be determined, the proportion to be paid in relation to the expense;

(f) the date on which the lump sum or first payment is payable and the day of the month or other time period on which all subsequent payments are to be made; and

(g) reference to the obligation under subsection 24.1(1) to provide updated income information no later than 30 days after the anniversary of the date on which the order is made in every year in which the child is a child within the meaning of this Regulation, unless the parties agree that the obligation shall not apply, as provided for in that subsection.

## VARIATION OF ORDERS FOR THE SUPPORT OF A CHILD

### Circumstances for variation

**14.** For the purposes of subsection 37(2.2) of the Act and subsection 17(4) of the *Divorce Act* (Canada), any one of the following constitutes a change of circumstances that gives rise to the making of a variation order:

1. In the case where the amount of child support includes a determination made in accordance with the table, any change in circumstances that would result in a different order for the support of a child or any provision thereof.

2. In the case where the amount of child support does not include a determination made in accordance with a table, any change in the condition, means, needs or other circumstances of either parent or spouse or of any child who is entitled to support.

3. In the case of an order made under the *Divorce Act* (Canada) before May 1, 1997, the coming into force of section 15.1 of that Act, enacted by section 2 of chapter 1 of the Statutes of Canada, (1997).

4. In the case of an order made under the Act, the coming into force of subsection 33(11) of the Act.

## INCOME

### Determination of annual income

**15.** (1) Subject to subsection (2), a parent's or spouse's annual income is determined by the court in accordance with sections 16 to 20.

### Agreement

(2) Where both parents or spouses agree in writing on the annual income of a parent or spouse, the court may consider that amount to be the parent's or spouse's income for the purposes of these guidelines if the court thinks that the amount is reasonable having regard to the income information provided under section 21.

### Calculation of annual income

**16.** Subject to sections 17 to 20, a parent's or spouse's annual income is determined using the sources of income set out under the heading "Total income" in the T1 General form issued by the Canada Revenue Agency and is adjusted in accordance with Schedule III.

### Pattern of income

**17.** (1)  If the court is of the opinion that the determination of a parent's or spouse's annual income under section 16 would not be the fairest determination of that income, the court may have regard to the parent's or spouse's income over the last three years and determine an amount that is fair and reasonable in light of any pattern of income, fluctuation in income or receipt of a non-recurring amount during those years.

### Non-recurring losses

(2)  Where a parent or spouse has incurred a non-recurring capital or business investment loss, the court may, if it is of the opinion that the determination of the parent's or spouse's annual income under section 16 would not provide the fairest determination of the annual income, choose not to apply sections 6 and 7 of Schedule III, and adjust the amount of the loss, including related expenses and carrying charges and interest expenses, to arrive at such amount as the court considers appropriate.

### Shareholder, director or officer

**18.** (1)  Where a parent or spouse is a shareholder, director or officer of a corporation and the court is of the opinion that the amount of the parent's or spouse's annual income as determined under section 16 does not fairly reflect all the money available to the parent or spouse for the payment of child support, the court may consider the situations described in section 17 and determine the parent's or spouse's annual income to include,

    (a)  all or part of the pre-tax income of the corporation, and of any corporation that is related to that corporation, for the most recent taxation year; or

    (b)  an amount commensurate with the services that the parent or spouse provides to the corporation, provided that the amount does not exceed the corporation's pre-tax income.

### Adjustment to corporation's pre-tax income

(2)  In determining the pre-tax income of a corporation for the purposes of subsection (1), all amounts paid by the corporation as salaries, wages or management fees, or other payments or benefits, to or on behalf of persons with whom the corporation does not deal at arm's length must be added to the pre-tax income, unless the parent or spouse establishes that the payments were reasonable in the circumstances.

### Imputing income

**19.** (1)  The court may impute such amount of income to a parent or spouse as it considers appropriate in the circumstances, which circumstances include,

    (a)  the parent or spouse is intentionally under-employed or unemployed, other than where the under-employment or unemployment is required by the needs of any child or by the reasonable educational or health needs of the parent or spouse;

    (b)  the parent or spouse is exempt from paying federal or provincial income tax;

    (c)  the parent or spouse lives in a country that has effective rates of income tax that are significantly lower than those in Canada;

    (d)  it appears that income has been diverted which would affect the level of child support to be determined under these guidelines;

    (e)  the parent's or spouse's property is not reasonably utilized to generate income;

    (f)  the parent or spouse has failed to provide income information when under a legal obligation to do so;

    (g)  the parent or spouse unreasonably deducts expenses from income;

    (h)  the parent or spouse derives a significant portion of income from dividends, capital gains or other sources that are taxed at a lower rate than employment or business income or that are exempt from tax; and

    (i)  the parent or spouse is a beneficiary under a trust and is or will be in receipt of income or other benefits from the trust.

### Reasonableness of expenses

(2)  For the purpose of clause (1)(g), the reasonableness of an expense deduction is not solely governed by whether the deduction is permitted under the *Income Tax Act* (Canada).

### Non-resident

**20.** (1)  Subject to subsection (2), where a parent or spouse is a non-resident of Canada, the parent's or spouse's annual income is determined as though the parent or spouse were a resident of Canada.

### Non-resident taxed at higher rates

(2)  Where a parent or spouse is a non-resident of Canada and resides in a country that has effective rates of income tax that are significantly higher than those applicable in the province or territory in which the other parent or spouse ordinarily resides, the non-resident parent's or spouse's annual income is the amount which the court determines to be appropriate taking the higher rates into consideration.

## INCOME INFORMATION

### Obligation of applicant

**21.** (1)  A parent or spouse who is applying for an order for the support of a child and whose income information is necessary to determine the amount of the order must include with the application,

(a) a copy of every personal income tax return filed by the parent or spouse including any materials that were filed with the return for each of the three most recent taxation years;

(b) a copy of every notice of assessment and reassessment issued to the parent or spouse for each of the three most recent taxation years;

(c) where the parent or spouse is an employee, the most recent statement of earnings indicating the total earnings paid in the year to date, including overtime, or, where such a statement is not provided by the employer, a letter from the parent's or spouse's employer setting out that information including the parent's or spouse's rate of annual salary or remuneration;

(d) where the parent or spouse is self-employed, for the three most recent taxation years,

(i) the financial statements of the parent's or spouse's business or professional practice, other than a partnership, and

(ii) a statement showing a breakdown of all salaries, wages, management fees or other payments or benefits paid to, or on behalf of, persons or corporations with whom the parent or spouse does not deal at arm's length;

(e) where the parent or spouse is a partner in a partnership, confirmation of the parent's or spouse's income and draw from, and capital in, the partnership for its three most recent taxation years;

(f) where the parent or spouse controls a corporation, for its three most recent taxation years,

(i) the financial statements of the corporation and its subsidiaries, and

(ii) a statement showing a breakdown of all salaries, wages, management fees or other payments or benefits paid to, or on behalf of, persons or corporations with whom the corporation, and every related corporation, does not deal at arm's length;

(g) where the parent or spouse is a beneficiary under a trust, a copy of the trust settlement agreement and copies of the trust's three most recent financial statements; and

(h) in addition to any information that must be included under clauses (c) to (g), where the parent or spouse receives income from employment insurance, social assistance, a pension, workers compensation, disability payments or any other source, the most recent statement of income indicating the total amount of income from the applicable source during the current year or, if such a statement is not provided, a letter from the appropriate authority stating the required information.

### Obligation of respondent

(2) A parent or spouse who is served with an application for an order for the support of a child and whose income information is necessary to determine the amount of the order, must, within 30 days after the application is served if the parent or spouse resides in Canada or the United States or within 60 days if the parent or spouse resides elsewhere, or such other time limit as the court specifies, provide the court, as well as the other spouse, an applicant under section 33 of the Act or the order assignee with the documents referred to in subsection (1).

### Special expenses or undue hardship

(3) Where, in the course of proceedings in respect of an application for an order for the support of a child, a parent or spouse requests an amount to cover expenses referred to in subsection 7(1) or pleads undue hardship, the parent or spouse who would be receiving the amount of child support must, within 30 days after the amount is sought or undue hardship is pleaded if the parent or spouse resides in Canada or the United States or within 60 days if the parent or spouse resides elsewhere, or such other time limit as the court specifies, provide the court and the other parent or spouse with the documents referred to in subsection (1).

### Income over $150,000

(4) Where, in the course of proceedings in respect of an application for an order for the support of a child, it is established that the income of the parent or spouse who would be paying the amount of child support is greater than $150,000, the other parent or spouse must, within 30 days after the income is established to be greater than $150,000 if the other parent or spouse resides in Canada or the United States or within 60 days if the other parent or spouse resides elsewhere, or such other time limit as the court specifies, provide the court and the other parent or spouse with the documents referred to in subsection (1).

### Failure to comply

**22.** (1) Where a parent or spouse fails to comply with section 21, the other spouse, an applicant under section 33 of the Act or an order assignee may apply,

(a) to have the application for an order for the support of a child set down for a hearing, or move for judgment; or

(b) for an order requiring the parent or spouse who failed to comply to provide the court, as well as the other parent or spouse or order assignee, as the case may be, with the required documents.

### Costs of the proceedings

(2) Where a court makes an order under clause (1)(a) or (b), the court may award costs in favour of the other spouse, the applicant under section 33 of the Act or an order assignee up to an amount that fully compensates the other spouse, the applicant or order assignee for all costs incurred in the proceedings.

### Adverse inference

**23.** Where the court proceeds to a hearing on the basis of an application under clause 22(1)(a), the court may draw an adverse inference against the parent or spouse who failed to comply and impute income to that parent or spouse in such amount as it considers appropriate.

### Failure to comply with court order

**24.** Where a parent or spouse fails to comply with an order issued on the basis of an application under clause 22(1)(b), the court may,

(a) strike out any of the parent's or spouse's pleadings;

(b) make a contempt order against the parent or spouse;

(c) proceed to a hearing, in the course of which it may draw an adverse inference against the parent or spouse and impute income to that parent or spouse in such amount as it considers appropriate; and

(d) award costs in favour of the other spouse, an applicant under section 33 of the Act or an order assignee up to an amount that fully compensates the other spouse, the applicant or assignee for all costs incurred in the proceedings.

### Annual obligation to provide income information

**24.1** (1) Every person whose income or other financial information is used to determine the amount of an order for the support of a child shall, no later than 30 days after the anniversary of the date on which the order was made in every year in which the child is a child within the meaning of this Regulation, provide every party to the order with the following, unless the parties have agreed otherwise:

1. For the most recent taxation year, a copy of the person's,

    i. personal income tax return, including any materials that were filed with the return, and

    ii. notice of assessment and, if any, notice of reassessment.

2. As applicable, any current information in writing about,

    i. the status and amount of any expenses included in the order pursuant to subsection 7(1), and

    ii. any loan, scholarship or bursaries the child has received or will receive in the coming year that affect or will affect the expenses referred to in subparagraph i.

### Notices of assessment

(2) If the person has not received his or her notice of assessment or notice of reassessment for the most recent taxation year by the date referred to in subsection (1), the person shall provide every party to the order with a copy of the notice as soon as possible after the person receives the notice.

### Change in address

(3) If the address at which a party receives documents changes, the party shall, at least 30 days before the next anniversary of the date on which the order was made, give written notice of his or her updated address information to every person required to provide documents and information under subsection (1).

### Failure to comply

(4) If a person required to provide a document or information under this section fails to do so, a court may, on application by the party who did not receive the document or information, make one or more of the following orders:

1. An order finding the person to be in contempt of court.

2. An order awarding costs in favour of the applicant up to an amount that fully compensates the applicant for all costs incurred in the proceedings.

3. An order requiring the person to provide the document or information to,

    i. the court,

    ii. the applicant, and

    iii. any other party to whom the person did not provide the document or information when required to do so.

### Exception

(5) Subsection (4) does not apply if the person who fails to provide the document or information is a child who is not a party to the order for support.

### Transition

(6) In the case of an order to which subsection (1) applies that is in existence on the day section 5 of Ontario Regulation 25/10 comes into force, if the first date by which a person must provide documents and information under that subsection occurs less than six months after the day on which the person provided documents and information under section 25, the person is not required to provide documents and information under subsection (1) in the first year in which he or she would otherwise have been required to provide them.

### Continuing obligation to provide income information

**25.** (1) Every parent or spouse against whom an order for the support of a child has been made must, on the written request of the other spouse or the person or agency entitled to payment under the order not more than once a year after the making of the order and as long as the child is a child within the meaning of this Regulation, provide that other spouse, or the person or agency entitled to payment under the order, with,

(a) the documents referred to in subsection 21(1) for any of the three most recent taxation years for which the parent or spouse has not previously provided the documents;

(b) as applicable, any current information in writing about,

>   (i) the status and amount of any expenses included in the order pursuant to subsection 7(1), and
>   (ii) any loan, scholarship or bursaries the child has received that affect the expenses referred to in subclause (i); and

(c) as applicable, any current information, in writing, about the circumstances relied on by the court in a determination of undue hardship.

### Below minimum income

(2) Where a court has determined that the parent or spouse against whom an order for the support of a child is sought does not have to pay child support because his or her income level is below the minimum amount required for application of the tables, that parent or spouse must, on the written request of the other spouse or the applicant under section 33 of the Act, not more than once a year after the determination and as long as the child is a child within the meaning of this Regulation, provide the other spouse or the applicant with the documents referred to in subsection 21(1) for any of the three most recent taxation years for which the parent or spouse has not previously provided the documents.

### Obligation of receiving parent or spouse

(3) Where the income information of the parent or spouse in favour of whom an order for the support of a child is made is used to determine the amount of the order, the parent or spouse must, not more than once a year after the making of the order and as long as the child is a child within the meaning of this Regulation, on the written request of the other parent or spouse, provide the other parent or spouse with the documents and information referred to in subsection (1).

### Information requests

(4) Where a parent or spouse requests information from the other parent or spouse under any of subsections (1) to (3) and the income information of the requesting parent or spouse is used to determine the amount of the order for the support of a child, the requesting parent or spouse must include the documents and information referred to in subsection (1) with the request.

### Time limit

(5) A parent or spouse who receives a request made under any of subsections (1) to (3) must provide the required documents within 30 days after the request's receipt if the parent or spouse resides in Canada or the United States and within 60 days after the request's receipt if the parent or spouse resides elsewhere.

### Deemed receipt

(6) A request made under any of subsections (1) to (3) is deemed to have been received 10 days after it is sent.

### Failure to comply

(7) A court may, on application by either spouse, an applicant under section 33 of the Act or an order assignee, where the parent or spouse has failed to comply with any of subsections (1) to (3),

(a) consider the parent or spouse to be in contempt of court and award costs in favour of the applicant up to an amount that fully compensates the applicant for all costs incurred in the proceedings; or

(b) make an order requiring the parent or spouse to provide the required documents to the court, as well as to the spouse, order assignee or applicant under section 33 of the Act, as the case may be.

### Unenforceable provision

(8) A provision in a judgment, order or agreement purporting to limit a parent's or spouse's obligation to provide documents under this section is unenforceable.

## PROVIDING INCOME INFORMATION FOR DOMESTIC CONTRACTS AND OTHER AGREEMENTS
### Annual obligation to provide income information

**25.1** (1) Every person whose income or other financial information is used to determine the amount of a child support obligation under a domestic contract or other written agreement shall, no later than 30 days after the anniversary of the date on which the contract or agreement was entered into in every year in which the child is a child within the meaning of this Regulation, provide every party to the contract or agreement with the following, unless the parties have agreed otherwise in a domestic contract or other agreement:

1.  For the most recent taxation year, a copy of the person's,
    i.   personal income tax return, including any materials that were filed with the return, and
    ii.  notice of assessment and, if any, notice of reassessment.
2.  If the contract or agreement provides for the payment of any of the expenses referred to in clauses 7(1)(a) to (f), any current information in writing about,
    i.   the status and amount of the expenses, and
    ii.  any loan, scholarship or bursaries the child has received or will receive in the coming year that affect or will affect the expenses referred to in subparagraph i.

### Notices of assessment

(2) If the person has not received his or her notice of assessment or notice of reassessment for the most recent taxation year by the date referred to in subsection (1), the person shall provide every party to the contract or agreement with a copy of the notice as soon as possible after the person receives the notice.

## Change in address

(3) If the address at which a party to the domestic contract or agreement receives documents changes, the party shall, at least 30 days before the next anniversary of the date on which the contract or agreement was entered into, give written notice of his or her updated address information to every person required to provide documents and information under subsection (1).

## Failure to comply

(4) If a person required to provide a document or information under this section fails to do so, a court may, on application by the person who did not receive the document or information, make one or more of the following orders:

1. An order awarding costs in favour of the applicant up to an amount that fully compensates the applicant for all costs incurred in the proceedings.

2. An order requiring the person to provide the document or information to,

    i. the court,

    ii. the applicant, and

    iii. any other party to the domestic contract or other written agreement to whom the person did not provide the document or information when required to do so.

## Exception

(5) Subsection (4) does not apply if the person who fails to provide the document or information is a child who is not a party to the domestic contract or other written agreement.

## Transition

(6) This section applies in respect of a domestic contract or other written agreement only if the contract or agreement was entered into on or after the day section 7 of Ontario Regulation 25/10 comes into force.

**26.** Omitted (provides for coming into force of provisions of this Regulation).

> **Note: The child support guidelines come into force with respect to cases to which the *Family Law Act* applies on the day the *Uniform Federal and Provincial Child Support Guidelines Act, 1997* is proclaimed in force. Proclamation date is December 1, 1997. See: O. Reg. 391/97, s. 26(1).**
>
> **Note: The child support guidelines come into force with respect to cases to which the *Divorce Act* (Canada) applies on the day the guidelines are specified by order of the Governor in Council as "applicable guidelines" within the meaning of that Act under subsection 2(5) of that Act. See: O. Reg. 391/97, s. 26(2).**

## SCHEDULE I

### Child Support Table For Ontario (Subsection 2(1))

**Notes:**

1. The child support table for Ontario sets out the amount of monthly child support payments for Ontario on the basis of the annual income of the parent or spouse ordered to pay child support (the "support payor") and the number of children for whom a table amount is payable. Refer to these guidelines to determine whether special measures apply.

2. There is a threshold level of income below which no amount of child support is payable. Child support amounts are specified for incomes up to $150,000 per year. Refer to section 4 of this Regulation to determine the amount of child support payments for support payors with annual incomes over $150,000.

3. Income is set out in the tables in intervals of $1,000. Monthly amounts are determined by adding the basic amount and the amount calculated by multiplying the applicable percentage by the portion of the income that exceeds the lower amount within that interval of income.

4. The amounts in the tables are based on economic studies of average spending on children in families at different income levels in Canada. They are calculated on the basis that child support payments are no longer taxable in the hands of the receiving parent and no longer deductible by the paying parent. They are calculated using a mathematical formula and generated by a computer program.

5. The formula referred to in note 4 sets support amounts to reflect average expenditures on children by a parent or spouse with a particular number of children and level of income. The calculation is based on the support payor's income. The formula uses the basic personal amount for non-refundable tax credits to recognize personal expenses, and takes other federal and provincial income taxes and credits into account. Federal Child Tax benefits and Goods and Services Tax credits for children are excluded from the calculation. At lower income levels, the formula sets the amounts to take into account the combined impact of taxes and child support payments on the support payor's limited disposable income.

# Child Support Table for Ontario, Number of Children: One

| Income ($) From | To | Basic Amount | Monthly Award ($) Plus (%) | Of Income Over |
|---|---|---|---|---|
| 12000 | 12999 | 0 | 4.1 | 12000 |
| 13000 | 13999 | 41 | 1.94 | 13000 |
| 14000 | 14999 | 60 | 1.92 | 14000 |
| 15000 | 15999 | 79 | 1.88 | 15000 |
| 16000 | 16999 | 98 | 1.96 | 16000 |
| 17000 | 17999 | 118 | 1.92 | 17000 |
| 18000 | 18999 | 137 | 1.7 | 18000 |
| 19000 | 19999 | 154 | 0.72 | 19000 |
| 20000 | 20999 | 161 | 0.74 | 20000 |
| 21000 | 21999 | 168 | 0.8 | 21000 |
| 22000 | 22999 | 176 | 0.78 | 22000 |
| 23000 | 23999 | 184 | 0.8 | 23000 |
| 24000 | 24999 | 192 | 0.72 | 24000 |
| 25000 | 25999 | 199 | 0.96 | 25000 |
| 26000 | 26999 | 209 | 1.36 | 26000 |
| 27000 | 27999 | 223 | 1.32 | 27000 |
| 28000 | 28999 | 236 | 1.08 | 28000 |
| 29000 | 29999 | 247 | 0.86 | 29000 |
| 30000 | 30999 | 256 | 0.82 | 30000 |
| 31000 | 31999 | 264 | 0.86 | 31000 |
| 32000 | 32999 | 273 | 0.88 | 32000 |
| 33000 | 33999 | 282 | 1 | 33000 |
| 34000 | 34999 | 292 | 1.22 | 34000 |
| 35000 | 35999 | 304 | 1.14 | 35000 |
| 36000 | 36999 | 315 | 1.06 | 36000 |

| Income ($) From | To | Basic Amount | Monthly Award ($) Plus (%) | Of Income Over |
|---|---|---|---|---|
| 61000 | 61999 | 566 | 1.02 | 61000 |
| 62000 | 62999 | 576 | 0.94 | 62000 |
| 63000 | 63999 | 585 | 0.98 | 63000 |
| 64000 | 64999 | 595 | 1 | 64000 |
| 65000 | 65999 | 605 | 1.02 | 65000 |
| 66000 | 66999 | 615 | 0.94 | 66000 |
| 67000 | 67999 | 624 | 0.96 | 67000 |
| 68000 | 68999 | 634 | 0.98 | 68000 |
| 69000 | 69999 | 644 | 1 | 69000 |
| 70000 | 70999 | 654 | 0.94 | 70000 |
| 71000 | 71999 | 663 | 0.96 | 71000 |
| 72000 | 72999 | 673 | 0.78 | 72000 |
| 73000 | 73999 | 681 | 1 | 73000 |
| 74000 | 74999 | 691 | 0.94 | 74000 |
| 75000 | 75999 | 700 | 0.86 | 75000 |
| 76000 | 76999 | 709 | 0.86 | 76000 |
| 77000 | 77999 | 718 | 0.88 | 77000 |
| 78000 | 78999 | 727 | 0.88 | 78000 |
| 79000 | 79999 | 736 | 0.9 | 79000 |
| 80000 | 80999 | 745 | 1 | 80000 |
| 81000 | 81999 | 755 | 0.94 | 81000 |
| 82000 | 82999 | 764 | 0.98 | 82000 |
| 83000 | 83999 | 774 | 0.94 | 83000 |
| 84000 | 84999 | 783 | 0.92 | 84000 |
| 85000 | 85999 | 792 | 0.9 | 85000 |

| Income ($) From | To | Basic Amount | Monthly Award ($) Plus (%) | Of Income Over |
|---|---|---|---|---|
| 110000 | 110999 | 989 | 0.8 | 110000 |
| 111000 | 111999 | 997 | 0.82 | 111000 |
| 112000 | 112999 | 1005 | 0.84 | 112000 |
| 113000 | 113999 | 1013 | 0.74 | 113000 |
| 114000 | 114999 | 1020 | 0.76 | 114000 |
| 115000 | 115999 | 1028 | 0.78 | 115000 |
| 116000 | 116999 | 1036 | 0.78 | 116000 |
| 117000 | 117999 | 1044 | 0.8 | 117000 |
| 118000 | 118999 | 1052 | 0.82 | 118000 |
| 119000 | 119999 | 1060 | 0.84 | 119000 |
| 120000 | 120999 | 1068 | 0.74 | 120000 |
| 121000 | 121999 | 1075 | 0.76 | 121000 |
| 122000 | 122999 | 1083 | 0.78 | 122000 |
| 123000 | 123999 | 1091 | 0.78 | 123000 |
| 124000 | 124999 | 1099 | 0.8 | 124000 |
| 125000 | 125999 | 1107 | 0.82 | 125000 |
| 126000 | 126999 | 1115 | 0.82 | 126000 |
| 127000 | 127999 | 1123 | 0.74 | 127000 |
| 128000 | 128999 | 1130 | 0.76 | 128000 |
| 129000 | 129999 | 1138 | 0.78 | 129000 |
| 130000 | 130999 | 1146 | 0.78 | 130000 |
| 131000 | 131999 | 1154 | 0.8 | 131000 |
| 132000 | 132999 | 1162 | 0.82 | 132000 |
| 133000 | 133999 | 1170 | 0.82 | 133000 |
| 134000 | 134999 | 1178 | 0.74 | 134000 |

# Child Support Table for Ontario, Number of Children: One   Concluded

| Income ($) From | Income ($) To | Monthly Award ($) Basic Amount | Monthly Award ($) Plus (%) | Of Income Over |
|---|---|---|---|---|
| 37000 | 37999 | 326 | 1 | 37000 |
| 38000 | 38999 | 336 | 1.06 | 38000 |
| 39000 | 39999 | 347 | 1.18 | 39000 |
| 40000 | 40999 | 359 | 1.14 | 40000 |
| 41000 | 41999 | 370 | 1.12 | 41000 |
| 42000 | 42999 | 381 | 1.26 | 42000 |
| 43000 | 43999 | 394 | 1.24 | 43000 |
| 44000 | 44999 | 406 | 1.22 | 44000 |
| 45000 | 45999 | 418 | 0.9 | 45000 |
| 46000 | 46999 | 427 | 0.88 | 46000 |
| 47000 | 47999 | 436 | 0.88 | 47000 |
| 48000 | 48999 | 445 | 0.68 | 48000 |
| 49000 | 49999 | 452 | 0.88 | 49000 |
| 50000 | 50999 | 461 | 0.88 | 50000 |
| 51000 | 51999 | 470 | 0.88 | 51000 |
| 52000 | 52999 | 479 | 0.96 | 52000 |
| 53000 | 53999 | 489 | 0.94 | 53000 |
| 54000 | 54999 | 498 | 0.92 | 54000 |
| 55000 | 55999 | 507 | 0.98 | 55000 |
| 56000 | 56999 | 517 | 1.02 | 56000 |
| 57000 | 57999 | 527 | 0.94 | 57000 |
| 58000 | 58999 | 536 | 0.96 | 58000 |
| 59000 | 59999 | 546 | 0.98 | 59000 |
| 60000 | 60999 | 556 | 1 | 60000 |

| Income ($) From | Income ($) To | Monthly Award ($) Basic Amount | Monthly Award ($) Plus (%) | Of Income Over |
|---|---|---|---|---|
| 86000 | 86999 | 801 | 0.88 | 86000 |
| 87000 | 87999 | 810 | 0.86 | 87000 |
| 88000 | 88999 | 819 | 0.68 | 88000 |
| 89000 | 89999 | 826 | 0.76 | 89000 |
| 90000 | 90999 | 834 | 0.64 | 90000 |
| 91000 | 91999 | 840 | 0.66 | 91000 |
| 92000 | 92999 | 847 | 0.76 | 92000 |
| 93000 | 93999 | 855 | 0.76 | 93000 |
| 94000 | 94999 | 863 | 0.78 | 94000 |
| 95000 | 95999 | 871 | 0.8 | 95000 |
| 96000 | 96999 | 879 | 0.8 | 96000 |
| 97000 | 97999 | 887 | 0.82 | 97000 |
| 98000 | 98999 | 895 | 0.74 | 98000 |
| 99000 | 99999 | 902 | 0.76 | 99000 |
| 100000 | 100999 | 910 | 0.76 | 100000 |
| 101000 | 101999 | 918 | 0.78 | 101000 |
| 102000 | 102999 | 926 | 0.8 | 102000 |
| 103000 | 103999 | 934 | 0.8 | 103000 |
| 104000 | 104999 | 942 | 0.82 | 104000 |
| 105000 | 105999 | 950 | 0.84 | 105000 |
| 106000 | 106999 | 958 | 0.74 | 106000 |
| 107000 | 107999 | 965 | 0.76 | 107000 |
| 108000 | 108999 | 973 | 0.78 | 108000 |
| 109000 | 109999 | 981 | 0.8 | 109000 |

| Income ($) From | Income ($) To | Monthly Award ($) Basic Amount | Monthly Award ($) Plus (%) | Of Income Over |
|---|---|---|---|---|
| 135000 | 135999 | 1185 | 0.76 | 135000 |
| 136000 | 136999 | 1193 | 0.76 | 136000 |
| 137000 | 137999 | 1201 | 0.78 | 137000 |
| 138000 | 138999 | 1209 | 0.8 | 138000 |
| 139000 | 139999 | 1217 | 0.82 | 139000 |
| 140000 | 140999 | 1225 | 0.72 | 140000 |
| 141000 | 141999 | 1232 | 0.76 | 141000 |
| 142000 | 142999 | 1240 | 0.72 | 142000 |
| 143000 | 143999 | 1247 | 0.78 | 143000 |
| 144000 | 144999 | 1255 | 0.74 | 144000 |
| 145000 | 145999 | 1262 | 0.78 | 145000 |
| 146000 | 146999 | 1270 | 0.74 | 146000 |
| 147000 | 147999 | 1277 | 0.7 | 147000 |
| 148000 | 148999 | 1284 | 0.76 | 148000 |
| 149000 | 149999 | 1292 | 0.72 | 149000 |
| 150000 | or greater | 1299 | 0.72 | 150000 |

# Child Support Table for Ontario, Number of Children: Two

| Income ($) From | To | Basic Amount | Plus (%) | Of Income Over |
|---|---|---|---|---|
| 12000 | 12999 | 0 | 9.5 | 12000 |
| 13000 | 13999 | 95 | 3.86 | 13000 |
| 14000 | 14999 | 134 | 3.6 | 14000 |
| 15000 | 15999 | 170 | 3.3 | 15000 |
| 16000 | 16999 | 203 | 3 | 16000 |
| 17000 | 17999 | 233 | 3.02 | 17000 |
| 18000 | 18999 | 263 | 3.34 | 18000 |
| 19000 | 19999 | 296 | 1.5 | 19000 |
| 20000 | 20999 | 311 | 1.3 | 20000 |
| 21000 | 21999 | 324 | 1.32 | 21000 |
| 22000 | 22999 | 337 | 1.26 | 22000 |
| 23000 | 23999 | 350 | 1.26 | 23000 |
| 24000 | 24999 | 363 | 1.28 | 24000 |
| 25000 | 25999 | 376 | 1.5 | 25000 |
| 26000 | 26999 | 391 | 1.86 | 26000 |
| 27000 | 27999 | 410 | 1.82 | 27000 |
| 28000 | 28999 | 428 | 1.68 | 28000 |
| 29000 | 29999 | 445 | 1.44 | 29000 |
| 30000 | 30999 | 459 | 1.52 | 30000 |
| 31000 | 31999 | 474 | 1.44 | 31000 |
| 32000 | 32999 | 488 | 1.48 | 32000 |
| 33000 | 33999 | 503 | 1.42 | 33000 |
| 34000 | 34999 | 517 | 1.46 | 34000 |
| 35000 | 35999 | 532 | 1.4 | 35000 |

| Income ($) From | To | Basic Amount | Plus (%) | Of Income Over |
|---|---|---|---|---|
| 61000 | 61999 | 930 | 1.52 | 61000 |
| 62000 | 62999 | 945 | 1.5 | 62000 |
| 63000 | 63999 | 960 | 1.48 | 63000 |
| 64000 | 64999 | 975 | 1.56 | 64000 |
| 65000 | 65999 | 991 | 1.54 | 65000 |
| 66000 | 66999 | 1006 | 1.52 | 66000 |
| 67000 | 67999 | 1021 | 1.5 | 67000 |
| 68000 | 68999 | 1036 | 1.48 | 68000 |
| 69000 | 69999 | 1051 | 1.56 | 69000 |
| 70000 | 70999 | 1067 | 1.54 | 70000 |
| 71000 | 71999 | 1082 | 1.52 | 71000 |
| 72000 | 72999 | 1097 | 1.2 | 72000 |
| 73000 | 73999 | 1109 | 1.5 | 73000 |
| 74000 | 74999 | 1124 | 1.48 | 74000 |
| 75000 | 75999 | 1139 | 1.46 | 75000 |
| 76000 | 76999 | 1154 | 1.44 | 76000 |
| 77000 | 77999 | 1168 | 1.4 | 77000 |
| 78000 | 78999 | 1182 | 1.38 | 78000 |
| 79000 | 79999 | 1196 | 1.46 | 79000 |
| 80000 | 80999 | 1211 | 1.52 | 80000 |
| 81000 | 81999 | 1226 | 1.44 | 81000 |
| 82000 | 82999 | 1240 | 1.46 | 82000 |
| 83000 | 83999 | 1255 | 1.48 | 83000 |
| 84000 | 84999 | 1270 | 1.44 | 84000 |

| Income ($) From | To | Basic Amount | Plus (%) | Of Income Over |
|---|---|---|---|---|
| 110000 | 110999 | 1594 | 1.22 | 110000 |
| 111000 | 111999 | 1606 | 1.2 | 111000 |
| 112000 | 112999 | 1618 | 1.18 | 112000 |
| 113000 | 113999 | 1630 | 1.26 | 113000 |
| 114000 | 114999 | 1643 | 1.24 | 114000 |
| 115000 | 115999 | 1655 | 1.22 | 115000 |
| 116000 | 116999 | 1667 | 1.2 | 116000 |
| 117000 | 117999 | 1679 | 1.28 | 117000 |
| 118000 | 118999 | 1692 | 1.24 | 118000 |
| 119000 | 119999 | 1704 | 1.22 | 119000 |
| 120000 | 120999 | 1716 | 1.2 | 120000 |
| 121000 | 121999 | 1728 | 1.18 | 121000 |
| 122000 | 122999 | 1740 | 1.26 | 122000 |
| 123000 | 123999 | 1753 | 1.24 | 123000 |
| 124000 | 124999 | 1765 | 1.22 | 124000 |
| 125000 | 125999 | 1777 | 1.2 | 125000 |
| 126000 | 126999 | 1789 | 1.26 | 126000 |
| 127000 | 127999 | 1802 | 1.24 | 127000 |
| 128000 | 128999 | 1814 | 1.22 | 128000 |
| 129000 | 129999 | 1826 | 1.2 | 129000 |
| 130000 | 130999 | 1838 | 1.18 | 130000 |
| 131000 | 131999 | 1850 | 1.26 | 131000 |
| 132000 | 132999 | 1863 | 1.24 | 132000 |
| 133000 | 133999 | 1875 | 1.2 | 133000 |

# Child Support Table for Ontario, Number of Children: Two   Concluded

| Income ($) From | Income ($) To | Monthly Award ($) Basic Amount | Monthly Award ($) Plus (%) | Monthly Award ($) Of Income Over | Income ($) From | Income ($) To | Monthly Award ($) Basic Amount | Monthly Award ($) Plus (%) | Monthly Award ($) Of Income Over | Income ($) From | Income ($) To | Monthly Award ($) Basic Amount | Monthly Award ($) Plus (%) | Monthly Award ($) Of Income Over |
|---|---|---|---|---|---|---|---|---|---|---|---|---|---|---|
| 36000 | 36999 | 546 | 1.26 | 36000 | 85000 | 85999 | 1284 | 1.42 | 85000 | 134000 | 134999 | 1887 | 1.18 | 134000 |
| 37000 | 37999 | 559 | 1.24 | 37000 | 86000 | 86999 | 1298 | 1.4 | 86000 | 135000 | 135999 | 1899 | 1.26 | 135000 |
| 38000 | 38999 | 571 | 1.3 | 38000 | 87000 | 87999 | 1312 | 1.36 | 87000 | 136000 | 136999 | 1912 | 1.24 | 136000 |
| 39000 | 39999 | 584 | 1.32 | 39000 | 88000 | 88999 | 1326 | 1.18 | 88000 | 137000 | 137999 | 1924 | 1.22 | 137000 |
| 40000 | 40999 | 597 | 1.36 | 40000 | 89000 | 89999 | 1338 | 1.26 | 89000 | 138000 | 138999 | 1936 | 1.2 | 138000 |
| 41000 | 41999 | 611 | 1.3 | 41000 | 90000 | 90999 | 1351 | 1.14 | 90000 | 139000 | 139999 | 1948 | 1.18 | 139000 |
| 42000 | 42999 | 624 | 1.54 | 42000 | 91000 | 91999 | 1362 | 1.18 | 91000 | 140000 | 140999 | 1960 | 1.16 | 140000 |
| 43000 | 43999 | 639 | 1.66 | 43000 | 92000 | 92999 | 1374 | 1.24 | 92000 | 141000 | 141999 | 1972 | 1.16 | 141000 |
| 44000 | 44999 | 656 | 1.76 | 44000 | 93000 | 93999 | 1386 | 1.22 | 93000 | 142000 | 142999 | 1984 | 1.1 | 142000 |
| 45000 | 45999 | 674 | 1.7 | 45000 | 94000 | 94999 | 1398 | 1.2 | 94000 | 143000 | 143999 | 1995 | 1.16 | 143000 |
| 46000 | 46999 | 691 | 1.68 | 46000 | 95000 | 95999 | 1410 | 1.26 | 95000 | 144000 | 144999 | 2007 | 1.2 | 144000 |
| 47000 | 47999 | 708 | 1.72 | 47000 | 96000 | 96999 | 1423 | 1.24 | 96000 | 145000 | 145999 | 2019 | 1.14 | 145000 |
| 48000 | 48999 | 725 | 1.34 | 48000 | 97000 | 97999 | 1435 | 1.22 | 97000 | 146000 | 146999 | 2030 | 1.18 | 146000 |
| 49000 | 49999 | 738 | 1.68 | 49000 | 98000 | 98999 | 1447 | 1.2 | 98000 | 147000 | 147999 | 2042 | 1.12 | 147000 |
| 50000 | 50999 | 755 | 1.72 | 50000 | 99000 | 99999 | 1459 | 1.18 | 99000 | 148000 | 148999 | 2053 | 1.16 | 148000 |
| 51000 | 51999 | 772 | 1.74 | 51000 | 100000 | 100999 | 1471 | 1.26 | 100000 | 149000 | 149999 | 2065 | 1.2 | 149000 |
| 52000 | 52999 | 789 | 1.72 | 52000 | 101000 | 101999 | 1484 | 1.24 | 101000 | 150000 | or greater | 2077 | 1.2 | 150000 |
| 53000 | 53999 | 806 | 1.72 | 53000 | 102000 | 102999 | 1496 | 1.22 | 102000 | | | | | |
| 54000 | 54999 | 823 | 1.6 | 54000 | 103000 | 103999 | 1508 | 1.18 | 103000 | | | | | |
| 55000 | 55999 | 839 | 1.54 | 55000 | 104000 | 104999 | 1520 | 1.26 | 104000 | | | | | |
| 56000 | 56999 | 854 | 1.52 | 56000 | 105000 | 105999 | 1533 | 1.24 | 105000 | | | | | |
| 57000 | 57999 | 869 | 1.5 | 57000 | 106000 | 106999 | 1545 | 1.22 | 106000 | | | | | |
| 58000 | 58999 | 884 | 1.48 | 58000 | 107000 | 107999 | 1557 | 1.2 | 107000 | | | | | |
| 59000 | 59999 | 899 | 1.56 | 59000 | 108000 | 108999 | 1569 | 1.18 | 108000 | | | | | |
| 60000 | 60999 | 915 | 1.54 | 60000 | 109000 | 109999 | 1581 | 1.26 | 109000 | | | | | |

## Child Support Table for Ontario, Number of Children: Three

| Income ($) From | To | Monthly Award ($) Basic Amount | Plus (%) | Of Income Over |
|---|---|---|---|---|
| 12000 | 12999 | 0 | 10.3 | 12000 |
| 13000 | 13999 | 103 | 4.12 | 13000 |
| 14000 | 14999 | 144 | 3.86 | 14000 |
| 15000 | 15999 | 183 | 3.6 | 15000 |
| 16000 | 16999 | 219 | 3.24 | 16000 |
| 17000 | 17999 | 251 | 3.22 | 17000 |
| 18000 | 18999 | 283 | 3.62 | 18000 |
| 19000 | 19999 | 319 | 4.12 | 19000 |
| 20000 | 20999 | 360 | 3.84 | 20000 |
| 21000 | 21999 | 398 | 3.96 | 21000 |
| 22000 | 22999 | 438 | 3.86 | 22000 |
| 23000 | 23999 | 477 | 2.34 | 23000 |
| 24000 | 24999 | 500 | 1.68 | 24000 |
| 25000 | 25999 | 517 | 1.98 | 25000 |
| 26000 | 26999 | 537 | 2.2 | 26000 |
| 27000 | 27999 | 559 | 2.26 | 27000 |
| 28000 | 28999 | 582 | 2.02 | 28000 |
| 29000 | 29999 | 602 | 1.86 | 29000 |
| 30000 | 30999 | 621 | 1.96 | 30000 |
| 31000 | 31999 | 641 | 1.92 | 31000 |
| 32000 | 32999 | 660 | 1.98 | 32000 |
| 33000 | 33999 | 680 | 1.94 | 33000 |
| 34000 | 34999 | 699 | 1.9 | 34000 |
| 35000 | 35999 | 718 | 1.88 | 35000 |
| 36000 | 36999 | 737 | 1.68 | 36000 |
| 37000 | 37999 | 754 | 1.64 | 37000 |

| Income ($) From | To | Monthly Award ($) Basic Amount | Plus (%) | Of Income Over |
|---|---|---|---|---|
| 61000 | 61999 | 1214 | 2.2 | 61000 |
| 62000 | 62999 | 1236 | 2.2 | 62000 |
| 63000 | 63999 | 1258 | 2.18 | 63000 |
| 64000 | 64999 | 1280 | 1.92 | 64000 |
| 65000 | 65999 | 1299 | 1.98 | 65000 |
| 66000 | 66999 | 1319 | 1.92 | 66000 |
| 67000 | 67999 | 1338 | 1.96 | 67000 |
| 68000 | 68999 | 1358 | 1.92 | 68000 |
| 69000 | 69999 | 1377 | 1.96 | 69000 |
| 70000 | 70999 | 1397 | 2 | 70000 |
| 71000 | 71999 | 1417 | 1.94 | 71000 |
| 72000 | 72999 | 1436 | 1.5 | 72000 |
| 73000 | 73999 | 1451 | 1.96 | 73000 |
| 74000 | 74999 | 1471 | 2 | 74000 |
| 75000 | 75999 | 1491 | 1.84 | 75000 |
| 76000 | 76999 | 1509 | 1.88 | 76000 |
| 77000 | 77999 | 1528 | 1.84 | 77000 |
| 78000 | 78999 | 1546 | 1.88 | 78000 |
| 79000 | 79999 | 1565 | 1.84 | 79000 |
| 80000 | 80999 | 1583 | 1.86 | 80000 |
| 81000 | 81999 | 1602 | 1.86 | 81000 |
| 82000 | 82999 | 1621 | 1.86 | 82000 |
| 83000 | 83999 | 1640 | 1.86 | 83000 |
| 84000 | 84999 | 1659 | 1.82 | 84000 |
| 85000 | 85999 | 1677 | 1.88 | 85000 |
| 86000 | 86999 | 1696 | 1.84 | 86000 |

| Income ($) From | To | Monthly Award ($) Basic Amount | Plus (%) | Of Income Over |
|---|---|---|---|---|
| 110000 | 110999 | 2078 | 1.54 | 110000 |
| 111000 | 111999 | 2093 | 1.58 | 111000 |
| 112000 | 112999 | 2109 | 1.6 | 112000 |
| 113000 | 113999 | 2125 | 1.54 | 113000 |
| 114000 | 114999 | 2140 | 1.56 | 114000 |
| 115000 | 115999 | 2156 | 1.58 | 115000 |
| 116000 | 116999 | 2172 | 1.62 | 116000 |
| 117000 | 117999 | 2188 | 1.54 | 117000 |
| 118000 | 118999 | 2203 | 1.58 | 118000 |
| 119000 | 119999 | 2219 | 1.6 | 119000 |
| 120000 | 120999 | 2235 | 1.52 | 120000 |
| 121000 | 121999 | 2250 | 1.56 | 121000 |
| 122000 | 122999 | 2266 | 1.58 | 122000 |
| 123000 | 123999 | 2282 | 1.62 | 123000 |
| 124000 | 124999 | 2298 | 1.54 | 124000 |
| 125000 | 125999 | 2313 | 1.58 | 125000 |
| 126000 | 126999 | 2329 | 1.6 | 126000 |
| 127000 | 127999 | 2345 | 1.52 | 127000 |
| 128000 | 128999 | 2360 | 1.56 | 128000 |
| 129000 | 129999 | 2376 | 1.58 | 129000 |
| 130000 | 130999 | 2392 | 1.62 | 130000 |
| 131000 | 131999 | 2408 | 1.54 | 131000 |
| 132000 | 132999 | 2423 | 1.56 | 132000 |
| 133000 | 133999 | 2439 | 1.6 | 133000 |
| 134000 | 134999 | 2455 | 1.52 | 134000 |
| 135000 | 135999 | 2470 | 1.56 | 135000 |

# Child Support Table for Ontario, Number of Children: Three    Concluded

| Income ($) From | To | Basic Amount | Plus (%) | Of Income Over |
|---|---|---|---|---|
| 38000 | 38999 | 770 | 1.7 | 38000 |
| 39000 | 39999 | 787 | 1.8 | 39000 |
| 40000 | 40999 | 805 | 1.8 | 40000 |
| 41000 | 41999 | 823 | 1.7 | 41000 |
| 42000 | 42999 | 840 | 1.6 | 42000 |
| 43000 | 43999 | 856 | 1.64 | 43000 |
| 44000 | 44999 | 872 | 1.64 | 44000 |
| 45000 | 45999 | 888 | 1.56 | 45000 |
| 46000 | 46999 | 904 | 1.56 | 46000 |
| 47000 | 47999 | 920 | 2 | 47000 |
| 48000 | 48999 | 940 | 1.66 | 48000 |
| 49000 | 49999 | 957 | 2.04 | 49000 |
| 50000 | 50999 | 977 | 2.08 | 50000 |
| 51000 | 51999 | 998 | 2.14 | 51000 |
| 52000 | 52999 | 1019 | 2.14 | 52000 |
| 53000 | 53999 | 1040 | 2.04 | 53000 |
| 54000 | 54999 | 1060 | 2.06 | 54000 |
| 55000 | 55999 | 1081 | 2.26 | 55000 |
| 56000 | 56999 | 1104 | 2.24 | 56000 |
| 57000 | 57999 | 1126 | 2.24 | 57000 |
| 58000 | 58999 | 1148 | 2.22 | 58000 |
| 59000 | 59999 | 1170 | 2.22 | 59000 |
| 60000 | 60999 | 1192 | 2.22 | 60000 |

| Income ($) From | To | Basic Amount | Plus (%) | Of Income Over |
|---|---|---|---|---|
| 87000 | 87999 | 1714 | 1.8 | 87000 |
| 88000 | 88999 | 1732 | 1.62 | 88000 |
| 89000 | 89999 | 1748 | 1.6 | 89000 |
| 90000 | 90999 | 1764 | 1.6 | 90000 |
| 91000 | 91999 | 1780 | 1.54 | 91000 |
| 92000 | 92999 | 1795 | 1.54 | 92000 |
| 93000 | 93999 | 1810 | 1.58 | 93000 |
| 94000 | 94999 | 1826 | 1.6 | 94000 |
| 95000 | 95999 | 1842 | 1.52 | 95000 |
| 96000 | 96999 | 1857 | 1.56 | 96000 |
| 97000 | 97999 | 1873 | 1.58 | 97000 |
| 98000 | 98999 | 1889 | 1.62 | 98000 |
| 99000 | 99999 | 1905 | 1.54 | 99000 |
| 100000 | 100999 | 1920 | 1.56 | 100000 |
| 101000 | 101999 | 1936 | 1.6 | 101000 |
| 102000 | 102999 | 1952 | 1.52 | 102000 |
| 103000 | 103999 | 1967 | 1.56 | 103000 |
| 104000 | 104999 | 1983 | 1.58 | 104000 |
| 105000 | 105999 | 1999 | 1.6 | 105000 |
| 106000 | 106999 | 2015 | 1.54 | 106000 |
| 107000 | 107999 | 2030 | 1.56 | 107000 |
| 108000 | 108999 | 2046 | 1.6 | 108000 |
| 109000 | 109999 | 2062 | 1.62 | 109000 |

| Income ($) From | To | Basic Amount | Plus (%) | Of Income Over |
|---|---|---|---|---|
| 136000 | 136999 | 2486 | 1.58 | 136000 |
| 137000 | 137999 | 2502 | 1.6 | 137000 |
| 138000 | 138999 | 2518 | 1.54 | 138000 |
| 139000 | 139999 | 2533 | 1.56 | 139000 |
| 140000 | 140999 | 2549 | 1.5 | 140000 |
| 141000 | 141999 | 2564 | 1.46 | 141000 |
| 142000 | 142999 | 2579 | 1.48 | 142000 |
| 143000 | 143999 | 2594 | 1.5 | 143000 |
| 144000 | 144999 | 2609 | 1.5 | 144000 |
| 145000 | 145999 | 2624 | 1.52 | 145000 |
| 146000 | 146999 | 2639 | 1.52 | 146000 |
| 147000 | 147999 | 2654 | 1.54 | 147000 |
| 148000 | 148999 | 2669 | 1.44 | 148000 |
| 149000 | 149999 | 2683 | 1.46 | 149000 |
| 150000 | or greater | 2698 | 1.46 | 150000 |

# Child Support Table for Ontario, Number of Children: Four

| Income ($) From | To | Basic Amount | Plus (%) | Of Income Over | Income ($) From | To | Basic Amount | Plus (%) | Of Income Over | Income ($) From | To | Basic Amount | Plus (%) | Of Income Over |
|---|---|---|---|---|---|---|---|---|---|---|---|---|---|---|
| 12000 | 12999 | 0 | 11 | 12000 | 61000 | 61999 | 1431 | 2.56 | 61000 | 110000 | 110999 | 2473 | 1.86 | 110000 |
| 13000 | 13999 | 110 | 4.5 | 13000 | 62000 | 62999 | 1457 | 2.52 | 62000 | 111000 | 111999 | 2492 | 1.9 | 111000 |
| 14000 | 14999 | 155 | 4.12 | 14000 | 63000 | 63999 | 1482 | 2.58 | 63000 | 112000 | 112999 | 2511 | 1.84 | 112000 |
| 15000 | 15999 | 196 | 3.8 | 15000 | 64000 | 64999 | 1508 | 2.54 | 64000 | 113000 | 113999 | 2529 | 1.9 | 113000 |
| 16000 | 16999 | 234 | 3.46 | 16000 | 65000 | 65999 | 1533 | 2.5 | 65000 | 114000 | 114999 | 2548 | 1.84 | 114000 |
| 17000 | 17999 | 269 | 3.44 | 17000 | 66000 | 66999 | 1558 | 2.56 | 66000 | 115000 | 115999 | 2566 | 1.88 | 115000 |
| 18000 | 18999 | 303 | 3.9 | 18000 | 67000 | 67999 | 1584 | 2.52 | 67000 | 116000 | 116999 | 2585 | 1.82 | 116000 |
| 19000 | 19999 | 342 | 4.34 | 19000 | 68000 | 68999 | 1609 | 2.58 | 68000 | 117000 | 117999 | 2603 | 1.86 | 117000 |
| 20000 | 20999 | 385 | 4.18 | 20000 | 69000 | 69999 | 1635 | 2.54 | 69000 | 118000 | 118999 | 2622 | 1.9 | 118000 |
| 21000 | 21999 | 427 | 4.32 | 21000 | 70000 | 70999 | 1660 | 2.5 | 70000 | 119000 | 119999 | 2641 | 1.84 | 119000 |
| 22000 | 22999 | 470 | 4.14 | 22000 | 71000 | 71999 | 1685 | 2.56 | 71000 | 120000 | 120999 | 2659 | 1.88 | 120000 |
| 23000 | 23999 | 511 | 4.04 | 23000 | 72000 | 72999 | 1711 | 2.02 | 72000 | 121000 | 121999 | 2678 | 1.82 | 121000 |
| 24000 | 24999 | 551 | 4.02 | 24000 | 73000 | 73999 | 1731 | 2.36 | 73000 | 122000 | 122999 | 2696 | 1.88 | 122000 |
| 25000 | 25999 | 591 | 4.38 | 25000 | 74000 | 74999 | 1755 | 2.32 | 74000 | 123000 | 123999 | 2715 | 1.82 | 123000 |
| 26000 | 26999 | 635 | 4.38 | 26000 | 75000 | 75999 | 1778 | 2.22 | 75000 | 124000 | 124999 | 2733 | 1.86 | 124000 |
| 27000 | 27999 | 679 | 2.88 | 27000 | 76000 | 76999 | 1800 | 2.2 | 76000 | 125000 | 125999 | 2752 | 1.9 | 125000 |
| 28000 | 28999 | 708 | 2.44 | 28000 | 77000 | 77999 | 1822 | 2.2 | 77000 | 126000 | 126999 | 2771 | 1.84 | 126000 |
| 29000 | 29999 | 732 | 2.24 | 29000 | 78000 | 78999 | 1844 | 2.2 | 78000 | 127000 | 127999 | 2789 | 1.88 | 127000 |
| 30000 | 30999 | 754 | 2.36 | 30000 | 79000 | 79999 | 1866 | 2.2 | 79000 | 128000 | 128999 | 2808 | 1.82 | 128000 |
| 31000 | 31999 | 778 | 2.34 | 31000 | 80000 | 80999 | 1888 | 2.28 | 80000 | 129000 | 129999 | 2826 | 1.86 | 129000 |
| 32000 | 32999 | 801 | 2.32 | 32000 | 81000 | 81999 | 1911 | 2.24 | 81000 | 130000 | 130999 | 2845 | 1.82 | 130000 |
| 33000 | 33999 | 824 | 2.28 | 33000 | 82000 | 82999 | 1933 | 2.28 | 82000 | 131000 | 131999 | 2863 | 1.86 | 131000 |
| 34000 | 34999 | 847 | 2.36 | 34000 | 83000 | 83999 | 1956 | 2.14 | 83000 | 132000 | 132999 | 2882 | 1.9 | 132000 |
| 35000 | 35999 | 871 | 2.24 | 35000 | 84000 | 84999 | 1977 | 2.16 | 84000 | 133000 | 133999 | 2901 | 1.84 | 133000 |
| 36000 | 36999 | 893 | 1.96 | 36000 | 85000 | 85999 | 1999 | 2.18 | 85000 | 134000 | 134999 | 2919 | 1.88 | 134000 |
| 37000 | 37999 | 913 | 2 | 37000 | 86000 | 86999 | 2021 | 2.22 | 86000 | 135000 | 135999 | 2938 | 1.82 | 135000 |

# Child Support Table for Ontario, Number of Children: Four   Concluded

| Income ($) From | To | Basic Amount | Plus (%) | Of Income Over |
|---|---|---|---|---|
| 38000 | 38999 | 933 | 2.02 | 38000 |
| 39000 | 39999 | 953 | 2.16 | 39000 |
| 40000 | 40999 | 975 | 2.2 | 40000 |
| 41000 | 41999 | 997 | 2.04 | 41000 |
| 42000 | 42999 | 1017 | 1.9 | 42000 |
| 43000 | 43999 | 1036 | 1.96 | 43000 |
| 44000 | 44999 | 1056 | 2.02 | 44000 |
| 45000 | 45999 | 1076 | 1.96 | 45000 |
| 46000 | 46999 | 1096 | 1.9 | 46000 |
| 47000 | 47999 | 1115 | 1.9 | 47000 |
| 48000 | 48999 | 1134 | 1.4 | 48000 |
| 49000 | 49999 | 1148 | 1.88 | 49000 |
| 50000 | 50999 | 1167 | 1.96 | 50000 |
| 51000 | 51999 | 1187 | 2.04 | 51000 |
| 52000 | 52999 | 1207 | 2.44 | 52000 |
| 53000 | 53999 | 1231 | 2.42 | 53000 |
| 54000 | 54999 | 1255 | 2.42 | 54000 |
| 55000 | 55999 | 1279 | 2.5 | 55000 |
| 56000 | 56999 | 1304 | 2.56 | 56000 |
| 57000 | 57999 | 1330 | 2.52 | 57000 |
| 58000 | 58999 | 1355 | 2.58 | 58000 |
| 59000 | 59999 | 1381 | 2.54 | 59000 |
| 60000 | 60999 | 1406 | 2.5 | 60000 |

| Income ($) From | To | Basic Amount | Plus (%) | Of Income Over |
|---|---|---|---|---|
| 87000 | 87999 | 2043 | 2.14 | 87000 |
| 88000 | 88999 | 2064 | 1.94 | 88000 |
| 89000 | 89999 | 2083 | 1.9 | 89000 |
| 90000 | 90999 | 2102 | 1.86 | 90000 |
| 91000 | 91999 | 2121 | 1.8 | 91000 |
| 92000 | 92999 | 2139 | 1.9 | 92000 |
| 93000 | 93999 | 2158 | 1.84 | 93000 |
| 94000 | 94999 | 2176 | 1.88 | 94000 |
| 95000 | 95999 | 2195 | 1.84 | 95000 |
| 96000 | 96999 | 2213 | 1.88 | 96000 |
| 97000 | 97999 | 2232 | 1.82 | 97000 |
| 98000 | 98999 | 2250 | 1.86 | 98000 |
| 99000 | 99999 | 2269 | 1.9 | 99000 |
| 100000 | 100999 | 2288 | 1.84 | 100000 |
| 101000 | 101999 | 2306 | 1.88 | 101000 |
| 102000 | 102999 | 2325 | 1.82 | 102000 |
| 103000 | 103999 | 2343 | 1.86 | 103000 |
| 104000 | 104999 | 2362 | 1.82 | 104000 |
| 105000 | 105999 | 2380 | 1.86 | 105000 |
| 106000 | 106999 | 2399 | 1.9 | 106000 |
| 107000 | 107999 | 2418 | 1.84 | 107000 |
| 108000 | 108999 | 2436 | 1.88 | 108000 |
| 109000 | 109999 | 2455 | 1.82 | 109000 |

| Income ($) From | To | Basic Amount | Plus (%) | Of Income Over |
|---|---|---|---|---|
| 136000 | 136999 | 2956 | 1.86 | 136000 |
| 137000 | 137999 | 2975 | 1.9 | 137000 |
| 138000 | 138999 | 2994 | 1.84 | 138000 |
| 139000 | 139999 | 3012 | 1.9 | 139000 |
| 140000 | 140999 | 3031 | 1.84 | 140000 |
| 141000 | 141999 | 3049 | 1.74 | 141000 |
| 142000 | 142999 | 3066 | 1.78 | 142000 |
| 143000 | 143999 | 3084 | 1.72 | 143000 |
| 144000 | 144999 | 3101 | 1.76 | 144000 |
| 145000 | 145999 | 3119 | 1.8 | 145000 |
| 146000 | 146999 | 3137 | 1.74 | 146000 |
| 147000 | 147999 | 3154 | 1.78 | 147000 |
| 148000 | 148999 | 3172 | 1.72 | 148000 |
| 149000 | 149999 | 3189 | 1.76 | 149000 |
| 150000 | or greater | 3207 | 1.76 | 150000 |

# Child Support Table for Ontario, Number of Children: Five

| Income ($) From | Income ($) To | Basic Amount | Plus (%) | Of Income Over | Income ($) From | Income ($) To | Basic Amount | Plus (%) | Of Income Over | Income ($) From | Income ($) To | Basic Amount | Plus (%) | Of Income Over |
|---|---|---|---|---|---|---|---|---|---|---|---|---|---|---|
| 12000 | 12999 | 0 | 11 | 12000 | 61000 | 61999 | 1613 | 2.84 | 61000 | 110000 | 110999 | 2803 | 2.08 | 110000 |
| 13000 | 13999 | 110 | 4.5 | 13000 | 62000 | 62999 | 1641 | 2.84 | 62000 | 111000 | 111999 | 2824 | 2.08 | 111000 |
| 14000 | 14999 | 155 | 4.12 | 14000 | 63000 | 63999 | 1669 | 2.82 | 63000 | 112000 | 112999 | 2845 | 2.08 | 112000 |
| 15000 | 15999 | 196 | 3.8 | 15000 | 64000 | 64999 | 1697 | 2.8 | 64000 | 113000 | 113999 | 2866 | 2.1 | 113000 |
| 16000 | 16999 | 234 | 3.46 | 16000 | 65000 | 65999 | 1725 | 2.78 | 65000 | 114000 | 114999 | 2887 | 2.1 | 114000 |
| 17000 | 17999 | 269 | 3.44 | 17000 | 66000 | 66999 | 1753 | 2.86 | 66000 | 115000 | 115999 | 2908 | 2.1 | 115000 |
| 18000 | 18999 | 303 | 3.9 | 18000 | 67000 | 67999 | 1782 | 2.84 | 67000 | 116000 | 116999 | 2929 | 2.1 | 116000 |
| 19000 | 19999 | 342 | 4.34 | 19000 | 68000 | 68999 | 1810 | 2.82 | 68000 | 117000 | 117999 | 2950 | 2.1 | 117000 |
| 20000 | 20999 | 385 | 4.18 | 20000 | 69000 | 69999 | 1838 | 2.8 | 69000 | 118000 | 118999 | 2971 | 2.12 | 118000 |
| 21000 | 21999 | 427 | 4.32 | 21000 | 70000 | 70999 | 1866 | 2.8 | 70000 | 119000 | 119999 | 2992 | 2.12 | 119000 |
| 22000 | 22999 | 470 | 4.14 | 22000 | 71000 | 71999 | 1894 | 2.78 | 71000 | 120000 | 120999 | 3013 | 2.12 | 120000 |
| 23000 | 23999 | 511 | 4.04 | 23000 | 72000 | 72999 | 1922 | 2.26 | 72000 | 121000 | 121999 | 3034 | 2.12 | 121000 |
| 24000 | 24999 | 551 | 4.02 | 24000 | 73000 | 73999 | 1945 | 2.8 | 73000 | 122000 | 122999 | 3055 | 2.12 | 122000 |
| 25000 | 25999 | 591 | 4.38 | 25000 | 74000 | 74999 | 1973 | 2.78 | 74000 | 123000 | 123999 | 3076 | 2.14 | 123000 |
| 26000 | 26999 | 635 | 4.38 | 26000 | 75000 | 75999 | 2001 | 2.76 | 75000 | 124000 | 124999 | 3097 | 2.14 | 124000 |
| 27000 | 27999 | 679 | 4.38 | 27000 | 76000 | 76999 | 2029 | 2.74 | 76000 | 125000 | 125999 | 3118 | 2.14 | 125000 |
| 28000 | 28999 | 723 | 4.36 | 28000 | 77000 | 77999 | 2056 | 2.74 | 77000 | 126000 | 126999 | 3139 | 2.14 | 126000 |
| 29000 | 29999 | 767 | 4.56 | 29000 | 78000 | 78999 | 2083 | 2.74 | 78000 | 127000 | 127999 | 3160 | 2.04 | 127000 |
| 30000 | 30999 | 813 | 4.62 | 30000 | 79000 | 79999 | 2110 | 2.72 | 79000 | 128000 | 128999 | 3180 | 2.06 | 128000 |
| 31000 | 31999 | 859 | 4.66 | 31000 | 80000 | 80999 | 2137 | 2.8 | 80000 | 129000 | 129999 | 3201 | 2.06 | 129000 |
| 32000 | 32999 | 906 | 3.9 | 32000 | 81000 | 81999 | 2165 | 2.8 | 81000 | 130000 | 130999 | 3222 | 2.06 | 130000 |
| 33000 | 33999 | 945 | 2.64 | 33000 | 82000 | 82999 | 2193 | 2.52 | 82000 | 131000 | 131999 | 3243 | 2.06 | 131000 |
| 34000 | 34999 | 971 | 2.68 | 34000 | 83000 | 83999 | 2218 | 2.46 | 83000 | 132000 | 132999 | 3264 | 2.06 | 132000 |
| 35000 | 35999 | 998 | 2.64 | 35000 | 84000 | 84999 | 2243 | 2.42 | 84000 | 133000 | 133999 | 3285 | 2.08 | 133000 |
| 36000 | 36999 | 1024 | 2.24 | 36000 | 85000 | 85999 | 2267 | 2.46 | 85000 | 134000 | 134999 | 3306 | 2.08 | 134000 |
| 37000 | 37999 | 1046 | 2.2 | 37000 | 86000 | 86999 | 2292 | 2.42 | 86000 | 135000 | 135999 | 3327 | 2.08 | 135000 |

# Child Support Table for Ontario, Number of Children: Five   Concluded

| Income ($) From | To | Monthly Award ($) Basic Amount | Plus (%) | Of Income Over |
|---|---|---|---|---|
| 38000 | 38999 | 1068 | 2.36 | 38000 |
| 39000 | 39999 | 1092 | 2.5 | 39000 |
| 40000 | 40999 | 1117 | 2.44 | 40000 |
| 41000 | 41999 | 1141 | 2.38 | 41000 |
| 42000 | 42999 | 1165 | 2.24 | 42000 |
| 43000 | 43999 | 1187 | 2.22 | 43000 |
| 44000 | 44999 | 1209 | 2.38 | 44000 |
| 45000 | 45999 | 1233 | 2.3 | 45000 |
| 46000 | 46999 | 1256 | 2.24 | 46000 |
| 47000 | 47999 | 1278 | 2.24 | 47000 |
| 48000 | 48999 | 1300 | 1.64 | 48000 |
| 49000 | 49999 | 1316 | 2.2 | 49000 |
| 50000 | 50999 | 1338 | 2.2 | 50000 |
| 51000 | 51999 | 1360 | 2.3 | 51000 |
| 52000 | 52999 | 1383 | 2.24 | 52000 |
| 53000 | 53999 | 1405 | 2.28 | 53000 |
| 54000 | 54999 | 1428 | 2.24 | 54000 |
| 55000 | 55999 | 1450 | 2.36 | 55000 |
| 56000 | 56999 | 1474 | 2.58 | 56000 |
| 57000 | 57999 | 1500 | 2.82 | 57000 |
| 58000 | 58999 | 1528 | 2.8 | 58000 |
| 59000 | 59999 | 1556 | 2.78 | 59000 |
| 60000 | 60999 | 1584 | 2.86 | 60000 |

| Income ($) From | To | Monthly Award ($) Basic Amount | Plus (%) | Of Income Over |
|---|---|---|---|---|
| 87000 | 87999 | 2316 | 2.36 | 87000 |
| 88000 | 88999 | 2340 | 2.18 | 88000 |
| 89000 | 89999 | 2362 | 2.16 | 89000 |
| 90000 | 90999 | 2384 | 2.16 | 90000 |
| 91000 | 91999 | 2406 | 2.04 | 91000 |
| 92000 | 92999 | 2426 | 2.1 | 92000 |
| 93000 | 93999 | 2447 | 2.1 | 93000 |
| 94000 | 94999 | 2468 | 2.12 | 94000 |
| 95000 | 95999 | 2489 | 2.12 | 95000 |
| 96000 | 96999 | 2510 | 2.12 | 96000 |
| 97000 | 97999 | 2531 | 2.12 | 97000 |
| 98000 | 98999 | 2552 | 2.12 | 98000 |
| 99000 | 99999 | 2573 | 2.14 | 99000 |
| 100000 | 100999 | 2594 | 2.14 | 100000 |
| 101000 | 101999 | 2615 | 2.14 | 101000 |
| 102000 | 102999 | 2636 | 2.04 | 102000 |
| 103000 | 103999 | 2656 | 2.06 | 103000 |
| 104000 | 104999 | 2677 | 2.06 | 104000 |
| 105000 | 105999 | 2698 | 2.06 | 105000 |
| 106000 | 106999 | 2719 | 2.06 | 106000 |
| 107000 | 107999 | 2740 | 2.06 | 107000 |
| 108000 | 108999 | 2761 | 2.08 | 108000 |
| 109000 | 109999 | 2782 | 2.08 | 109000 |

| Income ($) From | To | Monthly Award ($) Basic Amount | Plus (%) | Of Income Over |
|---|---|---|---|---|
| 136000 | 136999 | 3348 | 2.08 | 136000 |
| 137000 | 137999 | 3369 | 2.08 | 137000 |
| 138000 | 138999 | 3390 | 2.1 | 138000 |
| 139000 | 139999 | 3411 | 2.1 | 139000 |
| 140000 | 140999 | 3432 | 2 | 140000 |
| 141000 | 141999 | 3452 | 1.98 | 141000 |
| 142000 | 142999 | 3472 | 1.98 | 142000 |
| 143000 | 143999 | 3492 | 2 | 143000 |
| 144000 | 144999 | 3512 | 2.02 | 144000 |
| 145000 | 145999 | 3532 | 2.04 | 145000 |
| 146000 | 146999 | 3552 | 1.94 | 146000 |
| 147000 | 147999 | 3571 | 1.96 | 147000 |
| 148000 | 148999 | 3591 | 1.98 | 148000 |
| 149000 | 149999 | 3611 | 2 | 149000 |
| 150000 | or greater | 3631 | 2 | 150000 |

## Child Support Table for Ontario, Number of Children: Six or more

| Income ($) From | To | Monthly Award ($) Basic Amount | Plus (%) | Of Income Over |
|---|---|---|---|---|
| 12000 | 12999 | 0 | 11 | 12000 |
| 13000 | 13999 | 110 | 4.5 | 13000 |
| 14000 | 14999 | 155 | 4.12 | 14000 |
| 15000 | 15999 | 196 | 3.8 | 15000 |
| 16000 | 16999 | 234 | 3.46 | 16000 |
| 17000 | 17999 | 269 | 3.44 | 17000 |
| 18000 | 18999 | 303 | 3.9 | 18000 |
| 19000 | 19999 | 342 | 4.34 | 19000 |
| 20000 | 20999 | 385 | 4.18 | 20000 |
| 21000 | 21999 | 427 | 4.32 | 21000 |
| 22000 | 22999 | 470 | 4.14 | 22000 |
| 23000 | 23999 | 511 | 4.04 | 23000 |
| 24000 | 24999 | 551 | 4.02 | 24000 |
| 25000 | 25999 | 591 | 4.38 | 25000 |
| 26000 | 26999 | 635 | 4.38 | 26000 |
| 27000 | 27999 | 679 | 4.38 | 27000 |
| 28000 | 28999 | 723 | 4.36 | 28000 |
| 29000 | 29999 | 767 | 4.56 | 29000 |
| 30000 | 30999 | 813 | 4.62 | 30000 |
| 31000 | 31999 | 859 | 4.66 | 31000 |
| 32000 | 32999 | 906 | 4.6 | 32000 |
| 33000 | 33999 | 952 | 4.66 | 33000 |
| 34000 | 34999 | 999 | 4.7 | 34000 |
| 35000 | 35999 | 1046 | 4.54 | 35000 |
| 36000 | 36999 | 1091 | 3.98 | 36000 |
| 37000 | 37999 | 1131 | 4.02 | 37000 |

| Income ($) From | To | Monthly Award ($) Basic Amount | Plus (%) | Of Income Over |
|---|---|---|---|---|
| 61000 | 61999 | 1767 | 2.9 | 61000 |
| 62000 | 62999 | 1796 | 3.06 | 62000 |
| 63000 | 63999 | 1827 | 3.02 | 63000 |
| 64000 | 64999 | 1857 | 3.06 | 64000 |
| 65000 | 65999 | 1888 | 3.02 | 65000 |
| 66000 | 66999 | 1918 | 3.06 | 66000 |
| 67000 | 67999 | 1949 | 3 | 67000 |
| 68000 | 68999 | 1979 | 3.06 | 68000 |
| 69000 | 69999 | 2010 | 3 | 69000 |
| 70000 | 70999 | 2040 | 3.06 | 70000 |
| 71000 | 71999 | 2071 | 3 | 71000 |
| 72000 | 72999 | 2101 | 2.46 | 72000 |
| 73000 | 73999 | 2126 | 3 | 73000 |
| 74000 | 74999 | 2156 | 3.06 | 74000 |
| 75000 | 75999 | 2187 | 2.9 | 75000 |
| 76000 | 76999 | 2216 | 2.96 | 76000 |
| 77000 | 77999 | 2246 | 2.92 | 77000 |
| 78000 | 78999 | 2275 | 2.98 | 78000 |
| 79000 | 79999 | 2305 | 2.94 | 79000 |
| 80000 | 80999 | 2334 | 2.98 | 80000 |
| 81000 | 81999 | 2364 | 2.98 | 81000 |
| 82000 | 82999 | 2394 | 3.06 | 82000 |
| 83000 | 83999 | 2425 | 2.94 | 83000 |
| 84000 | 84999 | 2454 | 2.96 | 84000 |
| 85000 | 85999 | 2484 | 3 | 85000 |
| 86000 | 86999 | 2514 | 2.92 | 86000 |

| Income ($) From | To | Monthly Award ($) Basic Amount | Plus (%) | Of Income Over |
|---|---|---|---|---|
| 110000 | 110999 | 3082 | 2.26 | 110000 |
| 111000 | 111999 | 3105 | 2.26 | 111000 |
| 112000 | 112999 | 3128 | 2.28 | 112000 |
| 113000 | 113999 | 3151 | 2.28 | 113000 |
| 114000 | 114999 | 3174 | 2.28 | 114000 |
| 115000 | 115999 | 3197 | 2.28 | 115000 |
| 116000 | 116999 | 3220 | 2.28 | 116000 |
| 117000 | 117999 | 3243 | 2.28 | 117000 |
| 118000 | 118999 | 3266 | 2.28 | 118000 |
| 119000 | 119999 | 3289 | 2.28 | 119000 |
| 120000 | 120999 | 3312 | 2.3 | 120000 |
| 121000 | 121999 | 3335 | 2.3 | 121000 |
| 122000 | 122999 | 3358 | 2.3 | 122000 |
| 123000 | 123999 | 3381 | 2.3 | 123000 |
| 124000 | 124999 | 3404 | 2.3 | 124000 |
| 125000 | 125999 | 3427 | 2.3 | 125000 |
| 126000 | 126999 | 3450 | 2.3 | 126000 |
| 127000 | 127999 | 3473 | 2.3 | 127000 |
| 128000 | 128999 | 3496 | 2.32 | 128000 |
| 129000 | 129999 | 3519 | 2.32 | 129000 |
| 130000 | 130999 | 3542 | 2.32 | 130000 |
| 131000 | 131999 | 3565 | 2.32 | 131000 |
| 132000 | 132999 | 3588 | 2.32 | 132000 |
| 133000 | 133999 | 3611 | 2.32 | 133000 |
| 134000 | 134999 | 3634 | 2.32 | 134000 |
| 135000 | 135999 | 3657 | 2.34 | 135000 |

# Child Support Table for Ontario, Number of Children: Six or more    Concluded

| Income ($) From | To | Basic Amount | Plus (%) | Of Income Over | Income ($) From | To | Basic Amount | Plus (%) | Of Income Over | Income ($) From | To | Basic Amount | Plus (%) | Of Income Over |
|---|---|---|---|---|---|---|---|---|---|---|---|---|---|---|
| 38000 | 38999 | 1171 | 3.84 | 38000 | 87000 | 87999 | 2543 | 2.96 | 87000 | 136000 | 136999 | 3680 | 2.34 | 136000 |
| 39000 | 39999 | 1209 | 2.68 | 39000 | 88000 | 88999 | 2573 | 2.64 | 88000 | 137000 | 137999 | 3703 | 2.34 | 137000 |
| 40000 | 40999 | 1236 | 2.76 | 40000 | 89000 | 89999 | 2599 | 2.44 | 89000 | 138000 | 138999 | 3726 | 2.34 | 138000 |
| 41000 | 41999 | 1264 | 2.64 | 41000 | 90000 | 90999 | 2623 | 2.3 | 90000 | 139000 | 139999 | 3749 | 2.34 | 139000 |
| 42000 | 42999 | 1290 | 2.44 | 42000 | 91000 | 91999 | 2646 | 2.26 | 91000 | 140000 | 140999 | 3772 | 2.24 | 140000 |
| 43000 | 43999 | 1314 | 2.48 | 43000 | 92000 | 92999 | 2669 | 2.32 | 92000 | 141000 | 141999 | 3794 | 2.22 | 141000 |
| 44000 | 44999 | 1339 | 2.58 | 44000 | 93000 | 93999 | 2692 | 2.32 | 93000 | 142000 | 142999 | 3816 | 2.14 | 142000 |
| 45000 | 45999 | 1365 | 2.56 | 45000 | 94000 | 94999 | 2715 | 2.32 | 94000 | 143000 | 143999 | 3837 | 2.16 | 143000 |
| 46000 | 46999 | 1391 | 2.44 | 46000 | 95000 | 95999 | 2738 | 2.32 | 95000 | 144000 | 144999 | 3859 | 2.2 | 144000 |
| 47000 | 47999 | 1415 | 2.4 | 47000 | 96000 | 96999 | 2761 | 2.34 | 96000 | 145000 | 145999 | 3881 | 2.22 | 145000 |
| 48000 | 48999 | 1439 | 1.86 | 48000 | 97000 | 97999 | 2784 | 2.34 | 97000 | 146000 | 146999 | 3903 | 2.14 | 146000 |
| 49000 | 49999 | 1458 | 2.42 | 49000 | 98000 | 98999 | 2807 | 2.34 | 98000 | 147000 | 147999 | 3924 | 2.16 | 147000 |
| 50000 | 50999 | 1482 | 2.46 | 50000 | 99000 | 99999 | 2830 | 2.34 | 99000 | 148000 | 148999 | 3946 | 2.18 | 148000 |
| 51000 | 51999 | 1507 | 2.5 | 51000 | 100000 | 100999 | 2853 | 2.34 | 100000 | 149000 | 149999 | 3968 | 2.22 | 149000 |
| 52000 | 52999 | 1532 | 2.5 | 52000 | 101000 | 101999 | 2876 | 2.34 | 101000 | 150000 | or greater | 3990 | 2.22 | 150000 |
| 53000 | 53999 | 1557 | 2.5 | 53000 | 102000 | 102999 | 2899 | 2.34 | 102000 | | | | | |
| 54000 | 54999 | 1582 | 2.5 | 54000 | 103000 | 103999 | 2922 | 2.24 | 103000 | | | | | |
| 55000 | 55999 | 1607 | 2.68 | 55000 | 104000 | 104999 | 2944 | 2.26 | 104000 | | | | | |
| 56000 | 56999 | 1634 | 2.62 | 56000 | 105000 | 105999 | 2967 | 2.26 | 105000 | | | | | |
| 57000 | 57999 | 1660 | 2.66 | 57000 | 106000 | 106999 | 2990 | 2.26 | 106000 | | | | | |
| 58000 | 58999 | 1687 | 2.7 | 58000 | 107000 | 107999 | 3013 | 2.26 | 107000 | | | | | |
| 59000 | 59999 | 1714 | 2.64 | 59000 | 108000 | 108999 | 3036 | 2.26 | 108000 | | | | | |
| 60000 | 60999 | 1740 | 2.68 | 60000 | 109000 | 109999 | 3059 | 2.26 | 109000 | | | | | |

## SCHEDULE II
### Comparison of Household Standards of Living Test (Subsection 10(4))

**Definitions**

1. The definitions in this section apply in this Schedule.

"child" means,

(a) in cases where the *Divorce Act* (Canada) applies, a child of the marriage or a child who,

(i) is under the age of majority, or

(ii) is the age of majority or over but is unable, by reason of illness, disability or other cause to obtain the necessaries of life, or

(b) in cases where the Act applies, a child who is a dependant under the Act;

"household" means a parent or spouse and any of the following persons residing with him or her,

(a) any person who has a legal duty to support the parent or spouse or whom the parent or spouse has a legal duty to support,

(b) any person who shares living expenses with the parent or spouse or from whom the parent or spouse otherwise receives an economic benefit as a result of living with that person, if the court considers it reasonable for that person to be considered part of the household, and

(c) any child whom the parent or spouse or the person described in clause (a) or (b) has a legal duty to support;

"taxable income" means the annual taxable income determined using the calculations required to determine "Taxable Income" in the T1 General form issued by the Canada Revenue Agency.

**Test**

2. The comparison of household standards of living test is as follows:

*STEP 1*

Establish the annual income of each person in each household by applying the formula

$$A - B - C$$

where

A   is the person's income determined under sections 15 to 20 of this Regulation,

B   is the federal and provincial taxes payable on the person's taxable income, and

C   is the person's source deductions for premiums paid under the *Employment Insurance Act* and contributions made to the *Canada Pension Plan* and the *Quebec Pension Plan*.

Where the information on which to base the income determination is not provided, the court may impute income in the amount it considers appropriate.

*STEP 2*

Adjust the annual income of each person in each household by

(a) deducting the following amounts, calculated on an annual basis:

(i) any amount relied on by the court as a factor that resulted in a determination of undue hardship, except any amount attributable to the support of a member of the household that is not incurred due to a disability or serious illness of that member,

(ii) the amount that would otherwise be payable by the person in respect of a child to whom the order relates, if the pleading of undue hardship was not made,

(A) under the applicable table, or

(B) as considered by the court to be appropriate, where the court considers the table amount to be inappropriate,

(iii) any amount of support that is paid by the person under a judgment, order or written separation agreement, except,

(A) an amount already deducted under subclause (i), and

(B) an amount paid by the person in respect of a child to whom the order referred to in subclause (ii) relates; and

(b) adding the following amounts, calculated on an annual basis:

(i) any amount that would otherwise be receivable by the person in respect of a child to whom the order relates, if the pleading of undue hardship was not made,

(A) under the applicable table, or

(B) as considered by the court to be appropriate, where the court considers the table amount to be inappropriate, and

(ii) any amount of child support that the person has received for any child under a judgment, order or written separation agreement.

*STEP 3*

Add the amounts of adjusted annual income for all the persons in each household to determine the total household income for each household.

*STEP 4*

Determine the applicable low-income measures amount for each household based on the following:

**Low-income Measures**

| Household Size | Household Composition | Low-income Measures Amount |
|---|---|---|
| One person | One adult | $10,382 |
| Two persons | Two adults | $14,535 |
| Two persons | One adult and one child | 14,535 |
| Three persons | Three adults | $18,688 |
| Three persons | Two adults and one child | 17,649 |
| Three persons | One adult and two children | 17,649 |
| Four persons | Four adults | $22,840 |
| Four persons | Three adults and one child | 21,802 |
| Four persons | Two adults and two children | 20,764 |
| Four persons | One adult and three children | 20,764 |
| Five persons | Five adults | $26,993 |
| Five persons | Four adults and one child | 25,955 |
| Five persons | Three adults and two children | 24,917 |
| Five persons | Two adults and three children | 23,879 |
| Five persons | One adult and four children | 23,879 |
| Six persons | Six adults | $31,145 |
| Six persons | Five adults and one child | 30,108 |
| Six persons | Four adults and two children | 29,070 |
| Six persons | Three adults and three children | 28,031 |
| Six persons | Two adults and four children | 26,993 |
| Six persons | One adult and five children | 26,993 |
| Seven persons | Seven adults | $34,261 |
| Seven persons | Six adults and one child | 33,222 |
| Seven persons | Five adults and two children | 32,184 |
| Seven persons | Four adults and three children | 31,146 |
| Seven persons | Three adults and four children | 30,108 |
| Seven persons | Two adults and five children | 29,070 |
| Seven persons | One adult and six children | 29,070 |
| Eight persons | Eight adults | $38,413 |
| Eight persons | Seven adults and one child | 37,375 |
| Eight persons | Six adults and two children | 36,337 |
| Eight persons | Five adults and three children | 35,299 |
| Eight persons | Four adults and four children | 34,261 |
| Eight persons | Three adults and Five children | 33,222 |
| Eight persons | Two adults and six children | 32,184 |
| Eight persons | One adult and seven children | 32,184 |

*STEP 5*

Divide the household income amount (Step 3) by the low-income measures amount (Step 4) to get a household income ratio for each household.

*STEP 6*

Compare the household income ratios. The household that has the higher ratio has the higher standard of living.

## SCHEDULE III
### Adjustments to Income (Section 16)
**Employment expenses**

1. Where the parent or spouse is an employee, the parent's or spouse's applicable employment expenses described in the following provisions of the *Income Tax Act* (Canada) are deducted:

(a) Revoked.

(b) paragraph 8(1)(d) concerning expenses of teacher's exchange fund contribution;

(c) paragraph 8(1)(e) concerning expenses of railway employees;

(d) paragraph 8(1)(f) concerning sales expenses;

(e) paragraph 8(1)(g) concerning transport employee's expenses;

(f) paragraph 8(1)(h) concerning travel expenses;

(f.1) paragraph 8(1)(h.1) concerning motor vehicle travel expenses;

(g) paragraph 8(1)(i) concerning dues and other expenses of performing duties;

(h) paragraph 8(l)(j) concerning motor vehicle and aircraft costs;

(i) paragraph 8(1)(l.1) concerning *Canada Pension Plan* contributions and *Employment Insurance Act* (Canada) premiums paid in respect of another employee who acts as an assistant or substitute for the parent or spouse;

(j) paragraph 8(1)(n) concerning salary reimbursement;

(k) paragraph 8(1)(o) concerning forfeited amounts;

(l) paragraph 8(1)(p) concerning musical instrument costs; and

(m) paragraph 8(1)(q) concerning artists' employment expenses.

### Child support

2. Deduct any child support received that is included to determine total income in the T1 General form issued by the Canada Revenue Agency.

### Support other than child support and universal child care benefit

3. To calculate income for the purpose of determining an amount under an applicable table, deduct,

(a) the support, not including child support, received from the other parent or spouse; and

(b) any universal child care benefit that is included to determine the parent or spouse's total income in the T1 General form issued by the Canada Revenue Agency.

### Special or extraordinary expenses

3.1 To calculate income for the purpose of determining an amount under section 7 of this Regulation, deduct the support, not including child support, paid to the other parent or spouse and, as applicable, make the following adjustment in respect of universal child care benefits:

(a) deduct benefits that are included to determine the parent or spouse's total income in the T1 General form issued by the Canada Revenue Agency and that are for a child for whom special or extraordinary expenses are not being requested; or

(b) include benefits that are not included to determine the parent or spouse's total income in the T1 General form issued by the Canada Revenue Agency and that are received by the parent or spouse for a child for whom special or extraordinary expenses are being requested.

### Social assistance

4. Deduct any amount of social assistance income that is not attributable to the parent or spouse.

### Dividends from taxable Canadian corporations

5. Replace the taxable amount of dividends from taxable Canadian corporations received by the parent or spouse by the actual amount of those dividends received by the parent or spouse.

### Capital gains and capital losses

6. Replace the taxable capital gains realized in a year by the parent or spouse by the actual amount of capital gains realized by the parent or spouse in excess of the parent's or spouse's actual capital losses in that year.

### Business investment losses

7. Deduct the actual amount of business investment losses suffered by the parent or spouse during the year.

### Carrying charges

8. Deduct the parent's or spouse's carrying charges and interest expenses that are paid by the parent or spouse and that would be deductible under the *Income Tax Act* (Canada).

### Net self-employment income

9. Where the parent's or spouse's net self-employment income is determined by deducting an amount for salaries, benefits, wages or management fees, or other payments, paid to or on behalf of persons with whom the parent or spouse does not deal at arm's length, include that amount, unless the parent or spouse establishes that the payments were necessary to earn the self-employment income and were reasonable in the circumstances.

### Additional amount

10. Where the parent or spouse reports income from self-employment that, in accordance with sections 34.1 and 34.2 of the *Income Tax Act* (Canada), includes an additional amount earned in a prior period, deduct the amount earned in the prior period, net of reserves.

### Capital cost allowance for property

11. Include the parent's or spouse's deduction for an allowable capital cost allowance with respect to real property.

### Partnership or sole proprietorship income

12. Where the parent or spouse earns income through a partnership or sole proprietorship, deduct any amount included in income that is properly required by the partnership or sole proprietorship for purposes of capitalization.

### Employee stock options with a Canadian-controlled private corporation

13. (1) Where the parent or spouse has received, as an employee benefit, options to purchase shares of a Canadian-controlled private corporation or a publicly traded corporation that is subject to the same tax treatment with reference to stock options as a Canadian-controlled private corporation, and has exercised those options during the year, add the difference between the value of the shares at the time the options are exercised and the amount paid by the parent or spouse for the shares and any amount paid by the parent or spouse to acquire the options to purchase the shares, to the income for the year in which the options are exercised.

### Disposal of shares

(2) If the parent or spouse has disposed of the shares during a year, deduct from the income for that year the difference determined under subsection (1).

# Formal Requirements of the Continuing Record Under the Family Law Rules

Published by: The Family Rules Committee
Version Date: October 21, 2013
Effective Date: January 1, 2014
Available at: http://www.ontariocourtforms.on.ca

## I. Introduction

The "Formal Requirements of the Continuing Record under the *Family Law Rules*" is published by the Family Rules Committee and available at the following website: http://www.ontariocourtforms.on.ca. These requirements must be followed in all cases, governed by the *Family Law Rules*, except child protection cases The Family Rules Committee has the authority to make court rules for the practice and procedure in family cases, subject to the approval of the Attorney General.

The formal requirements of the continuing record for child protection cases are set out in the "Formal Requirements of the Child Protection Continuing Record under the *Family Law Rules*," published by the Family Rules Committee and available at http://www.ontariocourtforms.on.ca.

The substantive requirements of the continuing record are set out in Rule 9. There are provisions in Rules 13 and 17 that set out the types of documents that may be excluded from the record. The formal requirements for the preparation and maintenance of the continuing record are set out in this document, and in the following appendices:

Appendix A – Summary of Contents
Appendix B – Sample Cover
Appendix C – Sample Table of Contents

## II. Formal Requirements

### 1. Contents of the record

Unless otherwise indicated, a continuing record includes: an endorsements volume and documents volume.

The endorsements volume will contain a cumulative table of contents, an endorsements section, which would also contain reasons for judgment and minutes of settlement, and an orders section.

The documents volume will contain documents filed in the case, including applications, answers, replies, affidavits of service, financial statements, motions, affidavits and trial management conference briefs.

The applicant will file the endorsement volume at the same time as filing volume 1 of the documents volume of the continuing record. However, it is not necessary to start a separate endorsements volume in the following types of cases:

- Joint applications for divorce;
- Uncontested divorces in which the only claim is for divorce, when the respondent does not file an answer;
- When the applicant files a change information form (Form 15) and the respondent does not file an affidavit;
- Support enforcement proceedings;
- A consent motion for a final order.

The continuing records for these cases must include a separate section for endorsements and a minimum of three blank sheet on which the judge dealing with the case will note the disposition and the date.

The same endorsements volume must be used for all applications and motions to change that are filed in the same court file. Where a motion to change a final order is made a separate endorsements volume should not be created, unless there is no endorsements volume already in the court file.

A support enforcement continuing record consists of one volume, split into two sections, one called "Documents" which contains the table of contents and documents filed in the case. The second called "Endorsements" and contains endorsements, orders, reasons for judgment and minutes of settlement made in the enforcement proceeding, in the order in which they were made.

A summary of the contents of the continuing record is set out in a chart at Appendix A.

## 2. Preparation of the Record

### (a) Volumes

Each new application or motion to change a final order starts a new volume to the continuing record.

Where a new volume is started when a motion to change a final order is made, the new volume shall be numbered sequentially after the last volume filed. Only documents related to the motion to change shall be filed in the motion to change volume.

If the clerk determines that a volume is full, the party filing the next document must create a new volume, which will be numbered sequentially.

### (b) Record Cover

The endorsements volume will have a yellow cover, which will include the court file number and names of the parties to the case.

The documents volume will have a red cover. A sample record cover is attached at Appendix B. All elements of the sample cover must appear on a party's record cover. The title of the record (e.g. "Continuing Record") must appear in bold, font size 20, or an equivalent size, below the names of the parties to the case. The cover must identify the volume number of the record.

The support enforcement continuing record will have a green cover.

If separate continuing records are ordered, the respondent's document record will have a blue cover.

For the volume(s) of the record containing documents relating to a motion to change a final order, the cover must identify the order that is the subject of the motion. Below the title of the record state: "Motion to Change Final Order of Mr./Madam Justice……..…………, dated ……………, with respect to ……………".

### (c) Filing Documents

Documents must be filed in chronological order, with the most recently filed document at the back. All documents filed in the record must be punched in standard three-hole format.

Other than in a support enforcement continuing record, a numbered tab must identify each document filed. Tabs must be in sequential order. A new volume must start with a new tab sequence starting with tab 1.

Pages between numbered tabs must be numbered consecutively. Page numbers are not required to appear in the table of contents, unless there are no tabs as in the support enforcement continuing record.

### (d) Contents of Continuing Record

### (i) Table of Contents

A sample table of contents is attached at Appendix C. There will be one cumulative table of contents located in the endorsements volume or in the support enforcement continuing record. It will be used to list all documents filed, including documents filed in the motion to change a final order volume. The table of contents must list documents in the order in which they are filed, indicate the volume in which the document is located, the tab number or page number that locates the document, the kind of document, which party filed it, and the date it was filed. For an affidavit or transcript of evidence, the name of the person who gave the affidavit or the evidence must also be shown.

Affidavits of service must be listed in the table of contents including a notation as to the document(s) served and the party who was served.

For documents filed in the volume containing a motion to change a final order, the table of contents must clearly identify that the documents relate to the motion to change.

The table of contents must be updated every time a document is filed.

### (ii) Endorsements

The endorsements section of the endorsements volume, or of the support enforcement continuing record, must be identified by a tab or divider. The endorsements section must contain a minimum of three (3) blank sheets, on which the judge dealing with any step in the case will note the disposition of that step and the date. Any written reasons for judgment and minutes of settlement that form the basis of an order must be put in the endorsements section.

### (iii) Orders

The orders section of the endorsements volume must be identified by a tab or divider, except for the support enforcement continuing record. The court's file copy of each order made in the case must be put into the orders section.

### (iv) Documents

Documents filed in the case, including applications, answers, replies, financial statements, motions, affidavits and trial management conference briefs must be filed in the documents volume.

If the court has ordered separate records for the applicant and respondent, a report ordered by the court must be filed in the applicant's record. A report requested by a party must be filed in the record of the party who requested it.

A financial statement must be filed under its own numbered tab or page number in the support enforcement continuing record. Copies of income tax returns are not required to be attached to the financial statement in the continuing record, unless the court orders otherwise.

A motion for an order to refrain under s. 35(1) of the *Family Responsibility and Support Arrears Enforcement Act, 1996* must be filed in the volume containing the motion to change a final order.

## (v) Affidavits of Service

Affidavits of service must be filed within the tab of the document to which the affidavit of service relates, behind the document. If the affidavit of service relates to more than one document, it must be filed within the tab of the first document to which it relates (usually the main document in the package of documents, or the document claiming the relief).

### (e) Separate or combined records

Where the court orders that the continuing record be separated, or that separate court records be combined,

- court staff must supervise the separation or the combination of separate records;
- if the record is separated, the party requesting the separate records shall prepare an updated cumulative table of contents reflecting the contents of both records unless otherwise ordered by the court; and
- if separated records are combined, the party directed to combine the record, or the party that requested the combination, shall prepare an updated cumulative table of contents that reflects the contents of the combined record.

## 3. Additional requirements for support enforcement continuing record

The support enforcement continuing record will have its own cumulative table of contents, listing each document filed in the case. The support enforcement continuing record will be split into two sections: a documents section and an endorsements section.

The documents section must contain each document filed in the case, numbered consecutively and arranged in order, with the most recently filed document at the back. All affidavits of service must be filed in this section.

Endorsements, orders, reasons for judgment and minutes of settlement made in the enforcement proceeding are all filed in the support enforcement record, in numerical order under the second section.

## APPENDIX A – SUMMARY OF CONTENTS

| CONTINUING RECORD | | |
|---|---|---|
| **SINGLE RECORD** | **SEPARATE RECORDS IF ORDERED** | |
| | **Applicant's Record** | **Respondent's Record** |
| **Endorsements Volume** | **Endorsements Volume** | **Endorsements Volume** |
| Yellow cover | Yellow cover | |
| - Table of Contents<br>- Endorsements, incl. Reasons for Judgment and Minutes of Settlement<br>- Orders | - Table of Contents<br>- Endorsements, incl. Reasons for Judgment and Minutes of Settlement<br>- Orders | N/A |
| **Documents** | **Documents** | **Documents** |
| Red cover | Red cover | Blue cover |
| - All documents, including affidavits of service, in chronological order | - All applicant documents, including affidavits of service, in chronological order | - All respondent documents, including affidavits of service, in chronological order |

| SUPPORT ENFORCEMENT CONTINUING RECORD | | |
|---|---|---|
| **SINGLE RECORD** | **SEPARATE RECORDS IF ORDERED** | |
| | **Director's Enforcement Record** | **Payor's Enforcement Record** |
| **Documents and Endorsements** | **Documents and Endorsements** | **Documents and Endorsements** |
| Green cover | Green cover | Green cover |
| - Documents (including affidavits of service)<br>- Endorsements, incl. Reasons for Judgment and Minutes of Settlement<br>- Orders | - Documents (including affidavits of service)<br>- Endorsements, incl. Reasons for Judgment and Minutes of Settlement<br>- Orders | - Documents (including affidavits of service)<br>- Endorsements, incl. Reasons for Judgment and Minutes of Settlement<br>- Orders |

## APPENDIX B – SAMPLE COVER

*ONTARIO*

| Court File Number / *Numéro de dossier du greffe* |
| --- |
| |

_____

(Name of court / *Nom du tribunal*)

**at /** *situé(e) au* _____

Court office address / *Adresse du greffe*

**Volume /** *Volume* **:** _____

### Applicant(s) / *Requérant(e)(s)*

| Full legal name & address for service — street & number, municipality, postal code, telephone & fax numbers and e-mail address (if any). *Nom et prénom officiels et adresse aux fins de signification — numéro et rue, municipalité, code postal, numéros de téléphone et de télécopieur et adresse électronique (le cas échéant).* | Lawyer's name & address — street & number, municipality, postal code, telephone & fax numbers and e-mail address (if any). *Nom et adresse de l'avocat(e) — numéro et rue, municipalité, code postal, numéros de téléphone et de télécopieur et adresse électronique (le cas échéant).* |
| --- | --- |
| | |

### Respondent(s) / *Intimé(e)(s)*

| Full legal name & address for service — street & number, municipality, postal code, telephone & fax numbers and e-mail address (if any). *Nom et prénom officiels et adresse aux fins de signification — numéro et rue, municipalité, code postal, numéros de téléphone et de télécopieur et adresse électronique (le cas échéant).* | Lawyer's name & address — street & number, municipality, postal code, telephone & fax numbers and e-mail address (if any). *Nom et adresse de l'avocat(e) — numéro et rue, municipalité, code postal, numéros de téléphone et de télécopieur et adresse électronique (le cas échéant).* |
| --- | --- |
| | |

### Children's Lawyer / *Avocat des enfants*

| Name & address of Children's Lawyer's agent for service (street & number, municipality, postal code, telephone & fax numbers and e-mail address (if any) and name of person represented. *Nom et adresse de la personne qui représente l'avocat(e) des enfants aux fins de signification (numéro et rue, municipalité, code postal, numéros de téléphone et de télécopieur et adresse électronique (le cas échéant) et nom de la personne représentée.* |
| --- |
| |

# Continuing Record

(Title of record in bold, font size 20 or equivalent / *Intitulé du dossier en caractères gras; police de taille 20 ou l'équivalent*)

## APPENDIX C – SAMPLE TABLE OF CONTENTS

*ONTARIO*

| Court File Number |
|---|

_____
*(Name of court)*

at  _____
*Court office address*

**Cumulative Table of Contents
Continuing Record**

**Applicant(s)**

| Full legal name & address for service — street & number, municipality, postal code, telephone & fax numbers and e-mail address (if any). | Lawyer's name & address — street & number, municipality, postal code, telephone & fax numbers and e-mail address (if any). |
|---|---|
| | |
| | |

**Respondent(s)**

| Full legal name & address for service — street & number, municipality, postal code, telephone & fax numbers and e-mail address (if any). | Lawyer's name & address — street & number, municipality, postal code, telephone & fax numbers and e-mail address (if any). |
|---|---|
| | |
| | |

| Document<br>(For an affidavit or transcript of evidence, include the name of the person who gave the affidavit or the evidence.) | Filed by<br>(A = applicant or<br>R = respondent) | Date of Document<br>(d, m, y) | Date of Filing<br>(d, m, y) | Volume/Tab |
|---|---|---|---|---|
| Application | A | 11/10/06 | 20/10/06 | Volume 1, Tab 1 (page # in support enforcement continuing record) |
| Affidavit of Service of Application on Respondent | A | 18/10/06 | 20/10/06 | Volume 1, Tab 1 |
| Financial Statement | A | 11/10/06 | 20/10/06 | Volume 1, Tab 2 |
| Answer | R | 6/12/06 | 6/12/06 | Volume 1, Tab 3 |
| Affidavit of Service of Answer on Applicant | R | 6/12/06 | 6/12/06 | Volume 1, Tab 3 |
| Financial Statement | R | 6/12/06 | 6/12/06 | Volume 1, Tab 4 |
| Notice of Motion | R | 5/6/07 | 5/6/07 | Volume 1, Tab 5 |
| Affidavit of Service of Notice of Motion on Applicant | R | 5/7/07 | 5/6/07 | Volume 1, Tab 5 |
| Affidavit (name of person) | R | 5/6/07 | 5/6/07 | Volume 1, Tab 6 |
| Affidavit in Response (name of person) | A | 4/7/07 | 4/7/07 | Volume 2, Tab 1 |
| Affidavit of Service of Affidavit in response on Respondent | A | 4/7/07 | 4/7/07 | Volume 2, Tab 1 |
| Notice of Motion to change final order dated 1/08/07 | R | 1/02/09 | 10/02/09 | Volume 3, Tab 1 |
| Affidavit of Service of Notice of Motion on Applicant | R | 5/02/09 | 10/02/09 | Volume 3, Tab 1 |
| Financial Statement | R | 1/02/09 | 10/02/09 | Volume 3, Tab 2 |

☐  *Continued on next sheet*
*(Français au verso)*

# Marriage Act

RSO 1990, c M.3

**Definitions**

1. (1) In this Act,

"band" means a band as defined in the *Indian Act* (Canada);

"church" includes chapel, meeting-house or place set aside for religious worship;

"Indian" means a person who is registered as an Indian or entitled to be registered as an Indian under the *Indian Act* (Canada);

"issuer" means a person authorized under this Act to issue marriage licences;

"judge" means a provincial judge or a judge of the Superior Court of Justice;

"licence" means a marriage licence issued under this Act;

"Minister" means the minister responsible for the administration of this Act;

"prescribed" means prescribed by the regulations;

"regulations" means the regulations made under this Act;

"reserve" means a reserve as defined in the *Indian Act* (Canada).

**Application of Act to subsequent ceremonies**

(2) This Act does not apply in respect of any ceremony or form of marriage gone through by two persons who are married to each other by a marriage previously solemnized in accordance with this Act or recognized as valid in Ontario.

**Administration**

2. The administration of this Act is under the direction of the Minister.

**Delegation of powers and duties**

3. The Minister may delegate in writing any or all of his or her powers and duties under this Act to any person, subject to any restrictions set out in the delegation.

**Authority to marry**

4. No marriage may be solemnized except under the authority of a licence issued in accordance with this Act or the publication of banns.

**Who may marry**

5. (1) Any person who is of the age of majority may obtain a licence or be married under the authority of the publication of banns, provided no lawful cause exists to hinder the solemnization.

**Idem**

(2) No person shall issue a licence to a minor, or solemnize the marriage of a minor under the authority of the publication of banns, except where the minor is of the age of sixteen years or more and has the consent in writing of both parents in the form prescribed by the regulations.

**Giving of consent**

(3) The consent referred to in subsection (2) is not required in respect of a minor who was previously married and whose marriage was terminated by death or divorce.

**Idem**

(4) Where one of the parents of a minor is dead or both parents are living apart, the consent required by subsection (2) may be given by the parent having actual or legal custody of the minor.

**Idem**

(5) Where both parents of a minor are dead or are voluntary or involuntary patients in a psychiatric facility, the consent required by subsection (2) may be given by a lawfully appointed guardian or an acknowledged guardian who has brought up or who for the three years immediately preceding the intended marriage has supported the minor.

**Idem**

(6) Where a minor is made a ward of someone other than a parent by order of a court or under any Act, the consent required by subsection (2) may be given by the lawful guardian of the minor or person responsible for exercising the rights and duties of a guardian of the minor.

**Application to dispense with consent**

6. (1) Where a person whose consent is required by section 5 is not available or unreasonably or arbitrarily withholds consent, the person in respect of whose marriage the consent

is required may apply to a judge without the intervention of a litigation guardian for an order dispensing with the consent.

### Powers of judge

(2) The judge shall hear the application in a summary manner and may, in his or her discretion, make an order dispensing with the consent required by section 5.

### Persons lacking mental capacity

7. No person shall issue a licence to or solemnize the marriage of any person who, based on what he or she knows or has reasonable grounds to believe, lacks mental capacity to marry by reason of being under the influence of intoxicating liquor or drugs or for any other reason.

### Where dissolution of former marriage recognized in Ontario

8. (1) An applicant for a licence who has been previously married is entitled to be issued a licence if such marriage has been dissolved or annulled and such dissolution or annulment is recognized under the law of Ontario and the applicant otherwise complies with the requirements of this Act.

### Proof of divorce, etc.

(2) Subject to subsection (6), an issuer shall not issue a licence to a person whose previous marriage has been dissolved or annulled in Canada unless the person produces for inspection by the issuer,

(a) the final decree or judgment dissolving or annulling the previous marriage;

(b) a copy of the final decree, judgment or Act dissolving or annulling the previous marriage certified by the proper officer; or

(c) a certificate of divorce issued by the registrar under the Rules of Civil Procedure.

### Same

(2.1) Before issuing a licence, an issuer may require a person to whom subsection (2) applies to deposit with the issuer such material as the issuer considers relevant to the proof of the divorce or annulment.

### Where dissolution, etc., outside Canada

(3) Subject to subsection (6), no issuer shall issue a licence to a person whose previous marriage has been dissolved or annulled elsewhere than in Canada, unless the authorization in writing of the Minister is obtained upon the deposit of such material as the Minister may require.

### Review of refusal to issue licence

(4) Where an issuer refuses to issue a licence, or the Minister refuses to issue an authorization under subsection (3), the applicant may apply to the Divisional Court for judicial review under the *Judicial Review Procedure Act* and for an order directing that a licence be issued to the applicant and if the court finds that the applicant is so entitled it may make such an order.

### Parties

(5) The applicant, the Minister and such other persons as the court may order are parties to an application under subsection (4).

### Issue of licence under court order

(6) Where an applicant for a licence files with an issuer, together with his or her application, an order of the Divisional Court made on an application under subsection (4) directing that a licence be issued to the applicant, the issuer shall issue the licence.

### Order under *Declarations of Death Act, 2002*

9. (1) If an order has been made under the *Declarations of Death Act, 2002* declaring that a married person has died, the person to whom the deceased was married may, subject to the provisions of this Act, obtain a licence or be married under the authority of the publication of banns upon depositing a certified copy of the order with the person issuing the licence or solemnizing the marriage together with an affidavit in the required form.

### Exception

(2) Subsection (1) does not apply if the order is limited, under subsection 2(6) of the *Declarations of Death Act, 2002*, to specified purposes other than remarriage.

### Discretionary power of Minister

10. Despite anything in this Act, if the Minister considers that circumstances justify the issue of a licence in any particular case, the Minister may, in his or her absolute discretion, authorize the issue of the licence.

### Issuers

11. (1) Marriage licences may be issued by the clerk of every local municipality except a township.

### Interpretation

(1.1) In subsection (1) and clause (2)(a), "township" means a local municipality that had the status of a township on December 31, 2002 and, but for the enactment of the *Municipal Act, 2001*, would have had the status of a township on January, 1, 2003.

### Same

(2) If the Minister considers it expedient for the public convenience, the Minister may in writing appoint as an issuer,

(a) the clerk of a township, or a resident of a county or township adjacent thereto;

(b) a resident of a territorial district; or

> **Note: On a day to be named by proclamation of the Lieutenant Governor, subsection (2) is amended by striking out "or" at the end of clause (b). See: 2012, c. 8, Sched. 32, ss. 3, 9.**

(c) a member of a band, on the band council's recommendation.

> **Note: On a day to be named by proclamation of the Lieutenant Governor, subsection (2) is amended by adding "or" at the end of clause (c). See: 2012, c. 8, Sched. 32, ss. 3, 9.**
>
> **Note: On a day to be named by proclamation of the Lieutenant Governor, subsection (2) is amended by adding the following clause:**
>
> (d) any other person.
>
> **See: 2012. c. 8, Sched. 32, ss. 3, 9.**

### Deputy issuers

(3) An issuer may, with the approval in writing of the Minister or of the head of the council of the local municipality of which he or she is clerk, appoint in writing one or more deputies to act for him or her, and any such deputy while so acting has the power of the issuer appointing him or her.

### Notice of appointment of deputy

(4) The issuer shall, upon appointing a deputy, forthwith transmit to the Minister a notice of the appointment, and of the name and official position of the person by whom the appointment has been approved, and the Minister may at any time cancel the appointment.

(5) Repealed.

### Evidence on applications

**12.** (1) An issuer or the Minister may require evidence to identify any applicant or to establish his or her status and may examine, under oath if required, any applicant or other person as to any matter pertaining to the issue of a licence.

### Untrue information

(2) Where an issuer has reason to believe that any information set out in an application for a licence is untrue, he or she shall not issue the licence unless, on the production of such further evidence as the issuer may require, he or she is satisfied as to the truth of the information.

### Record of licences

**13.** (1) Every issuer shall keep in his or her office a record of the serial number and the date of issue of every licence issued by him or her, and the names and addresses of the parties to the intended marriage.

> **Note: On a day to be named by proclamation of the Lieutenant Governor, subsection (1) is repealed and the following substituted:**
>
> **Record of licences**
>
> (1) Every issuer shall keep in his or her office a record of every licence he or she issues and the record shall contain any particulars required by the regulations.
>
> **See: 2012, c. 8, Sched. 32, ss. 4, 9.**

### Searches

(2) Any person is entitled, upon application, to have a search made respecting any licence issued within three months immediately preceding the date of application.

### Information disclosed

(3) The search shall not disclose any information other than whether or not a licence has been issued and, if so, the date of issue of the licence.

### Documents to be forwarded to Registrar General

**14.** (1) Every issuer shall immediately upon issuing a licence and every person registered as authorized to solemnize marriage shall upon publishing banns forward to the Registrar General any documents required by the regulations.

### Interpretation

(2) In this section,

"Registrar General" means the Registrar General under the *Vital Statistics Act*.

### Oaths and affirmations

**15.** Issuers may administer oaths for the purposes of this Act.

### Indians

**16.** Where both parties to an intended marriage are Indians ordinarily resident on a reserve in Ontario or on Crown lands in Ontario, no fee shall be charged for the licence.

### Publication of banns

**17.** (1) Where a marriage is to be solemnized under the authority of the publication of banns, the intention to marry shall be proclaimed openly in an audible voice during divine service,

(a) where the parties are in the habit of attending worship at the same church, being within Canada, at that church; or

(b) where the parties are in the habit of attending worship in different churches, being within Canada, in each such church.

### Method and time of publication

(2) The banns shall be published according to the usage of the denomination, faith or creed of the church in which they are published and during divine Sunday service.

### Exception

(3) Where the usage of any denomination, faith or creed substitutes any other day as the usual and principal day of the week for the celebration of divine service, the banns shall be published on such other day.

### Proof

(4) The person or persons who publish banns shall certify proof thereof in the prescribed form.

## Where banns not to be published

**18.** Banns shall not be published where either of the parties to the intended marriage has been married and the marriage has been dissolved or annulled.

## Prohibited degrees

**19.** If the regulations prescribe a form setting out the relationships by consanguinity or adoption that, under the *Marriage (Prohibited Degrees) Act* (Canada), bar the lawful solemnization of marriage, the form shall be endorsed on the licence and on the proof of publication of banns.

## Who may solemnize marriage

**20.** (1) No person shall solemnize a marriage unless he or she is authorized by or under section 24 or is registered under this section as a person authorized to solemnize marriage.

## Application for registration

(2) Upon application the Minister may, subject to subsection (3), register any person as a person authorized to solemnize marriage.

## Who may be registered

(3) No person shall be registered unless it appears to the Minister,

(a) that the person has been ordained or appointed according to the rites and usages of the religious body to which he or she belongs, or is, by the rules of that religious body, deemed ordained or appointed;

(b) that the person is duly recognized by the religious body to which he or she belongs as entitled to solemnize marriage according to its rites and usages;

(c) that the religious body to which the person belongs is permanently established both as to the continuity of its existence and as to its rites and ceremonies; and

(d) that the person is resident in Ontario or has his or her parish or pastoral charge in whole or in part in Ontario; provided that in the case of a person who is in Ontario temporarily and who, if resident in Ontario, might be registered under this section, the Minister may register him or her as authorized to solemnize marriage during a period to be fixed by the Minister.

## Where no person authorized to solemnize marriage

(4) Despite subsection (1), where it appears to the Minister that the doctrines of a religious body described in clause (3)(c) do not recognize any person as authorized to solemnize marriage, the Minister may register a person duly designated by the governing authority of the religious body who shall, in respect of marriages performed according to the rites, usages and customs of the religious body, perform all the duties imposed by this Act upon a person solemnizing a marriage, other than solemnizing the marriage.

## Idem

(5) Where a person registered under subsection (4) performs the duties imposed by subsection (4), every marriage solemnized according to the rites, usages and customs of the religious body is valid.

## Rights of person registered

(6) A person registered under this section is not required to solemnize a marriage, to allow a sacred place to be used for solemnizing a marriage or for an event related to the solemnization of a marriage, or to otherwise assist in the solemnization of a marriage, if to do so would be contrary to,

(a) the person's religious beliefs; or

(b) the doctrines, rites, usages or customs of the religious body to which the person belongs.

## Definition

(7) In subsection (6),

"sacred place" includes a place of worship and any ancillary or accessory facilities.

## Register

**21.** (1) The Minister shall keep a register of the name of every person registered as a person authorized to solemnize marriage, the date of such registration, and such other particulars as the Minister considers advisable.

## Certificate of registration

(2) The Minister may issue a certificate of registration under this section in the prescribed form.

## Cancellation of registration

**22.** (1) Where it appears to the Minister that any person registered as authorized to solemnize marriage has ceased to possess the qualifications entitling him or her to be so registered, or for any other cause, the Minister may cancel the registration.

## Notice of change

(2) Every religious body, members of which are registered under this Act, shall notify the Minister of the name of every such member so registered who has died or has ceased to reside in Ontario or has ceased to be associated with such religious body.

## Publication of registration and cancellation

**23.** When a person is registered under this Act as authorized to solemnize marriage, and when any such registration is cancelled, the Minister shall publish notice thereof in *The Ontario Gazette*.

## Civil marriage

**24.** (1) A judge, a justice of the peace or any other person of a class designated by the regulations may solemnize marriages under the authority of a licence.

(2) Repealed.

### Form of ceremony

(3) No particular form of ceremony is required except that in some part of the ceremony, in the presence of the person solemnizing the marriage and witnesses, each of the parties shall declare:

I do solemnly declare that I do not know of any lawful impediment why I, AB, may not be joined in matrimony to CD,

Je déclare solennellement que moi, AB, je ne connais aucun empêchement légal à mon mariage avec CD,

and each of the parties shall say to the other:

I call upon these persons here present to witness that I, AB, do take you, CD, to be my lawful wedded wife (*or* to be my lawful wedded husband *or* to be my lawful wedded partner *or* to be my lawful wedded spouse),

Je demande aux personnes qui sont ici présentes d'être témoins que moi, AB, je prends CD comme légitime épouse (*ou* comme légitime époux *ou* comme partenaire conjugal légitime *ou* comme légitime conjoint(e)),

after which the person solemnizing the marriage shall say:

I, EF, by virtue of the powers vested in me by the *Marriage Act*, do hereby pronounce you AB and CD to be married,

En vertu des pouvoirs qui me sont conférés par la *Loi sur le mariage*, moi, EF, je vous déclare mariés(ées), AB et CD.

### Language

(4) For the purposes of subsection (3), it is sufficient to use only the English or only the French language.

### Attendance of parties and witnesses

**25.** Every marriage shall be solemnized in the presence of the parties and at least two witnesses who shall affix their names as witnesses to the entry in the register made under section 28.

### Proof of publication

**26.** No marriage shall be solemnized under the authority of the publication of banns unless proof of publication by the person or persons publishing the banns has been deposited with the person solemnizing the marriage.

### Time for solemnization

**27.** (1) Repealed.

### Idem: under banns

(2) A marriage shall not be solemnized under the authority of the publication of banns, earlier than the fifth day after the date of the publication of banns.

### Time within which marriage to be solemnized

(3) A marriage shall be solemnized only within the three months immediately following the issue of the licence or the publication of banns, as the case may be.

### Entry in marriage register

**28.** (1) Every person shall immediately after he or she has solemnized a marriage,

(a) where the marriage was solemnized in a church, enter in the church register kept for the purpose; or

(b) where the marriage was solemnized elsewhere than in the church, enter in a register kept by him or her for the purpose,

the particulars prescribed by the regulations, and the entry shall be authenticated by his or her signature and those of the parties and witnesses.

### Record of marriage

(2) Every person who solemnizes a marriage shall, at the time of the marriage, if required by either of the parties, give a record of solemnization of the marriage specifying the names of the parties, the date of the marriage, the names of the witnesses, and whether the marriage was solemnized under the authority of a licence or publication of banns.

### Supply of marriage registers

**29.** (1) Every person or religious body authorized to solemnize marriages may apply to the Minister for a marriage register, and the Minister shall thereupon supply the register.

### Property of Crown

(2) Every register supplied by the Minister is the property of the Crown.

### Protection of persons solemnizing marriage in good faith

**30.** No person who solemnizes or purports to solemnize a marriage is subject to any action or liability by reason of there having been any legal impediment to the marriage unless, at the time the person performed the ceremony, he or she was aware of the impediment.

### Marriages solemnized in good faith

**31.** If the parties to a marriage solemnized in good faith and intended to be in compliance with this Act are not under a legal disqualification to contract such marriage and after such solemnization have lived together and cohabited as a married couple, such marriage shall be deemed a valid marriage, although the person who solemnized the marriage was not authorized to solemnize marriage, and despite the absence of or any irregularity or insufficiency in the publication of banns or the issue of the licence.

### Breach of promise of marriage abolished

**32.** (1) No action shall be brought for a breach of a promise to marry or for any damages resulting therefrom.

### Application of subs. (1)

(2) Subsection (1) does not apply in respect of actions for breach of promise to marry or damages resulting therefrom commenced before the 1st day of August, 1978.

### Recovery of gifts made in contemplation of marriage

**33.** Where one person makes a gift to another in contemplation of or conditional upon their marriage to each other and the marriage fails to take place or is abandoned, the question of whether or not the failure or abandonment was caused by or was the fault of the donor shall not be considered in determining the right of the donor to recover the gift.

### Powers of Minister

**33.1** (1) The Minister may by order,

(a) set and collect fees for services that the Minister provides under this Act; and

(b) provide for the waiver of payment of those fees in favour of any person or class of persons.

### Orders are not regulations

(2) An order made under this section is not a regulation for the purposes of Part III (Regulations) of the *Legislation Act, 2006*.

### Regulations

**34.** The Lieutenant Governor in Council may make regulations,

(a) prescribing any matter required or permitted by this Act to be prescribed by the regulations;

(b) requiring the payment of fees in respect of any matter required or authorized to be done under this Act, other than for services provided by the Minister;

(c) providing for the retention of fees or a portion of the fees by issuers and persons solemnizing marriages or any class of either of them and for the commutation of such fees;

(d) prescribing the duties of issuers;

(d.1) respecting the particulars that shall be contained in a record under subsection 13(1);

(d.2) respecting the documents that shall be forwarded to the Registrar General under subsection 14(1);

(e) requiring persons authorized to solemnize marriages to furnish such information and returns as are prescribed;

(f) Repealed.

(g) designating classes of persons authorized to solemnize marriages under section 24.

### Penalty: false statements

**35.** (1) Every person who knowingly makes any false statement in any document required under this Act, in addition to any other penalty or punishment to which the person may be liable, is guilty of an offence and on conviction is liable to a fine of not more than $1,000 or to imprisonment for a term of not more than one year, or to both.

### Idem: general

(2) Every person who contravenes any provision of this Act for which no other penalty is provided is guilty of an offence and on conviction is liable to a fine of not more than $500.

**Form Repealed.**

# Civil Marriage Act

SC 2005, c 33

An Act respecting certain aspects of legal capacity for marriage for civil purposes

## Preamble

WHEREAS the Parliament of Canada is committed to upholding the Constitution of Canada, and section 15 of the *Canadian Charter of Rights and Freedoms* guarantees that every individual is equal before and under the law and has the right to equal protection and equal benefit of the law without discrimination;

WHEREAS the courts in a majority of the provinces and in one territory have recognized that the right to equality without discrimination requires that couples of the same sex and couples of the opposite sex have equal access to marriage for civil purposes;

WHEREAS the Supreme Court of Canada has recognized that many Canadian couples of the same sex have married in reliance on those court decisions;

WHEREAS only equal access to marriage for civil purposes would respect the right of couples of the same sex to equality without discrimination, and civil union, as an institution other than marriage, would not offer them that equal access and would violate their human dignity, in breach of the *Canadian Charter of Rights and Freedoms*;

WHEREAS the Supreme Court of Canada has determined that the Parliament of Canada has legislative jurisdiction over marriage but does not have the jurisdiction to establish an institution other than marriage for couples of the same sex;

WHEREAS everyone has the freedom of conscience and religion under section 2 of the *Canadian Charter of Rights and Freedoms*;

WHEREAS nothing in this Act affects the guarantee of freedom of conscience and religion and, in particular, the freedom of members of religious groups to hold and declare their religious beliefs and the freedom of officials of religious groups to refuse to perform marriages that are not in accordance with their religious beliefs;

WHEREAS it is not against the public interest to hold and publicly express diverse views on marriage;

WHEREAS, in light of those considerations, the Parliament of Canada's commitment to uphold the right to equality without discrimination precludes the use of section 33 of the *Canadian Charter of Rights and Freedoms* to deny the right of couples of the same sex to equal access to marriage for civil purposes;

WHEREAS marriage is a fundamental institution in Canadian society and the Parliament of Canada has a responsibility to support that institution because it strengthens commitment in relationships and represents the foundation of family life for many Canadians;

AND WHEREAS, in order to reflect values of tolerance, respect and equality consistent with the *Canadian Charter of Rights and Freedoms*, access to marriage for civil purposes should be extended by legislation to couples of the same sex;

NOW, THEREFORE, Her Majesty, by and with the advice and consent of the Senate and House of Commons of Canada, enacts as follows:

## Short title

**1.** This Act may be cited as the *Civil Marriage Act.*

## PART 1  MARRIAGE

### Marriage — certain aspects of capacity

**2.** Marriage, for civil purposes, is the lawful union of two persons to the exclusion of all others.

### Religious officials

**3.** It is recognized that officials of religious groups are free to refuse to perform marriages that are not in accordance with their religious beliefs.

### Freedom of conscience and religion and expression of beliefs

**3.1** For greater certainty, no person or organization shall be deprived of any benefit, or be subject to any obligation or sanction, under any law of the Parliament of Canada solely by reason of their exercise, in respect of marriage between persons of the same sex, of the freedom of conscience and religion guaranteed under the *Canadian Charter of Rights and Freedoms* or the expression of their beliefs in respect of marriage as the union of a man and woman to the exclusion of all others based on that guaranteed freedom.

### Marriage not void or voidable

4. For greater certainty, a marriage is not void or voidable by reason only that the spouses are of the same sex.

### Marriage of non-resident persons

5. (1) A marriage that is performed in Canada and that would be valid in Canada if the spouses were domiciled in Canada is valid for the purposes of Canadian law even though either or both of the spouses do not, at the time of the marriage, have the capacity to enter into it under the law of their respective state of domicile.

### Retroactivity

(2) Subsection (1) applies retroactively to a marriage that would have been valid under the law that was applicable in the province where the marriage was performed but for the lack of capacity of either or both of the spouses to enter into it under the law of their respective state of domicile.

### Order dissolving marriage

(3) Any court order, made in Canada or elsewhere before the coming into force of this subsection, that declares the marriage to be null and void or that grants a divorce to the spouses dissolves the marriage, for the purposes of Canadian law, as of the day on which the order takes effect.

## PART 2 DISSOLUTION OF MARRIAGE FOR NON-RESIDENT SPOUSES

### Definition of "court"

6. In this Part, "court," in respect of a province, means

(a) for Ontario, the Superior Court of Justice;

(b) for Quebec, the Superior Court;

(c) for Nova Scotia and British Columbia, the Supreme Court of the province;

(d) for New Brunswick, Manitoba, Saskatchewan and Alberta, the Court of Queen's Bench for the province;

(e) for Prince Edward Island and Newfoundland and Labrador, the trial division of the Supreme Court of the province; and

(f) for Yukon and the Northwest Territories, the Supreme Court, and in Nunavut, the Nunavut Court of Justice.

It also means any other court in the province whose judges are appointed by the Governor General and that is designated by the Lieutenant Governor in Council of the province as a court for the purposes of this Part.

### Divorce—non-resident spouses

7. (1) The court of the province where the marriage was performed may, on application, grant the spouses a divorce if

(a) there has been a breakdown of the marriage as established by the spouses having lived separate and apart for at least one year before the making of the application;

(b) neither spouse resides in Canada at the time the application is made; and

(c) each of the spouses is residing—and for at least one year immediately before the application is made, has resided—in a state where a divorce cannot be granted because that state does not recognize the validity of the marriage.

### Application

(2) The application may be made by both spouses jointly or by one of the spouses with the other spouse's consent or, in the absence of that consent, on presentation of an order from the court or a court located in the state where one of the spouses resides that declares that the other spouse

(a) is incapable of making decisions about his or her civil status because of a mental disability;

(b) is unreasonably withholding consent; or

(c) cannot be found.

### Exception if spouse is found

(3) Despite paragraph (2)(c), the other spouse's consent is required if that spouse is found in connection with the service of the application.

### No corollary relief

8. For greater certainty, the *Divorce Act* does not apply to a divorce granted under this Act.

### Effective date generally

9. (1) A divorce takes effect on the day on which the judgment granting the divorce is rendered.

### Certificate of divorce

(2) After a divorce takes effect, the court must, on request, issue to any person a certificate that a divorce granted under this Act dissolved the marriage of the specified persons effective as of a specified date.

### Conclusive proof

(3) The certificate, or a certified copy of it, is conclusive proof of the facts so certified without proof of the signature or authority of the person appearing to have signed the certificate.

### Legal effect throughout Canada

10. On taking effect, a divorce granted under this Act has legal effect throughout Canada.

### Marriage dissolved

**11.** On taking effect, a divorce granted under this Act dissolves the marriage of the spouses.

**11.1** Repealed.

### Definition of "competent authority"

**12.** (1) In this section, "competent authority", in respect of a court in a province, means the body, person or group of persons ordinarily competent under the laws of that province to make rules regulating the practice and procedure in that court.

### Rules

(2) Subject to subsection (3), the competent authority may make rules applicable to any applications made under this Part in a court in a province, including rules

(a) regulating the practice and procedure in the court;

(b) respecting the conduct and disposition of any applications that are made under this Part without an oral hearing;

(c) prescribing and regulating the duties of the officers of the court; and

(d) prescribing and regulating any other matter considered expedient to attain the ends of justice and carry into effect the purposes and provisions of this Part.

### Exercise of power

(3) The power of a competent authority to make rules for a court must be exercised in the like manner and subject to the like terms and conditions, if any, as the power to make rules for that court that are conferred on that authority by the laws of the province.

### Not statutory instruments

(4) Rules that are made under this section by a competent authority that is not a judicial or quasi-judicial body are deemed not to be statutory instruments within the meaning and for the purposes of the *Statutory Instruments Act*.

### Regulations

**13.** (1) The Governor in Council may make regulations for carrying out the purposes and provisions of this Part, including regulations providing for uniformity in the rules made under section 12.

### Regulations prevail

(2) Any regulations that are made to provide for uniformity in the rules prevail over those rules.

**14.** Repealed.

**15.** Repealed.

# Spousal Support Advisory Guidelines

July 2008

## EXECUTIVE SUMMARY

The **Spousal Support Advisory Guidelines** were developed to bring more certainty and predictability to the determination of spousal support under the federal *Divorce Act*. The Advisory Guidelines project has been supported by the federal Department of Justice. The Advisory Guidelines were released three years ago, in January 2005, in the form of a Draft Proposal and have been used across Canada since then. Comments and feedback were provided and some revisions made. This document is the final version.

The *Spousal Support Advisory Guidelines* are very different from the *Federal Child Support Guidelines*. They **have not been legislated** by the federal government. They are informal guidelines that will operate on **an advisory basis only**. The Advisory Guidelines will be used to determine the amount and duration of spousal support within the existing legal framework of the *Divorce Act* and the judicial decisions interpreting its provisions. The Guidelines are not legally binding and their adoption and use will be voluntary. They are intended as a practical tool to assist spouses, lawyers, mediators and judges in determining the amount and duration of spousal support in typical cases. The various components of the Guidelines—the basic formulas, restructuring, and exceptions—are intended to build upon current practice, reflecting best practices and emerging trends across the country. The process of developing the Advisory Guidelines is described in Chapter 2.

An overview of the structure of the Guidelines is found in Chapter 3.

The Advisory Guidelines do **not** deal with **entitlement**, just amount and duration once entitlement has been found. A mere disparity of income that would generate an amount under the Guidelines does not automatically lead to entitlement. As is set out in Chapter 4, there must be a finding (or an agreement) on entitlement, on a compensatory or non-compensatory or contractual basis, *before* the formulas and the rest of the Guidelines are applied. The basis of entitlement is important, not only as a threshold issue, but also to determine location within the formula ranges or to justify departure

from the ranges as an exception. Entitlement issues also arise frequently on review and variation, especially applications to terminate support.

Some limitations on the application of the Guidelines are dealt with in Chapter 5. The Advisory Guidelines have been developed specifically for use under the federal *Divorce Act*. **Provincial/territorial laws** differ in some respects and any use of these Guidelines in the provincial/territorial context must take account of these distinctive statutes, especially on matters of entitlement for unmarried couples and agreements. A **prior agreement** may limit the application of the Guidelines, as the Advisory Guidelines cannot be used to override existing agreements, especially agreements that time limit or waive spousal support.

There are two basic formulas in the proposal: the ***without child support* formula** and the ***with child support* formula**. The dividing line between the two is the absence or presence of a dependent child or children of the marriage, and a concurrent child support obligation, at the time spousal support is determined. Both formulas use **income sharing** as the method for determining the amount of spousal support, not budgets. The formulas produce **ranges** for the amount and duration of support, not just a single number. The precise number chosen within that range is a matter for negotiation or adjudication, depending upon the facts of a particular case.

The starting point under both formulas is the definition of **income** used in the *Federal Child Support Guidelines*, subject to some minor adjustments for spousal support purposes, explained in Chapter 6.

The ***without child support* formula**, set out below, is built around two crucial factors: the **gross income difference** between the spouses and the **length of the marriage**. Both the amount and the duration of support increase incrementally with the length of the marriage, as can be seen in the summary box below. The idea that explains this formula is **merger over time**: as a marriage lengthens, spouses more deeply merge their economic and non-economic lives, with each spouse making countless decisions to mould his or her skills, behaviours and finances around those of the other spouse.

The gross income difference measures their differential loss of the marital standard of living at the end of the marriage. The formulas for both amount and duration reflect the idea that the longer the marriage, the more the lower income spouse should be protected against such a differential loss. Merger over time captures both the compensatory and non-compensatory spousal support objectives that have been recognized by our law since *Moge* and *Bracklow*.

---

**The *Without Child Support* Formula**

**Amount** ranges from 1.5 to 2 percent of the difference between the spouses' gross incomes (the **gross income difference**) for each year of marriage (or, more precisely, years of cohabitation), up to a maximum of 50 percent. The maximum range remains fixed for marriages 25 years or longer at 37.5 to 50 percent of income difference. (The upper end of this maximum range is capped at the amount that would result in equalization of the spouses' net incomes—the **net income cap**.)

**Duration** ranges from .5 to 1 year for each year of marriage. However, support will be **indefinite (duration not specified)** if the marriage is **20 years or longer** in duration *or*, if the marriage has lasted 5 years or longer, when the years of marriage and age of the support recipient (at separation) added together total 65 or more (the **rule of 65**).

---

Chapter 7 contains examples of the application of the *without child support* formula and the ranges it produces for marriages of different lengths and incomes.

Cases with dependent children and concurrent child support obligations require a different formula, the **with child support formula**, set out in Chapter 8. These cases raise different considerations: priority must be given to child support; there is usually reduced ability to pay; and particular tax and benefit issues arise. The rationale for spousal support is also different. Where there are dependent children, the primary rationale is compensatory, as both *Moge* and *Bracklow* made clear. What drives support is not the length of the marriage, or marital interdependency, or merger over time, but the presence of dependent children and the need to provide care and support for those children. This **parental partnership** rationale looks at not just past loss, but also at the continuing economic disadvantage that flows from present and future child care responsibilities, anchored in s. 15.2(6)(b) of the *Divorce Act*.

There are three important differences between the *without child support* formula and the *with child support* formula. First, the *with child support* formula uses the **net incomes** of the spouses, not their gross incomes. Second, this formula divides the **pool** of combined net incomes between the two spouses,

not the gross income difference. Third, the upper and lower percentage limits of net income division in the *with child support* formula **do not change with the length of the marriage**.

Set out below is a summary version of the **basic *with child support* formula**, used to determine the amount of spousal support to be paid where the payor spouse pays both child and spousal support to the lower income recipient spouse who is also the parent with custody or primary care of the children.

---

**The Basic *With Child Support* Formula for Amount**

(1) Determine the individual net disposable income (INDI) of each spouse:

- Guidelines Income *minus* Child Support *minus* Taxes and Deductions = Payor's INDI
- Guidelines Income *minus* Notional Child Support *minus* Taxes and Deductions *Plus* Government Benefits and Credits = Recipient's INDI

(2) Add together the individual net disposable incomes. By iteration, determine the range of spousal support amounts that would be required to leave the lower income recipient spouse with between 40 and 46 percent of the combined INDI.

---

Net income computations like these require computer software. Basic to this formula is the concept of **individual net disposable income**, an attempt to isolate a **pool** of net disposable income available after adjustment for each spouse's child support obligations. This is done by deducting or backing out their respective **contributions to child support**. The details of these calculations are set out in Chapter 8, along with several examples.

**Duration** under this basic *with child support* formula also reflects the underlying parental partnership rationale. Initial orders are **indefinite (duration not specified)**, subject to the usual process of review or variation. The formula does, however, provide a **durational range** which is intended to structure the process of review and variation and to limit the cumulative duration of spousal support. The durational limits under this formula can be thought of as "soft" time limits. There are two tests for duration and whichever produces the longer duration at each end of the range is to be employed:

- First is the **length-of-marriage** test, which is modelled on the duration under the *without child support* formula, i.e. one-half to one year of support for every year of marriage, and which will likely govern for most marriages of ten years or more.

- Second is the **age-of-children** test. The lower end of the durational range is until the youngest child starts full-time school. The upper end of the durational range is until the last or youngest child finishes high school. This test will typically apply to marriages of less than ten years.

**Shared and split custody** situations require slight variations in the computation of individual net disposable income, as the backing out of child support obligations is a bit more complicated. There is also a different, hybrid formula for cases where **spousal support is paid by the custodial parent**. Under this formula, the spouses' Guidelines incomes are reduced by the grossed-up amount of child support (actual or notional) and then the *without child support* formula is applied to determine amount and duration. Finally, there is one more hybrid formula for those spousal support cases where the child support for **adult children** is determined under section 3(2)(b) of the *Child Support Guidelines.*

The formulas provide ranges for the amount and duration of spousal support. The location of a precise amount or duration within those ranges—what we refer to as **using the ranges**—will be driven by the **factors** detailed in Chapter 9: the strength of any compensatory claim; the recipient's needs; the age, number, need and standard of living of any children; the needs and ability to pay or the payor; work incentives for the payor; property division and debts; and self-sufficiency incentives.

**Restructuring** allows the amount and duration under the formulas to be traded off against each other, so long as the overall value of the restructured award remains within the total or global amounts generated by the formula when amount and duration are combined. Chapter 10 shows how restructuring can be used in three different ways:

- to **front-end load** awards by increasing the amount beyond the formula's range and shortening duration;
- to **extend duration** beyond the formula's range by lowering the monthly amount; or
- to formulate a **lump sum** by combining amount and duration.

**"Ceilings" and "floors"** in Chapter 11 define the boundaries of the typical incomes to which the formulas can be applied. The **ceiling** is the income level for the payor spouse above which any formula gives way to discretion, set here at **a gross annual income for the payor of $350,000**. The **floor** is the income level for the payor below which no support is usually paid, here set at **$20,000**. To avoid a cliff effect, there is an **exception** for cases where the payor spouse's gross income is **more than $20,000 but less than $30,000**, where spousal support may not be awarded or may be reduced below the low end of the range. An additional **exception** is also

necessary, to allow an award of spousal support **below the income floor** in particular cases.

Any formula, even with restructuring, will have its limits and there will always be exceptional cases. Because the Guidelines are only advisory, departures are always possible on a case-by-case basis where the formula outcomes are inappropriate. The Guidelines do contain a short list of **exceptions** in Chapter 12, intended to identify common categories of departures:

- compelling financial circumstances in the interim period;
- debt payment;
- prior support obligations;
- illness and disability;
- the compensatory exception in short marriages without children;
- reapportionment of property (British Columbia);
- basic needs/hardship under the *without child support* and *custodial payor* formulas;
- non-taxable payor income;
- non-primary parent to fulfil parenting role under the *custodial payor* formula;
- special needs of a child; and
- section 15.3 for small amounts and inadequate compensation under the *with child support* formula.

Self-sufficiency is a central concept in the law of spousal support and Chapter 13 draws together in one place all the aspects of the Advisory Guidelines that promote self-sufficiency, one of the objectives of the *Divorce Act.*

The formulas are intended to apply to initial orders and to the negotiation of initial agreements, including interim arrangements. Given the uncertain state of the current law, it is not possible to make the Advisory Guidelines apply to the full range of issues that can arise on **variation and review**, issues that are considered in Chapter 14. The Advisory Guidelines can be applied on applications to reduce spousal support because of changes in income, for example, when the payor spouse's income goes down or the recipient spouse's income goes up (or ought to have gone up). In some cases, one spouse may wish to apply to vary to **cross over** between the two formulas, mostly in longer marriages once the children are no longer dependent, where the *without child support* formula produces higher ranges.

More difficult issues arise where the payor's income increases or the recipient's income is reduced after separation. The most the formula can do is to establish an upper limit upon any increase in spousal support in such cases. At the present time, no formula can be constructed to resolve issues around the recipient spouse's remarriage or re-partnering, or subsequent children.

Quebec has different guidelines for determining child support, which have an impact on spousal support determinations. The application of the Advisory Guidelines to *Divorce Act* cases in Quebec raises special issues that are dealt with in Chapter 15.

## 3 AN OVERVIEW OF THE ADVISORY GUIDELINES

Spousal support guidelines can be structured in many different ways. For those who are interested, the Background Paper reviews in detail other models of spousal support guidelines. This chapter presents a structural overview of this scheme of Advisory Guidelines. Some of what you will find here has already been touched on, in a less systematic way, in Chapter 2. As well, many of the individual components of the Advisory Guidelines will be discussed more extensively in subsequent chapters. However, we thought it would be helpful for readers to have a sense of the big picture at the beginning.

We begin with a discussion of the basic concept of income sharing on which the Advisory Guidelines are constructed and then move into an organized, step-by-step review of the specific components of the Advisory Guidelines. We have divided this review into three main sections. First, we deal with the preliminary issues that arise *before* any consideration of the formulas—what might be called issues of application. Then we deal with the basic structure of the income-sharing formulas for determination of amount and duration of support that are at the heart of the proposed approach. The outcomes generated by the formulas are not necessarily determinative, however. The final section deals with the steps that can be taken *after* the formula calculations: locating a specific amount or duration within the ranges, restructuring the formula outcomes (by trading off amount against duration), and departing from the amounts and durations generated by the formulas, through exceptions.

### 3.1 Income Sharing

The core concept on which the Spousal Support Advisory Guidelines are built is **income sharing**. Under the Advisory Guidelines, budgets play a diminished role in determining spousal support outcomes. Instead the Advisory Guidelines look primarily to the incomes of the parties and rely on a mathematical formula to determine the portion of spousal incomes to be shared. Contrary to common perception, **income sharing does not mean equal sharing**. There are many ways of sharing income; it all depends on the formula that is adopted.

You will see below that other factors are also relevant in determining support outcomes under the Advisory Guidelines, such as the presence of dependent children or the length of the marriage. But the income levels of the parties and, and more specifically the income disparity between them, become the primary determinants of support outcomes. Under the Spousal Support Advisory Guidelines, as under the *Child Support Guidelines*, the precise determination of income, including the imputing of income, becomes a much more significant issue than it has been in the past.

**Income sharing here is a method, and not a new theory of spousal support.** As we have noted earlier, the Advisory Guidelines project has not been driven by a desire to theoretically reorder the law of spousal support. Rather it has been driven by the practical needs of family law practitioners and judges who deal with the daily dilemmas of advising, negotiating, litigating and deciding spousal support.

It is therefore important to emphasize that **the use of income sharing as a method** for determining the amount of spousal support does not necessarily imply adoption of the income-sharing theories of spousal support identified in the Background Paper. Some of these theories, which are admittedly contentious, rest upon a view of marriage as a relationship of trust and community, which justifies treating marital incomes as joint incomes.

The method of income sharing can be used, however, as a practical and efficient way of implementing many support objectives such as compensation for the economic advantages and disadvantages of the marriage or the recognition of need and economic dependency. Such use of proxy measures already exists in spousal support law—think of the prevalent use of standard of living and a "needs and means" analysis to quantify compensatory support.

The Guidelines do not commit to any particular theory of spousal support. As will become clear in the discussion of the different formulas under these Advisory Guidelines, they aim to accommodate the multiple theories that now inform our law and, to generate results that are in broad conformity with existing patterns in the law.

We now move on to an overview of the basic framework of the specific scheme of income sharing found in the Advisory Guidelines.

### 3.2 Preliminary Issues—The Applicability of the Advisory Guidelines

#### 3.2.1 Form and force

Unlike the *Federal Child Support Guidelines*, the Spousal Support Advisory Guidelines **have not been legislated**. Following the practice in some American jurisdictions, these are **informal guidelines. They are not legally binding. Their use is completely voluntary.** They have been and will be adopted by lawyers and judges to the extent they find them useful, and will operate as a practical tool within **the existing legal framework**. As non-legislated, informal guidelines, these Guidelines are **advisory only**. They are intended as a **starting point** for negotiation and adjudication.

#### 3.2.2 Entitlement

The Advisory Guidelines do **not** deal with entitlement. The informal status of the Guidelines means that they must remain subject to the entitlement provisions of the *Divorce Act*, notably ss. 15.2(4) and (6) as interpreted by the courts. Entitlement therefore remains a threshold issue to be determined before the guidelines will be applicable.

**On its own, a mere disparity of income that would generate an amount under the Advisory Guidelines formulas, does not automatically lead to entitlement.** There must be a finding (or an agreement) on entitlement, on a compensatory or non-compensatory or contractual basis, *before* the formulas and the rest of the Guidelines are applied.

The Advisory Guidelines were drafted on the assumption that the current law of spousal support, post-*Bracklow*, continues to offer a very expansive basis for entitlement to spousal support. Effectively any significant income disparity generates an entitlement to some support, leaving amount and duration as the main issues to be determined in spousal support cases. However, the Guidelines leave the issue of when an income disparity is significant, in the sense of signalling entitlement, to the courts. It is open to a court to find no entitlement on a particular set of facts, despite income disparity, and the Advisory Guidelines do not speak to that issue.

The basis of entitlement is important, not only as a threshold issue, but also to determine location within the formula ranges or to justify departure from the ranges as an exception. Entitlement issues also arise frequently on review and variation, especially applications to terminate support.

Entitlement is dealt with in Chapter 4.

### 3.2.3  Application to provincial/territorial law

The Advisory Guidelines have specifically been developed under the federal *Divorce Act* and are intended for use under that legislation. Provincial/territorial support law is governed by distinct statutory regimes. However, in practice there is much overlap between federal and provincial/territorial support laws.

The broad conceptual framework for spousal support articulated by the Supreme Court of Canada in *Moge* and *Bracklow* has been relied upon under both provincial and federal legislation. Indeed *Bracklow*, which combined claims under the *Divorce Act* and provincial legislation, made no real distinction between the two. Given this overlap, the Advisory Guidelines have been used under provincial/territorial support legislation.

There are some distinctive features of provincial/territorial spousal support laws that need to be taken into account when using the Advisory Guidelines. Many provincial/territorial laws have specific provisions governing entitlement, for example provisions determining which non-marital relationships give rise to a spousal support obligation. Like other issues of entitlement discussed above, this must be a threshold determination before the Advisory Guidelines are applied to determine amount and duration of support. We also note that the list of specific factors to be considered in determining spousal support does vary from statute to statute, with some provincial/territorial legislation making explicit reference, for example, to factors such as property and conduct, although the impact of these differences in wording on spousal support outcomes is unclear.

Provincial laws differ from the *Divorce Act* in their application to unmarried couples but this should not cause any difficulties with respect to the operation of the Advisory Guidelines. Although we conveniently refer to "length of marriage" as a relevant factor in the operation of the formulas, the formulas actually rely upon the period of spousal cohabitation (including any periods of pre-marital cohabitation), thus easily meshing with provincial/territorial legislation.

The application of the Advisory Guidelines under provincial/territorial legislation is dealt with in Chapter 5.

### 3.2.4  Application to agreements

The Advisory Guidelines **do not confer any power to reopen or override final agreements on spousal support**. This issue, like entitlement, is outside the scope of the Advisory Guidelines and will continue to be dealt with under the common law doctrine of unconscionability, provincial/territorial statutes and the evolving interpretation of the Supreme Court of Canada's recent decision in *Miglin*.[33] Agreements limiting or waiving spousal support may therefore preclude the application of the Guidelines.

If a final agreement is set aside or overridden under existing law, the Advisory Guidelines *may* be of assistance in determining the amount and duration of support, although the intentions of the parties as reflected in the agreement may also continue to influence the outcome.

As well, the Advisory Guidelines *may* be applicable if a spousal support agreement provides for review or variation.

Further discussion of the application of the Advisory Guidelines in the cases where there are spousal support agreements can be found in Chapters 5 and 14.

### 3.2.5  Interim orders

The Advisory Guidelines are intended to apply to interim orders as well as final orders. We anticipate, in fact, that they will be particularly valuable at the interim stage, which is now dominated by a needs-and-means analysis—budgets, expenses and deficits that require individualized decision making.

**Any periods of interim support clearly have to be included within the durational limits set by the Advisory Guidelines.** Otherwise, if duration were only to be fixed in final orders, there would be incentives in both directions—for some to drag out proceedings and for others to speed them up—and general inequity. Interim support is discussed in Chapter 5.

The Advisory Guidelines do recognize that the amount may need to be set differently during the interim period while parties are sorting out their financial situation immediately after

---

33  *Miglin v. Miglin*, [2003] 1 S.C.R. 303.

separation. To accommodate these short-term concerns, the Guidelines recognize an exception for compelling financial circumstances in the interim period, considered in Chapter 12.

### 3.2.6 Review and variation

The primary application of the Advisory Guidelines is to **initial determinations** of spousal support at the point of separation or divorce, whether through negotiated agreements or court orders. Ideally a truly comprehensive set of guidelines would apply not only to the initial determination of support but also to subsequent reviews and variations over time. However, these issues have proven the most difficult to reduce to a formula given the uncertainty in the current law concerning the effect of post-separation income changes, remarriage and repartnering, and subsequent children.

In the end, we chose a more modest course, identifying certain situations where the Advisory Guidelines can apply on reviews and variations, including increases in the recipient's income and decreases in the payor's income. We have left others, such as post-separation increases in the payor's income, re-partnering, remarriage and second families, to more discretionary determinations under the evolving framework of current law.

The application of the Advisory Guidelines in the context of review and variation is dealt with more extensively in Chapter 14.

### 3.3  The Formulas

### 3.3.1 Two basic formulas

The Advisory Guidelines are constructed around **two basic formulas**, rather than just one formula: the ***without child support*** formula and the ***with child support*** formula. The dividing line between the two is the absence or presence of a dependent child or children of the marriage, and a concurrent child support obligation, at the time spousal support is determined.

### 3.3.2 Determining income

Both formulas use **income sharing** as the method for determining the amount of spousal support, not budgets. Income-sharing formulas work directly from income, as income levels essentially determine the amount of support to be paid. Under the Advisory Guidelines, the accurate determination of income becomes a much more significant issue in spousal support cases than it has in the past, and there may be more incentives to dispute income. However, because the Advisory Guidelines generate ranges and not specific amounts, absolute precision in the determination of income may not be as crucial as under the *Federal Child Support Guidelines*. Many cases will involve combined claims for child and spousal support, where a precise determination of income is already required for child support purposes.

**The starting point for the determination of income under both formulas is the definition of income under the** *Federal Child Support Guidelines*, **including the Schedule III adjustments.** More details on the determination of income are found in Chapter 6.

The Advisory Guidelines do not solve the complex issues of income determination that arise in cases involving self-employment income and other forms of non-employment income. In determining income it may be necessary, as under the *Federal Child Support Guidelines*, to **impute income** in situations where a spouse's actual income does not appropriately reflect his or her earning capacity. In some cases the issue will be imputing income to the payor spouse. On variation and review the issue may be imputing income to the recipient spouse if it is established that the he or she has failed to make appropriate efforts towards self-sufficiency.

### 3.3.3 The *without child support* formula

In cases where there are no dependent children, the ***without child support*** formula applies. This formula relies heavily upon length of marriage—or more precisely, the length of relationship, including periods of pre-marital cohabitation—to determine both the amount and duration of support. Both amount and duration increase with the length of the relationship. This formula is constructed around the concept of **merger over time** which offers a useful tool for implementing both compensatory and non-compensatory support objectives in cases where there are no dependent children in a way that reflects general patterns in the current law.

**Under the basic *without child support* formula:**

- The *amount* of spousal support is 1.5 to 2 percent of the difference between the spouses' gross incomes for each year of marriage, to a maximum range of 37.5 to 50 per cent of the gross income difference for marriages of 25 years or more. (The upper end of this maximum range is capped at the amount that would result in equalization of the spouses' net incomes—the net income cap.)

- *Duration* is .5 to 1 year of support for each year of marriage, with duration becoming indefinite (duration not specified) after 20 years *or*, if the marriage has lasted 5 years or longer, when the years of marriage and age of the support recipient (at separation) added together total 65 or more (the "rule of 65").

The *without child support* formula is discussed in detail in Chapter 7.

### 3.3.4 The *with child support* formula

In cases where there are dependent children, the ***with child support*** formula applies. The distinctive treatment of marriages with dependent children and concurrent child support obligations is justified by both theoretical and practical considerations and is reflected in current case law.

On the theoretical front, marriages with dependent children raise strong compensatory claims based on the economic disadvantages flowing from assumption of primary responsibility for child care, not only during the marriage, *but also after separation*. We have identified this aspect of the compensatory principle as it operates in cases involving dependent children as the **parental partnership principle**, and have drawn on this concept in structuring the *with child support* formula. For marriages with dependent children, length of marriage is not the most important determinant of support outcomes as compared to post-separation child-care responsibilities.

On the practical front, child support must be calculated first and given priority over spousal support. As well, the differential tax treatment of child and spousal support must be taken into account, complicating the calculations. The *with child support* formula thus works with computer software calculations of net disposable incomes

**Under the basic *with child support* formula:**

- Spousal support is an *amount* that will leave the recipient spouse with between 40 and 46 percent of the spouses' net incomes *after child support has been taken out*. (We refer to the spouses' net income after child support has been taken out as Individual Net Disposable Income or INDI).

- The approach to *duration* under this formula is more complex and flexible than under the *without child support* formula; orders are initially indefinite in form (duration not specified) but the formula also establishes durational ranges which are intended to structure the process of review and variation and which limit the cumulative duration of awards under this formula. These durational limits rely upon both length of marriage and the ages of the children.

The *with child support* formula is really a cluster of formulas dealing with different custodial arrangements. **Shared and split custody** situations require slight variations in the computation of individual net disposable income, as the backing out of child support obligations is a bit more complicated. There is also a different, hybrid formula for cases where **spousal support is paid by the custodial parent**. Under this formula, the spouses' Guidelines incomes are reduced by the grossed-up amount of child support (actual or notional) and then the *without child support* formula is applied to determine amount and duration. Finally, there is one more hybrid formula for those spousal support cases where the child support for **adult children** is determined under section 3(2)(b) of the *Child Support Guidelines*.

The *with child support* formula is discussed in detail in Chapter 8.

### 3.3.5 Length of marriage

Under the Advisory Guidelines length of marriage is a primary determinant of support outcomes in cases *without* dependent children. Under the *without child support* formula the percentage of income sharing increases with length of the marriage; the same is true for duration of support.

Length of marriage is much less relevant under the *with child support* formula, although it still plays a significant role in determining duration under that formula.

Given the relevance of length of marriage under the Advisory Guidelines, it is important to clarify its meaning. **While we use the convenient term length of marriage, the more accurate description is the length of the cohabitation, which includes periods of pre-marital cohabitation, and ends with separation.**

### 3.3.6 Ranges

The Advisory Guidelines do not generate a fixed figure for either amount or duration, but instead produce **a range of outcomes** that provide a starting point for negotiation or adjudication.

Ranges create scope for more individualized decision-making, allowing for argument about where a particular case should fall within the range in light of the *Divorce Act*'s multiple support objectives and factors. Ranges can also accommodate some of the variations in current practice, including local variations in spousal support cultures.

### 3.3.7 Ceilings and floors

As with the *Federal Child Support Guidelines*, the Spousal Support Advisory Guidelines establish ceilings and floors in terms of the income levels to which they are applicable. Both the ceiling and the floor have been set by reference to the annual gross income of the payor. The ceiling has been set at a gross annual income for the payor of $350,000 and the floor at a gross annual income of $20,000. Ceiling and floors are dealt with more extensively in Chapter 11.

### 3.4 After the Formulas Have Been Applied

Under the Advisory Guidelines there is still much room for flexibility to respond to the facts of particular cases. First, there is considerable room for discretion in the fixing of precise amounts and durations within the ranges generated by the formulas. Second, there is the ability to restructure the formula outcomes by trading off amount against duration. Third the other is the possibility of departing from the formula outcomes by relying upon exceptions.

### 3.4.1 Using the ranges

The location of a precise amount or duration within those ranges will be driven by the factors detailed in Chapter 9: the strength of any compensatory claim, the recipient's needs, the age, number, needs and standard of living of any children, the needs and ability to pay of the payor, work incentives for the payor, property division and debts, and self-sufficiency incentives.

### 3.4.2 Restructuring

Although the formulas generate separate figures for amount and duration, the Advisory Guidelines explicitly recognize that these awards can be restructured by trading off amount against duration.

In *Bracklow* the Supreme Court of Canada explicitly recognized that the amount and duration of awards can be configured in different ways to yield awards of similar value (what the Court called quantum). Thus the Court noted that an order for a smaller amount paid out over a long period of time can be equivalent to an order for a higher amount paid out over a shorter period of time.

Restructuring can be used in three ways:

- to **front-end load** awards by increasing the amount beyond the formulas' ranges and shortening duration;
- to **extend duration** beyond the formulas' ranges by lowering the monthly amount; and
- to formulate a **lump sum** payment by combining amount and duration.

When restructuring is relied upon to resolve issues of inappropriate formula outcomes, awards remain consistent with the overall or global amounts generated by the Advisory Guidelines. **Restructuring thus does not involve an exception or departure from the formulas.**

Restructuring works best when duration is clearly defined, and will thus have its primary application under the *without child support* formula.

Restructuring is dealt with in more detail in Chapter 10.

### 3.4.3 Exceptions

The formulas are intended to generate appropriate outcomes in the majority of cases. We recognize, however, that there will be cases where the formula outcomes, even after consideration of restructuring, will not generate results consistent with the support objectives and factors under the *Divorce Act*. The informal, advisory nature of the Guidelines means that the formula outcomes are never binding and departures are always possible on a case-by-case basis where the formula outcomes are found to be inappropriate. The Advisory Guidelines do, however, itemize a series of exceptions which, although clearly not exhaustive, are intended to assist lawyers and judges in framing and assessing departures from the formulas. The exceptions create room both for the operation of competing theories of spousal support and for consideration of the particular factual circumstances in individual cases where these may not be sufficiently accommodated by restructuring.

The exceptions are listed and explained in Chapter 12:

- compelling financial circumstances in the interim period;
- debt payments;
- prior support obligations;

- illness or disability of a recipient spouse;
- a compensatory exception for shorter marriages under the *with child support* formula;
- reapportionment of property (British Columbia);
- basic needs/hardship under the *without child support* and *custodial payor* formulas;
- non-taxable payor income;
- non-primary parent to fulfil a parenting role under the *custodial payor* formula;
- special needs of a child; and
- section 15.3 for small amounts and inadequate compensation under the *with child support* formula.

## 7 THE WITHOUT CHILD SUPPORT FORMULA

Here we examine the first of the two basic formulas that lie at the core of the Advisory Guidelines—the ***without child support* formula**. This formula applies in cases where there are no dependent children and hence no concurrent child support obligations. Assuming entitlement, the formula generates ranges for amount and duration of spousal support.

The *without child support* formula covers a diverse range of fact situations, the only unifying factor being the absence of a concurrent child support obligation for a child or children of the marriage.[61] It covers marriages of all lengths where the spouses never had children. It also applies to long marriages where there were children, but they are no longer dependent.[62] The support claims in these cases involve a mix of compensatory and non-compensatory rationales.

It might seem impossible to develop one formula that could yield appropriate support outcomes over such a wide array of marital situations. In developing the formula we turned to the concept of **merger over time**, which incorporates both compensatory and non-compensatory rationales for spousal support. Put simply, the idea is that as a marriage lengthens, spouses more deeply merge their economic and non-economic lives, resulting in greater claims to the marital standard of living.[63] Using that concept, which relates support outcomes to the length of the

---

61  Support obligations to children or spouses from prior relationships are dealt with as exceptions under both formulas; see Chapter 11.

62  Some medium length marriages with dependent children in which support is initially determined under the *with child support* formula may cross-over to the *without child support* formula for a re-determination of amount after child support ceases. Crossover is discussed in Chapter 14, Variation and Review, below.

63  In developing this formula we drew in part on the American Law Institute (ALI) proposals referred to in Chapter 1, including the concept of merger over time. As we discuss further below, this concept—although not the terminology—is strongly anchored in our current law of spousal support.

marriage, we developed a formula that surprisingly generates results consistent with much of current practice, while bringing some much-needed structure.

In what follows we first introduce the basic structure of the *without child support* formula and provide an example of its operation. We then discuss the concept of merger over time that underlies the formula and its relation to existing rationales for spousal support. This is followed by a more detailed examination of the different parts of the formula and a series of further examples illustrating the formula's application in a variety of factual contexts.

---

**The *Without Child Support* Formula**

**Amount** ranges from 1.5 to 2 percent of the difference between the spouses' gross incomes (the **gross income difference**) for each year of marriage (or more precisely, year of cohabitation), up to a maximum of 50 percent. The range remains fixed for marriages 25 years or longer, at 37.5 to 50 percent of income difference. (The upper end of this maximum range is capped at the amount that would result in equalization of the spouses' net incomes—the **net income cap**).

**Duration** ranges from .5 to 1 year for each year of marriage. However support will be **indefinite (duration not specified)** if the marriage is **20 years or longer** in duration *or*, if the marriage has lasted five years or longer, when years of marriage and age of the support recipient (at separation) added together total 65 or more (the **rule of 65**).

---

## 7.1 The Basic Structure of the *Without Child Support* Formula

The *without child support* formula is set out in the box below in its most basic form. The formula is in fact two formulas—one for amount and one for duration. The formula generates **ranges** for amount and duration, rather than fixed numbers.

There are two crucial factors under the formula:

- the **gross income difference** between the spouses, and
- the **length of the marriage**, or more precisely, as will be explained below, the length of the period of cohabitation.

Both amount and duration increase incrementally with the length of marriage.

A simple example illustrating the basic operation of the *without child support* formula will be helpful at this point before we venture further into its more complex details. The primary purpose of this example is to show the basic calculations required under the formula and to give a sense of the outcomes the formula generates.

## Example 7.1

Arthur and Ellen have separated after a 20-year marriage and one child. During the marriage Arthur, who had just finished his commerce degree when the two met, worked for a bank, rising through the ranks and eventually becoming a branch manager. He was transferred several times during the course of the marriage. His gross annual income is now $90,000. Ellen worked for a few years early in the marriage as a bank teller, then stayed home until their son was in school full time. She worked part time as a store clerk until he finished high school. Their son is now independent. Ellen now works full time as a receptionist earning $30,000 gross per year. Both Arthur and Ellen are in their mid forties.

Assuming entitlement has been established in this case, here is how support would be determined under the *without child support* formula.

To determine the **amount** of support:

- Determine the **gross income difference** between the parties:

  $90,000 − $30,000 = $60,000

- Determine the **applicable percentage** by multiplying the length of the marriage by 1.5–2 percent per year:

  1.5 × 20 years = **30 percent**
  to
  2 × 20 years = **40 percent**

- Apply the applicable percentage to the income difference:
  30 percent × $60,000 = $18,000/year
  (**$1,500/month**)
  to
  40 percent × $60,000 = $24,000/year
  (**$2,000/month**)

**Duration** would be indefinite (duration not specified) in this case because the length of the marriage was 20 years.

**Thus, assuming entitlement, spousal support under the formula would be in the range of $1,500 to $2,000 per month for an indefinite (not specified) duration. This formula amount assumes the usual tax consequences, i.e. deductible to the payor and taxable to the recipient. It would also be open to the normal process of variation and review.**

An award of $1,500 per month, at the low end of the range, would leave Ellen with a gross annual income of $48,000 and Arthur with one of $72,000. An award of $2,000 per month, at the high end of the range, would leave Ellen with a gross annual income of $54,000 and Arthur with one of $66,000. In

Chapter 9 we deal with the factors that determine the setting of a precise amount within that range.

On first glance, this formula no doubt looks like an entirely new approach to spousal support, far removed both from the *Divorce Act* and its spousal support objectives and factors and from the principles of compensatory and non-compensatory support that the Supreme Court of Canada articulated in *Moge* and *Bracklow*. Before we examine the operation and application of this formula in more detail, we explain the concept of "merger over time" that underlies this formula and how it relates to existing theories of spousal support and the current law. We will show that the formula is a "proxy measure" for factors such as economic disadvantage, need, and standard of living that are currently used to determine spousal support outcomes.

## 7.2 Merger over Time and Existing Theories of Spousal Support

The idea that underlies the *without child support* formula and explains sharing income in proportion to the length of the marriage is **merger over time**. We use this term[64] to capture the idea that as a marriage lengthens, spouses merge their economic and non-economic lives more deeply, with each spouse making countless decisions to mould his or her skills, behaviour and finances around those of the other spouse. Under the *without child support* formula, the income difference between the spouses represents their differential loss of the marital standard of living. The formulas for both amount and duration reflect the idea that the longer the marriage, the more the lower-income spouse should be protected against such a differential loss.

Under this formula, short marriages without children will generate very modest awards, both in terms of amount and duration. In cases where there are adequate resources, the support could be paid out in a single lump sum. Medium length marriages will generate transitional awards of varying lengths and in varying amounts, increasing with the length of the relationship. Long marriages will generate generous spousal support awards on an indefinite basis that will provide the spouses with something approaching equivalent standards of living after marriage breakdown. The formula generates the same ranges for long marriages in which the couple have never had children as for long marriages in which there have been children who are now grown.

While the label may be unfamiliar, the concept of merger over time, which relates the extent of the spousal support claim to the length of the marriage, underlies much of our current law. Its clearest endorsement can be found in Justice L'Heureux-Dubé's much-quoted passage from *Moge*:

Although the doctrine of spousal support which focuses on equitable sharing does not guarantee to either party the marital standard of living enjoyed during the marriage, this standard is far from irrelevant to support entitlement ... . As marriage should be regarded as a joint endeavour, the longer the relationship endures, the closer the economic union, the greater will be the presumptive claim to equal standards of living upon its dissolution.[65]

Merger over time offers an effective way of capturing both the compensatory and non-compensatory spousal support objectives that have been recognized by our law since *Moge* and *Bracklow*. Under our current law, both kinds of support claims have come to be analyzed in terms of loss of the marital standard of living. Budgets, and more specifically budgetary deficits, now play a central role in quantifying this drop in standard of living. Under the *without child support* formula, the spousal income difference serves as a convenient and efficient **proxy measure** for loss of the marital standard of living, replacing the uncertainty and imprecision of budgets. The length of marriage then determines the extent of the claim to be protected against this loss of the marital standard of living.

Merger over time can have a significant compensatory component. One of the common ways in which spouses merge their economic lives is by dividing marital roles to accommodate the responsibilities of child-rearing. Compensatory claims will loom large in one significant segment of marriages covered by the *without child support* formula—long marriages in which there were children of the marriage who are now independent

Compensatory claims, in theory, focus on the lower income spouse's loss of earning capacity, career development, pension benefits etc. as a result of having assumed primary responsibility for child care. However in practice, after *Moge*, courts began to respond to the difficulties of quantifying such losses with any accuracy, particularly in longer marriages, by developing proxy measures of economic loss that focussed on the marital standard of living. When awarding spousal support in cases involving long traditional marriages, courts began to articulate their goal as providing the lower income spouse with a reasonable standard of living as assessed against the marital standard of living. And increasingly the standard for determining spousal support in long marriages has become a rough equivalency of standards of living.

Merger over time also has a significant non-compensatory component. In cases of long traditional marriages where the children are grown, it is now common to see spousal support justified on a dual basis. Non-compensatory support claims based on dependency over a long period of time are commonly relied upon to supplement compensatory claims based on

---

64  We have taken this term from the American Law Institute (ALI) proposals which are referred to in Chapter 1 above and discussed in more detail in the Background Paper.

65  *Moge v. Moge*, [1992] 3 S.C.R. 813 at 870.

earning-capacity loss. In marriages where the spouses have never had children—the other segment of marriages covered by the *without child support* formula—spousal support claims are usually non-compensatory in nature, based on need, dependency, and loss of the marital standard of living. Merger over time addresses these non-compensatory claims.

Giving precise content to the concept of non-compensatory or needs-based support has been one of the main challenges in spousal support law since *Bracklow*. One reading of *Bracklow* suggests that non-compensatory support is grounded in the economic dependency or, in Justice McLachlin's words, the "interdependency" of the spouses. It recognizes the difficulties of disentangling lives that have been intertwined in complex ways over lengthy periods of time. On this broad reading of *Bracklow*, which many courts have accepted, need is not confined to situations of absolute economic necessity, but is a relative concept related to the previous marital standard of living.[66] On this view entitlement to non-compensatory support arises whenever a lower income spouse experiences a significant drop in standard of living after marriage breakdown as a result of loss of access to the other spouse's income, with amount and duration resolved by an individual judge's sense of fairness.

Merger over time incorporates this broad view of non-compensatory support and provides some structure for quantifying awards made on this basis.[67] It takes account not just of obvious economic losses occasioned by the marriage, but also of the elements of reliance and expectation that develop in spousal relationships and increase with the length of the relationship.

The *without child support* formula generates the same ranges for long marriages in which the couple have never had children as for long marriages in which there have been children who are now grown. This result, which flows from the merger over time principle, mirrors what we find in the current law—lengthy marriages involving economic dependency give rise to significant spousal support obligations without regard to the source of the dependency.

We recognize that in some specific situations the *without child support* formula, based as it is on the concept of merger over time which gives significant weight to the length of the marriage, may not adequately satisfy either compensatory or non-compensatory (needs-based) support objectives. Rather than modifying the formula, which in general works well across a wide-range of fact situations and incomes, we have dealt with these problems through exceptions—the exception for disproportionate compensatory claims in shorter marriages; the illness and disability exception, and the basic needs/undue hardship exception in short marriages. These exceptions are discussed in Chapter 12, below.

We now turn to a more detailed examination of the operation and application of the formula.

### 7.3 Determining the Length of the Relationship

The *without child support* formula relies upon length of marriage for determining both amount and duration of support. While we use the convenient term "length of marriage," the actual measure under the Advisory Guidelines is the **period of cohabitation**. This includes pre-marital cohabitation and ends with separation. Inclusion of pre-marital cohabitation in determining length of marriage is consistent with what most judges do now in determining spousal support. This way of defining length of marriage also makes the Advisory Guidelines more easily used under provincial spousal support laws, which apply to non-marital relationships.

We have not set precise rules for determining the length of marriage. The simplest approach would be to round up or down to the nearest full year, and this is what we have done in our examples. Another, slightly more complicated, approach would be to allow for half years and round up or down to that. Because the formula generates ranges and not a fixed number, absolute precision in the calculation of the length of the marriage is not required. Addition or subtraction of half a year will likely make little or no difference to the outcome.

### 7.4 The Formula for Amount

Several aspects of the formula for amount should be noted. First, this formula uses **gross income** (i.e. before tax) figures rather than net (i.e. after tax). (The determination of income is dealt with more fully in Chapter 6.) While net income figures may be marginally more accurate, familiarity and ease of calculation tipped the scales in favour of using gross income figures.[68] As you will see in Chapter 8, net income figures are

---

66 Some read *Bracklow* as grounding non-compensatory support in a "basic social obligation" theory of spousal support. This somewhat questionable theory, which is discussed in more detail in the Background Paper, understands need in the absolute sense of an inability to meet basic needs and grounds the obligation to meet that need in the status of marriage itself.

67 Building as it does on the concept of merger over time, the *without child support* formula does not directly incorporate the "basic social obligation" theory of non-compensatory support that some read *Bracklow* as supporting, see footnote immediately above. The *without child support* formula produces awards that will go some way toward meeting basic needs where they exist, but limits the extent of any basic social obligation by the length of the marriage. However, some of the exceptions identified in Chapter 12, such as the illness/disability exception and the basic needs/hardship exception in short marriages do provide some accommodation for elements of basic social obligation.

---

68 In the revision process we introduced one small element of a net income calculation—an "equalization of net income" cap on the formula, which is discussed below.

used under the *with child support* formula because of the need to deal with the differential tax treatment of spousal and child support.

Second, this formula applies a specified percentage to the **income difference** between the spouses rather than allocating specified percentages of the pool of combined spousal incomes. In applying income sharing to the spousal income difference this formula once again differs from the *with child support* formula where the use of net income figures requires a model of income sharing that applies to a combined pool of spousal incomes.

Third, the formula for amount does not use a fixed or flat percentage for sharing the income differential. Instead, drawing on the underlying concept of merger of time, the formula incorporates a **durational factor** to increase the percentage of income shared as the marriage increases in length.[69] The durational factor is 1.5 to 2 percent of the gross income difference for each year of marriage.

The **ranges for amount** were developed by first determining the point when maximum sharing would be reached, which we set at 25 years. We also started with the assumption that maximum sharing would involve something close to equalization of incomes, or sharing 50 percent of the gross income difference. We then essentially worked backwards to determine what level of income sharing per year would be required to reach maximum sharing at year 25. The answer was 2 percent per year. In the course of developing the formula, we experimented with different percentage ranges, but the range of 1.5 to 2 percent provided the best fit with outcomes under current practice.

We chose income equalization (50 per cent of the gross income difference) as the **maximum level of income sharing**, potentially reached after 25 years of marriage and representing the full merger of the spouses' lives. Much time was spent considering the arguments for a somewhat lower maximum to take into account incentive effects and the costs of going out to work in situations where only the payor is employed. However, we also recognized that there would be cases where equalization of income would be appropriate. For example where only pension income is being shared after a very long marriage, where both spouses are low income, or perhaps where both spouses are employed after a long marriage, but with a significant income disparity. We drafted the formula to allow for that possibility.

After the release of the Draft Proposal we sought feedback on the issue of whether the maximum level of sharing should be set lower than 50 percent of the gross income difference.

We concluded that income equalization should be retained as the maximum level of sharing, but that it should be expressed as equalization of *net* incomes rather than of gross incomes. The formula has therefore been adjusted by capping the upper end of the maximum range at equalization of the spouses' net incomes—the **net income cap**.

### 7.4.1 The equalization of net income cap

In long marriages where the formula generates the maximum range of 37.5 to 50 percent of the gross income difference the recipient can end up with more than 50 per cent of the spouses' *net* income, notably where the payor spouse is still employed and subject to tax and employment deductions, and the recipient has little or no income. This result should never occur.

To avoid this result, shortly after the release of the Draft Proposal we began advising lawyers and judges to look closely at the net incomes of the spouses in these longer marriages when determining an appropriate amount within the range. We have now decided to modify the *without child support* formula itself by introducing a **net income cap. The recipient of spousal support should never receive an amount of spousal support that will leave him or her with more than 50 percent of the couple's net disposable income or monthly cash flow.**

Effectively, the introduction of the net income cap retains income equalization as the maximum level of sharing under the *without child support* formula. It simply provides for a more accurate calculation of income equalization. As for lowering the high end of the maximum range below equalization of net income, we concluded that the arguments that supported the initial choice of income equalization as the maximum level of sharing continued to be persuasive. As well, there was no obvious consensus around a lower percentage cap.

The software programs can calculate the "50 percent of net income" limit with precision and the formula range presented on the screen will reflect this limit at the upper end of the range. In computing "net income" for purposes of this cap, the permitted deductions would be federal and provincial income taxes, employment insurance premiums, Canada Pension Plan contributions, and any deductions that benefit the recipient spouse (e.g. medical or dental insurance, group life insurance and other benefit plans). Mandatory pension deductions are not permitted, for the same reasons as under the basic *with child support* formula, explained below in Chapter 8. Union dues and professional fees are already deducted from the spouses' gross incomes, consistent with the *Federal Child Support Guidelines* (see Chapter 6).

One of the advantages of the *without child support* formula is that the calculations can be done without a computer. For those without software, or more precise net income calculations, this net income cap can be calculated crudely by hand,

---

69   The concept of the durational factor is drawn from the ALI and Maricopa County guidelines; see Chapter 1.

at 48 percent of the gross income difference. This "48 percent" method is a second-best, but adequate, alternative.[70]

In thinking about the maximum level of sharing under this formula it is important to keep in mind that the formula does not **require** an award that would equalize spousal incomes after 25 years, but rather **permits** awards in the range of between 37.5 to 50 percent of the gross income difference (capped at net income equalization). Consistent with current law, the formula does not generate a general rule of income equalization; it simply provides for the possibility of equalization.

## 7.4.2 The problem of amount in short marriages

The feedback we received after the release of the Draft Proposal, combined with our continued reading of Guidelines cases, has confirmed that the ranges for amount generated by the *without child support* formula are "about right" and require no major adjustment beyond the net income cap.

We have generally found that the *without child support* formula works well, generating a reasonable range of outcomes across a wide range of cases from short to long marriages with varying incomes. The formula works extremely well for long marriages, which constitute the majority of the cases in which this formula is applied.[71] For medium length marriages, in some cases the monthly amounts need to be adjusted (i.e. increased) through restructuring (see Chapter 10), but we were well aware of this when we developed the formula. We placed heavy emphasis on restructuring to render the results of the formula consistent with current practice. These are also the cases—medium-length marriages without children—that frequently give rise to exceptions.

During the feedback process we did hear criticisms in some parts of the country that the amounts produced by the formula in shorter marriage cases were "too low."

In some of these cases, there was a failure to consider the **compensatory exception**—the exception for disproportionate compensatory claims in shorter marriages. In these cases, one spouse may have experienced a significant economic loss as a result of the marriage, by moving or by giving up employment, for example. Or, one spouse may have conferred an economic benefit on the other spouse by funding his or her pursuit of a professional degree or other education and training. This exception is considered in more detail in Chapter 12.

In other, non-compensatory cases, the formula was criticized as not providing enough support for the transition from the marital standard of living back to a lower standard of living based upon the recipient's earning ability. In these cases, involving marriages of less than 6 or 7 years, there is also little scope for much restructuring. This raised the issue of whether the structure of the formula needed to be fundamentally changed by increasing the percentage level of income-sharing in shorter marriages.

In the end, we concluded against any change to the basic structure of the formula. In the majority of cases across the country the formula works well for short marriages without children, which under current law typically give rise to very limited support obligations, if entitlement is found at all. The modest amounts generated by the formula are typically restructured into a lump sum or into a very short transitional award. In most of these cases, the recipient has a base income, which is supplemented by spousal support. In some parts of the country one does find more generous transitional awards providing the marital standard of living even after short marriages. This is a limited, regional pattern that is difficult to justify under the current principles that govern spousal support.

We do recognize, however, that there is a specific problem for shorter marriages where the recipient has little or no income. In these shorter marriage cases, the formula may generate too little support for the low income recipient even to meet her or his basic needs for a transitional period. The amount required to meet those basic needs will vary from big city to small city to town to rural area. Whether restructuring provides a satisfactory outcome, i.e. more support for a shorter time, will depend upon where the recipient lives. Thus the problem for these short-to-medium-marriage-low-income cases is most acute in big cities.

We did not wish to change the structure of the formula itself for this one sub-set of cases. The best approach to these cases was to create a carefully-tailored exception—the **basic needs/undue hardship exception for short marriages**—discussed further in Chapter 12 on Exceptions below.

### 7.5 The Formula for Duration

As with amount, duration under the *without child support* formula increases with the length of marriage. Subject to the provisions for indefinite support (duration not specified), the formula generates ranges for duration with the ends of the ranges determined as follows:

- **a minimum duration of half the length of the marriage and**
- **a maximum duration of the length of the marriage**.

---

70 The "48 percent" cap will work well in cases where the payor is working and the recipient is not. It will not necessarily be a good proxy for the equalization of net income cap where both parties are working; that will depend upon the spouses' respective tax rates and deductions.

71 This is true not only for long marriages/relationships in which there were children who are now adults, but also long marriages/relationships in which the parties had no children. See *Foley v. Girard*, [2006] O.J. No. 2496 (S.C.J.) which involved a 20 year same-sex relationship and *Long-Beck v. Beck*, [2006] N.B.J. No. 398, 2006 NBQB 317 which involved a 22 year marriage without children in which the wife quit work with the husband's consent.

**It is important to remember, as discussed in Chapter 5 on application, that any periods of interim support are to be included in the durational ranges.**

The ranges for duration under the *without child support* formula are admittedly very broad, allowing for an award at the top end of the range that is effectively double in value that at the bottom end. This will be particularly significant in medium-length marriages. Given the uncertainties in the current law on duration, it was not possible to come up with tighter ranges.

The formula also provides for indefinite support (duration not specified) in two circumstances:

- when the marriage has been 20 years or longer in length; or
- when the marriage has lasted five years or longer, **if the years of marriage plus the *age* of the support recipient *at the time of separation* equals or exceeds 65 and (the rule of 65).**

The "rule of 65" recognizes that length of marriage cannot be the only factor in determining the duration of spousal support in marriages without dependent children. Age is also a significant factor as it affects the ability to become self-supporting.

### 7.5.1 The tendency to ignore duration

Our monitoring of the use of the Advisory Guidelines since the release of the Draft Proposal has shown that **in practice the durational aspect of the *without child support* formula is often ignored.** The formula is used to determine the amount of spousal support, but not duration. In some cases awards are for shorter periods of time than the formula suggests. In other cases the durational limits are ignored in favour of indefinite orders.

To ignore duration is to misapply the *without child support* formula. Amount and duration are interrelated parts of the formula—they are a package deal. Using one part of the formula without the other undermines its integrity and coherence. If the durational limits were to be systematically increased, for example, by lowering the threshold for indefinite support, the formula would have to be redesigned and the amounts decreased. Within the scheme of the Advisory Guidelines itself, adjustment of duration beyond the formula requires restructuring and will involve a corresponding adjustment of amount.

In what follows we discuss in more detail four aspects of the formula for duration under the *without child support* formula: indefinite support, the "rule of 65," time limits in short marriages, and time limits in medium-length marriages. The real problem of duration under this formula has proven to be this last aspect, the use of time limits in marriages that are neither long nor short.

### 7.5.2 The meaning of "indefinite" support

In using the term "indefinite" we simply adopted a word that had been used for years in spousal support law to mean "an order for support without a time limit at the time it is made." Under the Advisory Guidelines **an order for indefinite support does not necessarily mean permanent support, and it certainly does not mean that support will continue indefinitely at the level set by the formula**.

Under the current law, orders for indefinite support are open to variation as the parties' circumstances change over time and may also have review conditions attached to them. The Advisory Guidelines do nothing to change this: **"indefinite" support means support that is subject to the normal process of variation and review**.

Through the process of review and variation the amount of spousal support may be reduced, for example if the recipient's income increases or if the recipient fails to make reasonable efforts to earn income and income is imputed. Support may even be terminated if the basis for entitlement disappears. It is true that current law supports the idea that after long marriages spousal support will often be permanent, even if the amount is subject to reduction to reflect the recipient's obligation to pursue self-sufficiency.

In practice, however, most orders for indefinite support after long marriages will be significantly modified, if not eliminated, after the retirement of the payor and the receipt of pension income by the payor and the recipient. "Indefinite" often means "until the payor reaches 65." Variation and review in the context of the Advisory Guidelines are discussed in more detail in Chapter 14.

After the release of the Draft Proposal we were very surprised to learn from our feedback sessions that the term "indefinite" in the Advisory Guidelines was being misinterpreted by many as meaning "infinite" or "permanent."

We realized that we would have to develop a new term to express the concept that indefinite orders are not necessarily permanent, that they are subject to review and variation and, through that process, even to time limits and termination. Our solution has been to add "duration not specified" as a parenthetical explanation whenever the term "indefinite" is used in the formulas, i.e. **indefinite (duration not specified)**.

### 7.5.3 The "rule of 65": the age factor and indefinite support

The *without child support* formula provides that indefinite (duration not specified) support will be available even in cases where the marriage is shorter than 20 years **if the years of marriage plus the *age* of the support recipient *at the time of separation* equals or exceeds 65**. In a shorthand expression, we described this as the **"rule of 65."**

Thus, if a 10-year marriage ends when the recipient is 55, indefinite (duration not specified) support will be available because years of marriage (10) plus age (55) equals 65. Note that this is only a "rule" about duration, as the amount of support would be limited by the length of the marriage, i.e. 1.5 to 2 percent per year or 15 to 20 percent of the gross income difference in a 10-year marriage.

In reality, given the ages of the parties in the cases covered by the rule of 65, there will likely be significant changes in the amount of support ordered upon the retirement of one or both of the spouses. This refinement to the formula for duration is intended to respond to the situation of older spouses who were economically dependent during a medium length marriage and who may have difficulty becoming self-sufficient given their age.

**The "rule of 65" for indefinite (duration not specified) support is not available in short marriages (under 5 years in length).** The assumption in the current law is that short marriages generate only limited support obligations.

In the Draft Proposal, we struggled with the issue of whether an age component should always be required for indefinite (duration not specified) support—i.e. whether the "rule of 65" should apply even in long marriages. Under a 20-year rule with no age requirement, for example, a 38-year-old spouse leaving a 20-year marriage would be entitled to indefinite (duration not specified) support. Some would argue that indefinite (duration not specified) support is not appropriate for a spouse who is still relatively young and capable of becoming self-sufficient. If the "rule of 65" were generally applicable, support would not become indefinite (duration not specified) even after a 20-year marriage unless the recipient were 45 years of age or older.

Several considerations led us to the conclusion that a 20-year rule without any age requirement was the more appropriate choice. First, a spouse who married young and spent the next 20 years caring for children could be more disadvantaged than someone who married when they were older and had been able to acquire some job skills before withdrawing from the labour force. As well, under the current law it would be very difficult to impose a time-limit on support after a 20-year marriage, even if self-sufficiency and an eventual termination of support were contemplated at some point in the future. The typical order would be an indefinite order subject to review and/or variation. An order for indefinite support (duration not specified) under the Advisory Guidelines is no different.

Despite the frequent misinterpretation of the meaning of "indefinite," there was no pressure to change either of the conditions for indefinite support. Most of the feedback about the "rule of 65" focussed on technical issues of its application, as there was general agreement on the "rule."

### 7.5.4 Time limits in short marriages

The current law of spousal support has no difficulty with time limits in short marriages without children. Time limits, or

lump sum orders, are common in these cases. Even in those jurisdictions where appeal courts have discouraged the use of time-limited support, discussed below, short marriages without children are identified as permissible exceptions. In practice, we were told in the feedback phase, these cases are not a problem.

### 7.5.5 Lowering the threshold for indefinite support?

In some parts of the country, it is very difficult to time limit spousal support, by reason of appellate decisions or local practices. For marriages of less than 20 years, the Draft Proposal incorporated time limits, although these were generous time limits. During the feedback phase, we did canvass the possibility of lowering the threshold for indefinite support, below 20 years.

We found little support for such a change. Even those who wanted to lower the threshold could not agree on what that new threshold should be. Many lawyers, mediators and judges expressed their frustration with the current law on duration, especially their perceived inability to use time limits in a sensible way. The durational limits in the Advisory Guidelines were seen as providing some structure for negotiations, initial decisions and variation or review. Lowering the threshold for indefinite support would not solve the problem and would in practice undermine the usefulness of the Guidelines.

### 7.5.6 The problem of time limits in medium length marriages

The real "problems" for time limits under the *without child support* formula are concentrated in marriages that are neither "long" (20 years or more) or "short" (under 5 years). For marriages that last 6 to 19 years, in every jurisdiction we were told, it becomes increasingly difficult to impose time limits on initial support orders as the marriage lengthens. At some point, in each jurisdiction, the time limits were seen as inconsistent with the current law on duration. At the same time, as we explained above, many lawyers, mediators and judges wanted to see more use of time limits.

It is certainly true that after *Moge* time limits fell into disfavour because of the associated problems of "crystal ball gazing" and arbitrary terminations of spousal support where self-sufficiency was "deemed" rather than actually achieved. Time-limited orders became less common. However, since *Bracklow*, some judges have brought back time limits, at least for non-compensatory support orders. While time limits are frequently negotiated by parties in agreements and consent orders, the law on time limits remains uncertain. In some parts of the country trial courts feel bound by appellate court rulings confining time-limited orders to a narrow range of exceptional cases, primarily short marriages without children.

It is in marriages of medium length that duration remains uncertain. Here practice varies and depends upon many factors—regional support cultures and the governing provincial appellate court jurisprudence; whether the context is negotiation or court-ordered support; and whether the support claim is compensatory or non-compensatory in nature. The most that can be said is that current law is inconsistent on the issue of time limits in medium-length marriages.

In practice the issue of duration in medium-length marriages is often put off to the future, to be dealt with through ongoing reviews and variations. In some cases this process of review and variation may eventually generate a time-limited order leading to termination. Under current practice uncertainty about duration can generate low monthly awards, as judges or lawyers fear that any monthly amount of support could continue for a long time, even permanently.

In developing the Draft Proposal, it was our view that reasonable time limits for medium length marriages would be an essential element of the scheme, under both the *without child support* and *with child support* formulas, especially if the Guidelines were to generate reasonable monthly amounts. *Bracklow* emphasized this interrelationship between amount and duration, recognizing that a low award paid out over a lengthy period of time is equivalent to an award for a higher amount paid out over a shorter period of time. As well, we were aware of the importance of providing structure in this area to facilitate negotiation and settlement. Recognizing that this was an area of law in flux, we saw a role for the Advisory Guidelines in helping to shape the developing law.

In assessing the compatibility of the time limits generated by the *without child support* formula with current law it is important to keep in mind that they are potentially very generous; in medium length marriages they can extend for up to 19 years. These time limits are thus very different from the short and arbitrary time limits, typically of between three to five years, that became standard under the clean-break model of spousal support for medium-to-long marriages and which *Moge* rejected. The time limits generated by the formula should be assessed in context—they are potentially for lengthy periods of time and, once marriages are of any significant length, operate in conjunction with generous monthly amounts.

As well, it is important to keep in mind that in the context of the *without child support* formula, support claims in medium-length marriages will typically be non-compensatory. In non-compensatory support cases, one strand of the post-*Bracklow* case law recognizes the appropriateness of time limited orders when the purpose of the support order is to provide a period of transition to a lower standard of living rather than compensation for lost career opportunities. Such use of time limits does not involve "crystal-ball gazing" and the making of arbitrary assumptions about future developments, but rather reflects the basis of entitlement.

In Chapter 8 you will see that we dealt with the issue of time limits in short and medium-length marriages with

children somewhat differently, because of the strong compensatory claims in such cases and the need for individualized assessment of recipients' challenges in over-coming disadvantage resulting from the assumption of the child-rearing role.

We recognize that some provincial appellate court jurisprudence may at this point create barriers to the use of the formula's time-limits by trial judges. We also recognize that the lengthy time limits potentially generated under the *without child support* formula—up to 19 years in duration—are very different from the typical kinds of time limits with which our law of spousal support is familiar and raise some distinct problems of foreseeability. In our view, the law around time limits will continue to develop and to respond to the durational ranges under the formula. We already see signs of this in the Guidelines case law since the release of the Draft Proposal which offers several examples of judges making somewhat novel time-limited orders for the lengthy durations generated by the *without child support* formula.[72] In assessing the feasibility of these orders, it is important to remember that time-limited orders are subject to variation. It is thus possible to avoid some of the problems of arbitrary "crystal ball gazing" while reinforcing expectations with respect to the eventual termination of the support order.[73]

As well, in cases where it is not feasible for courts to impose the time limits generated by the formula in initial orders, the time limits can still be used in a "softer," more indirect way to structure the on-going process of review and variation and to reinforce expectations of the eventual termination of the order. This is not dissimilar to the use of the time limits under the *with child support* formula where they establish the outside limit for indefinite (duration not specified) orders. The fact that courts are reluctant to make time limited orders on initial applications does not preclude the eventual use of time limits on subsequent reviews or variations. The Guidelines case law already offers several examples of this "softer" use of

---

72  See for example, *Hance v. Carbone*, 2006 CarswellOnt 7063 (Ont.S.C.J.) (17½ yr. marriage; spousal support ordered for 15 years in addition to 6 years time-limited provided under separation agreement) and *Bishop v. Bishop*, [2005] N.S.J. No. 324, 2005 NSSC 220 (N.S.S.C.) (13 year marriage; final order spousal support for 10 years in addition to 1 year interim). For an example under the *with child support* formula, discussed in Chapter 8, see *Fewer v. Fewer*, [2005] N.J. No. 303, 2005 NLTD 163 (N.L.S.C.) (16½ yr. marriage; 1 child 15 with wife; spousal support ordered for 16½ yrs from separation, subject to variation).

73  The variation of time-limited orders is explicitly discussed in *Fewer, ibid*.

time limits in subsequent variations or reviews to bring an eventual termination to what was initially an indefinite order.[74]

Finally, if the durational limits under this formula, even in their "softer" form, are found to be inappropriate in cases close to the 20 year threshold for indefinite support, restructuring can be used to extend duration. As is explained in Chapter 10, duration can be extended by restructuring so long as an appropriate downward adjustment is made to amount so as to keep the total value of the award within the global ranges generated by the formula.

## 7.6 Making the Formula Concrete—Some Examples

### 7.6.1 A short-marriage example

In cases of short marriages, marriages of less than 5 years, the *without child support* formula generates very small amounts for a very short duration. The formula will always generate time-limits in these cases.[75]

### Example 7.2

Karl and Beth were married for only four years. They had no children. Beth was 25 when they met and Karl was 30. When they married, Beth was a struggling artist. Karl is a music teacher with a gross annual income of $60,000. Beth now earns $20,000 per year, selling her work and giving art lessons to children. Entitlement is a threshold issue before the Advisory Guidelines apply. On these facts, given the disparity in income and Beth's limited income at the point of marriage breakdown, entitlement is likely to be found.

The conditions for indefinite (duration not specified) support do not apply and duration would be calculated on the basis of .5 to 1 year of support for each year of marriage.

To determine the **amount** of support under the formula:

- Determine the **gross income difference** between the parties:

  $60,000 − $20,000 = $40,000

- Determine the **applicable percentage** by multiplying the length of the marriage by 1.5–2 percent per year:

  1.5 × 4 years = **6 percent**

  to

  2 × 4 years = **8 percent**

- Apply the applicable percentage to the income difference:

  6 percent × $40,000 = $2,400/year **($200/month)**

  to

  8 percent × $40,000 = $3,200/year **($267/month)**

**Duration** of spousal support = (.5–1) × 4 years of marriage = 2 to 4 years

**The result under the formula is support in the range of $200 to $267 per month for a duration of 2 to 4 years.**

In practice, this modest award would likely be converted into a lump sum using **restructuring**, discussed in Chapter 10.

### 7.6.2 Some medium-length marriage examples

In medium-length marriages (5 to 19 years), the formula generates increasing amounts of support as the marriage increases in length, moving from relatively small percentages at the shorter end of the spectrum to relatively generous amounts after 15 years, when awards of 30 percent of the gross income difference become possible. Except where the rule of 65 is applicable, the formula generates time limits of varying lengths depending on the length of the marriage. The ranges for duration are, however, very wide, leaving much opportunity to respond to the facts of particular cases.

This category covers a diverse array of cases raising a variety of support objectives. Current law is at its most inconsistent in its handling of these cases. This area posed the greatest challenges to developing a single formula that would yield appropriate results. We concluded that our formula based on merger over time provided the best starting point. But not surprisingly, it is in these cases that there will be the most frequent need to rely upon restructuring to massage the formula outcomes and where there will likely be the greatest resort to exceptions.

---

74 One of the best examples is *Kelly v. Kelly*, [2007] B.C.J. No. 324, 2007 BCSC 227 (17 year relationship, no children, support paid for 9 years; wife remarried; on variation application support recognized as non-compensatory; time-limited to further 19 months, 10 years total.) Another good example under the *custodial payor* formula is *Puddifant v. Puddifant*, [2005] N.S.J. No. 558, 2005 NSSC 340 (S.C.F.D.) (12 year marriage, 1 child with husband, wife mental illness, support paid for 9 years; on husband's application to terminate support ordered for further 3 years, total 12 years.)

75 The "rule of 65," which allows for indefinite support to older spouses in marriages of less than 20 years in length, does not apply to short marriages (under 5 years).

### Example 7.3

Bob and Susan have been married 10 years. They married in their late twenties and Sue is now 38. Bob is employed as a computer salesman and Sue is a hairdresser. Both worked throughout the marriage. There were no children. Bob's gross annual income is $65,000; Sue's is $25,000.

Entitlement is a threshold issue before the Advisory Guidelines are applicable. An argument might be made that there is no entitlement to support: Sue is employed full time and could support herself, and there is no compensatory basis for support. However, Sue will suffer a significant drop in standard of living as result of the marriage breakdown and, at an income of $25,000, will likely experience some economic hardship. Current law would suggest an entitlement to at least transitional support on a non-compensatory basis to allow Sue to adjust to a lower standard of living.

The case does not satisfy the conditions for indefinite (duration not specified) support. The marriage is under 20 years and the case does not fall within the "rule of 65" for indefinite support because Sue's age at separation plus years of marriage is below 65 (38 + 10 = 48).

To determine the amount of support under the formula:

- Determine the **gross income difference** between the parties:

  $65,000 − $25,000 = $40,000

- Determine the **applicable percentage** by multiplying the length of the marriage by 1.5–2 percent per year:

  1.5 × 10 years = **15 percent**

  to

  2 × 10 years = **20 percent**

- Apply the **applicable percentage** to the income difference:

  15 percent × $40,000 = $6,000/year (**$500/month**)

  to

  20 percent × $40,000 = $8,000/year (**$667/month**)

**Duration** of spousal support = (.5–1) × 10 years of marriage = 5 to 10 years

**The result under the formula is support in the range of $500 to $667 per month for a duration of 5 to 10 years.**

Consistent with current law, the formula essentially generates modest top-up support for a transitional period to assist Sue in adjusting from the marital standard of living.

An award of $500 per month, at the low end of the range, would leave Sue with a gross annual income of $31,000 and Bob with one of $59,000. An award of $667 per month, at the high end of the range, would leave Sue with a gross annual income of $33,000 and Bob with one of $57,000. In a marriage of this length the formula does not equalize incomes.

Some might find the amounts generated by the formula too low, even at the high end of the range. An argument could be made that, consistent with current law, any transitional order should put Sue somewhat closer to the marital standard of living for the period of gearing down. As will be discussed in Chapter 10, a **restructuring** of the formula outcome is possible to produce larger amounts for a shorter duration.

### Example 7.4

David and Jennifer were married for 12 years. It was a second marriage for both. David was 50 when they met. He is a businessman whose gross annual income is now $100,000 per year. Now 62, he is in good health, loves his work, and has no immediate plans to retire. Jennifer was 45 when they met, while Jennifer was working in his office. She had been a homemaker for 20 years during her first marriage and had received time-limited support. When they met she was working in a low-level clerical position earning $20,000 gross per year. Jennifer, now 57, did not work outside the home during the marriage.

Entitlement is a threshold issue before the Advisory Guidelines are applicable. Given the length of the marriage and Jennifer's lack of income, entitlement to support on non-compensatory grounds would be relatively uncontentious.

The **amount** of support on an income difference of $100,000 and a 12 year marriage would be calculated as follows:

18 percent × $100,000 = $18,000/year (**$1,500/month**)

to

24 percent × $100,000 = $24,000/year (**$2,000/month**)

This is a case where the "rule of 65" would govern duration. Because Jennifer's age at separation plus years of marriage is 65 or over (57 + 12 = 69), the formula provides for indefinite (duration not specified) support, rather than the durational range of 6 to 12 years based on length of marriage alone. A variation in amount would, however, be likely when David retires.

**The result under the formula is support in the range of $1,500 to $2,000 a month on an indefinite (duration not specified) basis, subject to variation and possibly review.**

Support at the low end of the range would leave Jennifer with a gross annual income of $18,000 and David with one of $72,000. Support at the high end of the range would leave Jennifer with a gross annual income of $24,000 and David with one of $66,000. Again, because of the length of the marriage (12 years), the formula does not generate results that approach income equalization.

### 7.6.3 Some long-marriage examples

In cases of long marriages (20 years or longer) the formula generates generous levels of spousal support for indefinite periods, reflecting the fairly full merger of the spouses' lives. The long marriages covered by the *without child support* formula fall into two categories: those where there have been children who are no longer dependent and those where the couple did not have children.

Example 7.1 provides an example of the formula's application to a long marriage with children where the wife was a secondary earner. *Example 7.5*, presented below, involves the familiar scenario of a very long traditional marriage.

### Example 7.5

John and Mary were married for 28 years. Theirs was a traditional marriage in which John worked his way up the career ladder and now earns $100,000 gross per year, while Mary stayed home and raised their two children, both of whom are now grown up and on their own. Mary is 50 years of age and has no income. John is 55.

Entitlement to spousal support is clear on these facts and thus the Advisory Guidelines are applicable. Because the length of the marriage is over 25 years, the maximum range for amount applies—37.5 to 50 percent of the gross income difference (capped at equalization of net incomes).

The range for amount on an income difference of $100,000 after a 28 year marriage would be:

37.5 percent × $100,000 = $37,500/year (**$3,125/ month**)

to

50 percent × $100,000 = $50,000/year (**$4,167/ month, capped at $4048**[76])

---

76   This is based on an assumption of Ontario residence and the applicable tax rates and mandatory deductions in November 2007.

**Duration** is indefinite (duration not specified) because the marriage is 20 years or over in length.

**The formula results in a range for support of $3,125 to $4,048 per month for an indefinite (unspecified) duration, subject to variation and possibly review.**

An award of $3,125 per month, at the low end of the range, would leave Mary with a gross income of $37,500 per year and John with one of $62,500. An award of $4,048 per month, at the high end of the range, would equalize the net incomes of the parties.

As will be discussed further in Chapter 14, the order is open to variation over time in response to changes in the parties' circumstances, including increases in Mary's income or the imputation of income to her if she fails to make reasonable efforts to contribute to her own support. John's retirement would also likely be grounds for variation.

Example 7.6 involves a long marriage without children.

### Example 7.6

Richard is a teacher with a gross annual income of $75,000. He is in his late forties. His wife, Judy, is the same age. She trained as a music teacher but has worked as a freelance violinist for most of the marriage, with a present gross income of $15,000 a year. Judy has also been responsible for organizing their active social life and extensive vacations. They were married 20 years. They had no children.

Entitlement will easily be established in this case given the significant income disparity, Judy's limited employment income, and the length of the marriage.

The range for amount under the formula, based on income difference of $60,000 and a 20 year marriage is:

30 percent × $60,000 = $18,000/year (**$1,500/ month**)

to

40 percent × $60,000 = $24,000/year (**$2,000/ month**)

**Duration** would be indefinite (duration not specified) because the marriage was 20 years in length.

**The result under the formula is support in the range from of $1,500 to $2,000 per month for an indefinite (unspecified) duration, subject to variation and possibly review.**

An award at the lower end of the range would leave Judy with a gross annual income of $33,000 and Richard with one of $57,000. An award at the high end of the range would leave

Judy with a gross annual income of $39,000 and Richard with one of $51,000.

Judy will certainly be expected to increase her income and contribute to her own support. The issue in applying the formula will be whether a gross income of $30,000 a year, for example, should be attributed to Judy for the purposes of an initial determination of support. If so, support under the formula would be lowered to a range of $1,125 to $1,500 per month (or $13,500 to $18,000 per year).

More likely, Judy would be given some period of time (for example one or two years) before she would be expected to earn at that level, with support to be adjusted at that point, after a review.

### 7.7  After the Formula

As the examples in this chapter indicate, many issues remain after the application of the *without child support* formula—issues of choosing an amount and duration within the ranges, restructuring, and exceptions, all addressed in separate chapters below. It is important to keep these other parts of the Advisory Guidelines in mind, particularly in cases involving the *without child support* formula where restructuring and exceptions will frequently need to be used.

### 8  THE WITH CHILD SUPPORT FORMULA

The dividing line between the two proposed formulas under the Advisory Guidelines is the presence of a child support obligation.[77] Where the spouses have not had children or the children have grown up and are on their own, the *without child support* formula will apply. Where a spouse is paying child support, the *with child support* formula will apply.

From a technical perspective, there must be a different formula for spousal support in these cases, a formula that takes into account the payment of child support and its priority over spousal support as set out in s. 15.3 of the *Divorce Act*. Further, because of tax and benefit issues, we have to use net rather than gross incomes. Practically, the payment of child support usually means reduced ability to pay spousal support. And, theoretically, there are different rationales for the amount and duration of spousal support where there are still dependent children to be cared for and supported.

This category of cases dominates in practice, in support statistics and in jurisprudence. Any guidelines must generate a workable formula for amount and duration for this category, a formula that can adjust across a wide range of incomes and family circumstances. For the most part, marriages with dependent children will involve spousal support paid by a

parent who is also paying child support to the recipient spouse. The basic formula in this chapter is constructed around this typical situation. Variations on the basic formula are required to accommodate cases of shared and split custody. There are also a sizeable number of cases where the spouse paying spousal support has primary parental responsibility for the children. In these custodial payor situations, an alternative formula must be constructed. Finally, we have added one more hybrid formula, applicable in cases where the only remaining children are away at university or otherwise have their child support determined under section 3(2)(b) of the *Child Support Guidelines*.

The *with child support* formula is thus really a family of formulas, adjusted for different parenting arrangements.

### 8.1  The Compensatory Rationale for Spousal Support

Where there are dependent children, the primary rationale for spousal support is compensatory. After *Moge*, spouses must, as Chief Justice McLachlin put it in *Bracklow*, "compensate each other for foregone careers and missed opportunities during the marriage upon the breakdown of their union."[78] The main reason for those foregone careers and missed opportunities is the assumption of primary responsibility by one spouse for the care of children during the marriage. Where one spouse, in a marriage with children, has become a full-time homemaker or has worked outside the home part time or has worked as a secondary earner, there will be disadvantage and loss at the end of the marriage, usually warranting compensatory support. This compensatory rationale is encompassed by the first of the four objectives of spousal support, in s. 15.2(6)(a) of the *Divorce Act*.

Under compensatory theory, it is usually necessary to estimate the spouse's disadvantage or loss by determining what the recipient's career or employment path might have been, had the recipient not adopted his or her role during the marriage—not an easy task. The ideal evidence would be individualized economic evidence of earning capacity loss, but few litigants can afford such evidence and often it would be highly speculative. Some spouses never establish a career or employment history. For others, their pre-marital and marital choices were shaped by their future expected role during marriage. And there are short marriages, where past losses are relatively small and most of the spouse's child-rearing and any associated losses are still to come in the future.

As was explained in Chapter 1, after *Moge*, courts had to develop proxies to measure that loss where there was no clear and specific career or employment path. Need became the most common proxy, calculated through the conventional budget analysis. Sometimes standard of living was used, with

---

77  The child support obligation must be for a child of the marriage. A child support obligation to a child from a prior marriage or relationship is dealt with as an exception under both formulas, explained in more detail in Chapter 12 on Exceptions below.

78  *Bracklow v. Bracklow*, [1999] 1 S.C.R. 420 at para. 1.

the post-separation position of the recipient spouse measured against the marital standard or some reasonable standard of living. In practice, crude compromises were made in applying the compensatory approach.

More recently, what we have called the **parental partnership** rationale has emerged in the literature and in the case law. On this approach, the obligation for spousal support flows from parenthood rather than the marital relationship itself. It is not the length of the marriage, or marital interdependency, or merger over time, that drives this theory of spousal support, but the presence of dependent children and the need toprovide care and support for those children. Unlike the conventional compensatory approach, parental partnership looks at not just past loss, but also the continuing economic disadvantage that flows from present and future child-care responsibilities. For shorter marriages with younger children, these present and future responsibilities are more telling. Further, the parental partnership rationale better reflects the reality that many women never acquire a career before marriage, or mould their pre-marital employment in expectation of their primary parental role after marriage.

The parental partnership rationale is firmly anchored in one of the four statutory objectives in s. 15.2(6) of the *Divorce Act*, where clause (b) states a spousal support order should:

apportion between the spouses any financial consequences arising from the care of any child of the marriage over and above any obligation for the support of any child of the marriage.

The 1997 implementation of the *Federal Child Support Guidelines* has reinforced this rationale. Under the Guidelines, only the direct costs of child-rearing—and not even all of them—are included in child support. The indirect costs of child-rearing were left to be compensated through spousal support, as was recognized by the 1995 Family Law Committee's *Report and Recommendations on Child Support*. Principal amongst these indirect costs is the custodial parent's reduced ability to maximize his or her income because of child-care responsibilities. Now that child support is fixed under the *Child Support Guidelines* and determined by a different method than before 1997, spousal support has to be adjusted to reflect the concerns identified by the parental partnership model.

With the implementation of the *Federal Child Support Guidelines* came the increased use of computer software. The software regularly and graphically displays information like net disposable income, monthly cash flow and household standards of living. This information has made spouses, lawyers, mediators and courts more conscious of the financial implications of child and spousal support, in turn reflected in the use of these concepts in determining the amount of spousal support. Before the *Federal Child Support Guidelines*, and

even afterwards for a while, most courts were not prepared to award more than 50 percent of the family's net disposable income to the recipient spouse and children, leaving the single payor spouse with the other 50 percent. With the new software, many courts began consciously to allocate more than 50 percent of a family's net disposable income to the recipient spouse and children, and even as much as 60 percent, as in the Ontario Court of Appeal decision in *Andrews v. Andrews*[79] and in numerous trial decisions across the country.[80]

These cases also reveal a non-compensatory element found in some decisions where both child and spousal support are paid to the same parent. There is a household standard of living element within the parental partnership rationale that should be openly acknowledged. Both child and spousal support go into the same household, to support the standard of living of both parent and child. In some cases, spousal support is used as a residual financial remedy to shore up the standard of living that the children experience in the recipient's household.

## 8.2 Background to the Basic Formula

There is no simple way to construct a formula for spousal support where the support payor is also paying child support. First, child support must be determined, as it takes priority over spousal support in assessing the payor's ability to pay. Second, child support is not taxable or deductible, but spousal support is taxable to the recipient and deductible for the payor. Third, child and spousal support must be determined separately, but it is very difficult in any formula to isolate spousal finances cleanly from support of children.

This formula for cases with child support—the *with child support* formula—differs from the *without child support* formula set out in Chapter 7. First, the *with child support* formula uses the **net incomes** of the spouses, not their gross incomes. Second, the *with child support* formula divides the **pool** of combined net incomes between the two spouses, not just the difference between the spouses' gross incomes. Third, in the *with child support* formula, the upper and lower percentage limits for net income division **do not change with the length of the marriage**.

Unlike the *without child support* formula, this formula must use **net income**. While gross income would be simpler to understand, calculate and implement, nothing remains simple once child support has to be considered. Different tax treatment demands more detailed after-tax calculations, and

---

79  *Andrews v. Andrews* (1999), 50 R.F.L. (4th) 1 (Ont. C.A.).

80  See for example *Gale v. Gale* (2000), 6 R.F.L. (5th) 157 (Man. Q.B.), *Bastedo v. Bastedo*, [2000] P.E.I.J. No. 49 (S.C.T.D.), *Lyttle v. Bourget*, [1999] N.S.J. No. 298 (S.C.), *Tedham v. Tedham*, [2002] B.C.J. No. 1635 (S.C.), *Clark v. Cooper-Clark*, [2002] N.B.J. No. 41 (Q.B.).

ability to pay must be more accurately assessed. Net income computations will usually require computer software, another unavoidable complication.

Thanks to that same computer software, many lawyers had become familiar with net disposable income or monthly cash flow calculations before the release of the Draft Proposal. Judges were using such calculations to underpin their spousal support decisions. In the software programs, these numbers included child and spousal support to produce what can be called **family net disposable income** or monthly cash flow. This larger pool of net income is then divided between the spouses. Often, more than 50 percent of this family net disposable income is allocated to the recipient spouse and children by way of combined child and spousal support, or sometimes as much as 60 percent and occasionally even more. Under the formula proposed here for spousal support, we divide a different and smaller pool of net income, after removing the spouses' respective child support obligations—what we call **individual net disposable income** or **INDI**.

We considered using the more familiar family net disposable income as the basis for the *with child support* formula, rather than this newer variation of individual net disposable income. In the end we opted for individual net disposable income. First, the family net disposable income of the recipient spouse includes both child and spousal support, bulking up the recipient's income in a somewhat misleading fashion and masking the impact of spousal support upon the recipient parent's individual income. Second, allocating family NDI between spouses blurs the distinction between child and spousal support, between child and adult claims upon income. Individual NDI attempts to back out the child support contributions of each spouse, to obtain a better estimate of the income pool that remains to be divided between the adults. Third, after separation, the spouses see themselves, not as one family, but more as individuals with distinct relationships with their children and their former spouses. Fourth, separating out each spouse's individual net disposable income, after removal of child support obligations, produced a more robust and sophisticated formula, one that adjusted better across income levels and numbers of children.

### 8.3 The Basic Formula

Set out in the box below is a summary of how this basic *with child support* formula works. Remember that this formula applies where the higher income spouse is paying both child and spousal support to the lower income spouse who is also the primary parent. By primary parent, we mean the spouse with sole custody or the spouse with primary care of the children in a joint custody arrangement.

---

**The Basic *With Child Support* Formula for Amount**

(1) Determine the **individual net disposable income (INDI)** of each spouse:

- Guidelines Income *minus* Child Support *minus* Taxes and Deductions = Payor's INDI
- Guidelines Income *minus* Notional Child Support *minus* Taxes and Deductions *plus* Government Benefits and Credits = Recipient's INDI

(2) Add together the individual net disposable incomes. By iteration, determine the range of spousal support amounts that would be required to leave the lower income recipient spouse with between 40 and 46 per cent of the combined INDI.

---

#### 8.3.1 Calculating individual net disposable income

Basic to this formula is the concept of **individual net disposable income**, an attempt to isolate a **pool** of net disposable income available after adjustment for child support obligations.

The starting point is the Guidelines income of each spouse as is explained in Chapter 6 above. In the interests of uniformity and efficiency, we basically use the same definition of income as that found in the *Federal Child Support Guidelines*. Next, we deduct or back out from each spouse's income their respective **contributions to child support**.

For the child support **payor**, that is usually the table amount, plus any contributions to special or extraordinary expenses, or any other amount fixed under any other provisions of the *Federal Child Support Guidelines*. For the child support **recipient**, a **notional table amount** is deducted, plus any contributions by the recipient spouse to s. 7 expenses. In reality, the recipient will likely spend more than these amounts through direct spending for the children in her or his care. But by this means we make an adjustment, however imperfect, for the recipient's child support obligation. A formula could be constructed without this notional child support number, but such a formula would have adjusted to the number of children and income levels with less precision and with less transparency about the role of the recipient parent.

Second, **income taxes and other deductions** must be subtracted from the incomes of both the payor and the recipient to obtain net incomes. As spousal support is transferred from one spouse to another, because of tax effects, the size of the total pool of individual net disposable income actually changes slightly, which complicates these calculations. The current software does these calculations automatically, as differing hypothetical amounts of spousal support are transferred, a process called "iteration."

Clearly permissible **deductions** are federal and provincial income taxes, as well as employment insurance premiums and Canada Pension Plan contributions. Union dues and professional fees are already deducted from Guidelines income under the adjustments of Schedule III to the *Federal Child Support Guidelines*. Deductions should be recognized for certain benefits, e.g. medical or dental insurance, group life insurance, and other benefit plans, especially those that provide immediate or contingent benefits to the former spouse or the children of the marriage.

More contentious are **deductions for mandatory pension contributions**. We concluded that there should **not** be an automatic deduction for such pension contributions, but the size of these mandatory deductions may sometimes be used as a factor to justify fixing an amount towards the lower end of the spousal support range.

We reached this conclusion after considerable discussion. Like EI, CPP and other deductions, pension contributions are mandatory deductions, in that the employee has no control over, and no access to, that money. But, unlike other deductions, pension contributions are a form of forced saving that permit the pension member to accumulate an asset. Further, after separation, the spouse receiving support does not usually share in the further pension value being accumulated by post-separation contributions. Finally, there are serious problems of horizontal equity in allowing a deduction for mandatory pension contributions by employees. What about payors with non-contributory pension plans or RRSPs or those without any pension scheme at all? And what about the recipient spouse—would we have to allow a notional or actual deduction for the recipient too, to reflect her or his saving for retirement? In the end, we decided it was fairer and simpler **not** to allow an automatic deduction for pension contributions.

Third, we **do include** in each spouse's income the amounts identified for **government benefits and refundable credits**. Included are the Child Tax Benefit, the National Child Benefit Supplement, the GST credit, the refundable medical credit, the Child Disability Benefit, the various provincial benefit and credit schemes, and the new Universal Child Care Benefit. Under the *Federal Child Support Guidelines* these benefits and credits are generally **not** treated as income. For the reasons set out in Chapter 6 on Income above, a different approach is warranted for spousal support purposes.

### 8.3.2 The Basic Formula: Dividing Individual Net Disposable Income

Once the individual net disposable income (INDI) of each spouse has been determined, the next step is to add together these individual net disposable incomes. Then we have to iterate, i.e. to estimate hypothetical spousal support repeatedly, in order to determine the amount of spousal support that will leave the lower income recipient spouse with between 40 and 46 percent of the combined pool of individual net disposable income.

How did we arrive at the percentages for the range, from 40 to 46 percent of the individual net disposable income? This was a critical issue in the construction of this formula. In our earlier Sneak Preview in the summer of 2004, we had suggested a higher range, from 44 to 50 percent of INDI. We ultimately opted for a lower range, after much discussion with the Advisory Working Group, some limited feedback from the Sneak Preview, further reviews of the case law in various provinces, and some more hard thought about the upper and lower bounds for these ranges. Since the release of the Draft Proposal and after our meetings across Canada, we can confirm that this percentage range is appropriate.

We found that a range of 40 to 46 percent of individual net disposable income typically covered spousal support outcomes in the **middle** of the very wide range of outcomes now observed in most Canadian provinces. To capture the middle of the range on a national basis means that some areas will find the upper bound (46 percent) a bit low and other areas will consider even the lower bound (40 percent) at the higher end of their local range.

Prior to the Sneak Preview, we had experimented with a range of 40 to 50 percent of INDI. But that produced far too broad a range in absolute dollar terms. One of the objectives of the Advisory Guidelines is to develop more predictability and consistency in spousal support outcomes and a ten-percentage point range simply failed to do that. A narrower five or six percentage point range is about right.

The lower boundary of this range—40 percent of INDI—does ensure that the recipient spouse will receive not less than 50 percent of the family net disposable income in all cases involving two or more children, and slightly below that in one-child cases.

The upper end of this range—46 percent of INDI—falls short of an equal split, which would leave both spouses in the same individual position. Despite the intellectual attraction of a 50/50 split, there are a number of practical problems that convinced us that it was not appropriate to set the upper limit of the range there. First, very few courts are currently prepared to push spousal support amounts that high. Second, there is a live concern for the access-related expenses of the payor spouse, expenses that are not otherwise reflected in the formula. Most payors are exercising access and most are spending directly upon their children during the time they spend with their children. Third, there are concerns for the payor in the situation where the payor has employment-related expenses and the recipient spouse is at home full time and receiving large spousal support.

We should repeat here a central difference between this formula and the *without child support* formula: **the length of the marriage does not affect the upper and lower percentages in this *with child support* formula**.

We also wish to stress the inter-relationship between the percentage limits and the precise elements of our version of individual net disposable income. If a notional table amount were not removed from the recipient spouse's income, or if government benefits and refundable credits were excluded, then the formula percentages would have to change. Our objective throughout has been to develop formulas that can capture the bulk of current outcomes, while at the same time demonstrating robustness in adjusting across incomes and child support amounts and custodial situations.

As a result of computer software, lawyers and courts became accustomed to calculating net disposable income or monthly cash flow on a *family* basis: the payor's net disposable income after deduction of child and spousal support and taxes, and the recipient's after addition of child and spousal support (and deduction of taxes). How do these more familiar family net disposable income percentages compare to our range of individual net disposable income divisions? Typically, the 46 percent of INDI at the upper end of our proposed formula generates a family net disposable income for the primary parent spouse of 56 to 58 percent where there are two children. At the lower end of the range, a spousal support amount that leaves the recipient spouse with 40 percent of INDI will typically leave that spouse and the two children with 52 or 53 percent of the family net disposable income. For comparison purposes, we have provided family net disposable income proportions in the examples below.

We recognize that Quebec has a different scheme of determining child support, which in turn has implications for fixing spousal support. The application of the Advisory Guidelines in divorce cases in Quebec is dealt with in more detail in Chapter 15.

## 8.4 Amounts of Spousal Support: Examples of the Basic Formula

At this point it helps to give a few examples of the ranges of monthly spousal support generated by this basic formula. Then we will move to the issue of duration. For illustration purposes, we assume that these parents and children all live in Ontario, as the use of one jurisdiction simplifies the exposition of the formula's operation.

In the earlier Draft Proposal, the formula calculations were done partially with software and partially by hand. With the release of the Draft Proposal, Canada's three major family law software suppliers incorporated the Spousal Support Advisory Guidelines into their programs, so that the calculations can be done easily and with greater precision. In addition, the ranges for amount have changed since the January 2005 release of the Draft Proposal, due to changes in child support

table amounts in May 2006, various changes to federal and provincial taxes and changes in child benefits. The result is that the numbers in these examples are different from those set out in the Draft Proposal.

### Example 8.1

Ted and Alice have separated after 11 years together. Ted works at a local manufacturing plant, earning $80,000 gross per year. Alice has been home with the two children, now aged 8 and 10, who continue to reside with her after separation. After the separation, Alice found work, less than full time, earning $20,000 gross per year. Alice's mother provides lunch and after-school care for the children, for nothing, when Alice has to work. Ted will pay the table amount for child support, $1,159 per month. Alice's notional table amount would be $308. There are no s. 7 expenses (if there were, the spousal amounts would be lower).

**Under the formula, Ted would pay spousal support in the range of $474 to $1,025 per month.**

Using the family net disposable income figures (or the similar monthly cash flow figures) more familiar to current software users, spousal support of $1,025 monthly along with the child support would leave Alice and the children with $4,003 per month and Ted with $2,976 per month, or 57.4 per cent of the family's net disposable income in favour of Alice and the children. At the lower end of the range, with spousal support of $474 per month, the net disposable income of the family would be split 52.6/47.4 in favour of Alice and the children, leaving Ted with $3,326 monthly and Alice and the children with $3,684. The amount of spousal support is obviously affected by the **number of children**. If Ted and Alice had only one child, the spousal support range would be higher, from $888 to $1,463 per month. If the couple had three children, Ted's ability to pay would be reduced, bringing the range down to $79 to $626 monthly. Four children would lower that range even further, down to a range from zero to $222 per month.

The spousal support range will also be lowered by any payment of section 7 expenses. In our *Example 8.1*, if Alice were paying child care expenses of $8,000 per year for the two children and Ted paid his proportionate share of the net cost, the formula range would reduce to $319 to $925 per month for spousal support.

### Example 8.2

Bob and Carol have separated after eight years of marriage and two children, now aged 4 and 6, who are both living with Carol. Bob earns $40,000 gross annually at a local building supply company, while Carol has found part-time work, earning $10,000 per year. Carol's mother lives with Carol and provides care for the children when needed. Bob pays the table amount of $601 per month for the children. Carol's notional table amount of child support would be $61 per month. There are no s. 7 expenses.

**Under the formula, Bob would pay spousal support in the range of zero to $34 per month.**

Again, by way of comparison to the more familiar numbers, if Bob were to pay child support of $601 and spousal support of $34 monthly, at the upper end of the range, he would be left with $1,951 per month, while Carol and the two children would have *family* net disposable income of $2,325 monthly, or 54.4 percent of the family's net disposable income.

### Example 8.3

Drew and Kate have been married for four years. Drew earns $70,000 gross per year working for a department store. Kate used to work as a clerk in the same store, but she has been home since their first child was born. The children are now 1 and 3, living with Kate. Kate has no Guidelines income (and hence there is no notional table amount for her). Drew will pay the table amount of $1,043 per month for the two children.

**Under the formula, Drew would pay spousal support to Kate in the range of $908 to $1,213 per month.**

If Drew were to pay spousal support of $1,213 monthly, he would have $2,394 per month, while Kate and the children would have *family* net disposable income of $3,084 monthly, or 56.3 percent of the total family NDI. At the lower end of the range, spousal support of $908 per month would leave Drew with $2,604 in family NDI, while Kate and the children would have $2,780 monthly, or 51.6 percent of the family's NDI.

The formula generates ranges for the amount of spousal support. Chapter 9 below discusses the factors to be considered in fixing a particular amount within the ranges.

### 8.5 Duration under the Basic Formula

In most cases where there are dependent children, the courts order "indefinite" spousal support, usually subject to review or sometimes just left to variation. Even when the recipient spouse is expected to become self-sufficient in the foreseeable future, courts typically have not often imposed time limits in initial support orders. Where the recipient spouse is not employed outside the home, or is employed part-time, the timing of any review is tied to the age of the children, or to some period of adjustment after separation, or to the completion of a program of education or training. As the recipient spouse becomes employed or more fully employed, spousal support will eventually be reduced, to top up the recipient's employment

earnings, or support may even be terminated. In other cases, support is reduced or terminated if the recipient spouse re-marries or re-partners.

In practice, where there are dependent children, few "indefinite" orders are permanent. Many intervening events will lead to changes or even termination. Some of these issues are canvassed in Chapter 14, which deals with variation, review, remarriage, second families, etc. By making initial orders indefinite, the current law simply postpones many of the difficult issues relating to duration and recognizes the fact-specific nature of these determinations.

Under the *without child support* formula, discussed in Chapter 7, there are time limits keyed to the length of the marriage, i.e. .5 to 1 year of spousal support for each year the spouses have cohabited, subject to the exceptions for indefinite (duration not specified) support.

Under the *with child support* formula, one option was simply to leave duration indefinite in all cases, with no durational limits of any kind, thereby avoiding all of the difficult issues of duration where there are dependent children. Such an approach would, however, be inconsistent with our durational approach under the *without child support* formula. It would also be inconsistent with the underlying parental partnership rationale for spousal support. This rationale emphasizes the ongoing responsibilities for child-care after separation and the resulting limitations on the custodial or residential parent's earning abilities. When those responsibilities cease, there must be some other reason for support to continue, such as the length of the marriage.

Our approach to duration for marriages with dependent children maintains current practices, while introducing the general idea of a range for duration. **Initial orders continue to be indefinite (duration not specified) in form**, subject to the usual processes of review or variation. That does not change. What our approach adds is the acceptance of generally understood **outside limits** on the cumulative duration of spousal support that will inform the process of review and variation.[81]

The durational limits under this formula combine the factors of length of marriage and length of the remaining child-rearing period, under two different tests for duration. For longer marriages, it makes sense that a recipient spouse should get the benefit of the time limits based upon length of marriage that might be obtained under the *without child support* formula, as these will typically run well beyond the end

---

81  The approach to duration under this formula involves fairly extensive reliance upon review orders. We discuss review orders and the leading Supreme Court of Canada decision, *Leskun v. Leskun*, [2006] 1 S.C.R. 920 in more detail in Chapters 13 and 14. In our view, the role contemplated for review orders under this formula is not inconsistent with *Leskun*.

of any child-rearing period. More difficult are shorter marriages where the recipient parent has the care of young children. To deal with these cases we have, under this formula, developed additional durational limits based on the responsibilities of child-rearing and the age of the children.

In what follows we explain in more detail the different elements of the admittedly complex approach to duration under this formula, and then draw these elements together in a concise summation in s. 8.5.4.

### 8.5.1 The creation of a range for duration in the basic formula

In this final version we have made some changes to the language used to describe and present the two tests for duration under this formula. More importantly, we have also added a lower end for the range under the basic *with child support* formula.

In the Draft Proposal, we did not propose any minimum duration or lower end of the range for duration under the *with child support* formula, only a maximum outside duration. Through the feedback process, we became convinced that some range for duration was required, for three reasons. First, absent a lower end of the range, the maximum duration was not treated as an outside time limit, but instead as a default time limit, i.e. a recipient was seen as possessing an entitlement to receive spousal support for the length of the marriage or until the youngest child finished high school, no matter what. That was never our intention. Second, absent a lower end and following upon the default approach just described, there was no room created for negotiation around duration between the spouses, unlike under the *without child support* formula. Third, after further feedback across Canada and further research, we did get a strong sense of what the lower end of the range could be under the current law.

The real crux of any range is for shorter marriages with pre-school children, where we feared that these recipients might be seriously disadvantaged by creating a lower end of the range. This remains a concern, especially since it appears that the duration of support in these cases is lengthening, as the courts continue to develop an appreciation of the serious continuing disadvantage flowing from a spouse's ongoing childcare obligations.

We emphasise that the durational limits under this formula must be seen as "softer," more flexible than under the *without child support* formula given the prominence of the compensatory rationale under this formula. First, the durational limits are not intended to be implemented as time limits on initial orders, but rather to give structure to an on-going process of review and variation. Second, determinations of duration in cases with dependent children are very fact-specific and vary enormously based upon the education, skills

and work-experience of the dependent spouse, the ages of the children and the available arrangements for child-care. Our suggested durational range is at best a typical range that will not be appropriate in all cases. And third, this is an area of law in flux. We see the law over time giving increased emphasis to what we have termed the "parental partnership" concept, which recognizes the ongoing responsibilities for child-care after separation and the resulting limitations on the custodial or residential parent's earning abilities.

As we explain in more detail below, there are two tests that establish the range for duration under the basic *with child support* formula. We have renamed these test to clarify their rational and operation: the *length-of-marriage* test and the *age-of-children* test. Under these two tests the upper and lower end of the range in each case will be the **longer duration** produced by either test.

Before we explain the two tests for duration, it is import to remember that **the durational limits under the *with child support* formula include any period of spousal support paid at the interim stage**, the same treatment as under the *without child support* formula.

### 8.5.2 The *length-of-marriage* test for duration

The first test for duration is the same as the test for duration under the *without child support* formula. It will typically be the applicable test for longer marriages, marriage of ten years or more. The **upper end** is one of support for each year of marriage, subject to the provisions under the *without child support* formula for indefinite (duration not specified) support after 20 years of marriage. The **lower end** is one-half year of support for each year of marriage. If the children are already in school at the time of separation, then the lower end of the range will always be determined by this *length-of-marriage* test.

Once again, we emphasize that these "softer" time limits are intended to structure the process of review and variation of initial orders that are indefinite in form; they are not intended to give rise to time-limited orders, at least not initially.

We can use *Example 8.1* above to explain this test. Ted and Alice cohabited for 11 years during their marriage and are now in their late thirties or early forties, with two children, aged 8 and 10 at separation. The initial support order would be indefinite (duration not specified), but it would be expected that the ultimate, cumulative duration of the award would fall somewhere within the range of 5.5 years (lower end) to 11 years (upper end). The maximum outside time limit would be 11 years. Reviews and variations in the meantime may bring support to an end before 11 years, and certainly the amount may have been reduced significantly during this period. But if support is still in pay after 11 years, there would be an expectation, barring exceptional circumstances, that support would be terminated at that point on an application for review or variation.

In the longer marriage cases under the *with child support* formula, where the *length-of-marriage* test defines the durational range, most cases will tend towards the longer end of the durational range and few cases should see support terminate at the lower end, given the strong compensatory claims that are typically present in these cases. The age of the children will be a critical factor in location with the range. Consider *Example 8.1* again: if support terminated for Alice at lower end of 5.5 years, the children would be only 13 and 15, an age at which the demands of child care can still have considerable impact upon Alice's income-earning abilities. By contrast, if Ted and Alice had been married for 14 years, and the children were 10 and 12 at separation, the lower end of the durational range would see support last until the children were 17 and 19. The choice of a particular duration within this range would be affected by these and other factors set out in Chapter 9.

### 8.5.3 The *age-of-children* test for duration

The second test for duration under the basic *with child support* formula is driven by the age of the children of the marriage. It usually operates where the period of time until the last or youngest child finishes high school is greater than the length of the marriage. These are mostly short or short-to-medium marriages, typically (but not always) under 10 years in length. The current case law is inconsistent and erratic on duration for these marriages, ranging from indefinite orders without conditions, to indefinite orders with short review periods and sometimes stringent review conditions, and even occasionally to time limits. Despite the language of indefinite support, the reality in most cases is that support does not continue for long, as re-employment, retraining, remarriage and other changes often intervene to bring spousal support to an end.

We too have struggled with duration for this category of cases. On the one hand, many of these custodial parents face some of the most serious disadvantages of all spouses, especially mothers with little employment history who have very young children in their care, all of which militates in favour of no time limits or very long time limits. On the other hand, many recipient spouses do have good education and employment backgrounds, are younger, and are emerging from shorter marriages and briefer periods out of the paid labour market, all indicators of quicker recovery of earning capacity. Inevitably, as under the current law, this means that reviews are a critical means of sorting out the individual circumstances of the recipient spouses.

The **upper end of the range** for spousal support under this test is **the date when the last or youngest child finishes high school**. Relatively few cases will reach this outside time limit and those that do will likely involve reduced amounts of top-up support by that date. Hence, extensions beyond that date

would involve cases that fall within any of the exceptions described in Chapter 12, like the exception for the special needs of a child or the exception under s. 15.3 of the *Divorce Act*.

The **lower end of the range** under this test is also tied to the age of the youngest child and schooling, once again reflecting the parental partnership model. In shorter marriages, spousal support should continue at least until **the date the youngest child starts attending school full-time**. The school date will vary from province to province and from school district to school district, based upon the availability of junior kindergarten, the age rules governing school registration and the program the child takes.

Keep in mind that these tests for duration say nothing about the proper *amount* of spousal support during this period. That will be a function of the recipient's income-earning ability, her or his ability to undertake part-time or full-time employment. The amount of support may be significantly reduced over the course of any order, or even reduced to zero.

As with longer marriages with dependent children, **the initial support order in these shorter marriage cases will still be indefinite (duration not specified)**, as the determination of self-sufficiency remains an individualized decision. Any time limit will typically only appear after a review or variation hearing, especially in these cases involving young children. This appears to be the pattern in the current Canadian practice, as best as we can discern from the few reported decisions, the feedback we received since the Draft Proposal and the Advisory Working Group.

Take our *Example 8.3* where Drew and Kate have only been married four years, with two pre-school children aged 1 and 3 and Kate at home with them. The upper end of the range for duration would be 17 years, while the lower end would be 5 years, the latter assuming that children in their area start full-time school at age 6. In this typical case, any initial order would likely include a review provision, the review to occur at some point before the youngest child starts school.

### 8.5.4 The use of the two tests for duration: whichever is longer

In most cases, only one of the two tests, either the *length-of-marriage* test or the *age-of-children* test, will apply to determine both the upper and lower ends of the range. In general, the *length-of-marriage* test applies for longer marriages, marriages of ten years or more, while the *age-of-children* test applies for shorter marriages, those under ten years. But the two tests must be used together, **as it is the longer of the two tests that applies for each end of the range**. Remember that this is a **range** for duration, and that the actual outcome in any particular case will be worked out within that range over a series of orders or agreements, by way or review or variation of an initial order or agreement.

> **The Basic *With Child Support* Formula for Duration**
>
> **Initial orders indefinite (duration not specified)**
> Subject to cumulative durational limits implemented by review or variation:
>
> **Upper End of the Range: the longer of**
> - the length of marriage, or
> - the date the last or youngest child finishes high school
>
> **Lower End of the Range: the longer of**
> - one-half the length of marriage, or
> - the date the youngest child starts full-time school

Take our *Example 8.2* where Bob and Carol have been married for 8 years, with two children aged 4 and 6. The *length-of-marriage* test suggests a durational range of 4 to 8 years, while the *age-of-children* test would suggest a range of 2 to 14 years. The result for Bob and Carol would be a durational range where the lower end of the range is 4 years (from the *length-of-marriage* test) and of the upper end of the range is 14 years (from the *age-of-children* test). As can be seen, much turns upon the interaction of the length of the marriage and the age of the children.

### 8.5.5  The problem of short marriages with young children

Applying the two tests for duration under the *with child support* formula, the range for duration will be determined by whichever test produces the longer duration at both the lower and upper ends of the range. Where those bounds are determined by the *length-of-marriage* test, there seems to be little difficulty. The range is the same as that under the *without child support* formula. A durational range of half the length of the marriage to the length of the marriage is intuitively understandable.

The *age-of-children* test is not as simple. It is tied to the presence of children in the marriage, and the economic disadvantages that come with the obligation to care for children. Length of marriage alone no longer provides a measure of the duration of the spousal support obligation, as the case law increasingly demonstrates, even if some spouses think it should. The *age-of-children* test will usually apply in shorter marriages. For shorter marriages with young children, this test will generate a long potential duration at the upper end of the range, one that *can* run as long as the date that the last or youngest child finishes high school, an outcome that raised some concerns during the feedback process. For very short marriages with very young children, the lower end of the range under the *age-of-children* test, added in the revision process, has also raised some concerns.

Critical to understanding these durational issues is the compensatory rationale for spousal support in these shorter marriage cases. Most of the economic disadvantage in these cases is not in the past, but in the future; it is the continuing disadvantage that flows from the obligations of child care and their impact upon the ability of the recipient parent to obtain and maintain employment. Hence the importance of the age of the children in fashioning durational limits. Our understanding of the current law, based both upon reported cases and discussions with lawyers and judges in our cross-country consultations, is that the law applicable to these cases is in flux, showing increasing recognition over time of the on-going economic disadvantage flowing from post-separation child-care responsibilities.

The upper end of the range for duration under the *age-of-children* test—up until the last or youngest child finishes high school—may appear long in a shorter marriage case. Consider Bob and Carol again in *Example 8.2*, where spousal support could potentially last as long as 14 years after an 8-year marriage, if the children are 4 and 6 in Carol's primary care at the date of separation. If duration were tied to the length of the marriage alone, spousal support would otherwise terminate when the children were 12 and 14 years old. But at this point, Carol's employment position may still reflect continuing economic disadvantage and limitations placed on her ability to achieve full-self-sufficiency by her post-separation custodial responsibilities. It may only be as the children reach their teenage years that she can focus more on improving her employment position. Termination at this point might also fail, depending on the facts, to recognize Carol's continuing child care obligations. A good way to test this outside durational limit is to think about the labour market position of the primary parent if one of those children had special needs or developed problems in their teenage years.

Slightly different problems are raised by the lower end of the durational range under the *age-of-children* test—until the youngest child starts attending school full-time. In the majority of cases, as our consultations revealed, this lower end of the durational range will not be contentious. In marriages of even four or five years, the *age-of-children* test will begin to yield results similar to the lower end of the durational range under the *length-of-marriage* test. Indeed, the major concern raised by the introduction of the lower end of the durational range in cases of shorter marriages with children, whether defined by length of marriage or age of youngest child starting full-time school, has been that it will create a "ceiling" and stunt the progressive development of the law in this area.

However, in some cases, of very short marriages, the *age-of-children* test has raised concerns that it sets the lower end of the durational range too high—i.e., that it establishes a "minimum duration" that is too long because it exceeds the length of the marriage. The kind of case that raises this concern is a fairly extreme set of facts: a marriage as brief as one or two years, with an infant less than a year old. In this hypothetical case, assuming the child would start full-time school at age 6, the lower end of the range for duration under the *age-of-children* test would be five years, which some would suggest is too long for such a short marriage.

In responding to this concern, we note that there are a number of other important dimensions to spousal support in these cases, in addition to duration, that soften the impact of this lower end of the range for duration. First, the lower end of the range for duration does not guarantee any particular *amount* of support. The formula range is driven by the number and age of the children, the spousal incomes, the child custody arrangements, child support amounts, section 7 contributions and tax positions. Much will turn upon the employment status of the recipient, and the recipient's ability to return to the paid labour market. A recipient is always under an obligation to make reasonable efforts towards self-sufficiency, and, on particular facts, those efforts may be subject to scrutiny in a review scheduled well before the youngest child starts full-time school. Second, in some situations, income will have to be imputed to the recipient, either part-time or full-time, on an individualized basis, often through the process of review. Third, entitlement is always an issue, before reaching the questions of amount and duration under the Advisory Guidelines. In some cases of strong facts—i.e. a recipient with a strong connection to the work-force—there may even be a finding of no entitlement so that the lower end of the range for duration is not engaged. The lower end of the durational range does not create a "minimum entitlement." Finally, we have said all along that the durational limits under the *with child support* formula are "softer," less formulaic, than those under the *without child support* formula. In *Moge*, the Supreme Court of Canada emphasized the need for individualized decision-making on self-sufficiency in compensatory support cases and duration under the *with child support* formula must therefore not be too rigidly applied.

## 8.6 Shared Custody

The basic formula is constructed around the typical fact situation, where the higher income spouse pays child and spousal support to the lower income spouse who has the primary care of the children. Here we address custodial variations, the first being shared custody.

Where the spouses have **shared custody**, the starting point for the calculation of child support under s. 9(a) of the *Federal Child Support Guidelines* is the straight set-off of table amounts for the number of children subject to shared custody, as set out in the Supreme Court decision in *Contino v. Leonelli-Contino*.[82] That amount is then adjusted, usually upwards, but occasionally downwards, based upon s. 9(b) (increased costs

---

82  [2005] 3 S.C.R. 217, 19 R.F.L. (6th) 272.

of shared custody and actual spending on children by the spouses) and s. 9(c) (other circumstances, including relative incomes, income levels, assets and debts, household standards of living, any reliance upon previous levels of child support paid). The *Contino* decision was handed down after the release of the Draft Proposal, but the shared custody formula anticipated that outcome. The majority in *Contino* emphasised that there is no presumption in favour of the full table amount for the payor, nor is there any presumption in favour of the straight set-off, under section 9.

Under the basic *with child support* formula, child support is deducted from the payor's income and then that child support amount plus a notional amount for child support is deducted from the recipient's income, to obtain individual net disposable income. Shared custody requires some changes to this basic formula.

Assume for the moment that the payor is paying only the straight set-off amount of child support in a shared custody case. If we were only to deduct the smaller set-off amount of child support for the payor spouse in a shared custody situation, that would misrepresent and understate the payor parent's contribution to child support. Shared custody assumes that both parents spend directly upon the child in their shared care. The full table amount (plus any s. 7 contributions) is thus deducted from the payor spouse's net disposable income. For the recipient, the notional table amount (plus any contribution to s. 7 expenses) is deducted from his or her income. This would be done in the calculation of INDI, even though the child support paid by the payor and received by the recipient would be the straight set-off amount.

If the straight set-off of child support is calculated as above, it turns out that the spousal support ranges are basically the same in these shared custody situations as in sole custody situations. Shared custody arrangements do not result in any automatic lowering of spousal support. It was important that the shared custody formula not provide any false financial incentives to encourage shared custody litigation, while at the same time providing ample room within the range to adjust for the realities of shared parenting.

### Example 8.4

Peter and Cynthia have separated after nine years together. Peter works as a reporter at the local television station, earning $65,000 gross per year, while his wife Cynthia works for a local arts organization, earning $39,000 gross per year.

Peter and Cynthia share custody of their two children, aged 8 and 7 on a week about, 50/50 basis. In these circumstances, there could be entitlement issues, but we will assume entitlement here for exposition purposes.

First, assume Peter only pays the straight set-off amount of child support, i.e. $972 – $584 = $388. We would deduct from Peter's income the full table amount of $972, of which $584 is spent by him directly for the children in his care and $388 is paid as child support to Cynthia. Cynthia's income would still be reduced by her notional table amount of $584. If Cynthia receives the full amount of the child benefits, and assuming entitlement, then the range for spousal support would be **zero to $142 per month**.

### 8.6.1 Adjusting for rotating child benefits

Since the release of the Draft Proposal, there has been a change in policy governing the receipt of the Child Tax Benefit and the child portion of the GST/HST Credit. The Canada Revenue Agency (CRA) decided that parents in shared custody cases "will have their benefits rotated between them *only* on a six-month on, six-month off basis." According to the CRA policy, it is possible for only one shared custody parent to receive the full child benefits provided that the parents do not self-identify or otherwise come to CRA's attention. The same approach has now been extended to the Universal Child Care Benefit (UCCB) in shared custody situations. As with all tax matters, the CRA policy cannot be altered by the parents' agreement or by a court order.

Under the *with child support* formula, these child benefits are treated as income and thus the allocation of the Child Tax Benefit, GST Credit and UCCB can affect the spousal support range for amount. It is therefore critical to be clear on this income issue.

> In our *Example 8.4*, if the child benefits are rotated, thereby reducing Cynthia's income, the formula range would be higher, **from zero to $289 per month**.

### 8.6.2 Adjusting the ranges for child support that departs from the set-off

To make matters more difficult, in some shared custody cases, the amount of support is increased beyond the straight set-off amount, for various reasons: to reflect the increased costs of shared custody (or the respective abilities of the parents to incur those increased costs); to adjust for the recipient parent's larger share of actual child care costs; to reflect a parent's reliance upon a previous higher amount of child support, as in *Contino*; or to reduce disparities in the standards of living between the parental households. A central concern expressed in *Contino* was that the children not experience any dramatic change in standards of living as they move between the two parental households.

> To return to *Example 8.4*, what if Peter pays more than the straight set-off amount of $388 per month? Much depends upon why Peter pays more. If Peter pays a higher amount of child support because Cynthia spends more on the children or because of the increased costs of shared custody, no adjustment should be made.

> On the other hand, if Peter pays more child support simply to reduce the disparity in household standards of living, an adjustment should probably be made to the ranges for spousal support, as there is less need for the same function to be performed by spousal support. For example, if Peter were to pay child support of $569 per month on this standard-of-living rationale, rather than $388, then the range for spousal support would be **zero to zero** after adjustment (assuming the full child benefits are paid to Cynthia). At child support of $569 per month, Cynthia would have noticeably more of the family's net disposable income than Peter, leaving no room for spousal support under the *with child support* formula.

*Contino* emphasized the discretionary nature of child support in shared custody cases. Departures from the set-off can even sometimes go below the set-off amount. There can be a number of reasons for departing from the set-off amount, either above or below. A careful analysis of those reasons is thus necessary, to determine whether any adjustment should be made in calculating the formula ranges and, eventually, in choosing the appropriate amount within the ranges.

### 8.6.3 Adjusting the limits of the range

We received much feedback from mediators and lawyers working with shared custody parents, stating that these parents often opt for a 50/50 split of the couple's family net disposable income or monthly cash flow after the payment of child and spousal support (remember that this is a broader and different measure from INDI or individual net disposable income). This option leaves the children with roughly the same resources and standard of living in each household. We agree that this equal split of net income should be available as one of the normal range of outcomes—not mandated, just available—in every shared custody case.

The shared custody formula for spousal support usually includes this 50/50 split within the range, but in some cases this 50/50 split falls just outside the upper or lower end of the range. In these cases, the shared custody range has been broadened to include this 50/50 split. Take *Example 8.4* which shows a range of zero to $142 per month where Peter pays the set-off amount of $388 as child support (and assuming that Cynthia receives the full child benefits). At the upper end of the range, Cynthia would be left with 49.7 per cent of the family net disposable income. To increase her share to 50 per cent, the upper end of the spousal support range would have to be $179. Under our revised shared custody formula, the range here would become zero to $179 per month, to ensure that the 50/50 split falls within the range.

In what cases has the formula range been adjusted? In cases where parental incomes are lower or not that far apart (like Peter and Cynthia), the upper end of the range has been adjusted upwards a bit. In cases where the recipient parent has little or no income and there are two or more children subject to shared custody, then the lower end of the range has been adjusted downwards, to ensure that the 50/50 split falls within the range. These adjustments are made automatically by the software programs.

In these latter cases, where there are two or more children subject to shared custody and the recipient has little or no income, the formula will produce a range with a lower end that leaves the lower-income recipient with 50 per cent of the family's net disposable income and the rest of the range will obviously go higher. During the feedback process, some criticized this range of outcomes, suggesting that a shared custody recipient should never receive spousal support that would give her or him more than 50 per cent of the family's net disposable income. After all, they suggested, under this arrangement, both parents face the same ongoing obligations of child care going into the future, with neither parent experiencing more disadvantage.

The answer to these criticisms is that the past *is* relevant in these cases, as there is a reason the recipient has little or no income, usually explained by that parent's past shouldering of the bulk of child care responsibilities. In most shared custody cases, both parents have shared parenting during the relationship, so that there is less disadvantage and less disparity in their incomes at the end of the marriage. Where the recipient has little or no income, she or he will have a greater need for increased support in the short run. But the shared custody arrangement will reduce the impact of ongoing child care upon the recipient's employment prospects, such that progress towards self-sufficiency should occur more quickly. In these cases, spousal support will likely be reduced in the near future on review or variation, and the duration of support may be shorter.

## 8.7 Split custody

In a **split custody** situation, more significant changes to the basic formula are required. If each parent has one or more children in their primary care or custody, then s. 8 of the *Federal Child Support Guidelines* requires a set-off of table amounts, with each spouse paying the table amount for the number of children in the other spouse's custody. But this means that each parent will also be considered to support the child or children in their care directly, out of their remaining income. Thus, in the split custody situation, a notional table amount must be deducted from *each* parent, not just the recipient but the payor as well.

Since there is one child in each household, there are no economies of scale and accordingly larger proportions of their incomes are devoted to child support, leaving a smaller pool of INDI to be divided by way of spousal support. Again, as with shared custody, this would be done in the calculation of INDI, even though the child support paid by the payor and received by the recipient would be the set-off amount directed by the s. 8 formula.

### Example 8.5

Take the case of Peter and Cynthia again, and assume that each parent has custody of one child, same incomes, same facts. Peter's one child table amount would be $601 per month, Cynthia's $358 per month. Under s. 8 of the *Federal Child Support Guidelines*, these table amounts would be offset, with Peter paying Cynthia $243 per month. In calculating Peter's individual net disposable income, for spousal support purposes, the full one child amount is deducted, twice, once for the table amount effectively paid to Cynthia and once for the notional amount spent directly on the child in his care. Similarly, in calculating Cynthia's INDI, a double deduction of her one-child table amount is made, once for the amount effectively paid to Peter for the child in his care, plus a notional table amount for the child in Cynthia's own care.

The actual child support paid by Peter to Cynthia would be $243, the one-child set-off amount under s. 8. Using the split custody formula for spousal support, Peter would pay spousal support to Cynthia in the range of **zero to $445 per month**.

## 8.8 Step-Children

Under the *Divorce Act* and provincial family law statutes, a spouse can be found to stand in the place of a parent towards a child who is not his or her biological or adoptive child.[83] With that finding, a step-parent becomes liable to pay child support, in an amount that is "appropriate" under section 5 of the *Child Support Guidelines*, "having regard to these Guidelines and any other parent's legal duty to support the child." For the most part, the threshold for finding step-parent status is fairly high, not easily satisfied in short marriages except for very young children.[84] After the Supreme Court decision in *Chartier*,[85] some courts have lowered that threshold, making it more likely that a spouse will be found to stand in the place of a parent after a shorter marriage. In British Columbia, the *Family Relations Act* imposes a step-parent child support

---

83 *Divorce Act*, s. 2(2).

84 Carol Rogerson, "The Child Support Obligations of Step-Parents" (2001), 18 Can.J.Fam.L. 9; Nick Bala, "Who is a 'Parent'? 'Standing in the Place of a Parent' and Section 5 of the Child Support Guidelines" in Law Society of Upper Canada, *Special Lectures 2006: Family Law* (Toronto: Irwin Law, 2007) at 71.

85 *Chartier v. Chartier*, [1999] 1 S.C.R. 242.

obligation if "the step-parent contributed to the support and maintenance of the child for at least one year."[86]

During the feedback phase, especially in British Columbia, there were questions about which formula is appropriate to apply in short-marriage step-parent situations or whether there should be an exception under the *with child support* formula for step-parent cases. There were concerns that this formula generated spousal support obligations that were too substantial in such cases.

In the vast majority of step-parent cases, the *with child support* formula will apply with no difficulty. In many cases, the step-parent will treat the children as his or her own after the breakdown of the marriage. In some of these cases, there will be both step-children and biological children, with all of them treated alike. In other cases, the threshold for the finding of step-parent status will be high enough that the marriage will be a medium-to-long one, with substantial spousal support obligations.

In our view, the short marriage concerns are now resolved by the creation of a range for duration under this formula. Upon closer analysis, the difficulty in these step-parent cases was not the range for amount, but the potentially long duration under the *age-of-children* test for the upper end of the range and its use as a "default rule." An example can demonstrate how the addition of a lower end for the durational range allows for a reasonable range of outcomes in step-parent cases.

### Example 8.6

Art and Kathie have been married for 5 years. Art earns $80,000 per year and Kathie earns $20,000. Kathie had two children from a previous relationship at the time she and Art got married, two girls who are now 10 and 12. Assume that Kathie does not receive any child support from the girls' father and that she has sole custody of the girls.

Under the *Federal Child Support Guidelines*, Art could be required to pay as much as the table amount of child support, $1,159 per month. If Art pays the full table amount, **the basic *with child support* formula would produce an amount for spousal support in the range of $474 to $1,025 per month**.

As for the duration of spousal support, the order would be **indefinite (duration not specified), with a cumulative durational range of 2.5 years at the lower end to 8 years at the upper end**. The upper end of the durational range here is determined by the

*age-of-children* test, i.e. when the youngest daughter (now 10) finishes high school at age 18, or 8 years. The lower end, however, is fixed by the *length-of-marriage* test, as both children are older and in full-time school, i.e. one-half the length of the marriage, or 2½ years. Upon a future review or a variation application, a court could put a relatively short time limit on spousal support, depending upon the facts.

The facts of this simple example can be modified to strengthen or weaken the spousal support claim. If the girls are younger during their relationship with Art, so that they are only 6 and 8 at separation, then the durational range would be 2½ to 12 years and there would be strong factors pushing towards the upper end of the range. Contrast the effect of the low British Columbia threshold under the *Family Relations Act*. The girls are 6 and 8 at separation, but assume that Art was only married to Kathie for two years. The upper end of the durational range would still be 12 years, but the lower end would be reduced to one year, i.e. one-half year for each year of marriage.

Under section 8 of the *Child Support Guidelines*, it is possible for a step-parent to pay less than the table amount of child support if appropriate. A reduced amount is only ordered or agreed upon when the biological parent is already paying child support.[87] Where the amount of child support is reduced under s. 8, the *with child support* formula range should be calculated using the full table amount rather than the reduced amount.[88]

### 8.9  A Hybrid Formula for Spousal Support Paid by the Custodial Parent (The *Custodial Payor* Formula)

The basic formula for marriages with dependent children assumes that the higher income spouse pays both child and spousal support to the recipient parent, who also has sole custody or primary care of the children. The spousal support to be paid must then adjust for the payor's child support payments. The shared and split custody situations may change the math, but both still involve the higher income spouse paying both child and spousal support to the recipient.

A different formula is required where the higher income spouse paying spousal support is also the parent with sole custody or primary care of the children. Now spousal support and child support flow in opposite directions. The *without child support* formula does not apply, however, as it assumes

---

86  *Family Relations Act*, R.S.B.C. 1996, c. 128, s. 1 "parent." Section 1(2) requires that the step-parent be married to the parent or that they lived together in a marriage-like relationship for at least two years.

87  Sometimes a court will order the step-parent to pay less than the full table amount, leaving the custodial parent to take steps to obtain or increase child support from the biological parent.

88  Given the way the formula works, any reduction in the step-parent's child support would otherwise lead to an increase in the range for spousal support, an inappropriate result.

no dependent children. While we could have left this situation as an exception, with no formulaic solution, it is common enough that we constructed a formula to guide outcomes in this situation.

---

**Formula for Spousal Support Paid by Custodial Parent (The *Custodial Payor* Formula)**

(1) Reduce the payor spouse's Guidelines income by the **grossed-up notional table amount** for child support (plus a gross-up of any contributions to s. 7 expenses).

(2) If the recipient spouse is paying child support, reduce the recipient's Guidelines income by the **grossed-up amount of child support paid** (table amount plus any s. 7 contributions).

(3) Determine the **adjusted gross income difference** between the spouses and then quantum ranges from 1.5 percent to 2 percent for each year of marriage, up to a maximum of 50.

(4) **Duration** ranges from .5 to 1 year of support for each year of marriage, with the same rules for indefinite (duration not specified) support as under the *without child support* formula.

---

Either of the two formulas could be used as a starting point and then modified to accommodate custodial payors. We chose to start from the *without child support* formula for custodial payors. In this situation the recipient parent does not have the primary care of children and thus more closely resembles the single recipient in the *without child support* formula. The primary rationale for the payment of spousal support in these cases will be merger over time, rather than parental partnership. That said, a number of lower income recipient spouses in this situation will continue to play an important role in their children's lives and any formula must be able to adjust in such cases. The other advantage of the *without child support* formula is ease of calculation, but the formula will have to be modified to back out child support and to take into account tax implications.

Most of these cases will involve older children and longer marriages, where the husband is the higher-income payor and the parent with primary care. In many of these cases, the non-custodial wife may have a sizeable compensatory claim from her past role in child-rearing, which will be reflected in the range for spousal support, and the location of any amount within that range. In these cases involving older children and longer marriages, the children will cease to be children of the marriage within a few years and the wife will cross-over into the *without child support* formula, as is explained below in Chapter 14 on variation and review. In a subset of custodial payor cases, there will be illness or disability issues for the

non-custodial spouses, many of which can be accommodated within the ranges or restructuring, but exceptions will be made in some cases, as discussed below in Chapter 12 below. There is a small minority of custodial payor cases that involve young children, shorter marriages and husbands claiming spousal support from their wives.

In reducing gross incomes by grossed-up amounts for child support, this formula does the same thing conceptually as the basic *with child support* formula—it establishes the spouses' available incomes after their child support obligations are fulfilled. To gross up the child support will require a calculation of the gross value of the non-taxable child support, using the appropriate marginal tax rate for the payor or recipient spouse.

### Example 8.6

Matt earns $100,000 gross per year and has custody of two teenage children. Anna earns $30,000 gross per year. The spouses separated after 16 years together. There are no s. 7 expenses.

Assume entitlement to spousal support has been established.

First, Matt's income is reduced by the table amount for two children, $1,404, grossed-up to $2,525 per month or $30,300 annually. Matt's reduced income would thus be $69,700. Anna is required to pay child support at the table amount of $444 per month, grossed-up to $625 monthly or $7,500 annually. Anna's reduced income would be $22,500. After a 16-year marriage, Anna would receive a range of 24 to 32 percent of the adjusted gross income difference of $47,200.

**Under the *custodial payor* formula, Matt would pay spousal support in a range from $944 to $1,259 per month, for a duration of 8 to 16 years.**

There is one **exception** distinctive to this *custodial payor* formula, discussed in more detail below in Chapter 12. Where the recipient spouse and non-primary parent plays an important role in the child's care and upbringing after separation, yet the marriage is shorter and the child is younger, the ranges for amount and duration applied under this *custodial payor* formula may not allow that spouse to continue to fulfil that parental role. In our view, in such cases, under this **parenting exception**, it should be possible to exceed the upper limits on both amount and duration for that purpose.

### 8.10 A Hybrid Formula for Adult Children and Section 3(2)(b)

After the release of the Draft Proposal, we added another formula to this family of formulas, another hybrid formula, this time for adult children whose child support is determined under section 3(2)(b) of the *Federal Child Support Guidelines*.

In these cases of children who are the age of majority or over, the table-amount-plus-section-7-expenses approach is considered "inappropriate." Under the case law, these are usually cases where:

(i)  the adult child attends a post-secondary institution away from home;

(ii)  the adult child makes a sizeable contribution to his or her own education expenses; or

(iii)  there are other non-parental resources to defray education expenses, like scholarships or RESP's or grandparent monies.

Under section 3(2)(b), an individual budget is usually prepared for the adult child and, after the child and other contributions are deducted, the remaining deficit is then apportioned between the parents, based upon their incomes or some other arrangement. These child support amounts will differ significantly from any amounts using the table and section 7 expenses, almost invariably lower.

This *adult children* formula will *only* apply where the child support for *all* the remaining children of the marriage is determined under section 3(2)(b) of the *Child Support Guidelines* and there are no children for whom a table amount of child support is being paid under section 3(1) or section 3(2)(a). It should not be used, for example, where there is one older child away at university and another still at home in high school. In that case, the basic *with child support* formula would be used, with any necessary adjustment to the amounts of child support contributed by each parent for the child away at school.

Under this *adult children* formula, like the *custodial payor* formula, the framework of the *without child support* formula is used, but adjusted for the child support amounts paid, another hybrid formula. Once each parent's contribution to the child's budget has been allocated under s. 3(2)(b), those actual child support amounts are grossed up and deducted from each spouse's gross income. Then the *without child support* formula is applied, using the adjusted gross income difference and the length of marriage factor to determine amount and duration. The box above for the *custodial payor* can be used to describe the calculations, with one change: the actual amounts of each parent's contribution to child support will be grossed up, rather than table and section 7 amounts.

### Example 8.7

Take Matt and Anna from the previous *Example 8.6* and assume that there is only one child of the marriage, now 20 years old and attending university away from home. Matt earns $100,000 and Anna earns $30,000. Their son's tuition, books and living expenses total $20,000 and, through a mix of summer

employment and scholarships, he can contribute $5,000. The parents have agreed to divide the remaining $15,000 between them, $12,000 by Matt ($1,000 per month) and $3,000 by Anna ($250 per month).

Under this formula, Matt's gross income would be reduced by the grossed up amount of the child support, or $21,300, while Anna's grossed up contribution would be $4,100. The adjusted gross income difference would be $78,700 less $25,900, leaving $52,800.

**After a 16-year marriage, under this formula, the range for spousal support for Anna is 24 to 32 per cent of $52,800, or $1,056 to $1,408 per month, for whatever duration would remain of the original 8 to 16 years.**

Another practical advantage of this formula is that it eases the transition between formulas. Most of these cases are longer marriages and, once the last child ceases to be a "child of the marriage" and child support stops, the spouses will "cross over" to the unadjusted *without child support* formula, described briefly below. In *Example 8.7*, when the son ceases to a "child of the marriage" in a few years, Anna's spousal support would be determined by crossing over to the *without child support* formula, with no adjustment any longer for child support. The range for amount would be 24 to 32 per cent of the gross income difference of $70,000, or $1,400 to $1,867 per month, again for whatever duration would remain of the original 8 to 16 years.

### 8.11  Crossover to the *With Child Support* Formula

There is one last issue to be flagged here, that of crossover between the two formulas. The most frequent crossover situation will be in cases where child support ceases after a medium-to-long marriage, where the children were older or even university-age at the time of the initial order, as in *Example 8.7* above. At this point, either spouse can apply to vary, to bring spousal support under the *without child support* formula. In most cases, it will be the recipient making the application, to obtain an increase in support under the *without child support* formula, once child support is no longer payable and the payor's ability to pay is improved as a result. Specific examples of crossover are considered in Chapter 14 on variation and review.

**Source:** Publication: *Spousal Support Advisory Guidelines* prepared by Professor Carol Rogerson, University of Toronto, and Professor Rollie Thompson, Dalhousie Law School, with the support of the Department of Justice Canada, July 2008. http://www.justice.gc.ca/eng/rp-pr/fl-lf/spousal-epoux/spag/pdf/SSAG_eng.pdf.